# The British Welfare Revolution, 1906–14

# The British Welfare Revolution, 1906–14

John Cooper

Bloomsbury Academic
An imprint of Bloomsbury Publishing Plc

B L O O M S B U R Y
LONDON • OXFORD • NEW YORK • NEW DELHI • SYDNEY

**Bloomsbury Academic**

An imprint of Bloomsbury Publishing Plc

| | |
|---|---|
| 50 Bedford Square | 1385 Broadway |
| London | New York |
| WC1B 3DP | NY 10018 |
| UK | USA |

www.bloomsbury.com

**BLOOMSBURY and the Diana logo are trademarks of Bloomsbury Publishing Plc**

First published 2017

© John Cooper, 2017

John Cooper has asserted his right under the Copyright, Designs and Patents Act, 1988, to be identified as Author of this work.

All rights reserved. No part of this publication may be reproduced or transmitted in any form or by any means, electronic or mechanical, including photocopying, recording, or any information storage or retrieval system, without prior permission in writing from the publishers.

No responsibility for loss caused to any individual or organization acting on or refraining from action as a result of the material in this publication can be accepted by Bloomsbury or the author.

**British Library Cataloguing-in-Publication Data**
A catalogue record for this book is available from the British Library.

ISBN: HB: 978-1-3500-2573-8
ePDF: 978-1-3500-2574-5
eBook: 978-1-3500-2575-2

**Library of Congress Cataloging-in-Publication Data**
A catalog record for this book is available from the Library of Congress.

Cover image © Wellcome Library, London

Typeset by Fakenham Prepress Solutions, Fakenham, Norfolk NR21 8NN
Printed and bound in Great Britain

To find out more about our authors and books visit www.bloomsbury.com. Here you will find extracts, author interviews, details of forthcoming events and the option to sign up for our newsletters.

# Contents

| | |
|---|---|
| Acknowledgements | vi |
| Introduction | 1 |
| 1  The Rise of the Counter-Elite | 7 |
| 2  The Recruiting Grounds of the Counter-Elite | 15 |
| 3  Child Welfare | 39 |
| 4  Old Age Pensions | 61 |
| 5  Sweating and the Minimum Wage | 79 |
| 6  The Webbs and the Minority Report of the Poor Law | 105 |
| 7  Asquith at the Exchequer | 121 |
| 8  The Great Budget of 1909 | 133 |
| 9  National Health Insurance | 151 |
| 10  Unemployment Insurance | 165 |
| 11  Boy Labour and Continuation Education | 185 |
| 12  A Partially Reformed Poor Law | 209 |
| 13  First Steps Towards a Health Service | 215 |
| 14  Municipal Housing and Town Planning | 241 |
| 15  From Trade Boards to the Minimum Wage | 261 |
| Conclusion | 287 |
| Biographical Notes | 297 |
| Notes | 305 |
| Bibliography | 341 |
| Index | 353 |

# Acknowledgements

I have been working on the topic of the downfall of the Poor Law system and the emergence of a new form of society orientated to welfare goals for many years; and I would like to thank the team at Bloomsbury and beyond, who have enabled me to make my ideas more coherent and to put them into print. Many thanks go to the history editor Emily Drewe for her confidence in the project and to her assistant Beatriz Lopez; copy editor Moira Eagling; and to Kim Storry the project manager at Fakenham Prepress. I would also like to thank the anonymous reviewers of my book, whose criticisms I have tried to take on board and have I hope improved it.

No book of this kind could be written without the splendid assistance of the librarians of the British Library, the National Archives and the Parliamentary Archives, and of the special collections at the Weston Library at Oxford, the Cambridge University Library, the Cadbury Research Library in Birmingham and the London School of Economics Library. I would like to thank as well Mr Christopher Osborn for permission to quote from the diaries of Margot Asquith.

It has not always been possible to trace copyright holders and I beg the indulgence of any I may have missed.

Without the sustained support of my family, who spurred me on to finish the book, it would not have been completed. To my late father and mother Isaac and Kitty, my brother Martin, and my son Zaki I owe more than words can express; and to my wife Judy, who saw me over the final hurdle, I dedicate this book.

John Cooper
London
June 2017

# Introduction

Despite the limited objectives on which the Liberals fought the 1906 election, historians have concluded that a new variety of social politics was emerging under the Liberal governments of 1906–14 of Henry Campbell-Bannerman and his successor H. H. Asquith. Campbell-Bannerman had few striking qualities for the premiership which he occupied for just over two years, lacking in charisma, administrative competence, or skills as an orator. In the country he had gained standing for leading the pro-Boer campaign against the South African War. True that his election address at the Royal Albert Hall on 22 December 1905 spoke of the need for the modernization of the Poor Law, measures concerned with unemployment and sweating, the improvement of the waterways, but his principal emphasis was on the colonization of land. At the same time, he promised a massive reduction of public expenditure, a reiteration of the Gladstonian policy of retrenchment, indicating that he was not aware that social reform would inevitably lead to the need for a massive increase in taxation. G. R. Searle pointed out that '[a]n analysis of Liberal election addresses reveals that 69 per cent of them mentioned "Poor Law reform and pensions", but in order of rank this issue only came seventh, behind references to free trade, amendments to the Education Act [to placate the Nonconformists], licensing reform, Chinese labour, and Tory misuse of its 1900 mandate'. The Liberals in secret alliance with Labour swept to victory, winning 400 seats and reducing the Tories to 157. Successive election victories allowed the Liberals to implement reform in every area of social administration between 1906 and 1914. But is it possible to go further and ask whether this was tantamount to a Welfare Revolution? This I believe is a question well worth exploring and which I try to answer in the following pages.[1]

For almost three-quarters of a century from the advent of the Poor Law Amendment Act of 1834 until the Liberal government of 1906, relief for the destitute was governed by the principles of this Act. Instead of parishes being responsible for the day-to-day running of the Poor Law, they were grouped together in large unions with the benefit of better administration and greater financial resources to build workhouses. Contemporary opinion accepted that the aged, the infirm, widows and orphan children, who were placed in this position through no fault of their own, required some form of residential care; but what happened was that all these different classes of poor were haphazardly thrown together without any proper system of classification in a mixed workhouse. However, the chief bone of contention for the reformers was the able-bodied male labourer, who was to be provided with the choice of seeking work or entering the confines of the workhouse with a harsh regime – the deterrent workhouse. His condition was supposed to be made less eligible than that of the independent labourer. Formerly the poor, whose wages had fallen below subsistence level, had sometimes had them subsidized at the local level by payment of outdoor relief. This too was supposed to end. In reality it proved to be impossible to enforce such a restrictive law and the Poor Law Commission devised the labour test: so long as some work was done by the recipient, outdoor relief continued to be dispensed; this concession allowed popular opposition to the New Poor Law to ease. Poor Law legislation, which was designed to cope with the problems of rural distress, became increasingly out of step with industrial conditions prevailing in the towns, where sections of the labour force were thrown out of work by cyclical unemployment. Towards the closing decades of the nineteenth century some local boards of guardians began to improve the stultifying conditions in the workhouses, by providing better diets, better care for the feeble-minded and disabled, increased comforts for the elderly, soup kitchens for the unemployed, and the boarding-out of children – improvements due to the enlargement of the franchise after 1884. But even where material conditions improved, the inmates of the workhouse were subjected to 'the principles of "discipline" – the monotonous routine which should ensure the inmate's total [physical and mental] subjection'. In addition, legislation in 1867 allowed rates to be utilized to build infirmaries, with London and large towns taking the lead and providing facilities that rivalled the voluntary hospitals. Because of the rising cost of these improvements, Poor Law expenditure doubled between 1870-1 and 1905-6 both generally and on the amount spent per head, prompting Balfour's government to appoint the Royal Commission on the Poor Laws in 1905.[2]

Thus, despite an unpromising start to reform under Campbell-Bannerman, much of this Poor Law system was rendered redundant by successive Liberal administrations before 1914. Why did this happen and why did it happen so rapidly? Our answer would be in broad terms that from the 1880s until the advent of the Liberals in 1906 a counter-elite was forming and that members of this counter-elite, by a sociological approach to the various aspects of the problems of poverty, put forward radical remedial action which the government often accepted and implemented.

Turning now to the existing literature on the subject, while Bentley Gilbert undertook a broad survey of the emergence of National Insurance in 1966, there are many gaps in his account of other social services and some of his research is now outmoded. He presented the compulsory medical inspection of children and arrangements for possible treatment as secretly hidden in the Education (Administrative Provisions) Act 1907 by civil servants, when it was part of a wider campaign; and he underestimated the significance of Arthur Newsholme's tenure as chief medical officer of the Local Government Board, when steps were taken to establish state services for the treatment of tuberculosis and venereal disease and to promote infant welfare, as demonstrated by John M. Eyler. Thus, Gilbert's *The Evolution of National Insurance in Great Britain* should be supplemented by reading Eyler's *Sir Arthur Newsholme and State Medicine 1885–1935*, Simon Cordery's study of friendly societies and David Green on working-class patients and doctors. Also on social insurance there is E. P. Hennock's *British Social Reform and German Precedents: The Case of Social Insurance 1880–1914*, though he plays down Churchill's role in persuading Lloyd George to adopt an insurance policy, as he showed an earlier interest in the whole topic than his colleague.³ Apart from the previously cited works, there are a series of excellent monographs on specific topics, such as Jose Harris on unemployment, John Macnicol and Pat Thane on old age pensions, and Sheila Blackburn on the minimum wage, but these monographs sometimes make little attempt to gauge the individual significance of the factors responsible for poverty or to delineate the whole welfare scene and show how the different reforms fit into a larger framework.⁴ José Harris's wide-ranging book on *Unemployment and Politics*, like that of Hennock, tends to overlook the part played by Arthur Wilson Fox and W. H. Dawson in the drafting of the unemployment insurance legislation, and could possibly have had more to say on the role of the National Right to Work Council which exerted immense pressure on the government for action, the effectiveness of which has been well delineated by Kenneth D. Brown. José Harris has also published a superb biography of William Beveridge, the civil servant responsible for the implementation of a national network of labour exchanges and unemployment insurance.⁵

As far as the poverty surveys are concerned, there are biographies of Charles Booth by T. S. and M. B. Simey and of Seebohm Rowntree by Asa Briggs, but a study which puts the poverty surveys into a wider context by A. L. Bowley and A. R. Burnett-Hurst (1915) is still worth reading; and Ian Gazeley in his *Poverty in Britain 1900–1965* provides a balanced critical assessment of Seebohm Rowntree. Because the Liberal land campaign embraced the issues both of housing and the minimum wage, these two subjects are grouped together in the last chapters of this book. The confrontation between the Webbs and the Bosanquets over Poor Law reform is covered in a lively fashion in A. M. McBriar's *An Edwardian Mixed Double* (1987), but should be supplemented by looking at Jane Lewis's more nuanced portrait of Helen Bosanquet in her *Women and Social Action* (1991).⁶ Many of the issues connected with the restructuring of the British system of taxation are dealt with in Martin Daunton's *Trusting Leviathan* and Bruce K. Murray's *The People's Budget*, even if they could say more about the struggle between the radicals and their opponents in the Select Committee on Income Tax.⁷ The most comprehensive survey of housing was Anthony Wohl's *The Eternal Slum* (1977) and Kenneth Brown's biography of John Burns (1977) also had useful material, while for town planning Anthony Sutcliffe's *Towards the Planned City: Germany, Britain, the United States and France 1780–1914* (1981) should also be consulted.⁸ Although the land campaign was first covered by H. V. Emy, there is a fuller treatment by Ian Packer in his *Lloyd George, Liberalism and the Land* (2001). In addition to Emy, Chris Wrigley in *David Lloyd George and the British Labour Movement* (1976) and Duncan Tanner in *Political Change and the Labour Party 1900–1918* (1990) tackled the issue of the minimum wage; there is a masterly survey of the whole subject of sweated labour in Sheila Blackburn's *A Fair Day's Wage*.⁹

Since the early literature on the subject, a number of different approaches have developed to account for the formation of a welfare-orientated society, and while I do not utilize any one of these approaches, I hope to incorporate some of their insights. Critics from the right claim that there has been too much state expenditure on building the welfare state at the expense of the economy. Hence they have a much more benevolent view of the need for voluntary action and feel that the sacrifice of friendly societies by Lloyd George was unwarranted, as it dispensed with comradeship and mutual aid which would have improved the health of the working class more rapidly. Feminist critics have, too, denounced the National Insurance scheme for being over-reliant on the male breadwinner and neglecting wives and children and for overburdening the working-class mother with new obligations in the care of her children. Marxist critics such as John Saville argued that while 'the pace and tempo of social reform have been determined by the struggle of working class groups and organisations', welfare provision improved the efficiency of the workforce and promoted political stability. But despite the scale of social reform under Asquith between 1908 and 1911, there was massive labour unrest in the aftermath, as striking workers believed they could wring more concessions out of the government, making Saville's assertion questionable. From a Labour party perspective, Henry Pelling claimed that the working class was initially hostile to welfare reform because of their suspicion of state institutions allegedly set up for their benefit, though later historians, such as Pat Thane, have distanced themselves from this viewpoint.[10]

The book opens with two chapters starting in the late Victorian age dealing with the rise of the counter-elite, when important structural and attitudinal changes took place in British society; these created the preconditions for the welfare reforms. The actual reforms are treated at length in Chapters 3 to 15. Closer examination reveals that the Liberal welfare reforms occurred in three distinctive phases: a slow, almost concealed beginning under Campbell-Bannerman in 1906 to 1908 (Chapter 3); a momentous acceleration of the rate of change under Asquith and Lloyd George between 1908 and 1911 (Chapters 4–12); and a final widening of the government's agenda between 1911 and 1914 (Chapters 13–15).

In Chapter 1 I survey the rise of a counter-elite emerging from Oxford-educated graduates under the influence of T. H. Green's Idealist school of philosophy and its successors, also from the professions, and above all, the business class. Charles Booth, Seebohm Rowntree and the Webbs and their acolytes in the Ratan Tata Foundation at the LSE utilized applied sociology to present an overwhelming case for social reform, challenging the alliance between civil servants trained in the classical tradition at Oxford and Cambridge and the City-aristocratic governing elite; they had hitherto dominated politics and preached the virtues of low taxation, small government instead of a bloated bureaucracy and free trade. Because the Poor Law attached great weight to defects of character, individuals were blamed for their own fate and failures in life. The key figure in this blighted constellation was the able-bodied unemployed, who was offered the stark choice of the workhouse or starvation. Together with the able-bodied unemployed, the aged, the sick and children were crowded into the mixed workhouse. Under the prompting of the business group, the national debate shifted away from a discussion of pauperism and the various categories of pauper into an inquiry into the components of poverty – its dimensions and the multifarious factors behind it, such as low wages and old age. Once the individual factor had been isolated by sociological research, possible solutions could be put forward. Having traced the emergence of a counter-elite, I proceed in the next chapter to discuss their recruiting grounds: the university settlements, women's organizations and female social workers, the adherents of the social gospel, the land associations, the Fabian Society and the London School of Economics; all these groups helped to influence civil servants and MPs, who became responsible for what became known as the New Liberalism.

During the time he served as prime minister, Campbell-Bannerman encouraged an old-fashioned Liberal programme of education, land and temperance reform and was lukewarm towards social reform from 1906 until his retirement in early 1908. Nonetheless, in alliance with the Labour party, progressive Liberal MPs started a momentum which resulted in the first spate of social reforms covered in Chapter 3 – the provision of school meals and the start of medical inspection, children's courts and the probation service, and the Children's Act. While the first two reforms may be attributed to pressure groups associated with Labour and organizations in which women were active plus backbench clamour, the Children's Bill was an official government measure which was steered through Parliament by Herbert Samuel, then a junior minister associated with the New Liberalism, but became law some months after the sitting prime minister had left office.

With the resignation and death of Sir Henry Campbell-Bannerman early in 1908 and H. H. Asquith's succession as prime minister, added momentum was given to the movement for reform, and the second and most significant phase of the upheavals in the welfare system are considered in Chapters 4 to 12. Not only was the balance of the Cabinet changed by the promotion of Lloyd George as chancellor of the Exchequer and Winston Churchill as president of the Board of Trade, but Asquith strongly supported the implementation of a scheme for non-contributory and universal old age pensions and, while he was chancellor, set in motion reforms at the Treasury – reforms which ensured that the tax system was overhauled and modernized, so that the government was in a position to raise another £8 million in revenue to pay for old age pensions and many of the other innovative measures that followed. Moreover, Asquith not only publicly stated, after becoming prime minister, that the Poor Law would be remodelled completely but strongly supported ministers, such as Lloyd George and Churchill, who presented him with new initiatives. He encouraged them to go ahead with their proposals, whether it was the Great Budget of 1909, the Trade Boards Act, the scheme establishing a national network of labour exchanges, or the health and unemployment insurance schemes which became the Liberal answer to the Webbs' plea for the break-up of the Poor Law.

In Chapter 4 I show how Charles Booth made a convincing sociological case for the payment of non-contributory old age pensions; this was espoused by the Labour movement and received a friendly reception from Asquith, who was much more open to the ideas of the New Liberalism. Chapter 5 discusses the start of the anti-sweating campaign and the Trade Boards Act of 1909. Here again the case for minimum wage regulation was dependent on the sociological analysis, but this time supplied by Beatrice Webb and later by her spouse. After a strong campaign by the Women's Trade Union League and elements of the New Liberalism, Churchill prepared a bill as a government measure with the approval of Asquith. In Chapter 6 I show how the Webbs' Minority Report was in certain respects less radical than they thought, allowing Asquith to shelve the scheme for the dissolution of the Poor Law, as they retreated from the idea that low wages were the primary cause of mass poverty and embraced Beveridge's casual labour theory; but, on the other hand, by a scintillating sociological analysis they forced the issue of health reform to the forefront of the national debate, and Beveridge was invited to join the civil service to implement his scheme for a national system of labour exchanges. In Chapters 7 and 8 I deal with the Great Budget of 1909 which not only completed Asquith's financial reconstruction and introduced a graduated income tax and supertax, but challenged the opposition by providing a Liberal answer to the Webbs' campaign for the abolition of the Poor Law – health and unemployment insurance and the Development Commission plus minimum wage legislation. More than this, Lloyd George introduced the supertax and the imposts on land as a direct challenge to the City and aristocratic interests, who controlled the House of Lords and were trying to impede the Liberal reform programme. Chapters 9 and 10 cover Parts 1 and 2 of the National Insurance Act 1911, the health and unemployment insurance schemes, while Chapter 13 has additional sections on the expansion of school clinics and the school meals service, the inauguration of a state service to cover the treatment of tuberculosis and venereal disease, and the opening of infant welfare centres – the first tentative steps in the construction of a national health service. Chapter 11 completes the coverage of the topic of unemployment by exploring blind-alley occupations for juveniles and their subsequent difficulty in finding suitable work, known as the boy labour problem, and is rounded off by dealing with the topic of continuation schools touted as a possible solution to the problem.

In Chapter 12 I discuss why the pre-1914 Liberal governments were averse to abolishing the Poor Law, though they tried to remove many categories from its embrace, including the aged, the sick, able-bodied unemployed and children in Poor Law institutions. In the third phase starting in 1911, because of large-scale labour unrest over what the unions believed were falling living standards, Lloyd George, under the prompting of the sociologists L. T. Hobhouse and Seebohm Rowntree, set up a Land Enquiry Committee and devised a programme for the rural areas and urban reforms to deal with the housing shortage and low wages; because of the outbreak of war, however, the proposals were never finalized and remained tangled. At the same time, the growing inadequacies of the medical cover provided by health insurance encouraged the implementation of a wide variety of public health schemes for infants and children and the victims of tuberculosis and venereal disease more in line with the Webbs' way of thinking – subjects which are discussed in Chapter 13. Chapter 14 focuses on housing legislation, an important aspect of the urban land problem, showing the failure of town planning to relieve the housing shortage and a movement in both main parties towards subsidized housing. The final chapter tackles the problem of minimum wage legislation and the living wage which Lloyd George espoused in his land campaign.

Clearly sociological inquiry underpinned the case for old age pensions, trade boards, labour exchanges, the boy labour problem and its solution, radical health reform, housing subsidies, minimum wage regulation and so on. The reforms were achieved through the energy of the proponents of the New Liberalism aligned with the Labour movement, the Webbs and their followers and Edwardian women, who moved into and became activists in the public sphere in huge numbers.

1

# The Rise of the Counter-Elite

As mentioned previously, the first two chapters of this book describe the formation of a counter-elite with new ways of thinking and acting. One important element in this was the rise of the Idealist philosophy of T. H. Green which influenced undergraduates in certain universities, but this thought could lead in two different directions: one was towards the espousal of collectivism, to maximum state intervention; the other led to a more personal approach to individuals and a belief in minimal state interference. Other important influences moving opinion in a collectivist direction were post-Darwinian evolutionary theory, the visionary thought of Ruskin, and socialism. In 1887 Hubert Llewellyn Smith, a future top civil servant at the Board of Trade, asserted that he 'would rather be wrong with Karl Marx than right with David Ricardo'. Nevertheless, the crucial elements reshaping progressive opinion in response to socialism were the university settlements which allowed graduates to live among the poor, the sociological study of poverty, the women's pressure groups, the social gospel and the revitalized Liberal land reform organizations. Out of these diverse groups a movement known as the New Liberalism coalesced.

According to H. V. Emy, '[t]he business proportion of Liberal MPs dropped steadily throughout the period' 1892–1914, thus allowing the social radicals to come to the fore – a thesis that must be treated with some scepticism. G. R. Searle has shown, by reanalysing the data, that 'on Emy's own figures, it is hard to find evidence of a significant fall in the percentage of businessmen within the parliamentary party between the 1890s and 1910; indeed, the percentage actually rises between the 1906 and 1910 parliaments'.[1] Moreover, Emy's claim by implication glosses over the crucial role undertaken by businessmen in developing the study of sociology as a dissolvent of the cultural and practical values of the aristocratic–civil service alliance and as an agent for social change; and it does less than justice to the radical businessmen on the Liberal benches in Parliament or to radicals from prominent business families, such as W. H. Lever, Arthur Markham, D. A. Thomas, Alfred Mond, Sir John Brunner, H. J. Tennant, Jack Pease and Arnold Rowntree. Max Weber has perceptively illuminated the links between an aristocratic ruling elite and the intellectual community by remarking that,

> As soon as intellectual and aesthetic education has become a profession, its representatives are bound by an inner affinity to all carriers of ancient social culture, because for them, as for their prototypes, their profession cannot and

must not be a source of needless gain. They look distrustfully upon the abolition of innumerable ethical and aesthetic values which cling to these traditions. They doubt if the dominion of capital would give better, more lasting guarantees to personal liberty and to the development of intellectual, aesthetic and social culture which they represent than the aristocracy of the past has given.[2]

In Victorian England there were powerful pressures to conformity, which either drove the intelligentsia into a close alliance with the aristocratic and City ruling elite or isolated its maverick members; but when the general precipitous fall in agricultural prices engulfed the rentals of the British aristocratic elite from the 1880s onwards and sapped their economic power, the intelligentsia – and this includes the upper ranks of the British civil service – broke from its socially sanctioned moorings and regrouped with new allies from the business classes to form a counter-elite.[3]

More important than any other factor in changing the outlook of undergraduates at universities in favour of a more statist and a more caring outlook in the late nineteenth century was a philosophical school known as Idealism. Its presence was most strongly felt at Oxford and the Scottish universities. Its leading exponent in the first generation of this school of thought was Thomas Hill Green (1836–80), who was appointed as tutor in classics at Balliol College, Oxford in 1866 and in 1878 was elected to a chair of moral philosophy at Oxford. Idealism drew on the ideas of Hegel and in the Edwardian period Rousseau, but its primary source of inspiration was Plato. Benjamin Jowett, the Master of Balliol, had pioneered the translation of Plato into English (1871), so making his ideas more accessible. From Plato Idealists took the concept of 'society as an organic spiritual community', which harmonized with new liberal notions. A second Platonic ideal adopted by this British school of thought was the concept of a 'vision' of the ethical nature of citizenship, in which individuals did not find happiness in satisfying their material needs but in developing 'mind' and 'character' in the service of the community. Thirdly, the Idealists believed that the state had moral functions, that it should play a positive role and benefit all its citizens.[4] Green in his lay sermons to Balliol undergraduates preached Christianity without theology, positing the existence of a transcendent good in the universe, giving 'meaning to individual conduct'. Through the conviction of his former pupils in its importance, R. G. Collingwood observed, 'the philosophy of Green's school [and its successors] might be found, from 1880 to about 1910, penetrating and fertilizing every part of the national life'. Among the top politicians, who pushed the agenda of the New Liberalism and were influenced by Idealism, were H. H. Asquith, R. B. Haldane and Edward Grey. Another closer disciple of Green was Arnold Toynbee, the 'Apostle Arnold', in whose memory the Toynbee Hall Settlement was founded. An important Idealist philosopher of the second generation was Professor Bernard Bosanquet (1848–1923), who was taught by Green at Balliol, and like his mentor had an aversion to state intervention to effect a more equitable distribution of wealth. He was also notable for serving as the first secretary of the Charity Organisation Society, and was married to Helen Bosanquet, the compiler of the Majority Report on the Poor Law.[5]

This narrative of when Idealist influence reached its zenith has been qualified by

Michael Freeden, who traced a counter-narrative of the gradual ascendancy of the New Liberalism from the 1880s with a fresh ideology and a clearer set of reformist goals. He asserted that,

> At the very most, Idealism must be regarded as one element amidst a general progressive movement in ideology, philosophy, economics, science, and practical politics. We would add that in these decades liberalism had to confront the issues raised by the stirrings of socialism and the matchgirls strike at Bryant & May in 1888 and the London Dock Strike of 1889. Had Green not existed, liberalism would still have become collectivist and favourably orientated to progressive social reform. More influence on, and responsibility for, events and social trends has been ascribed to him than he actually exercised ... Oxford [in the form of evangelical Christianity] provided the *emotional* atmosphere and motivation to study social problems and undertake social work rather than the intellectual justification and framework for social reform.[6]

The ideology for adopting social reform was hammered out by a group of middle-class professionals, journalists, academics and publicists, who reinterpreted the liberal tradition, thereby providing an intellectually coherent framework for justifying progressive legislation. These new theories were transmitted through the ethical movement and the Rainbow Circle and through a lively press by, among others, L. T. Hobhouse, Chiozza Money and J. A. Hobson, who were frequent contributors to the *Manchester Guardian*, the *Daily News*, the *Nation* and periodicals read by the political class.[7]

L. T. Hobhouse (1864–1924) wrote a volume entitled *Liberalism* in 1911, drawing on the ideas of John Stuart Mill much more than Green and infused with post-Darwinian evolutionary theory. He promoted 'the organic conception of the relation between the individual and society', suggesting that the process of social evolution resulted in the emergence of the rational mind and increasing cooperation between individuals. Biological theory thus underpinned science with ethics and this was reinforced by invoking utilitarian ideas about encouraging the happiness of the greatest number. State regulation was permissible to restrain violence and economic behaviour that impeded individual or social rights, thus sponsoring liberty and encouraging human growth. Hobhouse supported the right to work, a living wage, the government insurance schemes, and a tax on the unearned increment from land.[8] Similarly his friend and colleague J. A. Hobson (1858–1940) regarded under-consumption as the cause of unemployment, believing it could be mitigated by a redistribution of wealth, which in turn necessitated a rethinking of the principles of taxation; and he put forward the notion of a minimum income beyond the mere subsistence level which was superior to the standard espoused by the Webbs and Hobhouse, by demanding in addition to shelter, food and clothing, 'art, music, travel, education, social intercourse' and recreation for all.[9]

While their cash resources made them the natural allies of the landed and financial interests, the low social status of the business classes (Lloyd Warner's lower-upper class) caused them to gravitate into the camp of the counter-elite. In 1948 Violet de Bunsen recounted:

The aura of Whig magnificence had somewhat faded and though the Liberals had their presentable leaders, the rank and file of the party were felt (by Conservatives) to be distastefully radical and lower middle class. Looking back indeed, it appears to me that Liberalism was much more socially taboo than Labour has been in recent years.[10]

However, Emy's hypothesis that businessmen were ceasing to play a prominent role in the Liberal party is misleading because he grouped the Labour party with non-business elements in the Liberal party, and if the figures in his own tables are recalculated by excluding the Labour party, it will be seen that whereas the business proportion of Liberal MPs was 37 per cent in December 1906, it rose to almost 40 per cent in December 1910.[11] In any case it was Jesse Herbert's opinion (in 1903) that most employers who remained after the Home Rule split were prepared to come to terms with Labour: 'The severe Individualists of the party who are wholly out of sympathy with the principles of the L.R.C. are very few.' Nonetheless, these simple computations do not bring out the real economic structure of the Liberal party in the 1906 Parliament, by depicting that it increasingly represented persons controlling huge concentrations of capital with a series of interlocking directorships, often in heavy industry or textile combines. The business classes were held primarily by the leadership of the Nonconformist clergy, who preached a social gospel, thus fostering an alliance with the deprived and underprivileged masses; by the increasing polarization of party politics after 1910, when the American ambassador remarked three years later that '[e]very dinner party is made up with strict reference to party politics of the guests' and that '[t]hey [the Liberals and Tories] are almost at the point of civil war'; and by their careful emulation of a group of dynamic business leaders, who founded the techniques and methods of applied sociology in Britain, pioneered model educational and welfare schemes in their factories, built model housing communities for their employees, manned the local Liberal constituency associations and sat in Parliament.[12]

Of Sir John Brunner, his biographer Stephen Koss has declared:

Service in Parliament exposed him to new currents of thought that helped make him a more Liberal employer, and his Parliamentary Liberalism was in turn, enriched by his experience as an entrepreneur ... The remedies he proposed – pensions and sick pay, housing and recreational facilities, free baths and paid holidays were the products of social conscience and not, as it may sometimes appear, as capitulations to pressure from below or above.[13]

Accordingly, the challenge to the supremacy of the aristocratic ethic had to come from persons outside Oxford and Cambridge, with the robust self-confidence developed from large-scale business operations that social problems would yield to the techniques of business management, and with sufficient private financial resources to carry out wide-ranging social investigations. Charles Booth's originality lay, above all, in his notion of the 'poverty line' to describe the limits below which fell that that portion of the population without the cash resources to meet basic human needs, and in his seemingly scientific confirmation that 30.7 per cent of the inhabitants of London were living in distressed conditions.[14] Rowntree's originality lay in devising a dietary scale based on the research of Atwater to calculate the minimum food intake necessary to achieve physical efficiency, thereby simplifying the task of estimating the level of a subsistence wage.[15] Both Seebohm Rowntree and Booth saw the poverty line through the distorting haze of the casual labour theory of pauperism, while Rowntree's more satisfactory classification of the various categories of poverty was muddied by his concept of secondary poverty, which attempted to pin responsibility for hardship on the failings of the individual. Rowntree drew attention in particular to low wages as a prime cause of poverty; but through the inability of other sociologists such as Lady Bell, E. Jebb, C. B. Hawkins and C. V. Butler to do any follow-up studies based on his model, until the publication of Bowley and Burnett-Hurst's *Livelihood and Poverty* (1915) with its sophisticated sampling techniques, his previous findings were not confirmed, so that social research only slowly undermined Poor Law assumptions. Hence the Royal Commission on the Poor Laws (1909) failed to incorporate Rowntree's findings in a satisfactory manner. The pioneering study of Booth and J. A. Spender into the condition of the aged poor and the early investigations of Booth and his associates, such as Beatrice Webb, Ernest Aves and Llewellyn Smith, into the multifarious aspects of poverty, of course, provided the essential models for the sociological surveys carried out by the new recruits to the counter-elite. If Booth moved into the Liberal Unionist party over Home Rule for Ireland, most of his followers were proponents of the New Liberalism or socialists. Moreover, the wholesale adoption of the sociological approach, for which no one had a greater claim to credit than Booth, had revolutionary political implications. Booth wrote to his old friend Canon Barnett on 22 October 1904:

> My wife sent on to me your letter … with Mr Beveridge's admirable article on the unemployed. If we of the older generation have done something to start such work as this, we have in it our reward. I must see the continuation. I do not mind how hopeless the outlook; if we can only get down to the facts, good must come of it.[16]

Like Booth, many of the early applied sociologists such as Seebohm Rowntree, Beatrice Webb, Victor Branford and E. D. Simon followed business careers, or were closely connected with business families like Lady Bell, the wife of the ironmaster Sir Hugh Bell, and benefited from a self-education or were given a scientific education in universities other than Oxford and Cambridge. Even classical economics was challenged by another businessman. A. F. Mummery 'entangled … [J. A. Hobson] in a controversy about excessive saving, which he regarded as responsible for the underemployment of capital and labour in periods of bad trade', later converting him to his viewpoint.[17]

As Harold Perkin pointed out, Booth relied on school attendance officers to monitor their impressions after visits to absentees' homes and the surrounding streets. Rowntree employed paid investigators, who visited all working-class households in York to enquire about wages and noted signs of neglect and impoverishment, indicators of secondary poverty. Not until Bowley and Burnett-Hurst utilized random sampling techniques in three towns and a mining community to prove that low wages were the chief cause of poverty were Rowntree's previous findings vindicated in 1915.

However, contemporaries 'misunderstood' Booth's and Rowntree's findings, believing that a third of the population of Britain lived in poverty, when Booth stated that 8.4 per cent of the London population lived in poverty and Rowntree found that 9.9 per cent of the population of York so fared. Bowley, using a higher standard to estimate the level of poverty than Rowntree, calculated that it varied from 6 per cent of the population living in poverty in Northampton to 15 per cent in Reading, giving an average level of destitution as 10.62 per cent in the four towns he surveyed. Booth was misunderstood because contemporaries lumped together his findings of those sections of the working class living in poverty and those above them, who were forced to struggle and endure 'lack of comfort', when the latter category had sufficient food and clothing. Rowntree, through inventing the concepts of primary and secondary poverty, was similarly misinterpreted.[18] Further, it was suggested by Ian Gazeley and Andrew Newell that Rowntree, by mistaken assumptions 'over the needs of children relative to adults' in relation to their diet, misinterpreted his data and that those living in primary poverty were 5 or 6 per cent of the population of York, not almost 10 per cent.[19] However, Seebohm Rowntree was important in one other respect. He was the first to observe that in the family life cycle, when there were young children to feed and clothe, the family's financial circumstances became straightened and that the parents and children were sometimes plunged into poverty – the remedy for this situation was the payment of family allowances now called child benefit.

From the 1860s there was an unprecedented increase in the number of Oxford and Cambridge undergraduates; in fact, it is estimated that the number of students at the two universities doubled between 1850 and 1887, on top of which there was the admission of female students and an expansion of the new civic universities from the turn of the century. Considerable significance must also be attached to the fact that the old stereotyped Oxford don, Canon Barnett's 'moral scarecrow', was disappearing, being replaced by the new type of married don as personified by J. R. Green, A. L. Smith, Arnold Toynbee and Sidney Ball, with family ties and warmer and wider public sympathies. By the 1890s Oxford tutors giving evidence before the Bryce Commission concurred in the view that with the spread of university education, 'the danger of an "academical proletariat" is a real one': 'Only in the case of students of special aptitude or promise can a university education be looked upon as a safe investment likely to be repaid by profitable employment in later years.'[20]

The recruiting organizations of the counter-elite outside the universities gave a pronounced sociological orientation to their programme of activities, while inside the universities branches of such bodies as the Guild of St Matthew, the Christian Social Union, the Fabian Society and the Social Science Club were formed to cite the example of Oxford to remedy the deficiencies of a university education. As a writer in the *Progressive Review* in December 1896 noted:

> The most finished result of University education is the First-Class 'greats' man; but his peculiarity lies in his 'power' of making the appearance of knowledge as effective as the reality ... the attempt to form a judgment upon political and industrial problems on general a priori principles has ceased to be even plausible.

Here this critic questioned the lacunae in the past higher education of the upper ranks of the British civil service and political class.

Behind the increasing political radicalization of university graduates can be discerned two principal operative factors, one was their exposure to a keener, more bracing blast of training in the social sciences than their teachers from the business world, which a series of modern enquiries well summarized by Seymour Lipset shows to have important consequences for radicalism; the other was their pressing need to carve out new careers and to revivify decaying professions. R. H. Tawney, in a more sceptical mood in his inaugural address in October 1913 on taking over as director of the Ratan Tata Foundation, could declare that '[s]ocial research has in the last ten years become an industry ... There are more [matters], perhaps, where our knowledge is sufficient to occupy us for the next 20 years, and where the continuance of social evils is not due to the fact that we do not know what is right, but to the fact that we prefer to continue what is wrong'.[21] Victor Branford warned:

> It is essential that the Emotionals of social reform unite with the Intellectuals of Sociology, towards the making of a new Spiritual Power required to give education and counsel to Chiefs; to offer a purpose to philosophers; to clarify the inspiration of poets and artists, and thereby to incorporate into the culture of the age the body of women and workers ... the sociologist may find that for which ... he is searching. The true metal, to wit, out of which may be forged anew the keys of whatever St. Peter has charge of the gates of our social heaven and hell.[22]

The freer Edwardian social character subtly altered Hegelian and Comtist doctrine, away from the highly abstract reorganization of society on scientific lines, away from certain arid welfare institutions, to the human intimacy of pragmatic sociology and welfare services, unclouded by Poor Law rigidities.

The more graduates the greatly expanded Oxbridge and the new civic universities turned out, the more hazardous grew their employment opportunities, thus giving the nascent counter-elite the motive force to produce change: change could have been simple political change, a mere circulation of elites, or social change, the creation of a new type of society with a new range of jobs. Accordingly, the Welfare Revolution was not just an exercise in altruism by the middle class for the working class but a battle by middle-class graduates to expand the career opportunities in the old professions, by starting a health service and a school medical service to absorb more doctors, and by supplementing the voluntary legal aid services by state-aided schemes to absorb more lawyers; it was also a brilliant exercise in innovation, for completely new types of personnel were required to superintend the new social services, such as the probation officer, the youth employment officer, and the lesser types of officials such as the school meals supervisor and the experts who ran the children's play centres. Richard Titmuss noted that 'compared with what had obtained before [the 1911 National Insurance Act], the material rewards for most general practitioners were approximately doubled'. When the departmental committee on the Probation of Offenders Act reported in 1910, it demanded the creation of a professional body, thereby stimulating the foundation of the National Association of Probation Officers in 1912, while the State Children's Association in its evidence laid stress on a properly paid chief probation officer giving his whole time to the work.²³ Above all, it required a greatly enlarged civil service to run the administration of the new social service departments; it has been estimated by Emmeline W. Cohen that the number of established civil servants (excluding industrial staff) more than tripled between 1902 and 1920, rising from 107,782 in March 1902 to 135,721 in March 1911 and then soaring to 368,910 in 1920. 'The Labour Exchange Act of 1909 embodied attempts to deal with employment and unemployment which entailed a vast amount of work in a new field and the employment of large staffs'; likewise the Ministry of Health, created in 1919, absorbed the staff of the three health insurance commissions, possessing 6,412 employees in 1928. According to Abramovitz and Eliasberg, who included categories of staff omitted in the previous survey, the civil service in Great Britain expanded from 325,000 in 1914 to 850,000 in 1918.²⁴ 'The Trade Boards Acts', Élie Halévy reported, 'had necessitated the creation of 800 posts whose salaries reached in some cases £1,000 a year.' Indeed, the whole subject of the sudden expansion of the civil service under Liberal administrations fascinated Halévy, who stressed again and again the great number of Labour and trade union leaders as well as energetic young Fabians who had been appointed to civil service positions, while the same trends were to be observed among women social reformers, who were engaged in increasing numbers.²⁵

Whereas businessmen adhered to the profit motive, many people in the professions were guided by an 'ethic of service', which was perhaps derived from those in holy orders. Elaborating on this concept, Harold Perkin observed that in a more advanced industrial society 'professions proliferated, their clients multiplied and, in certain cases, for example in preventative medicine and sanitary engineering, and central and local government generally, the client became the whole community'. Professional men and women 'became freer to act as critics of society, apologists for the emerging classes of the new industrial system, and purveyors of a new terminology [applied sociology] in which people came to think about the new class society'.²⁶ We would add that whether they were employed in the local authority or central government, the professional staff or civil servants felt obliged to subscribe to this same impartial 'ethic of service'.

2

# The Recruiting Grounds of the Counter-Elite

## The Settlements

'Undergraduates and graduates, long before the late outcry, had become conscious that social conditions were not right, and that they themselves were called to do something.' With these words, Canon Barnett addressed an earnest group of Oxford undergraduates in November 1883 and summoned them to dwell in dedicated communities in the slum quarters of the great cities. The initiative of Samuel Barnett (1844-1913) and his wife Henrietta bore fruit in the foundation of Toynbee Hall in the East End of London in 1884 because it synchronized with a spontaneous movement of undergraduates, aroused by the poverty, dreariness and misery in the great cities, whereas the teachings of earlier advocates had encountered a silent response. Perhaps it was the death of Arnold Toynbee, the historian of the Industrial Revolution, in March 1883 that finally prompted Barnett to formalize their joint social gospel in an institutional setting. 'May we four never be parted', the recently married Toynbee had written to Mrs Barnett in June 1879, 'in our efforts to achieve that work – may we to the very end, through light and darkness, glide forward hand in hand to hasten the kingdom of heaven on earth.'[1] At any rate, on being approached by a Cambridge undergraduate in May 1883 to suggest a novel, alternative path, when there was talk of setting up yet another college mission on conventional lines, Barnett replied with his idea of a university settlement: 'men might hire a house', he wrote, 'where they could come for short or long periods, and, living in an industrial quarter, learn to "sup sorrow with the poor". Otherwise social work had in the past been left mainly to 'good kind women, generally elderly' from the upper middle class, such as Clement Attlee's aunt.

More than being a mere instrument to harness an immense social dynamic, Barnett conceived of a university settlement as a community with a secular orientation capable of absorbing Oxbridge undergraduates of diverse religious background and mixed talent, now that the universities had dropped their exclusive entry clauses, but in his original formulation he had depicted the new institution as embodying asceticism, calling it a 'modern monastery'. Barnett's proposal was adopted by a committee of Oxford students and graduates, among whom we would single out James Bryce MP, a future member of the Campbell-Bannerman Cabinet and the Cambridge Committee for the Study of Social Questions. So lively 'was the interest awakened in both universities', the first annual report disclosed, 'that the London Committee felt justified in arranging for the reception of from fifteen to twenty residents, with guest rooms adequate to wider educational and social undertakings than had at the outset been contemplated'. In a lapidary phrase, probably coined by Barnett, the report ended by stating that '"the raising of the buried life" is that which best expresses our aim', buried because hitherto repressed.[2] One reason for the immediate success of Toynbee Hall was the friendship between Benjamin Jowett, the Master of Balliol College, Oxford, and the Barnetts. A never-ending stream of the brightest graduates from Balliol in particular and from Oxford generally were directed to take up residence in the settlement, and they later had a huge political impact (see the Biographical Notes).

Toynbee Hall and Oxford House both opened their doors in 1884, though they gradually developed opposing institutional ideologies, with Barnett advocating an 'aestheticized spirituality' and the founders of Oxford House an 'ascetic vision of Christian missionary work'. According to Seth Koven, most of the settlement work in London was more influenced by the sectarian vision of Oxford House than the all-embracing, more secular stance of Toynbee Hall, with the various denominations vying with each other in founding new houses. Toynbee Hall, a former industrial school, was redesigned to resemble 'a neo-Elizabethan manor house' and looked much like an Oxford college, but with superior accommodation for its residents and communal rooms decorated with paintings and sculptures. Further, Koven argued that the slums located close to the settlements 'functioned as sites of personal liberation and self-realization – social, spiritual, and sexual – for several generations of educated men and women'. Discussions 'about "social" questions such as homelessness, social hygiene, childhood poverty, and women's work were often sparked by and tapped into anxieties about sex, sexuality and gender roles'.[3]

The key concept in Canon Barnett's philosophy, which he shared with his wife Henrietta as they moulded and enlarged each other's opinions, was the simple act of friendship across class lines – a patent reversal of Victorian values. In 1883 he declared:

> Many have been the schemes of reform I have known ... but, out of eleven years experience, I would say that none touches the root of the evil which does not bring helper and helped into friendly relations. Vain will be higher education, music, art, or even the Gospel, unless they come clothed in the life of brother men.[4]

Contrast, however, his remarks about Oxford undergraduates 'sharing their fuller lives and riper thoughts with the poor' and his wife's aside about 'remembering always that the minds of the poor being emptier, more active entertainment was needed' with his viewpoint twenty years later:

> [Settlers] must live their own life. There must be no affectation of superiority ... They must not come as 'missioners', they have come to settle, that is, to learn as much as to teach, to receive as much as to give ... A settlement in the original idea was ... a means by which University men and workmen might by natural intercourse get to understand one another, and cooperate in social reform.[5]

Starting from an axiom about the inherent potentialities of each individual, Canon Barnett erected an intellectual superstructure resting on the three plinths of a common high culture, the mobilization of an educational machine capable of imparting the finer nuances of what was hitherto an elite culture to the masses, and the forging of intellectual and aesthetic criteria with which to evaluate the timbre and moral tone of any given society. The sparseness and poor quality of the leisure facilities which were available to the masses, soon to be the subject of much comment, was emphasized for the first time by the Barnetts:

> among the majority of Englishmen life is poor; ... among the few life is made rich. The thoughts stored in books, the beauty rescued from nature and preserved in pictures, the intercourse made possible by means of steam locomotion, stir powers in the few which lie asleep in the many.[6]

The Archbishop of York, Cosmo Lang, one of Barnett's earliest disciples, noted that he regarded culture as not being the sole 'property of any privileged classes. He was eager that the industrial population should learn and enter into its heritage.'[7]

Today it is easy to dismiss the patronizing attitude of Canon Barnett to such popular manifestations of working-class culture as football matches on Saturday afternoon, the cinema and sometimes the over-exuberance of trippers at the seaside, but what is forgotten are his efforts to bridge the two cultures. His notion of providing guided tours, perfected at the annual Whitechapel art exhibitions, was later commonly adopted by many museums and art galleries. Whereas the elementary schools throughout most of the nineteenth century kept their classroom walls unadorned, apart from maps and uninteresting animal charts, Barnett through his establishment of the Art in Schools Association popularized a new fashion of stimulating the working-class child's awareness of beauty and serious art by filling schoolrooms with bright, attractive wall-posters, designed by artists. His close associate T. C. Horsfall, the founder of the Ancoats Settlement, was the driving force behind the Manchester Art Museum Committee and similar bodies were also active in Bradford and Halifax. Again, it is quite probable that Barnett acted as the link between his two friends, when Sir John Gorst, as vice-president of the Board of Education, sanctioned Horsfall's plan of allowing visits by schoolchildren to museums and art galleries to qualify for state grants. Moreover, so far from Barnett's foundation of the Whitechapel Library and Art Gallery, the institution of Sunday concerts in his church in Stepney, and the setting up of the Hampstead Garden Suburb Institute being isolated episodes, all were viewed by him as pilot plants for a national scheme. 'In every locality', Barnett had affirmed in 1883 and he was to go on repeating this plea throughout his life, 'there might be a hall where music, or pictures, or the talk of friends would call, into action sleeping powers, and by admiration arouse the deadened life.' So too, in many other settlements, quite apart from the pleasure to be milked from communal singing and the thumping of an untuned piano, there was a genuine attempt to offer more thoughtful entertainment to a popular audience. At the Liverpool Settlement, where Frederick Marquis (Lord Woolton) was director, plays by Galsworthy, Pinero and Shaw were performed by local dramatic societies at cheap rates for neighbourhood audiences.[8]

After its great electoral advance in 1906, Canon Barnett predicted that '[t]he Labour Party, if it came to power tomorrow, would probably be set on its own advantage, just as the propertied class had been set on securing its property for itself. There would be change without progress.' In the new world which he [Barnett] told his younger friends that they 'would see', one such disciple, R. H. Tawney reminisced,

> he thought that there might be more affluence but less enthusiasm, and that those who had been crushed in the past by economic misery might be drugged by prosperity ... But it seemed to him an insult to offer immortal spirits more money or comfort, instead of more life ... He hoped for the growth of a new standard of social values which would subordinate the all-pervading economic calculus to art, religion, to a keener sense of human dignity. He looked to education as one of the powers which might bring about that moral transformation.[9]

Barnett's recognition of the need to nationalize luxury in an essay written in 1886, his role in the formulation of an open indictment of luxury expenditure signed by all the settlement heads in 1904, his encouragement of the publication by his protégé E. J. Urwick of *Luxury and Waste of Life* (1908), his increasing readiness to countenance the steep taxation of high incomes from the time of the labour unrest in 1911, marked his assumption of a position in the economic debate which favoured the increased taxation of the wealthy to pay for the new social services.[10]

At the same time, we would contend that the third essential strand in Canon Barnett's philosophy, his stress on the need for the highest educational opportunities to be accessible to the mass of mankind, entitled him to be classed as one of the founders of the egalitarian tradition in modern education. Tawney surmised:

> Like Ruskin, he thought that the main aim of education ought not to be only to enable the exceptionally industrious to climb into positions usually thought higher than that of workmen, but to raise the general level of society and to humanise industry. What he desired to see was not merely the creation of greater opportunities of higher education for working-class children, but the establishment of a system under which education of a University character would be accessible to adult working men and women.[11]

However, the effects of a lengthy period of residence at a settlement on men who later became prominent in educational reform and administration gave rise to a mixed response: one group consisting of Sir Cyril Norwood and Sir Cyril Burt had their anti-democratic sentiments reinforced. The other group, all from Toynbee Hall, gained a more democratic appreciation of the role of education in an industrial society from Barnett's own lips. Sir Cyril Jackson, chief inspector of schools 1903–6, whose career was ruined by Morant's hostility, in his special Poor Law Report on Boy Labour advocated the raising of the school leaving age to fifteen years or the introduction of compulsory continuation education, while Bolton King as an educational administrator stoutly defended the continuation education policy in the backwash of retrenchment after the First World War. J. H. Whitehouse was the leading Liberal backbench spokesman on education and secured the endorsement of his policy, which was ahead of its party, by the group of Liberal MPs interested in education. He advocated the building of a cluster of elementary schools near parks, where rich and poor children would mix to form socially integrated primary schools, the free circulation of teachers between secondary and primary schools, and the bringing of secondary education within the reach of all, partly by raising the school leaving age to fourteen and partly by instituting compulsory day continuation schools for children between fourteen and eighteen years without beneficial employment. Arthur Hope, a contributor to the symposium *Problems of Boy Life* (1912), declared in favour of a comprehensive type of secondary school, so that as boys developed they could be freely transferred, and from which the incompetent whether poor or rich would be excluded, but which otherwise would be an ideal mixing place for all classes; public schools were brusquely condemned; and universal continuation schooling was seen as essential, if the working class was not to be weakened by the siphoning off of scholarship holders. Tawney became the Labour party spokesman on education, expounding his revised policy in his book *Secondary Education for All* (1922), though his interest in educational advance was of pre-war origin.[12]

Barnett's own forays in the field of higher educational reform were directed to giving the public greater control over the administration of Oxford and Cambridge Universities and to fostering adult education for the working class, by giving aid and encouragement to his protégé Albert Mansbridge, the founder of the Workers Education Association. Despite his mounting an impressive press campaign for university reform, the assembling of a committee of Oxbridge MPs, tutors and Labour Party representatives, Canon Barnett was unable to secure the appointment of a Royal Commission to secure root and branch reform. On the other hand, his suggestion that the universities in conjunction with Labour organizations should provide tutorial classes for the mass of the population was adopted; and bolstered by a grant from the Board of Education, wrung out of a sympathetic Morant, the tutorial classes grew from 234 students split up among eight classes in 1908–9 to 3,234 students divided into 145 classes in 1913–14.[13]

Through the ideas which she shared with her husband about friendship across classes and integrated communities and their general egalitarian philosophy, Henrietta Barnett introduced fresh approaches to housing reform and child welfare. Octavia Hill, the housing reformer, was the Barnetts' mentor, assisting their housing schemes in the East End by securing financial support and helpful volunteers, though gradually they broke with her rigid Charity Organisation Society mindset.[14] When the underground was extended to Golders Green, Henrietta and a group of like-minded persons resolved to save the countryside from the encroachments of the builder by extending Hampstead Heath; but in the course of the campaign, it became apparent to Henrietta that here was an opportunity for housing a community on new lines, even if she was also stirred by the example of Bournville. The project was initiated in 1904, and a band of supporters, including Lord Crewe, Sir John Gorst, Raymond Unwin and later Alfred Lyttelton, translated the ideals into actuality. Only by the intermingling of different classes in mixed housing estates, Henrietta believed, could a socially healthy community be created. One day she remarked to her husband that '[i]f we could buy a huge estate and build so that all classes could live in neighbourliness together, the friendship would come about quite naturally, and the artificial efforts to build bridges need not be made'; and this she set out to achieve in the Hampstead Garden Suburb. So supreme a principle did she hold this intermingling of the classes to be that later she strongly suggested that council housing estates should be socially balanced communities. The Garden Suburb Institute was an educational and recreational centre where persons from different classes could meet and where an informed local public opinion could flower, serving as the prototype of the community centres which flourished on the model housing estates built between the wars. 'There will be, I hope', Henrietta wrote in 1905, 'the convalescent home, the cooperative rest-house, the training school and working lads' hostel – for the community should bear the needy and handicapped in daily mind.' Special efforts were made to house the handicapped of all ages and classes in the Suburb, while Mrs Barnett gradually came to appreciate the need for the state to provide housing for these categories of citizens, so that they could lead a normal life among their fellows and that the teachers of sympathy were not foolishly incarcerated in the workhouse.[15]

Henrietta Barnett, starting from a similar realization that children in the care of the local authority could only thrive under conditions of normalcy and protective love, founded the State Children's Association in 1896 to remove children from the huge barrack schools and house them in family units, in certain respects anticipating the psychological theories of John Bowlby. This is a subject that we will explore more fully in Chapter 12.

Against the simplistic view that settlements were founded with the express purpose of promoting social reform, we would maintain that settlements were originally set up to quicken the pace of reform. In the prospectus entitled 'Universities' Settlement in East London', probably written by Barnett in 1884, it was hinted that '[t]he universal testimony of those best acquainted with the squalor and degradation to which attention has lately been directed affirms that there is less need of legislation than citizens who will maintain the law and create a public opinion amongst the poor themselves'. Percy Alden, the warden of the Mansfield House Settlement, who was to be a prominent proponent of the New Liberalism in Parliament, could blandly forecast in a symposium on settlements in 1898 that '[m]y own view is that nearly all the most important reforms of the next ten years will come by way of the Town Council, the Vestry, the School Board, and the Boards of Guardians'. Moreover, he favourably cited Lord Rosebery to the effect that the then age was one of local rather than House of Commons government. The settlement residents made less impact on the town councils than expected because of the three-year residential qualification, somewhat more of an impact on local Boards of Guardians and on schools as managers and care committee workers. Alden, a professional settlement worker, sat on the West Ham Council, where he pressed successfully for public baths and a library. Dr Scott Lidgett, the warden of the Bermondsey Settlement, was a member of the St Olaves Union, where he strove to improve the nursing personnel and to provide more humane treatment in the workhouse sick wards, to raise the standard of education and sanitation in the Poor Law schools, and to allow the elderly a greater degree of freedom in their leisure pursuits. With the turn of the century, the limitations of local government action, which in any case could only be exploited by persons who had chosen full-time careers in settlement activity, were becoming only too apparent and disillusion was pervasive. 'I have been interviewing three coming men – Masterman, Grinling, and Alden', noted Canon Barnett in March 1902; 'all are at a loose end waiting for a call. To each I suggested Parliament in the future.'[16]

Whereas philanthropic agencies were dismissed as useless for sociological research by Arthur Sherwell, he was convinced that every settlement should have a statistical and investigatory bureau to analyse the housing of the people, seasonal and cyclical unemployment and local industries; 'for the attention of Settlement and other workers cannot too strongly be directed to the point that for the purpose of intimate and accurate investigation of sociological facts nothing more admirable could be devised than the machinery that already exists in every crowded district'. Earlier he argued that 'until our information concerning sociological facts is more complete and perfect than it is, unhappily, at the present time [1898], it is useless to look for those ultimate and far-reaching reforms to which the social student at the last analysis of the problem inevitably and irresistibly turns'. Although it is well known that Charles Booth located his field headquarters in Toynbee Hall when producing his monumental survey of poverty in London, not so well known is the series of solid sociological monographs that were minted at Toynbee Hall, among them *Studies of Boy Life in Our Cities* edited by E. J. Urwick and N. B. Dearle's *Problems of Unemployment in the London Building Trades*; and more important that the bulk of the sociological literature written in the Edwardian era on the problems of child labour, sweating and unemployment emanated from persons enjoying the facilities for research offered by the settlements or by full-time professional settlement staff. Accordingly, on being commissioned to prepare a study of boy labour at the national level by the Poor Law Commission, Cyril Jackson tapped the local knowledge of social workers and settlement residents, while Arnold Freeman stayed in the Woodbrooke Settlement to assemble data on the subject of boy labour in the Birmingham area. So too, in assessing the ramifications of the problems of sweating and unemployment, sociologically orientated settlement workers were again prominent, such as George Shann, E. G. Howarth and T. R. Marr, all wardens of houses.[17]

In 1914 there were some forty-six settlements in Great Britain, if Picht's figures are corrected by adding the Woodbrooke Settlement which he overlooked. Of these settlements, forty-one were situated in England and Wales but the overwhelming majority of the English settlements – some twenty-seven – were concentrated in London. No more than eighteen settlements were purely foundations connected with the universities. Attached to the settlements over the entire breadth of the country were 400 residents plus 1,700 non-resident helpers; but not only were twenty-two settlements – almost half the entire total for Great Britain – exclusively women's settlements, but with 246 female residents to 189 men (accepting Picht's figures without any correction), female volunteers were easily preponderant. Despite the fact that men's and mixed settlements shared certain common features, they were on the whole sharply differentiated from the exclusively women's settlements. All the former type of settlement ran adult education classes, promoted boys' clubs and units of the Church and Lads' brigades, to which was later added a boy scout troop, the staging of art exhibitions and musical evenings, and the provision of premises where clients could consult the Poor Man's Lawyer for advice on landlord and tenant disputes, matrimonial discord, accident claims and the collection of petty debts.[18]

Religious settlements, which were the majority of all settlements, placed their emphasis on strengthening the desirable traits in individuals, thereby perpetuating the hierarchical structure of society in the relationship between the social worker and his client. A minority of the settlements were bulwarks of the Charity Organisation Society (COS). Take the example of the Oxford House Settlement, where residents worked on the district committees of the COS in Hackney and Bethnal Green and to a lesser degree in Poplar and Mile End, and where one such resident could exclaim: 'we must also recognize ... that a vast amount of human suffering is due to those defects in human nature which we generalize under the name of pauperism, and that pauperism is directly and immediately the result of indiscriminate relief'. Nor was this the limit of the drag caused by the swelling of anti-social service sentiment within the settlement world, for even in settlements such as Bermondsey, where opinion broadly favoured experiments, there were peculiar sectors like the reform of the Poor Law schools where the forces of darkness were joined by some strange hosts. Because he was a governor of these schools, Dr Scott Lidgett mounted an exhibition in 1900 and 1901 to counteract the campaigning of the Barnetts' State Children's Association, which was demanding that the barrack schools should be dismantled.[19]

In contrast Toynbee Hall and some of the other settlements were being permeated by the tenets of Sociological Socialism. At Toynbee Hall and the Manchester University Settlement, most of the clubs and other societies were organized by non-residents, so that the residents who followed their professional careers by day were sometimes thrown into an impersonal relationship with the poor of their neighbourhood more in harmony with the other abstract relationships of an industrial society. 'There is also among the young', observed Sir John Gorst in 1895, 'a general desire for equality which finds its satisfaction in fraternizing with the poor'. Further, according to Gorst, the poor were sullen, prone to outbursts of violence, yet their general state was indifference to their economic misfortunes; the leadership to arouse the poor had to come from the university settlements, after sociological science discovered the answers. 'Roughly speaking', Picht claimed, 'Toynbee Hall has become a political settlement. It has become more interested in questions of public life than individuals.' Again, George Lansbury in 1928 castigated the occupants of Toynbee Hall for 'the filling up of the bureaucracy of government and administration with men and women who went to East London full of enthusiasm and zeal for the welfare of the masses, and discovered the advancement of their own interests'. As the settlement members were converted to a belief in Sociological Socialism or were imbued with a spirit of sympathy for its aims, they were led inevitably by a series of steps from egalitarianism, thinking of the poor in friendly yet abstract terms rather than as persons to be manipulated, a faith in the efficacy of the sociological method, into the zealous pursuit of welfare reforms, instead of extolling the virtues of charity. Socialists such as Tawney, Fred Wise, Clement Attlee and J. J. Mallon began to exert a greater influence in Toynbee Hall; and even Canon Barnett supported what he called 'Practicable Socialism' and was much influenced by the Poor Law reform scheme of the Webbs, regurgitating their ideas on medical reform. Mary Stocks has recounted how for a time the Manchester University Settlement took a turn to the left in politics and espoused the Webbs' scheme for the reform of the social services. Again, the Liverpool University Settlement was directed by Frederick Marquis, then a Fabian, and one of his chief supporters was a wealthy, socialist university lecturer, Edward Whitley, who abetted him in establishing a branch of the Webb organization to vindicate the proposals of the Minority Report. Wherever, in fact, legislative proposals were enunciated Fabians were active, whether it was Percy Alden or Pethwick-Lawrence at Mansfield House or the exponents of the New Liberalism sympathetic to Fabianism consisting of the Cadbury family and George Shann at the Woodbrooke Settlement.

In its short-term effects settlement activity was noticeably successful in the areas of unemployment, sweating and child labour reform, with the qualification that success depended on the conjunction of other auspicious social forces; and in the provision of legal aid by the coming into force of new rules in June 1914, whereby poor suitors could obtain legal assistance in the Royal Courts of Justice. The settlement movement also ultimately triggered long-term changes in government policy in the spheres of education, the care of the aged, the treatment of children in state custody, and housing reform in a marked egalitarian direction which are now becoming more discernible.[20] In sum, the settlement movement in part fostered the move away from concerns about the problems of pauperism, the failings of the individual, to investigating the causes of why large sections of the population fell below the poverty line and recommending remedies for each specific social problem.

## Sociological Socialism

It was suggested, particularly by A. M. McBriar and Paul Thompson, that the influence of the Fabian Society on the legislative achievements of the Liberal governments of 1906–14 was infinitesimal. 'Their claims to have laid the foundations of the welfare state are slightly more plausible', Eric Hobsbawm conceded. 'Yet, in fact, the specific Fabian proposals of social reform were rarely adopted and, when they were, "in no case reproduced Fabian plans in detail, where these had been set forth in their tracts" (McBriar).' If attention is solely concentrated on the ephemeral pamphlet literature published by the Fabian Society between 1884 and 1914, no doubt a powerful case to this effect can be built up, though it must be asserted that McBriar's examination of the literature produced by the society in relation to the Liberal government's record is not all that convincing: for while the grand themes, Fabianism and Empire, Fabian collectivism, Fabian economics and sociology were dilated upon with the result that massive conclusions were erected on ill-assembled foundations, there is no minute analysis of the changing ideas of Fabians on such subjects as housing, child welfare, agriculture and unemployment. Paul Thompson's conclusion that more ready support for labour exchanges, the state feeding of school children, and municipal housing was shown by the underrated Social Democratic Federation (SDF) was too sweeping, in that it carries the corollary that Hyndman's organization contributed more to the implementation of the social services than the Fabians. Often the resentful, quarrelsome policy of the SDF was ill conceived, as in the case of the Georgeist land values taxation movement, where Hyndman held out for the politically unrealistic goal of land nationalization, whereas the Fabians and Sidney Webb in particular harnessed the Liberal and socialist forces struggling for the legislatively feasible aim of land values taxation. At its highest evaluation, the SDF can be credited with the inauguration of a national school dinners service, though this rare legislative success would not have been attained without the spadework of the Bradford ILP and the campaigning zest of Sir John Gorst MP, Thomas Macnamara MP and Lady Warwick, and an energetic participation in the national Right to Work campaign, but again no more so than other sections of the Labour movement. Nevertheless, over a wide range of issues there is nothing comparable on the side of the SDF to the victories of the Fabians and their allies.[21]

However, if this somewhat rigid approach is eschewed and the influence of the Fabian Society is assessed in a broader, looser way grouped under the concept of Sociological Socialism, then it can be seen that its influence was paramount. Between them Sidney and Beatrice Webb through the agencies which they set up, particularly the London School of Economics and the *New Statesman*, and through their own voluminous writings and political contacts, vastly extended the sway and effectiveness of Sociological Socialism as an instrument for attuning the Liberal governments of 1906-14 to new goals in social legislation and administration; moreover, some attempt must be made to measure the impact of individual Fabians, both in their published researches and in their journalistic compilations on the social policy of the government, and here even crude yardsticks are preferable to none.[22]

By establishing branches of the Fabian Society at Oxford and Cambridge in 1895 and encouraging its spread to other provincial English universities after 1906, by utilizing the LSE as a centre where Oxbridge graduates carried out sociological research, the Webbs by the end of the First World War had captured the 'higher intelligentsia' for the Labour Movement, according to Charles Masterman.[23] Sidney Webb summed up his credo in 1913:

> It is no part of the Socialist argument that all the science required for the efficient conduct of society has yet been attained. On the contrary, it is the socialists who are in all countries prominent in demanding additional research and in themselves pursuing in the study and in public administration, those investigations and experiments by which science advances ... If there is anything in the expectations of those at work at them, the twentieth century will see as great an advance in the sociological sciences as the nineteenth century witnessed in chemistry and physics.[24]

Again, while the first generation of sociological research workers were predominantly Liberals, sometimes Conservatives, often of confused political identity, the second generation of Tawney, Keeling, Mary Stocks, Mildred Bulkley, Arthur Greenwood, Hugh Dalton, Clement Attlee, Frederick Marquis, Leonard Woolf and Arnold Freeman were mainly socialists. Even the one economist and sociologist who is regarded as the archetypical Liberal, William Beveridge, because of his membership of the party later in life, was for a few years an associate member of the Fabian Society and enjoyed a brief youthful flirtation with socialism. 'I was deeply impressed by the Fabian movement', he recalled, 'Sidney Webb and his associates gave me the sense that by taking sufficient thought one could remedy all the evils in the world.'[25] Above all, the fresh formulations of the Sociological Socialists, especially the Webbs, rather than Charles Booth 'led us', Tawney declared, to approach problems of poverty, as, in the first place at any rate, as problems of industry, to emphasize the fundamental economic contrasts common to numbers of men, rather than the individual peculiarities of earning and spending, to take the trade, the town, the school as a unit of enquiry rather than the isolated individual or family ... Whatever may be true of more primitive communities, the characteristic note of modern poverty is its association, not with the personal misfortunes peculiar to individuals, but with the economic status of particular classes and occupations.[26]

There is a tendency to regard the Webbs' theory of permeation, the science of winning friends and influencing governments, as something grotesque, and to hold that by being outsmarted by their own cleverness, they achieved nothing. To Malcolm Warner, who is on the whole sympathetic to the Webbs, their achievements must be reduced in scale, so that he stated: 'Nor did they found the Welfare State. More credit is due to the Rowntree/ Beveridge/Lloyd George connection. Yet they were indispensable.' On the contrary, given the labile, fluid state of Edwardian politics, it was possible for two austere sociologists to be the intimates of cabinet ministers and to exert an influence on government policy, crucially shaping its agenda. When Asquith assumed the office of prime minister at the start of 1908, the Webbs persuaded him to make the break-up of the Poor Law into the central issue of politics before Churchill and Lloyd George had become immersed in the rival policy of social insurance. Through their friendship with R. B. Haldane and Reginald McKenna, they hardened Asquith's resolve not to deviate from the non-contributory basis of his old age pensions scheme. During the time the Old Age Pensions Bill was being formulated by a Cabinet committee, they plied Asquith with memoranda until they were certain that his handiwork had not been vitiated by Poor Law encroachments. So too, without the Webbs' sociological groundwork in jettisoning the view that the middleman was the sweater, by shifting the responsibility onto the public, and their later elaboration of a theory of the growth of parasitic trades due to imperfect competition, the Liberal Trades Board Act of 1909 is unthinkable. Much evidence points to the conclusion that the Webbs, not Lloyd George, fashioned public health reform into a viable political proposition by their brilliant analysis of the contradictions in the existing provision for medical care, out of which they produced the synthesis of a national health service. Through their contacts with the Fabian Dr McCleary and important public health officials such as Dr Arthur Newsholme and Dr George Newman, they saw the beginnings of a free public health service for tuberculosis patients, those suffering from venereal disease, schoolchildren and infants. In the field of unemployment policy, they prevailed on Winston Churchill to implement their protégé Beveridge's scheme for a national system of labour exchanges, but had no luck with inducing the government to adopt A. L. Bowley's policy of contracting and expanding public works during a downturn in the business cycle to boost full employment until Herbert Samuel assumed office at the Local Government Board in 1914. Further, Beatrice Webb in 1887 produced the earliest analysis, apart from Mayhew, of the problem of casual labour at the London docks; and as T. S. Simey has suggested, her solution of decasualizing the dock labour force was merely recapitulated by Charles Booth and was at the root of the Wilson government's scheme.²⁷ 'The central idea underlying the whole argument, as it was of the Minority Report of the Poor Law Commission, is the necessity, in order to prevent injury to the community as a whole, of maintaining from one end of the Kingdom to the other a definite Standard Minimum of the conditions of civilized life, below which in the interests of the whole, no individual shall be permitted to fall', wrote the Webbs in 1913.²⁸ The Minority Report of the Royal Commission on the Poor Laws 1909, written jointly by the Webbs, was epoch-making in that it was the first ever formulation of a complete network of mainly free social services, dealing with all the problems attendant on old age, sickness, childhood and unemployment, unlike the previous Liberal forays which were partial in scope. The Webbs' goals of the abandonment of the Poor Law administrative apparatus became law in 1928 and goals of a national health service and full employment by government expenditure during times of trade depression were accepted by the Attlee administration. Nonetheless, the failure of the Webbs to force the Asquith government onto these goals even earlier was not merely due to the adroitness of Lloyd George, but to the intellectual prevarications of the Minority Report, its analysis of social problems in terms of pauperism, instead of poverty, its too ready acceptance of Beveridge's theory of under-employment, its perverse refusal to select low wages as the key factor behind mass poverty.

Established in 1895 by the persistence of the Webbs from the proceeds of a trust fund left to the Fabian Society, the London School of Economics (LSE) was the premier institution to place social science at the forefront of its curriculum. In 1912 Sir Ratan Tata made a gift to the Webbs to endow a Foundation at the LSE bearing his name devoted to the 'study and further knowledge of the principles and methods of preventing and relieving poverty and destitution' and favouring 'inductive and statistically based research methods'. Under its auspices and from the staff and pupils of the parent body emanated impeccable monographs, criticizing the administration of the new preventative social services and presenting the case for their extension.²⁹ Of significance here was the volume of Mildred Bulkley on the school meals service, the careful accounts of R. H. Tawney and Miss Bulkley on the working of the individual trade boards and the more general appraisal by Dorothy Sells, Arthur Greenwood's (later research director of the Labour party) study of the requirements of the school health service; and the work of Greenwood, Frederic Keeling and N. B. Dearle on juvenile employment problems. Whereas the early Fabians and the Webbs tended to neglect the various aspects of child welfare, the second generation of Sociological Socialists figured prominently in the campaigns to augment these embryo services, by editing journals read by the staff of preventative agencies, such as *School Hygiene*, the brainchild of the Fabian Dr David Eder, which espoused the cause of school clinics, and the *School Child*, which focused principally on juvenile employment questions, edited by another Fabian Mrs Townshend; and by writing incessantly like Dr Haden Guest on school clinics and Reginald Bray on juvenile labour questions. So too, the *New Statesman* was an offshoot of a publication known as the *Crusade* (against poverty), started in 1910 as the house magazine of the Webbs' organization, the National Committee for the Break-Up of the Poor Law; both opened their pages to the views of the social reformers, who staffed the new preventative agencies, the youth employment service, the minimum wage boards and the public health services. If the early Fabians contributed little towards the inception of a school medical service and school dinners, the Sociological Socialists eclipsed the other sections of the Labour movement in their efforts to found school clinics and promote juvenile employment exchanges, and assisted in the expansion of the school meals service. In the course of this study, we shall come to appreciate better the reliance attached to the cautious, yet radical estimates of national income by Professor Arthur Bowley of the LSE by Haldane and Asquith; his role as an innovator in the formulation of a theory of the necessity for state expenditure to counteract the effects of the cyclical trade depression; and his stark conclusion that the prime cause of poverty was low wages – a finding that was lost amid the turmoil of the First World War, when his volume on poverty in Northampton, Reading, Warrington and Stanley was published in 1915. Between them Chiozza Money MP, a Fabian and author of *Riches and Poverty* (1905), and Bowley furnished the critical estimates of national income on which the income and supertax reforms of Lloyd George's 1909 Budget were based. Just as the settlements played a crucial role in the Liberal administration's unemployment and minimum wage reforms, so the Sociological Socialists, who were often in both camps, duplicated these endeavours, even in urging unemployment insurance on the government like Percy Alden MP.

True that the Victorian pressure groups associated with the Labour movement either had limited aims or had not been particularly successful. For instance, the National Association for the Extension of Workmen's Trains – or rather its predecessor – had inspired the timid Cheap Trains Act of 1883. The Land Nationalization Society had been formed in the early 1880s, without as yet being able to notch up a single parliamentary success. So, far from accomplishing anything, the Legal Eight Hours League had watched its proposals fade from the political scene. Not only were the three national associations which had been recently set up far more successful, but they embodied a special working-class viewpoint on social reform and the National Anti-Sweating League, a middle-class body with strong links to the Women's Trade Union League, relied in part on organized labour for the prosecution of its victorious campaign for trade boards. The National Committee of Organized Labour on Old Age Pensions (1899) carried its campaign to a successful legislative conclusion in 1908, the Old Age Pensions Act following in its main lines what they had been advocating, while in the Commons debates they reinforced the efforts of the Webbs in securing the complete divorce of the scheme from Poor Law taints. The Right to Work National Council (1905) demanded state aid to enable the municipalities to provide work for the unemployed and the establishment of a national system of labour exchanges. Although it may be conceded that the Liberal legislation on unemployment did not exactly adhere to the principles laid down by the Council, without its agitation there would not have been such memorable legislation wrested from the government. While the National Workmen's Housing Council (1898) failed to secure government aid for subsidized municipal housing and rent control in 1909, the Parliament of 1910 was increasingly responsive and its ideas triumphed during the wartime Coalition government. Because of the backing of the miners' union, Herbert Gladstone ensured that the Miners' Eight Hour Day Act reached the statute book in 1908.[30]

Hence we would dispute any revival of the contention of Henry Pelling that 'the extension of the power of the state at the beginning of ... [the twentieth] century ...

was by no means welcomed by members of the working class, and may even have been undertaken over the critical hostility of most of them', and that this hostility was rooted in 'working-class attitudes of suspicion and dislike towards existing institutions [the Poor Law] which were the expression of national social policy'. Historians now accept that many of the Liberal welfare reforms would not have come about without labour pressure and that state intervention was necessary to ameliorate the condition of the most deprived sections of the working class. According to Pat Thane, organized labour after 1906 supported 'Liberal reforms while stressing their inadequacy, and pressing both for improvement and for maximum working-class participation in their administration to achieve further gains'. Old age pensions were popular from the first – villagers exclaiming 'God bless Lloyd George' for easing their living conditions. So too, although the contributions payable under the National Insurance Act of 1911 rendered it initially unpalatable, once the benefits became visible 'when the chief wage earner was sick or unemployed' it was regarded as a boon.[31] In fact, after the first batch of Liberal reforms were implemented in two waves between 1906–8 and 1908 to 1910–11, attempts were made to repair their failings which stemmed less from employer pressure than the existing financial constraints on the government.

## Women and Social Reform

Of all the sections of the community from which pressure groups for social reform sprouted, women have been consistently ignored and underrated by the reiteration of a spurious conjecture that the efforts channelled into their campaign for political emancipation in the Edwardian era 'absorbed the entire energies of the feminists of both sexes during the years immediately preceding the War', thereby sapping their resolve for social reform. Defining his wife's attitude to the suffragette movement, Ramsay MacDonald claimed that 'when she found in connection with her many activities of mercy that rich women were declaring that all their sympathies were dried up and all their charities withheld until they got the franchise, she almost ceased to do anything for the movement', but continued her career as a social reformer. Suffragists like Mrs Fawcett called for the feminization of democracy:

> Do not give up one jot or tittle of your womanliness, your love of children, your care for the sick, your gentleness, your self-control, your obedience to conscience and duty, for all these things are terribly wanted in politics.[32]

In fact, it is hard to imagine an age blessed with a more glittering array of feminine talent, zeal and ambition devoted to multifarious initiatives for social amelioration, boasting such names as Mary Ward, Sophy Sanger, Mary MacArthur, Constance Smith, Gertrude Tuckwell, Clementina Black, Beatrice Webb, Henrietta Barnett, Mrs Creighton, May Tennant, Dr Marion Phillips, Mona Wilson, Violet Markham, Rose Squire, Nettie Adler, Mrs Ramsay MacDonald, Lady Warwick, Elizabeth Cadbury, Eglantyne Jebb, Margaret Bondfield and Margaret McMillan. The principal women's organizations through which these social reformers operated were the Women's Trade Union League, the Women's Industrial Council, the National Union of Women

Workers, the Women's Cooperative Guild and the National Women's Labour League. According to Braithwaite, who had experience of receiving deputations from them,

> These bodies were, in modern parlance, very much organized by the bourgeoisie and intellectuals ... There were none of the old-fashioned women, nor did we ever get a deputation from them, for they remained ... wholly unorganized.[33]

Not all of these insiders had a rigid, stereotyped viewpoint, as can be seen in Lily Montagu's tribute to Mrs Ramsay MacDonald:

> She had a very proper horror of letting industrial bodies degenerate into mere middle-class organizations. She, however, welcomed suggestions from people belonging to other classes and encouraged them to take an interest. We sometimes wondered at her extreme patience with amateurish people.[34]

Whereas the number of unoccupied females in Great Britain was 5,294,000 in 1851, it had more than doubled to 11,375,000 by 1911. Many were middle-class ladies with ample leisure time to carry out good works. By the mid-nineteenth century they were being praised for instructing their domestic servants in 'lessons of vast utility, lessons of order, lessons of economy, lessons of cleanliness, lessons of the management of children, of household comfort and tidiness' and were being urged to impart these values to the wider class of the poor.[35] This is what happened a few decades later, when these ladies ventured into the urban slums; their impact was huge, particularly on infant and child welfare, as middle-class ideals of motherhood reached an ever-swelling audience. The first such organization was the Ladies' Sanitary Reform Association formed in Manchester in 1862, but later known as the Manchester Health Society. By 1893 it was reckoned that 'about 500,000 women laboured "continuously and semi-professionally" in philanthropy; another 20,000 supported themselves as "paid officials" in charitable societies'. Nor was this all. There were 20,000 qualified nurses and another 5,000 women in religious orders, much of whose work was 'devoted to alleviating poverty and distress'.[36]

The early women's settlements were closely linked to the movement for middle-class girls to receive the benefits of a more academic secondary and occasionally a university education. Helen Gladstone, the daughter of the former prime minister and the sister of the home secretary, was warden of the Blackfriars Settlement but earlier had served as vice-principal of Newnham College, Cambridge.[37] If the majority of women's settlements worked in close liaison with the local Charity Organisation Society and the district nursing branch, there were a few women's settlements imbued with COS dogmas and opposed to the growth of social services. Mostly the women's settlements pioneered the various sectors of child welfare work before they received official recognition by being incorporated into the state apparatus, though these schemes were somewhat neglected elsewhere in the settlement movement. From the Mary Ward Settlement sprang the special schools for crippled children and children's play centres, both adopted on a national scale, and vacation schools, even if other women's settlements participated in the early stages of these schemes. Here we would mention the assistance given by the Southwark Women's Settlement, the Liverpool Victoria Women's Settlement and the Canning Town Women's Settlement. At the

Chesterfield Settlement a school for mothers was started prior to the first state infant welfare clinics. Increasingly the women's settlements – sometimes at centres in London and Liverpool, more often in conjunction with the university, as in Birmingham, Bristol, Leeds and Glasgow – concentrated much of their effort in providing social work training courses for women. Once the social reforms of the New Liberalism had been passed, there were many openings for qualified women with diplomas, making them eligible for employment in juvenile labour exchanges, children's play centres and care committees.[38]

Only by an effort of memory is it possible now to recall the disapproval and even dismay with which the news was received among relatives and friends that a young woman of the family had become 'an inspector'. Rose Squire stated in her memoirs:

> It was not in my girlhood expected that daughters of professional men would take up a career. Indeed there was very little opening for them if need to earn a livelihood arose except teaching for the highly educated, and the dreadful dullness of a 'companion's' lot for the incompetent. When at seventeen or eighteen years of age we 'came out' we had a large circle of friends summer and winter seasons of entertaining and being entertained, and at other times no lack of occupation in parish and other social-service activities.[39]

It has been suggested by Roger Fulford that

> The Victorians always supposed that the circle of acquaintances of any individual in fairly affluent circumstances was bounded by relations and the established friends of the family. To form private friendships outside the circle was very rare in Victorian times, and still unusual in Edwardian times.[40]

With the rise of the new woman, the tendency to look for friends outside the family and across class barriers and for paid positions in the state social services spread tensions in the sexual sphere, where some of the younger Fabians searched for love outside marriage, and where Edward Carpenter, Havelock Ellis and Aylmer Maude challenged male dominance within marriage. All these sexual pioneers had links – even if somewhat tenuous – with the Fabian Society, which underscores how social and sexual emancipation intersected with each other. Whereas there were only a handful of women in the higher grades of the civil service in the 1890s, including Miss Mason, an inspector of Poor Law children, appointed in 1883 and the first women factory inspectors appointed by Asquith in 1893, there were over 300 top grade female civil servants in 1926. Again, few women served in a voluntary capacity on local government bodies, the figures for 1912 being twenty-one women town councillors and three county councillors, while 232 Boards of Guardians had no women sitting on them. 'Social service in every form was then attracting women of all classes and of various degrees of education in Manchester, Liverpool, Leeds, and Bradford', commented Rose Squire, reviewing her responsibilities as a factory inspector in the years 1908–12, 'and we of the Civil Service were eagerly consulted as experts on much that was agitating the awakening civic sense of the women of that period.'[41]

Since 1889 the Women's Trade Union League had been doing valiant service under the guidance of the Dilke circle, Lady Dilke and her niece Gertrude Tuckwell, later joined by Constance Smith and Mary MacArthur, who devised many ingenious expedients to attract women workers into unions. Close relations existed between the league and the Christian Social Union, particularly the research division of the latter, leading to much collaboration between the two bodies. For the purpose of keeping social workers abreast of the changes in factory law and regulations and for their better enforcement, as there were only sufficient factory inspectors to cope with the fringes of the problem, the league ran an industrial law bureau.[42]

In 1894 the Women's Industrial Council split from the league and was 'established on a broader basis, as a body whose aim it should be to watch over women engaged in trades, and in all industrial matters which concern women. It has confined itself to this its special duty, leaving to sister societies interest in professional woman, in the poor as such, and in children – except in so far as they are occupied in trades.' Its leadership was more obviously Liberal in complexion than the Women's Trade Union League, with fewer socialists and without an assortment of male Labour MPs, including among its officers Lady Meyer, Mrs George Cadbury, Mrs Herbert Samuel; its honorary treasurer in 1912–13 was Sydney Buxton, a member of the Asquith Cabinet. Having primarily an investigatory function and harbouring within its ranks one of the outstanding female sociologists of her generation, Clementina Black, and other capable ones like Mrs Ramsay MacDonald and C. V. Butler, the author of *Social Conditions in Oxford* (1912), the other committees of the Council, such as the legal and statistical committee and the education and technical training committee, were both subservient to and obtained their sense of direction from the investigation committee:

> This Committee, strengthened by volunteers drawn from the Settlements and elsewhere, undertakes from time to time to investigate the actual conditions in one of the chief centres of a given trade in which women are employed. This means visitation, with systematic enquiry of employers, factories, workshops, home-workers, employees, trade union and other officials, and then the drawing up of a report, with tabulations.[43]

By broadcasting the results of these researches in the pages of the *Economic Journal* and its own quarterly *Industrial News*, by sponsoring a series of important monographs on Home Industries of Women in London, by forming a joint committee with the Apprenticeship and Skilled Employment Association to report to a departmental committee on the hardship and frustrations of van boys, and by featuring pamphlets delineating the comparative labour laws affecting women, the Council had an impact on social policy; but since it concentrated its legislative efforts on bills concerned with sanitary and employment standards in women's trades, more peripheral matters were left to specialist pressure groups and more general matters were debated at the annual conferences of the National Union of Women Workers.[44]

The National Union of Women Workers was formed in 1895, based on a number of local societies which came into existence in Yorkshire in 1889, Liverpool and Birmingham in 1890. From 1898 to 1907, Elizabeth Cadbury, the wife of George Cadbury, served as honorary treasurer, and senior positions in the association were occupied by such other prominent Liberal women as Mrs H. Fawcett, Mrs A. H. Bright, Henrietta Barnett and the Hon. Lily Montagu. 'Questions of housing, of industrial welfare, and, above all, of education were the main problems with which the early Union or Council were concerned.' So too, after pleas had been made to the Agricultural Organization Society to widen the outlook of village women in keeping with the more emancipated, more imaginative image that urban dwellers were aspiring to, by founding Women's Institutes on the Canadian and Belgian model, 'the Society had got no further than experimenting with introducing women members into local Farm Co-operatives. The experiment had proved a complete failure, the women taking no part in the business or discussions for fear of being made fun of by the men.' Urged on by Liberal ladies such as Mrs Wilkins (Louisa Jebb) and Lady Denman under the stimulus of wartime conditions, the countrywomen responded so enthusiastically that the number of Women's Institutes rose from seven in 1915 to 760 at the end of 1918.[45]

Again, the impact of the women's organizations on the legislative record of the Liberal governments was much more dramatic than has so far been admitted. Without the resolve and direction furnished by the Women's Trade Union League, there would have been no coalition against sweating as embodied in the National Anti-Sweating League, nor any measure for Trade Boards on the statute book, while the later stages of the campaign when the question of extending the administrative framework was aired was marked by the swelling tide of support from the Women's Industrial Council and the National Union of Women Workers. Further, it was not so much the agitation of the Christian Union as the stern fighting spirit of the Women's Trade Union League against the use of heavily leaded glaze and colours in the potteries that resulted in several government enquiries and the implementation of regulations controlling their application. Nonetheless, even more significant than their efforts to improve the position of women in industry was the magnificent contribution of women social reformers in the movement for child welfare, for it was of wider dimensions and of a more enduring intensity than that of their male counterparts. Much effort was concentrated on the foundation of infant welfare centres, but also on the establishment of school clinics and feeding centres. Having emerged from its chrysalis within the confines of the Women's Industrial Council in 1899, the Committee on Wage Earning Children embarked on an energetic campaign to curb the employment of children outside school hours, after which it joined its newly formed sister organization the Apprenticeship and Skilled Employment Association (1906) in drives to upgrade juvenile employment conditions through the foundation of a national system of youth employment exchanges and the introduction of universal continuation education.[46]

## Christian Socialism and the Social Gospel

It has often been claimed that the contribution of the Churches in the movement for social reform was of negligible proportions because, it was argued, the Churches merely reflected the *zeitgeist* of the age rather than possessing innovatory and exploratory capabilities of their own. To set the issue in its proper perspective, it is necessary to contemplate a situation in which the British Churches would have acted like the South American Churches in the past as institutionalized forces curbing the expression of social reform sentiment; and if the power of the Anglican Church through the National Society to manipulate opinion is properly understood – as in the struggle over the 1906 Education Bill, which is said to have equalled the agitation promoted by the reformers in 1832, with sleepy country towns springing to life – then the weight of the Churches on the side of reaction or splendid inactivity would have clearly stifled even a robust campaign for social reform. That the Churches tipped the scales in the efforts of the counter-elite to promote the Welfare Revolution was thanks to the rise of two movements: one was the various Christian Socialist organizations in the Anglican Church; the other was the Social Gospel confined to the Nonconformist Churches. The census returns for church attendance for 1886 and for 1902–3 revealed that the Anglican Church had lost 140,000 members between these two dates, whereas the decline of the membership of the Nonconformist Churches was less precipitous, a draining away of 5,000 to 6,000 members. If Christian Socialism in the Church of England was a protest movement by clergy often with aristocratic connections, who were sometimes educated at Eton, Harrow and Oxford, affronted by a loss of status and fearful of dwindling captive audiences in their churches, the propagation of the rival doctrine of the Social Gospel among the Nonconformists, despite the departure of rich dissenters from the 1880s, was more the lively outburst of a hitherto depressed strata which was clamouring for and clambering into power.[47]

The story of Christian Socialism in the Anglican Church has been related so many times that we shall recount it in a brief fashion. The Guild of St Matthew (GSM) (1877–1909), whose enrolment never rose above the 400 level and about a quarter of whose members were clergy, was the earliest Christian Socialist group in the period of revival; but any proliferation of its branch organization was crippled by the autocratic rule of its founder, the Revd Stuart Headlam, a Fabian and a keen supporter of the Georgeist single tax movement, who rather than allow his organization to express pure socialist doctrines hastily disbanded it.[48] There is no doubt that the Christian Social Union (CSU), whose principal luminaries were Bishop Westcott, Bishop Gore and Canon Scott Holland, despite a London branch membership which overlapped considerably with the GSM, had a greater impact on the Church of England and the general community in the years of its ascendancy 1889–1919. 'By 1908 the C.S.U. had thoroughly permeated the Church of England, especially the hierarchy', its latest historian has crisply stated; 'it was a form of "socialism" for bishops. Its achievements were partly to be seen in the growing awareness of social problems and sympathy to labour shown by successive annual congresses.' 'The Oxford University Branch, with its method of group discussion in the Colleges, did, I am told, completely change the minds of ordination candidates of that generation – this was true also of Cambridge in perhaps a less degree', Ruth Kenyon recalled. '"Practically every person under forty whom one meets", he [an organizing secretary] said, "knows that the Church has a duty towards the social problem. The trouble is that they are too frightened of their congregations to say so."'[49]

Charles Masterman wrote twenty years later:

> I remember the days of the Christian Social Union, with the extraordinary wisdom and genius of Bishop Wescott at the head of it, and with Scott Holland and Gilbert Chesterton and myself and others conducting 'crusades' in the great

cities of England, where we would still fill the largest halls in, say, the railway sheds at Derby, or Saint George's Hall at Bradford, or the Great Public Hall at Leeds; in which, although our doctrines scared the local clergy out of their wits, the packed audiences of the common people heard us gladly.[50]

At its peak the CSU comprised fifty-four branches with a total membership of 4,000.[51]

Like the other recruiting centres of the counter-elite, the CSU were adherents of pragmatic sociology. As early as 1879 Scott Holland had formed a discussion group at Oxford known as PESEK (Politics, Economics, Socialism, Ethics and Christianity); later the Oxford branch of the CSU brought out the *Economic Review*, partly as a platform for disseminating different views on welfare politics, but also as a medium through which the results of the group's sociological research could be made public. The London branch created a sociological research unit, among whose members were Gertrude Tuckwell and Constance Smith, although the bulk of their voluntary activities were concentrated elsewhere; this carried out investigations, for example, into certain sweated trades and into the general features of employment undertaken by schoolchildren for a departmental committee in 1910. Hobbled by an air of timorousness, an instance of which was the refusal of the Bristol branch to join the local Right to Work Committee, the CSU was challenged by a more radical organization – the Church Socialist League, a full-blooded socialist sect drawing its strength from the clergy in the northern industrial towns; it was this group that was responsible for a vigorous demonstration in Trafalgar Square at the beginning of 1909 on behalf of the unemployed, at which Dr Clifford and Headlam spoke, yet this latter body ceased to influence thinking on welfare politics when it was infiltrated by guild socialist elements.[52]

To summarize the achievements of the Anglican Christian Socialists we would point to the labours of General Maurice in securing, with the medical officers of health and Margaret McMillan, medical inspection in schools, the invention of the theory of the connection between blind-alley occupations and juvenile unemployment by the Revd Spencer Gibb; and more importantly, the role of the self-same individual as the *Great Disseminator* of a national system of employment bureaux, and the support bestowed on the National Anti-Sweating League by distinguished Anglican churchmen, particularly in the final phases of its campaign for trade boards. Again, the bishops lent stalwart support in the House of Lords, actually saving the Unemployed Workmen Act in 1905, bravely espousing the time limit in the 1908 Licensing Bill, and vainly trying to insert a quinquennial housing register in the 1909 Housing Bill.

Probably the movement for social redemption among the Nonconformist Churches, known as the Social Gospel because of its alignment with the Liberal party, was more productive than the zeal of the Anglican Church in fostering the triumph of social reform. Dr Horton, a Congregationalist, in his presidential address to the Free Church Council in 1905 averred that they should identify themselves more closely with the interests and needs of the working class; that they should proclaim that the housing question together with reasonable conditions of work and play were their intimate concern. Hence the Free Churches appointed a Social Questions Committee to take up matters akin to those for which Labour strove, while the local Free Church Councils were encouraged to set up committees on the same lines. Under the direction of Dr John Brown Paton, the Social Questions Committee drew up a blueprint early in 1906, which anticipated much of the social reform legislation of the Liberal governments of 1906–14.[53] While it was true that all the outstanding national leaders of Nonconformity were now ardent social reformers, it was nonetheless the case that the Congregational ministers excelled their colleagues, apart from Dr Clifford and Scott Lidgett. Among the earlier leaders two deserve passing mention: one was the Revd Andrew Mearns, the author of *The Bitter Cry of Outcast London: An Inquiry into the Condition of the Abject Poor* (1883), which attempted a 'primitive' house-to-house survey and was one of the factors that stimulated Charles Booth to investigate the poverty in the London slums; the other was the Revd Benjamin Waugh, the founder of the Society for the Prevention of Cruelty to Children (1884). Dr J. B. Paton was the head of a training college for Congregational clergy in Nottingham. G. P. Gooch, a reform-minded Liberal MP, eulogized:

> He was the parent of more societies for what the Americans call social uplift than any man in his lifetime. His farm colonies for epileptics are perhaps the most widely known of his creations, but he was as zealous for the normal citizen as for the afflicted and those who fall by the wayside. He maintained that the organization of leisure was as vital as the organization of work, and the National Home Reading Union was one of his schemes. I was associated with him in the Social Institutes Union, a body for the provision of recreational facilities for adults in school buildings after the children had left, and in the British Institute for Social Service, a bureau of information and research.[54]

Paton's most lasting contribution was in his unflagging campaign for continuation education, a cause that was warmly espoused by all the Liberal educationists. Under his stimulus, the Revd Arthur Leonard set up the Cooperative Holidays Association to encourage working-class persons to take an energetic, bracing holiday in the Lake District with walking and bathing rather than the usual seaside trip.[55]

While the Revd Jowett helped to raise the funds for the Digbeth Institute in Birmingham, which opened in 1908, his friend the Revd C. Silvester Horne, another Congregationalist, established

> what were called 'Institutional Churches' in the heart of the great cities from which the middle classes had migrated, leaving behind them a stratum of population of working people and assistants 'living in' at the larger shops ... This revolt [of younger social enthusiasts in the Congregational ministry] had found expression in the creation of Mansfield House University Settlement at Canning Town and the Robert Browning Settlement at Walworth as well as the Institutional Missions at Claremont in Pentonville, Crossways in Southwark, and Whitefields ... in Tottenham Court Road. Similar movements had been started at Leeds, Manchester, and Bradford.[56]

One of the most dazzling of the new breed of Nonconformist ministers, Silvester Horne was the driving dynamo behind the Whitefields Central Mission, with its lectures, music and billiards, to the disgust of the hardcore Puritan elements still sheltering in Nonconformity – a man who could enthral an audience of 1,200 working men on a Sunday afternoon with a virtuoso address which subtly blended politics and religion. As Horne explains in his memoirs,

> I wanted to convince men that Christianity must either be capable of application to life and all its problems, or else we must find some other religion that is more authoritative and comprehensive … Let anyone consider the great outstanding problems of our time, international arbitration, the reduction of armaments, disestablishment, education, temperance and licensing, housing, poor law reform, divorce; and those questions which are greater than any other: the congested city and the deserted village. Who will say the Church ought to be prepared to say nothing at all about these matters?[57]

Through the Institutional Churches, through the Pleasant Sunday Afternoon Associations and Adult Sunday Schools, Nonconformity sank into the taproots of the working class, arousing the articulate local opinion leaders on behalf of social reform, particularly old age pensions and a measure to stamp out sweating, and these opinion leaders in turn converted their workmates. At any rate, the Revd Herbert Stead, a Congregationalist clergyman, mounted the final victorious campaign for old age pensions through a National Committee operating from headquarters in the Browning Hall Settlement, for which he must be classified as a *Great Disseminator*, at one and the same time utilizing both the forces of the Labour movement and effectively mobilizing Nonconformity. In contrast, Booth – who on account of his sociological researches on the link between poverty and the fact of old age also deserves recognition as a *Great Disseminator* – remained somewhat aloof from the hurly-burly of pressure group stage management.[58] Otherwise, apart from Dr Paton's momentous battles for continuation education, sporadic support for the climacteric struggles of the single taxers, and a choicely worded telegram vindicating an amendment to exclude children from pubs inserted in the 1908 Children's Act, the Free Church Council increasingly shrank from committing itself to specific campaigns: an approach from the National Housing Reform Council was rebuffed. Even in circles where enthusiasm for social reform was high, there were those like George Cadbury who endorsed the view that the Free Church Council should avoid the contagion of party politics, and after Dr Meyer became secretary this line increasingly prevailed. Moreover, not only were wealthy Nonconformist congregations such as Dr Horton's at Hampstead restless when he pleaded the cause of the people, but when the Revd R. J. Campbell became a socialist proselytizer all Free Church platforms were barred, apart from his own pulpit in the City Temple.[59]

## The Land Reformers

In its 1871–2 report the Land Tenure Reform Association bemoaned 'the entire absence of sympathy of most of the members [of the Commons] with the principles and objects of the Association, as well as the bitter hostility of many thereto, so far as they comprehend them'. The defection of the Whigs and the elimination of the

Birmingham radicals in 1886 enhanced the status of the reformist pressure groups in relation to the official leadership of the Liberal party, particularly on the land question, although it must be conceded that Gladstone was never an ardent English land reformer. At the annual meeting of the Allotments and Small Holdings Association, a Birmingham-orientated organization, held at the National Liberal Club in London in the late 1880s, the combined vote of Gladstonian Liberals and Irish MPs helped to remove Jesse Collings MP, one of Joseph Chamberlain's closest political colleagues, from the presidency. Earlier in 1885 the Free Land League had been formed to unite all the different sections of the land reformers, but until the mid-1890s the chief emphasis of the land reform movement was on the brisk provision of smallholdings and the destruction of the encumbrances of the aristocracy, such as entail and primogeniture in a free market with minimal concessions to the urban land reformers. However, the English Land Restoration League, representing followers of Henry George, and the Municipal Reform League, the political machine of the London Progressives, set up a united body to convert the recently established governing body in London to the taxation of land values as a substitute for a levy on the coal supplies. A quarter of a million copies of Fletcher Moulton's pamphlet on the taxation of land values were circulated among the London electorate, forty members of the United Committee were elected to the London County Council (LCC) and thirty other councillors were known to be sympathetic. One consequence was that the Conservative chancellor of the Exchequer was emboldened to abolish the London coal dues. Other indications of the growing popularity of the movement within the Liberal party were that William Saunders carried a resolution in favour of land values in the Commons in 1886 and that the Liberal party added the taxation of land values to its plank in 1889. The elder Harcourt later admitted that if he had remained longer at the Exchequer, he would have tried his hand at the taxation of land values.[60]

The embellished Liberal land reform programme in 1906 hoisted the Liberal party away from the petty, internecine squabbling of the past, and attuned the minds of the parliamentary party to the need for embarking on bold schemes of social reconstruction. The National Housing Reform Council, a group run by practical businessmen and town councillors rather than members of the higher intelligentsia, championed both the cause of town planning and ultimately state subsidies for municipal housing ventures. Within the Georgeist body, there was a shift of support since the 1890s away from the radical working men's clubs and socialist politicians to a leadership composed of upper-middle-class intellectuals like C. P. Trevelyan MP, Josiah Wedgwood MP and Phillip Morrell MP, to a grass-roots support among the Nonconformist regions of the country, and a middle band of support from municipal politicians. The United Committee for the Taxation of Land Values and the municipal campaign committee demanded the rating of ground rents as a means of cheapening the price of building land and of enlarging the revenue that could be applied to projects of social amelioration.[61]

The rural land reform movement was reinvigorated by the infusion of a new generation of recruits from the higher intelligentsia together with the very keen cutting edge supplied by the invention of the techniques of rural sociology by H. H. Mann, Maud F. Davies, and above all, Seebohm Rowntree. The Cooperative Small Holdings

Society and its successor group the Land and Home League – organizations centred on London and drawn from fresh generations of Oxbridge intellectuals as compared with the older associations, which derived greater strength from the provinces, from practical farmers and from a past generation of intellectuals – pressed for the creation by compulsory means of smallholdings for the agricultural labourer; later they demanded the fixing of minimum wage rates through the agency of trade boards and increased government intervention to obtain a better supply of rural housing. The Land Law Reform Association pleaded the cause of the farmer and, on being rebuffed in their attempt to obtain more freedom and security on his behalf, declared that he could only be fully protected by setting up rent courts.[62]

What general conclusions may be gleaned from our survey of the five recruiting grounds of the counter-elite? First, the bulk of the Liberal MPs were attracted into a commitment for social reform through the alignment of the land reform pressure groups with the Liberal party and through the proselytizing of the Anglican Christian Social Union, a group overwhelmingly Liberal in outlook, and the Nonconformist exponents of the Social Gospel. Secondly, there was an accelerated trend towards the secularization of social work, both as a positive response to the disintegration of the exclusive hold of the established Church over Oxford and Cambridge and as a deliberate gesture to prevent the Churches from being too deeply implicated in the daily currents of party politics. Attachment to class rather than religious affiliation was gaining in importance among the electorate in the 1910 elections. Thirdly, the Liberal MPs were a leaven on which the chief espousers of social reform in the country, ensconced in the interlocking directorate of the university settlements, the institutions of the Sociological Socialists and the women's organizations, could work, partly by vanquishing opposition by confident assertions engendered by the adoption of new and powerful sociological techniques for defining and resolving the hitherto meaningless and intractable problems of poverty. Fourthly, the university settlements and the Fabians and other Sociological Socialists were only successful in securing social reform when they permeated the central political institutions, although both groups of reformers had preached a similar tactic of engulfing the central state apparatus by activism in local government units. Fifthly, at the storm centre of the movement for social reform stood a body of persons of broadly similar views consisting of Sociological Socialists and upholders of the New Liberalism, particularly the group of persons around Canon Barnett and the Cadbury and Rowntree families; but insofar as the stimulus for child welfare was concerned, the Sociological Socialists and the women's associations and female settlements enjoyed an easy precedence over waves of support emanating from rival centres of opinion such as the university settlements staffed by men and the Christian social reform organizations. 'I have heard his friends say in later years that Barnett had turned Socialist, in a sense he was always a Socialist', observed J. A. Spender in 1913; and similar sentiments echoed from the Cadbury circle, so that George Cadbury could write: 'I have no interest in the Liberal party ... except in so far as it promotes the welfare of the millions of my fellow countrymen who are on or below the poverty line.'[63]

# 3

# Child Welfare

## School Meals and the Start of Medical Inspection

The first instalment of the social reforms 1906–8 covered in this chapter was largely confined to child welfare and roughly coincided with the tenure of Sir Henry Campbell-Bannerman at the head of the Liberal administration, as he stepped down as prime minister through ill health on 6 April 1908. As noted earlier, Campbell-Bannerman was an old-fashioned liberal with little interest in welfare reform, who was mainly concerned with repaying his debt to the Nonconformist wing of the Liberal party by supporting education and licensing measures and a limited campaign for rural regeneration: the Land Tenure Act (1906) for farmers and the Small Holdings Act (1907) for the agricultural labourer. Thus, the provision of free school meals and the establishment of medical inspection and treatment did not arise from government initiatives, but sprang from the action of the Labour party, now a powerful political force in the Commons when joined by progressive Liberal MPs in its campaigns. Outside Parliament Thomas Macnamara, Sir John Gorst, a Tory radical who switched party allegiance, and Lady Warwick, a socialist, headed the movement for free school dinners, while the cause of medical inspection and treatment was led by Sir Lauder Brunton, a consultant, with the support of the Medical Officers of Health (MOH) and progressive doctors within the British Medical Association (BMA) and the assistance of the McMillan sisters. At the Home Office, Herbert Gladstone and his deputy, Herbert Samuel, a progressive Liberal MP, responding to pressure from reformist children's organizations with many activist ladies, introduced the Probation of Offenders Act (1907) and the Children's Act (1908) which established new norms for children's behaviour in public and children's courts. But the Children's Act became law many months after Campbell-Bannerman left office and showed a new determination on the part of the Asquith government.

The view that the provision of a state-subsidized school meals service and scheme of medical inspection by the Liberals during the Campbell-Bannerman administration of 1906–8 was a response produced by the widespread unease over the fitness of recruits during the Boer War is one that has gained general acceptance. This interpretation was refurbished by Bentley Gilbert with a wealth of documentation and pugnacious flourishes of argument, who declared that the Boer War produced a mood of self-questioning by proponents of a national efficiency movement and that they narrowed down their quest for much greater efficiency in the use of the nation's resources to the prime objective of promoting the physical efficiency of schoolchildren.[1] On the contrary, we shall propose that the reform movement for school health may be interpreted partly as a means of coping with the special problems created by the entry of children from the slums into the elementary schools in the 1880s and 1890s – for which one response was the regulation of their employment outside school hours, the other a rigorous medical inspection and free dinners; and partly as a means of bringing the level of the services for the health of the schoolchild in the state primary schools up to the high standards already achieved in certain Poor Law institutions and in the industrial schools and into line with recent continental advances in their elementary school system. Accordingly, the public debate provoked by the recruiting returns in the Boer War was not the decisive factor behind the institutionalization of welfare services for the schoolchild but rather acted as a catalyst, crystallizing forces that were already stirring in the educational and public health sectors. The national efficiency hypothesis requires further qualification insofar as it leads to the erroneous conclusion that the impetus for the provision of school meals and medical inspection in elementary schools came from an inchoate group of imperialist social reformers rather than from specific sections of the Labour movement and medical opinion.

Nor is Bentley Gilbert's assertion any more convincing that since there had been compulsory attendance at elementary schools from the 1870s without medical inspection and school meals services for another quarter of a century, this was the final proof that there was no necessary connection between the two events. It has been shown by Gillian Sutherland that the teething troubles in the administration of universal elementary education were not resolved until an act in 1880 stipulated that school boards and attendance committees were to pass by-laws rendering school attendance compulsory and a further act in 1891, by deftly sidestepping the issue of school fees, provided grants to encourage the spread of free schools. Once local education authorities had made the compulsory education law reality by scouring out the deprived children from the slums in the 1880s and 1890s, it was realized by responsible opinion that this action would be futile unless the special medical and material needs of the children from the poorest class, then called the 'submerged tenth', could be attended to. A. J. Mundella, the Liberal minister of education, told the Commons in 1883 that 'anyone who takes up Mr Marchant Williams' Report [on the schools of London] and who will visit the schools in Whitechapel, Finsbury, Marylebone, Walworth or Bethnal Green, will be somewhat astonished at the wretched character of the surroundings of the children, and the wretchedly fed children who are to be found in these schools'. So too, Samuel Smith MP demanded in Parliament that necessitous children should be fed and that there should be medical inspection of children in schools; and although Dr Crichton-Browne, having been deputed by the minister of education to sift the evidence, concurred that there should be a periodical weighing and measuring of children, his report was received with derision.[2]

On the Continent, where likewise elementary schools were absorbing children from the slums, opinion both in regard to medical inspection and school dinners, particularly in the 1890s and the early years of the twentieth century, moved ahead of Britain. Between 1849 and 1882 Paris was covered by a network of *caisses des écoles*, bodies similar in function to the later English care committees, which with the assistance of a swelling municipal subvention were able to provide food and clothing for necessitous children; in one district of the city suppers were served to poor children and the children of widows. Towards the close of the century many French municipalities earmarked grants to voluntary societies giving meals to children, so that by 1909 it was reckoned that these *cantines scolaires* existed throughout the length and breadth of the land, mostly dependent on public support for their wherewithal. Holland was the first country to enact that municipalities were to supply shortages of food and clothing found among children by raising the necessary funds from the rates.[3] Brussels appointed its first school doctor in 1874, Paris in 1879 and Antwerp in 1882. Between 1873 and 1899 Austria, Sweden, France, Hungary, Norway, Switzerland, Japan and Russia instituted a system of medical inspection in their schools. While in the United States and Germany it was a matter left to the local organization in the different states, the Prussian government in 1900 demanded the inspection of all schoolchildren on the model of the Wiesbaden system inaugurated in 1896, under which there was a shift of emphasis away from a concern for the heating, ventilation and sanitary arrangements of the schools and onto the health of the child.[4]

In Britain the more enterprising Poor Law authorities were already supporting services for the children under their care which were in advance of the provision to be found in the state primary schools. In 1902 Dr Milson Rhodes declared that there was a time when the army had rejected children from the South Manchester Chorlton Union, but

> They did not like this, so they took means to prevent it, with the result that he did not remember for years a child being refused by the Army ... This proved that if they gave the children the proper environment and proper feeding they could be educated. If their teeth were bad a dentist must be secured to give them proper attention, and in after-life it would pay them, because these children would grow up healthy.[5]

In fact, a small number of other unions including Bradford, Merthyr and Lambeth also provided dental treatment to conserve their children's teeth. The Webbs in their Minority Report praised the excellent standards attained in the scattered homes, where 'the food, clothing, and housing are always adequate ... [and] regular medical inspection is provided for'. The London Metropolitan Asylums Board opened centres for treating Poor Law children suffering from ophthalmia at Swanley in 1903 and Brentwood in 1904, each institution housing 360 children in thirty cottages. Elsewhere the minor diseases of childhood were sometimes treated in special reception centres prior to the children being admitted into the home for a lengthy stay; sometimes they were treated in workhouse infirmaries, where ophthalmia cases were isolated and ringworm was cured by the usual x-ray treatment.[6]

Perhaps an even more significant model for progressive opinion in England was provided by the forty-four reformatory schools and the 145 industrial schools with 25,522 children at the end of 1912, while there were an additional 3,131 children enrolled in some twenty industrial day schools. Children from the worst slum areas were educated and fed for five and a half days a week in the day industrial schools, which the Physical Deterioration Committee suggested could be increased as an alternative to making new arrangements for school dinners in the elementary schools to stamp out underfeeding. One educational expert commented:

> On admission they are much below the average size and weight of children who are more fortunate in their upbringing, frequently emaciated, rickety, scrofulous, or tubercular. They have been underfed or improperly fed since birth.[7]

Nevertheless, the children soon recovered their deficiency in weight, though they stubbornly refused to grow any faster. Recounting his experiences of these schools, another observer in 1913 remarked:

> The Reformatory and Industrial Schools – certainly those I visited – are in advance, in the way of medical inspection and dental treatment, of the Ordinary Elementary Schools of this country, because it is only quite lately that we have had Medical Inspection of Children.[8]

At the best schools there was some form of periodic medical inspection, as exemplified by the practice of one school where 'every child is seen by the doctor weekly, he is stripped before him fortnightly and examined quarterly'. Moreover, at other schools 'the eyes and ears are periodically examined, and any necessary treatment provided … considerable advance has been made, at the instigation of the Home Office, in the provision of facilities for dental inspection and treatment, and most of these schools have the advantage of the services of a dentist.'[9]

Particularly doctors with a public health orientation voiced dissatisfaction with the prevailing methods of medical treatment for the working class. 'School inspection was to become a lively topic in the nineties', Jeannne L. Brand discovered, 'and some medical officers of health commented that they increasingly were carrying out personal inspections of schoolchildren on a regular basis, sometimes in the schools, sometimes even house-to-house.' In May 1898 the Metropolitan branch of the Society of Medical Officers of Health drew up a memorandum to the London School Board, urging the board to cooperate with medical officers in preventing the spread of infectious disease in the schools.[10] John F. Sykes, the MOH for St Pancras, declared in 1902 that

> The diseases –chickenpox, measles, whooping cough, mumps, the symptomatic ailments, sore throat, cough, and diarrhoea, and the affections, ophthalmia, ringworm and itch together with body vermin, form a large group of diseases and ailments that require much more serious attention devoted to them than they have hitherto received at the counsels of sanitary authorities not only for the purpose of protecting schools, but also for the purpose of assisting families of the poor whose children are often in sad plights to rid themselves of these complaints.[11]

To rectify these matters, he asserted that teachers should be able to send ailing children for examination and that isolation wards for communicable diseases of children not admitted to hospital should be opened. Arthur Newsholme, who was to be appointed chief medical officer to the Local Government Board in 1908, and C. C. Pakes wrote in their textbook *School Hygiene* (1903) that

Parents earning under 30s a week cannot be expected to call in a doctor for what they regard as trifling complaints ... This state of affairs as pointed out by one of us, can only be remedied by having medical aid, to a certain extent, available for the labouring classes gratuitously in every district, without any implications of pauperism involved in securing its advantages ... This will involve a State Department of medical aid for free diagnosis, if not treatment, in the first instance, at least.[12]

They recommended that a start should be made by instituting a medical examination of every scholar entering and leaving the infant school for the upper school.

As far as restrictions on juvenile employment were concerned, the Inter-Departmental Committee on the Employment of School Children (1902) advised that whereas occupations dangerous to health and morals should be closed to the employment of children, they should be required to furnish medical certificates as a general condition of employment under local by-laws, thereby equating their position to that of the children examined by factory surgeons; and it is no less noteworthy that persons who were to testify before the famous Physical Deterioration Committee which reported in 1904, for example Dr Eichholz and Thomas Macnamara, agreed with their civil service questioners as to the necessity of medical inspection in schools. Dr Eichholz testified that 'if the medical officer went round the schools and certified a child as obviously ill in health he ought to be excluded from further employment out of school', and agreed that his proposal would result in a medical man being engaged by every local authority. 'Personally I should be prepared to adopt a scheme for the medical examination of all children under all circumstances', Thomas Macnamara told his interlocutor. Further, in July 1902 the Third International Congress for the Welfare and Protection of Children meeting in London passed a twofold resolution, affirming that there should be a systematic weighing and measuring of children in school and that all education authorities should impose measures to secure 'the proper medical supervision of all children'.[13]

If there is any substance in the view that the school health movement was merely due to an interest in the children of the nation because of their potential as military manpower, we would expect conservative philanthropists and imperialists or Liberal imperialists such as Asquith, Haldane or Grey to be in the forefront of this movement. But this was not the case: no middle party under Rosebery's leadership ever materialized. The Fabians' nudging of this chimerical party onto the paths of social reform signified little, as the Fabians evinced a lack of interest in the sponsorship of such measures as medical inspection, despite a plea for school nurses in an 1894 pamphlet, or a school medical service for the betterment of child health. Not only was there no mention of medical inspection in Sidney Webb's famous tract in 1901 which charted the course for the party of national efficiency, but since Graham Wallas' adverse report in 1896 on school dinners for the poor in London the society had come to regard the policy as somewhat futile. Only through Shaw's insistence and Dr Sykes' invaluable help was half a page inserted on the work of a school medical officer in a Fabian pamphlet on the Education Act in 1903, yet Shaw had to battle to overcome the deeply ingrained prejudices of his colleagues, 'who are disposed to pooh-pooh any suggestion of the kind on the ground that there is no work for a M.O. to do in schools except to say that the light comes in at the proper angle'.[14]

In December 1901 the young Winston Churchill wrote:

> I have lately been reading a book by Rowntree called 'Poverty' ... It is quite evident from the figures which he adduces that the American labourer is a stronger, larger, healthier, better fed, and consequently more efficient animal than a large portion of our population, and this is surely a fact which our unbridled imperialists, should not lose sight of.[15]

Close scrutiny of two service journals, the *Army and Navy Gazette* and *The Broad Arrow. The Naval and Military Gazette*, for the years 1904–6 reveals little interest in the Inter-Departmental Committee's Report on Physical Deterioration and no comment on medical inspection of schools, apart from a regular insistence on the 'importance of physical training, and training and drill with arms up to the eighteenth year'. Of the Conservative political weeklies and monthlies, almost alone Maxse's extremist anti-German journal, the *National Review*, solidly supported a state meals service, though its references to medical inspection and school dinners were so sparse that they can hardly have been of more than marginal significance in the success of the two campaigns.[16] True that Haldane was the only Liberal prominent imperialist associated with the National League for Physical Education, yet even here his role was passive and his passionate interest in politics was reserved for the foundation of new provincial universities and the promotion of science and technology, particularly the establishment of Imperial College, so that Britain could keep pace with surging American and German competition. Again, Bentley Gilbert's point about social reformers adopting the argument of national efficiency when demanding measures to protect the schoolchild's health can easily be countered by the suggestion that they were angling their propaganda to attract Conservative opinion while the Balfour Parliament was in being.

Alone Margaret McMillan and her sister Rachel had been devising their own plans. In the opinion of Margaret, who had been elected as an Independent Labour Party representative on the Bradford School Board in 1894, where she worked closely with Dr James Kerr, the second elementary school doctor to be appointed in the country,

> The School Clinic is the embodiment of a movement which has gone on ceaselessly in England since the early nineties ... A sub-committee of the Bradford School Board was formed in 1895. The members of this small Committee made investigations, through its attendance officers and others, which left them in no doubt that a considerable proportion of school children were verminous, diseased, afflicted with many kinds of physical defect and ailment, and yet all was disregarded – or, if observed at all, taken as a matter of course ... Leaflets were printed which gave no offence, and school baths were built. Breathing exercises were introduced, and a teacher of voice production was installed at the pupil's centre ... There was no treatment whatsoever for the ailing ... The voice trainer resigned and no successor was appointed. The baths were handed over to County Councillors, who put in attendants to do the work instead of teachers. In short, the movement, to all intents and purposes, failed.[17]

When the sisters settled in Kent in 1902, they decided that Rachel's plan for school health centres was too far ahead of public opinion and that it would be easier to push Margaret's scheme to further remedial treatment, which would cover school baths, singing and speech training. Morant, the permanent secretary of the Board of Education, had Margaret's plan printed and circulated among his inspectors, but no school board or section of the press would take up the scheme. Instead the McMillan sisters were later drawn into the doctors' campaign for medical inspection in schools. Margaret was invited to speak at a big conference. She sadly recalled: 'The public received [the plans] coldly. The public was ice-cold.'[18] Even the Labour movement outside Bradford could not be stirred to trouble itself with the matter. So much for the bracing impact of the Physical Deterioration Report on public opinion.

Just as the economic depression in the winter of 1904–5 forced the Labour movement to demand that the state should make provision for unemployment, so in turn it led them and other progressive allies to question the validity of voluntary effort in the provision of school meals. With a series of good years between 1895 and 1902, the Fabians and their radical allies had a dwindling interest in the question until 1905. Not so the Social Democratic Federation (SDF), which sent memorials to the London School Board in 1892, 1896 and 1899, demanding that children of unemployed parents should be fed, without being able to carry a majority of the school board in the critical debate of 1899. This was because the brisk demand for labour deprived them of a mass following in the streets, which would have administered the necessary jolt to secure reform. Both socialists and Liberal progressives regarded the provision of free dinners for children as a crucial means of tiding the unemployed over a period of distress. When tendering evidence to the Select Committee on School Meals in 1906, Canon Moore Ede explained that his school board had arranged for the supply of dinners in the poorer parts of Gateshead in 1884, a year of bad trade, and that the school meals fund was revived again and again in periods of trade depression. So too, G. P. Gooch, a Liberal MP, when discussing various remedies for alleviating unemployment in 1906 advocated a 'resolute grappling with the problem of physical deterioration of the town child by better safeguarding the life of the child before and after birth, by medical examination on entering school and supervision throughout school life, and by some coherent policy as to the feeding of necessitous children'.[19]

In 1905 voluntary societies were providing meals for schoolchildren in fifty-five out of seventy-one county boroughs, in thirty-eight out of 137 boroughs, and in twenty-two out of fifty-five urban districts, but there were few of them in county council areas. Nor were dinners made available on a regular basis throughout the year or generally for five days a week.[20] Bradford provided a good example of the stirring of opinion at the local level. There the teachers forced the town council to appoint a sub-committee to investigate the situation; it revealed that there were 2,574 cases of underfed children and that 329 had attended school without breakfast. During the local council elections in 1904, the Bradford Independent Labour Party (ILP) campaigned on the issue of one free meal a day at each school for pupils. Frederick Jowett showed that of 166 children who went to school without breakfast, in sixty-eight cases the father was unemployed, in fifty-two cases he was on short time and inadequately paid, and in forty-six cases there was no male breadwinner. Between 1 September 1905 and 23 March 1906 the

Bradford guardians working in cooperation with the education authority provided 101,932 meals. Moreover, a paper prepared for Jowett showed that in forty-nine cases in which the guardians had sued parents for the recovery of the costs of meals, the average family income per head only amounted to 2s. 7³/₄d, whereas the Rowntree minimum scale required an average of at least 4s. 3¹/₄d. per head.[21]

At the national level Sir John Gorst MP, who had been vice-president of the Board of Education in the Salisbury government, and Dr Thomas Macnamara MP (1861–1931), one of the leaders of the National Union of Teachers, led a public campaign for the provision of school meals for necessitous children. Their first success was a favourable attitude which the Inter-Departmental Committee on Physical Deterioration evinced towards their proposal; it observed that while in many places the proper organization of voluntary effort would suffice, in others where poverty was too great there would have to be municipal aid. This was followed up by holding a National Labour Conference on 20 January 1905 with the aim of clarifying the fact that the Labour movement and teachers now supported the feeding of necessitous children by some municipal agency other than the Board of Guardians. The principal resolution promoted by the Social Democratic Federation (SDF) demanded the 'State Maintenance of Children as a necessary corollary of Universal Compulsory Education, and as a means of partially arresting that physical deterioration of the industrial population'. Will Thorne argued that all children in all schools should be fed. Dr Macnamara, a progressive Liberal MP, claiming that such a resolution would never be assented to by Parliament, called on the government to implement the recommendations of the Inter-Departmental Committee report, by allowing local authorities to provide meals for children who were unfit through under-nourishment; they were, however, to recover the cost from parents or guardians. Although Macnamara was supported by the president of the NUT, his amendment was lost by a large majority, but there was general agreement that the school meals service should be publicly funded. Afterwards Gorst and Dr Macnamara, the leaders of the national campaign for the provision of school meals, toured the chief industrial centres of the country in association with trade union leaders and socialists, including Will Thorne, J. R. Clynes and the Countess of Warwick, to publicize their case.[22]

Throughout 1905 the leaders of both the Conservative and Liberal parties remained obdurate, unrepentant and unconverted. The government appointed the Inter-Departmental Committee on Medical Inspection and School Feeding to divert pressure, by promising to increase the efficiency of the voluntary feeding agencies. On two occasions in 1905 when the matter was prominently debated in the Commons, the Liberal front bench absented itself – that is, on 27 March and 18 April. So long as the leaders of the two principal parties were unhelpful, it was of little use trying to push private members' bills through Parliament. Instead Arthur Henderson and Claude Hay agreed to withdraw their bills to allow Bamford Slack to introduce a resolution in the Commons which would indicate whether there was any change of opinion of late. Despite the fact that William Anson, the parliamentary secretary to the Board of Education, spoke against the resolution, it was passed by 100–64 votes. Claude Hay remarked in his speech that only the Conservative and opposition backbenchers had shown any real interest in the question. According to the terms of the resolution the local authorities were to be responsible for administering the school meals service, but the concession that Boards of Guardians were to recover the cost from parents who could not afford to pay still kept the new service partially harnessed to the Poor Law system.[23]

On the other hand, so long as the government was unwilling to move in the matter, it was worthwhile for the campaigners to scrounge what they could out of the Poor Law; moreover, should the Poor Law authorities not show much positive response, then it could be argued that they were not the requisite authority for coping with the problem and their bluff would have been called. Hence on 15 March 1905 there followed a surprise visit of Gorst, Macnamara, Dr Robert Hutchinson, a physician in the Great Ormond Street Hospital and others to the Johanna Street School in Lambeth as part of the ongoing campaign. Dr Hutchinson picked out twenty underfed boys and the party then proceeded to the Lambeth Board of Guardians to demand that these pupils should be fed immediately. When the case was brought to the attention of the Commons, the president of the Local Government Board declared that the children of the school were entitled to immediate relief irrespective of the conduct of their parents. Circulars were issued by the Local Government Board and the Board of Education in April calling attention to the rights of hungry children and directing teachers to take steps to enforce these rights. Unfortunately there was little cooperation between the teachers and the Boards of Guardians, so that apart from exceptional authorities, such as Bradford, the order was disregarded. Further, the officials of the two departments disliked the issue of the circulars and did nothing to ensure that they were implemented.[24]

The example of the municipal feeding of necessitous children, as practised in France or Holland, did not have much impact on Britain. There was no winning over of conservative philanthropic opinion to free feeding through the interchange of ideas, as happened in the case of infant mortality, school medical inspection and special children's courts. The papers read before a conference in 1906 convened by the British section of the International Congress for the Welfare and Protection of Children on the feeding of schoolchildren was conservative in tone and still refrained from recommending provision from public funds. True enough, when the matter was thrown open to general discussion, opinion was divided on this issue. This is just what we should expect, for it was natural that advanced reformers would support public provision; but the important point is that philanthropic opinion outside progressive circles remained unconvinced of the need for change. Sir Charles Eliott, the chairman of the Joint Committee for Underfed Children in London, asserted that when children thought by various school authorities to be necessitous had been examined by relieving officers employed by local Boards of Guardians, it had been found that three-quarters of the children were not under-nourished. Of course, there was a good deal of temporary pinching and insufficiency, especially in the winter months when employment was slack, but the voluntary agencies and charitable funds could quite competently deal with this.[25]

That the Poor Law could not be exploited sufficiently to provide food for necessitous children convinced the Labour party to introduce their own bill, setting up a new service under the local authority. Although the Marxist SDF had brought the issue of the state maintenance of children, both as to their nutrition and medical care, to the notice of trade councils and the TUC, the comprehensive nature of such a scheme made it unpalatable to the Labour politicians. They turned instead to the more politically feasible policy of a measure that would deal with 'the single issue of feeding schoolchildren'. Having received instructions from the Labour Representation Committee, the forerunner of the party, to promote a bill, Arthur Henderson introduced the Education (Provision of Meals) Bill on 29 March 1905, but it was not proceeded with. At the start of the 1906 session William T. Wilson, a newly elected Labour MP, tried again, and was able to introduce a private member's bill for the feeding of schoolchildren by local authorities. This was a new Parliament in changed circumstances with a Liberal government, many of whose backbenchers were associated with the New Liberalism, and with a much larger Labour contingent.[26] Sir William Anson for the Conservative front bench wanted a measure 'which would have enabled local authorities to provide meals subject to payment and boards of guardians to deal with necessitous cases'. Reluctantly the government agreed to allot parliamentary time for the bill referring it for further consideration to a select committee. Here it encountered widespread hostility from Conservative philanthropic opinion. The County Councils Association, a body dominated by stalwarts of county society and the scions of the gentry, refused to submit evidence to the select committee, declaring that even if state feeding was desirable, it was not practical except in large towns. As was to be expected, the Charity Organisation Society campaigned against the bill, but the opposition of the Society for the Prevention of Cruelty to Children was no less vehement. Its annual report for 1904–5 glibly commented that politicians were beginning to take an interest in the question of underfed children. Responsibility for the feeding of schoolchildren rested on parents and not on the school authorities or ratepayers, and it must be enforced on parents from the time of a child's birth. It crowned these words by giving evidence against the bill to the select committee. The Poor Law Unions Association regarded the bill as a bitter affront, for on no account was relief to be given to the destitute by a body other than the Board of Guardians. The president of the association tendered evidence against the bill before the select committee, while 108 Boards of Guardians urged their local MPs to oppose the bill in response to a circular from the executive.[27]

Not only did the select committee make the bill discretionary but in the recommendation to their report, they suggested that 'only in extreme and exceptional cases' was the local authority to contribute towards the cost of the food, and then only a maximum rate of $^1/_2$d. in the pound was to be levied. Further, Jackman, the president of the NUT, in his evidence stressed that teachers strongly favoured the recovery of the cost from those who could afford to pay. The select committee had intended that the Society for the Prevention of Cruelty to Children and the Boards of Guardians should recover the cost of the meals from the parents who could afford to pay for the local education and canteen committees, so that the new service would not become divorced from the Poor Law system. The Labour party, and Ramsay MacDonald in particular, stressed that the school meals service was only to be provided for those in need, and was to be utilized to bolster the family.[28] Unintentionally through the resistance of the Boards of Guardians themselves, the last remaining link between this new service and the Poor Law was severed. For the Boards of Guardians maintained that the proposal that when the parent failed to pay for the cost of the meal supplied to his child, the local education authority was to require the payment of the amount by the local Board of Guardians, who were to pay for it and to recover the cost where possible from the parents, was bad: for where Boards of Guardians recovered the money, the education authorities would recover twice over the cost of the meal. Hence the Poor Law Unions Association compelled the parliamentary secretary to the Board of Education to agree on the report stage of the bill that the debts incurred by parents for the meals should be recovered by the local education authorities, not by the Boards of Guardians.[29]

The Education (Provision of Meals) Act 1906 was a limited measure that permitted local authorities to provide meals for children attending elementary schools by associating themselves with canteen committees, which were to provide the food, and assist such committees by the provision of buildings, furniture and apparatus for the preparation of meals. If the voluntary contributions to defray the cost of food were insufficient, the education authorities were allowed to levy a rate for the purpose which was not to exceed $^1/_2$d. in the pound. It was also stipulated on the insistence of the Labour party that parents who failed to pay for the meals were not to be disenfranchised or to be deprived of their civil rights and privileges, while the debt was to be treated as a civil one. The act was one of the first material rewards of the tacit alliance between Labour and the New Liberalism.

The campaign for medical inspection in schools sprang from three separate sources: General Frederick Maurice, the McMillan sisters and Sir Lauder Brunton, who was indisputably the leader of the movement. Already in 1902 informal soundings were made among doctors by Sir Lauder Brunton (1884–1916), a consultant at St Bartholomew's famous for his researches on drug use, to form a league to coordinate the work of agencies concerned with the advancement of physical education and health. A draft scheme was prepared, but the formation of the league was delayed by the death of Lord Frankfort and Brunton's own ill health. In a letter to the *Lancet* in February 1903 Brunton called for the appointment of a government commission with the aid of the Royal Colleges of Physicians and Surgeons 'to inquire into the causes of physical deterioration of the people of this country as shown in recruiting statistics'. He went on to claim that the unfitness of recruits was not only 'serious because it prevents us from getting the number of soldiers we need when an emergency arises, it is serious also from the civil standpoint, for if men are unfit for military service what are they good for?' In 1903 Brunton became chairman of the English committee in connection with the First International Congress for School Hygiene held in Nuremberg in April 1904, and if he had sufficiently grasped the necessity for school meals to be provided cheaply or free, no doubt from this time arose a ripening of his interest in medical inspection.[30] General Frederick Maurice was the son of Frederick Dennison Maurice, the distinguished Christian Socialist. His mother having died when he was young, he was much into the company of his father and the band of Christian socialists around him, such as J. M. Ludlow, Thomas Hughes and Lewellyn Davies, absorbing their principles and ideals; 'though his life was to be spent in spheres of activity very different from theirs', his son wrote in his short memoir, 'his natural versatility enabled him to apply these principles readily to other conditions'. With the support of Sir William Taylor, the director-general of the army medical service, and Sir Lauder Brunton, who had been engaged in a similar campaign for some time, he interested Broderick, the minister for war, the Duke of Devonshire and Balfour in the problem, and a result of their combined efforts was the appointment of the Physical Deterioration Committee in September 1903. 'Both Sir William Taylor and Maurice had maintained that the medical returns for the army supplied evidence that there existed at the time a considerable stratum of the population which was physically inefficient, and that this inefficiency was due to remediable causes'.[31]

True that Maurice and Brunton joined forces in the National League for Physical Education and Improvement which held its inaugural public meeting on 28 June 1905, though its inception may be traced back to a gathering of medical men and others assembled by Brunton at the Athenaeum in July 1903; and the short study of Maurice makes it abundantly clear that he was absorbed into a fighting movement created virtually single-handedly by Brunton in the years 1902-5, who must rank as a *Great Disseminator* of the idea of school medical inspection. Around the inner core of the league consisting of medical men, including both leading medical officers of health such as Newman, Newsholme, Sykes and James Niven, and outstanding representatives of the Royal Colleges of Physicians and Surgeons, such as John Tweedy, president of the Royal College of Surgeons, William Osler, Professor of Medicine at Oxford, and Howard Marsh, Professor of Surgery at Cambridge and president of the Medical Officers of Schools Association, were a host of establishment figures drawn from the clergy, the law, the press, educational institutions and the aristocracy, plus well-known social reformers like Mrs Humphrey Ward, May Tennant and Dr Thomas Macnamara associated with the New Liberalism. Among the objectives of the league 'were the physical condition of the people, the need of medical inspection of children in elementary schools, the desirability of increasing the opportunities of gymnastic exercises, of forming cadet corps', and it was no doubt the prominence given to the latter aims that lured in conservative reformers rather than any newly awakened interest that they possessed for medical inspection in schools.[32] When he had finished giving evidence to the Royal Commission on the Poor Laws, Newman had a conversation with its chairman, Lord George Hamilton, who was also on the council of the league, which he recorded in his diary:

> I hope I converted him to interest in medl. Inspection. He advocated compulsory military service as a means of improving physically and morally the rising generation. I urged medl. inspection, & physical training. [33]

Nor was Augustine Birrell, the Liberal minister of education, who was under the influence of his departmental officials, any more receptive to the campaign for medical inspection, and only the doggedness of the campaigners, which ignited a backbench revolt, forced the government to change its attitude. In a briefing paper a civil servant warned Birrell that if only medical inspection was being demanded this could 'be arranged at no very great cost by the Local Authority', but if treatment was also to be undertaken, by providing medicines, 'spectacles, crutches and similar apparatus' then 'the cost would ... be a very serious matter'. At an interview with Birrell on 27 February

1906, the National League for Physical Education and Improvement headed by Sir Lauder Brunton asked for the compulsory medical inspection of children in schools. Birrell sympathized with the objects of the league but proceeded to prevaricate by asserting that the government could take no action in advance of public opinion, although when the league had sufficiently enlisted public support Parliament might act. He also rejected the league's suggestion of the formation of 'a Central Advisory Committee of medical men' to assist the Board of Education, thereby ensuring that there was uniformity in the methods of inspection throughout the country. Accepting Birrell's challenge, the league embarked on a furious, whirlwind campaign to whip up public sympathy. *The Times* lent its support in a leading article in response to letters from the chairman of the league and Professor Marsh, who was connected with the School Medical Officers Association; a host of kindred associations were prodded into activity, such as the Medical Committee for Promoting Hygiene and Health, the British Medical Association, teachers organizations, and the Society of Medical Officers of Health, all of whom shaped the league's thinking on the question of medical inspection.[34]

As part of a coordinated assault on the government, a hastily arranged deputation of the BMA and the Manchester and Salford Sanitary Association was sent to Birrell on 16 July 1906. It was introduced by Jack Tennant MP, the husband of May Tennant, the prominent factory inspector, who had persuaded her husband to become a social reformer. May Tennant sat on the council of the National League for Physical Education and Improvement. Jack Tennant pressed the minister to convert the government's clause for the voluntary medical inspection of schoolchildren into a compulsory one. T. C. Horsfall, the Manchester philanthropist, stated that the question of medical inspection was one that 'concerns not only the health and happiness of the children but also the industries and commerce of the country to a serious degree. We know that in our towns and in our country villages we have a large proportion of diseased children.' He drew attention to the advances which had been made overseas and cited evidence from Sweden and Denmark to show that after a medical examination, 30 per cent of the children were found to be sickly when they entered school. Through these investigations the town of Wiesbaden adopted a model system of medical inspection in 1896, which the majority of towns in Germany with a population of over 20,000 copied. He concluded by saying that inquiries in St Louis, Vienna and Berlin had established that children of twelve who 'possess the most mental ability, are found to be on average, much taller and much heavier than the children of the same age who have remained in lower classes'. Sir Victor Horsley on behalf of the doctors urged Birrell to extend the German system of inspection of a child when entering school and to set up a medical bureau within his department, staffed by a medical official with two assistants. Faced by a powerful deputation, Birrell concluded by saying that '[m]uch would depend on the course the debate took, but as at present advised, he could not say it would be a good step to make the duty obligatory on every local authority'. However, he promised to add another doctor to the Board's staff.[35]

Bentley Gilbert put forward the theory that the introduction of the school medical service aroused little controversy because it was concealed 'among more than a dozen other clauses dealing with uninteresting ... details of ... school administration', and that Sir Robert Morant, the permanent secretary of the Board of Education, at the beginning of 1907 'devised a form of words which left the door open for medical treatment, while only referring to medical inspection'. This account has been shown by a number of historians to be seriously flawed. As originally drafted, the 1906 Education Bill contained a clause allowing local education authorities 'to make such arrangements as may be sanctioned by the Board of Education for attending to the health and physical condition of the children educated in public elementary schools'. On 16 July 1906 Jack Tennant, a backbench MP, moved an amendment to the bill, probably on behalf of the National League for Physical Education and Improvement and the BMA, making it 'the duty of every local education authority to make arrangements, in accordance with the scheme to be made by the Board of Education, for attending to the health and physical condition of children in public elementary schools'.[36] He also pressed the government to agree to the establishment of a small medical department within the Board of Education to supervise the medical inspection of children in line with Sir Victor Horsley's recommendation. Every MP was circularized and as many MPs as possible were interviewed on this point by the league to make medical inspection compulsory. Moreover, the prolonged preparatory lobbying of Birrell and his PPS Illingworth by the McMillan sisters softened the minister's opposition and made him more susceptible to backbench wiles. Under pressure from progressive Liberal MPs such as Charles Masterman, Percy Alden, Thomas Macnamara and some Tories across the floor of the House, Birrell conceded the principle of compulsory medical inspection, though he reserved the right to frame the clause with his own wording. Morant questioned his minister's judgement, suggesting that the Board of Education was not ready for such a scheme. Both Masterman and Alden were familiar with the condition of deprived children in the slums, having been settlement residents, and Dr Macnamara was an outstanding educational reformer. According to N. D. Daglish,

> [what comes across] from the debates in the Commons, the educational press, and the correspondence in the Board of Education files is evidence of a widespread feeling that treatment was accepted as a component of medical inspection. The first requisite, however, was the creation of a compulsory national system of [medical inspection].[37]

Tennant made it clear in the course of the debate that his amendment did not 'intend to include treatment as well as inspection'. He did not envisage that the school doctors would enter 'the children's homes; but it was quite possible that they or the nurses could follow up the cases'. Alden praised the example of America, where trained nurses assisted the school doctors, which was much less costly.[38]

On 25 July 1906 Birrell introduced the government's amended clause dealing with medical inspection which went somewhat further than the original clause. It stated:

> [T]he powers and duties of a Local Education Authority ... shall include ... the duty to provide for the medical inspection of children before or at the time of their admission to a Public Elementary school, and on such occasions as the Board of Education direct, and the power to make such arrangements as may be sanctioned

by the Board of Education for attending to the health and physical condition of the children educated in Public Elementary Schools'.[39]

When the government's Education Bill was defeated in the House of Lords, the provision for medical inspection lapsed, but a clause was introduced in a new measure in the following year. In the House of Lords, the Bishop of Ripon, the chairman of the executive of the league, later proposed additional changes to the government clause, including the suggestion that children should be medically inspected on leaving school as well as entering it; that it should be made obligatory on local authorities to make arrangements for 'supervising the health and physical condition of children' in public elementary schools as agreed by the Board of Education; and in this way local medical practitioners would be protected by limiting the scope of the medical treatment to be provided. These amendments were rejected by the government.[40]

The government brought in the Education (Administrative Provisions) Bill in February 1907, which instituted compulsory medical inspection and made tentative provision for treatment. This was in response to a private member's bill with similar wording sponsored by a Liberal MP, Walter Russell Rea. Fearing that Rea would accept amendments that did not reflect its thinking, the government asked him to withdraw his bill and introduced their own measure which became law on 27 August 1907.[41] Historians have focused on isolated episodes in the specific campaigns for the medical inspection of schoolchildren and the provision of school meals for necessitous children rather than treating each one as a sustained campaign that lasted for a number of years. The movement for medical inspection depended on the political pressure of doctors led by Sir Lauder Brunton of the National League for Physical Education and Improvement and the McMillan sisters with their ties to the ILP. At its height, the opposition of conservative philanthropic opinion was neutralized, so making it easier for campaigners to wring concessions out of a Liberal administration which was far from enthusiastic. True that Sir Frederick Maurice was a military man and that Jack Tennant was associated with the Liberal Imperialist wing of the party, but both men through close family ties were ardent social reformers and this is how they should be viewed in these years. Sir John Gorst was a Tory reformer, but in 1903 he decided to sit as an independent MP because of tariff reform and the reluctance of his party's leaders to espouse the cause of social reform, and in 1910 he stood unsuccessfully as a Liberal. Despite the contention of G. R. Searle that the school medical service and 'subsidized school meals for poor children' was 'the institutionalized legacy of the anxieties felt in the Boer War period', the evidence for this is thin, as little support was received from military circles and conservative philanthropists.[42] Rather they should be viewed as a response both to coping with children in the slums, who were enrolled in primary schools from the 1880s, and to the need to keep up with the overseas innovations in social services for children. The campaign for school meals was headed by Sir John Gorst, Dr Thomas Macnamara and the Countess of Warwick, but more important was the priority given to this measure by the Labour MPs in the 1906 Parliament, aided as they were by the interventions of the new band of Liberal MPs, such as Percy Alden and Charles Masterman, with experience of living in close contact with the poor in the settlement houses and Dr Thomas Macnamara's experience in teaching in schools in a socially deprived area of Bristol. Here in the 1890s out of 250 boys, he discovered that 'especially in mid-winter, at least fifty of the poorest boys were daily ill-fed and suffering from malnutrition and twenty-five were absolutely hungry'. Charitable donations fluctuated and appeals were only effective in mid-winter. Credit for the medical inspection and treatment of children in schools should go to the National League and to Reginald McKenna, the new minister of education and less certainly to Dr George Newman, who was only appointed as chief medical officer of the department in August 1907.[43] Particularly on the issues of free school meals, old age pensions, and unemployment the Labour MPs were increasingly setting the political agenda in Parliament and the country generally.

## Sources of Child Welfare Reform

The child welfare movement must be seen as one facet of that wider movement, that almost mysterious transmutation of feeling, which demanded a new deal for the aged and unemployed. 'It is certain that in a few years', predicted the *Municipal Journal* in 1903, 'radical reform, perhaps carrying with it the abolition of workhouses, will have to be made in the Poor Law administration ... Public opinion is rapidly developing towards the point when the care of the poor, and not merely the destitute, will be looked upon as a national duty, when the existence of hungry and ill-housed people will be regarded as casting a reflection upon the national honour.' Secondly, the late nineteenth century saw a renewed parental and public interest in children and an increasing state concern for their welfare, so that the legislation of the Liberals was a natural extension of the legislative efforts of the Unionist governments of 1895–1905. Among the landmarks of Unionist rule were the 1899 Education of Defective and Epileptic Children Act, the limitations placed on child labour in the factories and mines in the 1890s, the 1903 act limiting the employment of children outside school hours, and the Midwives Act of 1902. According to José Harris, the Edwardian age had an 'enhanced sense of the child' and childhood was now seen as a separate stage in life with 'its own generic modes of behaviour and perception'. By the 1890s it was no longer becoming fashionable among middle class families to administer corporal punishment to children. Thirdly, many of the welfare activities of the state were carried out in cooperation with voluntary societies or were eagerly campaigned for by these associations. Before the state could extend its sphere of influence, a vital prerequisite was the flourishing of voluntary action. As far as child welfare was concerned, there was already a plethora of societies, as revealed in a list compiled by the British Institute of Social Service in 1907 with the names of fifty-one national organizations. Women through the settlements and voluntary associations carried these new middle-class ideals of childcare into the poorer neighbourhoods, thus eventually changing British society.

Next, if the movement was merely due to an interest in the children of the nation because of their potential as military manpower, how are we to explain the release of energy and interest along so broad a front? This period saw the start of the infant welfare movement, the removal of pauper children from the tentacles of the Poor

Law, the inauguration of a new mode of treatment for the child offender, the extended protection of children and youth in the Children's Act 1908, the revival of apprenticeship and so on. As we have seen, conservative philanthropists were not at the forefront of the movement for reform: Balfour's government made no hurried attempt to implement the recommendations of the Inter-Departmental Committee, nor were the Liberals under Campbell-Bannerman anxious to pass far-reaching measures. The child welfare movement was sustained by support from three principal sources: one was the growing strength of New Liberalism and Labour at the national and local levels, and the resulting campaigns for specific services on the national level and the endless experimentation of progressive local authorities; the third, as we have seen, was the massive entry of women into the public sphere in the late Victorian era and impact of the advances made abroad. The annual report of the Apprenticeship and Skilled Employment Association in 1908 mentioned that '[i]nformation has been sent in reply to inquiries from Paris, where considerable attention is being directed to the question of apprenticeship, and to America on several occasions, showing that other countries are interested in the same problems'. In 1903 the Committee on Wage Earning Children noted that a conference on home work by children had been arranged with the Child Labor Committee of New York, while there had been an active correspondence with Herr Agahd, who organized the successful agitation in Germany. Moreover, the impact was felt through the international congresses at which social workers gathered to read papers, to discuss their new methods, and to ensure that the more advanced states were keeping abreast of each other in regard to recent developments. Examples of these conferences were the International Congress for the Welfare and Protection of Children, the International Congress on School Hygiene, the International Congress on Infant Welfare and the International Congress on Children's Courts. The attendance of many of the most distinguished Poor Law workers at these gatherings resulted in their conversion to the state undertaking fresh welfare services, so that on multifarious issues social workers confronted the government with a solid phalanx in favour of reform. Added to this was the enhanced prestige of the British Medical Association, the Society of Medical Officers of Health and the National Union of Teachers, and the proliferation of pressure groups concerned with child welfare.

## The Juvenile Offender

Again, in the sphere of juvenile delinquency, as in so many of the sectors of child welfare, the impetus which impelled the British government to devise a fresh approach came from abroad. Children's courts were set up in Canada in 1894, in South Australia in 1895 and in New South Wales in 1905. From Canada the idea took root in the United States, where E. Fellowes Jenkins, the secretary of the New York Society for the Prevention of Cruelty to Children, and Mrs Dwight Sheffield promoted the establishment of a network of children's courts with the probationary system as its backbone. Then the new approach crossed the Atlantic: the Parisian municipality inaugurated a probationary system on the American model in 1905, and the authorities then appointed a committee of inquiry to decide whether they should also adopt the idea of children's courts.

Through the medium of the International Congress for the Welfare and Protection of Children, the State Children's Association and the Committee on Wage Earning Children, the idea of children's courts and a probationary service entered the range of practical politics in Britain. One of the resolutions of the International Congress which met in 1902 was that all offenders under sixteen years of age should be tried at a different time to other prisoners; Mrs Dwight Sheffield, then Miss Ada Eliot, also read a paper on the recent developments in the treatment of juvenile delinquency in the United States, though a resolution requesting a system of probation officers for everyone under sixteen years similar to America was rejected by 28–18 votes; and the Inter-Departmental Committee pleaded for the establishment of courts for children with specially selected magistrates. Under the leadership of the Committee on Wage Earning Children various child welfare and penal reform societies decided at a conference in November 1904 that if a new system of children's courts was to function efficiently, probation officers would have to be appointed. By 1906 even the British section of the International Congress for the Welfare and Protection of Children, which was dominated by members of the committee of the Poor Law Conference, agreed that it was desirable to open remand homes and children's courts and that this should be followed up by placing children found in need of care and attention under the supervision of probation officers. Underlying these reforms were two basic axioms: that children should neither come into contact with the prison system with the chance of corruption by adult detainees, nor should they be placed within the confines of the workhouse and be corrupted by degrading influences to be found there.

In the early nineteenth century children were tried and sentenced with adults. Since the mid-nineteenth century, with the setting up of reformatory and industrial schools and the wide discretionary powers conferred on magistrates, children were gradually accorded special treatment and separated from adult prisoners. The reformatory schools housed some 5,000 children, while the industrial schools held some 25,000 juvenile detainees; in the latter category of school were immured children found begging, wandering without means of subsistence, those in the company of criminals. All these institutions were deficient in that they meted out indiscriminately the same treatment for neglected children as for those found guilty of transgressing the law. So too, magistrates could prescribe various sentences for the children arraigned in front of them, from the imposition of small fines, the binding over of the parents and holding them responsible for the future good behaviour of their offspring, the sending of children to industrial and reformatory schools, to ordering them to be whipped: in 1904 2,381 children were birched, but only occasionally were children still committed to prison. In November 1904 the Committee on Wage Earning Children convened a conference, at which representatives of the LCC, the London School Board, the State Children's Association and the Howard League for Penal Reform were present, to modify the law affecting juvenile offenders. The conference resolved that all penal authorities should have to provide remand homes for children, that courts where they were to be tried should be set up in places separate and apart from courts for adults, and that probation officers should be appointed. A petition embodying these proposals was drawn up and sent to the home secretary. To test opinion, local authorities all over the country were circularized as to these proposals, with many municipalities responding favourably. As there was little expectation that the government would initiate reforms of its own accord, the Committee on Wage Earning Children in conjunction with the State Children's Association drafted the Summary Jurisdiction Children's Bill, which Jack Tennant MP – the husband of the noted social reformer May Tennant, who was himself active in child welfare activities – introduced in the Commons in 1905 and again in the following year. The bill stipulated that children should be tried in some place other than an ordinary courtroom; that the Youthful Offenders Act of 1901 should be extended, so that juvenile offenders could be put in a place other than a cell before trial; and following the provisions of the First Offenders Bill of 1887, which was approved by the Commons but vetoed by the Lords, children instead of being sentenced could be placed under the supervision of an official of the court, the court missionary or some society willing to undertake the work of probation. Although the Church of England Temperance Society had developed probationary work for adult offenders, no special attention as yet had been devoted by voluntary societies to children who came before the courts.

At the same time the State Children's Association attempted to stimulate progressive authorities to carry out these reforms by voluntary means. Lord Crewe, the president of the association, sent a letter to every petty sessional court in England and Wales, asking that the magistrates might allow the separate hearing of children's cases; and in 1905 he wrote to all mayors, inviting them to promote children's courts. Both letters attracted satisfactory responses. Altogether forty-one petty sessional authorities and boroughs in England and Wales, including such towns as Manchester, Birmingham, Bradford and Bolton, decided to put aside either special rooms or premises for hearing children's cases. In Scotland the authorities in Glasgow and Greenock instituted special sittings of the courts to hear children's cases, at which probation officers were present. In Birmingham Courtenay Lord, long interested in the problems of juvenile delinquency, was prompted by Lord Crewe's letter to initiate a special court for youthful offenders, where they were handed over to the care of probation officers. In the summer of 1905 a circular regarding the treatment of juvenile delinquents in police courts was issued by the Home Office to metropolitan magistrates and the chairmen of the provincial petty sessions. It suggested that children's courts should be taken first each morning and apart from other business, that children should be kept in a waiting room to which other prisoners should not be admitted, and that they should not be allowed to appear in court either before or after their own case was heard.

The innovations of Herbert Gladstone, when he was placed in charge of the Home Office, together with Herbert Samuel, who served as under-secretary, must be understood with this background in mind. In the first weeks of his tenure of the office, Gladstone received a memorial from the State Children's Association, asking him to take steps to ensure that probation officers were appointed. Thus it was not altogether an unexpected gesture when Gladstone advised Tennant to withdraw the bill he was sponsoring, as the government was preparing its own measure. Having been introduced in December 1906, the Probation of Offenders Bill became law in the next session. It gave courts powers to create probation officers and enabled them to release an offender on probation without proceeding to a conviction; it specified that children were to be released under recognizances, especially framed to meet the salient features of each individual case; it stated that probation officers should be appointed, whose duty it would be to visit offenders at intervals, to befriend the children entrusted to their care and to help them obtain employment, where this was necessary; it permitted special probation officers for children under sixteen years to be appointed.

Nonetheless, the leading child welfare organizations in this field were not satisfied that the government bill went far enough. Among the reforms listed by the Committee on Wage Earning Children in a memorandum to the home secretary were the establishment of children's courts all over the country, the appointment of special children's magistrates in London, and opening of places of detention other than police stations and prisons for children under sixteen years of age on remand. To lend force to this statement of policy, a deputation comprised of the principal child welfare and penal reform associations called on Gladstone on 17 January 1907. By way of reminder, it might be added that even the conservative British section of the Congress for the Welfare and Protection of Children had voiced similar demands when it met in June 1906. Out of this deputation came some of the impetus for the government to amend the whole range of children's legislation; soon the children's organizations were requested to submit their views as to what needed amending. Among other matters the State Children's Association reminded the government of the need to set up children's courts. Most of the recommendations put forward by the child welfare societies were in fact incorporated in the Children's Act 1908. Section 107 outlined eleven methods of dealing with young offenders. No child was to be sent to prison for any offence. No young person – that is, anyone between the ages of fourteen and sixteen years – was to be sentenced to death or penal servitude, whatever the case, or to imprisonment for any offence unless he was too unruly to be committed to a place of detention. Juvenile courts were to be held in a different building or at a different time to the courts for adult offenders; unless he was charged with a joint offence, a juvenile was not to appear in court with an adult. In London one or more separate juvenile courts were to be opened, and the LCC was to set up remand homes. Elsewhere the police authority was to establish remand homes for children. A few words of explanation need to be added about this last matter. In the middle decades of the nineteenth century it had been the custom to remand children under sixteen years awaiting trial in the workhouse. With the improved administration of the Poor Law this was seen to be inadmissible because the juvenile offenders were themselves liable to be corrupted by old inmates or wayward children in the workhouse. In 1895 the London guardians stated that they wished to be relieved of this duty, and as a result in 1897 the Local Government Board empowered the Metropolitan Asylums Board to open remand homes. At the conference of the British section of the International Congress for the Welfare and Protection of Children a resolution was passed against remanding any juvenile offender in the workhouse.

Implemented at a moderate pace, the provisions of the Probation of Offenders Act and the Children's Act did not meet the expectation of the social reformers. So far as the establishment of remand homes was concerned, there was a considerable advance. Of 154 authorities who replied to an inquiry, five admitted that they had set aside separate remand homes, twenty-four utilized accommodation in voluntary institutions, nineteen used houses of police constables, ten entrusted the children to the care of probation officers, nine utilized industrial schools, while fifty-five made use of workhouses and in fourteen other cases mostly arrangements with Boards of Guardians were pending. But a return of 1 July 1912 showed considerable progress, in that only in thirteen unions were children still sent by the courts to workhouses.

Apart from this area of concern, the new methods of dealing with juvenile delinquency only slowly ousted the old procedures. There was a failure to appoint special magistrates to hear children's cases; equally absurd was the retention of the methods and procedure of adult courts for children. So too, only in a minority of cases were the children put on probation: the register of probation officers published by the Home Office in April 1911 indicated that in 285 petty seasonal or borough courts no probation officer was appointed; in some instances the same individual was given control of from eight to twenty-one divisions and the same person acted as probation officer for both adults and children. The criminal statistics for 1911 showed that of 19,974 children and young persons dealt with, only 3,594 were placed on probation. At the suggestion of Mr Paterson of the Committee on Wage Earning Children, a conference of representatives of the LCC, the State Children's Association, the Penal Reform League, the Howard League and the Romilly Society met on 9 October 1912; they appointed a working committee which sent in a report with recommendations for improving the treatment of juvenile offenders to the Home Office in 1913.

## The Children Act

When Mrs M. R. Inglis, a Scottish Reformer, suggested the formation of a Ministry of Child Welfare, this prompted Herbert Samuel to review some twenty-two statutes and reports concerning children and prepare legislation codifying and modernizing the existing law. After the House of Lords had blocked a number of Liberal measures, it was decided to omit any controversial items so as not to imperil the bill. There was a tightening of the law concerning infant life protection. Any child under seven years of age in the care of a person other than a parent for payment of a lump sum or a recurring payment had to be registered within forty-eight hours. Inspectors could visit these homes and remove children who were being ill treated, with fines of £100 or two years' imprisonment being imposed for carers found guilty of such abuse or neglect. Safeguards were inserted in the Act to prevent the overcrowding of places of entertainment, particularly theatres for children, following a tragic accident in Barnsley with many child fatalities. Where the number of children attending such a place of entertainment exceeded 100 and there were stairs, the Act imposed an obligation on the providers of the show to have a sufficient number of attendants on the stairs to prevent more children being admitted than the place could safely accommodate. Fines of £50 were imposed for a first offence; a second offence merited a fine of £100 with the threat of a licence being revoked. Penalties were introduced for anyone over sixteen years of age in charge of a child, who left a child under the age of seven alone in a room without a fire guard, as accidents of this nature caused 1,600 deaths every year and many injuries, and for drunken adults, who accidentally when asleep suffocated a child under the age of three by lying on top of it. Police and uniformed park keepers were given authority to confiscate cigarettes from juveniles whom they caught smoking in the street or a public space, and penalties were imposed for selling cigarettes to a child under sixteen. No child under fourteen was allowed into the bar of a licensed premises during opening hours, though they were still granted access to railway refreshment rooms. Parents were forbidden, when short of cash, to send their children with some valuable to the local pawnbroker. Children found wandering on the streets with parents who were showmen, tinkers or vagrants were compelled to attend school throughout the whole year, instead of times of their parents' choosing. Where education authorities neglected their powers of sending children to industrial schools, the police were to be given authority to bring such children before the magistrates, who could if necessary commit them to an industrial school. Thus the Act established a whole new range of behavioural norms expected of children and their parents, and its effects would soon be seen on the streets and in public spaces.

# 4

# Old Age Pensions

## Introduction

The advent of H. H. Asquith in April as prime minister heralded a momentous shift in the pace of reform away from small-scale, often tentative experiments, to large-scale, national enterprises and the erection of a system of welfare outside the Poor Law. Asquith showed an enthusiasm for reform that had been lacking in his predecessor. He promoted a national scheme for non-contributory old age pensions, started the reconstruction of the financial system to pay for it, and in response to the forthcoming report of the Poor Law Commission, boldly declared that the problems of unemployment, poverty and infirmity were on the political agenda. He then wholeheartedly supported Lloyd George and Winston Churchill, whom he had singled out for promotion, by giving them the political backing to go ahead with a National Insurance scheme encompassing health and unemployment insurance as the Liberal alternative to the Poor Law. Nor was this all. He encouraged Lloyd George to continue with the reconstruction of the financial system, Churchill to establish a national system of labour exchanges and a scheme to stamp out sweating in trades with a large percentage of female employees. In addition, to cope with the problem of juvenile unemployment the government devised a network of special labour exchanges and attempted to institute a system of compulsory continuation education. We will cover the second instalment of the Liberal welfare reforms in the years 1908–11 in this and the following eight chapters (Chapters 5–12). Having gone so far and shrunk the Poor Law system and built alternative institutions outside its orbit, the government seems to have lost its collective nerve and allowed vestiges of the old system to remain. Why was this? We will attempt to grapple with this question.

## Old Age Pensions

The introduction of old age pensions in 1908 marked another victory promoted by the tacit alliance between the New Liberalism and Labour. Here the sociologist Charles Booth documented an overwhelming case for the provision of state assistance to the aged and undermined the arguments of those who favoured a contributory scheme. Nonetheless, the driving force in the movement for old age pensions were the trade unions through their vehicle the National Committee of Organized Labour on Old Age Pensions set up in 1899. Yet it was not until the victory of the Liberal party and Labour that there was the necessary shift of the political forces in Parliament for a scheme to be implemented. H. H. Asquith, as chancellor of the Exchequer, was the embodiment of the New Liberalism on this issue, not only playing a crucial role in its implementation but ensuring that it was the first step in the break-up of the Poor Law.

Although Britain was one of the most advanced industrial societies at the end of the nineteenth century, she lagged behind Bismarck's Germany, agrarian Denmark and her own colonies in Australasia in implementing social security schemes. Nor was she lacking in pioneers, for in Canon William Lewery Blackley she possessed a major theorist of constructive welfare action by the state, who was said to have influenced the formulation of the earliest experiments in Germany and New Zealand. Blackley had worked on the question for many years before he published his famous article in *The Nineteenth Century* on national insurance in 1878. Briefly his plan was that everyone between the ages of eighteen and twenty-one years should pay £10 into a national fund, from which all wage earners would receive in return 8s. per week in sickness benefit until they reached seventy years of age and thereafter a pension of 4s. a week for the rest of their lives. Attracting the support of philanthropic as well as Poor Law opinion, the scheme seemed certain to secure an early success. An association was formed in 1880 under the presidency of the Earl of Shaftesbury, having on its council the leading philanthropists of the day, for the purpose of educating the public on the subject of national insurance. True that Blackley's scheme would establish a network of services outside the Poor Law and would curtail the activities of the Boards of Guardians, but its implementation would cheapen the cost of administration and a majority of the unions favoured the scheme.[1]

However, when a select committee of the Commons was appointed to inquire into National Insurance in 1885, its report was so unfavourable that Blackley's scheme was ruled out of practical politics. To the hostility of the friendly societies must be attributed that assembling of expert evidence which challenged the actuarial soundness of Blackley's scheme, by pointing out that contributions were too small, while those who most needed inclusion – low-paid and casual workers – were excluded from the German insurance scheme. Additional reasons why Blackley's scheme was disregarded was the following: no statesman of the front rank could be induced to campaign on behalf of his proposals, and as Labour was so subservient to the Liberal leaders, there was no really powerful force to compel the latter to take an interest in the problems of social security. Secondly, Blackley failed to make much impression even on young Liberals, as they did not attach sufficient credence to his figures. Arthur Acland MP admitted that when he was on the committee of inquiry, he was convinced that Blackley's estimate of the number of aged poor was grossly exaggerated.[2]

During the early part of the 1890s, the political field was dominated by a scheme for contributory pensions. This was an offshoot of Blackley's ideas. The Commons select committee had concluded on the rather dampening note that there was not much to be said against the pensions part of the scheme, though some would object to the compulsory element, but everything would have to await a further ripening of public opinion. Through the agency of the National Providence League for Promoting Insurance against Pauperism, Blackley prepared a new, voluntary state-aided scheme; hence the National Providence League commenced an active agitation throughout England and Wales in 1891 and 1892 in support of an old age pensions scheme. One result of their campaign was the appointment of a Royal Commission on the Aged Poor in 1893. 'There cannot be a doubt', proclaimed a circular of the league, 'and it is generally admitted – that it has been through the action of our League, and of its chief Members, that the whole question of Provision for the Aged Poor has been brought to its present advanced stage.' Because his name has been linked to a modified version of this scheme, Joseph Chamberlain has received undue credit for his advocacy of old age pensions. In 1891 Sir James Rankin MP, who was chairman of the National Providence League 1886–1892, called a meeting of MPs in the Commons over which Chamberlain was induced to preside to prepare a pensions scheme on lines similar to that of the league. Although the scheme was entitled the Parliamentary Scheme for Old Age Pensions, it was popularly called the Chamberlain scheme. It, too, was a voluntary state-aided scheme, though the state subsidy was on a smaller scale than was the case with the league's scheme. A pension of 5s. per week was to be paid to men at sixty-five years, and 3s. a week to women, while specified payments were also to be made to widows and orphans.[3] Chamberlain did not advance much beyond this state-aided pensions scheme. As late as October 1905, Chamberlain reiterated that he had 'stated publicly on many occasions that I do not believe universal Old Age Pensions to be either practicable or desirable.'[4] Nor would he make the question of old age pensions part of the programme of tariff reform. In fact, Chamberlain used his advocacy of voluntary state-aided pensions as an excuse to thwart the demands of those who asked for universal free pensions.

By the close of the nineteenth century the case for a contributory pensions scheme had been completely demolished. In the first place, it was politically dead. The Liberals had appointed a Royal Commission on the Aged Poor (1893–5) and its recommendation of a further inquiry resulted in the setting up of a committee of experts presided over by Lord Rothschild in 1896. Two years later the latter committee reported that after considering over 100 contributory schemes, it could not find one that was satisfactory. Secondly, the entrepreneur and sociologist Charles Booth and his followers, notably the Liberal journalist and confidant of Asquith, J. A. Spender, undermined the intellectual foundations of the case for contributory pensions. Finally, when the National Pensions Committee of Organized Labour declared for Booth's scheme and rapidly won the accord of the trade unions, it was thought that it was only a question of time before the friendly societies were converted to their viewpoint.

In his first publication on the subject, *Pauperism, a Picture, and the Endowment of Old Age, an Argument* (1892), Booth challenged the fashionable theory that the root cause of all social malaise among the lower classes was the excessive consumption of alcohol; instead he insisted that old age was the principal cause of pauperism, followed some way behind by sickness and then drink.[5] Between them Booth and Spender, who collaborated with the former on the production of *The Aged Poor in England and Wales* (1894), built up a detailed and convincing picture of the condition of the aged poor. Something like 30 per cent of the aged poor who were over sixty-five years old in rural districts and large industrial centres had to seek some form of poor relief, but in semi-urbanized areas the figures for those seeking relief dropped to 25 per cent, as the principal factors making for both urban and rural poverty were not so operative in these areas. Booth further estimated that at least half the shop-keeping class and half the workers over the age of sixty-five years would be paupers or on the brink of pauperism.[6] If anything, the position of the aged in large centres of population had worsened over the last two decades, for men past the age of forty-five years found it increasingly difficult to obtain fresh employment, though it was customary for them to work until sixty years of age. Once he was fifty or fifty-five years old, the skilled worker was no longer paid full wage rates; the unskilled worker after forty years of age could not do heavy manual labour, drifted downwards into inferior occupations, and was subject to a heavy mortality rate. In the villages men could remain independent until sixty-two or sixty-three years of age, but after that they depended on some outside source of help and were always too poor to lay money aside for an annuity in old age.[7]

As the ancient remedies of help from children and charity could not meet the needs of old people, many persons suggested the inauguration of a contributory pensions scheme. Booth and Spender made a number of points against the efficacy of a contributory scheme. Those who needed pensions most, such as low wage earners and casual labourers, would least be able to afford to contribute towards such a scheme; nor would housewives without financial means of their own be able to scrape together the cash required for regular contributions. Again, there would be a considerable lapse of time before the first contributors would be able to benefit from the scheme.

Then there was the difficulty over the attitude of the friendly societies, which covered some 5.5 million of the adult male population in England and Wales at the end of the nineteenth century, towards state pensions. While they had been established with the primary purpose of providing their members with sickness benefit, they gradually became accustomed to paying their older members pensions.[8] Charles Booth had observed:

> It is impossible to conceive any plan by which contributions can be drawn from the masses of people alongside Friendly Society contributions without interfering with Friendly Societies; nor could the government enter into a sort of partnership with Friendly Societies without in some way interfering with them, which is not only undesirable but would never be accepted.[9]

Spender claimed that state subsidies to friendly societies were dangerous, as testified by the example of France, where the societies devoted a larger portion of their funds to the annuity business than they could afford from their current benefits. No such problems would arise if a free and universal old age pension scheme was adopted. For while friendly societies did not run any superannuation schemes of their own, the cash paid to sick members after a certain age was nothing other than an old age pension in a disguised form; moreover, these payments were a constant drain on the financial resources of the societies and tended to undermine their financial stability.[10] Pat Thane has questioned the assumption of previous historians that the friendly society movement as a whole was opposed to state pensions, by suggesting that in fact the leading societies favoured such a scheme. This was partly because they understood that the poor, especially women, could not afford to become members of their societies, and partly because they were concerned about an ageing membership.[11]

The trade unions had an essential interest in securing state pensions in order to prevent too many of their older members from taking on work below union rates. Some unions, such as the Amalgamated Society of Carpenters (ASC) and the Amalgamated Society of Engineers (ASE), ran their own superannuation schemes, but they were criticized as being actuarially unsound and were a prodigal waste of the unions' resources. Spender succinctly outlined the position of the trade unions in regard to the old age pensions question in the early 1890s:

> So far as our inquiries among Trade Unionists have gone we feel justified in saying that organized workmen are inclined to favour a national solution of the question as the only acceptable one. In more than one case we have met with the frank statement that the temptation to fall in with any scheme which promises security against the risks of old age is a distinct danger to the independence of the working class. The Unions are convinced that no scheme can be possibly started on the employers side which is not fatal to a man's liberty of quitting his employment at his own discretion, and they are further of the opinion that no authority but the State is in a position to start a scheme which will be absolutely safe and entirely removed from all questions of wages and labour. Notwithstanding the fact that the greater Trade Unions are to a large extent Friendly and Benefit Societies themselves, we have not so far met with any objection to State Pensions from Trade Unionists, corresponding to the objections which have been so freely raised by the leaders of the Friendly Societies pure and simple. Trade Unionists are aware that they can only deal with the question to a very limited extent, and they prefer that it should be settled in some permanent way by the State rather than permitted to remain open, and perhaps, be used as temptation to workmen to forsake the principles of Trade Unionism.[12]

Thus, opinion in trade unions was markedly friendly towards a state scheme, and they had been mobilized early in support of the idea. Charles Booth persuaded both the Fabian Society and in 1893 the Trades Union Congress to support a scheme for 'a national state-aided system of old age pensions', so that from 1899 onwards until the introduction of the pensions law in 1908 the TUC annually passed resolutions for the payment of universal non-contributory pensions at sixty.[13]

The rapid growth of the National Committee of Organized Labour on Old Age Pensions was due above all to the enthusiastic support it was able to evoke from the trade unions, which had enrolled 1.5 million members in Great Britain and Ireland by 1892. In November 1898 William Pember Reeves the agent-general of New Zealand, a Fabian socialist and an ex-minister of labour, addressed a meeting at Browning Hall on the colony's recent pensions scheme of a 7s. allowance for all needy persons over the age of sixty-five years. Someone asked Herbert Stead, the warden of the settlement, 'Could you not call a Conference to consider whether something could be attempted for our old people like what has been done in New Zealand?' After consulting his old friend George Barnes, the secretary of the ASE, which ran its own superannuation scheme, Stead agreed to call a small private conference of local friendly society and trade union representatives on the subject. Booth was to address the meeting. As some circulars were left over, Stead sent them to old friends in the Labour movement – not to invite them, but to tell them what he was doing. Quite unsolicited, forty trade leaders, representing a quarter of a million workers, decided to attend. So responsive were the trade unions that it was then resolved to continue the movement on a permanent footing and to enlist their support, a confidential report on the first conference was dispatched to trade union branches throughout the country. Trade union officials called further meetings at Leeds, Manchester and Newcastle, which in turn resulted in the formation of branches of the provisional committee centred on Browning Hall.[14]

The National Committee of Organized Labour on Old Age Pensions was formally constituted in May 1899. It then drew up a policy statement, having been granted a preview of Booth's latest publication on the subject. The committee opted for a free and universal pension of 5s. a week for all over sixty-five years of age, and most important of all, it emphasized that there should be no connection between the pensions scheme and the Poor Law authority. For if there was such a tie, a distinction would have to be drawn between the deserving and the undeserving poor, and there could be no universal pension; moreover, should the pensions scheme be dominated by Poor Law ideals, the very people who would most need them would be precluded from sharing in the benefits. In this respect the National Committee diverged from the proposals contained in Booth's most recent declaration and the report of the government Select Committee on the Aged Deserving Poor in 1899. Under Booth's revised scheme, a pension of 7s. a week was not to be paid until seventy years because of the cost; from sixty to seventy years there were to be smaller supplementary pensions for people who claimed to be in need: they were to appear before the local Boards of Guardians, who were to order the pensions authority only to grant pensions to selected candidates.[15]

Two factors were responsible for the reawakening of interest in the question of old age pensions on a national scale. First, after a preliminary conference at Newcastle, the proceedings of the inaugural meetings of the National Committee were thrown open to the press and the pensions issue gradually began to come to the fore. Secondly, there was pressure from within the ranks of the Conservative party, with more than a hundred Tory MPs declaring in July 1898 that a definite attempt should be made by the government to legislate in 1899 in fulfilment of their pledges. That was why Joseph Chamberlain promised in Parliament that the government would legislate on the question before it left office, and why a select committee was appointed in April 1899, which hastily reported three months later. The report of the Chaplin Committee made it likely that legislation would follow shortly. Its report represented a triumph for Booth in that it came down on the side of a non-contributory scheme to be paid not earlier than sixty or later than seventy. Still the National Committee criticized the report for failing to divorce pensions from the Poor Law, by proposing that the new pensions authority should consist almost entirely of members of Boards of Guardians and that there should be an inquiry into desert. To show proof of its good intentions, the government appointed a departmental committee under Sir Edward Hamilton, the permanent secretary of the Treasury, to cost the scheme. The Hamilton Committee carried out this task well, but the outbreak of the Boer War in October 1899 threatened to eclipse the campaign for old age pensions. Balfour retorted that 'Joe's war stopped

Joe's pensions'.[16] To halt the rapid progress of the National Committee among the working class, with both the TUC and the Cooperative Union having endorsed its proposals, Chamberlain tried to revive the bugbear of friendly society opposition. On 29 May 1901 Chamberlain addressed the annual conference of the National Order of Odd Fellows. He claimed that the idea of universal pensions was absurd, damaging to thrift, while no chancellor of the Exchequer could afford it. Therefore, he appealed to the friendly society leaders to consider the question afresh. He begged them to formulate a contributory pensions scheme through their branches, which would be assisted by a state subsidy.[17]

As Pat Thane has suggested, the large friendly societies increasingly approved of non-contributory pensions because they saw them as a more effective means of relieving the poverty of the poorest strata of the population, who could not pay regular contributions. To tap into the groundswell of support within the friendly society movement, the Old Age State Pensions League was established in 1898, which advocated the payment of a pension of 5s. a week at sixty-five to all long-standing members of such societies. But it failed to make much headway until the Charity Organisation Society managed to alienate many of its erstwhile supporters within the friendly society movement, by opposing a measure which was designed to assist members of benevolent societies and by insisting on an individual relying on self-help without recourse to state assistance. Thus, the Outdoor Relief (Friendly Societies) Bill that finally became law in 1904 was anathema to the COS. It ensured that individuals would be allowed to receive up to 5s. a week from friendly society funds without Poor Law administrators having to take this income into account, when relieving their needs.[18]

The National Committee's riposte in these changing circumstances was to embark on a determined propaganda campaign to win the approval of the friendly societies to their viewpoint. The officials of the friendly societies were middle-class and feared that the least interference with the business of the societies would jeopardize their positions; through their control of country lodges, they dominated the proceedings at the annual meetings of the orders and their views on old age pensions often won acceptance. Frederick Rogers, the secretary of the National Committee, decided not to rush into an open challenge of the leadership, but to wait until the cause made headway, when the friendly societies would come around of their own accord. Not quite. True that the rank and file of the friendly societies were the same as those in the unions and cooperative societies and that the majority of them supported the scheme of the National Committee, but some effort was required before the leaders yielded. However, the attempt of the TUC in 1901 to organize a triple conference of trade unions, cooperative and friendly societies was baulked of its complete purpose, as the latter refused the invitation. Nevertheless, the movement for state pensions was gathering such momentum that at the 1902 National Conference of Friendly Societies a resolution was passed by a majority of three to one, demanding a state pension of 5s. a week for all thrifty and deserving persons, which was renewed a year later.[19]

During the Boer War and the remaining years of Conservative rule, both parties were equally hostile to the campaign for old age pensions. After analysing the returns to a questionnaire that he had sent to all members of the new Parliament of 1900,

Frederick Rogers concluded that the younger members of both parties were sympathetic to the movement, but that this was not the case with old parliamentary hands. At the conclusion of the South African War in 1902 the National Committee staged a fruitless campaign to secure pensions before the repeal of the war taxes. If the Liberal party displayed a truly feline cunning, it acted in a more feeble fashion. In 1903 the Liberal headquarters contacted Stead to inform him that the Liberal party would not officially move a resolution in favour of old age pensions, but that if he could find a Liberal MP willing to do so then the attitude of the Liberals would be clarified. On a number of occasions Stead saw John Burns, a member of the executive of the National Committee, who promised to move such a resolution but failed to act. However, when a by-election took place in Horsham, where Stead was an elector, the Liberal candidate was induced to mention old age pensions in his manifesto, though on being apprised of this, Liberal party headquarters forced him to delete the reference.[20]

The apathy of the major political parties trammelled the efforts of the National Committee. The movement was run on a shoestring budget. According to George Barnes,

> The funds came mainly from working class organizations and a few friends, among whom Edward Cadbury was conspicuous, but beyond the modest salary of Mr Rogers and the cost of printing, we spent very little.[21]

As its meetings dwindled in the opening months of 1904, there was talk of discontinuing the campaign; its organizing secretary Frederick Rogers reluctantly went on a year's leave of absence without drawing a salary, focusing his efforts instead on working with Joseph Rowntree and Arthur Sherwell on temperance reform. Trade unions and trade councils began to withdraw their subscriptions; more serious was the fact that the movement was heavily dependent on middle-class patronage as far as its finances were concerned and that the Cadburys seemed to have intimated that they were going to discontinue their financial assistance. Only the forceful intervention of Stead prevented this catastrophe.[22] As a matter of fact, it is claimed that the Cadburys finally contributed as much as half the cost of the campaign that culminated in the passing of the Old Age Pensions Act. Moreover, it is estimated that over a ten-year period the National Committee received over £1,900 of its income of £2,600 from a few wealthy subscribers, under £650 from the Labour movement, and just £40 from the sale of its literature.[23] Nonetheless, it was a distinct advance when the Labour movement was able to free itself from undue dependence on the whims of private benevolence.

By their ardour and determination in times of stress, Francis Herbert Stead and Frederick Rogers ensured the ultimate triumph of the movement. What it lacked and needed was a national figure at its head; Charles Booth had been offered the presidency of the organization, but refused to accept, though he assisted it financially. Still Stead, the brother of the distinguished journalist W. T. Stead, was the moving spirit of the campaign; he was the warden of the Browning Hall Settlement, and an ardent supporter of numerous collectivist causes. 'He was full of a fiery, passionate and high souled enthusiasm, which he was for applying always and everywhere, and had in him something of the fervour of the Hebrew prophet.' Frederick Rogers had characteristics which exactly complemented those of Stead, thus making them a formidable combination. Rogers was the perfect organizer, able to become passionate or coldly practical as it suited him, and a superb platform orator; he was closely acquainted with all sections of the Labour world, and was chosen as the first secretary of the Labour party. His salary was £4 per week plus expenses, while the only other expenditure borne by the National Committee was the cost of printing its campaign literature.[24] Yet within the space of a few years the movement swept to a successful conclusion. How are we to account for this sudden upswing in its fortunes? Above all, to the pressure of the Labour movement and to the emergence of a powerful pro-Labour block vote in the 1906 House of Commons of fifty representatives. Old age pensions after 1904 became the first plank in the social programme of the Labour Representation Committee, while George Barnes, who was chairman of the old age pensions organization, was later appointed as Labour party spokesman on pensions. Altogether eleven members of the executive of the National Committee sat in the Commons in 1906 after the election, four as Lib-Labs and seven as Labour MPs. The Irish party, now numbering eighty-three MPs, swelled the voting power of the Labour block, and as early as 1902 assured the National Committee that on pensions, as on other domestic issues, they were on the same side as the Labour party. Through a steady build-up of propaganda, the National Committee infiltrated all sections of the Labour world. Thus, despite the fact that neither of the major parties mentioned old age pensions during the election campaign, the issue was forced on the attention of candidates. A. K. Russell in his survey of the 1906 general election concluded that 59 per cent of the Liberal candidates in their election addresses favoured old age pensions. Stead went further, claiming that no less than four-fifths of the MPs in the 1906 House were pledged to pensions.[25]

Next the accord between Nonconformity and Labour ensured that, in addition to the Radicals, there was a solid group of Liberal MPs who would take their election pledges on the subject seriously. In vain the Nonconformists had tried to link the question of pensions to that of disestablishment, but after the setback which this effort suffered they continued their policy of temporizing in regard to social reform. In October 1894 the National Old Age Pensions League was established in Birmingham, with Sir James Kitson MP as chairman, to provide pensions for the aged out of the funds of a disestablished Church. Apart from the Nonconformists, it attracted little support and soon sank into somnolence. At the turn of the century the National Committee tried to obtain the assistance of the Churches in its campaign; whereas their deputation was courteously received by Cardinal Vaughan and Archbishop Temple, it was rebuffed by Hugh Price Hughes, the leader of the Wesleyans. One result of the growing cooperation between Labour and Nonconformity after the Balfour Education and Licensing Bills was that Dr Horton, then president of the Free Church Council, signed an appeal which was then dispatched to all Nonconformist candidates at the 1906 election; it requested them not merely to give vague promises but to push the old age pensions question to the fore. No less than 140 of the 200 Nonconformists MPs were returned pledged to pensions.[26]

At the end of the 1906 session, the government boldly declared in favour of the policy of the National Committee. This was a tremendous step forward and was, indeed, a much more radical course than has been imagined. For despite the energy of Herbert Stead and Frederick Rogers, the pensions cause has been somewhat in eclipse since the report of the 1899 select committee. Moreover, it should not be forgotten that the Conservatives still hankered after contributory schemes. Lansdowne wrote to Lord Avebury on 20 September 1907:

> I am, I confess, profoundly alarmed at the outlook. The present Government have, in effect, committed themselves to the policy [in regard to pensions], which, in my opinion is a disastrous one. Asquith will, no doubt, try to discover a moderate solution of the difficulty, and it may perhaps be possible to do something in the way of encouragement of thrift by the State.[27]

He ended by asking where he could procure a paper of Blackley's. In the following month, Austen Chamberlain said something in a similar vein in a letter to Balfour:

> Asquith has committed himself to a universal non-contributory scheme. I believe this to be vicious in principle and impossible in practice on account of the cost. May we not say that we are prepared to impose a contributory scheme somewhat on the German [lines] – 1/3 from the workmen, 1/3 from the employer, 1/3 from the State?[28]

In fact, Austen Chamberlain recorded how the Conservative leaders decided that they would support a second reading of the Old Age Pensions Bill in 1908, so long as it was regarded as a temporary bridge to a complete scheme on a contributory basis.[29] That the government decided on such a bold course was due not only to the influence of the pro-Labour block vote in the Commons but to the ardour with which Asquith took up the question.

When the 1906 session of Parliament opened, the government displayed a fumbling and dithering attitude in regard to legislating on old age pensions. Prime Minister Sir Henry Campbell-Bannerman told a deputation of the TUC Parliamentary Committee on 15 February 1906 that if there was more care shown in the administration of the national finances and a less ambitious policy was followed, the money for pensions would become available, but for the present it was beyond their ken. On 14 March 1906 J. O'Grady moved a resolution on the subject for the Labour party, and the new temper prevalent in the House was shown by the fact that the government concluded that it would be best to accept the resolution without a division. Dissatisfied still by the vague nature of the government's pronouncements, the National Committee summoned a meeting, at which it was agreed to send a small private deputation to H. H. Asquith, on whom as chancellor of the Exchequer the burden of finding the money for old age pensions would devolve.[30]

Asquith was then at the peak of his powers, and in the years before the First World War successfully steered the nation through a series of relentless crises. We must strip away the over-coatings of these later years and see Asquith as he was in his prime. Nor should we fall victim of a myth propagated by Conservative politicians, as shown in the letter of Lansdowne which we have just quoted, that Asquith was a timid, moderate politician, and the later elaboration of the myth that he was goaded by

Lloyd George into the adoption of nasty, confiscatory measures. To justify his seizure of power during the war, Lloyd George also had to denigrate Asquith's reputation:

> He was always essentially the judge. When he accepted a plan he used his great authority to obtain for it Cabinet sanction ... Such a mind was invaluable in the conduct of affairs when peace reigned and there were no emergencies demanding originality, resource and initiative. It was especially useful for a Cabinet where there were several able men full of ideas to which they were anxious to give administrative or legislative effect.[31]

Sometimes he seemed to be lost, too slow to react, but most of the time he quickly recovered and saw the way ahead more clearly than his colleagues, leading them and the nation out of the path of political turbulence.

From early in his career, Asquith was an exponent of a New Liberalism with an emphasis on social reform, as distinct from Gladstonian Liberalism. He belonged to a different generation and by 1899 as part of this policy of social reform, 'Asquith was convinced in principle of the merits of "a national scheme of pensions", but was not satisfied that any one of the schemes yet put forward is either practical or adequate'.[32] So it was Asquith, as chancellor of the Exchequer, who initiated the reconstruction of the financial system, by introducing different rates of taxation for earned and unearned income to pay for social reform. As soon as it is appreciated that it was Asquith who plumped for a trenchant policy in regard to old age pensions, then we can begin to reassess his role in the initiatives taken in the reconstructed Liberal government for the break-up of the Poor Law.

Already when Asquith conferred with the deputation from the National Committee in June 1906, consisting of Thomas Burt MP, George Barnes MP and Leo Chiozza Money MP, his ideas were beginning to crystallize: he announced that old age pensions were one of the most urgent public issues, but he was not prepared to say whether the issue would be dealt with in the 1907 Budget until the select committee on income tax reported. Still not satisfied, the National Committee resolved to send a large-scale deputation to the government in the autumn.[33] There was to be no mere patching of the Poor Law, but instead a bold measure of social reconstruction was agreed. On 20 November 1906 the prime minister and Asquith privately received a deputation of seventy to eighty Liberal and Labour MPs. If anything, Asquith spoke with more crispness than the premier. Everyone was surprised by the energy and passion with which he addressed the question. Like the prime minister, he averred that the pensions scheme must be one of universal application, must thus be of a non-contributory nature, and must be free from the taint of the Poor Law. However, he ended by declaring that the government regarded the question as one of extreme urgency.[34] It was through no fault of Asquith that an earlier start was not made to an old age pensions scheme; we shall see how despite the opposition of McKenna and the permanent officials, Asquith submitted a plan for a supertax to pay for pensions to the Cabinet in March 1907, only to have it rejected. Without such a tax, it was not possible to make an early start to the payment of old age pensions. Concerning Asquith's attitude, the parliamentary correspondent of the *Daily News* commented on 1 March 1907 that his great anxiety to proceed in the matter was common knowledge

– his friends saying that he thinks of little else. That was why the Budget introduced by Asquith in 1907 not only differentiated between earned and unearned incomes, but between incomes in excess of £2,000 and those under this amount, with the intention of taxing them at different rates.[35]

As early as December 1906, Asquith had instructed a Treasury official, Roderick Meiklejohn, to prepare an elaborate memorandum on old age pensions, outlining a possible plan. Meiklejohn dismissed the contributory schemes and rehearsed the well-known arguments against the participation of friendly societies in any new plan. Booth's scheme, so the paper argued, was free from the disadvantages of the self-insurance schemes; the sole difficulty was one of money, as it would cost £15.5 million to implement the scheme for pensions starting at the age of seventy. Various alternative proposals which were cheaper were adumbrated: a modification of the scheme suggested by the 1899 select committee could be tried, or as a first step, the chancellor could set aside a certain fixed sum which would be distributed by the special bodies, on the basis of information supplied by Boards of Guardians, clergy and the local Charity Organisation committees. Asquith rejected these alternatives and decided to adopt Booth's scheme, which was similar to the policy advocated by the National Committee.[36]

While the constant pressure which the National Committee was able to exert through the Labour movement forced the government to speed up the pace of their introduction of the Old Age Pensions Bill, the National Committee did not have sufficient access to ministers to dictate more than the general design of the draft bill. Throughout 1907 and 1908 the National Committee tried to keep the question prominently before the public gaze: in 1907 a vigorous campaign was kept up by the National Committee and meetings were held all over the country; in October 1907 the TUC arranged meetings in eight towns with the cooperation of the local trades councils; and in January 1908 the Labour party conference resolved to make pensions the subject of a speedy agitation throughout the country. It was claimed that the two Labour victories in by-elections at Jarrow and Colne Valley in 1907 were in large measure due to their stand on the old age pensions question.[37] However, Reginald McKenna, who was charged by Asquith with the drafting of the measure because the latter wished to avoid too much interference from John Burns, did not consult the National Committee leaders at all. Among the Asquith Papers is a file on old age pensions which contains one solitary letter from Stead dealing with the subject of pensions in the most general sort of way.[38]

No sooner had McKenna begun work on the pensions scheme in April 1907 than Beatrice Webb was in communication with him, and there can be little doubt that she influenced him in drawing up a more far-reaching scheme than had originally been envisaged. She stiffened his resolve, preventing his plan from being unduly overawed by Poor Law principles. During the course of an interview, he told her that he would be laughed at if he started his pensions scheme at an age above sixty-five years. Still because of the difficulty of finding enough cash, he wanted to devise tests to limit the number of applicants as far as possible. Mrs Webb vehemently opposed his idea of a character test and a test of ability to earn, gradually winning him around to her viewpoint. The character test, she maintained, was useless apart from marking out people with criminal convictions. As for the prior receipt of relief, it showed nothing about a person's character – for instance, women who lost their husbands and had been forced to bring up large families would be discriminated against. Likewise, the test of ability to earn would entail the adoption of inquisitorial machinery, based on the Poor Law pattern. As to imposing limits on excessive incomes, the fairest method devised was the New Zealand sliding scale. But how were they to discover, McKenna protested, if a person was fit to live outside of an institution? Mrs Webb suggested that this 'must be settled by the public health authority – it was, in the last resort, a question of public nuisance, a dirty or neglected old person'. McKenna, while thanking Mrs Webb, admitted that he had not yet abandoned hope of finding some test less objectionable than ability to earn.[39]

On 18 July 1907, McKenna dined with the Webbs to discuss his old age pensions plan. Beatrice Webb noted:

> The scheme he thrashed out with us was universal non-contributory pensions to all over 65 with less than 10s. a week from property, with sliding scale from 5s. upwards, income under 5s. not to be taken into account. No disqualification from pauperism present or future, some contribution from the rates on account of potential paupers. To be administered evidently by a stipendiary. He calculates that it will cost the national exchequer £7,000,000 to £10,000,000.[40]

Working through Haldane, the Webbs kept up their pressure on the government to ensure that pensions were to be paid by the Exchequer, as they did not trust the discretion of local boards in awarding pensions and they insisted that it was administratively impracticable to exclude former paupers and past criminals. They favoured a graduated pension like that adopted in New Zealand, depending on a person's income, while there would be a smaller income for married couples. All these suggestions were eagerly embraced by McKenna and they undoubtedly stiffened his resolve to make his scheme free from the taints of the Poor Law and to resist the counter-pressures coming from John Burns at the Local Government Board.[41]

In November 1907 a Cabinet committee consisting of Asquith, McKenna and John Burns was set up to approve the preliminary scheme prepared by McKenna. The Treasury stipulated that only £7 million per annum would be available for pensions; the chief saving on McKenna's proposals was made by raising the pensionable age to seventy years. The pension was still set at 5s. a week with a reduced pension of 7s. 6d. a week for married couples, as the Webbs had suggested.[42] When the Local Government Board sent its memorandum to the Cabinet committee, it put forward the Poor Law point of view: all those who had received Poor Law relief in the last twenty years and all those who had failed to pass a thrift test should be deprived of the right to a pension, leaving some 686,000 persons over the age of sixty-five years entitled to pensions. Roderick Meiklejohn, the civil servant in charge of drafting the pensions measure, wrote to Asquith that such assumptions were unwarrantable; they should only exclude people who were actually in receipt of relief and habitual criminals, leaving 950,000 persons eligible. However, in an effort to trim further costs off the scheme, the Cabinet committee decided that all those in receipt of poor relief after 1 January 1908 were not to receive a pension; nor were criminals, lunatics and aliens, mostly Jewish immigrants, to be eligible. A National Committee circular sent to MPs in January 1908 declared that 'there is absolute unanimity of opinion that pensions must not be given to aliens, an opinion which rises into passion in districts where aliens congregate'. Despite the previous protests of the Webbs, all those unable to furnish some proof of thrift were excluded from the scheme. Local voluntary committees with a paid clerk were to administer the scheme subject to the supervision of inspectors of Customs and Excise; pension payments were to be handled by the Post Office. It was a wonderful exercise in keeping down administrative costs.[43]

Asquith kissed the king's hand on 8 April 1908 at Biarritz, where Edward VII was on holiday, and took over as prime minister from Sir Henry Campbell-Bannerman, who was ailing. Among the changes he introduced into the government was that Lloyd George became chancellor of the Exchequer and Winston Churchill moved to the Board of Trade, subtly shifting the balance in the Cabinet in favour of social reform. Despite attempts by the former leader to reinvigorate the Liberal party on a platform of land reform, the party had been drifting and faring badly with the electorate. Since their momentous victory in the general election of 1906, the Liberals had lost six seats to the Conservatives and four to Labour, while in the months that ensued the Conservatives captured four more seats. Edwin Montagu advised Asquith shortly before he became premier that Lloyd George 'is in favour of the Nationalising of railways, and ominously hints that we shall have to go to the country next time with something appetising as a substitute for Tariff Reform'. On 17 March 1908 he reported to Asquith that the Licensing Bill which was at the centre of the government's new programme was unpopular. 'That is the view universal in the Lobbies and universal in the constituencies where, not only Members, but Organisations are very, very frightened. There is no doubt that Old Age Pensions will completely alter the situation.' Asquith had adopted this new initiative in social reform and was fully behind his ministers, Lloyd George and Churchill, when they seized other opportunities for bold welfare experiments.[44]

Asquith outlined his plan for old age pensions in his budget address to the Commons on 6 May 1908. Pensions of 5s. a week would commence at seventy years and be collected at the Post Office, but would not be paid to paupers, criminals and lunatics. Personal incomes had to fall below £26 per annum and £39 for a married couple, if the elderly were to be eligible to apply for pensions.[45] Lloyd George, as chancellor of the Exchequer, was given the task of introducing the Old Age Pensions Bill on 15 June 1908. But despite all his adroitness, Lloyd George could not resist the pressure of MPs spearheaded by both Labour sections from wringing concessions in the Commons. Throughout the discussions Stead and Rogers of the National Committee sat in the gallery of the House, while George Barnes MP came up to discuss the line of action to be taken with them. The estimated cost because of the concessions rose from £7 million to £8 million. While the trade union group of MPs would have been content with a sliding scale instead of a fixed income limit, the Labour party wanted the abolition of the fixed income limit altogether. Further, the friendly societies objected to payments made to their members being considered when a person's income was estimated. Lloyd George advised that a sliding scale would meet their case. Both Labour groups took exception to his actual proposals, but Lloyd George forced through a sliding scale for incomes of 8s. to 13s. a week by 334 votes to 114. Thus, for example, those who received an income of less than 8s. 1d. a week would receive the full pension of 5s., while those in receipt of less than 12s. 1d. would receive a pension of 1s. Again, little time was left for the consideration of the age limit and it was forced through by 341 votes to 124. However, George Barnes, chairman of the National Committee and vice-chairman of the Labour party, was more successful when he insisted on the smaller pension for a married couple being scrapped; this time he was supported by the Women's Liberal Federation and the Liberal party was divided. McKenna for the government refused to make concessions, but the government whips were seen eagerly conferring with Asquith and Lloyd George and the government's resistance snapped.[46]

Above all, the National Committee worked for the disassociation of the scheme from the Poor Law. Nevertheless, some tainted concessions had crept into the bill, in spite of the vigilance of Beatrice Webb, and they did their best to have these clauses struck out. The Labour party objected so strongly to the idea of the resurrection of the character test that Lloyd George observed on the second reading that it would have to go; it was eventually altered into an industry test. A pension could be withheld from anyone who was guilty of 'habitual failure to work according to his ability, opportunity, or need, for his own maintenance or that of his legal relatives'. However, the habitual failure to work clause was regarded as being 'essentially unenforceable', so long as the government failed to issue guidelines to local officials for its enforcement.[47] The proposal to exclude persons who were in receipt of Poor Law relief or other relief was a dangerous concession – the latter phrase embodied Charity Organisation principles and would have made the receipt of charity a condition for losing a pension, but through Labour insistence it was omitted. Nothing much could be done to prevent people who had received Poor Law relief since 1908 from losing their right to a pension; Asquith admitted that only financial necessity had induced him to accept such a clause. Such was the pressure in the Commons on this issue that the government conceded that the receipt of Poor Law relief from 1911 onwards should not debar a person from receiving a pension.[48]

The attitude of the Lords showed the ambivalent feelings of the Conservative party. The Lords proceeded to mutilate the Old Age Pensions Bill; Lansdowne claimed that the Lords could amend money bills and this meant that they could challenge budgets. Balfour was annoyed at the acceptance of Cromer's amendment, limiting the operation of the pensions scheme until 1915; in the Commons he told the peers that the bill could not be altered, which was a rather piquant comment on his later attitude. To safeguard their privileges the Lords passed a resolution stating that they did not accept the reasons given by the Commons for the elimination of their amendments.[49]

To sum up, the coming of old age pensions in Britain was due to the confluence of a variety of forces: first, the example of the successful act in New Zealand provoked people in this island to wonder whether they could not obtain similar blessings. Secondly, Charles Booth presented an overwhelming sociological case for the necessity of non-contributory pensions to relieve the poverty of the elderly and he acted as the *Great Disseminator* of the concept of old age pensions. Finally, the settlement movement forged links between the best elements in the New Liberalism on the one side and the upsurgent Labour forces and the Webbs on the other, so that they joined hands in the campaign for old age pensions. In this campaign a critical role was played by Francis Herbert Stead of the Browning Hall Settlement and Frederick Rogers with multiple links to the Labour movement through the medium of the National Committee of Organized Labour on Old Age Pensions. So far from extinguishing all the poverty of old age, the 1908 Act made a slow start, as it did not cover individuals below the age of seventy years and 5s. a week was hardly enough to help people without additional sources of income. Aliens and their wives were debarred from claiming a pension, nor was any person who was convicted of a crime and ordered to be imprisoned without the option of a fine allowed to apply for a pension while in prison or for ten years following his release; but by an amending Act, if a woman marrying an alien was a British subject at the time of her marriage, she could apply for a pension if she was a widow or was separated from or deserted by her husband. Lunatics detained in an asylum or elsewhere were excluded from the benefits of the Act and persons above the age of sixty convicted by any court and liable for a detention order to be made against them under the Inebriates Act could have a disqualification order imposed on them by the court for up to ten years.

Thanks to the Labour movement and the Webbs, the severance of all ties of any importance between the new pensions authority and the Poor Law system was ensured. Indeed, the Old Age Pensions Act was superior in conception to all the other Liberal welfare legislation because it accepted that the poor, who were unshod, could not lift themselves up by means of contributory insurance schemes; and the Act pointed the way towards a fairer distribution of the national income. Women because of their superior longevity benefited more than men under the Act, as at its inception they comprised 62.5 per cent of the pensioners. With the Poor Law disqualification lapsing in 1911, the initial number of recipients of the old age pension rose from 647,494 in the financial year 1908-9 to 967,921 in 1912-13 out of a total United Kingdom population of 45.3 million.[50] Under an amending Act in 1911 the disqualification imposed on a man because his wife was in receipt of Poor Law relief was removed, as well as the disqualification through temporary residence abroad. The poverty of the elderly was a relatively minor factor in the total sum of poverty: at the most, basing our estimate on the above figures, it could only have affected some 3 per cent of the population. Thus, the caveat may be entered that there were certain other sectors of social reform requiring more urgent attention.

In our assessment Asquith played a much more positive role in the coming of old age pensions than he has hitherto been accorded by historians; and we shall see how through his friendship with Haldane and through him with the Webbs, he had become accustomed to accept that old age pensions was the first instalment of a broader scheme for the reconstruction of the Poor Law. John Burns reported to Asquith, following a visit to shopping areas frequented by the poor, that

> After chats with the butcher, the cheesemonger and the police the general view was that the five shillings to one [person] was a boon, but where the couple received the joint pension it meant a great deal to the honest and provident poor. So far there was no evidence of waste or spending on drink and from many

sources there were really grateful thanks for those who had brought this boon to the deserving poor.[51]

So too, as E. P. Hennock has suggested, the piloting of the Old Age Pensions Bill through the Commons was an overpowering learning experience for Lloyd George, a reluctant reader of briefing papers but a wonderful listener who absorbed new ideas rapidly. Because of the soaring costs of his concessions on old age pensions, Lloyd George was suddenly awakened to the potential of the German contributory schemes of health and invalidity insurance which his Cabinet colleague and political ally Winston Churchill espoused.[52]

5

# Sweating and the Minimum Wage

## The First Phase of the Anti-Sweating Campaign

Only with the application of the sociological approach to the problem of sweated labour by Beatrice Webb, when serving her apprenticeship as a member of Charles Booth's London Enquiry team, and the later joint propounding with Sidney Webb of the theory of parasitic trades, were the old sensational and sentimental myths about its nature bluntly extirpated, and the way opened for the conquest of sweating by the clinical principles of scientific legislation. Not everyone in the growing movement against sweating accepted the full implications of the Webbs' theoretical formulations. In fact, so many new lines of sociological research were developed, highlighting the disastrous consequences for the whole family of the casual employment of male breadwinners, the penury visited on workers dismissed because of regular seasonal fluctuations in demand, and above all, the plight of the widows and the mass of under-paid women workers, that the hardship of large numbers of male workers with inadequate pay packets was overlooked. Thus, after the *Great Disseminators* popularized the idea of adopting the Australian wage board legislation as a remedy, a sectional interest, the Women's Trade Union League – which was itself entrenched in the executive of the National Anti-Sweating League (NASL) – manipulated the campaign against sweating in the interests of the women workers whom they represented. At the same time, they stopped Churchill from broadening the campaign, by espousing the cause of minimum wage regulation generally. Like the successful campaign for old age pensions, it was again the tacit alliance between representatives of the New Liberalism, as exemplified by George Cadbury and his circle, and the Labour movement that allowed the NASL to secure the Trade Boards Act of 1909.

Compared, however, with the contentions of other contemporary critics that the middleman was the sweater and that sweating was confined to those industries in which the sub-contract system prevailed, the hypothesis that society as a whole was to blame for the evils of sweating was a notable advance.[1] In its old sense, the term sweating had been used as early as 1849 by Charles Kingsley, a Christian Socialist, in *Alton Locke*. On the other hand, Beatrice Webb, in her pathfinding essay on the East London tailoring trade, stated:

> we are told that there are a class of middlemen who stand between the wholesale or retail house and the master of the workshop – a series of parasites all of whom

'sweat' profit out of the actual worker at the bottom of the scale. This class of middlemen was a fact of the past; with equal certainty we may assert that it is a fiction of the present. That there exist isolated instances of middlemen who are not superintendents of labour, I could hardly deny ... but we have overwhelming evidence, that these individuals (if they exist at all) do not constitute a class, for though we have full particulars of shops in all sections of the coat-trade, we have in every case traced the work direct to the retail or wholesale house.[2]

She further pointed out that in typical sweated industries such as the coat and low-class boot trade, both exclusively in the hands of Jews, the sweater worked harder and often earned less than the persons he employed. Again, she continued that in such industries as the making of shirts, ties, umbrellas and juvenile suits, where English women were employed, the middleman was fast disappearing. Instead manufacturers had opened shops in the East End for giving outwork to be machined and finished at the same rates that were adhered to by middlemen in the past. Further, the manufacturer of common cutlery in Sheffield, the maker of nails in Halesowen, the cheap bootmaker in London, all bought their materials on credit, after which they sold the finished products direct to the customer and retailer.[3]

Once the middleman, stereotypically the immigrant Jewish master, was removed as the bogeyman behind sweating, two important conclusions followed. First, there was a need for a fresh definition of sweating which assimilated the implications of the new theory. Contemporaries attributed the coining of the definition to members of the House of Lords Select Committee on Sweating (1888–90), a parliamentary body which was appointed after agitation by Church social workers; but we now know from her diaries that it was broached by Beatrice Webb, who persuaded Lord Thring, the drafter of the majority report of the Committee, to incorporate it. Sweating consisted of bad conditions of employment, wherever they were to be found: 'earnings barely sufficient to sustain existence; hours of labour such as to make the lives of the workers periods of almost ceaseless toil; and sanitary conditions which are not only injurious to the health of persons employed but dangerous to the public'. Every well-known social commentator and sociologist accepted this broader definition without demure: it was flourished by Gertrude Tuckwell in her essay in the *Handbook of the Sweated Industries Exhibition* (1906); it was given further publicity by Clementina Black in her *Sweated Industry and the Minimum Wage* (1907); it was cited by Edward Cadbury and George Shann in *Sweating* (1907), a guide prepared for social reformers. Secondly, in place of the middleman, the nation was denounced as a sweater by Beatrice Webb in its capacity as a consumer, as a landlord who demanded double rent for a workshop and dwelling, as a shopkeeper who gave out goods on credit, as the person who gave out material to be worked up into the finished articles. Sociological enquiries later instigated by the Women's Industrial Council on the Home Industries of London and the Christian Social Union confirmed these conclusions. Independent testimony by Clementina Black supports the view that because of the rapidly rising rents of workrooms in the West End and East End, many outworkers moved their homes to the new suburbs, where they overcrowded the houses and quickly generated slum conditions.[4]

So too, the reluctance to touch the middleman on the grounds that he sometimes had useful functions to perform was fraught with grave consequences. Accordingly, there is much in the contentions of contemporary critics, such as Chiozza Money MP, who wanted to abolish the middlemen altogether, as was done in New Zealand, and drive the outworkers and small masters into factories. If the middleman was not the principal motivating factor responsible for sweating, he was nonetheless the instrument through which unchecked market forces encouraged sweating in many trades, and there were inherent dangers in this situation.[5] Home workers' premises consisted of three types of establishment: one was the use of the employer's own home while engaging staff from outside; the second was once again utilizing the employer's own home but employing only members of his own family. Both of these establishments defined as workshops and domestic workshops were fully protected by the provisions of the Factory and Workshop Acts. The third category of home work establishment consisted of outworkers engaged in labour for others in their own homes, without the assistance of other persons whether family or otherwise, which escaped the protection of the Factory and Workshop Acts, apart from the particulars clause.

Since the 1891 Factory and Workshop Act, local authorities – and this means the sanitary inspectors working under the direction of the medical officers of health – supervised the sanitary arrangements of the workshops in cooperation with the Home Office factory inspectors, who had powers of acting in the last resort, if the sanitary inspectors failed to remedy defects. By the 1901 Act the powers of the factory inspectors were somewhat diminished in regard to the enforcement of sanitary standards, while the powers of the local inspectors were enhanced. Rose Squire, an experienced factory inspector, detected some improvement in the sanitary conditions of workshops in London and the large manufacturing towns, especially after the passing of the 1901 Act; other witnesses before the Select Committee on Home Work (1908) had the contrary impression. Moreover, so long as the outworker lists, which were compiled twice a year, were incomplete and inaccurate, there was no sound operational basis for the system of inspection. While engaged on a social survey of West Ham, E. G. Howarth sifted through approximately 1,800 names on the medical officer of health's list and traced only 600 outworkers – the rest had moved or were dead. Proceeding in the reverse order, Clementina Black discovered in one London borough that half the outworkers were not on the official lists. One manufacturer of boxes candidly admitted to her that the lists were a farce. 'I may have six home workers one week ... and next week I may not have one of the same workers, or if I had the same six workers at least half of them might be living at a different address.' Even when the authorities had detected the use of unwholesome premises in 1,201 cases in 1906, only 816 notices were served and prosecutions were commenced in a mere three cases. Henry Mess, looking back in 1926, wrote:

> Local authorities vary much in keenness and efficiency. Whilst there is little to say against most of the great municipalities, it is unfortunately the case that many of the smaller local authorities, and these by no means always rural authorities are extremely slack and recalcitrant. Factory inspectors comment on the lowness of some of their sanitary standards.[6]

As opposed to the premises of outworkers pure and simple, the signs of improvement in the factories and workshops were becoming clearer. As far as the clothing trade was concerned, Mrs Carl Meyer and Clementina Black reported in 1909:

> There are factories in which every point of space, sanitation, light air and warmth, facilities for washing, and for the cooking of meals and comfort of the meal-room are satisfactory; there are many others in which some one or two of these details will be far from satisfactory; and there are a few in which every possible condition not fixed by law is unsatisfactory.[7]

In another survey in 1907 Clementina Black commented that paper-bag workshops were ill ventilated and lighted but admitted that, thanks to the women factory inspectors, sanitary conditions had improved in factories and workshops as well as the heating arrangements in winter with the enforcement of the law requiring a minimum temperature of 60°F.[8]

Commencing with the Factory Act of 1891, employers in the cotton and woollen industries were enjoined to supply their workers with written 'particulars' of the terms on which they were employed; gradually by the 1895 Act the 'particulars' clause was extended by order of the home secretary to any class of non-textile factory and workshop and by the 1901 Act it was applied to outworkers undertaking work for others in their own homes. Again, the 'particulars' section was poorly enforced: some employers presented their work people with printed 'particulars', precisely stating the hours of employment and the wages to be paid; others proffered illegible scrawls; yet others neglected this duty altogether. The Christian Social Union research committee carried out a general enquiry into the need for the extension of the 'particulars' section in 1904, investigating the artificial flower making, basket, boot, button-holing, matchbox and paper bag trades and reporting to Miss Anderson, the chief woman factory inspector: 'The price is fixed arbitrarily by the foremen and is lowered by heavy fines and deductions. The payments vary not only for the same work in the case of different workers, but also for the same workers on different occasions.'[9]

None of this legislation influenced the European anti-sweating movement, apart from the 'particulars' clause, which was adopted for certain classes of home work in France and Germany, though the International Association for Labour Legislation passed resolutions affirming the need for the application of the 'particulars' clause to all trades. In any case, the fact that the Centre, National Liberal and Conservative parties in Germany in 1906 could still have faith in the efficacy of the British system of registration and inspection as a means of stamping out sweating shows that Britain would have to look elsewhere than across the Channel for inspiration, after the failure of the legislative methods which she had tried for the protection of home workers.[10]

Blessed with superior links to the English communities transplanted overseas, Britain turned instead to a closer examination of American and Australian experiments. The New York Consumers League was formed in 1890 with the avowed object of ensuring that all workers received a fair living wage, fixed at $6 a week for experienced female hands at the very least, while consumers were not to purchase goods unless they had first ascertained that they had been made under decent conditions of employment. For the guidance of shoppers, a white list of approved manufacturing and retail establishments was published; later goods made under fair conditions were specially labelled. If the demand for goods with these labels was not overwhelming in New York, the president of the league in her travels found labelled underwear on sale in department stores as far away as cities in the Midwest and on the Pacific coast.[11]

Where the Consumers League was vigorously supported by women of wealth and position belonging to the ruling elite – as in New York, among whose patrons were Mrs Vanderbilt and Mrs Jacob Schiff – these voluntary methods of arresting sweating had a modicum of success; but in London the Consumers League was ostracized by society ladies and wilted without leaving a trace. After a suggestion thrown out by Clementina Black in the *Longmans Magazine*, an inaugural meeting was held on 19 November 1890 under the auspices of leading Christian Socialists, with Canon Scott Holland in the chair. From an analysis of its prospectus, it is clear that the programme of the English league was carefully modelled on its Yankee counterpart. Every step in the article's production and transmission had to be scrupulously noted, if a system of vetting by consumers was to be effective; and as trade unionism was particularly weak in the sweated trades, it was almost an impossible task. Even if the attempt in London to check sweating by a consumer boycott failed, the Oxford branch of the Christian Social Union drew up a list of twenty local firms with acceptable trade union wage rates in 1893, which grew to 146 firms by 1900; the Leeds branch drew up a similar list which contained 572 names in 1900, and the Labour Churches carried out the same policy in the Midlands, so that consumer regulation was not altogether a failure.[12] There was also an attempt to secure the adoption of a minimum wage rate on a voluntary basis in connection with the making of 'Fives' balls.[13] What this revealed was the sharper class divisions of English society in comparison with America and France, where consumer leagues flourished, and the insulation of those at the opposite ends of the social poles from awareness of each other's way of life; the Tory tradition of aristocratic philanthropy was dead and contributed little to the first stages of the Welfare Revolution. Next British reformers investigated the American licensing system, first adopted for the Massachusetts clothing trades by the laws of 1891, 1892, 1894 and 1898. Any home workers in these trades employed in a dwelling house had to obtain a licence from the district chief of police before permission was granted for them to commence work; every room in which wearing apparel was made had to be kept clean and was subject to inspection. Subsequently New York instituted a similar licensing system covering more trades and with a more elaborate code of regulations, which became the model code for the legislation of other American states. Although in 1895 and 1901 Sir Charles Dilke moved amendments to the Factory Acts in an attempt to introduce a licensing system into Britain, the Commons would not be swayed by his advocacy.[14]

More determined efforts were exerted to convert British opinion by Ramsay and Margaret MacDonald, who, on a trip to the United States to boost the proposed Hague Peace Conference, were conducted around the homes of outworkers by inspectors in Boston and Philadelphia and became convinced advocates of the licensing system. They induced the Women's Industrial Council and the Scottish Council for Women's Trades to sponsor a Home Industries Bill, introduced from 1898 onward, applying the licensing system to some ten trades. Despite some favourable support in private from the factory inspectors, the Home Office blocked the bill, as they thought that the scheme would involve too much paperwork; other critics outside official circles also seized on this point. Essentially the protagonists of wages boards maintained that the licensing system would tend to improve sanitary conditions, which was of secondary importance compared with the need to augment the wages of home workers. Few, however, disparaged the American licensing system in terms so brusque as Mary MacArthur. Relating what she had witnessed in New York, MacArthur confessed to the Select Committee on Sweating in 1907 that 'there I was informed by the very people who promoted it, that they were disappointed with its results, that it led to a great deal of corruption, and that the workers sub-let their licences to other workers'. Against this current of opinion, the MacDonalds claimed that once workers were persuaded to adopt a higher standard of cleanliness, they would demand higher wages – a questionable assumption, seeing that those American states enamoured of a licensing system were later forced to introduce minimum wage regulations.[15]

More advanced reformers looked across to Australia and New Zealand. Of his own accord, Pember Reeves, the minister of labour in the New Zealand Liberal government and a self-proclaimed Fabian socialist, brought in the Industrial Conciliation and Arbitration Act of 1894, which was amended in 1900. Conciliation boards composed of equal numbers of masters and men with an impartial chairman were set up in the seven districts into which the country was divided. Only recognized associations of employers and workers could select representatives to serve on these boards; but as a group of as few as seven workers could register themselves as a trade union, an immense fillip was given to the organizing of both sides of industry. However, once a dispute was referred to the area conciliation board, a strike or lockout was forbidden, though there was an appeal system. Moreover, under the terms of the Factory Act of 1901 it was explicitly stated that no school leaver working in a factory was to receive less than 5s. a week's pay, while from sixteen years onwards juvenile employees were to be awarded annual increments of 3s. until their twentieth year, when they would take home the national minimum wage of £1.[16] Just because of the implementation of the statutory wage, hardly any awards were made by the conciliation boards for women workers, though they were the lowest-paid section of the working class. While home workers were in any case few in New Zealand, sweating was almost completely obliterated by forbidding the intervention of the middleman. According to a report of a Californian state commissioner, the unskilled worker in New Zealand enjoyed the highest standard of living for his social category in the world. Probably the New Zealand legislation was also superior to the Australian experiments in that its machinery at the local level was simpler and in that it covered the whole range of unskilled labour.[17]

Although a newspaper, *The Argus*, had launched a crusade against sweating and a Royal Commission had reported in 1884, the movement to combat sweating in the Australian state of Victoria did not gather powerful momentum until the trade crisis of the early 1890s exacerbated the existing economic situation. During the severest phase of the commercial depression, wholesale clothing establishments in Melbourne encouraged the substitution of home for factory work, particularly among the small contractors, who supplied their stocks of ready-made clothing to secure economies.

Only with the formation of a pressure group in 1895, the Anti-Sweating League, was the government pushed into action of a startling novel kind, adopting an idea of John Stuart Mill that in cases where workers were poorly remunerated, boards of employers and workmen were formed to regulate wages, with compulsory powers if necessary. Syme, a well-known Australian journalist and politician, passed the suggestion on to Deakin, the prime minister of Victoria; Dilke likewise claimed that he had been thinking on these lines since the 1880s. These two men must be ranked as *Active Innovators* of the idea of wages boards.[18]

Under the 1896 Victorian Factory and Workshop Act wages boards were empowered to fix a minimum standard wage for factory and outworkers by time and piece rates, to adjust the hours of work and to curtail the proportion of apprentices to the adult labour force. Somewhat later the chief inspector of factories was allowed to grant special permits to aged and infirm persons, enabling them to continue working at reduced rates, after the initial displacement of labour in the boot and clothing trades on the formation of the boards. The amending Act of 1900 extended the jurisdiction of the boards over the entire colony, not just to Melbourne, and allowed Parliament to set up new boards by resolution. Again, the wages boards experiment was conducted on the assumption that sweating was not confined to home work or limited to women's work. By 1912 the wages boards covered ninety-one trades, including those with skilled artisans. Cross-examined by Stuart Samuel, Aves, the Home Office expert sent out to explore their working, had to concede that sweating had been virtually abolished in the colony.[19]

Harder to interpret were the actual advances in wages promoted by the establishment of the wages boards. Summarizing the position, Aves concluded that although on the whole in the men's trades advances had been greater in the board than the non-board trades, the differences were not very wide, but there were quite a number of cases where the boards had secured marked increases of wages in the men's trades. Nevertheless, Aves admitted that part of the wage rise secured in the non-board trades, quite apart from the effect of advancing prosperity, was attributable to the new spirit fostered by the boards. Advances in thirteen boards catering for male workers amounted to an average wage rise of 7.6 per cent; in nineteen other boards, after the determination, the average wage rise reached 16.5 per cent; in contrast, in twelve non-board trades the aggregate advance was 11.6 per cent. According to the estimates of the Revd John Hoatson in 1906, the average of the increments in eight of the trades principally employing female labour was 2s.; in the underclothing, shirt and clothing trades, the worst trades in which women were employed, it was 1s. 4d; in ten trades with better conditions of employment the excess of wages over the minimum was 2s. 3d. Among his concluding remarks, Aves averred that 'as regards wages the distinguishable effects of the Special Boards on total average remuneration has often been slight, and that, when compared, so far as women's earnings are concerned, with changes that had taken place in trades with Special Boards, they are in aggregate hardly appreciable'. Even so, despite the laborious assembly of data by Aves, we must not vest his figures with too much significance, because he went out to Victoria with a definite bias against the effectiveness of the trade boards experiment. The later figures over a much longer period put forward by Dorothy Sells, which point to an opposite conclusion, are to be preferred.[20]

## The National Anti-Sweating League and the Trade Boards Act

Britain had a distinct advantage over her rivals in imbibing the lessons of the minimum wage experiments in her Australasian domains because the imperial ties linking the two meant that there was a constant interchange of ideas and visitors. In Britain the take-off phase of the campaign for minimum wage regulation may be pinpointed to three sources: William Pember Reeves and his wife, the Webbs and the Dilke family circle. All had ample means of access to a national audience through such forums as Parliament, the press, and the more enduring types of publication, from whence other *Lesser Disseminators* were given a lead; all may be enumerated as *Great Disseminators* of the idea of minimum wage regulation. On his frequent trips to Britain, Deakin, the premier of Victoria, perfected and clarified his scheme for a wages board in discussions with the Dilkes; afterwards, when the wages board experiment had hardened into an administrative reality in 1896, he strengthened the resolve of the Dilke family circle to try out a similar experiment in Britain. Perhaps the very notion of mounting a pressure group campaign to secure the introduction of trade boards was borrowed from the Revd John Hoatson and Col. Rae, both of whom had prominent roles in staging the operations of the Victorian Anti-Sweating League and devoted much energy to assisting the British campaign. Again, when the wages boards became practical politics at the time of the Guildhall Conference in October 1906, Dilke sought the advice of the governor of Victoria and the Australian bishops on the administrative minutiae of the Victorian legislation.[21]

Pember Reeves, the New Zealand Agent-General in London, was – in addition to being the architect of the pioneering Industrial Conciliation and Arbitration Act of 1894 in his home country – the author of the classic account of the Australasian minimum wage legislation with the publication of *State Experiments in Australia and New Zealand* (1902). Mrs W. P. Reeves gave one of the earliest expositions of the working of the Victorian wage boards scheme in a collective volume of essays entitled *The Case for the Factory Acts* (1901) under the editorship of Mrs May Tennant. Naturally Pember Reeves deemed his own creation superior to the Victorian wages board system, but he was rightly sceptical about the likelihood of British trade unions accepting compulsory arbitration in more than a few trades to begin with. The Reeves had good contacts with the Webbs – they were on visiting terms with each other – and the Dilke circle through Mrs Reeves' membership of the executive of the Women's Trade Union League, their pet organization. Nonetheless, prior to the advent of the Liberal government in 1906 accurate knowledge of the details of the Australasian innovations had just about penetrated down to the secondary level of the social reformers, to those whom we have called the *Lesser Disseminators*, while the general public had scarcely been stirred. According to Pember Reeves, at this stage of the campaign 95 per cent of the population knew nothing of the remedial measures which had been introduced in New Zealand, and '[t]he remaining 5 per cent have learned about them from the attacks made on them in your great newspapers … laws which have tackled problems … do not get fair play, even chilly fair play, and do not get sympathy, even critical sympathy'.[22]

On the other hand, the contribution of the Webbs to the successful prosecution of the campaign for trade boards was twofold. By refurbishing Beatrice Webb's preliminary sociological theory explaining the intricacies of the economic mechanism responsible for the mass sweating of workers and delineating its social manifestations along the lines of Marshallian marginal utility theory, the Webbs produced a totally cogent and convincing economic analysis, to which the plea for the adoption of the Victorian wages boards legislation could be plausibly hitched. By embarking on a trip in 1898 to probe the functioning of the Australian experiments at first hand, the Webbs ultimately became convinced champions of the Victorian wages boards system, thereby winning the assent of some important *Lesser Disseminators* in the ranks of the Fabian Society and carrying the socialist intelligentsia with them. Reflecting on her visit to Victoria, Beatrice noted that 'the machinery has worked smoothly; that the constitution is superior to the New Zealand Arbitration Act because minimum and not maximum conditions are determined by the Wages Boards and do not interfere with the workman's right to bargain collectively if not satisfied with the legal conditions'.[23]

In their book *Industrial Democracy* the Webbs formulated their revolutionary theory of parasitic trades. Halévy's statement that it was derived from Marx's formula of the reserve of labour was true. At any rate, it was the centrepiece on which the arguments advanced in the favourable report of the Select Committee on Home Work (1908) hinged. Starting from the premise of the imperfect nature of competition in a free market economy, otherwise wages would soon be reduced to the level of the marginal man in the trade or community, the Webbs asserted that the manner in which the national income was divided depended on what emerged from the haggling between employers and workers. Each section of the community pressed into service special devices to increase its bargaining power. Trade unions relied on the device of the Common Rule with its stipulated rates of pay, working hours, sanitation and safety.

> The inadequate wages, excessive hours, and insanitary conditions which degrade and destroy the victims of the sweated trades are caused primarily by their own strategic weakness in the face of the employer, himself driven to take advantage of their necessities by the unconscious pressure described in our chapter on 'The Higgling of the Market'.[24]

Here a gloss supplied by Cadbury and Shann can be used to summarize what the Webbs understood by their reference to the latter process. Unless a worker found employment, he would go hungry; he had no means of studying the varying conditions under which he might offer his labour; he could not easily uproot his family to towns, where there might be lucrative vacancies; he had no reserve fund with which to bargain with employers for better conditions of labour; he had to face the competition of many other labourers for any vacant work. While the introduction of minimum standards, the Webbs maintained, forced employers to introduce long standing inventions and new processes, parasitic trades throve on cheap supplies of female and boy labour subsidized out of the pockets of adult male wage earners.[25]

One result of the extensive investigation undertaken by Cadbury, Matheson and Shann was to confirm the Webbs' view on the reasons for the delay in introducing machinery into the most inefficient home work trades. Although a machine had been built in Birmingham for carding hooks and eyes, the cheapness of women's wages militated against its general introduction. So too, despite the invention of efficient machines in the paper box, chain making, metal box, boot and shoe and paper bag trades, only fragmentary use was made of them. At the same time as they tended to cause the whole supply of labour to deteriorate, the parasitic trades checked the expansion of the self-supporting industries. As long as this cheap source of labour was at hand, employers had no incentive to produce articles in a modern factory with labour-saving devices. The one conclusion the Webbs drew from this hypothesis was that dockers, women and boy labour could not be saved by the devices of collective bargaining.[26]

In the Preface to the 1902 edition of *Industrial Democracy*, the Webbs extended their analysis and indicated the colossal dimensions of the problem of low wage earners, claiming:

> The pressing need in England of today is not any increase in the money-wages of the better-paid and stronger sections of the wage earners, but a levelling up of the oppressed classes who fall below the 'Poverty Line' … the unskilled labourer, the operatives whose organization is crippled by home work, and the women workers everywhere, can never in our opinion, by mere bargaining obtain either satisfactory Common Rules or any real enforcement of such illusory standards as they may set up.[27]

Already in the first edition of this volume, the Webbs had argued for the adoption of a national minimum of sanitary conditions of work, of leisure hours and of wages: the minimum wage would be determined by a practical inquiry into the cost of food, clothing and shelter; different rates might be determined for town and country workers, and for male and female operatives.[28] Soon afterwards their Fabian disciple Reginald Bray, in *The Town Child*, maintained that the enforcement of a minimum wage rate was the essential social reform; everything else – municipal housing, the state feeding of school children, more generous out-relief – was merely an indirect method of increasing wages. Further, he added, '[t]hey are bad because they give a man by way of favour what should be his by way of right. They add indeed to his income, but at the expense of his independence and character.'[29] Accordingly, the Webbs and their followers regarded the sweating of women workers, home workers and unskilled labourers not so much as separate social problems but as facets of grave disturbances in the underlying order of society which could only be rectified by raising the submerged, poverty-stricken strata of society through the wholesale imposition of minimum wage regulation. As the instrument for reaching this goal, the Webbs had concluded by 1902:

> 'We think experience in this and other countries confirms the economic conclusion that there is no way of raising the present scandalously low Standard of Life of these classes, except by some legal stiffening as that given by the Victorian law.[30]

Taken over from the Webbs by a host of *Lesser Disseminators*, buttressed by a series of fresh sociological investigations, the theory of parasitic trades – together with the need for minimum wage regulation – percolated through to the opinion leaders of the local voluntary associations and captured the imagination of the politicians. From 1906 onwards, there was a stream of literature reiterating and amplifying the Webbs' suggestions. Cadbury, Matheson and Shann, in *Women's Work and Wages* (1906), after approvingly quoting the Webbs' arguments about the parasitic industries and putting forward the remedy of a national minimum fixed by legislation, admitted:

> More and more strongly it has been borne upon us that just because the problem of women's wages is part of the problem of the remuneration of wage earners generally, any adequate treatment of the subject must go much wider and deeper than we have gone.[31]

Then followed a section on the distribution of the national dividend culled from Chiozza Money's researches. They ended:

> The national income is increasing by leaps and bounds, and yet the mass of our people are in poverty. The problem of the future is the problem of distribution, and the trend of things seem to indicate that the hope of the future lies in a wise collectivism.[32]

Explicitly the theory of parasitic trades was mentioned by the economist J. A. Hobson; implicitly it is found in the utterances of Clementina Black, the most vociferous expositor of the position of women in employment, whose analysis of the sweated labour problem reached similar conclusions to the Webbs and whose theoretical groundwork rested on similar considerations. Giving evidence to the Select Committee on Home Work, Black stated that in nine cases out of ten married women worked, as their husbands did not earn a sufficient wage to keep their families comfortable. There was thus a need for wages boards to be established in both the under-paid men's and women's trades. Elsewhere she claimed that to relieve the poverty of the parents was a step towards abolishing child labour, while the introduction of a minimum wage by rendering a child's labour no longer cheap would remove the temptation of the employer to exploit it.[33]

It is doubtful whether a frontal assault on the distribution of wages in relation to the unskilled and semi-skilled sections of the working class commanded much support outside socialist and some New Liberal circles. Even a confirmed socialist like Mary MacArthur, who had been deeply influenced by the Dilkes, when challenged on the issue of whether sweating was solely confined to women's trades at the 1906 Guildhall Conference on Sweating, replied that '[i]t was no doubt true that all trades were sweated industries – laughter – so she must say that the object was to deal with the super-sweated industries'. To Sidney Webb, Chiozza Money MP and J. A. Hobson, speaking at the same conference, the problem was of more general application. 'Even the average mechanic or factory operative', Sidney Webb affirmed, 'who earns from 20s. to 35s. per week, seldom obtains enough nourishing food, adequate amount of sleep, or sufficiently comfortable surroundings to allow him to put forth the full physical and mental energy of which his frame is capable'. With prophecies of the fire to come, Chiozza Money warned:

> As to the under-paid themselves, a true knowledge of the facts could not but lead to a very holy discontent ... the first application of the principle [of the minimum

wage] should be made in connection with those grossly under-paid industries which are commonly regarded as sweated, but which are only the worst examples of an underpayment which extends throughout almost the whole of the trades and industries of the United Kingdom.³⁴

He stated that sweated and casual labour received about 10s. a week in wages; if the wages of these workers were raised to 30s., it would cost the country £195 million, while the one-thirtieth who ran the nation would still be left with an annual income of £400 million. Hobson challenged the view that a rise in wages would inevitably increase unemployment. On the contrary, by transferring a certain proportion of the national income from profit to wages, the standard of consumption would enlarge and regularize the process of production, giving fuller and more continuous employment to labour. And insofar as sweating was due to the demand of the very poor for inferior goods, a rise in the lower level of wages would help to diminish sweating by checking the demand for sweated goods. 'An increase of the general purchasing power of the workers,' Hobson concluded, 'secured by a legal minimum wage, will thus enlarge the volume and regularize the character of employment.' Alone a small Labour pressure group, the Labour Protection League, whose records do not survive, clamoured for a minimum wage of 30s. a week at the annual conference of the TUC.³⁵

What can be said with more assurance is that Dilke and the adherents from his family primarily regarded wages boards as a means of forcing up the niggardly wage levels of the mass of unskilled female labour and of easing the task of enrolling them into unions. The recruitment drives of the Women's Trade Union League, in which Lady Dilke and her niece Gertrude Tuckwell held dominant positions on the executive, had hitherto met with so many rebuffs in organizing women workers that an alternative legislative remedy was sought to achieve the same ends. On the other hand, their deliberate rejection of the need for far-reaching changes in the distribution of national income as between the different classes meant that the Trade Boards Act of 1909 only marginally reduced the amount of poverty in Edwardian England. Numerous attempts at organizing women workers in unions had been spiked by the antipathy of the masters, ever ready to replace recalcitrant girls by more amenable persons from the glutted labour market, and by the apathy of the women, many of whom quit their jobs on marriage. Gertrude Tuckwell recounted how in about 1891-2 Lady Dilke and Mrs Tennant tried to organize women in the dying matchbox trade, though their efforts were not rewarded with much success; next a vain attempt was made to organize women home workers in the tailoring trade. So too, Clementina Black found the task of organizing women in the box-making trade to be beyond her powers. Equally unavailing were the efforts made in Birmingham between 1895 and 1906 to organize the girls in the bedstead, bookbinding, pianoforte, tailoring and leather trades. At one time, the women penworkers union, established by Lady Dilke and Gertrude Tuckwell in 1895, had a membership of 600, but it had since dwindled to a mere five members, despite its successes in abolishing the scandalous system of fines and marked improvements in sanitary conditions.³⁶

Under the leadership of Lady Dilke, the Women's Trade Union League had tried to skirt the difficulty of organizing women into unions, by encouraging some sixty men's unions which admitted female workers – among them the shop assistants' union, of which J. J. Mallon was an organizer, and the cotton unions – to affiliate. After Mary MacArthur was appointed secretary in 1903, she formed the National Federation of Women Workers on the model of a general labour union, whose membership at the end of 1906 totalled 2,000, divided among seventeen branches in England and Scotland.[37]

No real progress, though, had been achieved in organizing a wide range of women's trades. Therefore, at the request of the Women's Trade Union League, Sir Charles Dilke MP annually introduced a Wages Board Bill in the Commons from 1900 based on the pilot scheme functioning in Victoria. Deakin, the prime minister of Victoria, used to come on frequent trips to Britain. As early as 1887 Deakin and Dilke discussed the feasibility of wages boards composed of representatives of both employers and workers with compulsory wage fixing powers. Again, when Deakin came to Britain in 1898, there were discussions with the Dilke family about the Victorian wages boards for wearing apparel which had been set up in 1896. From this time Dilke, his wife and niece were determined to introduce wages boards legislation in Britain. Gertrude Tuckwell explained the rationale behind the Women's Trade Union League (WTUL) policy to the 1906 conference on sweating, by pointing out that trade unions raised wages and perfected conditions; all trade unions were affected by the mass of unorganized labour indirectly, who degraded the whole standard of living; as it was impossible for some to gain a higher wage by unionization, it should be secured by law. The 1901 report of the WTUL declared that

> [Dilke's] Bill proposes to give power to the Secretary of State –on the representation of employer or employed that such action is desirable – to appoint Wages Boards in sweated trades to settle the minimum rate of wages; the boards to consist of an equal number of employers and employed.[38]

Just because Dilke's campaign had reached an impasse, Mary MacArthur, the secretary of the WTUL, approached A. G. Gardiner, the editor of the *Daily News*, in 1906 and after a tearful interview, appears to have persuaded him to sponsor a sweating exhibition like the recent German one. To stimulate legislation, the Germans staged the first sweated industries exhibition in connection with the Congress for the Protection of Home Workers in Berlin in March 1904, while a second one had been organized by the *Bureau für Socialpolitik* with the cooperation of the trade unions as recently as January 1906. On a smaller scale the Revd J. E. Ditchfield, vicar of Bethnal Green, had assembled an exhibition in May 1904. Above all, it was the intention of the organizers of the exhibition to quicken public opinion and stir Parliament to legislate more speedily. While the cost of staging the exhibitions was shouldered by George Cadbury, the proprietor of the *Daily News*, the task of planning the exhibition was entrusted to Richard Mudie Smith in conjunction with a committee of leading humanitarians and social reformers, mostly drawn from the friends and protégés of the Dilke circle and the exponents of the New Liberalism in the employment of the *Daily News*. The 1905–6 report of the Women's Industrial Council stated:

> When it was found that the *Daily News* intended to have an exhibition of 'Sweated Industries', Mrs MacDonald brought the matter to the notice of the Committee,

and Miss Clementina Black, Mrs J. R. MacDonald, and others represented the Council on the committee, and the W.I.C. was able to supply a good many workers and specimens of work to the Exhibition.[39]

The Daily News Sweated Industries Exhibition, held at the Queen's Hall from 2 May to 13 June 1906, was opened by Princess Henry of Battenburg and was attended by 30,000 visitors. All the ingredients utilized in the previous exhibitions were shown once again: both examples of sweated goods and demonstrations of the actual process of manufacture were on display; a series of lectures delineating different aspects and advocating tentative solutions to the problems was arranged; an elaborate handbook of the exhibition was published. For the first time public opinion all over the country was momentarily aroused. Charles Fenwick MP told the Guildhall Conference on Sweating later in the year: 'I can bear testimony to the large amount of interest excited in the provinces by the exhibition recently held at the Queen's Hall. It was the subject of general talk.'[40]

Once the exhibition closed, it was felt that the interest evoked among the general public must not be allowed to dissipate; and in the summer of 1906, '[a]fter the Exhibition was over a meeting of the Committee was held and it was decided that they should form themselves into [the National] Anti-Sweating League to secure a minimum wage'. Close liaison was maintained between the women's trade union movement and the new league, as they shared premises in Mecklenburgh Square, the rent of which was paid by George Cadbury. Dominating positions on the general purposes sub-committee of the executive of the NASL were held by Gertrude Tuckwell, Mary MacArthur and Herbert Burrows, all of whom were, of course, extremely influential in the inner counsels of the WTUL. Other persons with overlapping membership were Mrs Pember Reeves and Mrs H. J. Tennant, whose husband became Churchill's under-secretary at the Board of Trade in December 1908. Jack Tennant was a Liberal Imperialist, but more important was the fact that he was married to May Tennant, an ex-factory inspector and prominent social reformer. Under her influence he had already played a crucial role in ensuring that the government implemented the medical inspection of schoolchildren. The 1908 report of the WTUL disclosed:

> The chairman and secretary are active members of the Executive Committee [of the NASL] and have shared largely in its work. There is now hope that our proposals for the institution of Wages Boards in sweated industries may become law, and this, we are convinced, will give a great impetus to the movement for the organization of women workers.[41]

Moreover, J. J. Mallon, who had worked closely with Mary MacArthur in recruiting women trade unionists, was invited to become the secretary of the new league. James Joseph Mallon was born in 1875 in Manchester of Irish parentage, educated at Owen's College, the precursor of Manchester University, and moved into social work in the Ancoats Settlement, where his experiences made him 'dedicate … the major part of his life to stamping out sweating in this country', as Lord Woolton, himself a former settlement worker, recalled.[42] Margaret Stewart and Leslie Hunter wrote:

> A master of detail, he could out-argue any opponent with irrefutable facts. His acute and penetrating thoughts were communicated with Irish wit and urbanity.

He had the supreme gift of self-effacement and could bring a committee of men and women with widely divergent views and beliefs to a common purpose without any of them suspecting they were acting under his guidance ... As an ardent socialist, Mallon was convinced that the best hope of the future lay in a stronger trade union organization to assist the growth of the infant Labour party in the political field.[43]

Not surprisingly, these persons whose views had been shaped by the vicissitudes of enrolling women trade unionists prevailed on the NASL to plump for the Victorian system of wages boards rather than the New Zealand scheme of compulsory arbitration, particularly as the latter idea was anathema to the TUC.[44] In any case, the main priority of the reformers was to harness the anti-sweating campaign in the interests of enhancing the recruitment drive of the WTUL, and they were determined to prevent it from spilling over into a general campaign for a minimum wage.

Compared to the responsibilities it had assumed, the income of the NASL was not large, though it was probably more than double that of the very effective pressure group, the National Committee of Organized Labour on Old Age Pensions. During its infancy the league's annual income hovered around the £700 mark, while its expenditure was restricted to £600. By 1912 its income had crept up to £868 8s. 6d., and its expenditure had risen to £732 3s. 5d. Although the salaries of its small professional staff totalled only £371 7s. 11d. in 1912, the active assistance from trade union officials and voluntary helpers which it could mobilize was considerable. Thus, when the 1909 Trade Boards Act came to be implemented, the women's trade union movement cooperated with the league in the fieldwork of setting the elaborate administrative machinery in motion, a relationship that was greatly aided by the fact that the offices of both organizations were situated in the same premises. Around a core of professional workers like J. J. Mallon, drawn from the solid middle class, were a band of voluntary workers, mostly of upper-middle-class origin, often of Anglican background, many of whom enjoyed private incomes, eked out by low-paid journalism and social work. Constance Smith, the daughter of a Church of England clergyman and the niece of a high court judge, not only wrote a tract entitled 'The Case for Wages Boards' but lectured up and down the country; other voluntary helpers of independent means were Clement Attlee, Lady Shena Simon and Miss B. L. Hutchins. Spurned in its early stages by the upper class, the aristocratic ruling elite, the anti-sweating movement finally secured its patronage. Just as the war broke out, the Duchess of Marlborough presided over a fund-raising conference at her home in order to secure the wherewithal for augmenting the office staff of the league.[45]

As far as it is possible to identify the social origin of the league's 600 members, from whom the bulk of its funds were raised, it can be inferred that they were supporters of the New Liberalism or wealthy socialists. Above all, it was necessary for the NASL to register the support of the Labour movement, if the campaign was not to flounder in its early stages. The conference at the Guildhall on the Minimum Wage in October 1906 was designed to wean the Labour party and the trade union movement away from a partisan sponsorship of the MacDonalds' bill for a licensing system and to rally them behind the league's campaign. Delegates dispatched by the Labour party and most of the newly elected MPs, the TUC, the General Federation of Trade Unions, the Social Democratic Federation and the ILP and 106 unions attended the meeting. Not counting the Labour party and the TUC, the aggregate membership of the labour organizations present was estimated at 1,955,296. The very fact that representatives of Labour attended in such large numbers underscores the point that in neither the trade union movement nor the Labour party did the MacDonalds enjoy a privileged position from which they could not be dislodged by determined opponents. Moreover, these representatives voted for a resolution endorsing the league's policy of securing a minimum wage in the sweated industries by legislative action. Objections voiced by the social democrats that the league's policy meant no more than a trimming operation on the edges of the problem – something rather different from sweeping changes in the distribution of national income which the situation required – were hastily overridden, particularly by Mary MacArthur; in other words, the cause of the women workers, as championed by the WTUL, was covertly reaffirmed.[46]

The MacDonalds were swiftly and easily outmanoeuvred and outsmarted by James Mallon and Mary MacArthur, both of whom in their recruiting campaigns all over England had superior connections with the secretaries of the national unions and the local leaders. When it came to choosing between the merits of the alternative New Zealand and Australian minimum wage schemes, '[t]he attitude of the large Trade Unions, which opposed schemes of compulsory arbitration, narrowed in fact the field of choice' of the pro-union stalwarts on the executive of the NASL to the wages board system of Victoria. Other members of the executive viewed the New Zealand scheme more favourably. Clementina Black argued in 1907 that in addition to creating wages boards, Britain should adopt a feature of the New Zealand scheme, whereby seven persons were allowed to form a trade union and ask for the creation of a wages board. Within the space of a year, almost all the large trade unions and trade councils in the country, under Mallon's prompting, passed resolutions in favour of the NASL's programme. Further, the 1907 TUC passed a resolution affirming that the low rate of wages in sweated industries was a constant menace to the organized trades and directly responsible for a proportion of unemployment, and called on the government to give facilities for legislation to establish a legal minimum wage in selected industries.[47]

So too, despite Ramsay MacDonald's secretaryship of the party, the Labour party supported the league's bill. Keir Hardie MP, the father figure of the party, was nominated as a vice-president of the league together with other august personages. George Barnes MP, a future member of the War Cabinet and an influential voice in all the other pressure groups connected with the Labour movement, was an early champion of the idea of wages boards and sat on the executive of the league, where he was later joined by Arthur Henderson MP. So friendly was the attitude of the Labour party towards the league's bill that not only was it placed fourth on the list of bills which they were striving for in the 1907 session, but Arthur Henderson, on winning a place in the ballot for private members' bills, introduced it on behalf of the league, though its passage was halted in the middle of its second reading. One of the most frequent speakers at the branch meetings of the league was J. R. Clynes MP. High praise was bestowed by the WTUL on the Labour party; its 1910 report insisted that '[i]t is impossible in this connection not to pay tribute to Mr Henderson and the

Labour party for the constant care and attention by which the Bill has been carried to a successful issue, and to Sir Charles Dilke, its original sponsor'.[48]

The Webbs' enthusiasm for the Victorian system of wages boards brought the intellectual wing of the Labour movement, the Fabian Society, into the league's camp. Sidney and Beatrice Webb were included among the vice-presidents of the league. Beatrice Webb was too deeply involved in her work on the Royal Commission on the Poor Laws to devote much time to the league's affairs. Sidney Webb, on the other hand, was a frequent speaker at the branches of the league, read a paper at the Guildhall conference, and addressed the prime minister when the league sent a deputation packed with public figures in November 1908. Two other well-known Fabians, Pember Reeves and his wife, held office in the league, the one as a vice-president and the other as a member of the executive. H. G. Wells likewise consented to becoming a vice-president of the league. Mrs Charlotte Shaw, a wealthy member of a landed family whom the Webbs introduced to G. B. Shaw, was a member of the executive of the league. One publicity technique employed by the league was to exploit the prestige of the famous. With H. G. Wells in the chair, Bernard Shaw addressed a fashionable audience at the smaller Queen's Hall in 1907 on the social policy of the league, at the same time raising £80 for the league's funds. 'What are you people here for?' he asked. 'To hear me gibe at you, not because you care a rap for the wretched victims of your social system. If you cared for them you would not come for amusement. You would go outside and burn the places of fashion and commerce to the ground.' Chiozza Money, another Fabian and progressive Liberal MP, who was a member of the steering committee of the league executive, was one of the most active speakers on the league's panel and had espoused the cause of wages boards in the sweated industries handbook. Miss Beatrice Hutchins, a research assistant of the Webbs, toiled zealously in the Hampstead branch of the league, in addition to writing a Fabian pamphlet on *Home Work and Sweating: The Causes and Remedies* in 1907.[49]

Next attention had to be devoted to soliciting affirmations of support from the other women's organizations, as the NASL was concentrating its campaign against those trades where there was a preponderance of cheap female labour. Immediate avowals of support were received from two political organizations, the Women's Liberal Federation and the Tariff Reform Women's Liberal Federation, both of which were admixtures of women from the aristocratic ruling families and the upper reaches of the swelling business class. More important, perhaps, was the assistance received from the Women's Cooperative Guild thanks to the efforts of Mrs Gasson, who served on the general purposes committee of the league's executive. Led by Margaret Llewellyn Davies, one of the most eminent women of her age, the Guild boasted a membership of 30,000, drawn from women of the shopkeeping and upper artisan class rather than from the wives of labourers; every year there was an annual conference of 650 working-class women.[50]

But the most prominent body of women social workers, the Women's Industrial Council founded in 1894, proved harder to win round, as it had sponsored the MacDonalds' bill based on the American licensing system since 1898. To keep its supporters from wrangling, the league decided to continue with its support of the licensing system, while prevaricating when it came to taking a definite stand on the question of minimum wage regulation. Hence it spurned an invitation to attend the Conference on the Minimum Wage held at the Guildhall in October 1906; it instructed its witnesses on the Select Committee on Home Work not to give evidence on the matter of the usefulness of introducing wages boards before Aves returned from his exploratory visit to Australia and New Zealand. When the sister body of the association, the Scottish Industrial Council, insisted on placing the duty of inspecting the sweated workshops on the local authorities rather than on the factory inspectorate, as the MacDonalds demanded, a split occurred over the terms of the English organization's bill and a number of leading members resigned from the executive. 'The question of Wages Boards was discussed', the 1908–9 report admitted, 'and after the [annual] meeting [on 20 January 1909] Miss Clementina Black resigned because the Council decided to take no present official action in the matter.' Although she quit the executive, Clementina Black remained chairman of the investigating committee. The other senior women's organization, the National Union of Women Workers, had postponed a resolution on sweating and wages boards for a year on 14 October 1908 because of the difficulties of the subject, a certain indication of deadlock in the Industrial Committee, which contained Mrs MacDonald and Clementina Black.[51] But as the NASL could boast the adhesion of the most prominent women social workers, such as Mrs Tennant, Mrs Humphrey Ward and Clementina Black, who graced the demonstration in the Queen's Hall in 1908 and the important deputation to Asquith at the close of the year, they crushed the MacDonalds' wavering hold on public opinion.

After this, the league made determined efforts to swing the Churches behind its campaign. Because there was an overlap of membership between the social research unit of the Christian Social Union, among whose members were Gertrude Tuckwell and Constance Smith, and the WTUL, it is hardly surprising that the Anglican Church was dragged into the campaign on the side of minimum wage regulation. A resolution of sympathy was elicited from the Christian Social Union; its leader, Canon Scott Holland agreed to become a president of the league. Other Anglican supporters of the Social Gospel who aided the league's campaign were Bishop Gore, Bishop Wakefield, the chairman of the Homeworkers Association, and Bishop Boyd Capenter, all of whom agreed to serve as vice-presidents of the league; also the Revd Watts-Ditchfield was coopted onto the executive. At the same time, the fact that the campaign was sponsored by George Cadbury and the *Daily News* brought the Nonconformist proponents of the Social Gospel into the picture. Among the Nonconformist celebrities, Dr Horton and Dr Scott Lidgett were nominated as vice-presidents, while the Revd Peter Thompson of the Wesleyan Mission in the East End joined the executive. The Wesleyan Conference also passed a resolution in support of the league's policy. Impressive representatives of the Churches packed the seats on the platform at the Queen's Hall demonstration; even more significant was their attendance in the deputation to Asquith at the end of the year, when the Archbishop of Canterbury spoke and Dr Clifford was present with other Nonconformist leaders. Support for the campaign was also obtained from the Catholic hierarchy and the Chief Rabbi.[52]

Difficulty was encountered in setting up a network of branch organizations, as so many reformist voluntary associations already existed that people suggested that the agitation should be carried out through these societies. At their peak, branches flourished in some ten centres in leading industrial conurbations like Manchester, Birmingham and Liverpool, in medium-sized towns like Leicester and West Hartlepool, in prosperous suburbs of London like Chislehurst and Hampstead, and in areas such as Woolwich and Oxford, where the Christian Social union had already prepared the ground. Maud Smith (Lady Woolton) toiled tirelessly in Manchester, building up an active organization with 150 members; Clementina Black and Miss B. L. Hutchins with the cooperation of Dr Horton led the Hampstead branch of the league, which possessed 250 members. Sustained in large measure by the local trade union movement and religious bodies together with social workers from the upper and middle classes, the local branches of the league husbanded their resources in winning over the opinion leaders from the upper ranks of the working class. Thus the Woolwich branch of the league was formed by the Cooperative Society, which invited trade unions, the Conservative Workingmen's Association and miscellaneous bodies to affiliate; the Birmingham branch was formed at a meeting of delegates representing labour organizations in the Midlands; and the Manchester branch kept in close touch with local trade unions, cooperative societies and religious groups, by sending speakers to meetings, and by convening a conference in 1907 which heard speeches from Clynes, Mary MacArthur and Mallon. Speakers for the branches were supplied by the central office, mostly being selected from the officers and voluntary helpers of the league, and to make the lectures more interesting they were illustrated by lantern slides. Branch activities consisted of undertaking investigations into local sweated trades at Leicester, where reports issued on the glove makers secured a 25 per cent rise in piece rates, organizing outworkers as in Machester and Liverpool and convening meetings and demonstrations. For instance, in 1907 there was a huge gathering at the Mile End Town Hall in support of the scheme, at which 5,000 tailors and tailoresses were present.[53] When Prime Minister Campbell-Bannerman was approached and asked to make the NASL's bill into a government measure, he stated that he could not promise this.[54] Even when the select committee reported in favour of the league's scheme in 1908, at the end of the session the new government of Asquith had still not made up its mind to act. Three factors were responsible for the change in the government's attitude: first there was the intensive nationwide, non-partisan campaign of the league; secondly there was the active support of Herbert Gladstone at the Home Office; thirdly, there was the friendly attitude of Asquith and Churchill.

On the whole, despite the contentious nature of the legislation they were trying to promote, the league avoided becoming embroiled in party controversy. When opening an exhibition staged by the league at Oxford, Lord Milner praised the league for refusing to allow 'the blighting and corrosive influence of party' to vitiate its propaganda. Fabian Ware, the editor of the *Morning Post*, which circulated among the Tory upper class, was also on the executive of the league and encouraged the campaign, by allowing William Beveridge as a leader writer to support trade boards. Likewise A. G. Gardiner, who presided over the executive, lent the campaign of the NASL positive support in the *Daily News*. Toulmin introduced the bill on behalf of the league in 1908, without having to divide the Commons on its second reading. 'Such unanimous acceptance of a measure which introduces a new and very important principle into industrial legislation was the cause of very general comment', proudly proclaimed the league.[55]

In its attempt to court the favour of the general public, the NASL exploited the shock symbol. Having been handed the effects of the sweated industries exhibition at the Queen's Hall by Cadbury, the league – witnessing how the horror evoked hung in the public consciousness – decided to dispatch the exhibits across the country. During the opening year of the campaign, important exhibitions were staged at Manchester, Birmingham and Leicester and smaller ones in Glasgow, Liverpool, and fifty other towns. In the next year, a major exhibition was staged at Bristol, where 1,000 visitors attended each day for two weeks. Because of the exhibition a shoe factory at Kingswood decided to increase wages. Smaller exhibitions were opened in the London suburbs at Forest Gate, Leytonstone and Woolwich, and in Norwich and many of the smaller provincial towns. After that a large exhibition was staged at Crystal Palace in connection with the Cooperative Exhibition and at Ilford, with smaller ones being sponsored elsewhere.[56] Until recently it was assumed that Winston Churchill, as president of the Board of Trade, foisted the Trade Boards Bill onto a somewhat reluctant Cabinet. Nothing lies further from the truth. Herbert Gladstone, the home secretary, who first had charge of the issue before a reshuffle of departmental duties at the end of 1908, took the matter out of his hands, cooperated in every move with the executive of the league. 'The question will arise: if there is to be legislation on what lines should it proceed, and should it be in charge of the Home Office or the Board of Trade? The latter question will be partly determined by the answer to the former', Sir Hubert Llewellyn Smith, Churchill's principal adviser at the Board of Trade told him on 11 August 1908. In other words, if sweating was to be combated by the agency of trade boards, the labour and industrial arbitration experts at the Board of Trade would have to be given charge of the bill, but if the reform involved the licensing system of inspection then the Home Office could safely be entrusted with the bill. Herbert Gladstone's wife was, in fact, a member of the executive of the NASL; he was himself a vice-president. He dispatched a high-ranking civil servant, Ernest Aves, one of Charles Booth's collaborators, to Victoria to inquire into the working of the wages boards. He also permitted the league to display an exhibition of sweated goods to instruct MPs in one of the committee rooms of the Commons in June 1907. 'For the appointment of the [select] committee [in the same year], your Executive feels that it owes acknowledgment to the Home Secretary, who has been consistently helpful and sympathetic.'[57]

Further, a letter from Gladstone to Churchill on 18 December 1908 convincingly shows that it was Gladstone rather than Churchill who was enthusiastic for wages boards from the very first, that he knew every facet of the campaign and that Churchill took over the drafting of the bill as a comparative outsider. Gladstone declared:

> Last July I saw George Askwith K.C. on the sweating question ... He knows more about the possibilities of a Wages B[oar]d than any man alive in this Country. I hope that you will consult him ... The creation of a public opinion has been largely due to the anti-sweating League, headed by G. Cadbury and Gardiner of the D.N. [*Daily News*]. I venture to hope you will take them into counsel for all they are worth. The Sec[retar]y [Mallon] is a little man of energy who knows the ropes of

the public movement and it will be worth your while to see him. On the other side is Ramsay MacDonald whose opposition to the minimum wage has long ago reached the personal stage. But he stands alone among his fellows.[58]

In addition, the subscription list of the league for 1907 shows that the wives of two other cabinet ministers, Birrell and Sydney Buxton, also paid the league's membership dues.

The select committee in its report rebutted the alarmist conclusions of Aves, the Home Office investigator, who had been sent to Australia and New Zealand. He was sceptical whether the minimum wage agreements could be adequately enforced in Britain, where industries were organized on a much greater scale; he thought that the incompetents, the aged and the infirm would be unfairly driven out by wages boards, while large quantities of cheap juvenile labour would be substituted for adult employees; he feared the effects of competition between different areas and from overseas. The crux of the select committee's case was summed up in reasoning borrowed from the Webbs:

> If a trade will not yield such an income [a living wage] to average industrious workers engaged in it, it is a parasitic industry, and it is contrary to the general well-being that it should continue ... Low-priced labour is a great obstacle to improvement ... The direct and early result of prohibiting unsatisfactory conditions in industrial life is almost invariably to direct the attention of the most competent minds ... to the introduction of improvements.[59]

George Shann and Mary MacArthur specifically gave evidence on behalf of the NASL; other prominent members of the league who testified before the select committee were Sir Charles Dilke, Gertrude Tuckwell, Clementina Black and Margaret Irwin; in addition Mary MacArthur and Gertrude Tuckwell shepherded in eight outworkers, whose evidence had a great impact on members of the select committee. Partly because of the way the league marshalled its evidence, and partly because certain members of the league served on the select committee, such as G. P. Gooch MP and Chiozza Money MP, it concluded that wages boards went to the root of the problem by tackling the home workers' poverty but that sanitary reforms assuredly did not do so. Again, George Askwith, an arbitrator for the Board of Trade, having settled piece rates in many industries, told the select committee that as home work was paid on a piece rate basis, he thought that wages boards were practicable. On the other hand, the select committee echoed the views of the leaders of the women's trade union movement in its description of the low wage problem:

> We have had quite extensive evidence to convince us ... that the earnings of a large number of people – mainly women who work in their homes – are so small as alone to be insufficient to sustain life in the most meagre manner, even when they toil hard for extremely long hours.[60]

So too, Asquith on becoming prime minister in 1908 was instrumental in assuring the league that the government would legislate, and it is worth remarking that his sister-in-law Mrs Tennant was on the executive of the league, while her husband was

Churchill's underling at the Board of Trade. When questions in the Commons failed to elicit a convincing reply as to the government's intentions, despite the favourable report of the select committee, on 14 December 1908 the league promptly dispatched a high-powered deputation to Asquith, who was accompanied by Churchill, Buxton and Herbert Gladstone. Churchill with other Lancashire MPs had consented to becoming a vice-president of the Manchester branch of the league on its foundation while he was still an under-secretary at the Colonial Office; the Gladstones were earnest supporters of the league; Sydney Buxton had championed the cause of the sweated workers as a young MP and his wife had subscribed to the league's funds. Anxious to seize the responsibility for bringing in minimum wage regulation, Churchill prevailed on Asquith to listen to the deputation. 'He had an amplitude of spirit, Mallon was heard to say, which saw at once how right and just the case was. Mallon recalls how "with his characteristic magic way" Churchill interceded with Asquith and arranged a meeting with the Prime Minister.' One account of the deputation, evidently based on the recollections of Mallon, suggests that Sidney Webb was chosen as the sole spokesman of the deputation, that he needlessly provoked Asquith into an argument, so that the deputation broke up on an inconclusive note. Contemporary accounts of the deputation show not only that the case for wages boards was put by several speakers, but that Asquith's reply was most encouraging. Asquith stated that 'so far as I myself am concerned, I am in sympathy with the proposal to proceed by way of the establishment of Wages Boards'; he had not yet consulted his colleagues; he promised them a careful consideration of the matter. Going back into the room to retrieve a hat left by a member of the departing deputation, Mallon overheard a discussion between the assembled ministers: Churchill asked Asquith to let him play with the question, to which Asquith consented.[61]

There is rather an extraordinary account of a meeting a few days later between Churchill and a small working party from the league, consisting of Mallon, Mary MacArthur and Clementina Black, to clarify what action the government should take, again based on the recollections of Mallon but without confirmatory evidence from the Board of Trade records. If it is true, it would show that Churchill held far more advanced views on the question of a living wage than Asquith and Lloyd George, and that the Board of Trade experts were keener on the necessity for a living wage than has hitherto thought to have been the case. Churchill instructed his experts to plot the level of wages on a graph:

> He wanted advice on what was a 'reasonable wage'. He proposed to draw a line across his graph at this level and to ask Parliament to give him power to deal with all industries in which wages were 'below the line'. This would have involved at least one-third of the working population.

Further:

> To objections from the deputation that, much as they would welcome so glorious a crown to all their efforts, it would be impossible to get this revolutionary plan through Parliament, Churchill replied with an impatient gesture towards the lower half of his graph, 'I would call all these sweated trades. If you would give me a word like sweated to use I will guarantee to ride down any opposition.'[62]

Those like Mallon, who had spent years in pushing, prodding, intriguing, cajoling and proselytizing, were convinced that they were in danger of losing a prospective small, but real, victory if an attempt was made to leap at a bound towards these larger and more distant horizons. They sought allies in their efforts to curb Churchill's overmastering enthusiasm. It was Arthur Henderson who finally persuaded the impetuous president of the Board of Trade to adopt the principles of the Dilke bill which, like its author, had by now become almost respectable.

There is some evidence that seems to bear out the authenticity of this account. As far back as March 1908 Churchill had written in the *Nation*:

> The House of Commons has unanimously approved the institution of Wages Boards in certain notoriously 'sweated industries', and this principle may be found capable of almost indefinite extension in the those industries which employ parasitically underpaid labour.[63]

Moreover, in conversations between Churchill and Riddell for a Grand Coalition in March 1913, Churchill made much of the idea of a minimum wage for agricultural labourers and those in other trades. What is clear is that Churchill, having imbibed the Webbs' concept of a national minimum, took it very seriously.[64] It was also true that all along the NASL had a limited objective of raising women's wages and that they did not want their campaign disrupted by any widening of the horizons.

At any rate, Churchill intimated to Asquith that he intended returning to London for the new year so as to prepare a Sweated Industries Bill for presentation to Parliament. On 12 January 1909 he informed Asquith that a workmanlike scheme had been hammered out with the help of Llewellyn Smith, which could be brought before the Cabinet whenever he wished. Although Llewellyn Smith had previously opposed Dilke's bill, the new regime of Churchill and Tennant at the Board of Trade made him more amenable to the idea of wages boards.[65]

In the anticipatory period before the shape of Churchill's proposals were known, the NASL maintained its pressure on the government by holding large meetings in Liverpool, Leeds and Manchester. In the main the government bill introduced by Churchill on 24 March 1909 followed the NASL's own proposals, which in turn adhered to the design of the legislation from Victoria. As Dilke's original bill did not earmark any trades in which the trade boards experiment was to commence, it was decided to place the tailoring, dress and shirt trades in the schedule of the bill. Influenced by the pleas of witnesses who testified before it, the Select Committee on Home Work (1908) chose five trades, three of which differed from the league's choices, namely under-clothing, baby linen and the finishing processes of machine-made lace. The government's Trade Boards Bill departed from these suggestions, including instead the ready-made and bespoke tailoring trade, cardboard box making, machine-made lace and the ready-made blouse trade, for which chain making was later substituted. 'Most of us can remember', recalled Miss Irwin in 1912, 'the surprise and keen disappointment felt by the omission of this [the shirt making] trade when the Act was passed.'[66]

Following the practice in Victoria, the boards were to be composed of equal numbers of employers and workers representatives with an impartial chairman.

Whereas the league's bill set out to adjust wages to local conditions, by allowing them to vary with the cost of living in the district, the government bill created district wage boards to fix the minimum time and piece rates before sending their proposals for approval to the central trade board. Although not embodied in the league's bill, this last point had arisen after discussions between Miss Rose Squire, the other factory inspectors and the promoters of the league's bill; it also figured among the select committee's recommendations. Once the trade board had prescribed these rates, the Board of Trade on the application of the individual board could make these rates obligatory in law. One important concession that the league wrung out of the government was the inclusion of both factory and home workers in the scope of the boards, even if the select committee had not appreciated the advantages of bringing factory workers within the orbit of the trade boards scheme. Because the text of the government bill showed that the enforcement and inspection clauses were inadequate, Sir Charles Dilke MP and J. W. Hills MP, a progressive Conservative, pressed a second reading of the league's bill until satisfactory assurances were squeezed out of the government. 'During the Committee stage of the Bill the Secretary of the Women's Trade Union League and the Secretary of the Anti-Sweating League attended all meetings, and supplied information to members acting on the League's behalf', the 1910 report of the WTUL disclosed.[67]

Churchill's aim was to establish trade boards only in industries where the 'wages [were] *exceptionally* low' and where 'conditions prejudicial to physical and social welfare' existed, though if the experiment proved to be successful, they were later to be extended to additional trades. During the progress of the bill through the Commons, chain making, which was concentrated in a compact area, was substituted for shirt making, as an industry to be covered by a trade board. Churchill admitted:

> It is not because there is no great sweating about the shirt-making industry, but because to serve the cause of anti-sweating legislation we had better choose the ground on which we can rely to meet with the fairest possible prospects of success.[68]

Although Mary MacArthur and the NASL attributed the inclusion of chain making in the bill to the strength of their campaigning, there are strong grounds for believing that this victory was achieved by successful pressure from the Chain Manufacturers' Association.[69] Costs of administration were pared down to the minimum. Churchill claimed:

> £15,000 a year will cover the salaries and expenses of official members and inspectors, expenses of representative members, and incidentals such as postage, printing and light, heat, etc. I should like to point out to the House that by utilizing the premises of the Labour Exchanges, and having those as the places in which the Trade Board would meet there will only be a small expenditure on rent and staff.[70]

Despite cross-party support for trade boards, the passing of the 1909 Act marked another triumph of the tacit alliance between exponents of the New Liberalism, such as George Cadbury, A. G. Gardiner and Chiozza Money MP, and the two wings of the Labour movement: the trade unions and the Sociological Socialists. However, the NASL campaigners espoused the cause of women workers and were opposed to a minimum wage for all sections of the working class, as they believed that females were most discriminated against financially and needed the most protection. The implementation of old age pensions by Asquith and Lloyd George in 1908 and Churchill's sponsorship of the Trade Boards Act and the Labour Exchanges legislation marked a decisive shift in the Asquith administration towards a bold programme of social reconstruction and away from some of the Liberals' tired old panaceas, which were losing their appeal for the electorate. Whereas Campbell-Bannerman had not been enthusiastic about social reform, Asquith was prepared to encourage ministers such as Lloyd George and Churchill who showed initiative, and he had a much more positive attitude to measures for alleviating poverty. In the view of the Liberal journalist A. G. Gardiner, once installed as prime minister, Asquith commanded

> in a rare degree the confidence of his party, and his handling of the Parliamentary machine, at once masterful and adroit, has won universal admiration. He is slow to take up adventurous courses, but, once convinced, he has unequalled power to give them shape and, in doing so, to carry the conviction that comes from his own secure and impassioned intellect to that timid public who see the dread form of 'Socialism' in every effort after a more just and therefore more firmly-rooted State.[71]

# 6

# The Webbs and the Minority Report of the Poor Law

All the reforms which we have so far discussed were put forward by pressure groups with one specific aim in mind, which they continued to agitate for until the government agreed to find parliamentary time for its embodiment in legislation. In contrast to these reformers, Beatrice and Sidney Webb were prominent socialists and elitists, who cultivated leading politicians from the Conservative and Liberal parties with the aim of changing political opinion at the highest level, while remaining aloof from the Labour movement. Having worked well with the Conservatives in educational reform, Beatrice remained under the spell of Arthur Balfour, with his tantalizing hints of an interest in Poor Law reform. Deluded into believing they would implement a national minimum standard of life to foster an imperial race, the Webbs struck up friendships as well with the Liberal imperialists. Hence Sidney founded a 'bizarre' dining club, the Co-efficients, where he preached both the cause of imperialism, the superiority of British civilization, and that of social reform. Here he established good relations with Richard Haldane and Edward Grey.[1] The Webbs believed in a policy of permeation, of implanting their ideas for social reform in the governing elite before they realized they had imbibed them. Only with the failure of the policy of permeation did the Webbs turn to pressure group politics, by founding the National Committee for the Relief of Destitution, which united socialists and the exponents of the New Liberalism.

Among the fresh features introduced by the 1902 Education Act was the abolition of school boards and the transfer of their powers to counties and county boroughs. In 1903 there were rumours in the press that the Cabinet wished to abolish the boards of guardians and transfer their responsibilities to the county councils. In this the Conservative government was influenced by their recent destruction of the school boards and the presumed administrative efficiency that it was deemed to have accomplished. When Walter Long at the Local Government Board voiced his proposal to abolish the long-established administrative system for the needy, the outcry of the Poor Law Unions Association with its supporters was so great that he was forced to drop it.[2] Instead the government decided to assemble the evidence so as to smooth the path for this major administrative upheaval. Long's successor, Gerald Balfour, the brother of the prime minister, Arthur Balfour, appointed the Royal Commission on the Poor Laws and the Relief of Distress which deliberated between 1905 and 1909. Through her friendship with the Balfour brothers, Beatrice Webb was appointed as a member of the Commission which numbered among its members five guardians of the poor, the three permanent heads of the Local Government Board of England, Scotland and Ireland, and six influential members of the Charity Organisation plus the ailing Charles Booth, the most distinguished social investigator in Britain. These members were reinforced by the addition of two orthodox political economists, a few clerics, and a labour and socialist representative, Francis Chandler and George Lansbury, apart from Beatrice Webb herself. All served under the debonair and charming chairman, Lord George Hamilton, a former Conservative cabinet minister.[3] When Asquith became prime minister in April 1908, the Liberals had hardly breached the Poor Law, despite the fighting talk of Churchill and others in their election addresses in 1906 of reforming the Poor Law. What this meant, exclaimed *The Poor Law Officers' Journal*, was hinted at in

> vague generalities about 'the removal of the badge of pauperism from the unfortunate poor', and such like expressions, grounded all of them on the belief ... that the grant of State-aid ought to be conceived rather in the spirit of the Unemployed Act than that of the law we have so long known and worked under. This view holds that as it is no disgrace to the unfortunate poor to apply for relief from the public at large, such applications ought not to carry with them ... the disability of disenfranchisement.[4]

Because the Asquith administration adopted health and unemployment insurance as the Liberal answer to the Poor Law, the Webbs later believed that they had utterly failed to push the government along the road of Poor Law reform. In this Beatrice Webb was quite wrong. What we wish to assert is that the influence which Beatrice and Sidney Webb were able to exert over Asquith, Haldane and Churchill for a brief period in 1907 and 1908 was profound. Through the persistence of the Webbs, the government was driven to adopt an old age pensions scheme along non-contributory lines without being weakened by Poor Law intrusions, when the bill was lost to the input of the Labour-orientated National Old Age Pensions Committee during the vital drafting stage. More important, the non-contributory pension scheme – divorced as it was from the Poor Law – was the first major legislative measure of the Liberal administration that challenged the philosophical basis of the Poor Law system. Moreover, as José Harris has suggested, 'into the vacuum in unemployment policy created by the rejection of the Right to Work Bill, however, it was the Webbs who introduced a new fourfold programme, based on labour organisation, reformatory training, subsidized insurance, and public works', which the Liberal government appropriated in the autumn of 1908 as the cyclical trade depression deepened.[5] Beatrice Webb attempted to steer the Royal Commission in a new direction. But because of her failure to evolve a sufficiently radical critique of the problems of unemployment and casual labour and her inability to grasp the full dimensions of the problem of poverty, she could not propound a distinctive enough set of ideas with which to rip apart the whole fabric of the Poor Law system. Nevertheless, the government was brilliantly cajoled by her into promising a large-scale health reform, and the Webbs wheedled and needled Asquith into bringing the question of the break-up of the Poor Law onto the centre of the political stage.

Partly because the mass of unskilled workers were only eager to protest about their conditions of labour in times of exceptional distress, and partly because the legislative proposals put forward by the Labour movement represented on the whole the ideas of the skilled sections of the working class, organized in unions and the branches of the ILP and the Social Democratic Federation, the attention of the Liberal administration was focused on the problem of unemployment rather than on the broader issues of poverty. As Trevor Lummis has pointed out,

> This permanent poverty was the first and most crucial problem. Eight, 10, or even 15 per cent unemployment due to the trade cycle with the accompanying poverty for a few weeks, or even ... months [was] a less pressing evil [than those] in permanent poverty.[6]

From another angle, Beveridge and other Edwardian researchers showed that casual labour or under-employment was not only an enduring phenomenon but that it was the principal cause of unemployment and pauperism or perhaps even of poverty. The argument was carried a stage further by Sidney and Beatrice Webb, when they demonstrated in their Minority Report that the bulk of pauperism, apart from sickness and old age, or in other words the Poor Law system itself was produced by casual labour. Edwardian critics spoke in sweeping terms of millions of casual labourers, creating the illusion that the drastic reduction in their numbers by the organization of the labour market through the establishment of a national system of labour exchanges was the foremost task of social reformers. There is now a consensus among historians that the Edwardian social critics incorrectly stigmatized a section of the unemployed as unemployables, who could only be removed from society by detaining them in labour colonies, but they disappeared quickly with the upsurge in demand with the coming of the Great War.[7] We would, however, go further and question the staggering estimates of casual labour bandied about by Edwardian sociologists, projections which have been uncritically accepted by historians and which in turn served to preserve the Poor Law system from fundamental reform. There was a common misconceived opinion that the number of able-bodied paupers, both those inside the workhouse and those receiving outdoor relief, was of formidable dimensions, when this was not the case. On 1 January 1908 there were 11,413 men and 9,147 women immured in workhouses in England and Wales, while there were 16,213 men receiving outdoor relief, the majority of whom were mentally or physically unfit to do a full day's work.[8]

Beatrice Webb's most formidable protagonist on the Poor Law Commission was Helen Bosanquet (1860-1925), who drafted most sections of the Majority Report. A graduate of Newnham College, Cambridge, she completed the Moral Sciences Tripos in 1889, after which she went to work as the district secretary of the Charity Organisation Society in Shoreditch. She stayed for a few years in the Women's University Settlement before taking up residence in Hoxton, where she developed warm feelings towards the poor and their concerns. In 1895 she married the leading idealist philosopher Bernard Bosanquet, with whose views she was already in agreement, and wrote a series of books on the problems of poverty which were widely utilized in the training of social workers. She grounded her approach to social work in Idealist philosophy, placing an emphasis on the mind and will, and believing that only by changing an individual's behaviour could character development and progress be achieved. Helen tried first of all to understand individuals, by unravelling their family dynamics and their place in the community, including the workplace. Whereas Beatrice Webb saw intervention by the state as the solution to the problem of poverty, Helen believed in strengthening the character of the family, particularly that of the working-class wife and mother – a social casework viewpoint. Jane Lewis has asserted that not only did Helen empathize with poor women because of her feminist sentiments but that she wanted to 'empower the poor' and that her understanding of them 'was in many ways more profound' than that of Beatrice Webb. Although she contested the necessity for a school meals service and for the medical inspection of schoolchildren, seeing this as a dereliction of family responsibilities, she favoured many of the interventions by the state that were contemplated by contemporaries.[9] More than this, as the compiler of the Majority Report she approved of a number of collectivist recommendations and with C. S. Loch added a memorandum to the report, accepting 'the necessity of making some provision for meeting exceptional distress, if it should arise in the transitional period, before the system of Public Assistance has been actually established'.[10]

Imbued with a sense of superiority, sly and manipulative, and at times uncooperative, Beatrice Webb needlessly alienated other members of the Poor Law Commission, though their views often coincided, and hence she was unable to gain many adherents from her fellow commissioners. Thus, most of the members of the Commission signed the Majority Report, while Beatrice, supported by three other members, signed a Minority Report which was written by Sidney, who was not a member of the Commission. The Majority Report supported the transfer of welfare services to the county councils and county boroughs and insisted that 'pauperism was to be treated, not tested', thereby relinquishing the 'less eligibility' principle of the existing Poor Law system. Most of Beatrice's fellow commissioners declared:

> What we are aiming at is, instead of a system of allowances, granted capriciously and irresponsibly to meet a constantly increasing demand to substitute a system of careful and varied assistance, in which the allowance, will be only one of many forms of help, and which will be directly designed to raise the recipients, or where it is not possible the children of recipients, to a position of independence.[11]

Further, it recommended 'a substantial extension of the social services, under or outside the Poor Law, for the sick, the aged, children and the mentally defective'. It advocated a national system of labour exchanges to assist the unemployed, and recognized the 'necessity for a great extension of insurance against unemployment', particularly among the unskilled and unorganized labour, while at the same time indicating a willingness to provide a state subsidy to trade unions and other voluntary bodies to encourage enrolment in a scheme. On the other hand, it was opposed to any compulsory scheme of insurance.[12] It opposed 'making medical assistance gratuitous for all who cared to apply for it, and for transferring to the Sanitary Authorities the work of Guardians in connection with medical relief'; instead handing over medical treatment to a committee of the Public Assistance Authority which would be helped by representatives of the local Health Committee and doctors and would be able to co-opt additional representatives from hospitals, dispensaries and friendly societies

– a complicated and unworkable arrangement. Wage earners were expected to take out insurance to become members of a provident dispensary, but the aged and widows with children would obtain free membership, as their fees would be paid by the Public Assistance Committee.[13]

A crucial matter on which the two reports disagreed was that the Majority wished to utilize the services of the Public Assistance Authority to deal with the residuum of persons always seeking help, whom they believed would need 'continuous treatment'. Falling into this class were neglected children, frail elderly persons incapable of looking after themselves, unmarried mothers, the feeble-minded, persons suffering from infectious tuberculosis and venereal disease; and among the able-bodied, the loafer and those persons who neglected their families 'owing to habits of gambling, drink, or idleness'. Men in this last category were to be 'submitted to a course of severe discipline or training, which even if it does not restore the[m] ... to a comparative state of industrial efficiency, will at least for a certain period prevent ... further demoralisation'. Nonetheless, the Public Assistance Authority, which the Majority Report contemplated to vet applicants, was so dependent on the services of a vast number of volunteers that the scheme was flawed and unsustainable.[14]

Beatrice Webb, too, was concerned about finding a curative form of treatment to tackle the problem of the able-bodied unemployed. At first when she broached the subject to Reginald McKenna, she proposed attendance at an industrial school inculcating compulsory technical training and also providing recreational activities. When this proposal was rejected, she decided to set up a committee of enquiry into the unemployed outside the Poor Law Commission, consisting of Canon Barnett, William Beveridge and R. H. Tawney, to suggest remedies.[15] Beveridge's proposals soon came to dominate these discussions. In July 1904 Beveridge as an innovation had conducted a follow-up survey of 467 unemployed East End labourers given relief work in the winter of 1903–4 at the Hadleigh farm colony, discovering that seventy-two (or 26 per cent) had obtained regular employment since the closure of relief works in February or March, 102 (36 per cent) had obtained casual employment during one month in four or five, while 107 (38 per cent) had been unemployed or had found meagre casual jobs. From this followed the development of Beveridge's theory of under-employment and the reserve of labour, the latter almost certainly borrowed from the Webbs, which was developed in lectures and articles, his evidence to the Poor Law Commission, and finally elaborated in his *Unemployment: A Problem of Industry* (1909). He also served as secretary of the Charity Organisation Committee on Unskilled Labour, which mainly focused on casual employment in the London docks. During a visit to the Webbs in August 1907, he converted them to the need for a national system of labour exchanges, which they supplemented with unemployment insurance, technical education and penal colonies for the needlessly idle.[16]

Behind Beveridge's theory of under-employment and the reserve of labour was an attempt to reformulate common assumptions about the unemployed into the intellectually more tenable form of a sociological hypothesis, by reworking material contained in the researches of Booth and the Webbs. First there was the viewpoint shared with the Webbs and Booth that '[t]he industrial demoralisation of East London is ... caused mainly by the two factors of home work and intermittent dock labour, and even the existence of so large a class of irregularly employed dock labourers is, to a large extent rendered possible only by the home work done by their wives' – an early statement by Beatrice Webb. But in their volume *Industrial Democracy* (1898), the Webbs, on the strength of the additional researches of the Booth survey team in London, were able to draw wider conclusions about the industrial conditions in the metropolis:

> The facility of obtaining 'large supplies of low-paid labour', says Mr Charles Booth, 'may be regarded as the proximate cause of the expansion of some of the most distinctive manufacturing industries of East and South London – furniture, boots and shoes, caps, clothing, paper bags, and cardboard boxes, matches, jam etc. ... They are found in the neighbourhood of districts largely occupied by unskilled or semi-skilled workmen, or by those whose employment is most discontinuous, since it is chiefly the daughters, wives and widows of these men who turn to labour of this kind.'[17]

Further, the Webbs were of the opinion that because of the built-in weaknesses of their position in the labour market, dockers, women and boy labour could not be saved by the introduction of collective bargaining procedures:

> There is, in fact, for unspecialised manual labour ... a practically unlimited 'reserve army' made up of temporarily unemployed members of every other class. As these form a perpetually shifting body, and the occupation of 'general labouring' needs no apprenticeship, no combination, however co-extensive it might be with labourers actually employed at any one time, could deprive the employer of the alternative of engaging an entirely new gang.[18]

In contrast to Booth, the Webbs regarded the free market as a crude mechanism, producing unemployment which was wasteful and destructive to the individuals concerned.

Beveridge in his *Unemployment* (1909) extended and vulgarized these conclusions relating to the London trades, by arguing from the distress committee returns, a third or half of which came from London – a procedure fraught with risks of bias in the statistical sample – that the unemployed mainly consisted of casual labourers, who not only existed in large numbers but were heavily distributed throughout the length and breadth of the land; by asserting that every industry had its own special reserve of labour; by adopting Booth's proposal to the 1892 Labour Commission of labour exchanges as a remedy for the evils of casual riverside employment in London; and by declaring with increasing conviction that until a national system of labour exchanges was inaugurated to drain the swamps of casual labour, no other reform for dealing with the remaining hazards of unemployment was feasible. The distribution of employment would be regulated in such a way that regular work would be given to a portion of casual labourers, while the rest would be helped to emigrate to Canada or directed to farm colonies. Once the labour exchanges had been organized then other measures would be set in motion for dealing with cyclical unemployment. Chief among these was unemployment insurance. So too, Beveridge completely took over Charles Booth's strictures on the foibles and failings of men in classes B and C in London, though he linked the character weaknesses of these unskilled men in the labour market to the demand of employers for a reserve of labour, claiming that

> Employers want men only irregularly; men have learnt to fight against irregularity of earnings as they have learnt to fight against low rates of pay; as a consequence they submit to sweating by under-employment far worse than the more familiar sweating by under-payment. These are two sides of the problem of normal poverty which is being forced on public attention in the shape of the problem of unemployment.[19]

Nonetheless, Beveridge's emphasis on character was not something he merely derived from Booth, nor did his theory of under-employment stand or fall by such pronouncement, but was the considered articulation of a wider assumption that he shared with contemporaries, particularly those who served on the local Charity Organisation committees, and it should be noted that Beveridge went as a frequent visitor and admirer to the Whitechapel branch office.[20]

To provide a critical evaluation of Beveridge's casual labour theory, we shall attempt to assess as accurately as possible as we can from contemporary sociological literature the geographical distribution of casual labour and its exact significance in contributing to poverty in Edwardian England. Above all, it is clear from Bowley and Burnett-Hurst's examination of the problem in four industrial communities just before the First World War and Seebohm Rowntree's survey of York in 1899 that neither unemployment nor casual labour was a major cause of poverty. The percentage of poverty attributable to the casual employment of the chief wage earner was in the industrial towns of Warrington 3 per cent, Reading 4 per cent, and York 3 per cent, while in neither Northampton nor Stanley, a mining community, was the factor an immediate cause of poverty. The percentages relating to unemployment in these places was similar, with 3 per cent of the poverty in Warrington and York and 2 per cent in Reading being attributable to this factor, while Northampton and Stanley showed no indications of unemployment at the time of surveys. Hence the suspicion must be strong that casual labour was confined to certain towns with trades in which casual labour was endemic, such as work in the docks, or trades being revolutionized by new technological processes, as in the boot industry. This suspicion is confirmed by the findings of an enquiry undertaken by Rose Squire and A. D. Steel-Maitland for the Poor Law Commission, which vindicates the general drift of the conclusions of the poverty surveys. Casual labour was found to be exceptionally prevalent in London; to be common in commercial and distributive centres such as Manchester, Newcastle and Liverpool, but on nothing like the London scale; to be of minute proportions in the manufacturing towns; and to be practically non-existent in country towns.[21]

If the combined weight of these poverty surveys points to the conclusion that under-employment was a relatively minor sore in Edwardian England, then Sidney Webb's estimate in 1913 of 700,000 male casuals with another 100,000 female casuals in the UK must in all probability be scaled down to something like the German return of 356,000 casuals in a much larger population, which is approaching the figure of half a million casuals put forward by Bowley in 1907. The estimate of the Webbs of 1.2

million casuals mentioned in the Minority Report must be rejected, as must Seebohm Rowntree's suggestion in 1914 that there could be as many as 2.5 million casuals.[22]

The Webbs embraced the gamut of Beveridge's ideas, repeating them in a much more extreme form in part 2 of the Minority Report. As early as 22 May 1906 Beatrice Webb gleefully reported in her diary that the Poor Law Commission was on her side:

> What makes him [C. S. Loch, the COS representative] angry is that the enquiry is drifting straight into the *causes of destitution* instead of being restricted to the narrower question of *granted destitution is inevitable, how can we best prevent pauperism?* And the answer is being extracted by our enquiry into the causes of destitution takes the form of *more regulation and more public provision without the stigma of pauperism* – probably compulsory provision which *must* be given and *cannot* be refused.[23]

Retreating from the position which they had adopted in *Industrial Democracy* of laying down national minimum standards of welfare provision and suggesting that low wages were the principal cause of poverty, Beatrice Webb, in an ill-conceived attempt to win over her fellow commissioners, omitted mentioning these contentions in the Minority Report, after alienating them by her arrogant and intemperate behaviour. Previously the Webbs had suggested in 1902:

> As a nation we are becoming keenly conscious of the fact that the existence of whole classes who are chronically underfed, ill-clothed, badly housed, and over-worked constitute [a] ... serious drain on the vitality and productivity of the community as a whole. The only effective way to prevent the national loss involved in the existence of `parasitic' trades is seen to be the compulsory extension to them of those Common Rules which the stronger trades got for themselves. The idea of a compulsory enforced `National Minimum' – already embodied in our law as regards sanitation and education – is now seen to be applicable as regards rent and subsistence.[24]

Further, they added that Booth estimated that of the eight million adult males in the United Kingdom, one million in London lived on less than £1 a week.

> Even the average mechanic or factory operative, who earn from 20s. to 35s. per week, seldom obtain enough nourishing food, or adequate amount of sleep, or sufficiently comfortable surroundings to allow him to put forth the full physical and mental energy of which his frame is capable.[25]

But instead of emphasizing the need for national minimum standards in the Minority Report, the Webbs toned down their conclusion in a forlorn attempt to achieve consensus. Hence Kathleen Woodroofe conceded that '[a]lthough it is nowhere specifically mentioned, the underlying principle of the Minority Report, and to a lesser extent of the Majority Report, is clearly that of a "National Minimum"'.[26]

Despite Beatrice Webb's disclaimers, she must receive the credit not only for forcing some forms of medical reform on the government, but for developing the concept of a national health service, in contrast to the older idea of paying out sick benefit, with rare acuity and a stunning power of argumentation; it was a major sociological insight. Moreover, she approached nearer to winning the Cabinet to her proposals than she ever realized. In July 1906 when listening to the Charity Organisation Society members of the commission say that all medical relief should be restricted to the technically destitute, Beatrice Webb decided to adopt the opposite view – that is, of treating illness as a public nuisance to be suppressed in the interests of the community. When cross-examining witnesses she brought out the conflict between the Poor Law and public health authorities because of the divergence of attitude as to what were the requisite functions of the state in combating illness. For advice on how to obtain expert testimony in favour of her proposition that the Poor Law medical service should be merged with the public health authority, she turned to Dr George McCleary. As a leading public health authority, he was well acquainted with the idiosyncrasies of the medical officers of health and thus able to advise Beatrice Webb as to the doctors who were likely to supply helpful evidence, if summoned before the commission; dinner parties were held for the purpose of briefing witnesses, so that they would lend the weight of their testimony to the lines of thought along which Beatrice wished to persuade her fellow members on the commission to proceed.[27]

To arouse the interest of the MOHs throughout the country, Beatrice drafted a questionnaire on the relation of the Poor Law medical service to the public health authority. In January 1907 there was a protest against calling any more MOHs, as '[t]hey are all for one scheme, we know their view now'. Beatrice 'compromised on printed précis for eight more – two only to be cross-examined. And apparently, I am to have choosing of both of those who send in their statements and those who are to be called.'[28] By September 1906 over 100 replies had been received, most favouring her viewpoint. Some of this correspondence is still extant; their gist was that the medical work of the Boards of Guardians should be transferred to the public health authority. Not surprisingly, after having taken such precautions, no fewer than fifty-one MOHs testified before the commission that the policy of restricting the use of Poor Law doctors was responsible for the excessive infant mortality and the unnecessary ill-health and premature invalidity among wage earners.[29] Nonetheless, there was a significant minority of MOHs who objected to the thrust of Beatrice's proposals, such as the MOH for Sunderland, Dr H. Renney. He denounced the reference to the 'grudgingly doled out bottles of physic' as a 'gratuitous libel' and the absurdity of the suggestion that 'almost every case of illness may be regarded as a "public nuisance"'. In October 1907 Mrs Bosanquet challenged Beatrice, demanding that she hand over to the commission the replies from the MOHs on which she based her report on the reconstruction of the medical services. Although willing to do so, Beatrice removed some of the most hostile replies before she handed over the correspondence to the commission, justifying her own stricken conscience with Jesuitical posturing. Having called Dr Arthur Newsholme, whom she acknowledged as the 'most impressive and emphatic' of her witnesses, Beatrice regarded the battle for 'medical relief ... fought and won as far as I can win it'. In addition, her allies Robert Morant and Dr George Newman were installed at the Board of Education, while she assisted Newsholme's candidature when he applied to become the chief medical officer at the Local Government Board.[30]

Having harried her fellow commissioners until they were practically distraught, Beatrice now switched her attention to the Liberal administration. On 30 April 1907 she wrote to Reginald McKenna:

> Here are two or three statements that will show you the trend of evidence in favour of the transfer of Poor Law medical relief to the public health authority, with a view to organizing in each locality the discovery and prevention of disease. The evidence from all parts of the kingdom is becoming so overwhelming that I believe there is already a clear majority in favour of the consolidation of medical assistance under the public health authority.[31]

When she later sent him her paper on the break-up of the Poor Law, he replied:

> It would be presumptuous in me to praise your memorandum but at least I may express its effect on my mind as the most complete and I am disposed to think only satisfactory solution of the Poor Law problem which is open to us.[32]

Copies of the brief were also given to Asquith, Haldane, Churchill, Lloyd George, Buxton, Runciman, Harcourt, Burns and Samuel. Meanwhile, though the chairman of the commission favoured her proposals to some extent and though Beatrice had expected victory in this one matter, the commission in February 1908 voted against removing medical relief from the Poor Law, but such were Beatrice's contacts with the government that such momentary failures did not seem to matter much.[33]

The Webbs seized on public health reform and shaped it into a practical political proposition. Between them Beatrice and Sidney Webb had drafted a paper by the middle of 1907 which embodied Beatrice's new ideas on the functions and scope of a public health service. Richard Burdon Haldane was sounded out on the scheme, and then having read the Webbs' paper, promptly passed it on to Asquith. Do not let us underestimate the interest shown by Haldane and Asquith in Poor Law reform. Asquith was the individual in the government most involved in the whole question of Poor Law reform, as he had overall charge of the old age pensions scheme, about which he was most enthusiastic. If this was the case, perhaps his whole position as regards Poor Law reform can be viewed in a new and more favourable light. Haldane devoted all his spare time to the Poor Law question and was given charge of Poor Law reform by Asquith, who had just become prime minister and had more than an inkling that John Burns was a hindrance to reform. Among the Webb Papers is a rather mysterious letter from Haldane to Mrs Webb dated 30 May 1908, which seems to refer to Burns. One by one Asquith agreed to hand over Burns' departmental duties as regards Poor Law reform to other members of the Cabinet: public health to Lloyd George; unemployment to Winston Churchill; and general Poor Law reform to Haldane.[34]

Asquith was favourably impressed by the paper of the Webbs on public health reform and decided to set up a Cabinet committee on Poor Law reform in the autumn of 1907; presumably this committee and that on old age pensions were one and the same. Haldane prepared a memorandum to serve as a preliminary basis for discussion, which was deeply influenced by the Webbs' ideas. He began by stating that a pensions scheme must involve a comprehensive classification of individuals and of the modes of relieving them, and that this in turn would involve a sweeping reform of the Poor Law.

The sick, the aged and children would all be removed from the baneful influence of the Poor Law. Now follow two typically ideas of the Webbs: children would be entrusted to the care of the local education authority; and whenever sickness had the character of being a menace to society, it was to be dealt with by the public health authority outside the framework of the Poor Law.[35] The results of this Cabinet investigation are not entirely clear, even if one thing is certain: Lloyd George's taking up the question of health insurance must be linked to this in some way. When the Webbs sent Haldane some further papers in December 1907 on the break-up of the Poor Law and old age pensions, Haldane handed them over to Asquith, remarking that 'they have a bearing on what we are working out'. Further, Lloyd George's conversion to the need for a health insurance scheme is rather mysterious. As late as 18 June 1908 Lloyd George, when replying to a deputation of friendly societies on the Old Age Pensions Bill which he had to shepherd through Parliament, remarked that if adopting the German scheme of dealing with workmen's infirmities would destroy the friendly societies, this would be wicked, and that was one reason why the German scheme was inapplicable to Britain. Yet one week later Churchill, speaking in Dundee, declared that sickness and unemployment insurance had come within the range of practical politics.[36]

How are we to explain Lloyd George's conversion? Perhaps something may be attributed to Asquith. Haldane had told Beatrice Webb earlier in 1907 that Asquith had some of his own ideas on Poor Law reform.[37] Then it should be borne in mind that the intention of the government was still to graft a health insurance scheme on a unified public health service. It is interesting to note that when the Webbs breakfasted with Lloyd George accompanied by William Blain at the Treasury in October 1908 to discuss his health insurance scheme, the only other minister present was Haldane, who tried to act as peacemaker. According to Beatrice, they

> had a heated discussion with the Chancellor about the practicability of insurance against invalidity; tried to make him see that the state could not enter into competition with the friendly societies and insurance companies, that it could hardly subsidise a voluntary scheme without becoming responsible for the management, and that any insurance scheme would leave over all the real problems of public assistance. I tried to impress on them that any grant from the community to the individual, beyond what it does for all, ought to be conditional on better conduct and that any insurance scheme had the fatal defect that the state got nothing for its money – that the persons felt they had a right to the allowance whatever their conduct. Also, if you did all that was requisite for those who were uninsured, there was not much to be gained by being insured, except more freedom.[38]

Haldane, by way of compromise, 'suggested that insurance had to be a big part of the scheme with conditional relief for those at the bottom and insurance for those struggling up'. Finally, it should be remembered that the famous trip to Germany of Lloyd George in August 1908 was to decide whether a scheme of health insurance was practicable and that as late as December the scheme remained in a tentative state, as it was still uncertain whether the cooperation of the friendly societies could be secured.[39]

Through their friendship with Haldane, the Webbs once again struck up an acquaintanceship with Asquith, and at the beginning of 1908 there was considerable contact between the Webbs and Asquith, both socially and by letter. The diary of Beatrice Webb records at least three meetings between her and Asquith at the start of the year. Some correspondence also passed between them, so that among the Asquith Papers is Beatrice's scheme for the break-up of the Poor Law. She asserted that there was a need to end the overlapping and confusion between the different social services; there was a need to substitute a curative mode of treatment for that of deterrence, at least with regard to the sick and children, and public opinion accepted this; both demands would require a fresh classification and regrouping of the old Poor Law services to be made. To the local education authority would go Poor Law schools, cottage homes and whatever was decided on for the apprenticeship of boys and girls. To the public health authority would be given the task of providing medical treatment for the whole population. To the newly constituted pensions authority would be transferred the care of the aged. To a Ministry of Labour would be handed the care of the unemployed, but Beatrice's plans for dealing with unemployment was only tentatively sketched. In a letter that Beatrice dispatched to Asquith, she referred to the fact that he was in possession of a copy of her scheme. On 30 May 1908 J. Vaughan Nash, the private secretary of the new prime minister, sent Beatrice a letter appealing for a further memorandum, stating that the matter was pressing.[40]

Beatrice Webb's first impressions of Lloyd George were misguided; she seriously underestimated his abilities, regarding him more as a preacher than a statesman, when he was deeply interested in the plight of the poor. In 1908 he wrote to his confidant Herbert Lewis:

> Take [the example of] the man who works at the Llechwedd Quarry. He risks his life ... The death rate of the quarry is very high. What does he get for his work? 25 shillings a week, often having to live away from home in uncomfortable lodgings or barracks. When there is no work it means starvation.

He was thus genuinely interested in raising the standard of living of the 'poorly organized' sections of the working class, and was always open to new ideas, but Mrs Webb's hectoring manner and superior airs were counterproductive and off-putting. In contrast he later worked well with Dr Christopher Addison MP and Dr George Newman, when constructive proposals for the reform of the medical services were put to him.[41]

What were the results of this social contact between the Webbs and Asquith? On the one hand, it encouraged Asquith to accept the Webbs' contention that the Poor Law must be broken up. Sidney, when enclosing two of Beatrice's schemes to Haldane in December 1907, dropped in the remark: 'Yet, it seems to me that the C. of Ex. will almost necessarily want to adumbrate something for Poor Law reform, in unfolding his Pension scheme.' This idea seems to have stuck in Asquith's mind and he asked Beatrice if he should adumbrate the break-up of the Poor Law in his Budget speech when he introduced his pensions scheme. Later Beatrice wrote to Asquith, pleading with him to take this course, as this would spur the Poor Law Commission into adopting a more radical report. Asquith remained very cautious when he came to the matter in the Budget:

> I think that we may assume it [the Poor Law Commission] will give effect in some shape or other to what has long been regarded by careful observers as the most urgent of all reforms – namely, the reclassification of the vast heterogeneous mass of persons, young and old, sound and infirm, undeserving or unfortunate, who at present fall within one province or another of the area of Poor Law administration.[42]

Instead, Asquith returned to this theme in two major addresses which he delivered in 1908, after becoming prime minister. In his inaugural speech to the Liberal party he stated the need to turn to another group of questions: those connected with poverty and unemployment, with their cause and remedies, with the classification of the helpless and hopeless, and with the organized treatment of old age and childhood. In June he again took up this theme in an address delivered to the National Liberal Club: the Pensions Bill was the first step towards the general reconstruction of the organized dealing of the state with the problems of old age, poverty, infirmity and unemployment. Within a year or two the whole Poor Law would be completely remodelled. A few days later, on the second reading of the Old Age Pensions Bill, Lloyd George hinted that the government meant to deal with the subjects of sickness and unemployment. Under Asquith's leadership the government was moving in a totally new direction.[43]

Although the Majority and Minority Reports of the Poor Law Commission were published in mid-February 1909, it was almost a month later that Asquith circulated a memorandum that had been prepared for him to his Cabinet colleagues, summarizing the two Reports.[44] More important was a second memorandum dated 7 April 1909 but not circulated to the Cabinet until June 1909, which tried to amalgamate the findings of Beatrice Webb and her colleagues and was on the whole more favourable to the Minority Report, particularly with regard to the inmates of the workhouse. The compiler of the second memorandum, who was probably Harold Baker, quoted Professor Marshall in a crucial passage to the effect that 'the problem of the modern Poor Law is one not of pauperism but of poverty'. He went on to argue:

> The view that distress should be regarded as a whole and treated by a single body lends itself to a dangerous degree to the perpetuation of the Poor Law spirit and practice, which has proved a complete failure as regards, cure, prevention, and scientific relief.[45]

If the demand for indoor relief came mainly from the three principal classes of the aged, the sick who were often elderly or were able-bodied men who were mentally or physically ill, and orphan children, they could be entrusted to the health, education and employment authorities to deal with. This would leave 'the difficult question of the administration of *out-relief*, a sphere in which a stronger case for the single authority dealing with different classes of persons can be made out'. The drafter of the memorandum suggested

> a Committee administering the new system of public assistance, with the addition of co-opted members, aided by an officer of standing, who would supervise the relieving officers and be in touch with medical officers, school attendance officers, sanitary inspectors, and others concerned in administrative work.[46]

Here the emphasis was on family-based social work, much as the stance of the Charity Organisation members, who framed the Majority Report; and in addition he advocated a three-year transitional period before the new regime was fully implemented.

The Webbs also played a pivotal role in helping to secure the introduction of the Trade Boards Act of 1909, which regulated minimum wage rates in a number of trades as an experiment. First there was Beatrice Webb's sociological theory that the whole of society was responsible for sweated labour as consumers, landlords and shopkeepers, not just the fast-disappearing middleman; this was extended by their joint concept of the flourishing of parasitical trades with low wage rates which required government intervention. Without the Webbs' sociological theories, which were accepted by parliamentary committees of enquiry as central to their thinking, there would not have been any minimum wage regulation, and Sidney Webb played a prominent role in the campaign for the Trade Boards Act.

At any rate, the forthcoming 1909 Budget which Lloyd George was preparing outlined the Liberal master plan for the sick and the unemployed, the government having already provided for the aged by their universal non-contributory pension scheme introduced in 1908. We shall briefly summarize how this plan came into fruition, leaving a detailed exposition over to a later chapter. Because of the trade depression in the winter of 1908–9, there had to be an acceleration of the government's employment plans and Churchill and Lloyd George were provided with an opportunity of submitting their own plans to cope with the problem; but in addition to this the Poor Law Commission was due to report early in 1909 and Beatrice Webb had opened up the whole question of the reform of the health services – another huge challenge to which the chancellor responded magnificently. Whatever the Poor Law Commission pronounced and whatever happened to the Budget in its passage through Parliament, the government had the intention of going to the country on its own scheme for breaking up the Poor Law. Having taken over the task of reforming the Poor Law administrative apparatus from Burns, Haldane informed Beatrice Webb in mid-November 1908 that he had been deputed by Asquith to take up the whole subject and to draw up a comprehensive scheme of reform. Some portions of it would be implemented within the following two years, namely the health insurance measure of Lloyd George and Churchill's Labour Exchanges Bill; the government would then fight the election on the whole of their scheme.[47] Meanwhile taking up the suggestion of W. H. Dawson, a civil servant who had prepared an unemployment insurance scheme for the Board of Trade, Churchill and Lloyd George agreed with his suggestion that their two schemes should be harnessed together and presented as the Liberal alternative to the Poor Law. Further, Lloyd George had borrowed the Labour party plan for tackling unemployment, only to have it whittled down by other members of the Cabinet; this too in an attenuated form was incorporated in the Budget, after being remodelled to fit in with some ideas of the Webbs. At this point it still seemed as if the government would go ahead with an amalgam of the Webbs' proposals for administrative reform and the insurance schemes, though for reasons set out later this was not to occur. A by-product of this scheme was the Development Commission fund to aid forestry and rural industries. But now the government had additional ammunition in their arsenal: minimum wage regulation. In short, these plans held out the hope that the allegiance of the working class could be regained by the Liberal party, so that the Labour and New Liberal alliance could be resuscitated, which could give Liberals victory at the polls.

# 7

# Asquith at the Exchequer

## Indirect Taxation

If the voice that that elaborated the proposals of the 1909 Budget was that of Lloyd George, the hand that shaped the political strategy to throw the Lords off balance was that of Prime Minister Asquith, a masterful politician in his own right. According to A. G. Gardiner in a penetrating analysis of how contemporaries viewed him:

> Asquith's ... is incomparably the most powerful intellect in the ... Commons today – not the finest, nor the subtlest, nor the most attractive, but the most effective ... The sentences of his orderly speech march into action like disciplined units, marshalled and drilled ... Violence and recrimination find in him no response ... This detachment from the pettiness and meanness of controversy is largely the source of the growing authority he has established over the House ... His power of work is unequalled, for the strength of his mind is backed by a physique equal to any burden ... His succession to the premiership was a matter of course.[1]

Really the Budget grew out of the stresses and skirmishes with the House of Lords. Its basic features were shaped by pressure groups closely aligned to the Liberal party: the land value reformers, the temperance advocates, and an inchoate group of neo-Liberal economists, such as Leo Chiozza Money MP, A. L. Bowley and J. A. Hobson, who first argued the case for the redistribution of incomes. Within these limits, Asquith and Lloyd George devised the political strategy for the struggle with the Lords; both played equally significant roles in ensuring that these three features were incorporated in the Great Budget.

All the Liberals were convinced that a lighter burden of taxation should fall on the working class. Addressing the Financial Reform Association, Campbell-Bannerman asserted that tea and sugar duties weighed heavily on the working class. In 1902 Herbert Samuel estimated that the working class formed four-fifths of the population and paid four-fifths of the indirect taxes. Since the inclusion of the free breakfast table in the Newcastle programme, the Liberal leaders had committed themselves to a policy of lowering indirect taxation. Guided by the City, Unionist chancellors of the Exchequer had in part financed the expenditure entailed by the Boer War by steeply increasing the level of indirect taxation, and even after the war had come to a close, evinced a marked reluctance to repeal the new taxes.[2] Only the unleashing of three distinctive campaigns by the producers and users of the raw materials concerned, combined with the enhanced political prestige of the Labour movement, achieved a reduction in the duties.

On the other hand, the alterations in the level of indirect taxation engineered by Asquith meant that the structure of direct taxation had to be considered afresh. In all, the repeal of the coal duties, the lowering of the tea and sugar duties and the differentiation of income cost the Exchequer £8 million; naturally higher taxation was required to cover the resultant deficit. Further, Herbert Samuel noted that since a free breakfast table would only reduce the percentage of working-class taxation from 6.9 per cent to 6.2 per cent, it was necessary to raise taxes on higher incomes as well as lowering them on smaller incomes. Nor should it be forgotten that behind the concessions in taxation allowed by Asquith was the overriding purpose of making the fiscal system more equitable. In short, the changes in direct taxation decreed by the 1909 Budget flowed naturally from the alterations in the structure of indirect taxation as wrought by Asquith and from the increased charges demanded by social reform, as against the view propounded by Peter Rowland that 'the "People's Budget", luridly depicted by both its supporters and opponents as a Radical measure in every sense of the word, owed more for the need for Dreadnoughts than a desire to invade the bastions of property'; and further, that it was 'brought about more by the force of events than the forces of radicalism'.[3]

Because of the transcendent influence of the coal owners and shipowners and the added support of the miners, the anti-coal tax campaigners had no need to appeal to the general public against the export duty of 1s. per ton of coal imposed in 1901. Their campaign swept to an inevitable conclusion. In innumerable ways both parties humbled themselves before the force of an irresistible pressure. Hicks-Beach agreed to the appointment of a Royal Commission on Coal Supplies in 1901, which would among other objectives examine the effect of the duty on the export of coal. With five members of the executive of the Mining Association, the employers body, sitting on the commission, it was not altogether surprising that it reported that although the figures did not conclusively prove it, the commission could not doubt that an export duty must limit the tonnage which was shipped overseas. Even Austen Chamberlain, the new chancellor of the Exchequer, was conciliatory in the debates on the Finance Bill in May 1905, asserting that the tax would have to be watched. Clearly this was intended to silence the opponents of the tax; for Austen admitted in 1909 that his father Joseph was under a misapprehension and that if he had stayed longer at the Exchequer, he would not have abolished the coal duty.[4] The Committee of the Coal Exporting Districts, a body linking coal owners, exporters and shipowners, received replies from 133 Parliamentary candidates in 1906, to whom they had addressed circulars; most were prepared to vote for its immediate abolition, the others were sympathetic. Even before he had finished making the arrangements for his first Budget, Asquith assured a deputation from the Coal Exporters Committee that the tax would not form part of the permanent fiscal arrangements of the country and the tax was repealed without any delay.[5]

The agitation against the tea duty was promoted by planter interests, the Indian and Ceylon Tea Association, through a propaganda organization called the Anti-Tea Duty

League which they set up in January 1905. Only after the tea duty had been augmented twice since 1901 were the planter interests stirred into action. Even so, their aims were strictly limited; they had no intention of agitating for free tea because this would lead to increased exports from China and because the resultant competition would end with lower prices for the public. In fact, the planters wanted higher prices, only desiring so much to be knocked off the 8d. duty of 1904 that would help them realize this ideal. Compared to the other campaigners, they were politically and economically innocuous, with a capital of £40 million and a mere five representatives in Parliament; and while they employed two million workers, the fact that this huge labour force was resident in the colonies robbed them of electoral influence.[6] On account of these shortcomings, the tea interest was unable to exert much direct pressure on the government; the result was that they were forced to win the general public onto their side, and the league was compelled to embark on novel methods of publicity. Herbert Compton, its secretary, who had followed the calling of tea planter on and off for twenty-three years and later worked as a leader writer in the literary department of the Tariff Reform League, introduced a remarkable innovation in the employment of posters: he purchased an enormous amount of hoarding space for a brief period prior to the Budget, arranging his posters in sets of eight, each cartoon being slanted to appeal to a different shade of social and political opinion, so that they rammed their way into the public's imagination. Their effect was instantaneous, for Chamberlain reduced his tea duty by 2d. in 1905. Likewise the Anti-Tea Duty League mounted a gigantic poster display before the 1906 Budget, to which Asquith responded by taking a further 1d. off the duty. Unwisely the league questioned whether a continuation of Compton's poster display would have much effect on the government. In consequence they decided to act in a more sedate manner in future, so that their influence vanished overnight. Sir Roper Lethbridge informed the *Weekly Times of Ceylon*:

> As a member of the Carlton Club, and at the time knowing something of the inner workings of my party, which was, of course, then in power, I know that, if not for Mr Compton's marvellous energy and power of organization and initiative, we should never have got that reduction [in 1905].[7]

No attempt was made by the confectionery trades to organize their labour force in the campaign against the 4s. 2d. per cwt duty on sugar until 1904, despite the fact that it was realized from the first that their support could determine the outcome of the tussle. Still, even if the representation of the sugar trades in Parliament was poor, not only did the Cadburys and the Rowntrees hold dominant positions in the Liberal party in the country, but they also possessed substantial holdings in the popular Liberal press. Together the Confectioners' Association of the United Kingdom and the Manufacturing Confectioners Commercial Travellers Association established the Free Sugar Auxiliary to enlist the aid of their shopkeepers and employees. Because of the top-heavy membership dues, no more than 460 supporters had been collected by the end of 1905 out of an estimated 125,000 persons engaged in the manufacture of confectionery and another 100,000 in its retail distribution. And although sugar consumption per head had declined from 89lbs in 1901 to 82lbs in 1903 – the working class relied on a diet of cereals and sugar and went without meat – the confectionery trades decided to allow their case to the general public go by default, as they claimed there were too many organizations fulminating against the government's sugar policy. Nor was the interest evinced in the contest by the biscuit, cake and mineral water manufacturers anything but intermittent.[8] Hence Austen Chamberlain coolly disclosed to a deputation in 1905 that in the present financial situation the sugar tax could not be rescinded and that he could not think of a tax that was fairer. Hence whereas Asquith respectfully listened to the supplications of the coal exporters and tea planters, he brusquely turned aside the entreaties of the sugar users because it was felt that they could not bestir any vital sectors of opinion. Reporting to the king on 29 April 1908, Asquith implied that the surplus of £4 million in the current year would be wholly earmarked for old age pensions, but in his next missive he announced that half the surplus would be used to reduce the sugar duty: it seems that the government changed its mind at the last moment at the dictation of the Whips, who declared that only old age pensions and the repeal of the sugar duty could stem the adverse drift of working-class opinion.[9]

F. W. Kolthammer showed that before the 1914 war, despite a series of Liberal budgets, the taxes on food were still regressive as far as the working class was concerned, and where the family was small or the number at work large, consumption often exceeded the normal. Accordingly, Kolthammer concluded that the consumption of taxed foods by middle-class families did not exceed that prevailing in working-class families:

> The lower the standard of comfort, the larger the percentage of food expenditure which is taxed. When the cheaper jam displaces the dearer butter or margarine, as also when the cheaper condensed milk displaces the dearer cow's milk, a portion of the family income which was before untaxed automatically becomes taxed.[10]

So Kolthammer estimated that whereas a family with an income of 20s. per week consumed 2.56 per cent of it on the various food taxes (sugar, cocoa, coffee, tea and dried fruit), families with an income of 22s. paid 2.33 per cent and families with 25s. expended 2.09 per cent on food taxes, those earning 30s. paid a mere 1.71 per cent, those earning 40s. expended 1.28 per cent and those earning 100s. were mulcted of 0.51 per cent of their income.[11]

## Direct Taxation

Fundamental changes in the level of direct taxation were expected when the Liberals were returned to power. Soon after the new Liberal administration took office, Asquith appointed a select committee in 1906 to inquire into the two related problems of the differentiation and graduation of income tax under the chairmanship of Sir Charles Dilke. Dilke, the leader of a group of Radical MPs, asserted that a majority of MPs in the 1906 House of Commons believed in the principle of a graduated income tax. Nor were these ideas particularly new to Liberals: Harcourt in his Great Budget of 1894 had thought of levying a supertax, but the Board of Inland Revenue had reported against this. In fact, ever since the 1880s, advanced men had been clamouring for a graduated income tax to be secured by a series of abatements; and this is what Harcourt implemented, by raising the basic rate of income tax to 1s. 8d. in the pound and helping those with low incomes with abatements and exemptions, while at the same time imposing a single estate duty on all forms of property, whether landed or otherwise, by means of a graduated scale.[12] Chiozza Money, part of the new intake of Liberal MPs in 1906, assured a meeting of the parliamentary group of the National Committee on Old Age Pensions that the report of the committee was bound to be favourable.[13] The reason why no such bold declaration of policy was adopted by the select committee was quite simple. During the framing of the report, the opponents of the drastic taxation of large incomes played the advocates of a supertax and the proponents of a graduated income tax off against each other, so that the final report was riddled with anomalies and ringed by qualifications and equivocations. Before examining the work of the select committee in detail, it is necessary to pay some attention to the formulations of New Liberalism on the redistribution of incomes. While it was true that the academic world in the 1890s and the early twentieth century was dominated by the classical economists' heirs, through the piquancy of their writings and their provocative lectures J. A. Hobson and John M. Robertson MP propagated a new unorthodoxy which bestirred the Liberal party in the country and the socialist intellectuals, but was at best a marginal factor which helped create a more receptive climate of opinion for Chiozza Money and A. L. Bowley to produce their more radical estimates of national income that ultimately converted the Liberal politicians.

Hobson concentrated on exposing the defects of classical economics in accounting for the fluctuations of the industrial system, and in his first book, *The Physiology of Industry* (1889), written with A. F. Mummery, a businessman, he argued that the undue exercise of the habit of saving could cause an excessive accumulation of capital.[14] In Hobson's later works, particularly in *The Industrial System* (1910), he switched his approach to stressing that the unequal bargaining power between employers and workers was the cause of the economic surplus, which in turn resulted in the maldistribution of income, which further caused over-saving and industrial depressions. To an audience at the National Liberal Club on 9 November 1908, Hobson gave a preview of the chapter on social income in this book, asserting that society created such surpluses as the unearned increment on land, all dividends above the current rate of interest, monopoly values and all extortionate demands on the profits of workers; that these surpluses had the ability to bear increased taxation without interfering with the normal processes of industry and commerce; and that ground values, licence duties and all high incomes came under this classification.[15] John M. Robertson MP, a friend of Hobson and a fellow lecturer at the South Place Ethical Society, had already read a seminal paper on taxation to a conference of radical organizations summoned by the Fabian Society in 1886. In his *The Fallacy of Saving* (1892), in which more emphasis was placed on the demolition of the theoretical premises and internal contradictions of the classical economists, he unlike Hobson unequivocally denounced Say's law – the law which proclaimed that aggregate production created an equal quantity of aggregate demand – as 'a tenacious fallacy'. His solution was to suggest that:

Either (a) the principle of parsimony must be generally abandoned, and the majority must demand high-class goods or services which should be more or less providable by those who formerly provided nominally high-class goods or services for the fundholders; or (b) the State or the municipalities must institute important public works such as civic reconstruction, with good working-class houses, or comprehensive sewage schemes, which should extensively employ and train inexpert labour ... the workers must consume if production is to be kept up.[16]

Dilke failed to draw the majority of the select committee along with him, and Asquith resisted Dilke's plea for Chiozza Money to become a member of the committee. Dilke 'did his best to repair what he considered a blunder, by asking me to take a special seat by him at each sitting, and by calling me as the first unofficial witness', Money recalled in his memoirs.[17] It was supposed to be an expert committee, but only six of the seventeen members knew very much about finance. Hence the Liberals who served on the committee were easily influenced when Sir Henry Primrose of the Board of Inland Revenue, which advised the chancellor on matters of taxation, and Reginald McKenna, the financial secretary to the Treasury, spoke out against taxing the wealthy more severely. Primrose tried to control the lines of the inquiry, so that a report in harmony with his own viewpoint was drawn up. He made his purpose transparent in a letter which he addressed to Dilke on 2 May 1906. Although Primrose outlined two schemes to the committee for a progressive supertax, he made it clear that he was opposed to the levying of such a tax: he gave an extremely low estimate of the aggregate of incomes of over £5,000, putting it at £121 million, only half Chiozza Money's figure, while Bowley estimated it at something between £220 and £180 million. Not much reliance could be placed on Primrose's figures, for the Treasury had no statistical department of its own, and there was little reason to suppose that it would be able to compile more reliable estimates of the national income, as it was shared between the different classes from the imperfect data that was then available, than Bowley, who was a brilliant innovating statistician. On the whole, Bowley, after subjecting Money's figures to various tests such as Pareto's law to check incomes of under £10,000, found himself in agreement with Professor Cannan's appraisal of Money: his 'figures hold the field and those who dislike the reflexions which they suggest should endeavour to refute them if they are not prepared to accept them'. Further, Primrose insisted that evasion would be encouraged by such a tax and that there would be only a small total gain.[18]

Reginald McKenna, the financial secretary to the Treasury, supported Primrose. This was rather embarrassing as McKenna was a protégé of Dilke, the latter numbering him among his personal friends. Partly McKenna's attitude may be attributed to his narrow accountant's outlook, partly as an attempt to break free from Dilke, who was trying to dominate every corner of his life. Already in the opening stages of the inquiry McKenna had made up his mind against an increase in taxation; on 8 May 1906 he wrote to Dilke reiterating that he had an open mind on the subject, but he was forced to admit that he had said in conversation to Dilke that all the evidence he had seen was adverse, though he did not go beyond this. McKenna cross-examined every witness so as to leave no doubt that he was opposed to the progressive taxation of large incomes, opposed to personal declarations of income, and of the opinion that no considerable addition could be obtained for the revenue by reforming the income tax.[19]

From the radical point of view, the most important persons to testify before the Committee were A. L. Bowley, T. A. Coghlan and Leo G. Chiozza Money. Coghlan, a former statistical adviser to the Australian government, presenting evidence on graduation and differentiation of the income tax in the Australian states and New Zealand, noted how in Australia the population were more used to making returns to the government than in England and how statistics were more utilized than here; once again, we see how the close ties between Britain and her empire facilitated the adoption of experimental legislation, whether it was old age pensions or minimum wage controls. Of the English witnesses, Chiozza Money, a journalist, Fabian, and a radical Liberal MP, deserves the bulk of the credit for the successful promotion of the cause of the graduated income tax. To his magnificent role as a publicist through his many vantage points for moulding public opinion as a columnist on the *Daily News*, writing a 'daily article entitled "Life and Labour" dealing with seasonal and industrial questions', and as a resourceful MP harrying the chancellor with questions and resolutions must be added his primary role as the pioneering author of *Riches and Poverty* (1905). The newspaper articles formed the basis of this study which was divided into two parts, one dealing with the errors in the calculation and distribution of the national income, the other highlighting the social reforms which were necessary to rectify this, including a plea for the taxation of land on its sale value and a graduated income tax. By 1906 the book was into its third edition. The extent of Money's achievement can only be measured when the ramshackle condition of the government apparatus and the meagreness of the existing statistical compilations are thrown into contrast. Of the three sets of figures which were required to be known to quantify the division of the national income between the different classes, Money boldly conjectured estimates of the number of income tax payers with incomes under £700 and the number of persons with high incomes, while the total income which was taxed was on record. To estimate the number of tax payers with high incomes, Money utilized the estate duty returns – an approach which was commended and followed by Bowley – calculating that if £300 million flowed into the Treasury every year, two-thirds or some £200 million was left by 4,000 individuals; assuming that there were thirty living persons for every dead property holder, this left a total of 120,00 wealthy persons.[20] Although a departmental committee in 1881 had reported in favour of a central statistical department at the Treasury with a qualified statistician at its head, the only result was that a committee under Giffen was appointed in 1898 to advise on the form in which statistics should be presented to Parliament.

Dilke wrote a summary of the evidence with conclusions attached in the summer recess and expected his draft report to be adopted. In France the national revenue drawn from direct taxation and applied for national purposes was proportionately higher than in the United Kingdom. Dilke favoured a graduated income tax which was to be secured by degression: this meant collecting a given rate of taxation at the source and then making an allowance for those whose total net incomes were below a certain specified amount; a natural corollary of this system would be the compulsory declaration of income by all tax payers, as individuals would have to declare what their incomes were to receive an abatement. Two objections were raised against Dilke's scheme: banking opinion was convinced that taxation by degression would result in the locking up of a huge amount of money in the hands of tax collectors, which would have to be returned. To this Coghlan, the agent-general for New South Wales and a tax expert, replied that the locking up of money was largely a paper problem rather than a real one. He informed the committee that it was possible to combine a system of a graduated income tax with taxation at the source. Accordingly, Dilke concluded that the objection that a graduated income tax with its attendant compulsory declaration of incomes would involve a huge leakage of revenue was groundless. Nevertheless, even Chiozza Money conceded that Dilke's report was 'vague' and somewhat muddled, causing Whittaker to exclaim that 'Dilke is so loaded with information that he can't sort it out'. Because of the hostile attitude of Primrose and McKenna, the Liberals on the committee were divided and a clear majority could not be obtained for Dilke's draft report when it was submitted to them. His report was rejected by nine votes to five, the Irish MPs siding with Dilke, while four Liberals voted against him; two other MPs with a view akin to Dilke's were away absent.[21]

The radicals who favoured a properly graduated income tax believed that there was no need for differentiation between earned and unearned incomes. Chiozza Money, who put in an appearance before the committee, was wont to argue that graduation was the most effective means of securing differentiation: as income rose in the scale, the property element attached to it increased. Dilke reluctantly conceded the need for differentiation as long as it was limited to incomes of up to £2,000 per annum.[22] Surprisingly Labour party spokesmen supported the need for further differentiation. Philip Snowden submitted a scheme to the committee for graduation and differentiation of all incomes up to £50,000 per annum; incomes above that level would be subject to a straight graduated tax; when this was going well, he would extend his scheme for differentiation and graduation to lower incomes. Keir Hardie could speak of differentiation as 'a distinction which finds great favour today, is eminently reasonable and has actually been adopted in several of our colonies': his own plan was to tax all incomes between £1,000 and £5,000 which were derived from investments, land and property of all kinds on a higher scale than incomes that accrued from personal effort; once this level had been reached, a straight graduated tax would soak up superfluous wealth. The committee concluded it was not easy to distinguish between earned and unearned incomes, especially in regard to business enterprise, where it was hard to estimate how much of any income was due to the skill of the proprietor and how much was a return on capital. As the Liberal right-wingers agreed on the need for differentiation, it was decided to allow differentiation for incomes not exceeding £3,000.[23] McKenna persuaded Sir Thomas Whittaker MP, a member of the committee and the chairman of a great building society with many other business interests, to draft a report against the increased taxation of the wealthy. His report repeated the evidence of Primrose, its general tenor being adverse to the steeper taxation of large incomes – a point reiterated in an article he wrote for the *Financial Review of Reviews*.[24] Thus by omitting any reference to a compulsory declaration of incomes in their report, McKenna and Whittaker hoped to invalidate both the case for a supertax and a graduated income tax. Five of the seventeen members of the select committee had voted for Dilke's draft report, including two of the Liberals, Rose and McCrea, the two Irish representatives, and one Labour MP, Keir Hardie; two other MPs who favoured the report, Samuel Evans and Brace, the representative of the trade union group, were away absent. Thus when they returned to take part in the deliberations of the committee, the protagonists of a graduated income tax had seven supporters. Dilke, as acting chairman, was only allowed a casting vote; therefore, it only required one member of the other side to vote with this group on a specific issue to tip the balance of opinion in the committee. That was precisely what happened. Sir Charles Trevelyan MP, though opposed to a graduated income tax because he thought that this would interfere with taxation at the source, had in previous sessions of Parliament advocated the imposition of a graduated supertax on great incomes which was to be based on declarations of total income by tax payers. Such a tax had been raised in the United States during the Civil War. To facilitate the introduction of a supertax, then, Trevelyan was prepared to accept the necessity for a compulsory declaration of income to be completed by all those whose total income amounted to more than £5,000 per annum. Hence there was a majority on the committee in favour of the stringent taxation of large incomes and of the compulsory declaration of total incomes within certain well-defined limits. Nonetheless, by making vague pronouncements in favour of a supertax, the opponents of the greater taxation of the affluent aggravated the division between Trevelyan and the other progressives on the committee. On the other hand, to forestall the coming of a supertax, these opponents of the greater taxation of the wealthy sided with the progressives in their fight against a supertax and deliberately left in qualifying clauses questioning the validity of supertax in peacetime.

When paragraph 24 was reached, Evans introduced an amendment in favour of the universal declaration of total incomes which was passed by the chairman's casting vote. McKenna added a clause, stating that 'the compulsory declaration of income should only apply to the total income on which the recipient himself paid tax'. After two Liberals, Rose and Trevelyan, voted for McKenna's proviso, this was swiftly agreed to, but at this juncture McKenna had to leave the committee hearing and return to the Commons. Now Dilke and his allies on the committee tried to take control and added the words 'on which a system of graduation and differentiation could be based to McKenna's amendment', thereby nullifying it. The final version of the committee's report was thus ambiguous in meaning: on the one hand, appearing to countenance a graduated income tax combined with a compulsory declaration of income; on the other hand, in the summary of conclusions in the report it appeared to distance itself from such an objective.[25]

Bernard Mallet, who served on the Board of Inland Revenue, advised Dilke that,

> on the whole you have gained your point and nothing feasible has been shut out of the recommendations, & nothing too urgently recommended even as regards differentiation which now stands in the way of the more important object, better graduation ... I expect differentiation up to £3000 would cost a great deal & therefore if carried out put a spoke in the wheel of (degression) graduation ... Everything now depends on the Chancellor of the Exch. & the House of

Commons. He can do pretty much what he likes with the Committee's findings before him.[26]

When it came to devising the 1907 Budget, Asquith had to surmount considerable opposition from Edward Hamilton, Primrose and McKenna. All looked askance at the idea of introducing a supertax. McKenna seized various points at random from the report of the select committee, trying to convince Asquith that it had reported against the imposition of a supertax except in the case of an emergency; that the advocates of a graduated supertax on large incomes seemed to be influenced by a gross overestimate of the revenue to be obtained; and that the differentiation of the income tax was far more worthy of concern than the introduction of a supertax. McKenna's account of the proceedings of the committee was tendentious in that he failed to convey the fact that a majority of the committee were agreed that the wealthy should contribute a greater proportion of the national revenue to the Exchequer. Primrose, like McKenna, pleaded with Asquith to concentrate on the differentiation of the income tax rather than on the imposition of a supertax: 'This cod. be an opening of your door by the handle and hinges ... To use a supertax cod. be to apply dynamite as a means of opening, with much danger of destruction in various directions.' Both agreed that the income tax on earned incomes below the level of £2,000–3,000 per annum should be reduced from 1s. to 9d., and that the general rate of income tax should otherwise be increased to 13d. to pay for the differentiation.[27] However, in his 1907 Budget Asquith kept the 1s. rate on unearned income and confined the differentiation of the income tax at 9d. on earned income up to £2,000. To pay for this concession, death duties were increased on estates of over £150,000 and on estates of £1 million from 7.5 to 10 per cent, while a supertax of 1 per cent was levied on the first £500,000 in excess of this last sum and an additional 5 per cent on estates above the £3 million level. Pointing out the divergence of opinion within the select committee, Asquith told the Commons that 'it would not be possible for administrative reasons to introduce any change in graduation simultaneously with the already sufficiently complicated alterations of a differentiated tax', though he had an open mind on the question; privately he had clashed with his advisers on the feasibility of a supertax which he had wanted to incorporate in the 1907/8 Budget. Asquith also regained control of imperial revenue flowing into the coffers of local authorities, such as the proceeds of licence duties and a motor tax, by compensating them for this loss of income.[28] Asquith's Budgets of 1907 and 1908 paved the way for a wholesale reconstruction of the financial system, but because old age pensions would not come into operation until 1 January 1909 they were initially forecast to cost in their first year £1,200,000 before swelling to £6,000,000 per annum. When taken together, the increased cost of paying for old age pensions and the need to build more battleships, dreadnoughts, would mean introducing wholesale changes in the system of taxation in 1909. In his Budget statement in May 1908, Asquith, newly installed as prime minister, declared:

> In my judgement there cannot be a greater mistake than to suppose that a free trade Finance Minister has come to or is nearly approaching the end of his resources in the matter of new taxation. My solitary contribution in that direction during my three years of office [as Chancellor] has been a comparatively trivial

addition to the death duties last year, because ... I regarded it as my first and main duty to do what I could to reduce the national liabilities. The field is open to [Lloyd George], and I have the most complete confidence in his ability, if he should be in need – I do not know that he will – to make it yield a fruitful and abundant crop.[29]

Sir Edward Hamilton retired from the Treasury in 1907, followed by Sir Henry Primrose as chairman of the Board of Inland Revenue in the same year and Sir George Murray as secretary of the Treasury in 1911. A new generation of officials – John Bradbury, Bernard Mallet, Robert Chalmers, William Blain, the last three with strong Liberal sympathies – swept to the fore and were promoted and utilized by Asquith and Lloyd George. Hamilton in February 1907 wrote to Primrose, professing to be 'startled' at the memoranda emerging from the Treasury, which went much further than the report of the select committee.[30] Various papers were submitted by Asquith to the Cabinet on the incidence of taxation in the United Kingdom and on the conflicting estimates of the number of tax payers of different classes and their aggregate income, which had been prepared by Primrose and Chiozza Money. More important, William Blain drafted a superb memorandum, controverting the arguments against a supertax on incomes in excess of £5,000 and making a strong case in its favour. It opened by arguing that the poor contributed an excessive share of the UK's revenue, as taxes on articles of consumption hit the working classes the hardest:

> The present Government have recognized the pressing need for social reforms which must entail heavy expenditure. No one expects that the reductions of existing expenditure will provide the necessary means. A good deal has already been done, and more perhaps may be possible, in the way of reduction on Army and Navy Votes. But the automatic growth of the Civil Services, and the constant extension of their scope are only too likely to absorb the bulk of these savings.[31]

It ended by asserting that there was no other country in which so large a proportion of the total national income took the shape of big incomes in the hands of the few. It would take a few years for the machinery to be built up for the levying of a supertax. Afterwards the department could levy a higher rate of taxation for incomes above £5,000 and for lower incomes if it wished, so that a scientific graduation throughout the scale of incomes could be imposed.[32] Asquith thus left all his options open for a graduated income tax and supertax should the need arise in the future.

Moreover, it was Asquith who compelled Lloyd George to accept the necessity of a large-scale reconstruction of the national finances. In his final 1908 Budget Asquith lowered the duty on sugar from 4s. 2d. to 1s. 10d. per cwt, thus giving away an annual income of £3.4 million. The money had originally been earmarked for financing the cost of old age pensions; only about £1.24 million had been put aside for meeting their cost, and after various concessions had been made in the Commons, the estimated annual cost of the scheme rose to £7 million or more. Having listened to his criticism of the 1908 Budget, Lloyd George confessed to Chamberlain: 'I agreed with a good deal of what you said – with more perhaps than you would think and with more than I can say. I wanted to keep the sugar duty on and use it for pensions.'[33] Further evidence that an additional member of the Cabinet was in agreement as to the need for drastic reforms at the Exchequer was a memorandum Haldane sent to Asquith in August 1908. Haldane declared that a much greater toll had to be taken from the national income by means of direct taxation. He accepted Bowley's calculations as to national income and thought that the money was definitely available. He assumed Asquith had been thinking on the same lines:

> In this condition of things my suggestion is one over which you have probably thought much – that we should boldly take our stand on the facts and proclaim a policy of taking, mainly by direct taxation, such toll from the increase and growth of this wealth as will enable us to provide for (1) the increasing cost of Social Reform; (2) National Defence; and also (3) to have a margin in aid of the Sinking Fund.[34]

In his memoirs Haldane recounted that 'Asquith was doing good work. He had decided, overruling some of his advisers at the Exchequer on a graduation of the income tax and on a better distribution of the burden of taxation, and this was being carried out.'[35] Moreover, we should remember that it was Asquith who was instrumental in pushing the Cabinet to adopt a scheme for universal old age pensions, despite its cost.

# 8

# The Great Budget of 1909

## Lloyd George's Apprenticeship

Lloyd George became chancellor of the Exchequer after the Cabinet reshuffle when Asquith became prime minister on 8 April 1908, having earned the promotion because of his legislative achievements as president of the Board of Trade and his skills in debate. Under his inspired direction, the Board of Trade hummed with activity; a series of important measures poured out of it – the Merchant Shipping Act, the Patents Act, the Port of London Authority Act, the Companies Act, the Census of Production Act – all vital to ensure there was no further decline in Britain's commercial and industrial prosperity.[1] We will focus on the Merchant Shipping Act 1906 because in the drafting and passage of this measure through Parliament, Lloyd George honed his skills as a negotiator – a learning process that was to stand him in good stead when he had to prepare his Budgets and coerce powerful interest groups to accept his health insurance scheme.

When Lloyd George entered office, he was faced with an unpropitious situation, with discontent mounting from both the shipowners and seamen. To examine their grievances, a previous administration had appointed two committees of inquiry: one to examine certain questions affecting the merchant marine, particularly the rising numbers of foreign seamen employed on British ships, for which it recommended better conditions of service for seamen on board ships; the other was the Select Committee on Foreign Ships which examined whether the regulations concerning cargo and life-saving apparatus carried on British ships should be applied to foreign vessels.[2] On the plus side, since the formation of the Shipowners Parliamentary Committee in 1893, as the supreme negotiating body for the shipping community, and Walter J. Howell's accession to the command of the marine department of the board, a warmer relationship had been forged between them and there was an interchange of confidences. Relations were also good between Howell and J. Havelock Wilson of the Sailors' and Firemen's Union. Wilson had commended a draft bill in 1903, saying that 'it does not go so far as I should like … I am nevertheless prepared to accept a small instalment of what I am asking for.'[3]

To settle the details of his Merchant Shipping Bill, Lloyd George opened negotiations with both the shipowners and seamen, with the aim of persuading the shipowners to make quite far-reaching concessions to the men. In return British safety regulations would be applied to foreign shipping and the seamen would be asked to consent to a lowering of the British load-line standards so as to bring them into conformity with the best foreign standards. Before the bill was launched in the Commons Lloyd George spent some weeks haggling over its details, for his object was to award neither side the substance or appearance of victory. When the seamen still remained disgruntled, he had to make further concessions in the way of altering the composition of the local marine boards so as to augment the position of the men; and when the shipowners became aggrieved at such sweeping concessions, he had to repair the damage by bestowing fresh awards on them.

Lloyd George went through the draft of the bill line by line with Cuthbert Laws and Norman Hill, the secretaries of the Shipping Federation, the employers' organization, and the Liverpool Steamship Owners Association. He also exchanged views with the Shipowners Parliamentary Group of MPs which tended to act on its own initiative, conferring with Ropner and Austin Taylor. All ships trading at United Kingdom ports were to be subjected to the laws and rules governing loading, stowage, life-saving appliances and passenger ship regulations enforced by the Board of Trade and such regulations enforced by foreign nations as would be equivalent in safety value to those enforced in Britain. A prime necessity, if British regulations were to be applicable to foreign shipping, was to bring the international load-line regulations into harmony. After a committee of the Lloyd's Register reported in favour of a revision of the freeboard tables in 1905, the Board of Trade held its own inquiry and in February 1906 announced its own revised tables. These modifications in the tables were due to an improvement in the strength and arrangement of sections on the upper deck, such as the poop and forecastle, while another consequence of the revisions was that a further one million tons of carrying capacity was added to the British merchant fleet. The class of ship which derived the most benefit from these arrangements were tramp vessels carrying coal and heavy cargo homewards, but so too, passenger and emigration ship regulations were revised to bring them more into accord with modern requirements. Finally, an advisory committee on shipping was appointed to frame fresh regulations after due consultation with the interested parties. So well pleased were the shipowners with the form of the bill as originally drafted by Lloyd George that the shipping group of MPs decided not to meet until after the second reading.[4]

Despite numerous improvements in their living conditions on board merchant ships, the bill's compelling purpose being to force a reluctant minority of shipowners to adhere to the standards of the better class in their trade, the seamen were not completely placated. True enough their living accommodation had been substantially increased up to 120 cubic feet per man, instead of the previous limit of 72 cubic feet and 12 superficial feet. 'It seems clear that such accommodation', remarked the Jeune Committee, 'has improved in recent years, and it is much better in the newer classes of vessel. Nor have many complaints been made of accommodation in larger vessels and liners', though they conceded that they had listened to 'evidence of a varying and conflicting character'. Every British foreign-going vessel of 1,000 tons or more leaving a UK port was required to have a competent cook on board. Still the main subject of contention during the preliminary negotiations was the food scale and the seamen thought that the board had shown them a grudging attitude. During most of the

Victorian age there was no statutory victualling scale, and when the board decided to adopt such a scale for insertion in seamen's articles, it was not 'adhered to except as a punishment or in answer to complaints'; besides it was criticized for not being 'sufficiently ample or varied'. In 1893 a special committee of the Shipping Federation recommended an improved scale, but the Jeune Committee put forward a revised scale, trusting to its adoption by voluntary means, which passed with little subsequent alteration into the scale enshrined in the 1906 Merchant Shipping Bill. For the seamen, J. Havelock Wilson MP, a Lib–Lab, contended that bacon, cocoa and bananas should be restored to the items listed in the food scale, though there were graver weaknesses in the suggested statutory scale because of the absence of proteins in the form of milk, cheese and eggs and the absence of healthy foods in the guise of fruit and vegetables. According to Wilson, the food on liners was good, even if 'there was great dissatisfaction amongst the men with regard to tramp steamers generally, some of them feed the men exceedingly well, others, again, strictly adhere to the scale of provisions which the men sign for, and that scale is generally the scale that the men get on board sailing ships'. Moreover, some 39,000 foreigners were employed in the British mercantile marine, whose numbers increased by 5,168 in the period 1896–1901, with an additional increase in the number of Lascars (Indian seamen) and Asiatic seamen by 9,250; the British seamen, against the wishes of the shipowners, tried to curtail foreigners' employment opportunities on board British ships so as to augment their own opportunities for work and to strengthen their bargaining powers against the masters. As a compromise, it was decided that no foreign seaman could sign on if he did not know enough English to understand orders which might be given to him, but this restriction was not to apply to a British subject nor to Lascars, a hereditary class of sailor from Bengal whose own shipping had been vanquished by British competition. Other clauses in the bill modified the law in regard to the relief and repatriation of distressed seamen.[5]

On 28 May 1906, the seamen sent a deputation to Lloyd George. A question of the utmost importance was raised by the deputation, when they declared that they required trade union officials to be present at the hearing of disputes between the men and company representatives by the superintendents in the mercantile marine offices; they pressed for the abolition of local marine boards which controlled the local marine offices, as they were dominated by the shipowners. In sum, these changes would have brought about a decisive shift in the balance of power between masters and men, forcing the shipowners to recognize the seamen's union. In Lloyd George's estimation, the Board of Trade was quite indifferent to the matter of the local marine boards, unlike the shipowners, who would strongly resist any change in their character, but he was of a mind to allow seamen's representatives to be present at the settling of disputes. Wilson harried Lloyd George in the standing committee, compelling him to place further restrictions on foreign labour: the language tests for foreign seamen were extended from home ports to all ports between the Elbe and Brest; and Lloyd George promised to consult the India Office as to whether there could be a limited proportion of Lascar labour in the British merchant marine.[6]

On 12 July various minor amendments which the government was going to move were settled at a conference attended by Havelock Wilson MP and Austin Taylor, the secretary of the shipping group of MPs. The next day the Shipowners Parliamentary Committee requested Lloyd George to receive a deputation, for while they were content with the concessions that he had seen fit to grant them, they thought that what had been conceded to the men outweighed these advantages. Unless a compromise was reached, a stiff fight was promised over the report stage of the bill. But surprisingly enough, the points which the deputation wanted to raise skirted the major issues of contention; in particular, no reference was raised to the proposed alteration in the composition of local marine offices. A very large deputation from the Shipowners Parliamentary Committee, studded with distinguished names from the industry, assembled before Lloyd George on 3 August. He used both cajolery and flattery to soften them up, praising them for accepting the new burdens, telling them that they had much to be thankful for in the bill. On the whole, he was prepared to agree that the deputation had made a good case on most of the points raised and assured them that he was prepared to take appropriate action. A £10 deposit was to be left in the hands of the master as a guarantee against desertion; the fact that a seaman had passed the language test was to be endorsed on his certificate; and the total loss to a ship on account of desertion was to be set off against the total gain from uncollected wages of deserters. However, if the compulsory food scale was not to be applied in the case of Asiatic seamen, he remained adamantly opposed to any lowering of the standard for British seamen.[7]

Meanwhile the changes which Lloyd George had proposed in regard to local marine offices when responding to the seamen's deputation in May were causing some of the leading shipping organizations, including the Shipping Federation and the Chamber of Shipping, to seethe with discontent. The Shipping Federation protested that the entry of union officials into local marine offices would facilitate the intimidation and molestation of seamen who refused to join the union. The merchant officers' association urged that if trade unions could support men in cases where wages were deducted for infringements of rules, discipline on board the ships would collapse. Nevertheless, the Board of Trade issued circulars allowing trade union officials admittance to the local marine offices, even if the proposed alterations in the function of the local marine boards were to be incorporated in the bill.[8]

At the beginning of November, Lloyd George consented to receive a deputation from the Chamber of Shipping, on which there were also representatives from the shipping associations and local marine boards. Lloyd George immediately counter-attacked, after hearing the deputation present their case, stating that he would have been willing to meet a deputation from the local marine boards months earlier. Instead of contacting him, some seven or eight marine boards had passed defiant resolutions to the effect that they would not implement the new orders; this was a flagrant breach of the law, yet they had the effrontery to talk about the need for preserving discipline at sea. Lloyd George cleverly put the deputation in the wrong, and then with an air of magnanimity remarked that he would make them a generous offer, which they could take or leave. Whatever happened, the powers of the local marine boards would be clipped, but as a concession the new regulations might first be discussed with him by an advisory committee of shipowners.[9]

On the following day, 3 November, Lloyd George met a small group of shipowners, from which the more intransigent representatives of the local marine boards had been excluded, enabling them to settle down to some hard bargaining about the future constitution of the local marine boards. In addition there was much trading between Lloyd George and the shipowners at this interview, as other outstanding points were sorted out. In future the superintendents of the local marine offices were to be selected and removed by the Board of Trade; the fact that neutral administrators were to be in control of the local marine offices gave a tremendous fillip to trade union morale and authority at the local level. In the past the shipowners had contributed in part to the payment of these superintendents, but since 1889 the board had paid their salaries, so that it was only right – as Lloyd George put it – that he who pays the piper should call the tune. Howell had desired to abolish the disciplinary powers of the local marine boards, as they had been very negligent in the case of captains found drunk while on duty. For the time being Lloyd George was willing to delay precipitate action, but he warned the shipowners that if disciplinary cases were tried in so lax a manner in future their jurisdiction would be countermanded. Again, the shipowners wanted a special advisory committee on local marine boards, but Lloyd George insisted that they would have to act through a special sub-committee of the new shipping advisory committee. During these negotiations the shipowners were induced to help the Board of Trade with statistics of freight returns to aid them in their census of production; and as a final softener, Lloyd George agreed to adapt the timber deck cargo regulations under which such consignments were carried in modern vessels, so that in future greater loads could be transported. Further, the shipowners undertook to persuade their representatives not to oppose Lloyd George's amendments in regard to changed structure of the local marine boards.[10]

These further concessions to both the shipowners and seamen enabled Lloyd George to steer the bill through Parliament rapidly. Nonetheless, it would be wrong to assume that either the conditions of service for seamen or their living conditions on board ship had yet reached a very high standard in that the average wage for an able-bodied seaman of £4. 10s. a month was still far too low, especially when it is borne in mind that the seaman was often a casual worker. Even so, the standard wage rate was so inadequate that it would have been impossible for a seaman to bring up a family in decent accommodation and to provide them with enough food. On tramp steamers of medium size fourteen men would sleep, live and eat in the forecastle, where there could be no fire in winter as the ventilators had to be kept closed and no awning in summer, if there was a rough breeze. Although the food was standardized, we have seen how this diet was grossly deficient in certain essential nutritious items, while because the board had failed to stipulate how the food should be served, the cooks continued to hand the meals to the men in the galley in shoddy utensils, often in old coffee tins, after which they had to carry them on deck in the open, braving the cold and spray for half the length of the ship. The Jeune Committee commented in 1903: 'We think that in matters such as the provision of proper stoves, the provision of tables for meals, or even a separate place for meals, it would be a wise step on the part of the shipowners to see that their ships are well furnished, as in many cases they undoubtedly are.' According to the reminiscences of one merchant seaman, in the past crew were crammed four into a small room, where there were now only two bunks, while they had to provide their own bedding and blankets. Loss of life at sea was still of huge proportions: some 1,079 persons perished, one-third of the total in Plimsoll's heyday, so that there was a tendency among seamen to regret the lowering of the load-line and pressure was exerted on Parliament for an inquiry. On the other hand, the change in the balance of power in the local marine offices was of the utmost significance, ultimately compelling the shipowners to recognize the seamen's union in 1911 and to pay the men a wage of £5–£5. 10s. a month by 1914, which was somewhat closer to a living wage.[11]

Lloyd George decided to resolve the conflict between the traders and the railway companies in a similar fashion to that by which he had adjusted the differences between shipowners and seamen. Each side would relate its specific complaints at a private conference, and concessions to one side would be counterbalanced by concessions to the other. At any rate, the Railway Companies Association was informed by the Board of Trade on 11 December 1907 that its president was

> about to make an enquiry by means of an informal Committee, including representatives of the Railway Companies, manufacturers and traders, as to the possibility of arriving at a general agreement with regard to such modifications of the existing law and of the relations subsisting between the Companies, traders and general public, as may conduce to economy and elasticity of railway working, and also provide for the equitable division of any advantages accruing there from among the various parties interested.[12]

To a deputation from the railway companies, Lloyd George clarified that the conference would deliberate as to whether it might be possible to obtain an accession of revenue from Parliament for them, in return for which the companies would grant the traders increased facilities or reduced rates, probably hinting that there was to be some relaxation of passenger duty.[13]

Among the members of the conference was the distinguished journalist J. A. Spender, who observed:

> [Lloyd George] was a first-class chairman, and nothing could have been more skilful than his handling of these diverse elements. He always got up his subject beforehand, and though he knew exactly what he was driving at, he generally kept his intention veiled until opponents had been drawn three-quarters of the way he wanted them to go, then he cut off their retreat. He had almost an uncanny way of persuading men in opposite camps that they really meant the same thing – which was the thing he wanted them to mean – and before a few weeks were over the supposed irreconcilable difference of railways and traders were dissolving into incredible unity.[14]

On 4 March 1908, when answering a question in Parliament, Lloyd George blundered badly by admitting that railway nationalization would be on the agenda, when he had assured the companies that this would not be the case. Although he tried to repair the damage, he was unable to retrieve the confidence of the railway companies, making it impossible for his successor at the Board of Trade, Winston Churchill, to persuade the interested parties to agree to an amalgamation of the companies. Lloyd George meant to make the railway question a significant election issue, but now he was promoted to the office of chancellor of the Exchequer other contentious subjects came to the fore.[15] As president of the Board of Trade, he showed great initiative; he was a man who was primed for action and was developing brilliant skills as a negotiator. At the same time, Lloyd George's talks with the railway companies highlighted another less pleasant characteristic – his deviousness and the lack of trust that often surrounded his actions.

## Land Taxation

If the Liberals wished to convey anything by the phrase social reform, they meant principally the reform of the land. It was one of the leading tenets, perhaps the central feature, of the Liberal creed. Young Liberals of advanced views enhanced their reputations by labouring on behalf of the land reform associations: C. P. Trevelyan and Josiah Wedgwood helped to carry the ideas of the English Land Values League to a successful legislative conclusion; Herbert Samuel, as honorary secretary of the Land Law Reform Association, infused new life into its organization; Charles Roden Buxton was the moving spirit behind the Cooperative Small Holdings Society. Indeed, a Liberal enthusiast for social reform as representative as Charles Masterman could exclaim that land reform was more important than the new plans for health and unemployment insurance.[16]

At the turn of the twentieth century the Liberal land reform programme broadened, especially in regard to its urban aspects. Coinciding with the clash between the Liberals and the Lords over the Education Bill in November 1906, Massingham, then lobby correspondent of the *Daily News*, reported a hardening of opinion in the ranks of government supporters over the land question. Many MPs considered that instead of going in for piecemeal land reform, it would be wiser to prepare a great land bill for the whole of Britain, to devote all of the government's third session to it, and to make it the subject matter of the final quarrel with the Lords. Sir Walter Foster MP, speaking at the annual meeting of the Land Law Reform Association in March 1907, repeated this analysis of the situation and posited the same cure. Some members of the Cabinet appear to have discussed the feasibility of adopting such a scheme.[17]

Further, after the proposal had first been mooted in December, a committee composed of representatives from the main land reform associations met in April 1907 to plan a national land and housing demonstration for the end of the month. Now that the government was in so precarious a position, because the Upper House was whittling away their legislative programme, the land reform societies thought that an opportune moment had arisen for rallying it with the battle-cry of land reform. Campbell-Bannerman, the prime minister, addressed a luncheon at the Holborn Restaurant in the presence of ninety-eight Liberal MPs, while Winston Churchill delivered the principal speech to a Liberal rally in the Drury Lane Theatre. The essentials of the programme were that local authorities were to be vested with powers for the provision of smallholdings, for the purchase of housing sites in town and country, and for the planning and regulation of urban areas; there was to be separate valuation of land, apart from building and improvements, and its rating on such a valuation; and there was to be a compulsory acquisition of land by public authorities at a price based on this valuation.[18] Accordingly, in 1907 it appeared as if the Liberals were going to challenge the Lords on this question; even Conservatives expected this. Austen Chamberlain informed Balfour: 'It is to the land question that the Radicals are looking to destroy both us and the House of Lords. They avow it freely in private conversation.'[19]

Under the auspices of the Land Law Reform Association, the Land Tenure Bill was introduced in 1906 to protect farmers, which the government decided to take over. When the bill was sent to the Lords, it was so thoroughly amended that the land reformers were incensed and put forward a motion for its withdrawal. Whiteley, the chief whip, advised Campbell-Bannerman that a conflict with the Lords was imminent, and that the sooner the Liberals commenced the struggle in earnest, the better: '[The Lords'] practical destruction of the Land Tenure Bill by impossible amendments would increase that difficulty and place the whole of the farming interests in the country in opposition to them.' Moreover, if the government wished to take up the gauntlet against the Lords they should stand by the motion to consider the Lords' amendments this day three months. However, if the government did not wish to fight, it should take what it could and allow the bill through.[20] Inasmuch as the government did not relish a fight with the Lords at this juncture, they meekly submitted to the ignominies which had been thrust on them. So too, the 1907 Smallholdings Bill was emasculated by a landlord group led by Aldwyn in the Lords, but nevertheless the government allowed it to go through in this attenuated form.

As early as 1 May 1908, Shaw, the Scottish Lord Advocate, had advocated taxing land values in the Budget, without this idea crystallizing into a determined policy. With the mutilation of the Scottish Land Values Bill and the delay in introducing the English one, the situation was completely altered. The United Committee for the Taxation of Land Values, embracing the English, Scottish and Irish leagues, immediately after the destruction of the Scottish bill opened a vigorous campaign in Scotland, and sponsored resolutions at meetings calling on the government to incorporate the Scottish Land Values measure in the Budget. When Asquith announced that as a consequence of what had happened to the Scottish bill, the introduction of the English one would be postponed yet again, the land taxers were furious. They now decided that the Lords could be overcome by tacking land values onto the Budget. Josiah Wedgwood MP, the parliamentary leader of the campaign, suggested this in an interview with the *Daily News* on 16 October 1908; Francis Neilson, a prominent Liberal organizer and land taxer, passed on the idea to Alec Murray, recently promoted from being the Scottish Liberal whip, who conveyed this helpful piece of information to Lloyd George. By October the land taxers in the Commons were in open rebellion until they received adequate assurances from the government. On 19 October the land values group in the Commons sent a deputation to Asquith. Within the next few days Wedgwood, the leader of the parliamentary group, secured an interview with Lloyd George; T. Hart Davies MP, speaking a few days later, announced that the chancellor of the Exchequer was sympathetic to the movement, so that it was quite possible that the taxation of land would appear in the next Budget. Again, on 24 November the leading land taxers in the Commons had a private interview with Asquith and Lloyd George about taxing land values in the Budget. From this account it does not seem that Asquith required any special prompting, nor that Lloyd George took his own initiative in the matter.[21]

The United Committee began a national campaign in earnest in November to ensure that the government fulfilled its promises, concentrating on three targets: the Liberal MPs and party organizations; the Labour movement; and the general public through the press and meetings. Perhaps the most outstanding feature of the campaign was the studied attempt of the single taxers to garner the support of the Labour movement for their campaign and this was due to the influence of Joseph Fels, the left-wing American soap millionaire, who bankrolled this public relations exercise. All along he had insisted that until the Labour movement was interested in the campaign, nothing profitable could result. Wedgwood set about securing signatures from Liberal and Labour MPs for his memorial, calling on the government to insert a land values tax in the 1909 Budget; 246 MPs appended their names to it, forty-nine parliamentary secretaries and ministers could not sign the petition, while other Liberal MPs thought that the government could be trusted to honour its assurances without any outside pressure. Nearly all the Labour MPs signed the petition; Barnes, who was an ardent land taxer, persuaded the bulk of them to attach their names; only the insistence of Fels forced Ramsay MacDonald and Snowden to sign the manifesto, though they placed an asterisk against their names to show that they were not single taxers, but desired the tax for revenue purposes.[22] Under the auspices of the United Committee, a big conference was held in England with the cooperation of the Liberal and Labour parties in February 1909 to demand the inclusion of land values in the Budget. Four hundred and fifty-five representatives attended from local Liberal associations, trades councils, trade unions, Labour party branches, cooperative societies and rating bodies. Similar conferences were held in Scotland and Wales. Meetings were held across the country; in some places new branches of the United Committee were set up, and the prime minister was inundated with resolutions. All the leading Liberal dailies ran a series of articles on land values taxation, including the *Daily News*, the *Manchester Guardian*, the *Morning Leader* and the *Daily Chronicle*, advocating it as the leading economic and financial measure of the 1909 session.[23]

A high maintenance campaign was required from the United Committee both to awaken public opinion and to enable Lloyd George to overcome the resistance of some of his Cabinet colleagues. P. W. Wilson MP, who was close to Lloyd George, reported in January 1909 that '[u]pon the taxation of land, it is true to say that some ministers are more convinced than others, and that the opinion of the government as a whole is not as fully instructed as that of the party'. In addition, the whole shape of the land tax proposals that the Cabinet would adopt depended on unrelenting pressure being exerted by the United Committee. The supporters of the United Committee wanted a straight tax of 1d. in the pound on site value, which would have destroyed the sale value of land, thus making it cheap. McKenna, who had made a close study of the question and given evidence to the Royal Commission on Local Taxation, led the opposition to this scheme within the Cabinet and persuaded his colleagues to reject it. The complaint ventilated by the single taxers – that Lloyd George only wanted the money for revenue purposes and, not being a follower of Henry George, did not put up a stiff enough fight in the Cabinet – was not altogether fair. 'In the main Lloyd George got what he wanted, except for a tax on the ground rents of land already built upon', Bruce Murray has suggested.[24]

Even so, an attempt was made by the opponents of land taxation within the Liberal party to water down the proposals still further. The opposition came principally from the Liberal MPs, who sat for rural divisions; for while they admitted the necessity for some form of land values taxation, they held that rural land was already heavily taxed and that the proposal was not applicable in the countryside. Asquith received many communications on the subject, inserting three of them in a paper for circulation among members of the Cabinet. One MP asserted that all practical Liberal workers in rural districts maintained that if a land values tax was levied in country districts, the party would lose every purely agricultural seat, much land would be driven out of cultivation and the small holdings movement would be ruined. When Wedgwood announced at the English land conference on 9 February 1909 that rural land would be omitted from the scheme, the assembly bitterly denounced this move, declaring that it would, on the contrary, obstruct small holdings and rural housing reform.[25]

Moreover, the government-sponsored temperance reform, a Licensing Bill was introduced in 1908 under the covering fire of high licence duties and there was a clear warning from Asquith that if the bill was trampled underfoot, high licence duties would follow in the next Budget in 1909.[26] By clawing back the somewhat overgenerous compensation paid to brewers by the Kennedy Judgment when licensed premises were closed, the measure ignited a political storm. The more retail outlets were concentrated in the hands of the big brewery companies, the fiercer grew competition between them; and this threat to the value of the properties owned by the big brewers alarmed debenture holders and other investors. Soon the exponents of 'gentlemanly capitalism' in the City of London and their allies in the aristocracy were arraigned in vociferous opposition to the measure, thereby encouraging the House of Lords to throw out the government bill.[27] Hence the idea of inserting the licence duty and land values taxation in the Budget to avoid the stranglehold of the Lords did not originate with Lloyd George, but was the considered policy of the government led by Asquith. By November 1908 Lloyd George was taking the new government policy forward, writing to his brother: 'I am thinking out some exquisite plans for outwitting the Lords on Licensing'. So too, Asquith had already convinced his Treasury officials of the necessity of imposing a graduated income tax and supertax should the cost of non-contributory old age pensions and increased expenditure on the navy warrant this.[28]

## The Great Budget

There are some pairs of politicians, such as Asquith and Lloyd George, Stephen Koss remarked, 'who require the responsibilities of office to cement their relationship'. Kenneth Morgan summarized their partnership as follows:

Asquith's judicious leadership, backed by stern partisanship, Lloyd George's radical passion, supported by tactical flair, provided a massively effective partnership. It brought Liberal England, not to its 'death' as once was mistakenly claimed, but to its glorious high noon.[29]

In some fourteen meetings between mid-March and the end of April 1909 the Cabinet discussed the contentious issues raised by the chancellor's Budget.[30] Throughout the prime minister stood behind his colleague, so much so that Lloyd George maintained that without his support the Cabinet would never have approved his financial proposals. Without doubt Lloyd George, who was no expert on the niceties of the fiscal system and relied heavily on the advice of his professional advisers in the civil service, allowed himself to be guided by Robert Chalmers, the new head of the Board of Inland Revenue. Despite her obvious intention of belittling Lloyd George's reputation, Mrs Asquith's comment in her autobiography that 'the famous Budget of that year was largely the creation of Sir Robert Chalmers' was in the main true. But in her unpublished diary, Margot claimed that the Budget 'was created by [John] Bradbury ... ornamented by Lloyd George & pruned by my husband'.[31] Both Chalmers and Bradbury assisted Lloyd George at the Treasury in the reconstruction of the nation's finances; both men, it should be noted, had been picked and promoted by Asquith: Chalmers to the chairmanship of the Inland Revenue in October 1907; Bradbury from being Asquith's private secretary, when he was chancellor of the Exchequer, to becoming head of the Treasury first (finance) division in 1908, when Lloyd George took office. Like Asquith, Chalmers had been educated at the City of London School and Oxford, though unlike the prime minister he had supplemented this by doing voluntary work for Canon Barnett and living in the East End. In fact, because of the strained relationship between Lloyd George and Sir George Murray, the head of the Treasury, Chalmers generally acted as the chancellor's factotum.[32]

Lloyd George was an inveterate risk taker both in his private life and in politics – the audacious risk-taking move held an attraction for him, the excitement propelled him forwards. An article insinuating an indiscretion with the fair sex appeared in the *Bystander* on 29 July 1908, forcing him to sue the paper for libel and win token damages. Following this the *People* published a series of articles alleging an affair with a lady, possibly the wife of Charles Henry MP or the actress Edna May, whose husband was going to cite Lloyd George in a divorce suit, compelling him once again to sue for libel. The chancellor briefed Rufus Isaacs MP, F. E. Smith MP and Raymond Asquith, the prime minister's son, and he appeared in court on 12 March 1909 with his legal team. His wife accompanied him ready to testify on his behalf, Lloyd George swore on oath that there was nothing in the story, the *People* withdrew their allegations and agreed to pay damages. Instead of a hostile reaction, when Lloyd George next visited the Commons, he faced none of the expected sniping from critics, and was in fact cheered when he answered his first question, making him feel that he had outflanked and outfaced established opinion.[33] The encounter whetted Lloyd George's appetite for taking even bolder steps against the City and landed elite in his Budget, while protecting his supporters, the hard-working middle class and the industrious working class. Although Lloyd George estimated his Budget deficit at £17 million in March

1909 and this had fallen to £16 million by early April, it once again had to be revised upwards at the end of the month because of an anticipated shortfall in the existing taxes of £510,000. The Cabinet first turned its attention to an examination of the land taxes. Unless his land valuation clauses were coupled with the raising of revenue, Lloyd George warned his colleagues, they could not be incorporated in a finance bill. After prolonged discussions in the Cabinet, he was forced to drop his 1d. tax on the capital value of land worth over £50 per acre and base his scheme on the German model, not on the more Georgeist proposals of Australia and New Zealand. Indeed, the United Committee was not over-enthusiastic about the land taxes outlined in the Budget; their journal for August 1909 bluntly stated that 'the [Finance] Bill was of the weakest possible nature so far as the Taxation of Land Values is concerned'. Only the intention that all the land of the United Kingdom was to be revalued fanned their ardour for the Budget. Henry George had stated that there should be a tax on the capital value of land, a proposition which the government appeared to have accepted when they first began thinking about the subject. Now Lloyd George's advisers revived an idea first suggested by John Stuart Mill that a tax should be levied on the unearned increment from land; the city of Frankfurt had adopted this policy and Chiozza Money had been one of the first persons in Britain to disinter Mill's original proposal.[34]

In all the land taxes were expected to yield a revenue of £500,000. Under the provisions of the Budget, any land which could be inherited had its value determined in five different ways: gross value, full site value, total value, assessable site value, and the value of land for agricultural purposes – a needlessly complicated scheme. Starting from the existing level of the value of the land as at 30 April 1909, at every transfer of an estate on death or the sale of land, 20 per cent of the increase in the site value was to be taxed. There was also a reversion duty, a 10 per cent tax 'on the benefit accruing to a lessor' on 'the determination of a lease'. Under intense Cabinet pressure, Lloyd George had to forgo the tax 'of a penny for every £ capital value tax in land assessed at over 50l. an acre' and settle for something far less. The third tax was $1/_2$d. in the pound levy on the site value of undeveloped land, though land used exclusively for agricultural purposes was excluded from this provision. The tax was deemed by one critic to be ridiculously small and was hamstrung by so many allowances and deductions that it became difficult to collect. Finally, there was a mineral rights duty, an annual 1s. in the pound tax on the rental value of all rights to work minerals. Originally the mineral duty was not on the extracted coal or ore, but was an estimate of what a company would pay to commence mining operations on an estate. When this was shown to be an unworkable concept, Lloyd George substituted a tax on mining royalties on the German model.[35] What made these taxes so controversial on one side and so popular on the other was that they enabled Lloyd George to clothe them in inflated rhetoric to attack the aristocratic and City elite that had for so long governed Britain.

Once the land taxes had been agreed upon, Lloyd George turned his attention to an upwards revision of the licence duties on public houses and stamp duties on house sales and imposed a heavier tax on stock and share transactions, but with the help of Lord Rothschild and City interests a proposal to double the duty on bills of exchange was squashed.[36] Already in December 1908 Sir Samuel Evans MP, who had played a notable role in the proceedings of the select committee on income tax and was a confidant of the chancellor, announced that the forthcoming Budget would contain both a graduated income tax and increased death duties.[37] Still the Cabinet forced Lloyd George to temper his demands: by £1 million on the increased income tax and supertax to £3.5 million, and by £1.65 million on the death duties to £2.85 million. Various schemes seem to have been considered by Lloyd George as far as increasing the rate of income tax was concerned: his first plan was to raise the general tax on unearned incomes to 1s. 2d., then to tax all incomes over £3,500 at 1s. 4d. and all incomes over £5,000 at 1s. 6d.; his second plan evened the burden of taxation, by raising the general income level on all unearned income over £700 to 1s. 2d., while the same rate was to apply to all earned incomes of over £2,000. The aim of the Cabinet's revisions was to help the solid middle class: a general tax of 1s. 2d. was retained for all unearned incomes, but that for earned incomes was only raised from 9d. to 1s. in the pound and on earned incomes of over £3,000 to 1s. 2d. Within the Cabinet, Louis Harcourt, the commissioner for works, strongly objected to this scheme which spread the burden of taxation on moderate as well as large incomes, taking the attitude that the money should be collected from individuals with incomes over £5,000, and submitted a plan based on material utilized by Milner when he produced a graduated supertax scheme for the elder Harcourt. As the supertax of 6d. in the pound was only levied on that part of the income which exceeded £3,000, it had the effect of a graduated supertax.[38] Having overcome this criticism, Lloyd George had to agree to a reduction of the new rate of settlement duty. Moreover, though the increased death duties brought in an extra £2.85 million, the average scale had not risen all that much: it was 4.5 per cent under the elder Harcourt, 5.5 per cent under Asquith and 6.5 per cent under Lloyd George.[39] After a clash with Chalmers, who objected to a complicated system of abatements, Lloyd George had to agree to his adviser's income tax scheme, but the chancellor insisted on tax relief of £20 per child under sixteen years of age for a maximum of three such children to help 'the professional classes like Solicitors and Doctors', when the taxpayer's income was below £500. Thus, while many radicals asserted that the income tax levels below £5,000 should be increased by gradual stages, they also suggested that the tax level above that mark should equally be increased in stages. Lloyd George and the Cabinet accepted this plan in part. Their main aim was 'to avoid directly antagonizing the bulk of the middle classes', Bruce Murray suggested; 'the increases in direct taxation were aimed mainly at the wealthy, and at unearned sources of income'.[40]

Joseph Rowntree, the father of the sociologist Seebohm Rowntree, and Arthur Sherwell MP, a sociologist and one of the exponents of the New Liberalism, claimed in a study that 'the matter of [high licence taxation] is one of national rather than of party importance, and it cannot be overlooked in any wise and comprehensive attempt to re-organize the bases of taxation'. Quite apart from any effects it might have in promoting temperance, they maintained that it could be justified on economic and fiscal grounds. They argued that after the licensing legislation of 1869 and 1872, there was a decline in the number of retail outlets, though at the same time the per capita consumption of liquor increased. Hence the Budget of 1880 altered the scale of licence taxation. Since then there had been a further reduction in the number of retail outlets and a rise in the per capita consumption of liquor. In 1881 there were 2.6 publicans' licences per 1,000 of population in England and Wales; by 1908 the proportion had fallen to 1.8 per 1,000. On the other hand, the expenditure on alcohol in the United Kingdom had risen by £21.5 million between 1881 and 1907.[41] Finally, if the degree of taxation of alcohol in the United States and Britain was compared for say 1896, it was apparent that the Americans paid an extra 1s. $8^1/_4$d. per gallon in tax, thus demonstrating that the British liquor industry had the resources to bear a heavier burden of taxation.[42]

Although in detail the new scale of licence duties did not follow the scheme of Rowntree and Sherwell, in broad outline it adhered to their ideas. All on and off-licence premises were to pay higher duties: Rowntree and Sherwell agreed that villages and small towns were inadequately taxed as compared with corresponding districts in America. Above all, the Budget struck at the highly rated public houses which had escaped their due measure of taxation, partly because the greater the annual value of the pub, the less it paid proportionately in taxation, with the added advantage for all houses worth over £700 per annum paying a flat rate of £60 – partly because while a large number of small pubs had been shut down, there had been an increase in the number of houses worth over £700 per annum. The 122 licensed towns in the United States with a population of over 30,000 paid £7,395,000 in licence duties, against which the 164 towns in Britain with an equivalent population paid £816,000. The Budget provided that where the annual value of a pub was higher than £700, the duty could be charged on half the compensation value or value reckoned roughly in terms of profit, the minimum duty being about £350. Clubs had a licence duty levied on them for the first time, as failure to have included them within the scheme would have resulted in the rapid multiplication of drinking clubs; the duty charged was 3d. in the pound on the sale of alcohol. Higher duties were likewise imposed on hotels and restaurants. It was estimated that these duties would produce another £2.6 million in revenue. So far from Lloyd George being vindictive, he introduced amendments, lowering the proposed duty on highly rated pubs: the limit of £700 was reduced to £500, and the minimum duty from half to a third of the compensation value. Moreover, in London it was later found that the increased licence duty entitled the publicans to corresponding reductions in their assessments, since the annual value of the house would be depreciated by an increase in the duty.[43]

Despite the fiscal innovations, perhaps the centrepiece of the Budget was the Liberal answer to the recommendations of the Poor Law Commission, health and unemployment insurance in a linked package, as suggested by William Harbutt Dawson and the Development Commission. All of these new proposals were proudly announced by Lloyd George in his Budget address, which was lengthy, rambling and badly read. Having stated how impressed he was by the benefits conferred by the German invalidity insurance scheme, Lloyd George said that there were in this country 'several millions who either cannot be persuaded or perhaps cannot afford to bear the expense of the systematic contributions' to the voluntary schemes of friendly societies. Any government proposals would therefore have to be comprehensive and compulsory with contributions by employers, workers and the state, though the scheme would be operated through the existing benefit and provident societies. Provision had been made for the aged over seventy. 'All we have now left to do in order to put ourselves on a level with Germany – I hope our competition with Germany will not be in armaments alone – is to make some further provision for the sick, for the invalided, for widows, and orphans.' The chancellor went on to say that Churchill at the Board of Trade had anticipated the recommendations of the Poor Law Commission on unemployment, by formulating a scheme, 'which, while encouraging the voluntary efforts now being made by trade unions to provide unemployment benefit for their members, will extend the advantage of insurance to a very much larger circle of workmen, including labourers' whose lack of work was due to seasonal and cyclical trade fluctuations. A few selected trades would be chosen for the experiment, while 'the national system of labour exchanges promised in the King's Speech will afford the necessary machinery' for the insurance scheme. Again, contributions would have to be forthcoming from employers, the employed and the state.[44]

Further, to boost employment opportunities, the chancellor proposed to set up a Development Commission with an additional state grant of £200,000 in the first year to prepare waste land for afforestation, to encourage

> scientific research in the interests of agriculture, experimental farms, the improvement of stock ... the equipment of agencies for disseminating agricultural instruction, the encouragement and promotion of cooperation, the improvement of rural transport ... the facilitation of all well-considered schemes and measures for attracting labour back to the land by small holdings or reclamation of wastes.[45]

The commission would be invested with borrowing powers so far as afforestation was concerned because this initially required heavy capital expenditure. A Road Board was also to be instituted with a fund drawn upon a graduated tax on car licences and a 3d. tax on each gallon of petrol consumed by motor vehicles to construct new roads and improve existing ones. As Lloyd George evaluated the situation, there was '[n]othing that a Government can do, at any rate with the present organization of society, [which] can prevent the fluctuations and changes in trade which produce unemployment'; nor was it was 'the function of a Government to create work' but it could better utilize its national resources and resettle 'deserted and impoverished parts of its own territories'.[46] This was in contradiction to the evidence that Professor A. L. Bowley had tendered to the Poor Law Commission, when he had suggested that it was possible to take action to counter cyclical trade depressions; the Development Commission as framed by the chancellor was more a scheme to revitalize British agriculture and rural poverty than to deal seriously with urban unemployment.

Once his Budget address was concluded and its details were scrutinized in the Commons, Lloyd George encountered growing opposition to his financial reforms from the City and a chorus of disapproval from their allies among the landed interest, culminating in the formation of the Budget Protest League in mid-June 1909. Throughout the opening weeks of July, the policy of the Unionist party was to tear out the land clauses from the Budget, while leaving the rest of it intact.[47]

The brunt of the oratorical campaign against the Lords was borne by three men: the prime minister, Lloyd George and Churchill. While it is true that the force of the Unionist campaign against the land taxes compelled the Liberals to devote much attention to their defence, they did not confine themselves to this issue; in fact, it seems probable that the Liberals had not at first intended to exploit this issue so fully, but rather wished to concentrate on the issue of social reform. The first major theme taken up by Asquith in his early speeches was a challenge to the Unionist party; money was needed to pay for the navy and social reform. He challenged the Tariff Reformers to present their alternative Budget. Secondly, there were the schemes of national insurance which were the Liberal alternative to the Poor Law. In particular Asquith emphasized the issue of social reform in his first speech to the country at Sheffield. Likewise, Churchill devoted his opening address after the Budget's introduction to a lengthy exposition of the insurance principle.[48] Admittedly the next few speeches by this group of politicians were principally a defence of the land taxes, but Lloyd George returned to the question of insurance. Even when he spoke at Limehouse on 30 July 1909, lambasting the dukes as greedy landlords, he did not entirely neglect the insurance issue. Besides defending the land taxes at length, Lloyd George proclaimed that the Budget provided for the aged and deserving, that it was shameful that the wealthiest nation in the world's history had done nothing for them. At the overflow rally he spent his time giving some details on the proposed health and unemployment insurance schemes. At Norwich on 26 July Churchill paid as much attention to the insurance schemes as the land taxes and in his speech at Bournemouth on 31 July he confined himself solely to this issue.[49]

Whereas the campaign of the Liberal land associations misfired in 1907, they enjoyed an unparalleled success in 1909. The Conservative attack on the land taxes, combined with the fears as to wavering within the Liberal ranks, compelled the land societies to defend the Budget. The Land and Housing Joint Committee took a series of steps to strengthen the hands of the government over the land taxes. On 20 May the committee heard that Asquith had agreed to attend the luncheon it was arranging. On 24 June over 100 MPs listened to Asquith expounding a detailed defence of the land taxes.[50] As early as the beginning of May the land societies decided to hold a demonstration in Hyde Park in favour of the land taxes but it did not take place until 24 July. There were twelve platforms with 140 speakers; a marked feature of the rally was once again the cooperation between the Liberal land associations and Labour. A memorial was drawn up which was signed by Liberal and Labour MPs and then despatched to all Liberal and Labour organizations, so that they could put pressure on their local representatives. Finally, the Budget League, a Liberal party organization set up to rally support, arranged a meeting at which Asquith defended the land taxes before an audience of City members of the party. Lloyd George's speech at Limehouse was the culmination of this campaign; the important point about it was that he went over to the offensive. Other Liberal leaders concentrated on a rational defence of the land taxes; Lloyd George showed the huge profits that were being made from the sale of land, directing some choice barbs against the landowners. The speech became notorious being constantly reprinted for mass circulation.[51]

Peter Clarke asserted that in the two general elections in 1910 the Liberal party, by utilizing a programme of social reform based on the land taxes and health and unemployment insurance schemes, revitalized the progressive alliance between Liberal middle-class voters and the working class with particular success in industrial areas such as Lancashire and London, even if they alienated some businessmen.

Similarly Neal Blewett argued that the Liberals ran their election campaigns superbly, maintaining their ascendancy in Scotland and Wales, though they witnessed the defection of middle-class supporters in the suburbs.[52] Reduced to 275 seats after the January 1910 election and dependent on Labour and the votes of Irish Nationalists, the Liberals nevertheless secured a comfortable working majority. Asquith asked the king to give him a secret undertaking to create peers at the behest of the Liberal party should they prevail at the next election in order to curb the veto power of the House of Lords over legislation; and after some government resolutions on constitutional reform were passed, the 1909 Budget was also given parliamentary approval. Meanwhile, before the necessary undertakings from the Crown were obtained and amid discussions between the parties to settle their differences amicably, Lloyd George, buoyed by the success of his Budget, floated the idea of a grand coalition between Unionists and Liberals with the intention of secretly displacing Asquith from the premiership – a duplicitous move unsuspected by the prime minister. When talks broke down over the grand coalition, Asquith obtained the necessary undertakings from the king and new elections were scheduled for December 1910. Each party returned 272 MPs, a loss of one seat for the Liberals and three seats gained by the Unionists, though there was still an overall Liberal majority with support forthcoming from the Labour party and the Irish Nationalists, enabling Asquith to pass legislation removing the Lords' power of veto.[53] Churchill lavished praise on Asquith, whose star was on the rise again:

> [E]veryone feels ... that your leadership was the main and conspicuous feature of the whole fight ... You seemed to be far more effectively master of the situation and in the argument than at the Jan election, and your speeches stood out in massive pre-eminence whether in relation to colleagues or opponents.[54]

Not having the implicit trust in Lloyd George which her husband bestowed on him, Margot Asquith at the beginning of the second 1910 election campaign sent him a letter of rebuke, saying 'don't when you speak on platforms, arouse what is low and sordid and violent in your audience. It hurts the members of your party that are fighting these elections.' Annoyed at this unsolicited advice, Lloyd George sent her a reply, whose undertones she did not understand, forcing her into an abject apology and leaving her exhausted and racked with guilt: 'Hurting people's feelings seems to be my prevailing vice.'[55]

What Lloyd George had set out to achieve was to tap additional sources of revenue, particularly the new more graduated income tax and supertax, to pay for social reform, instead of raising the money by way of new tariffs, as the Unionists set out to do. It was essential that free trade should be preserved. Opting for increased direct taxation and eschewing more indirect taxation ensured that the burden of the new taxes would thus fall on wealth rather than wages.[56] Nor was this all. By making employers and workers pay weekly contributions to health and unemployment insurance schemes with a state contribution, Churchill and Lloyd George opened up further new vistas for social reform. For, as Chiozza Money pointed out in 1914,

> we see that it is far from true that the main increase in national expenditure in the last decade has been in respect of armaments, as is commonly alleged and

supposed. The chief cause of the increase is found in the new positive policy of social reform. Old Age Pensions, Insurance and Labour Exchanges account for over £22,000,000 of the increase.[57]

H. V. Emy drew attention to the crucial importance of the financial provisions contained in Lloyd George's 1914 Budget, a response to the inequalities exposed by the industrial unrest, which was designed to produce the revenue for a marked acceleration in the growth of the health and child welfare services. Not only were there to be increases in imperial grants-in-aid to local authorities amounting to £11 million, but they were now to be distributed according to the efficiency rating of the service maintained by the local authority and to those areas with the greatest need. Lloyd George brought in a graduated income tax of 1s. 4d. in the pound on earned incomes over £2,500, the overall limit was lowered from £5,000 to £3,000, while at the same time the rate of tax was raised, rising to a maximum of 2s. 8d. for all incomes over £9,000. Yet Chiozza Money still regarded the degree of support given by the Budget to the social services as modest and looked forward to £15 million being added to expenditure on continuation education and more being spent on providing adequate housing.[58] As the United Committee had never much cared for the hybrid land taxes in the 1909 Budget, apart from the valuation scheme, it was comparatively easy for the Land Union to secure the repeal of the land taxes in the 1920 Finance Act, though the mineral rights duty was left intact.

# 9

# National Health Insurance

In the summer and autumn of 1908 Lloyd George became converted to the necessity for a national scheme of invalidity insurance, which would also entail various medical benefits for the population within its scope. During conversations in 1911 William Braithwaite noted that the chancellor was constantly referring to the committee stage of the Old Age Pensions Bill in 1908 when he had totalled the cost of amendments at £62 million, although the total income of the government was only £200 million. This had been a salutary lesson and 'had turned his mind to contributory insurance'. In this he had received powerful intellectual support in discussions with his new Cabinet colleague Winston Churchill, who had already grasped that the working class in Britain needed to be underpinned by a nationwide system of national insurance for unemployment and sickness, as already existed in some measure in Germany. In addition, Lloyd George's interest in the working of the German invalidity scheme and the sanatoria had been reinforced by his trip to Germany in August 1908 with a group of Young Liberals. Although he had not as yet read the Poor Law Commission Reports (he was an inveterate non-reader), his sensitive political antennae had already picked up that the reform of public health was becoming a major concern thanks to the analytical and muckraking talents of Beatrice Webb.[1] David Lloyd George was a political genius with brilliant negotiating skills, honed from his years of apprenticeship at the Board of Trade in reconciling conflicting interests, particularly in the case of the Merchant Shipping Act 1906 and in his dealings with the railway companies. Robert Chalmers, then a senior official at the Board of Inland Revenue, while briefing Braithwaite, mentioned that all political manoeuvring should be left to Asquith and Lloyd George, who were 'masters at it', though 'the little man' was perhaps the greater and 'the most under-estimated man in the United Kingdom'. Affectionately known to the civil servants serving under him as 'the goat' because his political initiatives and reforming zeal leapt 'from bolder to bolder', the chancellor also merited this nickname because, although married, he took dangerous risks in liaisons with lady friends.[2] First and foremost Lloyd George had to overcome the antagonism of the friendly societies and to conciliate a cluster of other interest groups, notably the doctors and the industrial insurance companies, and this is what he set out to do.

On the other hand, the Labour movement was much more interested in insurance against accidents than in the wider aspects of public health reform. After much pressure the TUC obtained the Employers Liability Act of 1880, which only covered half the accident claims and the onus of proof rested on the worker. While the 1897 Workmen's Compensation Act extended compensation to all accidents, it only applied to a limited number of trades. When the Liberals brought in a bill to extend the various earlier Acts in 1906, they did nothing to endanger its enactment and their measure was a moderate one. Herbert Gladstone, the home secretary, went out of his way to conciliate business groups: it was bad enough that he had to coerce the powerful shipping interest to agree to coming within the ambit of the Act; what was worse was that he had to overcome the qualms of the officials at the Board of Trade. Unlike Asquith in his abortive bill of 1893, Gladstone no longer attempted to abolish contracting out, though the TUC demanded it, as it would alienate those employers who had devised their own schemes. Accompanying a deputation of various chambers of commerce to Gladstone in May 1906, Joseph Chamberlain stated that he would like to see further extensions to those contained in the Liberal bill, to which Gladstone replied that he did not wish to make the bill top-heavy and would consider proposals for extending the categories at the committee stage. By introducing two new principles, compensation for diseases of dangerous occupations and coverage for trivial accidents, the Act made the establishment of a health service more necessary.[3]

Once the 1906 Workmen's Compensation Act was passed, the TUC resumed its campaign for a compulsory state insurance scheme against accidents, and this explains to some degree why it did not itself initiate the plan for a national health service. Having interviewed Dilke at the beginning of 1908, the Parliamentary Committee of the TUC appointed a subcommittee to consider the question of state insurance for workers' compensation. It first prepared a questionnaire to obtain information which was circulated among trade unions; it then conferred with Herbert Gladstone, who agreed to appoint a Royal Commission on the subject in the autumn. But with the coming of the government's health and unemployment insurance schemes, everyone's interest in the subject waned.[4]

No one in fact knew where the Labour movement was going to turn for inspiration in regard to social security measures. Addressing the Associated Chambers of Commerce in 1907, James Taylor of Birmingham hazarded the guess that the Labour party would press for the insurance of all workers by their employers against accidents and sickness and the provision of funds out of income tax to provide state pensions for the aged and infirm men. He was wrong. The Labour movement was divided on the issue, distrusting bureaucratic intrusion into people's homes, particularly by health visitors.[5] Further, as yet doctors had little contact with the Labour movement: the Medical Practitioners Union, which was affiliated to the TUC, was not set up until 1914, and the Socialist Medical Association, which was affiliated to the Labour party and whose concern was the broad aspects of public health policy, was formed in 1930. The Labour party leaders knew little and cared little for medical reform; everything was left in the hands of the Webbs, who relied on their informal contacts with the progressive spirits among the doctors, especially Dr George McCleary, an early Fabian. Neither Newman nor Newsholme were collectivists and only the advocacy of Beatrice Webb won them round to her scheme.[6]

The business classes felt more certain about the direction which future social security legislation should take. Edward Cadbury and George Shann, in the concluding sections of their handbook on sweating, published in 1907, stated that the present industrial system tended to recruit the ranks of the inefficient from the class above them, that their wages were so low that they were not left with any margin to make provision for sickness, unemployment and old age, and that 'a living wage secured upon the lines suggested, possibly accompanied by a system of State Insurance, would enable the worker to meet hard times without the loss of physical or moral efficiency'.[7]

Speaking to the Associated Chambers of Commerce, J. S. Taylor warned that if the commercial classes did not face up to a comprehensive accident, sickness and old age pensions scheme on the German model, they would be forced to by the march of events. Up to the present all legislation imposed liabilities on the employers, but the workers ought to contribute something, so that the spirit of thrift and enterprise was encouraged. While the German employers paid out something in the region of £10 million, the English employers were mulcted of a larger sum, if the cost of Workmen's Compensation and the Poor Law were added together. At the September 1907 conference of the chambers a resolution was passed calling on the government to take into consideration the subject of national insurance against accidents, sickness, invalidity and old age on the lines of the comprehensive scheme in operation in Germany; and for a memorial to be sent to the prime minister and the home secretary, urging them to receive a deputation to push the inquiry now being held on the working of the Poor Law and to extend its term of reference to include an examination of the working of the system in Germany and the subject of pensions and national insurance against accidents and sickness. Prime Minister Campbell-Bannerman, in answer to their request, related that he had consulted the home secretary and the president of the Local Government Board: it was too late to extend the commission's terms of reference now; and as the subjects of old age pensions and insurance against accidents and sickness were receiving the attention of the government, no purpose could be served at the present by sending a deputation.[8] Exactly how much consideration the government was giving to national health insurance at this stage is still a moot point. In addition, there was hardly any mention of the topic in the Liberal press. If anything, the source of the impetus which drove the government on to public health must be sought in Beatrice Webb's role inside and outside the Poor Law Commission and Lloyd George's response, when a new administration was formed under Asquith.

On account of the fact that the bountiful dispensation of medical relief by the state was looked on askance by Poor Law inspectors and guardians, the only hope for impoverished members of the working class seemed to lie in grafting some form of state sickness insurance onto the Poor Law system; but when they attempted this, would-be reformers ran up against the equally intractable opposition of friendly societies. It was reckoned that the friendly societies just prior to the enactment of the National Insurance Act Part 1 had enrolled some six million members; the National Conference of Friendly Societies (NCFS) boasted a membership of 5,801,135 in 1909, while there were some additional members in the Holloway Societies, which stood outside the conference. There was a small sprinkling of the middle class in friendly societies, though they tended to predominate among the leadership. Against this total membership the German compulsory health insurance scheme had a coverage of 10 million persons, and it was superior to the British voluntary-run scheme in that it provided for the poorest artisans and their children. Moreover, the friendly societies were the most important of the organizations furnishing medical care on a contract basis; the local branches employed one or more doctors, who were paid according to the number of persons registered in the society's books; sometimes all the friendly societies of a town combined to run full-time dispensaries.[9]

From every point of view the system of medical care supplied by the friendly societies for the working class had serious defects. The doctors not only deprecated the inadequacy of the pay that they received from the friendly societies which threw open the employment to those doctors who charged least for their services, but also the unfairness of giving a few doctors exclusive rights, so that they gained admittance to the families of members of friendly societies and could increase the scale of their practice at the expense of colleagues. At least three-quarters of the population were disregarded by friendly societies; they included the poor risks among the males, and the poorest class of workers together with their wives and children, though of late there had been a tendency to extend the right of medical treatment to the families of members.[10] It was equally doubtful whether weekly contributions could be collected from millions of unskilled labourers and women workers without inflicting a serious financial strain – it was after all a regressive tax.

More important, as Sir John Gorst rightly pointed out, it may be contended that the aims of the friendly society movement were completely irrelevant to the question of decent standards of medical care.[11] Even if the provision of medical care was no longer to devolve on friendly societies, they would still have the function of providing cash payments to tide a family over a breadwinner's illness. Friendly societies paid a variety of benefits. In addition to the ordinary sickness benefit, whose exact amount depended on the age of entry of the member, most societies also provided a lump sum on the death of a member and smaller ones on the death of his wife; sometimes the societies dispensed various extras, such as maternity benefits and pensions; even so, after a certain age sickness payments were apt to glide into pensions of between 2s. 6d. and 3s. 6d. per week. The whole concept of a health service associated with the friendly society movement was ill-conceived, as it placed its main emphasis on cash benefits: contemporary critics alleged that the doctors employed by the friendly societies had their patients call at their surgery, instead of visiting them in their homes, where they could have judged conditions for themselves and urged them to adopt higher standards of personal and home care; so poor was the doctors' pay that they could only carry out the most cursory examination of their patients.[12] Again, because of the connection between the friendly society movement and the health scheme, there was no comprehension of the need for an integrated health service; the National Insurance Act Part 1 failed to provide specialist and midwifery services for the insured person and his family.

As early as the 1870s a memorial had been dispatched to the Royal Commission on Friendly Societies, signed by thirty-five MPs, seventeen peers and eight bishops, requesting that a government scheme of voluntary insurance through the Post Office for sickness, death and old age should be started. The displeasure of the friendly societies blocked this project; they also broke the back of the campaign of the National Providence League for a state health and pensions scheme in the 1880s and 1890s.[13] Only the political astuteness of Lloyd George prevented the friendly societies from consigning his health insurance scheme to an equally swift oblivion; when rumours grew stronger after the interview given by Lloyd George to the press on the results of his trip to Germany in August 1908 to explore the administration of their health insurance and old age pension schemes, the NCFS meeting in October 1908 condemned the idea of state insurance against sickness, as the cost of running voluntary institutions was 'infinitesimal compared with the cost of working a scheme of State insurance'.[14] Soon after the conference Lloyd George invited the friendly society leaders to have breakfast with him at his official residence to talk about 'insurance against sickness, invalidity, &c.' on an informal basis. 'Further meetings were held, and altogether the proceedings were of a most interesting and pleasant character. Both the Chancellor and ourselves profited by the meetings', stated the president of the NCFS – once again showing Lloyd George's masterly touch. The only sour note in the proceedings was that, as a result of press leaks, the leaders of the friendly society movement were denounced as renegades on the look-out for government jobs and fears were expressed that the societies would disintegrate.[15]

A. G. Gardiner, in a memorable portrait of his hero, observed:

Talking about the perils of the poor from insolvent friendly societies ... [Lloyd George] will tell you how, when he was a boy, he used to take his uncle's shilling a week to the friendly society. 'And when he fell ill the society had failed.' Out of the memory largely came the Insurance Act.[16]

Thus the chancellor was instinctively aware of the defects of friendly societies and, because of his compassion, was determined to take action, though the presumed long-term financial insolvency of friendly societies has been dismissed by one historian as a 'political red herring'. Chris Wrigley cited A. J. P. Taylor's remark that Lloyd George 'remained closer to the people than any other Liberal Minister, including John Burns'. His sympathy above all was for those outside the organized working class, whether excluded from the friendly societies or trade unions. Lloyd George observed that the latter 'are very cruel to the workmen below and outside them. Keir Hardie never forgot that class. He sympathised with them whereas Burns had no sympathy for them.'[17]

Meanwhile at the same time as he ordered his Treasury team to prepare the 1909 Budget with the supertax, licensing duties and land tax, the chancellor asked a brilliant young civil servant, William Blain to start work on the state health insurance scheme in the autumn of 1908. William Harbutt Dawson, the expert on German state insurance, noted in his diary on 8 October: 'At [Wilson] Fox's request saw Mr Blain of the Treasury. I gave him my ideas of workman invalidity insurance and unemployment insurance. He wanted me to give him more information later. The question is coming up.' They were in correspondence afterwards and it was planned that they would meet again to discuss the arrangements of the insurance scheme, but unfortunately Blain died suddenly in December.[18] In his Budget address on 29 April 1909 Lloyd George commented:

At present there is a network of powerful organizations in this country, most of them managed with infinite skill, whose main business is to induce workmen to insure themselves against the ordinary troubles of life. In spite of all the confidence which these Friendly Societies command, unfortunately there is a very considerable margin of people, aggregating several millions, who either cannot be persuaded or, perhaps, cannot afford the expense of systematic contributions which alone make membership effective in these Societies. Experience shows no place short of a universal compulsory system can ever hope to succeed in adequately coping with the evil.[19]

The chancellor outlined four principles, by which he would be guided. No plan could succeed without

an element of compulsion. For financial, as well as other reasons, success is unattainable except on the basis of direct contributions from the classes more immediately concerned. There must be a State contribution, substantial enough to enable those whose means are too limited and precarious to sustain adequate premiums to overcome that difficulty of throwing undue risks on other contributors, and ... in this country ... no scheme would be profitable or tolerable which would do the least damage to those highly beneficent organisations [the benefit and provident societies]. On the contrary, it must be the aim of every well considered plan to encourage and work through those organisations.[20]

He wanted to cooperate with approved friendly societies, meaning those societies which submitted 'their financial affairs for actuarial valuation every five years'.[21]

Despite a placatory letter from Lloyd George to the president of the NCFS, reiterating his statement in the 1909 Budget that he would safeguard the interests of their societies and that the state would like to ensure their active cooperation in carrying out the scheme, the Whitsun round of meetings of the individual friendly societies showed a pronounced coolness on the part of their leaders. For instance, the President of the Independent Order of Odd Fellows launched an attack on the idea of a state insurance scheme, and the Manchester Unity of Odd Fellows passed a resolution opposing compulsory state insurance for persons eligible to become members of friendly societies; if the government prepared a scheme for those who on account of their health could not be admitted to the membership of friendly societies, that would be feasible. Yet some friendly societies evinced more enthusiasm for the whole project: Mr McDiarmid of Glasgow, speaking for the Conference of Ancient Shepherds, welcomed the state scheme, stating that the people of his lodge had been waiting for such a scheme for years. Writing to the *Daily News*, George Cronin remarked that if a plebiscite was held of friendly society members, they would vote for state insurance; the recent Manchester resolution was a case in point; originally, there had been a resolution against state insurance altogether, but such was the strength of the dissent that a compromise resolution had to be found.[22] Accordingly, we can appreciate that while the bulk of working-class members would have been delighted by a state insurance scheme, the directors of societies offered resistance, as they felt that the security of their positions was being undermined or at least threatened; nonetheless, by promising the minority of moderate leaders that their interests would be protected by the state, Lloyd George was able to wear down the opposition of the intransigents.

Because there was friction between the chancellor and Sir George Murray, the head of the Treasury, Lloyd George relied increasingly on Robert Chalmers, who replaced Murray in 1911, on matters other than revenue. Under his auspices a memorandum was drawn up by John Bradbury of the Treasury and Ralph Hawtrey incorporating a draft health insurance scheme which was sent out for independent actuarial evaluation.[23] The scheme was intended to embrace all persons between the ages of sixteen and seventy years but would exclude all persons having an annual income of £160 and upwards, members of the armed services, civil servants and municipal employees, married women, and dependants. Among the proposed benefits were medical attendance and medicine for each contributor, a payment in respect of the confinement of his wife, a weekly allowance for every widow until her youngest child reached sixteen and a provision for orphans until they attained the age of sixteen. During a period of temporary illness not exceeding twenty-six weeks, each contributor would receive the sum of 5s. a week and the same sum in cases of permanent invalidity. Widows with dependent children under sixteen would also receive a sum of 5s., and fatherless orphans, whether or not their mother survived, would be given an allowance of 1s. 6d. per week. Married women dependent on their husbands would not have to pay any contributions, though they would be excluded from benefit during their husband's lifetime. As long as the husband enjoyed good health and was able to work, it was believed that the needs of the family were well provided for irrespective of the wife's health – a somewhat questionable assumption. There were also contributions towards the building of sanatoria and allowances for the maintenance of members in such institutions. The approved societies included in the scheme would retain the right to reject applicants 'on certain specified grounds of character, &c. (to be defined)'; and exclusion on grounds of health was 'only to be permitted in cases of specific weakness or disease appearing likely to lead to material and permanent impairment of capacity as a wage-earner'. Rejected applicants would have their needs covered by the Poor Law. A central administrative body would be established of representatives of the government, the societies and employers to advise on general issues arising under the scheme.[24]

The independent actuaries, George Hardy and Frank Wyatt, made their observations on the government scheme in two reports submitted on 21 March and 27 August 1910. In their second memorandum the actuaries commented that there should be uniform contributions for men of 1s. a week and 6d. a week for women. The allowance during incapacity should be fixed at 10s. a week for men and 7s. 6d. a week for women because of their reduced earning capacity. They suggested that the weekly allowance for widows should be reduced to 3s. 6d. with an additional payment of 1s. 6d. for each child under sixteen. If the government decided to provide one quarter of the benefits as they accrued and cover the cost of administration, they estimated the expenditure incurred by the state would be £5,112,000 in 1911–12, rising to £6,663,000 in 1916–17.[25]

After the December 1910 general election at which the Liberal party were again returned to office and a resolution of the constitutional crisis with the House of Lords seemingly at hand, Lloyd George was able to devote more time to his health insurance scheme, and William Braithwaite (1875–1938), a young high-flying official at the

Inland Revenue, was chosen to add flesh to what had hitherto been an outline plan. Educated at Oxford, Braithwaite was a product of Toynbee Hall with some experience of social work while acting as a volunteer with the Charity Organization Society in Whitechapel; he also had some first-hand knowledge of the Stoke and Melford Friendly Society, as his family had close links to it. Apart from the chancellor, Braithwaite was the constructive genius behind the health insurance scheme. His first assignment was to be sent on a trip to Germany to make an intensive study of their system of insurance, reporting back to the chancellor a few days later on 3 January 1911.[26]

In April 1911 W. H. Dawson (1860–1948) came in from the Board of Trade to help Braithwaite and John Bradbury and convinced Lloyd George that his scheme was small in comparison with the German one, thereby inducing him to make employers contribute another 1d. and opening the way for 'maternity benefits and decent doctoring'. Dawson was described by a senior civil servant as 'industrious' but 'without too much sense of proportion', yet in this particular case his intervention was important.[27] Maternity benefit amounted to a lump sum payment of 30s. made to married women whose husbands were insured and to women who were insured persons themselves; in these cases the woman, when confined of a child, was also entitled to sickness benefit or disablement benefit in respect of her confinement in addition to the maternity benefit due to herself or her husband, but was not entitled to sickness or disablement benefit for a period of four weeks following her confinement unless suffering from a disease or disablement not connected with her confinement. Women were allowed free choice of midwives, though Lloyd George believed that it was '[m]ost undesirable to require the attendance of a doctor in every case', as they were 'in a hurry'. Medical benefit expressly excluded 'any right to medical treatment or attendance in respect of confinement', though under the Insurance Act, 'in the case of insured persons entitled to maternity benefit, if a midwife has attended the confinement and in accordance with the rules under the Midwives Act summons the aid of a doctor, the prescribed fee shall ... be recoverable as part of the maternity benefit'. In Germany maternity benefit was allowed for six weeks and sometimes wives were entitled to the free services of a doctor or midwife.[28]

Lloyd George provided the political muscle and propagandist flair without which the friendly societies, the insurance companies and the doctors would have killed the plan. On 4 May 1911 he introduced his health insurance scheme to the House of Commons. Where the Insurance Act 1911 Part 1 National Health did not follow German precedent, it was shaped by Braithwaite and the chancellor taking into account its flaws and deliberately setting out to follow a different course. Thus, whereas in Germany there were four or five classes of invalidity contributors and for sickness every man paid according to his income and there were separate branches for sickness and invalidity insurance, the British scheme included everyone in one branch and opted in favour of a uniform scheme of deductions from wages and uniform benefits. Weekly deductions from wages were proposed for men of 4d. and for women of 3d. with a lower scale of contribution designated for low wage earners, while employers would pay 3d. for a man and woman alike. Lloyd George estimated that in the United Kingdom 9,800,000 men and 4,100,000 women would join the scheme together with 800,000 voluntary contributors. These were frequently self-employed persons such as the village blacksmith, publican, schoolmaster and small tradesmen, and persons who had hitherto been employed, though they were now working on their own account. But to all these categories 800,000 persons under sixteen would have to be added, 'consisting of 500,000 boys and 300,000 girls'. This made a grand total of 14,700,000 individuals covered by the insurance scheme.[29] As far as the state was concerned, the Treasury would contribute £3,359,000 in 1913–14 and an estimated £4,563,000 in 1915–16. In the first year of the scheme contributors would pay nearly £20 million, of which £9 million would be provided by employers and £11 million by their employees. The expenditure on benefits and administration would be £7 million in 1912–13, rising to £20 million by 1915–16.[30] Whereas before the Act the friendly societies embraced almost six million members and did not always provide medical benefit, state health insurance provided fourteen million British men and women with general practitioner medical care and sickness benefit of 10s. a week for twenty-six weeks, followed by 5s. a week invalidity benefit. Likewise in Germany medical attendance and appliances were given for twenty-six weeks with sickness benefit, after which an invalidity pension was paid. Following the German scheme, sanatorium benefit was instituted to treat any of the insured suffering from tuberculosis.

The industrial insurance companies had been alarmed by talk of the government scheme providing state funeral benefit and pensions for widows and orphans, thus directly competing with their business. Of the seventy-five industrial organizations, fifty were small and run as collecting friendly societies, while among the rest were twelve powerful corporations, monopolizing some 90 per cent of the market. The Prudential was the largest private owner of freehold land in the UK as well as the largest owner of Bank of England stock. At their command the insurance companies had an army of 100,000 collectors, of whom 70,000 worked full-time collecting payments from householders and canvassing for new clients. Such was the strength of the Association of Industrial Assurance Companies and Collecting Friendly Societies, known as the Combine, that at the December 1910 election they obtained pledges from 490 members of the new House of Commons for no action to be taken on these contentious issues. Hence the government quickly dropped the payment of funeral benefit from its plans and after a meeting on 12 January 1911 the provision of benefit payments to widows and orphans was discarded. Once these concessions had been made, Bradbury proposed increasing the sickness benefit from 5s. to 10s. a week; the concessions were not enough to satisfy the Combine, however, who now demanded to be allowed to participate with friendly societies in the new business generated by the state health scheme. Despite the opposition of the friendly societies and the disquiet of Braithwaite, Lloyd George forced the friendly societies in the summer of 1911 to accept this, thus changing the whole character of the state scheme; for whereas members exerted some measure of democratic control in friendly societies and laid great stress on mutual aid, insurance companies were run on autocratic lines.[31]

In a great speech delivered in Birmingham in June 1911, Lloyd George admitted that he was

> not putting [National Insurance] forward as a complete remedy. It was one of a series. We are advancing on the road, but it is an essential part of the journey.

> I have been now some years in politics and I have had, I think, as large a share of contention and strife and warfare as any man in British politics today. This year, this Session, I have joined the Red Cross. I am in the ambulance corps. I am engaged to drive a wagon through the twisting and turnings and ruts of the Parliamentary road ... I *am* rather in a hurry, for I can hear the moanings [sic] of the wounded, and I want to carry relief to them.[32]

But first he had to circumvent the opposition of certain sections of the Labour party and the doctors. During the committee stage of the bill, Philip Snowden and George Lansbury had obstructed it, necessitating the sitting of an autumn session. To obviate these difficulties, the chancellor had arranged with MacDonald that in return for Labour party support for the Insurance Bill, the safe passage of a measure for the payment of members of the Commons would be ensured.[33]

In addition to the insurance companies and doctors, employers were a third group who had misgivings about the government bill and had to be conciliated. Many large employers, foremost among them the companies represented by the Railway Companies Association, insisted on their employees joining their own company friendly society. Employers were permitted to contract out of the national insurance scheme, so long as the benefits offered in their own closed company shop club were equal to or superior to those provided by the state. But while employers were allowed to make membership compulsory for their staff in these shop clubs, only a quarter of the members of the committee running them could be employers' representatives.[34]

At the committee stage of the insurance scheme, the bill was fundamentally altered in the Commons through the insistence of the doctors, who inserted an amendment which took the arrangements between them and the friendly societies out of the hands of approved societies and transferred the administration of the medical benefit to local health committee (later called insurance committees). The Webbs had incorrectly forecast in 1910 that compulsory health insurance was beyond the realm of practical politics. There would be 'the strongest opposition, not only from those doctors who have large medical clubs of their own, but also from the whole Trade Union movement' – which was very much in the health insurance business – 'from all the friendly societies and from tens of thousands of agents and collectors and the millions of policyholders of the individual insurance companies'.[35] Lloyd George and his new political protégé Christopher Addison, who was elected as an MP in 1910, proved them to be misguided. The chancellor, with the support of the doctors and the insurance companies, was able to rein in the friendly societies and undermine their ability to dictate the format of the state insurance scheme. Percy Rockliff, a leader of the dividing societies, had a promise from Lloyd George conveyed through Dr Addison that neither the dividing societies nor the deposit societies would be barred from participating in the new administrative apparatus. To a parliamentary question raised by Addison on 16 June 1910, Lloyd George gave the same reply. Rockliff was a close ally of Kingsley Wood, the solicitor acting for the industrial assurance companies. Dr Addison successfully moved an amendment to the bill on 1 August 1911 transferring medical administration to the local health committees and away from the friendly societies, and a further amendment setting up a panel of doctors in the community from those doctors who chose to apply, any one of whom the insured could then select as his own practitioner. The panel system of doctors was another feature borrowed from the German insurance scheme.[36] Thus the free choice of doctors by patients remained intact. Addison also moved the 'local option' amendment which granted 'discretion to local health committees with regard to the limit of income for the doctors' contract system'.[37] Contract practice between doctors and friendly societies appeared to have ended, though the Harmsworth amendment, which made concessions to medical associations or institutes, preserved certain features of this system which was abhorrent to the majority of doctors. These medical institutes were formed by an amalgamation of branches of various friendly society orders in the same area to provide medical attendance and treatment for members. In most of these bodies the benefits of medical cover were extended to the wives and children of the insured. Altogether there were 100 of these medical associations with about 400,000 members, which hired one or two full-time doctors for their members, thus undermining the principle of the free choice of doctor. What a conference of Lloyd George and representatives of the British Medical Association and the friendly societies had to sort out was what to do with members of these associations over the age of sixty-five, chronically ill members under the age of sixty-five, and those members over the income limit of £160, all of whom were excluded from the national insurance scheme. By way of a compromise the existing elderly members over the age limit and the chronically ill members were allowed to remain members for their lifetime, while these categories were excluded from membership of the institutes in future, as were persons over the income limit. Bowing to the pressure of the insurance companies, the chancellor allowed them under clause 18 to participate in the scheme on flexible terms and, to Braithwaite's disgust, scrapped the notion of self-government by members.[38]

Owing to the adroit manoeuvring of Sir Victor Horsley and Dr Cox, the growth of a breakaway movement was prevented from developing in the British Medical Association some years earlier and it was reformed from within so as to give greater power to the advocates of reform, but this also made it a more turbulent organization to control. Thus authority was vested in the annual meeting, instead of the council, so that the society might adhere more closely to the wishes and aims of the rank and file; by establishing larger primary units called divisions, it was hoped that more attention would be paid to medical politics in the localities; the post of medical secretary was created to take charge of all committees dealing with medico-political concerns.[39] As a first step in 1904–5 a thorough investigation was conducted into contract practice. It was discovered that conditions of pay varied from 2s. to 6s. per patient; some 23 per cent of the doctors surveyed were paid under 4s. and an equal percentage were paid over 5s. per patient; of the 393 doctors who answered the question as to what constituted adequate pay, 145 said a fee of 5s. Doctors' incomes averaged £200 to £250 per annum. Bad debt varied among doctors, according to the district, from 20 per cent to 50 per cent. The situation of the profession was summed up by the Webbs as follows:

> A very large proportion of its members earn incomes which can only be described as scandalously inadequate, whilst many of those who now enter its ranks after a long and expensive education fail altogether to secure a footing.[40]

The report of the BMA on contract practice concluded in June 1905 that the control of the profession over the conditions of service could only be exercised through the creation of a public medical service, directed by local representative bodies of the profession, and that the service should be open to all doctors.[41] With such preoccupations among the rank and file of the profession, the situation was potentially explosive, and doctors felt that their concerns had not been sufficiently addressed by Lloyd George's concessions – so much so that they thought that by refusing service in the new insurance scheme throughout 1912, the government would eventually capitulate. An independent accountant's report by Sir William Plender on doctors' remuneration in six towns agreed between Lloyd George and the BMA concluded that the 6s. annual fee per patient offered by the chancellor to the profession was a considerable hike to their existing rates of pay. To counter the resistance to his scheme, Lloyd George threatened either to reconstitute friendly society control over doctors' pay or to establish a state medical service, but at the same time he tried to win over the profession by offering as an inducement to raise the total cost of medical benefit to 9s., including drugs and appliances. This would leave doctors with a minimum income of 7s. for each patient per annum, apart from drugs – even better than the conditions envisaged by the Plender report. Yet on 21 December 1912 a representative meeting of doctors voted by a wide margin to reject these terms. At the same time, buoyed up by these enhanced prospects, doctors flocked to join the panels and by 10 January 1913 almost 15,000 doctors had entered into contracts with the insurance committees. Addison campaigned across the country urging doctors to join the panels and he aligned himself with the newly formed National Insurance Practitioners organization, which endorsed the state scheme.[42]

From a free market perspective, David Green has criticized the agitation of the medical profession over the National Insurance Act, seeing their protest as being selfishly motivated: he declared that 'they freed themselves from lay control, insinuated themselves into the machinery of the state, and nearly doubled their incomes' at the expense of the insured, claiming that there was a transfer of income from the working class to wealthier middle-class professionals. Feminists have noted that these welfare reforms reinforced patriarchal attitudes, and 'brought only limited benefits to women because they have been predicated on the persistence of traditional assumptions about the primacy of the male breadwinner'.[43]

When Lloyd George introduced his health insurance scheme, he had so little understanding of public health issues that he discarded the local health committees that were an integral part of his bill and replaced them with insurance committees to regulate the medical benefit in order to appease the medical profession. An accompanying memorandum stated: 'The new authority [the local health committee] will have an invaluable amount of statistics at its disposal which will enable it to locate any "black spots" in any trade or district very quickly.' But when the bill was amended, the duty 'to consider generally the needs of the county or county borough with regard to all questions of public health' was dispensed with, so that the scope for action was blunted.[44] At Masterman's instigation Robert Morant, a senior civil servant, was drafted in to run the English Health Insurance Commission in 1912, with an agenda that was closer to the ideas of the Webbs, and William Braithwaite was callously sidelined by the chancellor and made a Special Commissioner of Income Tax. Ironically it was also Masterman who had become so incensed by an investigation of the county councils' sabotage of the 1906 Small Holdings Act that he deemed it the gravest folly to entrust them with additional responsibilities in the sphere of public health, and he had persuaded Lloyd George to set up the local health committees under the Insurance Commission, so long as ratepayers did not contribute financially.[45] Nonetheless, fundamental deficiencies in the health insurance scheme soon became apparent, paving the way for the introduction of a whole new range of public health services. Among these deficiencies was the gender bias of the Act – the assumption that women relied on men for their economic survival, so that wives who did not themselves work were on the whole excluded from the services of a doctor; and that hospital treatment was not provided for the insured who were paying contributions, let alone for their dependants.

# 10

# Unemployment Insurance

## Unemployment Insurance

The unemployed returns from the trade unions, then the best statistical indicator of the level of unemployment, climbed sharply to 8.2 per cent in August 1908 and to 9 per cent in September. Despite a joint whip signed by Liberal, Lib–Lab and Labour MPs, including the millionaire industrialist D. A. Thomas, the Commons in March 1908 refused a second reading to a bill embodying a right to work policy by 265–116 votes, the primary purpose of the measure being to provide suitable work for skilled workmen bereft of employment. While the leading socialists sat on the executive of the Right to Work National Council – G. N. Barnes was chairman, George Lansbury was treasurer, and other members included Ramsay MacDonald, J. R. Clynes, Edward Pease and Mary MacArthur – it was not an extremist body. Both sections of the Labour MPs accepted its policy, and when there was some money remaining from an unemployed demonstration account the Labour party executive voted to hand over the proceeds to the council.[1] As soon as the employment situation started to darken in 1908, the National Council communicated with 1,500 head offices of trade unions, 250 trade councils and 1,400 branches of socialist and labour bodies, begging them to take action. Demonstrations of the unemployed erupted all over the country in September and October. Sometimes there were spontaneous outbreaks of violence, as when 5,000 socialists and jobless workers rioted against Prince Arthur of Connaught in Glasgow; more often the meetings were stage-managed by local action groups of the National Council and passed off without incident. On Saturday 10 October 1908 and the following day the National Council sponsored rallies of the unemployed in London and 600 provincial centres, with the unemployed marching to the local churches on Sunday. On the succeeding Monday evening, deputations of workers tramped through the lobbies at Westminster. In the Commons the Labour party harassed the government, by urging the levying of a penny rate to enable distress committees to pay wages on an increased scale, and by affirming that they would be introducing the Right to Work Bill again. 'J. A. Pease, the Liberal Chief Whip, told Asquith ... that by introducing a measure to deal with unemployment, "we shall be able to resist Tory reaction and Socialism and to drive a wedge between the practical and impractical labour politicians".'[2]

John Burns was outvoted when the Cabinet met in mid-October 1908 after the summer recess, and practically superseded by the appointment of a Cabinet committee on unemployment. Burns maintained that nothing was the matter and that nothing should be done; Churchill counter-attacked, asserting that it was a burning question and that action was imperative. Arthur Henderson persuaded Churchill and Sydney Buxton, who were serving on the Cabinet committee, to adopt the Labour party's policy: that a special supplementary estimate should be voted and that permission should be given during the year for the payment of wages by the levying of a special local rate. Armed with statistics which they could not dispute, Burns partly outwitted Lloyd George and Churchill on the narrow front of palliatives to tide the country over the existing emergency, but could do nothing to prevent the government from speeding up its plans for permanent measures of relief. Burns claimed that the payment of wages out of funds subsidized by a locally levied rate would place a burden on 'poorer districts with a low rateable value', a point which Churchill and Sydney Buxton could not dispute.[3]

Nevertheless, the intervention of the Labour party was not entirely devoid of results, for Asquith told the Commons on 21 October that during 1908–9 an extra grant of £300,000 would be voted to the distress committees, exclaiming that the unemployed had a right to consideration at the hands of the community. Thus, although the campaign failed in its immediate aim of persuading the government to create the necessary conditions for maintaining full employment, it forced Asquith, recently installed as premier, to speed up his plans for dealing with unemployment and presented Churchill with a favourable opportunity for pressing schemes from his own department on more cautious Cabinet colleagues. To an anxious House, Asquith announced that the government had measures for dealing 'with the permanent causes and conditions of unemployment' on the stocks, though he refused to spell out the details.[4]

During the opening months of 1908 Winston Churchill, now installed as president of the Board of Trade, was questing for fresh approaches to social reform, and outwardly was most friendly to the Webbs, whatever his inner reservations. To his private secretary Edward Marsh, Churchill confessed that he did not want to go to the Local Government Board when Asquith formed his Cabinet, as 'I refuse to be shut up in a soup-kitchen with Mrs Sidney Webb'. But his ambition surpassed his discretion. When Sidney Webb attended a dinner of Churchill's in February, the latter made him sit next to him and 'was most eager to assure me that he was willing to absorb all the plans we could give him; that he would read anything we sent on to him and so on'. On 11 March Beatrice noted: 'Winston Churchill dined with us last night together with Masterman, Beveridge, Morton: we talked exclusively shop. He had swallowed whole Sidney's scheme for boy labour and unemployment, had even dished it up as an article in the *Nation* the week before'; and in May Sidney Webb sent Churchill not only their scheme of Poor Law reform, but copies of all the evidence on unemployment presented to the Royal Commission including statements touching on unemployment insurance. Apart from Haldane, more serious consideration was given by Churchill to the practical possibilities of social reform throughout 1908 than any other Liberal minister; and it was he, rather than Lloyd George, who forced the government to embark on the Welfare Revolution by advocating a package of measures including unemployment and health insurance, labour exchanges to eliminate casual labour, the expansion of certain state industries to counterbalance the oscillations of world trade, continuation and technical education for the nation's youth, and trade boards to assist low wage earners.[5] The evidence does not support E. P. Hennock's contention that Churchill had shown no interest in unemployment insurance until after the chancellor of the Exchequer's conversion to an insurance policy following his trip to Germany in August 1908.[6]

Churchill's interest in the wider issues of social reform was stimulated by the government's old age pensions scheme, but his apprenticeship in the Conservative party made him more intellectually receptive to the German model of social insurance than his fellow ministers; his fleeting contact with Sir John Gorst and the writings of his constituent T. C. Horsfall probably influenced him in this direction. While on a visit to Africa at the end of 1907, Churchill declared in a letter to J. A. Spender, the editor of the *Westminster Gazette*, that '[m]inimum standards of wages and comfort, insurance in some effective form or other against sickness, unemployment, old age – these are the questions, and the only questions, by which parties are going to live in the future'.[7] To Arthur Wilson Fox, the director of the Commercial, Labour and Statistical Department of the Board of Trade, Churchill elaborated his ideas on 4 January 1908:

> In Germany where the industrial system was developed under State control with all the advantages of previous British experience, uniform & symmetrical arrangements exist for insurance of workmen against accidents and sickness, for provision for old age, and through Labour bureaux etc. for employment. No such State organization exists in England. Its place is supplied by an immense amount of voluntary private machinery ... But in one respect the German system has an enormous advantage. It catches everybody. The meshes of our safety net are only adapted to subscribers, & all those who are not found on any of these innumerable lists go smashing down on the pavement. It is this very class, the residue ... for whom no provision exists in our English machinery, who have neither the character nor the resources to make provision for themselves, who require the aid of the state.[8]

Although he had not aired these views publicly, Churchill on 14 March 1908 avowed to Asquith that '[u]nderneath, though not in substitution for, the immense disjointed fabric of social safeguards & insurances which has grown by itself in England, there must be spread – at a lower level – a sort of Germanised network of State intervention & regulation'.[9]

Once he was promoted to the position of president of the Board of Trade in April 1908, Churchill with the assistance of the Webbs and their protégé William Beveridge set in motion the machinery for the establishment of a national network of labour exchanges. The Webbs advised Churchill that '[i]f you are going to deal with unemployment, you must have the boy Beveridge'. Beveridge wrote to his mother on 3 July 1908:

> On Wednesday I went by invitation to a conference on the unemployed – the President (Winston Churchill), Sidney Webb, Llewellyn Smith, Wilson Fox and me. The upshot of this was that the President expressed his intention of taking

up Labour Exchanges seriously and wanted a memorandum to back his views – which I undertook to prepare (voluntarily). However, on Thursday I was called up again by telephone to see Wilson Fox – who is I think second in command – and he gave me to understand that the President was passing sleepless nights till he should obtain my paid services.[10]

The result was that Beveridge started work in the department on a permanent basis shortly afterwards. As Churchill candidly informed Beatrice Webb in a letter dated 6 July 1908: 'You should not suppose that my interest in Labour Exchanges arises out of any decision of Government policy. I have not consulted my colleagues on the subject, nor shall I do so until I can put my case in all its strength before them.' Further, he continued, his absorption in the problem of labour exchanges arose not so much out of the intrinsic interest of the subject, but was a tactic designed to enlarge the responsibilities of his department, so that it could advance solutions to the problem of unemployment and thus get a larger enterprise under way.[11]

Beveridge produced a memorandum by 13 July 1908, rehearsing his familiar arguments about how labour exchanges would assist in the solution of the casual labour problem and outlining a scheme of local authority exchanges 'encouraged and co-ordinated by the Board of Trade with grants-in-aid'. Churchill overruled this cautious approach, opting instead for a national network of exchanges directly under the board's control. In practice the labour exchanges and the insurance scheme were indispensable to each other. Beveridge asserted:

> An insurance scheme involving contributions from employers makes it to the interest of employers to reduce unemployment or keep it from growing in order to secure a diminution or avoid an increase in their contributions … it gives them a financial motive for the use of Labour Exchanges … On the other hand, no public insurance scheme can hope to stand unless backed by an efficient Labour Exchange organisation. The insurance fund has to be protected against unnecessary claims, that is to say, it must have some absolute certain way of preventing men from drawing allowances as unemployed when they might be at work.[12]

In April 1909 there was a conference between the board's officials and the Parliamentary Committee of the TUC, at which the latter insisted on their proper representation on the councils which would have overall charge of the registries. Hence the country was divided into ten areas each with a council to manage the three classes of exchange; labour and capital would be equally represented on the councils, which would have a salaried and impartial chairman. Another deputation from the TUC met Churchill in July 1909, when it was decided that the exchanges could offer jobs below the standard rate of pay and in strike-bound firms, but in each case they had to make the position clear and the worker was left with the free choice of determining whether or not he should accept their offer. The 1909 Labour Exchanges Act permitted the Board of Trade to establish and take over existing bureaux, while the national Exchequer was to pay the costs of maintaining the new employment service.[13]

After moving to the Board of Trade, Churchill acquainted himself with the evidence of his officials, including Wilson Fox, William Harbutt Dawson and David Schloss, to the

Poor Law Commission, especially that dealing with the feasibility of a state-sponsored scheme of unemployment insurance. This accounts for the new emphasis in his public addresses as compared with his remarks earlier in the year. In a speech delivered to his constituents in Dundee at the end of June 1908, Churchill had boldly declared that labour exchanges, unemployment and health insurance were all questions lying at no great distance from practical politics. Insofar as the treatment of unemployment and sickness in Britain was concerned, he advised, they would have to incorporate the voluntary agencies into their schemes. In August, prior to Lloyd George's trip to Germany, Churchill returned to the same theme in another platform address, by exclaiming that

> our arrangements for insurance and safeguards are not complete [referring to the apparatus provided by friendly societies and trade unions]. In some respects they are better than those in Germany, but in one respect they are much inferior. They do not provide for the people most in need of assistance. Our existing organization does not cover the poorer people of the land ... the proper direction in which our legislation should move is not to sweep away the existing safeguard, but to try to weave them into a comprehensive system of safeguarding which shall make them really inclusive of the whole masses of people ... and result in relieving the working classes to some extent from the chances of infirmity and unemployment and from the harassing evils of casual labour.[14]

While Churchill should receive a due measure of credit for plunging his department into energetic action on the subject of a compulsory unemployment insurance scheme with the intensification of the employment crisis in the autumn of 1908, the plan which eventually emerged – a tripartite arrangement whereby the state, the employers and workers were all made responsible for maintaining the solvency of a central fund – was not of his doing.[15]

Since the autumn of 1908, Lloyd George had been shaping the essentials of a revolutionary Budget, so that it is doubtful whether he had time to play more than a secondary role in the creation of Churchill's social reform package. To Asquith, Churchill declared on 26 December 1908:

> The insurance policy must be presented as a whole ... and the ... policy could receive legislative form either as one half of a big Infirmity Insurance Bill or (if that fails) as the second part of the Labour Exchanges Bill. Nothing will be lost by getting the Labour Exchanges under way ... This is the course of action wh[ich] Lloyd George and I after much debating think best.[16]

On 11 January 1909, Asquith replied to Churchill:

> I have thought on your two letters, & took the opportunity of discussing their main points with Edward Grey, Haldane, & Gladstone, who were all here together last week. I am heartily at one with you as to the supreme importance of pressing on with our social proposals, particularly as they affect the various aspects of unemployment – e.g. Labour Exchanges, Boy Labour, Insurance.[17]

Accordingly the dramatic transformation in the posture of the Liberal Administration in 1909 as regards social reform by the rapid establishment of labour exchanges, juvenile employment bureaux and trade boards, together with the campaign for social insurance, was almost single-handedly the work of Churchill.

The initial shaping of the unemployment provisions of the National Insurance Act of 1911 was due neither to the initiative of a pressure group sponsored by the Labour movement, nor to the advice of experts outside the civil service, most of whom passed the European experience under an uncritical review and had soon become steadfast advocates of state-aided voluntary insurance plans. Percy Alden MP, in his 1905 and 1908 unemployment studies and in numerous parliamentary interventions, demanded government assistance for the trade union unemployment insurance schemes, as did David Schloss in 1909; but in July 1908 the latter had observed that it would be a 'mistake ... to suppose that the considerable sums asked for Labour Exchanges are to be followed by a demand for incomparably larger amounts for insurance against employment'. When Alden requested the TUC Parliamentary Committee in November 1906 to give an expression of opinion on the subject of government aid for voluntary unemployment insurance arrangements, he was rebuffed with a non-committal answer; and it was not until the deepening of the cyclical depression in September 1908 that the TUC was prepared to pass a resolution on these lines. The Webbs in the Minority Report announced that they favoured the continental method of subsidizing trade unions rather than a compulsory state system, partly because the latter plan foisted the burden ultimately on the consumer, partly because it was inequitable to demand high weekly contributions from the mass of casual labourers. On the other hand, many radical Liberal MPs were opposed to insurance schemes. G. P. Gooch MP wrote that '[w]hile the resources of the country are still far from being fully developed, it is premature to talk of the necessity of "making work", and unnecessary to have recourse to such doubtful expedients as municipal insurance'. In September 1908 Masterman informed his wife that 'the German system [of insurance] is merely ... a tax on wages which employer and employed pay, while the drone and unearned increment-drawer get off scot-free. Quite the most wasteful and unjust form of taxation.' 'One of his [Dilke's] last pencillings on the margin of an article reviewing the Government's forecast of the scheme for sickness insurance includes a note of regret and indignation at the apparent omission to make any provision for the lowest – paid classes of workers.' However, such Liberal publicists as Alden, T. C. Horsfall and Edward Cadbury and such Liberal sympathizers in the civil service as Beveridge and William Harbutt Dawson espoused an unemployment insurance scheme.[18]

To our mind, the most likely candidates in the civil service who pressed for the adoption of so radical a measure as compulsory unemployment insurance on their more staid colleagues were Arthur Wilson Fox (1861–1909) and William Harbutt Dawson (1860–1948). In the civil service hierarchy Wilson Fox was second in command at the Board of Trade under Hubert Llewellyn Smith and, when he was not settling trade disputes, had a crucial role in overseeing the new labour exchange and unemployment insurance legislation. For example, a conference was held on 29 July 1908 of Board of Trade officials presided over by Wilson Fox to draft the terms under which skilled workers would be included in the operations of the labour bureaux, after which trade union representatives could be approached.[19] Because he died in January 1909, Wilson Fox's work in helping to formulate these social reforms has been forgotten. Giving evidence to the Poor Law Commission in April 1908, Wilson Fox, comptroller-general of the Commercial, Labour and Statistical Department of the Board of Trade, advised that:

> It would be a good thing if you could get a system of insurance in this country, and run your insurance and labour bureaux together ... But if you have a big national compulsory insurance scheme, there is a great deal of money in 4d. per employee ... but if every worker paid 2d. a week and every employer paid 1d., and the State paid a halfpenny, and the municipality a halfpenny, you would then get 4d., and that would give you a fund of about £9,000,000 a year, which is a large sum for dealing with unemployment. You would then be able to give about 430,000 or 440,000 people 7s. a week through the year, and you would have about £1,000,000 over for expenses.[20]

Further:

> I do not say I am particularly in favour of compulsion; but I say we have got the trade unions who have done great work, but, who, although they have got a voluntary system, have not dealt with the question over a very wide area. After all, there are 2,000,000 trade unionists, and we have only 440,000 of those who are paying unemployed benefit mainly to the skilled trades; they have not covered the unskilled people, and one large union, which contains a great number of unskilled men, the gasworkers, have not got any unemployment fund at all, because they cannot afford it.[21]

He added: 'Of course, the building trade is the very trade in which these men ought to insure, because they are so liable to be thrown out of work by the weather'; and W. H. Dawson suggested that an insurance scheme could also cover dockers who worked for four days a week. Wilson Fox admitted that he 'had never worked any scheme out because there may be several ways of doing this ... but that a scheme could be worked out at a certain price I have very little doubt'. As far as trade union schemes were concerned, Wilson Fox concluded that 'there is some argument for subsidising them to some extent, but not to a large extent'.[22]

Wilson Fox generously praised his junior colleague to the Poor Law Commission, declaring that,

> as regards the foreign information much of what I know I have learnt from Mr W. H. Dawson ... he has been abroad so much and knows Germany so thoroughly, and has seen some of these schemes actually in work there and in other countries, so that he can tell you about it much better than I can.[23]

Dawson told the Poor Law Commission 'that the system which Mr Wilson Fox developed this morning of taking trade by trade and possibly trusting to a combination with the trade unions, as they find it to their interest, might be made to work if the proper encouragement was given'. Under Wilson Fox's proposals the employers would contribute 1d. per man to the scheme in addition to the employees' contributions, while the state and municipality would pay $^1/_2$d. each, to which Dawson added that the municipality would contribute because of a saving on Poor Law expenditure.

According to Robert Chalmers, Dawson was 'without too much sense of proportion', a characteristic which would incline him to favour the grandiose. Dawson had been one of the first to demand an old age pension open to all financed out of income tax. His future father-in-law Emil Muensterberg, with whom he had many conversations, was one of the greatest experts on the German system of social security. When employed as a part-time investigator for the Board of Trade, Dawson had conceived the daring notion of running the health and unemployment bills in harness as a grand design, after a talk and correspondence early in October 1908 with William Blain, the brilliant Treasury official who had been chosen by Lloyd George to sketch a health insurance scheme. This idea of presenting the insurance policy as a whole was avidly seized on by Churchill and Lloyd George 'after much debating', Churchill explained to Asquith, to awaken the slumbering sympathies of the electorate.[24]

On 30 September 1908 with the unemployment situation darkening, Dawson produced a memorandum on '[a]ssisted unemployment insurance in conjunction with labour registries' for Wilson Fox, which the latter assured him Churchill had found of 'great value'; Dawson noted in his diary on 24 October 1908: 'Unemployment Insurance is to be taken up.'[25] This was the key memorandum which propelled Churchill into opting for a scheme of unemployment insurance. Dawson declared that his aim was to suggest the broad principles of a scheme rather than to discuss the details of its actual working: 'It has been assumed that Unemployment Insurance would be (a) assisted, (b) voluntary, (c) locally organised, and (d) worked in conjunction with Labour Registries.' Further, Dawson noted:

> Insurance according to Trade is now accepted as the only sound and business-like principle. Only when that condition is complied with is it possible to adjust the cost of insurance, even approximately, to the risk of unemployment involved, and to create amongst the insured a substantial reciprocity of interest ... if Labour Registries are essential to the efficient and economical working of Unemployment Insurance, the latter is no less the natural complement of labour registration, in that it offers the opportunity of alleviating hardships which for the time being may be incapable of abatement.[26]

The unemployment insurance fund would cooperate with the labour registry 'in endeavouring to find work for unemployed members in receipt of benefit'. Dawson pointed out that 'all the experiments of recent origin now in operation in Belgium, France, Germany and Norway' encouraged collective and voluntary providence 'by subsidising organisations which give unemployment benefit to their members'. He asserted that subsidies contributed by the state and local authorities 'would be offered to all associations of both sexes regularly engaged in industry and trade ... no distinction would be made between labour organisations in the narrower sense and organisations of a purely provident character'; and he thought that it might be expected 'that many employers would be willing to assist such factory or trade union funds'. He concluded by stating:

> Should the experiments [on a voluntary basis] lead to a very large increase in the number of workpeople insuring themselves in different organisations against

unemployment, it might be found desirable to apply some form of pressure with a view to taking in the mass of workers belonging to certain specified trade groups. It is an advantage of the experimental methods proposed that they could at any time be made to serve as the basis of a more comprehensive system of insurance on obligatory lines, and could equally be combined with other systems of insurance (as, for example, insurance against sickness and invalidity).[27]

Lloyd George sedulously fostered the myth that he was the real author of the government's scheme of unemployment insurance, but this is unlikely to have been the case for a number of reasons. At the start of 1908 his interest lay elsewhere. As we have seen, in February 1908 Edwin Montagu confided to Asquith that Lloyd George 'is in favour of the Nationalising of railways, and obviously hints that we shall have to go to the country next time with something appetising as a substitute for Tariff reform'. True that at the end of February 1908 Lloyd George sent William Harbutt Dawson on a secret mission to Germany to ascertain how they were tackling their unemployment problems, yet he did not order his permanent officials at the Board of Trade to prepare an insurance scheme. Nor did Churchill borrow from Lloyd George's arsenal of ideas, when the hard fact is that Churchill twice publicly spoke of the possibility of unemployment insurance long before Lloyd George mentioned the matter privately. Even at his famous press interview on 26 August 1908 after his visit to Germany to study its health insurance scheme, Lloyd George did not broach the idea of unemployment insurance. On 8 October 1908, Dawson noted in his diary: 'At Fox's request saw Mr Blain of Treasury. I gave him my ideas of German invalidity insurance – and unemployment insurance – He wanted me to give him more information later. The question is coming up.' Lloyd George's first utterance on the subject was in a letter to Herbert Lewis on 8 September 1908 in which he proposed an insurance scheme which would cost the Treasury £2 million per annum and a confidential discussion he had with Riddell at the end of October 1908. 'His idea is to form a board in each trade', Riddell noted, 'which will make a levy in prosperous times upon employers and workmen, and apply the sums contributed to alleviate distress in times of depression.' However, we now know that at this time Churchill and Lloyd George were coordinating their policy on unemployment and invalidity insurance through their officials; the most likely explanation of Lloyd George's sudden interest in unemployment insurance is that he was relaying information gleaned from Churchill's officials or from an earlier talk with Wilson Fox or Dawson, for it is improbable that Lloyd George, whose ideas on social policy were then somewhat shallow, could have conjured up a brand new type of insurance plan.[28] Dawson mentioned in his diary on 27 December 1908: 'I had one long talk with Mr Blain about two months ago on the Insurance question … also correspondence later. I was to have talked with him again over the working and wh[at]not when I met him.' Unfortunately, William Blain, who was coordinating Lloyd George's invalidity insurance scheme with Dawson, died suddenly at the age of forty-seven.[29]

Although some of the earliest memoranda on unemployment insurance have been lost, we can reconstruct the thinking of the civil servants, as Harold Spender, the Liberal publicist, at the invitation of Wilson Fox met Dawson on 19 November

1908 to discuss the latter's ideas on unemployment insurance. It was suggested that Britain should apply the model of the German sickness and invalidity insurance scheme as a solution for dealing with unemployment. The drain on their funds to deal with unemployment was straining the finances of the leading British trade unions. Without a scheme of labour exchanges to reduce unemployment as much as possible, unemployment insurance would not be practicable. It could be started by a large experiment on the Ghent model, whereby the community subsidized trade union insurance schemes. But if workers outside the trade unions were to be covered, it would have to be converted into a scheme of universal compulsion. Harold Spender, echoing Dawson, asserted:

> Then, once more, it is obvious that in any State scheme of insurance the employer must be brought in ... But no system exists, save in a few exceptional German workshops, which provides us with any guidance for the establishment of a system of general compulsory insurance worked through employers and with the assistance and cooperation of the trades affected. Such a system, as we have conceived it, would be organised by the municipalities and local councils under the supervision of the State. It would follow the model of the German accident insurance system, and would be accompanied by the formation of labour registries on the Bavarian model. It might start by a large experiment on Ghent model, but if the workmen outside the Trade Unions are to be included in its benefits, it must necessarily be converted finally into a system of universal compulsion. The contributions would be small and would be levied by employers on the stamp or book system.[30]

Dawson also recorded that Spender approved of his proposal to bring unemployment and invalidity insurance together.[31]

Put into a more complete form by Llewellyn Smith, assisted by Beveridge, in the winter of 1908 and throughout 1909 and confined to a few trades because of its highly experimental nature, the British plan of unemployment insurance initially selected shipbuilding, engineering and the building industries for membership of a state-sponsored unemployment insurance fund which was to be raised from employers, workers and the state. Between them Llewellyn Smith and Beveridge recast Dawson and Wilson Fox's outline of an insurance scheme in the light of the national system of labour bureaux, giving employers a more central role in the running of the scheme. José Harris pointed out that Beveridge, in a memorandum to the Poor Law Commission,

> had suggested that insurance contributions should be collected and paid to the State by employers rather than workmen; and Churchill and Lewellyn Smith carried this principle a stage further by proposing that the employers' share of responsibility for unemployment insurance should not only be administrative but financial.[32]

Unlike Dawson's original proposals, the municipalities were not expected to make any contribution to the state fund and did not participate in the scheme. A third of the labour force of those engaged in purely industrial occupations, or two and a quarter million adult workers, was covered by this safety net of unemployment insurance. Those trades which were found to be most affected by seasonal and cyclical fluctuations were the trades in which the scheme was to be introduced first. Another third of the labour force consisted of railway workers, coal miners and textile operatives, who were put on short time during periods of depression but not discharged, thus making their need for insurance less imperative. Hence this left one third of the workers in industrial occupations uncovered by state insurance. Nonetheless, Churchill asserted on 22 May 1909 at Manchester that if the initial scheme were a success, there would be no stopping until the whole industrial population was protected by it.[33]

However, there was a two-year delay before the scheme reached the statute book because of the clash between the Commons and the House of Lords over the Budget. Under Part 2 of the National Insurance Act 1911, unemployment benefit payments were limited to 7s. a week for a fifteen-week period in the trades that had been selected. Beveridge, like Dawson, was troubled about the inequalities of risk between different trades and insisted on separate funds as between engineering, shipbuilding and house building. He suggested the insertion of an important provision limiting the period of benefit paid 'both to so many weeks in each year as a maximum and by reference to the total number of contributions paid by the individual ... one week of benefit for every five contributions paid'. When a Cabinet committee scrutinized the draft bill in April 1910, concern was expressed about malingering and Beveridge drafted a clause to prevent bogus claims. Churchill objected to moral criteria being used to vet the insurance claims of employees, but Beveridge showed that such rules were common in the voluntary schemes run by unions. Treasury officials had such a poor grasp of the insurance scheme's ability to curb seasonal trade fluctuations that they led a move to reduce payment of benefit in the building trade, a move that was later frustrated by trade union and Board of Trade opposition. Resistance within the parliamentary Labour party from leftwing MPs who opposed the payment of contributions by lower-paid workers was overcome by Ramsay MacDonald with the support of MPs who represented the skilled trades. Care was taken that the trades initially chosen for the scheme hardly included any women, 'so that the problem of insurance of women after marriage did not arise'.[34]

Under section 103 of the National Insurance Act 1911, Part 2 unemployment insurance could be extended to fresh trades by special decree. In November 1913 Sydney Buxton, the reform-minded president of the Board of Trade, envisaged bringing in 850,000 more workers within the insured trades by these means. Among the trades which he earmarked for selection were woodworking and furnishing, miscellaneous metal trades and electrical engineering, as well as works of construction, exclusive of roads and the permanent-way of railways and roads. By the end of February 1914, the Board of Trade officials under a new and weak minister, John Burns, were in full retreat, as the Treasury ordered them to scale down their proposals because of budgetary constraints.[35] Charles Masterman advised Lloyd George on 10 February 1914 that he doubted whether the time was 'propitious for any immediate substantial extension of Unemployment Insurance'. At the end of February 1914, Masterman noted that the chancellor of the Exchequer had 'decided that no provision in respect of [the] proposed extension of Unemployment Insurance is to be made in the original Estimate for 1914–15'. Lloyd George defeated Burns when the matter was considered by the Cabinet in March, and Llewellyn Smith decided to press for modest extension orders for men in the repair of works of construction and sawmilling, a proposal which Lloyd George accepted. Blacksmithing was dropped from the extension orders due to the opposition of Lord Crewe and Herbert Samuel. The number of new workmen now covered by the Act was a mere 50,000, a far cry from the original proposals. Lloyd George emerges from the constant departmental wrangling as a minister with a peevish attitude towards rival ministers and a somewhat limited understanding of the complex issues of unemployment.[36]

## Decasualization of Dock Labour

In England and Wales in the Edwardian era there were just over 100,000 dock and wharf labourers, whose existence was precarious, apart from a small number of permanent men, because of the casual basis of their daily engagement. 'At one call' which Henry Mess attended,

> there were some sixty men waiting. The foreman stood on the raised ledge of a warehouse and eyed the crowd over as if it were a herd of cattle. Then very deliberately he beckoned a man with his finger, and after a considerable interval a second and a third, until he had taken ten in all. There was an evident enjoyment of a sense of power.[37]

Again:

> It is during the later stages of a heavy call that disturbances are most frequent. The men begin to fidget, and to push; those who are small are shoved aside by the more burly ... Occasionally a foreman will toss a tally to a man at the rear of the crowd, just as a morsel of food might be thrown to a dog.[38]

Grace Foakes, the daughter of a docker, recalling her childhood remarked:

> If one ship berthed alongside the wharf the other was anchored out in the river. At such a time men would have to work all day and all night so that one could sail and the other come alongside at the next highwater ... Sometimes Father would come home after working all day, saying he must work all night. This he would do, returning for breakfast in the morning. There was no day off next day. He would go back and work until tea-time. Imagine it: two days and one night without stopping.[39]

Despite the fact that sociologists had been analysing the problem for over two decades by 1914, one contemporary wrote: 'To those of us who belong to a younger generation these records of twenty-five years ago are rather sad reading. So much seems unchanged.' Opposition to reform came from the docker, who 'like most men whose lives are hard and whose outlook is narrow, is very suspicious of any change the exact effect which he cannot foresee'; from the foreman, who objected 'to anything which would take the choice of men out of their hands'; and from the employers, who 'are very much afraid of possible shortages of labour which would mean expensive delays' and were fearful of allowing the men to become more independent and powerful.[40] According to David Wilson:

> The early unions thus opposed permanency as a threat to their existence and for a more basic reason: so long as the permanency was partial, the work available to casuals would decrease in proportion to the amount given to regularly employed men.[41]

Dockers' earnings in London fluctuated from an average of £91. 9s. in 1908 to £73. 10s. 4d. in 1912, but a surprising number of men at the docks did not earn on average 10s. a week, and there were many who were fortunate if they got as much work as a day in every week. In Liverpool, out of a sample of 600 dockers, 45 per cent earned less than £1, while 31 per cent earned less than 15s. a week.[42]

Gordon Phillips and Noel Whiteside argued that any proposal to eliminate casualism foundered over the issue of who was to regulate the supply of labour in the docks:

> Upon the possession of such power employers felt their managerial functions to rely; upon its acquisition, union leaders saw their bargaining capacity to depend. These rival claims to hegemony in the labour market long barred the way to decasualization.[43]

In 1891, at the suggestion of the shipowner and sociologist Charles Booth, a reform was instituted by the London and India Docks Company to regularize employment. This was perhaps the earliest attempt on a voluntary basis to apply sociology – the casual labour problem described in Booth's *Labour and Life of the People [in] London* – to the cause of social reform and specifically to eradicating casualism from the work of dockers, where it was most prevalent. Under Booth's scheme the port labour force in London was to be headed by a 'permanent staff', who were paid weekly, given a paid holiday, sick benefit and a benevolent allowance of up to 10s. a week after fifteen years of service'. Next lists of 'A' and 'B' men were compiled, who were given preference over irregulars if work was available, after the superintendent of each dock sent a statement of the following day's requirements to a central office. Men on the 'A' list, who had preference over 'B' men and casuals, were almost continuously in employment and were paid weekly. Booth hoped that after the implementation of his scheme the number of dockers employed on a casual basis would be drastically reduced by natural wastage. Phillips and Whiteside, however, concluded that

> the joint committee's measures may well have exacerbated casualism in the port [of London] as a whole. Not only did the enlargement of the shipowners' responsibilities compel the [dock] companies to curtail their weekly staff, but in addition the effect of regularizing one sector of a labour market which remained otherwise casual was to intensify underemployment elsewhere.[44]

Their criticism appears to be too sweeping, for as pointed out by David Wilson,

> By 1913 the PLA [Port of London Authority] had 3,000 permanent men, 47 per cent of its average daily requirement, and 40 per cent A men – a peak which was not going to be passed again until the 1950s.[45]

Richard Williams, a divisional official in charge of labour exchanges, suggested that advantage could be taken of section 99 of the National Insurance Act 1911 Part 2, which allowed the Board of Trade to undertake the custody of cards and the deduction of insurance contributions on behalf of employees, provided they engaged their casual labour in the manner prescribed by the labour exchange. In August 1911 a Joint Committee was set up in Liverpool at the behest of Williams, and in July 1912 every docker was registered and issued with a metal tally. Whereas 30,000 men registered, wages were never paid to more than 22,000 individuals in any week. Six clearing houses were established, linked by telephone to employers' offices and to the other clearing houses to place surplus labour from the fourteen surplus stands, where men without work for the day assembled. The capital cost of the clearing houses, tallies and salaries of the staff were borne by the Board of Trade, but a charge was imposed on employers for the use of these offices for payment of wages and the keeping of insurance cards. After James Sexton and George Milligan of the Dock Labourers Union urged the men to accept the scheme, a strike erupted, as the dock labourers were imbued with the mistaken idea that the proposals would deprive some of their number of a living, though it was swiftly crushed with imported blackleg labour. Williams believed that men might be made permanent in two ways: one was for each employer to keep a fixed number of permanent men; the other was for employers as a body to pool their demand and guarantee permanent employment to as large a group of men as they could support financially.[46]

The flaws in the scheme were that men did not like to travel long distances through fear of blacklegging, that the employers would telephone for extra hands from the surplus stands and then engage other men at the dock gates, that men from the surplus stands failed to report to an allocated job or refused to undertake the specific task allotted to them, and that many dockers wished to work a traditional two- or three-day week and earn 15s. Once the Dockers' Union had been given the task of distributing tallies to the men, it 'resisted any development of registration involving the appointment of permanent or preference men by individual firms'. David Wilson observed: 'In the 1920s and the 1930s, the register was repeatedly pruned back – to 24,300 in 1922 and 21,500 in 1929. But the onset of the Depression and bulk-handling of commodities cut back the demand for labour even faster.' Both employers and dockers boycotted the surplus stands, which were allowed to lapse after the First World War. Lawrence Holt, lord mayor of Liverpool in 1929, 'said ... the scheme has indeed mitigated the degree of casualness but it has so far not changed its nature'.[47]

Apart from Liverpool, there were earlier experiments under section 99 of the National Insurance Act 1911. The hope was that the employers would only engage casual labour through the exchange. Local decasualization schemes were taken up in 1912 for dock labourers in Goole and among ship repairers in South Wales, corporation labourers in Birmingham and cloth porters in Manchester and so on, covering some 130,000 workers before Treasury parsimony resulted in tighter, prohibitive regulations being issued in December 1912. This checked a further expansion of the existing schemes.[48] While Sydney Buxton was the minister in charge of the Board of Trade, the solution of the casual labour problem was treated as a matter of great urgency and in November 1913 he circulated a memorandum to the Cabinet, outlining a proposed expansion of unemployment insurance to more industries and dealing with the elimination of casual labour at great length. A Treasury official dismissed this, noting: 'The proposals of the B[oard] of T[rade] dealing with Casual Labour are in too inchoate a stage for useful criticism or for any approximate estimate of cost.'[49] Nevertheless, Beveridge devised a clause in the 1913 Insurance Amendment Act at the request of the insurance commissioners to protect casual labourers, by enabling them 'to issue special orders to regulate the collection of contributions in areas and industries subject to casualism. This clause allowed workers to be charged on a daily rather than a weekly basis, so that only after completing four days' work would they have paid a normal contribution of 4d.' The first location in which this innovative decasualization scheme was tried was the Port of London. Although when the Port of London Authority was set up in 1908, Board of Trade officials inserted a clause to promote the more regular engagement of casual labourers, it was not utilized to any great extent. At the end of 1913 the Board of Trade with the assistance of the insurance commissioners prepared a special order for the London docks, which again was never implemented. Under the scheme, special clearing houses were to be set up in London under the control of the labour exchange division. These centres were to distribute tallies to dockers, assess employers' contributions and do all the clerical work in connection with contributions. Beveridge blamed John Burns, who was the minister responsible, for the failure of the scheme to be pushed through, though he underrated the determined opposition of the employers.[50]

## The Development Commission

On the one hand, the Webbs in their Minority Report, swayed by the evidence of Professor A. L. Bowley of the London School of Economics, recommended that the sum of £40 million which was spent on public works over each decade by the government should be set aside for use exclusively in the lean years of the trade cycle. Works of afforestation, coast protection and land reclamation were to be included in the ten-year programme. Of the members of the government, only Churchill took any abiding interest in these proposals, but he unfortunately failed to convert Lloyd George when the latter was devising his Development Commission. In October 1908 Mrs Webb commented in her diary that a recent speech of Churchill had shown a mastery of the Webbs' scheme for unemployment. Churchill emphasized that there was a lack of a central agency for coordinating ordinary government work and local relief work, and that the Board of Trade should be able to foretell the amount of unemployment in the winter: the demand for labour should be stimulated in periods of unemployment by distributing more contracts. Further, the relief works such as afforestation should be contracted and expanded at will. Although unemployment could not be abolished in this way, Churchill suggested, its scale could be considerably limited. After prolonged discussions with Lloyd George at the end of 1908, Churchill remarked to Asquith that special expansive state industries were needed, such as roads and afforestation. In June 1909, Churchill

> proposed to Lloyd George the establishment of a Committee of National Organization, 'analogous in many respects to the Committee of Imperial Defence', chaired by the chancellor of the exchequer. Such a body could become responsible for forecasting the degree of unemployment, distributing treasury funds between the various development bodies, and investigating the merits of proposals for constructive expenditure on roads, afforestation, canals or municipal relief.[51]

The plan came to nothing.

In February 1911 Churchill told the king that he had 'always felt that it ought to be possible with our present science and civilization to mitigate the violent fluctuations of trade by some recourse to public works of a reproductive character wh[ich] could be carried on placidly in good times and actively in bad'. A. L. Bowley calculated that between 100,000 and 300,000 men were thrown out of work by cyclical trade depressions, rendering the problem one of easily manageable dimensions. He noted that '[it seems] that funds might be set aside in the prosperous years, earmarked for works of construction which need not be done at a particular time e.g. dock schemes, great building works, public parks, improvements of national roads'. However, Churchill somewhat bowdlerized this public works programme by omitting the building projects and lending it the surface appearance of an innocuous back-to-the-land scheme.[52]

Lloyd George's ideas on unemployment, on the other hand, were the complete antithesis of Churchill's, with an emphasis on the revival of agriculture rather than the introduction of sophisticated machinery to regulate the cyclical fluctuations of trade. Like Burns, Lloyd George held out little hope of being able to arrest cyclical trade fluctuations, asserting that '[y]ou might as well promise to flatten the Atlantic Ocean'. The afforestation schemes in his 1909 Budget were commended by Lloyd George for their utility as adjuncts to a system of small holdings rather than as a large-scale source of employment for town labourers ejected onto the labour market by a cyclical downturn in trade. Lloyd George wanted to create a Development Board with wide powers of initiative for promoting afforestation, agriculture, road improvement and canal and harbour construction, in sum a super Ministry of Lands, but the body which emerged from the Development and Road Improvement Funds Act 1909 had only truncated powers. Moreover, the Development Commission not only failed to set up adequate machinery for the implementation of the schemes, but decided to limit them only to the skilled workforce and utilized only a small fraction of the available funds. Under Part 2 of the Act a Road Board was instituted to construct new roads and keep them in good order. Lloyd George conceded that the Development Act was designed to exploit the natural resources of the country with only the incidental purpose of relieving unemployment.[53]

Despite the fact that in 1912 his adviser, Seebohm Rowntree, and other Liberal social theorists wanted to increase the demand for labour in times of unemployment by nationalizing the railways and regularizing 'the work of construction of new lines and rolling stock' and by allowing public authorities to undertake works of national or local improvement when the labour market was sluggish, Lloyd George hardly adjusted his approach to unemployment during the land campaign. He was able to adopt this attitude by emphasizing certain retrogressive features in Rowntree's approach that coincided with his own ideas. Seebohm Rowntree suggested that

> the provision of men working in the town of a home in the country, with a plot of land attached to it, would as in Belgium, provide them with a subsidiary means of support, minimize the hardships of unemployment, and produce in the next generation a race of men capable of working either in town or country.[54]

Following Rowntree, Lloyd George declared that he wished to curb unemployment at the root of which was the problem of casual labour 'by opening up the resources of land'. During the land campaign of 1913, Lloyd George asserted somewhat perversely that the prosperity of agriculture could determine employment prospects in towns:

> If they increased the cultivation of the soil there was greater demand for agricultural implements, for building material, a greater demand for transport facilities, railways and tramways. These were produced, not in the country, but in the great industrial districts. Not only that, they improved the market for labour. Once they freed the land the cultivation would improve, and improved cultivation necessarily meant more labour ... Instead of the towns drawing labour from the country they would have the country drawing labour from the towns.[55]

Much of Lloyd George's thinking from the Development Commission onwards appeared to be a rehash of public works schemes that had been expounded by some of the Young Liberals and Labour party pamphleteers.[56] The most persistent exponent of this type of programme was George Lansbury, the Labour party representative on the Poor Law Commission. According to an address given by Lansbury to the Christian Social Union in May 1907, industry was so organized that there was a margin of workers for whom no work could be found, but the labour exchanges would not relieve their plight: 'I have very little faith in the efficacy of these exchanges.' What the present situation called for was national department of public works. It would have control over all the main roads together with the Crown lands; it would be invested with compulsory powers of purchase over waste land, on which it could start up suitable projects such as afforestation; it would set up labour colonies, among whose objects would be the preparation of land for use as small holdings and the training of unemployed workers in agricultural skills. British agriculture was the only industry that was not over-extended; however, it required to be reorganized on cooperative lines based on the Danish model with more emphasis on dairy products and horticulture. So far as British agriculture being braced to receive the unemployed from the towns was concerned, this analysis was unsound, as there was already a surplus population living in the countryside; so far as the suggestions for reinvigorating agriculture were concerned, they were eminently sensible.[57]

Consistently the Webbs criticized the Unemployment Insurance Act and assembled an influential deputation, which pressed Asquith to appoint a departmental committee in 1913 to decide whether or not the government could phase their orders to regularize the demand for labour. Prophetically the *New Statesman* demanded:

> Are we to meet the next years of the trade slump, when hundreds of thousands of labourers will be out of work, and crowds of men outside the door of every Labour Exchange will, for all our transient doles, be sinking steadily into a demoralising unemployability, with nothing more preventive than insurance?[58]

In February 1914 when Herbert Samuel replaced Burns at the Local Government Board, it was reported 'on good authority that the Treasury is actually engaged with the appointment of a Committee to enquire into the possibility of regularising the demand for labour by a considered distribution of public works'.[59] It is almost certain that the pressure for this new initiative derived from Samuel, who had warmly congratulated Churchill in October 1908 on his exposition of unemployment policy which was on the Webbs' lines, and who agreed that a standing organization was required and 'that [in] addition to whatever localities may do, useful works should be organized on a national scale, set in operation in times of bad trade and reduced to a minimum in times of good trade'. In 1914 Edmund Harvey sponsored a Commons motion demanding the national and municipal regulation of the demand for labour, to which Samuel replied by announcing that the Treasury was appointing a departmental committee.[60]

Just after the outbreak of war on 6 August 1914, the Webbs gave an important interview to the *Daily News* in which Beatrice Webb declared that 'the Local Government Board should at once issue a circular to all local authorities calling upon them to do everything in their power to increase employment instead of economising, as many people are likely to suggest just now', while Sidney Webb advocated the establishment of a cabinet emergency committee to tackle the expected employment crisis. Anticipating that unemployment in the building trade would be severe, Samuel introduced an emergency measure in the Commons two days later to stimulate the building of workers' houses, informing the Commons that local authority schemes 'will be aided under this Bill according to the amount of distress or unemployment which prevails in their localities. If there is no unemployment the schemes will not be proceeded with, but where unemployment is acute preference will be given.' Privately to Lloyd George, Edwin Montagu, the financial secretary to the Treasury, accused his cousin Samuel of a 'craving for advertisement and a fear of Sidney Webb which is leading to blazing indiscretions'. Between August and September 1914, the government, following a flurry of circulars from Samuel, who was praised by the socialist press for his 'welcome recognition of the prevention of unemployment', sanctioned loans of £3.5 million as compared with £1,928,000 for the same period in 1913, including loans of £332,000 for working-class housing. Treasury orthodoxy soon prevailed when many building workers were absorbed into the army and the local authorities were instructed to curtail their schemes, despite the pleas of the National Housing Council.[61]

Samuel had already been warned in October 1914, when Montagu chided him: 'it is of the utmost importance that we limit expenditure … Surely the employment figures do not justify anything like the expenditure about which you swank.' The crux of the unemployment problem was the government sponsorship of state building programmes, a subject on which Samuel and the rest of the government had reservations. Having previously considered as postmaster-general whether or not the building of post offices could be staggered to times of trade depression, Samuel conceded that it was difficult to postpone such buildings because 'they are only erected when really urgently required'. Samuel was too prone to rely on road building schemes and projects of the Development Commission, including the improvement of rivers and the construction of light railways, a scheme for which was under consideration by the Cabinet. Critics denounced Samuel's schemes as inadequate because the government had not provided subsidies for the building of houses by the local councils, nor had the Board of Education created a special grant for the erection of schools or colleges. With the onset of the war enormous labour shortages developed, surplus manpower was absorbed into the army and Samuel's schemes to stagger the demand for employment over the trade cycle became irrelevant for the duration of the conflict.[62]

# 11

# Boy Labour and Continuation Education

## The Limitation of Child Labour

Since the decay of the apprenticeship system, social reformers had gradually been constructing a new network of agencies for supervising the mental and moral development of the nation's youth and for providing openings in which a definite training was supplied or the preparation for a future career was assured. As sociologists at the beginning of the twentieth century carefully unravelled the causes of unemployment and poverty, they began to apprehend that they were closely linked to the paucity of educational facilities which were available to the majority of the nation's youth and to the inadequate guidance which was offered to help them find really useful occupations, instead of blind-alley jobs which they would have to quit on reaching manhood. The reformers worked through two organizations, the Committee on Wage Earning Children, and the Apprenticeship and Skilled Employment Association; through their contacts at the Board of Trade, Llewellyn Smith and Beveridge, both of whom served for a time on the council of the latter association; and through the Webbs, who provided a platform for their ideas in the Minority Report and the National Committee for the Break-Up of the Poor Law. Among those reformers who were particularly interested in the problem of boy labour were three of the most brilliant young Fabians, R. H. Tawney, Frederic Keeling and Reginald Bray, a host of Liberal progressives such as T. Edmund Harvey MP, John Howard Whitehouse MP and G. P. Gooch MP; Cyril Jackson, a chief inspector of the Board of Education; Lord Henry Cavendish Bentick, a Tory progressive and brother of the society hostess Lady Ottoline Morrell; and quite a number of Jewish social workers such as Nettie Adler, the Hon. Lily Montagu and Ernest Lesser. While the Apprenticeship Association had aimed at an annual income of £500, despite the state increasingly taking over its functions, it could never keep to this target and its income slipped from £235. 5s. 6d. in 1911 to £174. 3s. 6d. in 1913. Thanks to the devoted services of the Misses Adler, Franklin, Pease and Jevons, the Committee on Wage Earning Children managed to perform quite well on a modest budget of £50. In fact, even if the means of the three associations were meagre, they contained the leading socialist and Liberal youth workers and progressives in their ranks; they cooperated with the National Education Association, the National Union of Teachers (NUT), the Romilly Society, the National Union of Women Workers, the Women's Industrial Council and the Joint Committee for the Abolition of Half-Time

Labour; they were thus by no means a politically insignificant force. Moreover, the Committee on Wage Earning Children, by having provincial members serving on its executive and general committee, such as Canon Moore Ede of Gateshead and Miss Geare of Exeter, and by maintaining a steady correspondence with them, was able to extend the sweep of its operations into provincial England.[1]

Perhaps the most deplorable consequence of the under-payment of adult labour was the fact that children from an early age were expected to contribute their mite to the family income – for tired children languished educationally, thereby manufacturing the next generation of paupers in slum districts. Especially in the most poverty-stricken neighbourhoods, there was a high proportion of children working outside of school hours, as was shown by Nettie Adler in a study of Hackney, where a quarter of the girls attending a school were engaged in such local sweated occupations as matchbox making, steel covering, fish basket sewing and making baby shoes. Moreover, interviews later conducted by Arnold Freeman in Birmingham among teachers and social workers confirmed the opinion that the bulk of the children employed outside school hours were drawn from impoverished households. As if the fact that their homes were too cramped and too squalid to provide an atmosphere congenial to study or the pursuit of attractive hobbies was not bane enough, children from these homes were driven to toil for long hours on empty stomachs before and after school, thereby exhausting their nervous and physical vitality. Suffering from fatigue, they also limped intellectually and filled the lowest standards in the elementary schools; further, because the majority of these boys ran errands of some kind for their employer, they naturally gravitated on leaving school into the most insidious blind-alley occupations after their initial experience of this type of work. Blighted mentally and physically and ejected onto an over-stocked labour market on reaching manhood, these youths, if fortunate, acquired some steady but ill-paid job; otherwise they drifted into the ranks of the casual labourers, slowly sinking into permanent unemployment and becoming virtually unemployable. Not enough individual biographies were compiled to prove this thesis conclusively, but one South London headmaster had formed the impression that '[i]rregularity, dullness and employment out of school hours (milk and newspaper distributing) causing slow progress through the standards, all make against due progress in after-life. (Boys answering to the above are holding poor positions as a rule.)' Constance Smith summed up the evidence of teachers on the effects of street-trading, which conceded that the boys so employed became quick-witted, but

> they lose their power of application, and they lose all interest in their school work. They become early full of the idea that you need not work to make a living, and that you can pick it up, and anything like regular industry becomes very distasteful to them. They also dislike the discipline of school and there is an additional factor to be taken into consideration that they come into school very often extremely exhausted and over-tired, and unable to work their brains.[2]

In 1897 the Women's Industrial Council set in motion an enquiry into the problem of wage earning by school children, the results of which were published in *The Nineteenth Century*. Mrs Hogg then asked for an investigation of children's work all over England, and although the Board of Education acceded to the request, the Local Government Board and the Home Office prevented any action being taken. In 1898 when a Liberal MP asked for a return of the number of children who worked for wages while attending school full-time, it was found that 144,000 children were regularly employed, though later over 3,000 extra names were added to the total. Only 1,120 children were employed between the ages of six and seven, but after that the number rose steeply. Some 39,355 children were employed for ten hours a week; 60,268 worked from ten to twenty hours a week; 27,008 children were engaged from twenty to thirty hours a week; 9,778 toiled from forty to fifty hours, while 793 children laboured for more than fifty hours a week. Different though was the position of children who were protected by the Factory and Mines Acts. Under the Factory and Education Acts children could obtain partial exemption from attending school at twelve years or total exemption at thirteen years, provided that certain educational standards had been attained; moreover, no children under the age of fourteen years worked for more than ten or six-and-a-half hours per day, depending on whether they were employed on the alternate or half-day system; in any event, before being taken on in the first place they had to be examined by a doctor. Under the Mines Acts the age limit under which boys were not to be employed below ground was raised to thirteen years in 1900 and fourteen in 1911; at the same time, their hours of labour were also restricted.[3]

In order to spur the government into action, Mrs Hogg and her friends from the Women's Industrial Council set up the Committee on Wage Earning Children in 1899 to consider reforms with regard to the labour of children of school age not covered by the Factory or Mines Acts. The committee met at the offices of the London School Board and Sir Charles Elliott, despite an attachment to old-fashioned philanthropic ideals, was induced to become chairman. After appealing in vain for the government to accept a clause limiting child labour in their 1900 Education Bill, the committee obtained the appointment of an Inter-Departmental Committee in 1901.[4] This committee estimated that 200,000 children were employed outside the Factory and Workshop Act in England and Wales and called for legislation. Quite a number of witnesses before the Inter-Departmental Committee testified that moderate amounts of work were not only non-injurious but positively beneficial. Although most witnesses agreed that twenty hours was a safe limit for such work, the committee concluded that if the work outside school hours was concentrated on two days a week, even fewer than twenty hours could be harmful to health. The committee recommended that child labour should be regulated by local by-laws rather than be totally prohibited. Already they were convinced that street-trading was the worst aspect of the child labour problem:

> Street trading sharpens the boys' wits, and notwithstanding in many cases the late hours and exposure to all sorts of weather, there is no evidence that it is generally injurious to health. Its most serious aspect is its effect on character. Where carried on in a quiet suburb by the children of respectable workmen, who sell evening papers for an hour or two, it does no great harm. But in the centres of large towns, where it is carried on by children drawn from the lowest classes in the poorest quarters, it is represented as a hotbed of vice and crime; [for the children learn]

to drink, to gamble, and to use foul language, while the girls are exposed to even worse things.[5]

For alleviating these ills, the committee suggested that all local authorities should be granted similar powers of licensing juvenile street-traders to those obtained by Manchester, Liverpool, Bradford and Halifax under private acts. Among other locations singled out for sharp criticism were barber shops, where boys worked five hours per evening and as many as fifteen hours on Saturdays in an insanitary atmosphere, made heavier in the eyes of reformers by the frequent gambling talk. Furthermore, children in industrial and reformatory schools had ample means of physical education and training, whereas the children in large towns lacked such facilities.[6]

As a result, the Employment of Children Act was passed in 1903. It gave local authorities permissive powers to frame by-laws, prescribing for all children the age below which their employment was illegal, and prohibiting absolutely or permitting subject to conditions the employment of children under the age of fourteen years in any specified occupation; it stipulated that by-laws could be made, allowing or prohibiting street-trading by young persons under the age of sixteen, while it banned street-trading outright for children under eleven years; it stated that children were not to work between the hours of 9.00 p.m. and 6.00 a.m. or between such times as local authorities should decide; it allowed these authorities to authorize a maximum number of working hours for children; stipulated that children were not to carry heavy weights, nor to be employed in any occupations which were fraught with dangerous risks to their health – the first regulations to protect the health of the school child. Not satisfied with the government bill, the Committee on Wage Earning Children tried without avail to strengthen it in committee, by conferring compulsory powers on local authorities, by debarring girls under sixteen years from street-trading, and by withdrawing the exemptions granted to young theatrical performers.[7]

The Committee on Wage Earning Children wanted to see a threefold policy enforced in the administration of the Act: the prohibition of street-trading for boys under fourteen years and girls under sixteen years; the restriction of the employment of children in laundries, barber shops and pubs; the enforcement of the limit of a twenty-hour week and an eight-hour working day on Sundays for such children. In conjunction with the State Children's Association, the NUT, the British section of the International Congress on the Welfare and Protection of Children and the Howard and Romilly societies, the committee sent a deputation to Herbert Gladstone on 17 January 1907 with considerably wider objectives. Among the reforms suggested were that the Employment of Children's Act should be made compulsory, that street-trading by children should be abolished, and that the age for half-time employment should be raised to thirteen years in 1909 and prohibited in 1910. Henceforth all these three objectives – the banning of employment of school children, the closing down of blind-alley occupations, and the abolition of half-time – became inextricably interlinked. None of these reforms was inserted in the Children's Act of 1908, but as a concession the government appointed a Departmental Committee on the Employment of Children Act and an Inter-Departmental Committee on Partial Exemption from School Attendance.[8]

## Youth Employment Exchanges and After-Care

Meanwhile, with the formation of the Apprenticeship and Skilled Employment Association in 1906, an additional fillip was given to the movement that was campaigning to prevent the exploitation of child labour. The second annual report of the association commented:

> We ... are encouraged by noting the evidence on all sides of a growing general interest in the question of better industrial training of boys and girls, and a recognition of the importance of the bearings of this question on the larger problem of poverty and unemployment.[9]

The whole movement seems to have sprung from those social workers who had started the first youth clubs in the poorer districts London and who, in following the progress of children under their care, noted how they were blindly flung onto the labour market. 'There is in all districts', the 1907 report observed, 'especially among the poorer working class, great ignorance as to the industrial opportunities, and the need for advice and help is found to be very great.' The report of the Higher Education Sub-committee of the London County Council stated that among boys leaving elementary schools in 1906–7, 67.9 per cent went into unskilled occupations; the 1907–8 returns from a larger number of schools showed a slight improvement in the position, with 61 per cent of the boys moving into unskilled jobs. In some measure the association aimed at making good the deficiency in knowledge as regards the placing of boys in industrial situations. Often club managers mulled over the idea of starting up employment bureaux for the youths under their charge, but the projects started chiefly in London and Manchester were none too successful, as the managers wished to cater exclusively for their own club members, and unless these exchanges were conducted on a large scale there was little hope of their achieving anything. At any rate, the pioneer body was the Industrial Committee of the Jewish Board of Guardians, which began to apprentice children from 1873, for which purpose a loan fund was instituted to lend money to parents who could not afford the usual premiums, with the money then deducted weekly from the apprentice's wages: later many of the skilled employment committees ran loan schemes on similar lines. Other features of the scheme were after-care, under which a member of the special committee supervised the progress of the boys and encouraged them to attend technical colleges, with fees being paid for evening classes from 1884. Two years later the East London Apprenticeship Fund was established to work among gentile children, whereupon the movement spread to other parts of London and to other industrial centres.[10]

The local committees of the association in London, of which there were already ten in 1907, in touch with the various boys' and girls' clubs and the elementary schools, found vacancies and then apprenticed suitable applicants, making certain at the same time that the conditions of employment were fair. Usually the skilled employment associations tried to secure binding agreements for five years, with the stipulation that the contract could be terminated on good cause being shown. An important feature of the methods adopted by the association was the elaborate attention devoted to after-care work: each apprentice was placed under the surveillance of a visitor, who called on his parents and employer at intervals, and also kept a careful watch over the boy's progress at trade classes; as far as was possible the skilled employment associations inserted a clause in the agreement, enjoining the employer to grant his apprentice one or two afternoons off a week to attend technical classes; moreover, the visitor encouraged the boys whom he was supervising to develop worthwhile leisure pursuits by joining a youth club and to acquire habits of thrift by becoming a member of a friendly society, and for those in need, a short holiday in the country might be arranged. The central office of the association pooled the information as to the vacancies collected by the local committees and later a comprehensive scheme of cooperation was hammered out to prevent local committees from encroaching on each other's preserves, and from contacting the same employer too often. Further, when labour exchanges were set up in London in 1906, a scheme of cooperation was arranged with them: children suitable for apprenticeship and the more skilled trades were referred by the labour exchanges to the local skilled employment associations; representatives of the associations served on the advisory committees of the labour exchanges, and often the superintendent of the exchange was a member of the local skilled employment association. Having published authoritative handbooks on trades for London boys and girls, the association consented to the Board of Trade quarrying in them to collect material for their own series of career guides. In addition, about ten provincial apprenticeship associations became affiliated to the central association, while education committees and social agencies throughout the country made requests for information. In 1908, 1,009 boys and girls plus 174 improvers and assistants were placed in London alone, but many other enquiries about jobs were dealt with.[11]

Of equal significance in stimulating the emergence of a sound public opinion and in presenting social reformers with a clear objective as to where best they should concentrate their efforts next was the clarity with which sociologists elucidated the connection between enrolment in blind-alley occupations in the formative years of adolescence and unemployment and casual labour in manhood. Charles Booth had already noticed this phenomenon, though he incorrectly drew the conclusion that only the most humble sections of society were affected by it rather than the bulk of the working class. He declared:

> Boys of the very poor ... are pitchforked into working life with more than a usual lack of care, as errand boys, as van boys, or as street sellers. An idle father, an empty cupboard, leads to many a false step for children – false, because either taken too soon, or on the wrong road. In this way the seed is sown of a future crop of unemployed adult labour.[12]

Again, the Webbs, in their volume entitled *Industrial Democracy*, seized on another aspect of the problem of boy labour. With the decay of the system of apprenticeship, they asserted, employers no longer felt themselves under an obligation to teach boys under their care; to garner rich profits quickly, it was customary to keep the boys absorbed in some routine and specialized task for which little training was required. When employers had such an abundant supply of cheap labour at their disposal, they ceased to have much interest in the perfection of machinery, preferring the yields to be gathered from a low-cost but scarcely productive labour force. As a solution, the Webbs recommended that the half-time system should be greatly extended from fourteen to eighteen years to permit juveniles to attend compulsory technical schools and continuation classes. By this means adults would be able to fill the places vacated by a boy labour force now down to half its original size. Whereas Booth's insights were too isolated for him to evolve any tenable theory, the Webbs sidetracked by harping on the theme of the constant replacement of adult labour by less expensive boy labour as a prime cause of unemployment.[13]

To the Revd Spencer J. Gibb of the Christian Social Union must be accorded the credit of being the first person to appreciate that the widespread engagement of youths in blind-alley occupations was conducive to unemployment and unfitness for employment in later life. In his pioneering tract *The Irregular Employment of Boys* (1903), Gibb claimed:

> Large numbers of boys, leaving school, embark on forms of employment which, involving no skill, and imparting none, are without definite promise of future settlement; and, liable to end absolutely with boyhood, leaving a youth resourceless at an age when he is too old to embark upon a trained career, and thus tend to convert him into an economic cripple.[14]

Among the range of reprehensible occupations which he specified were the huge class of errand boys and messengers, newsboys, the great multitude of office boys, page and door boys in shops, and the host of boys trapped in such unrewarding tasks as fastening labels on bottles and filling packets of tea. In fact, the majority of boys who left school opted for this type of work. Also noteworthy was the circumstance that Gibb, in his book *The Problem of Boy Work* (1906), besides insisting on the need for continuation education, advocated before anyone else in England that a national system of employment registries should be established in connection with each school or group of schools and he deserves recognition as a *Great Disseminator* of this idea. The function of the teachers would be to compile data on the capabilities and personality of each child, while the registries would assemble particulars on the condition and requirements of the local industries and would endeavour to place each boy in the most appropriate trade.[15]

More important, Mrs Ogilvie Gordon in 1904 placed a national scheme before an audience in Glasgow for the organization of juvenile employment bureaux under the control of school boards in Scotland and local education authorities in England. During the following years she led a persistent campaign which resulted in these powers being conferred on the Scottish school boards by the Education (Scotland) Act 1908 and culminating in the model scheme adopted by the Edinburgh school board from the proposals enunciated by Mrs Gordon in her *Handbook of Employment* (1908), whence she must be classified as an *Active Innovator*. At about the same time in England, the Nottingham education committee started a scheme on similar lines, in which they were soon followed by Wigan, though teachers had always been used as unofficial juvenile employment exchanges by children, employers and parents. So too, the leading authority on the subject explained:

> The revelations of the Poor Law Commission awakened public attention with a

start to the economic dangers of boy-work. The subject was widely discussed in reports, books and pamphlets. It became commonplace.[16]

Meanwhile many witnesses, including Cyril Jackson and George Lansbury, converted the Consultative Committee on Attendance at Continuation Schools (1909) to a national system of youth employment exchanges organized in conjunction with the schools, but in England the air was singed by the controversy between the advocates of youth employment bureaux and the proponents of the school-centred exchange.[17]

Crucial in the development of the theory of the nexus between an unwise choice of vocation at boyhood and future unemployment was a paper by R. H. Tawney, which the Webbs drew on in their Minority Report. Sidney remarked that Tawney's memorandum on unemployment was almost wholly confined to the training of boys.[18] So long as apprentices in engineering, building, joining and sawmilling were not accepted until fifteen to seventeen-and-a-half years, Tawney proclaimed, boys on quitting school, especially the less firm of purpose, would be diverted into low-paid and casual jobs through being ensnared by the emoluments offered in most blind-alley occupations. To cut off this source of future disaster, the school leaving age would have to be raised to fifteen years so as to permit direct entry into apprenticeship. True that over half the youths ceasing to attend school became errand and van boys, but once they had reached sixteen this was no longer the case. Quite a number were by then engaged as general labourers in foundries, in sawmills, in the docks. However, the majority were employed in factories, performing some simple task, often as the assistant of an adult machine operator: some were loom-boys, ensuring that the supply of yarn did not run short; others laboured in a soap factory, wrapping and filling packets of soap powder; still others toiled in sawmills, carrying wood to and from cutting machines; yet others were engaged by cloth-finishing works, fetching the cloth to and from the machines and so on. Nearly all the boys from the above-mentioned categories were summarily dismissed when they demanded adult wages, for there was little point in retaining their services if the employers had a constant supply of cheap boy labour to tap. Tawney went on to insist that the only way to stop boys flooding into low-paid and casual employment was to make their labour dear and scarce, by compelling those not taken on as apprentices to attend a trade school in order to acquire an all-round industrial training. Compulsory continuation education, combined with a reduction in the working hours of juveniles to enable them to arrive fresh from their period of study, would heighten and sharpen their potential and talents, thus drying up the mass of helpless workers adrift in the labour market in normal times.[19]

Against Tawney it can be contended that blind-alley occupations in youth would not in many cases lead to unemployment and low-skilled jobs in manhood, so long as there were proper employment opportunities in the town for adult workers. Even so, casual employment and low wages were due more to the effects of industrial fluctuations, inelastic demand, one-industry towns being undermined by foreign competition, and poor unionization of workers. In Liverpool many blind-alley occupations ended at eighteen years, but there was a big demand for adult labour in the mills for oil-seed crushing and flour making, in the warehouses, and in those trades which worked day and night shifts and which could only employ labour over eighteen years old. Arnold

Freeman observed that Birmingham was relatively immune from blind-alley situations, because there was a great demand for boys in the engineering, brass, jewellery and silversmith's trades, all of which offered permanent employment to adult workers, with only a small minority of boys being squeezed out on reaching manhood into the ranks of the unemployed and reserves of casual labour.[20] Again, in the centres of heavy industry, such as Middlesbrough, boys did not develop the physique to be employed in the iron and steel plants until they were in their late teens. Lady Bell wrote:

> The boy of the ironworking district ... when he leaves school, at the age of fourteen at latest, is in a part of the world where the principal industry offers hardly any occupations for boys. He is therefore between the ages of thirteen and sixteen ... simply turned loose, either to do nothing, or else to take on one odd job after another of a temporary kind leading to nothing, running errands, selling newspapers until he is old enough to take a job at the works, for which he is usually unskilled.[21]

Again, in Sheffield the value of the yard-men and barrow-men depended on their physique, pluck and judgement rather than on acquired skill, so that an unskilled labourer at twenty-one years was not necessarily doomed for life.[22]

Turning now to those urban centres with sparse employment opportunities, the majority of those who applied to the Oxford distress committee for relief in 1910 were men between the ages of twenty and thirty-five years, emboldened to join the building trade in its boom period, and ex-army men without skills; but because of the general lack of industry in the city, boys, on leaving the blind-alley occupations at seventeen or eighteen years, drifted into the services and the railway company. In the Lancashire cotton towns where everyone did their own carrying, there were, in fact, few errand boys, but nine out of ten boys could not hope to become cotton spinners and weavers on reaching maturity and the results were spelt out in the lack of diversification of industry, low wages, unemployment, and a great quantity of women's work. So too, the distress committee returns for Stepney in 1907 showed that 130 out of 270 men between the ages of twenty-one and thirty-five had never been in regular employment. Cyril Jackson asserted that enlistment in the army or navy was a means of slipping through the employment bottleneck at adulthood, as both the army and distress committee returns readily revealed.[23] Fred Marquis asserted:

> It is to be emphasized ... that in the growing family of a working-class home the supplement of the wages of a child of fourteen is considerable. In normal times, a small proportion of the working-class population is dangerously near the borderline of want. It is with difficulty that children are supplied, until they leave school, with the food and clothing which the growing boy and girl requires.[24]

Contrary to what was so often said, blind-alley occupations were well regarded by both employers and parents.

One aspect of the problem that the Webbs failed sufficiently to address through their rather dogmatic belief in the efficacy of a workshop training was the imperfect instruction retailed to apprentices and to the shortage of skilled apprentices; these factors curbed Britain's competitive power in the export markets. In the big houses in London the boys were not assisted to master a trade; they picked up the information, becoming experts in one branch; they were unable to work from drawings. Not surprisingly a high percentage of skilled workers in London were recruited from outside, thereby aggravating the housing scarcity in the metropolis and swelling the ranks of the unemployed. A meticulous investigation undertaken by Tawney of the trades in Glasgow showed much the same defects. Here it was found that few workers had any all-round skill: boys were kept in their own departments; they were not taught; they were ordered to work. It was also discovered that men trained in small country workshops were drained into the metropolitan area, where there was a constant shortage of skilled artisans, particularly in the bread making, tailoring and building trades. Moreover, a widespread belief among the teaching staff of the London trade schools was that a workshop training was narrow and not enterprising, and that for anything of value a trainee was compelled to go elsewhere. In Germany whenever there was an industry of importance, special higher trade schools, numbering some two hundred in all, were built; Britain had nothing comparable. Inasmuch as the number of skilled workers in Britain was probably larger than ever before and the number of semi-skilled hands was indubitably very much larger, the poor quality of the technical instruction available to workers was a matter of no small moment.[25] Only Haldane among the senior politicians had an inkling of this and an interest in the problem.

Having received encouragement from the reports of the Poor Law Commission, the Apprenticeship and Skilled Employment Association and the Committee on Wage Earning Children renewed their attack on child labour, though now attention shifted to the wider tasks of plugging blind-alley occupations and persuading the state to assume the responsibility for directing juveniles into useful employment. Finchley was the premier local authority in the country to open a youth employment bureau in 1907, and with the model voluntary scheme in London initiated at the behest of the Apprenticeship Association functioning well, it was obvious that government intervention could not be delayed much longer. Beveridge in his study of *Unemployment*, whose preface was dated December 1908, referred to the need for juvenile labour exchanges. On 18 March 1909 a deputation from the association met Winston Churchill at the Board of Trade to explain what it was striving to accomplish and to ask that in the event of his department setting up labour exchanges for juveniles, they should be kept informed of the proposed arrangements. Whether through the prompting of the association or through the original intention of Beveridge, on whom the task of drafting the bill fell, a clause was inserted in the Labour Exchanges Act, providing for the institution of juvenile advisory committees with representatives of the educational interest. After pressure from the two child labour organizations, the Board of Trade speedily organized the appointment of the new committees. As far as London was concerned, an intricate scheme of cooperation was entered into with the Apprenticeship Association, while some of the provincial committees were also absorbed into the new agencies created by the government. Juvenile advisory committees (JACs) were established in London for every labour exchange; many members of the affiliated local skilled employment associations served on these juvenile advisory committees for their neighbourhood; through the local associations, the advisory bodies placed children in situations where an adequate industrial training could be procured.[26]

Already in October 1907 the education section of the National Union of Women Workers, whose members included Nettie Adler, Mrs Barnett and Mrs Cadbury, secured the adoption of a resolution more from the standpoint of educationalists 'to consider establishing under each education committee an information bureau where boys and girls and their parents may be guided into the choice of suitable occupations'. Despite pressure from this and other organizations on the Board of Education in 1910, the government rejected their plea for a special grant to those education authorities that wished to commence schemes under the Choice of Employment Act 1910. Framed on the lines of the experimental Education (Scotland) Act, at the suggestion of these groups, the English legislation allowed educational authorities to continue their work on advising and guiding children who were leaving school as to 'the choice of suitable employment'. Under the terms of a joint memorandum concluded between the Boards of Education and Trade in June 1911, if the local education authority (LEA) desired to retain control, it could only do so by coming to an agreement with the Board of Trade officer in charge of the exchange before the end of the year; after the expiry of this period, the board would assume responsibility for the area. By 1914 some seventy juvenile advisory committees under the Board of Trade had been instituted in the provinces and another seventeen in the Greater London area, while fifty to sixty LEAs opened choice of employment bureaux for adolescents. However, a government report of 1916 disclosed that twenty county boroughs, some great industrial centres with a population of over 200,000, and 130 smaller towns and large urban districts had failed to create registries for the juvenile population of their area.[27]

Partly through the failure of the managers of the Board of Trade labour exchanges to take the local education experts into their confidence, there was much infighting between the two groups when the new voluntary advisory committees were being created. According to a correspondent in the *School Child* in 1912:

> An enormous controversy has raged for over two years with regard to the constitution of these bodies ... It appears to me that most of those who have advocated most strongly the establishment of Juvenile Labour Exchanges by Local Education Authorities working practically in complete independence of the national system of Labour Exchanges, have exhibited an extra-ordinary ignorance of the actual conditions of the juvenile labour market, and the results which can be produced by any sort of labour exchange, no matter who controls it.[28]

London possessed the most finely wrought after-care system in the country, consisting of three elements: the juvenile department of the labour exchange, the juvenile advisory committee and the care committee. The exchange canvassed local employers and compiled a list of vacancies, though some of the care committees unwisely tried to usurp these functions of approaching the employers, for which they were condemned by one experienced social worker. The juvenile advisory committee, supported by a secretary and permanent staff, interviewed the school leavers and their parents, sometimes in the presence of the care committee concerned. By separating the teacher from direct involvement in the choice of a pupil's job, the protagonists of the London system discerned the advantages of overcoming a teacher's biased assessment of a pupil's abilities and his usually meagre knowledge about local industrial conditions. As far as possible, the care committees by home visitation tried to ensure that 'all children leaving school do, in fact, come before a Juvenile Advisory Committee, or some analogous body, or give good reasons for not doing so'. In order not to incur the odium of the elite of the working class capable of making their own arrangements for their offspring and resentful of any intrusion on their privacy, voluntary helpers were not accustomed to follow up a boy placed by his own parents after the second visit, unless there was a good reason. Notwithstanding these efforts there was a leakage caused by families not yet prepared to use the resources of the labour exchange for job placement and the unwillingness of youths to re-register at the exchange whenever they changed their jobs. Nor were all the schools in the city covered. By March 1914, 786 of the 900 school care committees in London cooperated with the juvenile advisory committees, leaving a significant number of schools out of the system.[29]

To start with, the care committees tried to implement a threefold policy. If the youth was not going to succumb to the degrading influence of the street gang, the care committee helper had to persuade him to join one of the many recreational bodies that flourished at this time: the Scouts, the Boys' Brigade, old scholars' clubs, organizations sponsored by the Churches, and clubs run by his own committee. Whatever the intention of the founders, these clubs tended to be rapidly overrun by boys from the superior class of home to the detriment of the street-corner urchins, who would have benefited far more from their civilizing embrace; and similar difficulties were encountered in another aspect of after-care work, when visitors tried to induce the lads from the depths of society to enrol for a continuation course. Above all, the old axiomatic policy of withholding juveniles from all blind-alley occupations was gradually abandoned, as the care committee workers were forced into a more realistic appraisal of the employment situation. One care committee helper wrote in December 1912: 'One is bound to admit that in a number of cases we hear that a child's work is hard and his prospects poor, and are quite unable to do anything but tell him to make the best of it.' Another, writing a few months later, commented that

> children placed in jobs with 'no prospects' need supervision too. The old plan for dealing with places of this class was to dissuade the children from taking them up, to starve the bad places, to get all possible boys into trades, to give them 'a trade in their hands' and to create openings for skilled work by rousing London employers to train their own workmen.[30]

One respect in which care committee policy had an impact on recruitment in trades was its tendency to look askance at the pitiful prospects of a clerk's career, as compared with the high earnings of skilled manual employment, so that by 1918 the old interest of the working class in a clerk's career was waning.[31]

Before the First World War the two child labour organizations also initiated a campaign to block the entry of juveniles into the worst blind-alley occupations, or at least to curtail their hours of labour in the more controversial ones. The Departmental Committee on the Employment of Children Act of 1910 devoted its attention exclusively to the problem of street-trading. Constance Smith gave evidence before it on behalf of the Committee of Wage Earning Children, and details of a wide-ranging investigation into street-trading in London and several provincial cities handled by the association were reprinted in the departmental committee's report. Although by-laws were in force in England and Wales covering some eight and a half million persons, some large centres, such as Leeds, Nottingham and Salford, possessed no regulations dealing with street-trading and of the smaller boroughs, only forty-one out of 191 introduced them. It was estimated that of the 37,000 licensed children in England and Wales, some 26,000 were under fourteen years of age, while many towns, it should be noted, did not have any licensing system in force. By far the commonest mode of street-trading was newspaper selling by children under sixteen years of age, the number of licence holders being 16,000. In opposition to the reformers, the newspaper proprietors urged the necessity for the employment of boys for the sale of $^{1}/_{2}$d. evening newspapers on the streets, claiming that if boys were banned from this occupation their sales would fall drastically. While the Committee on Wage Earning Children calculated that the vendors of newspapers earned 1s.–1s. 6d. per week, Constance Smith put this figure more realistically at 2s.–2s. 6d., but added that 'in a great many of these cases, especially in the cases where the boys were unruly and came from bad homes, very little of the money was brought home'. Averring that the evils of street-trading were mostly moral, as newspaper sellers engaged in frequent gambling, while others fell into vagrancy, crime and prostitution, the departmental committee demanded the prohibition of street-trading for boys under seventeen years and girls under eighteen, but dismissed the dangers to health from fatigue and inclement weather.

At any rate, the Committee on Wage Earning Children introduced a bill to implement the findings of the departmental committee in 1911, and, after it was blocked by Banbury, again in 1912. For a time because of Winston Churchill's less than friendly attitude to the movement, there was talk in reform circles of transferring the administration of children's employment to the Board of Education, but the sympathy shown by Reginald McKenna when he took over the Home Office made this step unnecessary. A deputation of MPs from the executive interviewed Asquith in March 1913, at which he agreed that the Home Office should foster the government bill, which bore a close resemblance to the private member's bill. The latter extended the by-law making powers of the local authorities to prohibit employment or sanction it subject to certain conditions to cover the case of young persons between fourteen and sixteen years of age; it banned street-trading for girls under eighteen years of age and for boys under fourteen years; it exempted municipal boroughs and urban district councils with a population of under 10,000 and rural areas, however, from its provisions; it permitted a local authority to make the attendance of a boy at a continuation class a condition of his holding a licence, if he had left his elementary school. It is significant, though, that the Committee on Wage Earning Children was trying to protect exploited boy labour, by ensuring that while the youth was engaged in employment he was also receiving an education which would qualify him later for some worthwhile job. In 1912 Beck and Denman fought hard in the Commons to retain the essentials of the bill; the chief point of contention was the lowest permissible age for street-trading in the case of boys; the newspaper proprietors agreed in writing to accept fourteen years as a maximum. In the following year, owing to the objections of the newspaper proprietors, who thought that the bill had gone too far even though they had previously entered into a concordat, and certain branches of the NUT, who doubted whether the bill went far enough, the government decided that the bill was too contentious for the limited time of the Commons.[32]

At the same time the Apprenticeship and Skilled Employment Association put pressure on the government to tighten the regulations affecting certain blind-alley occupations. In cooperation with the Committee on Wage Earning Children, it attempted to insert a clause in the Employment of Children Bill to restrict the hours of van boys. Together with the Women's Industrial Council it tendered evidence to the departmental committee set up at its request on van boys. The departmental committee gathered evidence to show that there were 1,555 van boys, whose function was to accompany the drivers of delivery vans, guard the consigned goods against theft, watch the horses and assist in the delivery of parcels. The committee recommended that local authorities were to be given powers under by-laws to regulate the employment of van boys until the age of eighteen years, and their working hours, if they were under sixteen years, were not to extend for more than seventy hours a week. Through the coming of the war, these ideas were never implemented, but they were taken up again by the 1918 Education Act.[33]

In conclusion, we would suggest that the blind-alley hypothesis of the link between poor types of employment and subsequent unemployment after the threshold of adult status had been crossed was probably an untenable theory, apart from trades like van boys and street-traders; but a wrong hypothesis was better than no hypothesis, and the controversy and interest evoked by the new sociological viewpoint hastened the progress of reform. Although the only contemporary sociological criticism of the theory was by Arnold Freeman in 1914, we have adduced much other contemporary evidence to controvert it, while the pages of the *School Child* bristled with increasingly sharp condemnations of so simplistic a viewpoint from practical experience gleaned by care committee volunteers, who numbered 8,000 in London by 1914. On the other hand, the fact that there were 1,748 prosecutions under the Employment of Children Act and 250 under the Shops Act 1910 showed that the government was treating the subject of the employment of children seriously.

## The Struggle for Compulsory Continuation Schools

Like so many of the Liberal proposals for social reform, the idea of continuation schools was borrowed from Germany. As early as 1887 Samuel Smith MP, an early exponent of the new Liberalism, visited Switzerland and Germany to explore the workings of their educational institutions, and returned home more than ever convinced that the introduction of an extensive network of continuation schools was an urgent necessity. Two decades later he was followed by Robert Best, a Birmingham businessman, and C. K. Ogden, the distinguished philosopher, editor and inventor of Basic English, who introduced their volume on the continuation school in 1914 with the observation that 'the object of this book is to show that we can save ourselves a vast amount of painful experience of doubt, and perhaps of failure, by learning a few simple lessons from Germany'.[34] Elsewhere the movement for compulsory continuation education also relied heavily on German experience. Hitherto in the United States more attention had been lavished on prolonging the full-time education of children, so that in twenty-one states they stayed in school until fourteen, in seven states until fifteen, in five states until sixteen and in two states even longer. Much of what was being attempted in New England in the way of providing continuation schools with an emphasis on practical work was inspired by the writings of Dr Kerschensteiner, the outstanding educational director of Munich. In France, though reliance had been placed on the voluntary provision of educational facilities for adolescents, there was now a strong movement for making part-time education compulsory until seventeen years of age. In addition, the French possessed day training schools in Paris and the provinces to teach apprentices and training courses run by the unions, which condemned the *écoles professionnelles* for their rigid methods.[35]

Of the twenty-six states which comprised the German Empire, twenty-one had decreed that continuation schools were compulsory for boys; the remaining five states with voluntary schemes only contained an infinitesimal fraction of the country's population. Under the German Industrial Law of 1891, it was stipulated that town and district councils could make further education obligatory for males until they were eighteen, and that where local authorities required such attendance, employers were to grant their young workers time off. Restricted at first to the evenings between 8.00 and 10.00 p.m., these classes were gradually convened earlier and earlier until a system of day release had been built up in the more progressive areas, a process speeded up by ministerial edicts in 1900 and 1904. Behind the movement for the spread of continuation schools was the agitation of the masters of workshops in small towns, who hoped to call in the aid of technical education to resist the spread of the factory system; the movement then seeped into the factory areas.[36] Within the German Empire, continuation education had reached its apogee in Munich, a town of 600,000 inhabitants, just experiencing the first onrush of industrialism. According to Michael Sadler, Dr Kerschensteiner, the director of the town's school system, had synthesized the work of previous educational reformers: of the German Professor Natorp, who emphasized the necessity of a close relationship between education and life; of Professor Dewey with his experimental school at Chicago, where there was instruction in the occupations of the larger society and where the child was trained to be a member of his local group; of Dr Armstrong and Sir Philip Magnus in England, who spearheaded the movement for practical studies in elementary and secondary schools. At the base of the Munich system was the elementary school, which under the impact of the continuation school movement was being impelled to refashion its curriculum, by instituting metal workshops and instruction in science and drawing in the 8th grade, but they avoided the narrowness of some English schools despite an emphasis on training for specific trades. From fourteen to eighteen years there was compulsory daytime continuation schooling for all youths twice a week for a period of eight hours in all. While practical work was carried out in well-fitted classrooms and workshops in connection with the actual trade followed by the pupil, whether he was a butcher, waiter or shoemaker, which occupied the chief place in the curriculum, instruction in citizenship and hygiene and the wider aspects of education were not neglected and there was also a strong emphasis on arithmetic and drawing. The management of the fifty-six trade schools having been shared between the unions, the municipality and the school, half the cost of the upkeep of these schools was contributed by the municipality. In the trade schools there was a distinct workshop atmosphere with time, price and the newest methods of time saving and production being given prominence. Nonetheless, if the solemnity with which these youths were encouraged to regard their calling in life, however humble, had its ludicrous side, it also had a more dangerous side in that it rendered them curiously fearful of any loss of status and the somewhat narrowness of their training militated against job mobility.[37]

As the compulsory provisions of the Education Act of 1870 for primary schoolchildren were enforced, the attendance at evening classes in England, apart from Nottingham where the Revd Dr John Brown Paton was active, dwindled from 73,375 in that year to 24,233 in 1884. Hitherto evening classes had concentrated on rectifying a defective elementary education, but now the prime need was for some agency to supply children of the labouring classes with that extra intellectual edge bestowed by secondary education, which was naturally the lot of the middle-class child. Paton expounded the rationale behind the new system of evening schools which he had established in Nottingham to audiences of educationists. On the one hand, the evening class courses had to be given a much greater technical content; if the lads were to become better equipped for local trades, they would have to be taught the elements of drawing including design and mechanical craftsmanship, while the basic scientific principles and mathematics connected with their trade should also not be beyond their grasp. On the other hand, the bulk of working-class youth would not relish frequent attendance at these night schools unless their recreational features were developed and expanded; such activities as music, singing, drama and magic lantern slide lectures on history, science and literature deserved to be added to the curriculum. With the help of the trade unions, Paton founded the Recreative Evening Schools Association in 1885 to stimulate local authorities in regard to the provision of continuation schools; the religious and labour press were utilized for the insertion of telling propaganda; the trades councils zealously petitioned their district school boards. Proof of the success of the league's proselytizing activities was furnished by the education code of 1893, under which the regulations governing the conduct of evening classes were framed along the lines which the association had been advocating, and the growth of evening classes held in London under the auspices of the association, where the number of pupils enrolled increased from 4,350 in 1887 to 12,500 in 1892.[38]

Throughout the last two decades of the nineteenth century, the self-doubts about the technological basis on which British industry rested and the self-questioning as to whether her prosperity was transient – a gilded dream which would vanish under the harrying of her trade rivals – permitted the educational reform movement to sweep to the fore. One example of this was the activity of the National Association for the Promotion of Technical and Secondary Education (1887–1907), of which Llewellyn Smith was the first secretary, and whose executive included Canon Barnett, Philip Magnus, Dr Garnett and Sidney Webb, to whom must be credited the creation of a national system of technical education administered by the county and borough councils and the slow conversion of public opinion to the need for a steep increase in the number of places at secondary schools. The other was the campaign that Samuel Smith MP waged for the adoption of a universal system of continuation education, by annually introducing bills from 1887; on his retirement from Parliament, these were sponsored by the Bishop of Hereford. Even if his efforts were not particularly well rewarded, Smith's work was important in that it acclimatized trade union opinion to economic realities, undermining their fears of the dilution of the skilled labour force by state-sponsored trainees. George Howell MP distributed plentiful propaganda among the unions, emphasizing that Britain was falling behind Germany and Switzerland as regards technical instruction and that commercial enterprise would contract unless there was a change of mood among the working class.[39]

At the turn of the century there had been no noticeable advance in public opinion. Professor E. J. Urwick, writing the concluding chapter of *Studies of Boy Life in Our Cities* (1904), offered one answer as to why secondary education was not offered to every child, as was already being advocated by the TUC:

> either the day school education must be prolonged beyond the age of fourteen, or the evening school must be made compulsory. Of the two alternatives the former is for the present out of the question; public opinion is not likely to agree to raise the age-limit still further for some years to come.[40]

In fact, a myth has grown up that only the cotton industry with its interest in the question of half-timers impeded the progress of educational advance, but really the problem was of much wider dimensions. Altogether there were 31,140 children employed in England and Wales in 1914 as half-timers under the Factory Acts. Nonetheless, there were many more children under the age of fourteen years who were engaged in some form of labour, both those who were still at school and those who had obtained exemption from further attendance, and it was still very difficult to curtail this labour, whatever their occupations. There were 55,000 children in England and Wales employed full-time under the Factory Act; there were another 4,740 children employed in the mines; then there was a grand total of 136,424 children employed full-time outside the Factory and Mines Act with another 8,961 half-timers employed outside those Acts; and finally, there were 240,000 children attending school full-time employed outside school hours.[41] All these children, it should be noted, were under fourteen years of age. Nor was the business world as yet enamoured of providing full-time compulsory continuation schools for all; when B. F. Stiebel moved such a resolution at the spring gathering of the Associated Chambers of Commerce in 1907, it was rejected in favour of a watered-down counter-resolution.[42]

Hence it was a series of sociological investigations into the link between boy labour in blind-alley occupations and adult unemployment prepared for the Poor Law Commission and the report of the Inter-Departmental Committee on Partial Exemption (1909) that suddenly breached the apathy of the public and brought the question of compulsory continuation schools to the forefront of the political debate. It is worth mentioning that while all the economic ramifications of the subject were scrupulously explored, the notion that the problem could never be reduced to these stark terms, that it was a question of preventing the moral and physical deterioration of adolescent youth, was always borne in mind. Of course, the voluntary provision of places at evening schools had now reached a formidable total, though it still lagged behind the needs of the situation.[43] According to Michael Sadler, it was estimated by the Board of Education that 147,191 pupils in England and Wales attended the continuation schools in 1902–3, but a 1907 estimate showed a commendable increase, particularly in London. The Consultative Committee on Attendance at Continuation School conjectured that of the two million boys and girls in England and Wales aged between fourteen and seventeen years, 1,500,000 were untouched by continuation education, including 750,000 boys. Again, the overwhelming majority of children who registered for continuation courses were drawn from the lower middle class or the more comfortable sections of the working class; the slum dwellers remained immune from these educational influences.[44]

So too, if the majority of employers resisted the advance of universal continuation education, the pre-war period was nevertheless marked by an upsurge of interest in the more scientific training of apprentices, starting with the engineering industry and spreading to the building, textile leather and cabinet making trades, and by the inauguration of works schools, particularly in firms controlled by Liberal industrialists. As Michael Sadler notes:

> Many men of the foreman class make difficulty in the way of lads in the works getting opportunities for technical instruction. And in the course of our inquiry we heard of cases in which boys had been threatened with dismissal if they went to evening school.[45]

Public interest in the continuation school movement was strong in Cheshire, Lancashire and the West Riding, so that four out of five school leavers attended continuation classes in Widnes, in Rochdale 55 per cent of the boys under seventeen years attended, and in Halifax 58 per cent of school leavers. As far as the shipbuilding and engineering industries were concerned, a Manchester sponsored survey showed that out of thirty-four firms, eighteen excused day work to apprentices to allow them time off to attend technical classes. Since 1884 Messrs Brunner, Mond and Co. had been encouraging the attendance of their apprentices in evening classes and at the turn of the century such attendance was made compulsory for all employees under seventeen years. So too, the United Alkali Company insisted on all apprentices of fourteen to eighteen years attending classes. Both these leading chemical manufacturers had a great influence on other companies in their neighbourhood. Messrs Joseph Crosfield, makers of soap at Warrington, ended work at 5.00 or 5.30 p.m. to ensure that all boys under seventeen years attended classes. Messrs Lever Brothers endowed and equipped a technical institute, which was subsequently taken over by the local authority. Messrs Rowntree opened a domestic economy school at their works for all girls under seventeen years, where three teachers instructed them in cookery, dressmaking and hygiene. At the prompting of George Cadbury Junior, classes were set up by Cadburys; in 1913 when the LEA assumed the responsibility for running the school, attendance for the equivalent of one day a week became compulsory for all employees between fourteen and eighteen; moreover, all the younger workers had to participate in compulsory swimming, gymnastics and Swedish drill.[46]

At the end of February 1909 a deputation of child welfare organizations called on Asquith, Buxton, Samuel and Runciman, the minister of education, and urged them to adopt a bold policy in regard to the child labour question. They thrust a three-point programme on the government: the adoption of a system of compulsory attendance at continuation schools up to seventeen years of age, accompanied by a reduction in the length of the working day, together with the development of full-time trade schools; secondly, the raising of the school leaving age, together with the abolition of the half-time system, and modification of the existing elementary curriculum in the direction of providing some preparation for practical work during the last few years of school life; and finally, the prohibition of street-trading for all children under seventeen years of age. Asquith's reply was none too hopeful: in reference to raising the age of exemption and the principle of compulsory attendance at continuation schools, there was little that could be done. A poll among Lancashire operatives – incidentally, the vast majority of half-timers employed under the Factory Acts were hands in cotton mills – showed 34,000 in favour of raising the age for half-timers and 150,000 opposed to this course. Thus they could not introduce any statutory compulsion. Under the 1908 Education Act they had done something for continuation schools in Scotland and action on similar lines was contemplated for England. This was despite the fact that Churchill had swallowed Sidney Webb's scheme for boy labour, dishing it up as an article in the *Nation* and referring to it as a problem which needed attention in a public speech in October 1908; a few months later, he included part-time compulsory continuation education up to seventeen years as one of the items in his social reform programme with which he badgered Asquith.[47]

In accordance with the recommendations of the Inter-Departmental Committee on Partial Exemption, Walter Runciman introduced the School and Continuation Class Attendance Bill in 1911 to stimulate attendance at continuation schools. Among the reforms which he wished to see taken up were the abolition of half-time, permission for LEAs to compel attendance at continuation classes until sixteen, and in areas where there was no compulsion, to make fourteen the normal school leaving age. The bill required all children to attend school until thirteen. Beyond that age children were compelled either to attend school until fourteen, or in areas where continuation classes were made compulsory until sixteen, to obtain special exemption from attending school on grounds that they were about to enter into beneficial employment. Nonetheless, local authorities could pass by-laws making it compulsory to attend school between the ages of fourteen and fifteen years, and children who were employed in agricultural areas could be exempted from school attendance at thirteen, even if there was no obligation in the district to attend continuation classes.[48] The bill abided by the recommendations of the report, which had been signed by educationalists, workers and employers.

Soon after the publication of the report, a Joint Committee for the Abolition of Half-Time Labour was set up, on which the Committee on Wage Earning Children was represented and with which the National Union of Women Workers was connected, to awaken the interest of Southern England in a question which was supposedly of concern only to Yorkshire and Lancashire. Whereas the Lancashire cotton industry was heavily dependent on half-timers, the Yorkshire worsted industry drew on the services of a relatively small number of juveniles. A. D. Lewis, the honorary secretary of the joint committee, asserted that to allow a child under fourteen years to do half a day's school work and half a day's factory work was wrong, for it would be better to devote the time expended in some blind-alley occupation to manual training at school. Nor did he believe that the half-time system was the result of the poverty of the parents, as half-time labour increased where poverty decreased. Both the joint committee and the Wage Earning Children organization condemned the 1911 bill for its unfairness, because it would make children who had performed a full day's work in a factory attend educational sessions in the evening. If the bill became law, it would became necessary for the Board of Education to secure an additional £500,000 in grants, a point which Runciman would have to raise in the Cabinet. The minister's adviser remarked: 'I gather from you that your desire is rather to stimulate discussion and to ascertain from what quarters opposition will be made to the proposals to apply compulsion to Continuation Classes and to discover the strength of the opposition than to get this particular Bill made law.' Nor within the Cabinet was a reluctant Runciman a match for the persuasive powers of Lloyd George and Winston Churchill, who turned the government's attention to health and unemployment insurance as the principal domestic political issue once the House of Lords crisis was coming to a resolution. Because of lack of parliamentary time, the Education Bill 'forecasting [in many essentials] the later ... [Fisher Education Act of 1918] was withdrawn'.[49]

Meanwhile the joint committee kept up a constant barrage of propaganda. From a cautious optimism, the reformers of half-time sunk into despondency when a new ballot among cotton operatives in December 1911 unexpectedly voted in favour of retaining the old wastage of juvenile workers and the thriving cotton industry called on increasing numbers of half-timers in 1912 and 1913. Again, an attempt by the West Riding Council to amend the child employment by-laws so as to abolish half-time in 1912 was overruled by the courts, to the chagrin of educationalists.[50] Sir T. G. Coats, a leading cotton manufacturer, claimed that '[u]nless hours of work of all employees were reduced – which would greatly handicap manufacturers in the competition with foreign countries – the restriction of the hours of those under seventeen would thoroughly disorganise the work ... An arrangement of shifts and relays would not be feasible.' In cotton spinning mills, half-timers were usually engaged in replacing empty bobbins with full ones. Between fourteen and seventeen boys were employed as assistants to men in charge of spinning mules, while girls acted as assistants on the frames or in the card rooms. In weaving mills children assisted weavers in charge of looms or helped with the fetching and carrying and delivering messages. They became weavers at the age of fifteen. Abbot, one of the inspectors, disputed the assertion that releasing children from work to attend school during the day would dislocate the cotton industry, provided they were released in shifts.[51] A. H. Gill, the Labour MP for Bolton, who had worked in cotton mills as a boy of ten, wrote to Jack Pease, the new minister of education:

> the textile trade in Lancashire and Yorkshire employs the great majority of half timers ... That the provision for Continuation Classes is not compulsory, and that too much latitude is left to the Local Education Authority as to whether the classes

shall be day or evening classes ... That so far as the cotton trade is concerned, the provision of attendance at day classes is impracticable.[52]

What the union leaders would do was to induce the operatives to agree to raising the school leaving age to thirteen.

Under Nonconformist pressure, particularly from Dr Clifford, to rectify their grievances over education and the intervention of Jack Pease, the new minister of education, who placed the outlines of a short measure before the Cabinet, the government was forced to act; Haldane also fought to enlarge the scheme in the education consultative committee, of which he was chairman. Meanwhile Lloyd George, having successfully steered the Insurance Bill through Parliament, was formulating his proposals for the land campaign as the next major domestic political issue for the government to concentrate on. But on 9 January 1913 Haldane informed Pease that he had spoken to Asquith, who wanted him to make a big speech 'about the decision of the Liberal Govt. to take up, in succession to Old Age Pensions & Insurance, a great education policy as a foremost item in its policy for the future'. Lloyd George was furious, because Haldane was trying to make the cause of educational reform the centrepiece of government policy, knocking his land campaign badly off course. He denounced Haldane's speech as 'interminable verbiage' to C. P. Scott, the editor of the *Manchester Guardian*, denied that the latter had consulted the Cabinet, and in a withering description of Haldane's corpulent physique, called him 'a barrel of tallow' which when set alight could produce no flame, only smoke – a further dig at Haldane's propensity to obscure an argument by use of convoluted language. Nevertheless, the King's Speech in March 1913 announced that 'Proposals would be submitted ... for the development of a national system of education', modifying Asquith's original formula of 'dealing with certain fundamental aspects of the problem of national education'.[53] During the 1913 session Pease placed a scheme before the Cabinet to raise the school leaving age to fourteen and in some cases fifteen, to require attendance at continuation schools on 'a basis of local option', and to build new schools in single school areas to appease Nonconformists. He added that 'for the great majority of the youth of the country, part-time instruction after the age of fourteen or fifteen is all that economic conditions will allow'. He also promised grants of £2 million in 1914–15 to education authorities, rising thereafter to £7 million in 1920, together with provision for an extension of the school health services. As the parliamentary timetable became overcrowded, it was decided to defer the introduction of the bill until the next session. But because of continuing pressure from the Nonconformists, Pease decided to introduce a short bill in 1914 stipulating that from September that year, all grants-in-aid in single school areas were to be to state schools.[54]

When Christopher Addison joined the department in 1914, Pease confessed that

> he did not pretend to be an expert on matters of education, but that, as Minister of Education, he meant to do whatever he could give to our children and young folks a better chance – that he expected me to do what I could to help him, and that he would back me up if I did.[55]

Speaking in the Commons on 22 July 1913, Pease introduced the Education (No. 2) Bill giving a grant-in-aid of £150,000 to local education authorities partly to assist them in the building and improving of their schools, and partly to help them with medical treatment. This was in addition to the £80,000 that had already been allocated for medical treatment, but he promised a more comprehensive scheme the following year. He deplored the 'sectarian' obstacles and difficulties of 'class feeling' which impeded educational reform, and the 'lack of co-ordination and completeness in the system'. Matters had to be taken in hand,

> to avoid stagnation [and] to enter into healthy rivalry with other nations on the Continent of Europe and possibly across the ocean [the United States], who, at any rate in regard to higher education, are further advanced in their educational systems than we are. A well-organised system of education is the most powerful means we have of developing the social life of the nation. If the present generation can attend to the physical condition of their children, enlarge their occupations, widen their sympathies, increase their intellectual freedom, and encourage them to use their gifts in mutual service, it will have done the best thing it can do to ensure the peace, the prosperity, and the independence of our country.[56]

Pease's arguments were couched in conciliatory and moderate language and stressed above all the deficiencies in British higher education; nowhere did he use the words 'national efficiency', despite Geoffrey Sherington reading this phrase into his speech. Even if it is conceded that the speech could be read as a whole in this way, it gained little traction with his parliamentary colleagues, and because of sectarian difficulties educational reform was not given priority before 1914, so that the argument for the importance of this concept as a significant factor in social reform is hardly compelling.[57]

At last time was found in 1914 to introduce a more stringent private member's bill against child labour which also extended the educational instruction available for the nation's youth. Jack Pease commended the main principles of the bill that he was most willing to support. Under the provisions of the School (Employment and School Attendance) Bill 1914 sponsored by Richard Denman and the Committee of Wage Earning Children, local education authorities were empowered to raise the school leaving age to fifteen instead of fourteen, when the Board of Education consented. All exemptions from school attendance under thirteen years of age were abolished, and 'also half-time exemptions above the age of thirteen'. The power of local education authorities to prohibit or sanction employment subject to conditions was extended from fourteen to sixteen years. Street-trading was forbidden for boys under fifteen years and for girls under eighteen years. Local authorities were authorized to require attendance at continuation schools as a condition of employment. Having secured a second reading by 187 votes to 35, the bill was blocked on the report stage. An attempt was made by the MPs in charge of the bill to curb the opposition to it by dropping the school attendance and continuation class courses; but this was to no avail, because the enemies of the bill, headed by the Lancashire MPs, talked it out. The fear of losing additional seats in Lancashire, which was a key electoral area with a general election approaching, made the government wary of offering too much assistance to the promoters.[58]

Behind the scenes, Haldane kept up the pressure for increased expenditure on all sectors of education. On 20 April 1914, he wrote to Selby-Bigge:

> I drove the P.M. to Downing Street. So after dinner I had a talk ... I think he will agree to [a supplement of] £500,000 for [19]14–15, £3,500,000 (with a carry over) for [19]15–16 & £4,250,000 for [19]16–17 ... But an inspiration came to me & I proposed to offer £20,000 a year a piece to Oxford & Cambridge for Science.[59]

Selby-Bigge replied: 'I have no doubt we can manage Oxford and Cambridge (is it not high treason to corrupt the Prime Minister) if they will take it.'[60] In May 1914 Lloyd George announced that in 1915–16 the grants to elementary education were to be increased to £2,750,000, while an extra £500,000 was earmarked for school meals and to aid the poorest areas. Pease later clarified that an additional £1 million was to be made available for secondary schools, technical education, special schools, teacher training, universities and the development of health services among children.[61] Pease told the Commons on 28 July 1914:

> There are many defects in our system of education which can only be remedied by attention of the law. These include a compulsory continuation system and the abolition of the religious difficulty which exists in our schools ... Our prosperity, from an educational point of view, is, I think, assured also our future as a nation if only we put our house in order.[62]

Their indifference to general educational advance was the gravest defect of the pre-war Liberal administration. Sir Henry Roscoe, the distinguished scientist and educational reformer, exclaimed with pardonable exaggeration in 1900:

> The cry that we are being outbid on all sides by Germany and America is no new one but it becomes louder and louder every day, and it is now admitted by all those best qualified to judge that, unless some drastic steps are taken to strengthen our educational position in the direction long ago taken by our competitors, we stand not merely to lose our industrial supremacy, but the bulk of our foreign trade ... our children and grandchildren may see England sink to the level of a third-rate power, for upon education, the basis of industry and commerce, the greatness of our country depend.[63]

The Liberals despite the efforts of Haldane and Pease failed to remove Britain's endemic backwardness in educational reform: this was a serious matter, as the expansion of each educational tier is dependent on the rate of growth of each lower grade in the educational structure. In the years before the First World War, Lloyd George had become too powerful a figure in the Cabinet and country for Haldane, a politician handicapped by sitting in the Lords, and Jack Pease, a junior cabinet minister, to seize the political agenda from him and make educational reform the central feature of domestic politics.[64] In fact, Philip Snowden assured Selby-Bigge that 'Labour Members were rather wooden on the subject [of an Education Bill], they would back the new scheme on the lines of the latest article in "The Nation".'[65] In essence the Fisher Education Act of 1918 differed little from the last pre-war bill, which we have seen was the result of the fusion of efforts from two sources, from the child welfare organizations and from educationalists within the factory, but because of government-enforced cuts in public expenditure after the war its provisions for continuation education were never implemented.

# 12

# A Partially Reformed Poor Law

## Poor Law Reform

Although Beatrice Webb tended to exaggerate the differences between the signatories of the Majority and Minority Reports on the Poor Laws, they shared much common ground in their analysis of the issues of pauperism, sickness, unemployment and under-employment. They also both wished to abolish the Poor Law administrative unit, the Boards of Guardians, and to transfer their powers to the county councils, but where the supporters of the Majority Report differed from the Webbs was that they favoured keeping intact a destitution authority staffed by professionals to supervise in the main a team of voluntary social workers, who would utilize the family casework approach. In contrast the Webbs wished to transfer problems such as sickness, unemployment, and child welfare to specialist committees of the county council, such as the health and education committees.[1] Early in February 1909, Asquith favoured

> removing the mentally defective and the sick from the Poor Law and transferring them to the Health authorities, and removing also the vagrants who were to be placed in Detention Colonies in charge of the Home Office; he also at first favoured the Majority plan of transferring all the remaining categories of paupers ... to statutory committees of the counties and county councils.[2]

Asquith rejected the establishment of a Ministry of Labour, worrying that it would impose an additional onerous obligation on the state, the duty of drastically minimizing unemployment, and in turn this would enshrine the principle of the 'Right to Work' – or what later came to be called the right to full employment. By June, he doubted whether there was any need for a new Public Assistance Authority, as various categories of past recipients were being removed from the Poor Law.[3] By chance, on 22 June 1909 Beatrice Webb met Churchill on the Embankment, when she questioned him as to whether or not the government was going 'to do anything with the poor law, to which he replied: "You must talk to Haldane about it, he has a hand in it. We are going in for a *classified* poor law." I muttered something about that not being sufficient ... I had obtained the clue to Haldane's displeasure. He and Asquith have decided against *the break-up of the poor law*.'[4]

To facilitate the acceptance of the ideas embodied in the Minority Report, the Webbs founded the National Committee to Promote the Break-Up of the Poor Law in April 1909 on a cross-party basis. Under the editorship of Clifford Sharp, a Fabian, it launched a journal, the *Crusade Against Destitution*, and encouraged a Liberal MP, Sir Robert Price, to sponsor the Prevention of Destitution Bill, which he introduced into Parliament in 1910. On learning of this new organization, the supporters of the Majority Report rallied and created a new body, the National Poor Law Reform Association, headed by Lord George Hamilton, the former chairman of the Poor Law Commission. Yet their proposals went too far for some of those who still adhered to the non-eligibility principle of the 1834 Commission, so that they set up the National Committee for Poor Law Reform. Charles Booth was an influential figure in this third organization, publishing his proposals in a well-received pamphlet *Poor Law Reform*, in which he argued against the distribution of the functions of Boards of Guardians to the county councils and for enlarging Poor Law areas; and he successfully lobbied John Burns at the Local Government Board and Asquith for his idea of retaining much of the existing administrative structure.[5] When the Prevention of Destitution Bill was introduced in the Commons in April 1910 Asquith denounced the conclusion of both reports, remarking that they

> both pronounced sentence of death on boards of guardians. Let us assume that they are right, I think you will find that the boards of guardians will die very hard. They are very powerful bodies. With all their defects and shortcomings they after all represent an enormous amount of gratuitous and public spirited service ... we could ill spare from the sphere of local administration. I confess I am old-fashioned in that matter.[6]

The prime minister then went on to plead for a rather more accurate estimate of the cost of the legislative changes envisaged by the bill, which were put at 'something like £3,000,000 or £4,000,000'. Since the Poor Law Commission was appointed,

> very large steps have been taken ... in the direction in which we all desire to move. Old age pensions enormously mitigate, if they have not completely transformed the problem so far as it relates to old age. That large provision which both parties are now absolutely agreed ought to be maintained, and, indeed, developed it must be by the removal of the Poor Law disqualification, has ... if not solved, gone some way towards removing one of the most dangerous, if not one of the most urgent aspects of the case ... We have got still to deal with invalidity and sickness, and some of the other hazards of industrial life ... old age pension committees have no relation to Poor Law administration – and when you come to deal with those other developments of an insurance scheme, I am sure there will be equal care to see that they shall lie outside the province of this institution in the sense in which it is commonly understood ... when you have provided, as we have during the last year in the Labour Exchanges, a satisfactory answer to the recommendations ... both of the Majority and the Minority [Reports] ... when you consider that in the establishment of Trade Boards we have done something, not only for the cure of destitution, but for its prevention with regard to sweated trades – if you take all those things into account, the problem, large as it is, has been very largely curtailed in dimensions, and a very considerable advance has, at any rate, been made towards dealing with particular cases.[7]

In October 1910, before the second election of that year, Beatrice Webb discerned that Haldane was 'favourable to the Minority Report'. He assured her that

> 'Both Asquith and Lloyd George want me to go on the Local Government Board, if there is another Liberal administration, and to carry out a large reconstruction.' He would evidently be prepared to give us the substance so long as he could keep some semblance of compromise with those favourable to a poor law authority.[8]

Asquith, replying to a parliamentary question in May 1911 posed by Robert Harcourt, a radical MP sympathetic to the aims of the Webbs' National Committee, stated that Burns in a speech had expressed the opinion that in view of what the government was doing,

> with such matters as old age pensions, labour exchanges, land and housing reform, and insurance against invalidity and unemployment – measures which admittedly affect the treatment of destitution – the character of the problems remaining to be dealt with has been in some important respects modified. But ... [Burns] and the Government quite realise that the necessity for Poor Law legislation, when time and opportunity permit, will not have been removed by these actual and contemplated reforms.[9]

Over a year later, when the question was asked again in December 1912, Asquith gave the same evasive reply.[10] Poor Law reform had been submerged by other issues, such as invalidity insurance, minimum wage legislation, land and housing reform, and had drifted out of practical politics for the time being. In any case the Liberal administration was not prepared to inflict increased financial burdens on the county councils through Poor Law reform without better sorting out the 'tangled' relationship between local and national taxation and was in no position to do this until a Treasury Departmental Committee reported in 1914.[11]

Asquith concluded his remarks in 1910 thus:

> [concerning] the all-important question which lies at the very root of the Poor Law administration, the abolition of the mixed workhouse, that is not a very easy thing to do ... They have been allowed to grow up; they cost a great deal of money; they employ very large staffs; and the whole local system of administration of the last fifty years has been based on the assumption that they will continue to exist. You cannot abolish them – no Administration can – by a stroke of the pen or by the wave of a wand. All you can do is what ... [Mr Burns] is and has been for the last four years doing, to encourage guardians everywhere to adopt the system of classification in institutions in substitution for the general mixed system. In all these ways – first, by legislation, actual and contemplated; next, by administration, strenuously and persistently pursued, as it has been by ... [Burns] – I think we may fairly claim ... to have somewhat diminished the dimensions of the problem with which Parliament four years ago was faced.[12]

Despite Asquith's defence of his minister, Kenneth Brown pointed out that Burns 'lacked the ability and the drive to do anything ... very quickly' and was out of touch with the modern approach to social problems, unleashing a barrage of protest when he tried issuing orders in 1911 and 1913 restricting outdoor relief, particularly medical provision.[13]

Feeling that their campaign had lost momentum, the Webbs strove for less ambitious goals and changed the name of their organization to the National Committee for the Prevention of Destitution, later reduced its staff and ceased publication of the *Crusade* in February 1913. However, it was replaced by the *New Statesman*, a review of politics and literature that also contained sociological supplements. In addition, between the summer of 1911 and May 1912, for almost a year, the Webbs, who were in need of recuperation, went on an extended tour of Asia, when the movement they had started began to lose it sense of direction, and saw that it could not be resuscitated on their return. Nonetheless, in the propaganda battle to convince public opinion of the merits of the Minority Report and their anti-destitution campaign, the Webbs triumphed over the Charity Organisation Society, winning the adhesion of the youthful intelligentsia for socialism rather than the Liberal party.[14] During the First World War Beatrice Webb served on the Maclean Committee, in which she adroitly negotiated a compromise with her opponents from among the supporters of the Majority Report to transfer the guardians' powers, particularly those of institutional relief to existing committees of the county and borough councils, while at the same time agreeing that a newly created Home Assistance Committee could be in charge of disbursements from the rates. Not until the Local Government Act of 1929 were the Boards of Guardians abolished and their powers transferred along the lines suggested by the Webbs.[15]

## The Child Under the Poor Law

In 1896 the State Children's Association was set up by Henrietta Barnett and her brother-in-law Ernest Hart, who died in the following year. She became honorary secretary of the organization and was its inspirational driving force. In December 1905 Lord Crewe resigned as its chairman on securing office in the new Liberal government, but the organization retained excellent links with a number of Liberal MPs and was a robust campaigning body.[16] Our primary interest in the association stems from the fact that it was the first body to demand a complete disassociation between the Poor Law and the child, albeit in this case the pauper child. Its programme commenced with the axiom that on no account was there to be any connection between children and the workhouse and its officials, who dealt with the pauper class. Special receiving centres were to be set up for children outside the workhouse. The large barrack schools for pauper children were to be dissolved, so that children could be nourished with love and treated as individuals. So accustomed were the children in these schools to being treated as automatons that it was said that they did not know how to walk singly. The best method of enabling children to secure the benefits of family life was to board them out with foster parents; if this was not possible, the next best option was for the Boards of Guardians to establish scattered homes on the Sheffield model; as a last resort, suitable children could be sent to Canada, where the government had put in place the appropriate machinery to look after their welfare. The older boys and girls were to be sent to trade training schools and technical education establishments.[17]

Mrs Barnett's influence on Parliament was considerable – so much so, that the clerk of one Board of Guardians under financial pressure was overheard to remark in 1904: 'We could of course crowd the children, but one can't put two in a bed without Mrs Barnett and her Society coming down on us with a question in the House, or a note to the Local Government Board.'[18]

Only after a long and persistent campaign did the State Children's Association persuade the Local Government Board to renounce its policy in regard to pauper children. At last in 1913 it induced John Burns, the minister responsible, to prohibit the retention of children over the age of three years in workhouses. In 1900 the Local Government Board issued a circular to the effect that all children should be removed from workhouses and sent to cottages and scattered homes, boarded out or assisted to emigrate, but little action followed. In 1903 there were still some 22,240 children in workhouses, a third of the 60,000 state children. In 1910 the Local Government Board brought out a new circular, urging that the Boards of Guardians should cease to maintain children of school age in workhouses. Nevertheless, a White Paper published in June 1912 revealed that it had taken six years to remove 2,343 children from workhouses, and besides the 8,729 children over the age of three years in workhouses on 1 January 1912, there were 5,483 children in sick infirmaries.[19]

Although the State Children's Association and other children's organizations favoured the extension of the boarding out of children, more progress was made in persuading Boards of Guardians to set up scattered homes rather than village communities for these pauper children. At the same time the number of children in the barrack schools only fell from 11,809 at the start of 1907 to 10,851 in 1912. Burns noted that Henrietta Barnett felt 'cocksure' about the deficiencies of these massive institutions, implying that he was of the opposite opinion. He was a significant brake on the progress of reform for these unfortunate children, so long as he remained at the Local Government Board until he was transferred to the Board of Trade. The State Children's Association encountered difficulties when they tried to make Boards treat the children as individuals, as 'Boards with an ambition to do something, and anxious to impress their constituents, readily commence building operations; they think by means of the small block system or a village community they escape the evils of barrack schools'.[20] While the boarding out of children was a widespread practice in Scotland, Australia and New Zealand, in Britain there was only fitful progress in this direction. But the State Children's Association compelled the Local Government Board to improve the system of inspecting boarded-out children; it pressed successfully for the appointment of more inspectors, preferably women, to visit the homes of the children boarded out beyond the union, though on the whole these children were well-supervised by voluntary committees of local residents, untarnished by any connection with the Poor Law; it forced the Local Government Board to issue a number of orders in 1900 and 1911, taking the inspection of boarded-out children within the union out of the hands of relieving officers and placing them under the charge of new boarding-out committees of the union, a third of whose members were to be women, while in future these children were only to be inspected by women. The perfecting of the system of inspection was marked by the slow rise in the number of boarded-out children; those boarded out beyond the union increased from 1,910 in

January 1900 to 2,158 on 1 July 1912; those boarded out within climbed from 6,580 in January 1904 to 8,897 in July 1912.[21]

Much more rapid, though, was the adoption of the Sheffield system of scattered homes by the Poor Law unions. Under this system that originated in 1893, children lived in ordinary houses which were scattered about the town, each containing about sixteen children of both sexes and presided over by a foster-mother; not only was there an authentic family atmosphere, but the boarders were allowed to mix freely with other children. By 1903, thirty-four Boards of Guardians had opened these homes and by 1912, 116 unions had followed suit.[22]

Inevitably Sidney Webb served on the committee of the State Children's Association, but the policy advocated in the Minority Report was a sharp critique of the ideas of the State Children's Association. Of course, the Webbs found it necessary to transfer the control of pauper children to the local education authority, but otherwise their ideas were curiously old-fashioned and outdated. Boarding out was somewhat surprisingly condemned as an unfeasible idea, although the system had worked well outside England and Wales. The Webbs concluded that there was not a large number of suitable foster parents and that the number of boarded-out children could not be greatly increased. Part of the difficulty here no doubt was that it was commonly believed that children should be boarded out in rural areas and that the sanitary condition of so many country cottages was low; but there must have remained a vast potential of suitable homes in towns which went untapped. So far from condemning the barrack schools, the Webbs claimed that the scant evidence available showed that they were not as bad as depicted by their opponents and that great improvements had recently taken place in their organization and education.[23]

Yet the strictures of contemporary critics on these massive establishments were too damning to be brushed aside so lightly. No proper home influence was provided by them; they were a happy breeding ground for infectious diseases; the children at the age of fourteen years were rudely cast out into the world with a deficient industrial training. Indeed, despite the criticisms levelled by the Webbs, it can be asserted that the policy of the State Children's Association stood for a sharp cleavage between the pauper child and the Poor Law, whereas the Webbs would have retained much of the Poor Law apparatus intact, only transferring its control to the education authority. To a certain extent the Webbs' policy prevailed. It was agreed after the Second World War that wherever possible children should be boarded out; yet the national average for the boarding out of children in the early 1960s was only 48 per cent and the LCC managed as late as 1962 to retain five large homes intact, each accommodating over 250 children.[24]

# First Steps Towards a Health Service

In the final phase of the pre-war Asquith administration from 1911 to 1914, against a background of domestic unrest stoked by striking workers and militant suffragettes, the government tried to correct some of the failures and gaps in its welfare programme. Urged on by a group of Liberal publicists including the sociologists L. T. Hobhouse and Seebohm Rowntree, Lloyd George set up the Land Enquiry Committee in 1912 to devise new policies for reviving the countryside, solving the shortage of affordable housing for the working class and implementing a minimum wage in the basic industries, including agriculture. At the same time, once the government insurance scheme was implemented its deficiencies in the area of public health became more obvious, and remedial action came from a number of quarters. A health service started to emerge akin to that proposed by the Webbs. Sir Robert Morant moved from the Board of Education to oversee the National Health Insurance Commission in 1912. The first contributions to the national insurance scheme were collected in July 1912 and the first medical benefit was dispensed in January 1913. We will cover the issues of public health, housing and the minimum wage and the widening of the government's welfare reform programme in this and the following two chapters.

## School Clinics and School Meals

In a preface to a guide to *National Insurance* (1912) the chancellor proudly declared that ten million workers hitherto not provided for had been swept into his health insurance scheme, but that '[m]uch remains to do, and in the coming years much may be done, but here at least is a beginning made in a broad and comprehensive plan'.[1] Lloyd George learnt quickly on the job. His newly forged friendships with Christopher Addison and Sir George Newman, head of the Board of Education's medical department, widened his conception of health reform beyond improving the pay and working conditions of the GP, and alerted him to the necessity of alleviating a serious shortcoming, by providing medical care of the nation's children. Further, the health insurance measure stimulated Arthur Newsholme, chief medical officer of the Local Government Board, into much greater efforts in implementing a national anti-tuberculosis programme and in fostering the infant welfare movement; clinics to combat venereal disease followed later. As Addison remarked in 1914:

For medical men at any rate, at this time, political life affords unusual opportunities for useful service ... They are improvement of the organization of the services, the provision of earlier and more effective treatment, and an increase in the prevention of sickness.

The result was a whole range of new services from 1912 until 1918, including a school medical service, infant welfare clinics, a national anti-tuberculosis campaign and clinics for venereal disease, under the control of the medical officer of health (MOH), with an emphasis on domiciliary visitation, the screening of contacts, and the integration of new forms of medical care in a public health service. Prior to the 1914 war, plans were announced for insured persons to have access to consultants and diagnostic services and the government announced its intention to establish a Ministry of Health.

The Education (Administrative Provisions) Act 1907 introduced the compulsory medical inspection of schoolchildren and made provision for their treatment. Morant, still at the Board of Education, decided to invite Dr George Newman to become head of its new medical department. Newman, a lecturer at St Bartholomew's Hospital, was a brilliant young doctor, whose thinking was partly derived from his experience in the field of preventative medicine in Finsbury and partly shaped by his beliefs as a practising and fervent Quaker. He had served as the president of the Westminster adult school for ten years, was for a time honorary secretary to the National Council of Adult Schools, and was a convinced social reformer and proponent of the Social Gospel with a background similar to such ardent exponents of the New Liberalism as Arnold Rowntree MP and T. Edmund Harvey MP, who were his close personal friends. In a circular issued 22 November 1907, Newman suggested that children should be examined by the school doctor when they entered school, again at the ages of seven and ten and before finally leaving. The 1908 report of the board stated that in 224 out of 307 areas the school medical officer appointed was the MOH of the area, while in seventy-six of the other local education authorities the school medical officer worked under or in cooperation with the MOH. This harmony between the school medical officer and the public health authority was a 'further step in the direction of a simplified and unified State Medical Service'.[2] When giving evidence to the Poor Law Commission in February 1908, Newman observed that the Poor Law medical service

> fails to touch the medical needs of children, only the glaring cases of disease are submitted and then only after delay. I have repeatedly found children in poor tenements in Finsbury suffering from incipient disease wholly untouched by the Poor Law medical service though the family are under observation. I am satisfied that we have in the past made the fatal error of neglecting far too much to treat incipient disease in childhood.[3]

Moreover, his previous circular prepared with the assistance of Newsholme and Morant proposed the preparation of schemes for 'the establishment of school surgeries or clinics, such as exist in some cities of Europe, for further medical examination, or the specialized treatment of ringworm, dental caries, or diseases of the eye, the ear, or the skin', but stressed that he favoured using the existing facilities provided by voluntary agencies to the full before embarking on a vigorous expansion of school clinics, as the results derived from school medical inspection were as yet too inconclusive to formulate a coherent policy.[4]

What gave a fillip to the movement for school clinics were the model centres set up in Bradford and Bow. The first general school clinic was started in Bradford, where the Independent Labour Party was influential, by 1911 comprising a full-time staff of three doctors, one dentist, two nurses and two clerks. According to Dr Lewis Williams, the medical superintendent of the Bradford education authority, the advantage of the scheme was that it

> ensures the minimum of leakage, that it provides for the following up of the cases, that it secures due attention to the educational as well as the medical aspects of the work, that inspection and treatment are closely linked together; in short, that the treatment scheme as such is closely connected with the education system of the authority as one piece of machinery.[5]

With the backing of the ILP Committee for Promoting the Physical Welfare of Children and the financial assistance of Joseph Fels, a millionaire soap magnate, socialist and single taxer, the Bow clinic was opened by Margaret McMillan in December 1908. Clara Grant, the headmistress of Devons Road School, made a room available for use as a clinic, where Dr Tribe and Dr Eder each treated children on one afternoon a week, giving medical attention over the course of two years to 450 children out of the 1,000 pupils in the school plus another twelve young patients sent along by other schools. As in all school clinics, the key figure was the school nurse, applying dressings and treatment prescribed by a doctor, for it was found to be useless just giving lotions to parents with instructions.

> Firstly, [as the treatment was carried out in the school] it ensured the regular attendance day by day of the children for dressing, ear-syringing etc.; to this we must ascribe the cure of several cases that had been treated for many years by hospitals in vain. Secondly, it took the children away from their class-work for the minimum of time.[6]

When the Greenwich Borough Council offered Margaret McMillan a rent-free house, she moved the clinic to Deptford in June 1910, as the expansion of the facilities offered by the Bow clinic was impeded both by the cramped working conditions and a perpetual shortage of cash.

> At Deptford an eye-witness records Eder's unfailing cheerfulness and ingenuity when eye-testing had to be done in a little dark back-cupboard of a room, tonsils operated on when beds must be improvised on the spot, extra money collected here, there and everywhere, when it was found that the open-air life inaugurated by Miss McMillan so increased these slum children's appetites that the ... usual 'institution diet' became totally impossible.[7]

After deliberation it was decided that conjunctivitis, a contagious eye disease, could only be effectively stamped out by extending treatment to the parents and siblings of affected children, while many children were fitted with spectacles through the munificence of the care committee and the Association for the Supply of Spectacles. A dentist from Bradford was added to the staff and was engaged on a full-time basis in January 1911, when the LCC agreed to subsidize the activities of the dental department, and grants followed in the next year for the treatment of eye, ear and minor ailments.[8]

Between them Margaret McMillan and Dr David Eder spearheaded the campaign for school clinics which began in 1909 and gathered pace in 1910 and 1911. Once the experiment in Bow had demonstrated the value of the methods adopted in the school clinic, McMillan wrote to Lady Warwick on 23 August 1909, appealing to her to use her influence with the TUC Parliamentary Committee and the Labour party to secure action in the Commons, as it was easier for them to do this than advanced Radicals:

> I want to say that in my opinion not much progress can be made in elementary education till we get school clinics ... There is not the smallest use in asking for clinics everywhere. What is wanted now is some more clinics *at once*.[9]

From 1911 onwards, Margaret McMillan seized every opportunity to state the case for school clinics: by describing in detail the work of the earliest school clinics in her book *The Child and the State* (1911), her own efforts at Bow and Deptford, the Bradford clinic, the three state-supported dental clinics, particularly the pioneering work at Cambridge; by speaking on every available occasion at conferences, whether organized by the British Institute of Social Service or the Women's Labour League; by writing in all the child welfare journals; and by lobbying influential persons like Morant behind the scenes, although much of the evidence that survives is fragmentary and patchy. In 1911 she suggested a £500,000 subsidy to build up a network of school clinics; by 1912 she was urging that school clinics should treat babies and that they should be made compulsory in certain areas.[10] Dr David Eder (1866-1936), a socialist, early Fabian, co-founder of the London Labour party, frequent contributor to Orage's *New Age*, psychoanalyst and Zionist, frequently utilized the columns of his journal *School Hygiene* to demand a more positive response from Dr George Newman at the Board of Education. Even if he condemned Newman's second report for its temerity in not giving his blessing to any particular form of treatment, he conceded in February 1911 that 'the natural tendency of the Board's policy upon the question of treatment is towards the establishment of School Clinics'.[11]

Backbench Conservative MPs introduced the Local Education Authorities (Medical Treatment) Bill which was adopted by the government and became law in 1909. Its aim was to recover the medical cost of treatment for children from parents who could afford to pay, and not shift it onto the shoulders of reluctant ratepayers. When the bill was debated in the House of Lords, the Earl of Crewe made a commitment on behalf of the Board of Education that could not be retracted, but many authorities found the cost of administrating the scheme prohibitive.[12] The Labour party in particular was criticized in the school doctors' journal for helping to promote the Medical Treatment Act of 1909, arguing in the March 1911 issue that there was no more reason for parents to pay the cost for dental treatment than for mains drainage.[13]

Within a matter of months, Newman was making an approach to Lloyd George for a government subsidy for the expansion of school clinics, quickly winning his confidence, and was dazzled and electrified by offers of career advancement dangled before him. During the negotiations over the Insurance Bill, Newman was inevitably drawn into the discussions and became friendly with Dr Christopher Addison MP, who rapidly became the chancellor's principal confidential adviser on medical politics, and Arthur Sherwell MP, a sociologist and former settlement worker who also participated in these talks because he was disturbed about the ill-health of the nation's children – an important group not covered by the medical provisions of the insurance scheme. Through the good offices of Walter Runciman, the president of the Board of Education, Newman was introduced to Lloyd George on 3 August 1911. 'He recd. me kindly', Newman jotted in his diary, 'and we had a long talk on the Insurance Bill & School Children.' At this meeting, Lloyd George appears to have been willing to listen to a request for a grant for schoolchildren, and it was agreed that Newman should prepare a memorandum for him. Further discussions took place in October. On 25 October an elated Newman noted a wonderful day with the chancellor:

> Ll. Geo & Tuberc. Children. He offered me the Vice Chairmanship of the Insurance Commission. We discussed the Bill – Sanatoria, Health Committees, Children. He wished me to start the Ins. Scheme & afterwards go to the L.G.B. as Chf. M.O ... I said I wd. only go to the L.G.B. if I cd. take the chn. w[ith] me.[14]

Sherwell was present at this meeting with Lloyd George. Reflecting on these events, Newman wrote: 'I had my great talk w[ith] Lloyd George ... in which I discussed ... Children as the basis of his Bill.'[15] In what must have been a deliberately contrived manoeuvre planned with Newman beforehand, Sherwell with a group of MPs, T. Edmund Harvey, Arnold Rowntree and Percy Alden, all the medical official's friends and exponents of the New Liberalism, launched a blistering assault against the chancellor, demanding an Exchequer subsidy to second the efforts of the local authorities in the area of child health. In December 1911 Lloyd George told the Commons that the Board of Education was framing regulations for Treasury approval and that he hoped to make a grant for medical treatment in 1912.[16] On 1 February 1912 Newman recorded in his diary: 'Lloyd George, Masterman, and Sir R. Chalmers & Pease & I – a long wrangle over money. Ll. Geo. wanted us to have 40,000 only – we fought for 100,000, probably we shall get £60,000.' Despite a further interview between Newman and Chalmers, the grant for £60,000 was all that Newman could squeeze in the first instance – a fact which indicates that it took Newman and Addison several years of determined persuasion before they could awaken Lloyd George to the gravity of the situation surrounding children's health.[17]

In 1912–13 the government gave a grant for the medical treatment of schoolchildren to local authorities on a sliding scale, with the most active authorities reimbursed for 60 or 66 per cent of their expenditure, while less zealous authorities received 50 per cent or less. In August 1913 a consolidated grant of 50 per cent of recognized expenditure on both the medical inspection and treatment of children was made to robust authorities and, at the same time, the grant was withheld from underperforming authorities. Expenditure by local authorities on the medical inspection and treatment of schoolchildren rose from £285,933 in 1912–13 to £325,735 in 1913–14.[18]

Most of the school clinics originated in a suggestion of the local MOH or the school medical officer, who was nearly always a MOH with a wide-ranging preventative philosophy of public health, or from more zealous members of the local education committee; although sometimes the care committees, which were offshoots of the education committees, played a vital role in bringing about the provision and equipment of additional clinics. To promote the opening of more clinics, the National League for Physical Education, in which a section of MOHs were entrenched, commissioned Dr Cruickshank to prepare a survey of the gaps in the existing medical provision for children and indicate how this could be rectified by the improvisation of school clinics; its 1914 annual report claimed a measure of success in stimulating local authorities in this direction.[19] Otherwise the principal impulse behind the creation of school clinics came from persons influenced by the New Liberalism or members of the ILP and Fabian socialists, such as Arthur Greenwood and Dr L. Haden Guest. In his memoirs the then warden of the Liverpool University Settlement, a Fabian socialist, related how he and a group of fellow school managers after starting an experimental dental clinic in December 1910, closed it shortly before the local elections in 1913 to focus attention on the duty of the municipality to provide such centres everywhere.[20] In June 1914 the Fabian educational group, the Medical Officers of Schools Association and the Women's Industrial Council organized a conference on the 'Next Steps in Educational Progress', at which Dr Lewis Cruickshank read a paper exploring the merits of the school clinic. An MP with strong connections to the settlement movement, J. H. Whitehouse, in his volume entitled *A National System of Education* (1913) – a work endorsed by the executive of the education committee of Liberal MPs – pleaded for a vast programme of clinics.[21] Women's organizations, especially the National Union of Women Workers and the Women's Industrial Council, hurled their influence behind the campaign. Elizabeth Cadbury, having been asked to serve as the chairman of the newly constituted hygiene subcommittee of the Birmingham Council in December 1911, pushed her fellow members to agree to the institution of a series of dental and eye clinics, and despite the reluctance of the full council, baited them until they agreed to a nose and throat operating hospital and a central school clinic complete with baths and X-ray apparatus.[22] Whereas it has been estimated that there was a total of ten voluntary and state sanctioned clinics in 1909, to which sixteen were added in 1910, by 1914 350 treatment clinics had been opened, so that almost all the local authorities secured the treatment of children under their care directly or by using voluntary facilities.[23]

Towards the end of 1913, Christopher Addison MP and Waldorf Astor MP urged Newman to become the secretary of the newly created Medical Research Council as a step towards coordinating the public health activities of different government departments, thereby laying the foundations of a Ministry of Health. The Medical Research Council arose from a clause in the Insurance Act, for which Lloyd George credited Addison as being 'mainly responsible'.[24] Advised by Morant and by his departmental chief Jack Pease to remain at the Board of Education, Newman intimated to Pease that he was willing to stay at his post, provided 'the Govt. wished it so & meant progress of Med. Department particularly in regard to sch.[ool] for mothers & physical training'; he was trying to expand his activities in the area of infant welfare which had hitherto mostly belonged to the Local Government Board. On 12 February 1914 Lloyd George sent for Newman ostensibly to discuss the Welsh medical department, but Newman noted that 'he wanted to see me on the Prov. of Meals for sch. chn.'. Later that day Newman lunched with Lloyd George and Seebohm Rowntree, chatting among other things about 'Burns, L.G.B., Sch. for Mothers, Meals, Quakerism, Dentist etc.'. The next day Newman spent a quarter of an hour privately closeted with the chancellor:

> Said he was keen on helping medl. treatment & sch. feeding & asked me to write to him fully on the whole question of financial needs of Medl. Dept. He said he did not believe in ordinary educatl. methods but was prepared to help on medl. side – feeding, phys. training, m[edical] t[reatment], sch. for M ...[25]

At a commemoration dinner a few years later, Lloyd George admitted that he had depended upon Dr Addison almost as much as he had done upon any member of the House of Commons: 'With Sir George Newman he was almost entirely responsible for committing the Government to the medical treatment of school children, which had committed the country to one of the biggest propositions it had ever undertaken.'[26]

> [Newman, Addison and Morant] put together the health schemes that were first introduced in the 1914 Budget. They were the subject of many discussions after breakfast with Lloyd George as the process of elaboration went on. [The chancellor] was of course, not blind to the electioneering advantages of social services directed towards helping the people in their everyday life, but he was keen on them for their own sake, and was an alert and helpful critic.[27]

Addison and Newman in particular broadened Lloyd George's conception of the scope of remedial measures to improve the nation's health. In April 1914 there were further discussions between Newman and Lloyd George at the Treasury, at which the latter 'raised money for Provis. of Meals from £100,000 to £150,000 – Epid. Grant £30,000–£50,000. Health, work from £25,000 to £50,000'. Despite the government's generosity, this was still a far cry from Newman's ambitious plans, which he had unburdened to Pease, as his diary reveals: 'Talk abt. whole position of Medl. work and the financial needs. I asked for a million.'[28]

On 4 May 1914 the chancellor in his Budget speech announced a new health programme with special attention devoted to children, promising a government subsidy of £150,000 for school meals, £27,000 for special schools, an epidemic grant of £55,000 'to help local authorities close the schools where there is an epidemic in the neighbourhood', and £50,000 rising to £90,000 in 1915 to be shared between encouraging physical training in schools, the creation of schools for mothers and subsidizing open air schools, making a total grant of £282,000 plus an epidemic grant of £100,000 concealed among the general consolidated grants. For the first time, grants were made for public health that were to be given or withheld from local authorities for their work in this area. Further grants were made to encourage the growth of nursing services, particularly in country districts, and for laboratory assistance. Through the intervention of Addison and Masterman, it was proposed to start a system of consultants for insured persons and, where possible, clinics to assist with early diagnosis, but with the coming of the war the opening of clinics and laboratories was abandoned.[29]

Turning now to the growing movement for the wider provision of school dinners, we have seen that the underlying motive was to sustain necessitous children during periods of trade depression. Coinciding with the development of the Edwardian casual labour theory of unemployment, sociologists, when investigating the reasons why parents sought free meals for their offspring, concluded that the bulk of the families applying to the canteen committees for meals comprised those in which the male head of the household was unemployed or in casual occupations or were families dependent on the earnings of a woman because her husband was ill, had deserted her or was dead. Hence Phyllis Winder and Mildred Bulkley seemed to fasten onto the preponderant number of children with fathers out of work, in casual employment or on short time: 336 out of 718 families or 49 per cent of the total number of families. The figures for those families with disabled fathers, deserted wives and widows were roughly the same: 357 out of 718 families, again 49 per cent of the total number of families. By way of contrast only 2 per cent of the total comprised families whose heads were in regular work but on low wages. This was virtually to ignore the problem of low wages, which was the main cause of poverty in Edwardian Britain, by accepting the poverty test for sorting out applicants for school meals, a test embodying Poor Law assumptions which resulted in a set of statistics buttressing the casual labour theory of unemployment and pauperism.[30] In an important reappraisal of working-class diets culled from six surveys between 1887 and 1901 and drawing on 151 family budgets, Derek Oddy declared that even families with an income of between 21s. and 30s. a week (group C) had an average nutrient intake of 2,113 calories, only reaching a satisfactory level of 2,537 kilocalories in a family with an income of 30s. or more a week. His principal conclusion was that '[t]he gap between inadequate and adequate diets was rather to be found between group C families – the regularly employed unskilled workers – and group D who, in terms of income, were equivalent to skilled workmen's families', not as Booth suggested between those families earning less than 21s. and those earning more.[31] After the discovery of vitamins by Gowland Hopkins in 1912 and the proof of the connection between the deficiency in vitamin D and rickets by Mellanby after the 1914–18 war, a new consensus developed among experts such as Sir John Boyd Orr, Dr G. C. M. M'Gonigle and Dr J. Kirby, and C. E. McNally, who in a series of volumes published in the 1930s more accurately posited that quantitative and qualitative deficiencies in diet were the predisposing factors behind malnutrition, that rickets and caries were generated through dietetic lacunae, and that there was a clear link between unbalanced diets and poverty.[32]

The 1906 Act failed to bring significant change in its wake. Out of 322 local education authorities in England and Wales, 131 made some provision through the rates or voluntary funds to feed children. Only ninety-five of these spent money on food, where they were seriously hampered by the $^1/_2$d. rate limit. The extent of this activity lagged far behind the needs of the nation's schoolchildren. According to an estimate of the chief medical officer of the Board of Education, 10 per cent of these children were suffering from malnutrition, with Arthur Greenwood putting the figure at 20 per cent. Dr Letitia Fairfield, who served on the Education and Public Health Committees of the LCC for thirty-seven years, agreed that the malnutrition rates for schoolchildren varied between 10 per cent and 20 per cent. What is more certain is that out of a total school population of 5.36 million, only 230,000 children benefited from meals. Voluntary funds for the school meals service shrank rapidly, reaching a mere £3,064 in 1911–12 out of a total expenditure of £157,127. Further, because the recovery of debt was left in the hands of the local education authorities, which did not possess the necessary machinery, only 1 per cent of the cost was recovered from parents. Most authorities still used a means test for selecting children and less than a dozen in 1909 left the final selection of the children to the school doctor.[33]

One beneficial consequence of the 1906 Act was the rise of the care committee system. Since 1896 a few schools in London had been providing destitute children with food and clothing, after Margaret Frere, a social worker who had imbibed the pristine Charity Organisation Society ideology, had organized what was in effect the earliest care committee in the Seven Dials district. But it was not until the care committees had been started up all over London in connection with schools designated as necessitous to fulfil the obligations imposed by the 1906 Education (Provision of Meals) Act that the movement was lifted into public prominence. Gradually the care committees were extended to all the schools in the twilight areas; gradually they blazed forth in fresh directions along the whole perimeter of child welfare, becoming the clearing house for all the statutory and voluntary bodies entwined in the movement.

Less than 40 per cent of the local authorities provided school meals before 1914, with scant provision in rural areas, and even among permissive authorities, the rising cost of school meals made some look towards retrenchment.[34] At the behest of F. W. Jowett, the Labour party introduced bills between 1908 and 1914 with the purpose of abolishing the $^1/_2$d. rate limit on expenditure for food, legalizing the feeding of children in the school holidays, removing the onus of deciding which children were to be fed from the local education authorities and shifting it onto the school doctors, and giving the Board of Education powers to coerce recalcitrant authorities to put the Act into force. Supported in 1914 by influential Conservative spokesmen like Anson and Col. Lockwood, despite criticism from Conservative backbenchers like Banbury and Sir Henry Craik, who reflected COS views, Jowett's bill evoked a favourable response from the Liberal president of the Board of Education, Jack Pease. He stated that while the present time was not ripe for compulsion, it would shortly become so and that in the meantime the government intended to make a contribution to the rates to encourage those authorities that had hitherto been somewhat remiss. Asquith in 1913 expressed a desire that Jowett's bill should pass onto the statute book after the contentious portions had been removed.[35] Under persistent Labour party pressure, Lloyd George, Newman and Jack Pease were awakened to the need to assist those local authorities financially providing school dinners, even if the government Act of 1914 was still not far-reaching enough. In fact, with the coming of the First World War, the government bill was rushed through the Commons amid concerns expressed by Newman of mass unemployment and starvation; for although the bill abolished the $^1/_2$d. rate limit on food expenditure and permitted the provision of meals during the school holidays, it retained the restrictions on the school doctor's activities as far as the selection of children was concerned.[36] Pease announced in the Commons that the government would allocate a subsidy of £77,000 in 1914 for school meals, increasing it to £150,000 in the following year. The medical criteria adopted by Newman for assessing levels of nutrition were so vague that rates varied considerably across the country, making the findings useless. Newman continued with his old-fashioned advice, adhering to the view that 'persistent, kindly, and skilled missionary effort' would persuade people to change their eating habits, and he suggested that LEAs and local authority public services should promote health education and encourage parents to make their homes 'suitable training grounds for children of good nutrition and sound physique'. Thus without adequate support from the centre between 1914–15 and 1918–19 the number of local education authorities providing meals dropped from 134 to eighty-six, while the number of children benefiting fell from 422,401 to 53,742 – hardly an outstanding achievement on Newman's part.[37] On the other hand, feminist historians have criticized the establishment of school clinics and a school dinner service for throwing additional burdens on the over-stretched working-class mother, who weekly had to juggle with the family budget and time to ensure the smooth running of this unit.[38]

## The Campaign to Combat Tuberculosis

At the beginning of the twentieth century the majority of doctors, including MOHs, opposed the compulsory notification of persons infected with tuberculosis on the grounds that the communicability of the disease was 'of a lower order' than other infectious diseases, and that even when a patient went promptly for treatment, the disease had already been incubating in him for some time. Dr J. C. McVail claimed:

> It is true that hospitals and sanatoriums, in dismissing a patient, explain to him that he is to take precautions with his sputum and to keep his window open, and so forth; also many public health authorities issue prints of instructions, or send an officer to call at the house of the patient. But even where voluntary notification is in force, some medical officers do not appear to intimate cases to the medical officer of health, and as a matter of fact, domestic prevention is, up till now, very little more than a name. Precautions are not properly understood, and only half practised, and are hardly at all enforced ... Under the Poor Law there is practically no sanitary supervision of phthisis in the home of the patient ... Such consumptive patients as I found in rural workhouses were being treated side by side with other patients in ordinary wards, not suited for modern methods of dealing with consumption.[39]

Even in urban areas, where the disease was much more prevalent, in some workhouse infirmaries the precaution was not taken 'of ranging the consumptive patients on one side of the ward and the rest on the other'.[40]

On his exploratory trip to Germany in August 1908, Lloyd George was surprised by the number of hospitals and sanatoria supported by insurance funds. Grants were readily available for municipal hospitals and voluntary dispensaries which diagnosed the disease, disinfected homes of patients and examined other members of their family for signs of the spread of the infection. If the patient was well enough to remain at home, he was visited by doctors and nurses, who advised him as to what steps he should take to protect his health, such as ventilation, food, clothing, exercise, and the adaptation of the accommodation to the hygienic needs of both himself and his family. Curable cases were despatched to sanatoria, mostly in pine forests, if they required treatment. In Germany in 1909 there were 135 sanatoria with 13,241 beds, including ninety-nine sanatoria for the working class with 11,066 beds, whereas in Britain there were ninety-six sanatoria for tuberculosis and other diseases with 4,081 beds, but only forty of these sanatoria charged less than 25s. per week, thus putting the overwhelming number of them well beyond the resources of the working class.[41] In the United Kingdom there were between 60,000 and 70,000 deaths every year from tuberculosis and at least 200,000 cases at any one time, but there were only 2,000 beds in sanatoria available for treatment. If a minimum of three months' treatment was provided, this would mean only about 8,000 people could be treated properly each year, when at least ten times that much accommodation was required.[42]

The Finance Act 1911 Section 16(1) and the National Insurance Act 1911 Section 64(1) allowed the distribution of sums for the purposes of the provision or making grants to sanatoria or other institutions for the treatment of tuberculosis or such other diseases as the Local Government Board with the approval of the Treasury agreed. On 7 July 1911, Lloyd George announced in the Commons:

> If this experiment [with sanatoria] is a success, and it becomes perfectly evident that it is effectively stamping out consumption, it will be a great mistake for the State not to face any liability within reason in order to effectively stamp out this scourge altogether ... but it is an experiment. There are doctors in this country of great experience who are not quite so confident of this being the best method of stamping out consumption ... I invite the House to try this experiment on this very considerable scale – £1,500,000 towards building [sanatoria] and £1,000,000 towards maintaining them.[43]

Throughout 1911, the chancellor had a persistent sore throat and his interest in alleviating tuberculosis, Braithwaite noted, 'was particularly lively and personal'.[44] Sanatorium treatment consisted 'especially in spending as much time in the open air as possible, together with adequate and appropriate diet, suitable exercise, rest, and medical care'. Although such a method of treatment was considered highly beneficial for the wealthier classes, who led a healthy outdoor life afterwards, many MOHs asserted that working-class patients could derive little of permanent value from this form of treatment, so long as they had to return to bad home conditions. Because the new provision was somewhat clumsily drafted, the insurance committees spent what they were empowered to on sanatorium benefit and were unable to spend it on anything else. This arrangement was castigated by Waldorf Astor, a progressive Unionist MP and a spokesman for the anti-tuberculosis movement, who in a brilliant speech in the Commons advocated a four-point programme: educational propaganda, diagnosis with the aid of dispensaries, treatment of the curable victims of the disease and isolation of advanced cases and after-care to prevent a relapse. From the other side of the house, Sherwell demanded that the extension of the sanatorium benefit to the wives and dependants of the insured should only be made by means of a Treasury grant.[45]

At the same time as Lloyd George was inaugurating this new policy at the Treasury, Dr Arthur Newsholme, who had joined the Local Government Board as its medical officer on 4 February 1908, was also not slow in initiating measures to restrict the spread of the disease. In his memoirs he recalled that by 1907 he had 'become convinced that in the interest of the community and as a means of preventing both poverty and continued sickness, free medical aid should be given at the communal expense to all who lacked it'.[46] Already when he had previously served as MOH for Brighton, he had insisted on a policy of both the voluntary notification of tuberculosis and preventative measures within the patient's family combined, if necessary, with institutional treatment for the patient. He was now ready to extend this policy, by making it compulsory and by launching it on a national basis.[47] In January 1909, LGB regulations made the notification of pulmonary tuberculosis compulsory in all cases attended by Poor Law medical officers, while new orders extended the scope of the scheme to all hospitals and dispensary patients in May 1911 and to all the remaining victims of this form of consumption on 1 January 1912. The first notification order led to a great increase in notification in towns in which voluntary measures were in place. Some towns followed Brighton and used the empty wards of isolation hospitals, others such as Manchester admitted tuberculosis patients into empty smallpox hospitals. John Eyler pointed out that once Newsholme grasped that the sanatorium benefit in the chancellor's health insurance scheme presented a challenge to certain public health aspects of his policy, he accelerated the issuing of orders in 1911 in order to salvage his control over the anti-tuberculosis programme. On 19 December 1912 the Local Government Board under Newsholme's direction passed a consolidated order, extending compulsory notification to the non-pulmonary aspects of the disease with effect from 1 February 1913, thus earning the praise of a newly appointed government committee who were 'glad to find that they have been anticipated by the action of the Local Government Board'.[48] Newsholme was supported fully by his minister John Burns and F. J. Willis, the assistant secretary, when he devised this series of orders.[49] The Local Government Board, however, not having been consulted in the preparation of the Insurance Bill until a late stage, were presented with the sanatorium benefit as a fait accompli, though they doubted the wisdom of this policy. More importantly, noted Newsholme,

> it soon became evident that tuberculosis being an infectious disease, provision for its control under the above provisions could not be limited to insured persons; and rigorous representations to this effect were made by the Local Government Board and Associations of Local Authorities.[50]

On 22 February 1912 the Treasury, under pressure from the Local Government Board, at last relented and agreed to the appointment of the Departmental Committee on Tuberculosis under the chairmanship of Waldorf Astor MP to advise on national policy, its members included Newsholme, Newman and Addison. In the interim report it recommended that the treatment of tuberculosis should apply to the whole population, as the National Insurance Act failed to provide financially for the maintenance and treatment of persons who were not insured or for the dependants of the insured. Once again Newsholme anticipated the findings of the committee, by making the first moves towards establishing facilities for treatment on a national basis. In a memorandum on 'Administrative Measures against Tuberculosis' dated February 1912, Newsholme declared:

> When the National Insurance Act has come into full operation the provision of adequate treatment of tuberculosis will be within the reach of a very high proportion of the total population, and it will be in the power of local authorities to organise this treatment both for insured persons and for the general population. In considering such provision, it is essential to remember that since pulmonary tuberculosis is a communicable disease, its control cannot satisfactorily or safely be treated as a separate problem for the insured and non-insured.[51]

After outlining the proposed new machinery for treating tuberculosis, the memorandum concluded:

> The additional measures now rendered practicable for the prompt and adequate medical care of cases of pulmonary tuberculosis provide means for securing the reduction of tuberculosis at an accelerated rate; and given active and continuous cooperation between Local Authorities and Insurance Committees in the provision of the sanitary and medical measures necessary for the control of tuberculosis, it may be confidently anticipated that this end will be secured.[52]

The Astor Committee envisaged a plan for dealing with tuberculosis which would include dispensaries to serve as a clearing-house after diagnosis and later as centres for after-care and for institutional treatment to be provided principally by way of sanatoria, all to be administered by county boroughs and county councils in cooperation with insurance committees and sanitary authorities. The committee regarded 'with some anxiety the smallness of the funds available under the National Insurance Act for the maintenance of dispensaries and institutions'.[53]

Having estimated that the cost of sanatorium treatment for the whole population of England and Wales would total £2,682,000 per annum, of which £1 million would come out of insurance funds, Newsholme confidentially suggested that the remainder of the cost of treatment should be shared equally between the Treasury and the ratepayers.[54] Railing against Treasury frugality, John Burns wrote to the chancellor backing Newsholme's contentions with the suggestion that 'we should take sanatorium treatment out of the Insurance Act, and make it a duty of local authorities to provide, to the satisfaction of the Local Government Board, adequate institutional arrangements, giving them a maintenance grant of half the costs'.[55] On 31 July 1912 Lloyd George, following Newsholme's advice, wrote to Henry Hobhouse, the chairman of the County Councils Association, offering to place at the disposal of the Local Government Board a sum which would represent half the estimated cost of treating the non-insured and the dependants of insured persons, for under the insurance scheme the local authorities were authorized to provide sanatoria and dispensaries but were not obliged to take such action. Immediately after this decision, the board prepared a further circular announcing the chancellor's decision and stimulating the local authorities to take action, but because of some outstanding queries the Treasury would not allow it to be issued until December.[56]

Nevertheless, the local authorities remained unhappy with the proposed funding by the chancellor and in this they were supported by the Local Government Board. John Burns wrote to Lloyd George on 24 January 1914:

> Seeing how far we have gone in the direction of getting the Local Authorities to work, I feel we can scarcely let our action in this direction drop and if as seems rather likely from present indications the Authorities will not move unless the Treasury guarantee them 75 per cent of the total maintenance charge it may be necessary to make this concession. With this inducement and a grant of the full capital expenditure for any building ready for occupation within a limited time we should probably get the best immediate results at the minimum of cost.[57]

The County Councils Association, the Association of Municipal Corporations and the Borough Councils announced in a deputation to Lloyd George on 6 February 1913 that they were willing to undertake the burden of the complete schemes if they received from sources other than the rates 75 per cent of the cost of maintenance. Cleverly in his reply Lloyd George downplayed his refusal to accept this request, by praising the deputation for their moderation, their reluctance to present their demand as an ultimatum. He reiterated that the only definite obligation undertaken by the government was to provide sanatorium benefit for insured persons. What was difficult was to provide sanatorium benefit for insured persons and their dependants as well. Under Clause 17 power was given to the Insurance Committee of any county,

> if they saw fit, to extend sanatorium treatment to dependants ...; [and] there was a further provision that enabled the representatives of the ratepayers to find half the expense, on the condition that the Treasury found the other half. That does not impose an obligation on any of the three authorities that are mentioned there. It is purely a matter for arrangement and agreement amongst them, and what we are considering now is the possibility of effecting an arrangement which enables these three authorities to cooperate for the purpose of stamping out this great evil, not merely amongst insured persons, but amongst every class.[58]

Six months previously a deputation had asked him to provide sanatorium benefit not only for the insured and their dependants, 'but for uninsured persons as well'. He made an offer that 'the Treasury should find 50 per cent of the deficiency after deducting the contribution made by the Local Insurance Committees', a concession that had been rebuffed by the county councils and municipalities. Why did they not try out his offer on an experimental basis for a year or two, when they would be in a better position to evaluate its merits?[59]

To have a complete scheme to counter tuberculosis, Morant maintained in a subsequent memorandum prepared for the chancellor that it was desirable that the insurance committees should extend the sanatorium benefit as far as institutional treatment was concerned to the dependants of insured persons, and should hand over to local authorities the sums available for institutional treatment. In this way local authorities would become responsible for the treatment of all classes whether insured or dependants or non-insured. The Local Government Board would grant half of the net cost of county councils and county boroughs for treatment in dispensaries, sanatoria and hospitals less money from the insurance committees and sums from non-insured persons. While the grants included in the estimates for 1913 for treatment of tuberculosis amounted to £125,000, it was anticipated that they would rise to £500,000 per annum. To cope with the shortage of accommodation in sanatoria the government set aside a capital grant of £1,500,000, at the same time urging the local authorities and insurance committees to cooperate. Soon, however, the insurance committees were in financial difficulties as far as the sanatorium benefit was concerned, because 6d. had been deducted from the per capita grant of 1s. 3d. per insured person given to the insurance committees for panel doctors. Morant declared that after 6d. was deducted from the insurance committees' per capita grant,

> [the] Insurance Committees in many instances complained that they would not have sufficient income left for the provision of institutional treatment, while many Local Authorities hesitated to proceed with schemes which on the financial side depended to a considerable extent on the revenue received from the Insurance Committees.[60]

Morant predicted that the English Health Commission would have a shortage of accommodation for the next six months to a year. This could be overcome 'by stimulating the provision and use of dispensaries and thus limiting the demand for purely Sanatorium treatment'. He recommended that insurance committees should only permit a short stay of two to three months unless the medical officer ordered otherwise.[61] S. P. Vivian, the assistant secretary of the English Health Insurance Commission, warned Lloyd George on 27 April 1914 that the insurance committees were spending in excess of their income.[62]

During 1913 and the beginning of 1914, Newsholme devoted much of his attention to developing a national anti-tuberculosis programme based on dispensaries and sanatoria. Whereas the Local Government Board approved the appointment of tuberculosis doctors and inspected and approved sanatoria and dispensaries which, if new, were set up with government financial assistance, the Health Commission merely exercised control over the insurance committees. Under the Public Health (Prevention and Treatment of Disease) Act 1913 county boroughs and county councils were empowered 'to make such arrangements as may be sanctioned by the ... Board for the treatment of tuberculosis'. Six of the sixteen medical inspectors in the Local Government Board were allocated by Newsholme to review schemes and to inspect dispensaries and residential institutions.[63] Further, he pressed for the application on a national scale of the policy which he had instituted in Brighton of keeping tuberculosis patients in sanatoria for a short stay in order to inculcate hygienic habits; then on their returning home, advocating the use of a separate bedroom, good nutrition and elementary hygiene. On account of their lack of experience of this type of work, Newsholme refused to appoint GPs as assistant tuberculosis officers, even if he encouraged them to send samples of sputum to laboratories for free examination and was willing to employ them as clinical assistants as long as they were not given responsible charge of the patients. By May 1913 complete schemes for residential institutions had been submitted by seventy-three of the county councils and county boroughs and partial schemes by forty-eight councils, including all the more important county councils and the larger municipalities. At the same time, the board had approved 'for the treatment of insured persons suffering from tuberculosis, *204* sanatoria and institutions, containing over 7,200 beds, and *189* dispensaries'. By June 1914, according to John Eyler, the Local Government Board had approved 255 dispensaries in England, 'of which 216 were new, and the appointment of 177 Tuberculosis Officers'; and by the autumn the schemes submitted covered almost the whole of the English population.[64] Again, by the board sanctioning arrangements with existing institutions and hospitals, the number of beds available had increased to 8,846.

In London nine voluntary dispensaries and two out-patient departments of hospitals were included in local schemes by 1914, while five municipal dispensaries were already functioning and eight hospitals had opened dispensaries or were shortly to do so, but every dispensary referred difficult cases to hospitals.[65] Newsholme was deeply critical of the voluntary dispensary movement because many of the tuberculosis doctors concentrated their efforts on clinical work, to the detriment of the wider public health aspects of the problem. The London voluntary dispensaries were municipalized to augment their efficiency, just as tuberculosis work in county councils and county boroughs outside London was placed in charge of the MOH, who was assisted by tuberculosis officers.[66]

The National Association for the Prevention of Consumption (NAPC) was founded in 1898 with the encouragement of Edward, then Prince of Wales, and a group of leading consultants including Sir William Broadbent and Sir Malcolm Morris, who were joined by many of the principal MOHs in the campaign against tuberculosis. When he was appointed to his post at the Local Government Board, Newsholme with his background as a provincial MOH was sympathetic, rendering assistance to the organization on several occasions, and was a vice-president of the association for many years together with aristocrats like the Duke of Bedford and the Duke of Newcastle. For 1914 the expenditure of the organization reached £6,833. 19s. 1d., a considerable sum for a voluntary body. The establishment of sanatoria was one of the chief policies of the association and through its branches, which had grown to twenty-six by 1913, seventeen sanatoria for the working class were set up.[67]

The bulk of the National Association's efforts before the outbreak of the war was otherwise devoted to fostering the growth of after-care and providing without much success the first tentative steps in voluntary care for advanced tuberculosis cases and children, categories hitherto neglected by the state. The After-Care Committee of the association reported that Newsholme had been invited to join its ranks and that 'his assistance and advice have been most useful, and have been much appreciated'. At the sanatorium, according to the model scheme, the medical officer would interview the patient and advise him on his mode of life and his future work, embodying his conclusions in a memorandum for the tuberculosis officer attached to the dispensary. This latter place would be the centre for the after-care committee, consisting of members of the local insurance committee, the phthisis nurse, health visitors and the local Charity Organisation Society, who would keep in touch with patients treated solely by the dispensary or those referred by the sanatorium. A memorandum incorporating this plan was forwarded to 196 insurance committees, 1,748 MOHs and the superintendents of working-class sanatoria; the National Association of Industrial

Assurance Approved Societies also approached the association for guidance in after-care work, while 'thanks to the Approved Societies ... new openings for visits of the Tuberculosis Exhibition were being made in many quarters in the industrial cities of the North'. When the MOHs were circularized as to the progress which had been made in instituting permanent tuberculosis schemes and initiating after-care, their answer was that 'much advance in these matters has been made in the Counties and in the Boroughs but that much remains to be done'. Where the association's branches were active, marked progress was achieved after 1900. The Oxfordshire branch, for instance, maintained six dispensaries, where the tuberculosis officer examined new patients unless he first saw them in their homes with their general practitioner, providing all the treatment other than institutional, including shelters, medicine and food, and in one year despatched sixty-three tuberculosis children to convalescent homes.[68] It also set up a central fund for the promotion of dispensaries in London, as a result of which four were opened, with plans to open another four shortly after.

During the war years 1914–18 the staff of the medical department of the Local Government Board engaged in tuberculosis work was reduced, the local authorities' programme of capital expenditure was curtailed, and certain forms of tuberculosis work were abandoned, such as the systematic examination of home contacts. From an expenditure of £6,833. 19s. 1d. in 1914, the National Association's budget sank to £788. 12s. 4d. in 1915; its report for that year admitted that 'in common with other philanthropic societies [the association] has suffered from the war, in consequence of which anti-tuberculosis work in many directions has been curtailed'.[69] In London the Insurance Committee reduced tuberculosis beds from 932 to fewer than 500, admitting that they could no longer fulfil their obligations to insured consumptives. In 1916 the association noted:

> Many schemes which were getting under way in the early part of 1914 have been blocked, or, at least, seriously crippled ... Tuberculosis officers of different grades have been hurried off to other work. Institutions for the treatment of tuberculosis have been vacated for war purposes, while new buildings, already sanctioned or actually in the course of erection, have been held up.[70]

Again, Newsholme declared in 1918:

> Owing to the shortage of medical staff it has been impossible in most areas to carry out a fully dispensary service. The amount of home visitation of patients by the tuberculosis officers has been curtailed, and the important work of examination of contacts in many areas has been restricted.[71]

As a result, the average increase in deaths from tuberculosis in England and Wales during the years 1914–17 was nearly 1,500, a trend followed in other Western countries.[72] Nonetheless, the many tuberculosis schemes in embryo and the unabated blasts of propaganda by the association throughout the war conserved a solid base for a rapid post-war recovery. Newsholme designed a national free tuberculosis service with an additional emphasis on alleviating the poverty of stricken families by improving their food intake and accommodation, which his successor Newman inherited. According to Newsholme, '[n]otwithstanding all difficulties, however, a great amount of dispensary work has been carried on and a number of new dispensaries have been opened'. In the year 1917-18 the number of beds available for the residential treatment of tuberculosis increased from 11,884 to 12,441. After the war, there was a rapid expansion of existing facilities for combating tuberculosis. 'The Councils have in many cases taken over the administration of the Sanatorium Benefit, though in some cases the Insurance Committee carry out the work themselves'. By 1919 there was 'a scheme of some sort in every County or County Borough, but none are complete; none cover all forms of tuberculosis'.[73] By the time Newsholme retired in March of that year, he had created the enduring foundations of a national preventative anti-tuberculosis scheme, allowing for a rapid post-war expansion of facilities. While the National Insurance Act of 1920 permitted insured persons to retain the right to domiciliary treatment as a medical benefit, the Public Health (Tuberculosis) Act in the following year gave everyone equal entitlement to sanatorium treatment – the long-standing rationalization goal of many reformers – the cost being shared by local authorities and the Exchequer. In 1921 the tuberculosis service in England and Wales consisted of 381 tuberculosis officers, 441 tuberculosis dispensaries and twenty-four visiting stations plus 20,395 beds in hospitals and sanatoria, with another 2,664 beds in preparation.[74]

## The Treatment of Venereal Diseases

With the advent of the Wasserman test in 1906 for diagnosing syphilis – if clinical evidence was dubious – and Paul Ehrlich's discovery of Salvarsan to treat it in 1910, medical science at last developed the techniques to vanquish venereal diseases. Because in the past the disease was regarded as a divine punishment for sin, little effort was made to treat it. Describing conditions in the Edwardian era, it was alleged that '[s]everal … honorary staff of general hospitals testified that those suffering from the earlier forms of venereal disease were not encouraged to attend' them to seek treatment. 'In some hospitals it is contrary to their statutes to admit venereal disease [patients] into the institution', though advanced cases were treated. In 1912 Newsholme appointed Dr Ralph Johnstone to prepare a report on the adequacy of the facilities for the treatment of venereal disease in England and Wales, which was published in August 1913. As far as Poor Law institutions were concerned, Johnstone

> visited in all thirty-five workhouses and their infirmaries, mostly in the provinces. In these institutions special wards were in all cases provided for infective venereal cases (primary and secondary syphilis and gonorrhoea), sometimes at the infirmary, but much more often at the workhouse … Salvarsan treatment for syphilis has been given on a small scale in one or two infirmaries, and occasionally Wasserman tests are undertaken.[75]

Later that year a Royal Commission on Venereal Diseases was appointed under the chairmanship of Lord Sydenham. He accepted the assignment, provided only the question of prevention but not the moral and social issues were discussed.

Due to the care and moderation with which the Royal Commission reported in February 1916, its recommendations were welcomed by Walter Long, the president of the Local Government Board. The moving spirit in the commission was Newsholme, whose recommendations in the main were adopted, apart from a measure of disagreement as to the role of general practitioners. His experience in the administration of sanatorium benefit shaped his ideas on the control of venereal diseases. Whereas the commission was willing to allow general practitioners to administer Salvarsan, despite a conflict of expert evidence as to their competence to do so, Newsholme wished to limit the GPs' function to sending specimens for analysis to the free state laboratories and to following up treatment at the clinic by administering drugs such as mercury.[76]

Newsholme pressed the recommendations of the Royal Commission on Walter Long, convincing him to receive a deputation from the National Council for Combating Venereal Diseases, of which again Lord Sydenham was chairman. In July 1916 the Local Government Board issued compulsory regulations authorizing the universal treatment of venereal diseases. In this, he secured the backing of F. J. Willis, the assistant secretary and H. C. Monro, the permanent secretary of the board.[77] When testifying to the Royal Commission two years earlier, Newsholme suggested that the state could allow diagnosis of venereal diseases and provide facilities for treatment, although to qualify they would have to be recognized as infectious diseases, and that what was required was for the commission to seek clarification from the board on these points.

> This promptitude was in part due to the urgency caused by war conditions; but to ... Walter Long, then President of the Local Government Board, must be ascribed the chief credit for the prompt and effective action taken ... I was deeply impressed with the need for immediate action and was fearful that there might be official delay ... he received an urgent personal letter from me ... In my letter to Mr Walter Long I stated that on Monday he would receive my proposals for immediate action. On that morning I had a 'chit' from him: 'put forward your recommendations at once'. The proposals recommended by the Royal commission set out that 75 per cent of the cost should come from the National Treasury, leaving only 25 per cent to come out of local rates in counties and county boroughs. This I had urged on the Royal Commission, as I realized that without liberal help the local authorities might hesitate to act vigorously and some of them might refrain from action. Mr Long minuted to the effect that the Treasury should pay the full cost, but was persuaded to adhere to 75 per cent. He walked over to the Treasury the same day, and came back with the Chancellor's sanction to the proposed expenditure.[78]

Both the BMA and the National Health Insurance Commission insisted that the counties and county boroughs should consult with local doctors when drawing up their schemes, but all Newsholme would concede was that two doctors might be invited to attend their local venereal disease advisory committee.

In his memorandum to the Royal Commission Newsholme recommended that the treatment of venereal disease by unqualified persons should be curbed. He followed this up with a second memorandum to Lord Rhondda, the new president of the Local Government Board, dated 30 September 1916, after conferences with Lord Sydenham and Sir Thomas Barlow of the National Council, urging him to prohibit the treatment of venereal diseases by unqualified persons and to ban advertisements promising quick cures by patent medicines. Resolutions in support were passed by the Royal College of Physicians, the Association of Municipal Corporations and the County Councils Association. The Venereal Disease Act 1917 gradually suppressed treatment by unqualified practitioners, by stipulating that this section of the Act was to be enforced in areas where treatment schemes sanctioned by the Local Government Board had come fully into operation; there was a further clause proscribing advertisements for the treatment of venereal diseases and banning the advertising of drugs for the diseases. In their fourth annual report the National Council announced:

> Latterly, and owing to our activity, several cases [of prosecuting unqualified persons] have been taken up with complete success. Dr May in particular, with great energy, secured one very important conviction, and our branches have secured others.[79]

After the promulgation of orders from the Local Government Board in July 1916 authorizing local authorities to prepare schemes for the treatment of venereal diseases, a multitude of plans poured in for approval. By 1918 Newsholme had approved 127 schemes giving free treatment, after conferences between the board, medical inspectors and the local authorities, many of which were in operation, while another eighteen schemes were in the pipeline. Despite the impression conveyed by Newsholme's memoirs that a chain of clinics had been rapidly established, progress was slower and actually more patchy. By June 1918 sixty-nine clinics had been opened; a year later this had jumped to 148 for the whole of Great Britain, after which there was a much slower rate of increase, so that only twenty-four more clinics had been added by June 1920. Where possible special departments were started in general hospitals in order not to focus attention on the nature of the patient's illness; otherwise a few special clinics were set up when certain general hospitals would not cooperate. Although the BMA opposed the gratuitous treatment of all at first, their opposition was soon stilled by the generous provisions of the LGB regulations drawn up by Newsholme with the assistance of Dr Coutts and Dr J. P. Chandler. In the past, '[t]he well-to-do classes could consult specialists who kept abreast of the knowledge of the day, but the poorer classes were either left untreated, or were at the tender mercy of quack medicines'. Under the new regulations not only were all qualified doctors permitted to avail themselves of the free laboratory facilities by sending material for examination, but doctors were supplied with free Salvarsan for treating their private patients. A point emphasized by Newsholme in his regulations was that training centres should be made available for GPs to enable them to administer the new drug. Two London centres were opened as well as clinics at Nottingham and Newcastle.[80] John Eyler praised Newsholme for creating 'a public service unusual in its universality, in its reliance on treatment as the primary means of disease prevention, and in its aim of restricting treatment to qualified medical practitioners and of concentrating it in the hands of salaried medical officers'.[81]

## Infant Welfare

Between 1910 and 1916 Newsholme published five lengthy, groundbreaking reports on the causes of infant, childhood and maternal mortality. When he was the MOH of Brighton, he studied diarrheal diseases in infants and adopted measures to reduce them. On his promotion to medical officer of the Local Government Board he gave priority to his investigations of this subject before trying to implement a national scheme for infant welfare. First he rebutted Karl Pearson's suggestion that high infant mortality rates weeded out the unfit, by demonstrating that high mortality rates in the first year of life were not succeeded by lower rates in the following years. Next he dismissed the suggestion that high infant death rates were principally determined by low income levels, by pointing out that Durham mining areas had relatively high incomes and high infant mortality rates, while Jews living nearby in poorer neighbourhoods had lower infant mortality rates. Newsholme considered that there were five causes of excessive infant deaths: 'childhood infectious diseases, diarrheal diseases, bronchitis and pneumonia, convulsions and a miscellaneous category of wasting and developmental diseases'. Among the environmental conditions which undermined the health of infants to which Newsholme attached much importance were 'defective scavenging and retention of excremental matters in privies and pail closets [which] are always accompanied by excessive infantile diarrhoea'. He did not blame married women working outside the home for excessive infant deaths nor maternal ignorance and fecklessness, dismissing these as significant factors. As far as high maternal mortality was concerned, Newsholme believed that the primary factor was poor care during pregnancy and childbirth.[82]

Because manpower was a key factor in the French confrontation with Germany, the French pioneered the establishment of infant welfare centres from 1894 onwards with the objectives of the systematic supervision of infant rearing, the encouragement of breast-feeding, and the provision of sterilized milk where natural milk could not be provided.[83] At the turn of the century milk depots were set up by Seebohm Rowntree in York, Dr Newman in Finsbury and Dr McCleary in Battersea, where John Burns was the MP. Expensive to maintain, the milk depots failed to take root everywhere. In a few of these depots babies were supervised, weighed on a weekly basis for the first two years, and provided with sterilized milk in cases where mothers could not feed their infants naturally. After attending the first International Congress on Infant Welfare in Paris in 1905, a group of MOHs persuaded certain representatives of public health authorities to summon the National Conference on Infant Mortality in 1906. From a private act passed by Huddersfield in the same year sprang the movement which obtained the Notification of Births Act 1907, under which local authorities could compel parents to notify every birth within 36 hours of its occurrence to the local MOH, thus enabling health visitors to pay visits at effective times and acting as a stimulus to the foundation of new infant welfare centres, which now spread rapidly. In 1915 the Act was made compulsory, though it already covered 80 per cent of the population. Following the example of Huddersfield, fifty towns by 1905 had appointed female health visitors, who went into working-class homes to instruct young housewives in mothercraft; by 1914 their numbers had increased to 600. In 1907 another

MOH, Dr John Sykes, feeling that instructional leaflets on infant care would be unintelligible to working-class mothers, many of whom were illiterate, devised a School for Mothers in St Pancras. In 1908 the Board of Education made a grant to this school, and by 1913 twenty-seven such schools were receiving grants, though the board was hampered by restrictive regulations governing such schools.[84]

With the support of the Association of Schools for Mothers and Infant Consultations founded in 1911, Newman pressed Pease and Lloyd George early in 1914 for government grants for these voluntary centres under threat of resignation. Newsholme saw this as a stratagem which would have wrested the whole area of infant welfare away from the control of his own department in a series of carefully contrived raids. He was particularly incensed by one clause in an Education Bill which 'would have empowered Education Authorities to provide consultation centres, to make home visits, or otherwise to give medical assistance to mothers with regard to the care of their children from birth onward'. Already there had been a clash between the Local Government Board and the Board of Education over the administration of the sanatorium grant for children and despite an agreement that sanatoria for children requiring prolonged treatment should come under the Board of Education, the dispute was still smouldering in October 1914. Originally there had been a degree of cooperation between Newsholme, who was the more senior figure as a leading epidemiologist, and Newman, but during the negotiations involved in the framing of the National Insurance Bill in 1911, which was sharply criticized by Newsholme, relations between the two men deteriorated. In addition, as principal administrative secretary, Newman had direct access to his minister and outstripped his colleague in rank and political savvy and influence.[85] Whereas the Board of Education stressed that poor health in infancy and childhood could only be eradicated by the better teaching of mothers, Newsholme argued that adverse conditions in working-class homes could in addition be 'improved by public health measures, improved domestic sanitation, separate water supply for each tenement, etc., and by more adequate aid in the relief and prevention of poverty'. In 1913 Newsholme 'hoped that ere long Infant Consultations will be more generally established, and that their work will be extended so as to include the continued attendance for inspection and advice of children who have passed their first year'.[86]

Since Herbert Samuel had replaced Burns at the Local Government Board in February 1914, Newsholme was blessed with a departmental chief who was honestly intent on promoting a big development of public health, who was on good terms with Lloyd George and Christopher Addison MP, his chief adviser on health reform, and who could outmanoeuvre and outgun Pease, the president of the Board of Education, when the growing interdepartmental disputes came before the Cabinet. Meeting them at the opera one evening, Samuel had also rekindled his relations with the Webbs, intimating that he was open to their ideas. Samuel fought strongly in the Cabinet when Newsholme demanded grants-in-aid to be administered by the Local Government Board for maternity centres, infant consultations and health visitors. Added support for Newsholme came from the National Association for the Prevention of Infant Mortality, set up by Benjamin Broadbent in 1912, on which there were many representatives of health authorities, and the MOHs, while even Addison became disgusted at the interminable length of the departmental feuding and thought that Newman was prone to exaggerate the intractability of the problems being encountered. On the dispute being referred to Haldane, now Lord Chancellor, for arbitration, he awarded schools for mothers to the Board of Education and the remainder of infant welfare work to Newsholme's department. Not until 1917 was the dispute finally resolved when it was agreed that all the maternity and child welfare services should be transferred to the Ministry of Health, once it was set up.[87]

Added to the pressure to establish infant welfare centres were incessant demands for the care of children under five years of age, voiced at first solely by the Women's Labour League, which opened a baby clinic in North Kensington in 1911. Later Margaret McMillan recounted how doctors at her Deptford clinic had detected rickets in children of two or three months and how there was a need for a clause in the next Education Bill, ensuring treatment of babies in school clinics.[88] So too, Newman in 1913 drew attention to the need for the treatment of children below school age. No doubt as he developed his programme, Newman clarified his ideas in discussions with Christopher Addison, who personally elaborated these ideas to Lloyd George and who had little patience with the intransigent attitudes adopted by rival government departments.

> The point is, that, between the stage of the Infant Welfare Centre and the time children enter school, there is a mass of disability – adenoids, ears, eyes etc. – which a little sensible oversight might prevent or treatment cure, and the proposal that I originally put up to L.G. and which he is keen on developing and for which he is prepared to find the money – was to extend the facilities available for advice and help to mothers from the Infant Welfare Stage to the time when the child comes under the School Medical Service, and so fill the gap.[89]

With Haldane, Addison drew up a compromise formula, which resulted in the Board of Education having to drop proposals to be in charge of the children's welfare services after the age of two for a lesser jurisdiction of superintending children once they entered a nursery or primary school. At the behest of Herbert Samuel, the Treasury enabled the Local Government Board to give grants to local authorities to the extent of 50 per cent for approved expenditure as outlined in a circular of July 1914, including ambitious antenatal and maternity schemes, the provision of systematic advice and treatment for infants at baby clinics or infant dispensaries and the continuance of clinics for the pre-school child.[90]

Under the 1914 Budget the government was able to pay half the salary of sanitary officers, including health visitors. In 1915 the Notification of Births Act was passed, under which the notification of births and health visiting was made compulsory for the whole country and which gave county councils the powers alone possessed by sanitary authorities to make arrangements for the care of expectant and nursing mothers and young children. The infant welfare centres increased from 650 in 1915 to 1,278 in 1918; the number of health visitors employed by local authorities quadrupled from 600 in 1914 to 2,577 in 1918; and the support funds provided by the Local Government Board to local authorities climbed from £11,000 in 1914–18 to £218,000 in 1918–19.[91] From being aimed solely at the working class, health visiting was gradually extended to all households with a newborn baby. But Jane Lewis has criticized the infant and antenatal clinics as being concerned with 'the welfare of the infant[s] rather than the mother[s]', whether it was their nutrition or health, because most married women were not covered by health insurance.[92]

## Towards a Ministry of Health

By the outbreak of war in 1914, the government health insurance scheme was running into serious financial difficulties because the government actuary omitted to consider the risk of pregnancy in his calculations. Mary MacArthur contended that

> (apart from normal physical reasons) this extra sickness [in women] is due to their greater poverty, and to the character of their employment. Long hours, long standing, lack of fresh air, long intervals without food, are undeniably, especially in the case of young anaemic girls, detrimental to health, and the low wages which attach to most women's employment involve insufficient and often improper food.[93]

The Webbs at once grasped that this was an opportunity to refashion health insurance in the shape of a national health service, by transferring 'medical care connected with birth, pregnancy, and tuberculosis to a local government public health authority'. As a result of being shown a draft of a detailed critique of the insurance scheme which appeared in the *New Statesman*, Morant brought the Webbs 'a great scheme for taking the Birth and Pregnancy benefit out of insurance in order to make complete provision under the Public Health Authority at the cost of seven millions a year'. Although Lloyd George was prepared to listen to the Webbs' proposals, which were supported by Herbert Samuel, they were shelved because Masterman, whose influence over Lloyd George was still very strong, was an opponent of the existing local authorities. Only the 700,000 women who were insured under their own right were entitled to medical and sickness benefit, though the confinement period was excluded from this provision. Thanks to the efforts of Mary MacArthur and a number of women's organizations, women earning less than 1s. 6d. per day were exempted from making health insurance contributions. Whereas the working-class women's organizations, such as the Women's Trade Union League and the Women's Cooperative Guild, favoured the institution of a maternity service outside the insurance scheme, the powerful middle-class National Union of Women Workers bitterly condemned proposals to remove maternity insurance from the operation of the Act. A deputation from a conference sponsored by the Women's Trade Union League requested Masterman to make 'adequate provision from National Funds ... for women during pregnancy and when incapacitated as a result of complications arising out of confinement'. When the Departmental Committee on Sickness Benefit Claims reported in 1914, Mary MacArthur, one of its members, pleaded for 'the immediate appointment of a Royal Commission to inquire into the whole question of care, treatment, and provision before, during, and after confinement'. According to Frank Honigsbaum, the approved societies spearheaded the opposition to a municipal maternity service, as they feared that this 'could spell the end of the N.H.I.'s maternity benefit but threaten the existence of the approved society system itself'.[94]

Newsholme, once a Webb protégé, but now unfairly denigrated by them and Newman as 'weak & vain' and as a poor administrator, began pushing his own maternity schemes forward in conjunction with the expansion of the infant welfare centre. He explained in the LGB circular issued in July 1914 that government subsidies would be allotted to local authorities which made arrangements for supervising midwives, introduced antenatal clinics for expectant mothers, and provided assistance to ensure that mothers had skilled attendance at home confinements, and if necessary hospital care, where the birth involved complications.[95] Spurred by Newsholme, however, the Local Government Board in 1915 fostered the growth of antenatal clinics housed in maternity centres offering the full range of care to all, whether insured or not – and without the financial penalties imposed by the National Health Insurance Commission's tie with private practice. By 1918 there were 120 of these antenatal clinics in existence. In 1916, again under Newsholme's auspices, a bill was introduced to stimulate the development of municipal maternity services for pregnant and nursing mothers and pre-school children, but it did not become law until 1918 as the Maternity and Child Welfare Act, when local authorities were given permissive powers. With the emergence of the qualified midwife, there came greater pressure for the summoning of a doctor in emergency cases, whose fee would be paid by the local authorities, a step permitted in 1918. Apart from antenatal and postnatal care, the minor illnesses of working-class housewives were neglected by the state – perhaps the most serious defect in the state health services.[96]

The ranks of the public health reformers were split. Newsholme, the greatest proponent of the expansion of state health services for infants and those afflicted with tuberculosis and venereal disease, was isolated from Lloyd George so long as Burns remained at the Local Government Board and had forfeited the friendship of the Webbs, because of the aspersions cast by Newman. The opportunities unfolded in the 1914 Budget for establishing pathological laboratories for the free examination of samples forwarded by GPs, for the institution of nursing services, and for the inauguration of a consultancy service, where specialists attached to a clinic would give GPs a second opinion in a difficult case, were squandered – partly because of wartime cuts in government expenditure, but partly because Masterman was so determined to keep control of the new services, even the laboratories, that he wrecked the Morant–Webb scheme for a state maternity service. The Webbs' campaign for a rationalization of the health services, the empire building of members of the National Health Insurance Commission, and the increasing friction between Newman and Newsholme and their departments, all stimulated those with expertise to demand the formation of a Public Health Ministry. Already there was talk of this before the war. When Newman called on Lloyd George to discuss the School for Mothers judgement on 8 July 1914, he recorded that the chancellor 'wished me at the L.G.B. – spoke of the need of a Ministry of Health uniting Insurance & L.G.B'. On 26 July 1914, Haldane in a great public address demanded the setting up of a Ministry of Health embracing insurance and children.[97]

To Newsholme it was obvious that his own department already played such a role, but what he feared was that his rivals would use the call for a Ministry of Health to usurp the functions of his department. With the removal of Herbert Samuel's robust supportive spirit from the scene, and with the hardening of Addison's and Morant's opinions against public health authorities as they identified increasingly with the interests of the departments which they served, Newsholme became more politically isolated and vulnerable; and his department was absorbed into the new ministry before its unbridled growth rendered it too formidable to be dismembered.

Before the outbreak of the First World War, new ideas were circulating about the need for the reform of public health, both for a Ministry of Health and for a national or public health service. On 6 July 1914 Newman noted that he had a talk with Morant about the Haldane arbitration award, portending: 'The coming of a P[ublic].H[ealth]. Ministry wh. must begin by combining Insurance w[ith]. L.G.B.' Two days later he was discussing the same issue with Lloyd George.[98] The chancellor had moved a long way since 1908 when he decided to institute a national health insurance scheme based on the German model. Through the encouragement of Christopher Addison and Dr Newman, he had taken an interest in school clinics and infant welfare and Arthur Newsholme had reshaped the sanatorium benefit into a national anti-tuberculosis scheme. Addison was inclined to harp too much on the political obstacles to reform, so much so that he dismissed the suggestion that 'for £4,400,000 paid during the last year for medical benefit it would have been possible to have set up a complete medical service for insured persons, let alone dependants. It is utter nonsense.' But Lloyd George had a vision of possibilities beyond this, telling the Insurance Advisory Committee on 3 January 1913 that

> He was considering a scheme for a national medical service which might have been set up in place of the panel system, and ... [imagined] what could have been done in Bradford ... [which had a population of] 100,000 persons ... You have 7s., or 7s. 6d., that is [giving you an annual income of] £37,500. We proposed to engage fifty doctors at £500 a year; then we thought it would be necessary to have a certain number of consultants and specialist surgeons, so it was proposed that the service should include three specialist surgeons, one of them being an oculist, and that at the head of the service there should be a consulting physician, a superintendent, at a salary of £1,200 a year. The specialist surgeons were to receive £1,000 a year. We proposed to get other assistance for the doctors with the remaining £8,000. We proposed that the service should include a staff of skilled nurses. We proposed that there should be fifty nurses. You will find that there is something to spare, especially on the 7s. 6d. basis, for the provision of aids for exact diagnosis which pathology and bacteriology have placed at the disposal of modern medical science. This is what we could have done.[99]

So too, during the war years 1914–18, Newsholme added a wide-ranging anti-venereal programme and a national infant welfare service to his anti-tuberculosis programme, compelling him to recognize the need for the inauguration of a national public health service.

# 14

# Municipal Housing and Town Planning

One answer to the housing problem was to encourage the development of municipal enterprise. The principal planning advantage which municipalities enjoyed over the private builder was that they could borrow money on more favourable terms, as they could always fall back on the security of rates. Yet so little use had been wrung out of this advantage that nationally only 0.25 per cent of the houses had been erected by them. The cost of slum clearance and reconstruction was thought to be prohibitive. Only very large bodies could undertake such schemes, working expenses were high, and a huge price was paid for land and as compensation to slum owners. Until the rise of the New Liberalism, and more importantly the Labour movement, the housing question figured little in local politics. All schemes for slum demolition had to be paid for out of the rates, and the publicans and the shopocracy, who occupied premises of a value disproportionate to their net income, felt that an undue share of the burden fell on them and used their preponderant influence on the local town councils against the implementation of schemes under the Artisan Dwellings Act.[1] Then there were those who condemned the municipal building of houses as unfair competition with private enterprise. For instance, there was a group on Manchester City Council who were so convinced of the superior methods of the speculative builder in constructing working-class houses that when the Public Health Committee purchased a large site for development in 1900, they blocked scheme after scheme, allowing a mere 150 houses to be built; the greater part of the site lay derelict for twenty years and the interest on the money borrowed became a punitive charge.[2]

The formation of the Workmen's National Housing Council in 1898 presaged a new era. The fact that its income barely exceeded the £100 level makes it easy to underestimate its significance. In particular, the widespread support of trades councils – by 1909 no fewer than sixty-six had taken out subscriptions – created a strong opinion at the local level for better housing, while everywhere, in the words of its 1913 report, 'it has helped to strengthen the Labour movement on the constructive side with knowledge and initiative'. Exclusively a working-class organization, with a power base of national union organizations, some thirty of which were adherents by 1912, trade union branches and trades councils, it both contributed to the rise of the Labour party and gained in thrust and prestige at the centre of affairs as the Labour party's electoral support widened. Alderman Fred Knee, the individual who rapidly built up the Labour party in London, was its energetic secretary; George Lansbury, a future leader of the parliamentary Labour party, served as one of its vice-presidents; C. W. Bowerman MP, the chief Labour party expert on housing and transit questions and later general secretary of the TUC, was its formidable president. Another important figure was W. C. Steadman, who was vice-chairman of the parliamentary committee of the TUC, and also served as its president before 1914. By the turn of the century, housing councils were active in Liverpool, Leeds, Sheffield, Greenock, Oxford and Hastings; at the LCC elections in 1904, of forty-eight recommended candidates, thirty-two were returned; annually meetings were arranged with the National Association for the Extension of Workmen's Trains to coincide with LCC conferences.[3]

Behind the various measures advocated by the Workmen's Council was the overriding object of enabling municipalities to undertake large-scale building operations. The government was to lend the municipalities money at a ridiculously low rate of interest, at some 2 per cent per annum for 100 years; an additional source of revenue was to be provided by taxing ground rents; from 1905 onwards, increasing emphasis was placed on Exchequer grants-in-aid to local authority sinking funds. Land was to be obtained by local authorities both inside and outside their districts at a price based on twenty-five times the annual value fixed for taxation purposes. The slums were to be eradicated not by buying up substandard housing, but by setting up a strong counter-attraction which would rob them of their value; moreover, rents were to be controlled by fair rent courts to protect tenants from unscrupulous private landlords.[4] When the Housing Bill was before the Commons in 1908 and 1909, the Workmen's Council tried without avail to insert an amendment creating an imperial subsidy for housing; earlier the prime minister and Burns had begrudged them an interview on the subject. One concession of importance was extracted from the government: in future persons in receipt of Poor Law grants were not to be disqualified from becoming municipal tenants. Nonetheless, the ideas of the Workmen's Council triumphed with a dazzling swiftness; soon after the failure of the 1909 Housing and Town Planning Act, most of the housing and land societies slowly became converted to the policy of municipal housing, and during the First World War the government introduced the equivalent of fair rent courts by passing the Rent and Mortgage Restriction Act in 1915, which froze the rents of dwellings with a low rateable value.[5]

The other answer to the housing problem was controlled suburban development. As George Cadbury asserted, it was the work of generations to remedy the evils of the past, but they could at once prevent their multiplication. Land in cities was expensive – hence the houses in working-class areas were packed closely together, running up to forty houses per acre in comparison with a maximum of fourteen houses per acre in garden cities. Nevertheless, the rents for this type of house were high, for the more people were squeezed into an area, the steeper the ground rents tended to become, while the higher rates of large towns comprised anything from 20 per cent to 40 per cent of the rent charge. Because the bulk of the working-class houses were crammed together in narrow streets, they could easily degenerate into slums, a process that was being duplicated all over again in the working-class housing boom on the perimeter of the great cities which reached its peak around 1902, though in some parts of the country there was no downswing in house building until 1914.[6] Outside London, for example, an outer ring of villages at the end of the tram routes in West London, Leytonstone, Clapton, Stoke Newington, Finsbury Park, Edmonton, Tottenham, Finchley and Acton, utilized by persons ejected from town centres due to the population explosion, were becoming transformed into sordid and grim slums; in one place the yet unfinished rows of mean houses ended in green fields, where all the sports facilities were going to be built over; elsewhere each room in spacious houses was occupied by different families, and in streets not ten years old drunks wandered about before midday.[7]

The need, as the Land Enquiry Committee recognized, was to obtain cheap building land outside the towns for carefully planned suburban development; such land could easily be purchased near small towns, but ingrained habit had prevented its use. Cheap building land would be difficult to procure in the proximity of large centres of population, but given adequate transit facilities, could have been brought within reach. So far there was little conscious opening up of new areas; the Cheap Trains Act of 1883 did not throw upon the railways the duty of tapping fresh neighbourhoods, but merely of providing trains where a demand existed. What was required was the deliberate colonization of new areas, either through the instrumentality of a publicly controlled transport system or through the tighter supervision of the great railway companies. Among the earliest objectives of the National Housing Reform Council was the increase, cheapening and quickening of the means of transit by tram and rail through the exercising of public ownership, while mention should be made of the National Association for the Extension of Workmen's Trains, a sister body of the Workmen's Housing Council. Reconvened in 1907, the Browning Hall Conference through pressure on the LCC persuaded the Liberal government to grant the rudiment of a Traffic Board, thereby adopting a long-standing proposal of Charles Booth. Housing reformers averred that every opportunity donated for the freer growth of the city in the suburbs would tend to reduce congestion at the centre, causing the rents to drop, thereby stimulating slum clearance.[8]

At any rate, the housing and town planning reform movement in Britain, so far as the middle-class reformers were concerned, sprang from the Liberal land associations. When housing experts connected with the Liberal party wished to formulate their ideas on the housing of the poor in 1890, they had to summon a mixed assemblage of radical and land reform associations. Under Fabian influence the key financial and compensation committee of the conference, of which both Sidney Webb and Graham Wallas were members, decided that slum property should be purchased at its break-up value and that municipalities should be permitted to levy a special local income tax and death duty to scrape together the funds for housing projects; the rural committee of the conference, despite the fact that it lacked Fabian representatives, concluded that so long as private enterprise did not find it profitable to provide rural housing, the task must devolve on the state out of the proceeds of the probate duty, a sum amounting to £2 million.[9] Yet what is clear is that in the 1890s, because of the failure of the Fabians to develop a convincing policy for municipal housing and the equal failure of the Social Democratic Federation to excite interest in council housing by specific campaigns, the municipal socialists in the ranks of the parliamentary Liberal party were swamped by land reformers. After the Liberal debacle at the 1895 election, there was a gradual crystallization of interest among land reformers in the housing question. In 1895 the

Land Law Reform Association added prompt legislation to provide the workers in town and country with suitable housing accommodation to its programme. Both the Garden City Association and the National Housing Reform Council were nursed in their infancy by the Land Nationalization Society: the Garden City Association was born in 1899 in the offices of the society and drew its leading members from the parent body; the National Housing Reform Council, which came into being in 1900, long continued to use the society's offices as its London headquarters, and its initial propaganda campaign was arranged by the society. Besides, measures of land reform and control predominated among the objects of the National Council when they were drawn up, as we should expect to be the case, because most of its founders were well-known Liberals.[10] Another connecting link between the land reform movement and the Liberal party was the campaign for the taxation of ground values.

Just because the housing reformers were so intimately connected with the land reform movement, they considered the housing problem in its widest possible aspects. Essentially town planning comprised two ideas: control by the state and municipalities of land use in general; and control by the public authorities of particular areas that had been specifically designated for building purposes. By the turn of the century many housing reformers advocated a rapid suburban development as a means of solving the housing problem; a conference called by the Land Law Reform Association in 1901 would not go beyond recommending a simpler and cheaper procedure for their acquisition of land by public authorities and an improved means of transit. Lough added, though, that municipalities should be allowed to buy land a few years before it was needed, if it was cheap – a step in the direction of planned land use. Herbert Samuel declared in 1902 that the housing shortage should be relieved by encouraging workers to move out to the suburbs so as to leave room at the centre; Parliament and the local authorities were to cheapen the means of transit by running more workmen's trains and by augmenting the tramway services; moreover, local authorities were to be permitted to buy the land when it was cheap and hold it for future needs. In 1905 a committee of young Liberals, including C. R. Buxton and Masterman, in their manifest entitled 'Towards a Social Policy' argued for the implementation of similar proposals and held out little hope of municipal housing coping with the demand for homes occasioned by population growth. However, the National Housing Reform Council went further and listed among its aims the conferring on local authorities the power to acquire and hold land compulsorily, both within and beyond their borders, at a price based on the assessment of such land for local and imperial taxation. So too, in actual fact, if not in name, the housing societies were already proposing the planned development of new working-class housing estates. The Workmen's Council wanted the development of these estates to be entrusted to the municipalities, as they would not indulge in jerry building and the misdemeanours of the speculative builders; the National Council considered that the land acquired by the municipalities should be leased under stringent by-laws which would render impossible the overcrowding of people in houses or the overcrowding of houses on the land.[11]

T. C. Horsfall acted as the marriage broker between the land reform movement and the German town planning tradition, and must be classed as the *Great Disseminator* of the concept of town planning in Britain. Originally the National Housing Reform

Council tried to win over an inter-party group of MPs interested in housing to a policy ranging from the granting of loans by the Treasury at the market rate of interest, and the modification of building regulations to meet local needs, to the appointment of a central Housing Commission, but this policy was so obviously ill-designed to solve a problem of daunting dimensions that it was quickly shelved. Nor could the National Council look to the Workmen's Council for inspiration, as the middle-class reformers disliked both fair rent courts and cheap government loans for local housing projects, while the Labour men were suspicious of the National Council's proposal for allowing local authorities to lease back land which they had acquired to private building firms. At the end of 1903 the National Housing Reform Council was urgently searching for ideas on how to prevent the building of new slums on the borders of large cities in response to the unprecedented rash of working-class suburban housing development, as the long building cycle commencing in 1890 reached its peak in the years 1902–3. Just as the 1890 Housing Act crystallized out of the deliberations of the Royal Commission on Housing of 1885, which followed in the wake of the earlier housing boom from the mid-1860s to 1876, so the 1909 Housing and Town Planning Act was the by-product of the 1890 housing boom. Horsfall, a settlement enthusiast with an entrée to Canon Barnett's circle of social reformers based at Toynbee Hall and himself an influential member of the National Council, was meanwhile writing his book on *The Example of Germany* (1904) and publicizing his ideas by an address to a civic group in Manchester and by confidential discussions with housing experts in Liverpool and other towns. His own study, undertaken at the behest of fellow members of the Manchester and Salford Citizen's Association for the Improvement of Unwholesome Dwellings and the Surroundings of the People, one of the many local housing associations springing up in this period, was complementary to T. R. Marr's sociological survey of the housing problem in Manchester and set out a course of remedies. During the winter of 1903–4 Horsfall converted his associates on the National Council, principally Alderman Thompson and Henry Aldridge, to the need for town planning on the lines of the German achievements; after carefully sounding out MPs and other public figures, the latter reconvened the inter-party group of MPs interested in housing, headed by Sir John Gorst, Thomas Macnamara and Claude Hay, to win their approval for the new policy.[12]

The National Council was now ready to carry its proposals to a wider public, embracing the local opinion leaders within the municipalities and the trade union world, and sponsored a housing conference in Bournville on 9 July 1904, attended by 200–300 delegates from the health and housing committees of many English towns, representatives of rural district councils and trade unions. Here a resolution was passed calling the attention of the president of the Local Government Board to the need for a measure to enable local authorities to plan all new housing areas in order to ensure that there was an ample provision of air, light and space, and gardens, thus rendering impossible the development of new slums. This was the first public acclamation of the idea of town planning in Britain and thus there is no need to seek the origins of the town planning movement in Britain in the report of the Inter-Departmental Committee on Physical Deterioration, whose publication date was 29 July, some three weeks later – quite a few months after a host of *Lesser Disseminators*, who were active in propagating the lessons gleaned from the experience of the German municipalities, had undergone a thorough exposure to Horsfall's credo. In any case, Horsfall's evidence was responsible for the favourable outcome of the Inter-Departmental Committee's deliberations.[13] So too, the report failed to galvanize public opinion. At the end of 1904 the National Council expressed regret that despite all the publicity of the past year, their financial position and membership figures had not improved. Even more important, the report failed to convert the Conservative government, although while Walter Long remained at the Local Government Board he expressed sympathy towards the idea of town planning. However, his successor Gerald Balfour, when replying to a deputation from the National Council in July 1905, could only promise minor improvements in the local authorities' attention to their sanitary duties and fobbed off the plea for town planning with trite phrases about German bureaucratic methods being inapplicable to English conditions.[14]

Again, it is important to stress that Britain, like the United States and her Australasian Dominions, where towns were laid out on a gridiron pattern, was slipping behind the rest of Continental Europe, especially Germany, Austria, Switzerland, Holland and the Scandinavian countries in regard to town planning. However, nineteenth-century town planning was confined to giving old urban centres cosmetic treatment, that is, to constructing grandiose palatial buildings in magnificent surroundings as a means of bolstering autocratic regimes and to developing spacious quarters for the fashionable and wealthy.[15] Here great landlords built estates to house the affluent in Edinburgh, Bath and in the famed London squares; but as John R. Kellett has remarked, in dismissing an attempt to instal the great landlord in a 'creative role as a town planner', 'the whole idea of the great estate was, in fact, to deny that the lower orders, retail trades or public transport existed, and no rational planning could be carried out on this basis'.[16] Apart from the work of some German municipalities in the closing decades of the nineteenth century, Aldridge asserted,

> it must ... be recognized that the type of town planning adopted in most continental towns is fundamentally bad, for the people are closely packed in tenement houses, with the result that behind the spectacular boulevards and imposing streets of Berlin, Vienna, and many other cities, conditions in regard to housing exist which are truly appalling.[17]

According to Horsfall, under the Prussian law of 1875, German municipalities could prepare extension plans dealing with the chief streets and other public places that would be necessary within the space of a few years, and adopt a policy for new estates and street improvements that would result in the provision of wide and tree-planted boulevards for the main traffic flows; and under a 1901 law, towns could buy up tracts of land on the cheap and hoard them for future needs. Moreover, the land around the old urban core was zoned, so that the further out of town one proceeded, the fewer were the number of houses that could be erected per acre and the more sacrosanct were the restrictions on the heights of buildings.[18]

Since housing conditions differed so much in Germany, where the poor and the rich shared large tenement blocks, with the bourgeoisie living on the lower floors and the working class on the upper storeys at the back of the flats overlooking sunless courtyards, the function of town planning had the purpose of creating a salubrious environment for tenement dwellers, and it is possible to conclude that Horsfall's borrowing of the German town planning lore was genuinely creative and innovatory, in that he proposed its use against the new slums created by the 1875 Public Health Act and the small, high-density houses of the English worker.[19]

No clearer estimate of Horsfall's role in the early town planning movement can be found than that contained in a letter written by Henry Aldridge, the secretary of the National Council, to George Cadbury in 1909:

> the real and effective work which has produced legislative action (as distinct from private effort) in the town planning clauses of the bill [the 1909 Housing and Town Planning Act] had been done first, and absolutely foremost of all, by the strenuous educational efforts of one good man – Mr Horsfall. By the publication of his book on *The Example of Germany*, he performed the national service of showing how the creation of new slums could be prevented by legislative effort. The great honour belongs to Mr Horsfall. By persistent effort and personal sacrifice – for his books have always been published at a loss – he has educated us all.[20]

Similarly, Horsfall told Cadbury:

> so far as I know, the Council took ground which had never been occupied in this country in urging that the power of planning which had given such good results at Bournville, Letchworth & c. in this country and in many foreign towns, should be given TO ALL TOWN COUNCILS in this country.[21]

All outstanding housing reform advocates belonged to the National Housing Reform Council, a body founded in 1900, including Horsfall, George Cadbury, W. H. Lever, Seebohm Rowntree, William Thompson, Henry Aldridge, Harold Shawcross and John Nettlefold. Above all, it drew into the service of the community a group of middle class town councillors and businessmen, who might otherwise have devoted their talents exclusively to the amassing of private fortunes. When Alderman Thompson died, Horsfall described his death as a 'loss of one of the great workers for improving the lives of the people', and Shawcross praised the founder of the National Council, declaring: 'That determination to solve the question of Housing and Town Planning possessed his heart and soul, and he went on his way with high courage and unconquerable resolution.' Until 1913 the National Council did not acquire permanent headquarters in London but was run from its secretary's house in Leicester, which was within easy reach of other provincial centres such as Manchester, Derby, Liverpool, Sheffield and Newcastle, where its main body of supporters were found to be in charge of a flourishing network of some nineteen middle-class local housing associations in 1907. In Manchester, where a comparatively small set of people cared greatly about the housing conditions of the poor, their society was 'partly the cause of every improvement that has been affected. It has cooperated with most public-spirited members of the Town Council.' The National Council was in receipt of a sizeable income and with many of its principal figures being bigwigs in the local Liberal party organizations, it was politically very potent; in 1907–8 its income rose to £2,500, usually it was in the region of £1,000. In 1912–13 its income equalled that of all the other housing and land societies combined. Even so it only managed to strike a financial balance through the munificence of Cadbury and Lever, since such additional sources of income as drawing room meetings were not open to the National Council because of the unglamorous nature of its work. Increasingly the National Council looked to local authorities for sustenance; by 1910–11 with a contribution of £570. 4s. 6d., they formed the largest group of subscribers to the National Council.[22]

What appeared to be a growing national interest in town planning shown by a widening circle of bodies was really the result of propaganda projected by *Lesser Disseminators* in the ranks of the National Council operating in these organizations, so that it was undoubtedly true that it was almost exclusively the magnificent political campaigning of the National Council which placed a town planning measure on the statute book. Deputations were sent to the Free Church Council and the Archbishop of Canterbury to win their support; some success was achieved here in that the bishops made strenuous efforts in the Lords to reintroduce the vital registry of housing clause on behalf of the council. While a few national unions, such as the Boilermakers Union and the Amalgamated Society of Engineers, were affiliated to the National Council, the cooperative and friendly societies would not respond to its overtures; and to keep working-class opinion on its side, apart from a particularly harmonious relationship which it enjoyed with the Northumberland Miners' Association, it was left to operate stealthily through the Workmen's Council, by staging a joint conference to coincide with the annual gathering of the TUC; the adoption of town planning reform led to more cordial relations between it and the workers' society from 1904 onwards.[23] Probably its greatest triumph was in coaxing the aid of the municipalities to town planning, by paying for a column in the *Municipal Journal* to publicize its activities, by holding special conferences in the main urban centres from 1904, and by opening a bureau of housing in 1908 which published papers on the various aspects of town planning and on the latest designs and materials for house building. One consequence was that the Association of Municipal Corporations, under the vigorous prompting of Councillor Nettlefold, dispatched a deputation to the government in August 1907 to stress the urgency of town planning reform. Also through their revival of the inter-party group on housing, the National Council mobilized a group of 130 MPs, mainly Liberal and Labour, who were sympathetic to the cause of town planning.[24]

The 1909 Act owed little to the influence of the Garden City Association; as Alderman Thompson, himself a founder member, explained to George Cadbury:

> we always thought that [it] was established not to do municipal work, but to develop Garden Cities as advocated by Mr Ebenezer Howard on voluntary and cooperative lines, and to extend those ideas by the promotion of new and improved building areas on commercial lines.[25]

Unless it was formulated in conjunction with an ambitious land policy, there was little hope for controlled suburban development. But on this vital point the association refused to endorse the policy of the National Council. Aldridge in his capacity as joint secretary of the Land and Housing Reform Committee, which organized the 1907 land demonstration to stiffen the resolve of Campbell-Bannerman's government, asked them to send representatives, but they refused because they disagreed with the suggested land policy. Nor was Letchworth of much use as a model housing estate, as hardly any houses had been constructed at the start of 1906. If people wished to see town planning in practice, they went to Bournville, as did Walter Runciman, then Burns' under-secretary, or better still were conducted on a tour of the German municipal projects under the auspices of the National Council. Although the Garden City Association began to take an increasing interest in town planning along German lines in 1907, their activities were but a fraction of the effort expended by the National Council and their zeal was stimulated by the ubiquitous John Nettlefold.[26]

At the end of 1906 the National Council sent an important deputation of housing reformers to present their scheme to the Local Government Board. 'I do not think that it can be doubted', Horsfall wrote to Cadbury, 'that it was the deputation to Sir H. Campbell-Bannerman and Burns which led the Government to prepare the Housing, Town-Planning &c. Bill.' Transport, housing, land – all were seen as facets of one problem, and at both the central and local level they were to be handled by a single authority. A Central Commission would map out a series of town planning areas; for each of the districts they would establish a statutory committee, two-thirds of whose members would be nominated by the local authorities, while the remainder would be experts chosen by the commissioners. The statutory committees would induce local councils to draw up plans for urban expansion, dealing especially with the belts of land surrounding the towns and prepared in good time so as to meet future needs on the lines adopted by the German towns and combined districts. The Central Commission and the statutory committees would buy or help local councils to purchase large tracts of land at a value fixed by the tax commissioners, which would be held for future needs. In addition, town planning methods would cheapen expenses by relaxing by-laws relating to the construction of small streets and the use of new building materials.[27] Unremitting pressure was maintained on the government by the National Council throughout 1907 until a bill was introduced in the following years, when they organized a conference of municipal and trade union representatives to discuss the bill at length.[28]

Both the housing and town planning provisions of the 1909 Housing and Town Planning Act were insubstantial. When the bill was referred to a standing committee in 1908, Burns, time and time again siding with his departmental officials, clashed constantly with the housing reformers on it, such as Dickson-Poynder, Vivian, Morrell and Lyttleton, who were briefed by Aldridge, the secretary of the National Council, in the committee room. The entries in Burns' diary betray his attitude quite clearly. 'Reformers sulky and indifferent. Worked and worried through.' Again, 'Literally revelled in repelling and winning agst H[ousing] R[eformers] who resent a workman knowing more than they.'[29] The housing provisions were ruined by the opposition of the local authority associations, so that progressive MPs like A. H. Scott, an influential voice in the Association of Municipal Corporations, bitterly attacked the efforts of the housing reformers; granted that the government would not concede a system of house-to-house inspection by local authorities, they nevertheless reluctantly agreed to the compilation of a quinquennial housing register in 1909, when the National Council firmly pressed this proposal on them. After securing the withdrawal of this concession with the help of Burns, the local authorities next knocked out the clause granting MOHs security of tenure. Added together, these amendments completely blunted the effectiveness of the inspectorial system and were a serious blow to those who proclaimed that the state should assist a vast programme of house construction because no assessment of housing needs as a basis for future action was envisaged.[30]

Over fifty trades councils and other bodies were induced by the Workmen's Council to set up a special local committee to spur the local authorities into action; the influence of these bodies was most marked in Lancashire, Yorkshire, the Midlands, Wales and London. During the first year of the Act's operation representations were made in respect of more houses than in two years under the previous legislation. However, a majority of the councils remained inactive: in the year ending 31 March 1913, 58 per cent of the urban authorities issued no closing orders under the 1909 Act, and 54 per cent did not deem it worthwhile sending notices ordering landlords to maintain their dwellings in a reasonable condition. So long as large-scale municipal house building remained expensive, local authorities temporized about proceeding against the stock of inferior housing when there was an appalling shortage of accommodation.[31]

Equally disastrous was the failure of town planning reform to make much headway. In part this was due to the unimaginative outlook of Burns, to his stolid qualities that impaired his grasp of the need for comprehensive reform, and to his distinctive incapacity for handling big issues. Thus the idea of regional town planning authorities was brushed aside with vapid phrases about the unsuitability of ad hoc authorities; town planning was to be piecemeal and fragmentary. Nonetheless, a major portion of the blame for the nebulousness of the planning provisions of the Act must be loaded on the Cabinet as a whole. It is idle to pretend that the question of planning could be entirely divorced from controlled land use and from means to facilitate the acquisition of cheap agricultural land for suburban development; it was questionable whether the government was prepared to implement sweeping proposals conferring on local authorities powers to acquire land compulsorily for the future expansion of towns and it is certain that they thought that by whittling down the bill, they could avoid a collision with the Lords on the land issue.

Nothing was more foolish: the bill did not escape the spleen of the Lords and the propertied interests, while – deprived of its essential pivot – town planning reform never moved much beyond the starting line. Indeed, so rampant was timorous counsel among the land reformers that Alderman Thompson had to defend most strongly the essential power of land purchase by municipal authorities in connection with planning schemes, which others wished to omit from the bill through fear of losing everything. A vital concession was squeezed from the government by the landowners in the standing committee of the Commons in 1908, whereby local authorities were saddled with the obligation of consulting landlords frequently and in the most minute detail in regard to town planning schemes. When the bill was sent to the Lords in 1909, they made it optional for local authorities to draw up planning schemes. Between them the Act and the 1909 Budget did something to render land cheaper for building purposes: the latter forbade landowners to claim compensation, if their land was used for housing of low density. Further, the parsimony of the Exchequer held up the formation of a separate housing department, without which local authorities could not be stirred to attend to their housing and planning duties, and even Burns had expressed the desire to expand the old housing department of the board. Among a series of further concessions demanded by the Lords was the abandonment of a clause limiting the number of houses per acre, a point which Burns had only yielded after relentless pressure by the National Council. To stiffen the resistance of the government, the National Council called a conference, which demanded that the administration drop the measure rather than accept it in so mutilated a form – a protest that stiffened the government's resolve. Apart from passing a weak resolution and sending telegrams to peers, the Garden City Association did nothing.[32]

The National Housing Reform Council, now renamed the National Housing and Town Planning Council, devoted most of its energy until the outbreak of the war to exhorting the local authorities to prepare planning schemes, instructing them by means of pamphlets and conferences. In all this the Garden City Association played a subordinate role, despite their protests, merely nominating six persons to serve on the advisory town planning committee of the former body. Unable to approach anywhere near their target of a £5,000 fund for town planning or to pump much life into its new branch organization, the National Council still succeeded in fanning the enthusiasm of the localities for planning reform, by holding, for example, nine conferences in 1911–12 attended by 1,400 representatives from local authorities. On the other hand, the local workmen's associations soon gave up trying to do anything about town planning, as they found the Act too intricate.[33] Then again, the newly hatched projects were savaged by local vested interests. J. S. Nettlefold asserted:

> The Act applies to undeveloped districts and it is the land and building speculators who are chiefly interested in such districts. It is worth their while to spend money and take trouble to obtain influence on local councils. Even in larger places they have great weight and this accounts in no small degree for the very inadequate results achieved up to the present. They are looked upon as experts, and doubtless they are experts in the old discredited method of estate development, but they do not understand and do not want to understand the new method ... Local officials have long been accustomed to working with men of this stamp and their influence is too often seen in a number of arrangements in the interests of property.[34]

Of course, the paramount obstacle to a vigorous administration of the Act was the Local Government Board itself. Hampered by lack of requisite staff, the board slowly plodded through schemes which had been submitted for its endorsement. By 1914 some sixty-six schemes were under various stages of consideration by the board and 125 local authorities informed the board that they had schemes pending. Only two of the sixty-six schemes had been approved by the board. On the other hand, the total area covered by the sixty-six schemes was 110,962 acres, which amounted to less than a fifth of the area under the control of the local authorities.[35] Worse still, the sullen, mean-spirited attitude of the board prevented a flexible administration of the Act. By insisting that they must state the exact purpose for which each parcel of land was required, by paying too much attention to details, the board stopped authorities from buying huge tracts of land on the cheap. The whole efficacy of the town planning scheme hinged on the provision of adequate means of access; yet the board would not permit tramway extensions to be incorporated in town planning schemes on the grounds that tramways came under a different department. So too, the new estates had to offer advantageous terms so as to attract industry, but the board would not sanction the linking up of railway sidings in factory areas with the company lines in the East Birmingham scheme, and was equally obdurate in declining to relax antiquated by-laws in town planning schemes. Incredibly enough through the imposition of a number of warrantless conditions, the board abnegated the right of local authorities to collect half the betterment from the properties improved by their scheme. Just prior to 1914 the National Council formulated a demand for fresh legislation, whereby town planning would be made compulsory in urban areas and rural planning would be introduced to prevent the growth of urban streets in these areas, but despite winning the sympathetic ear of Herbert Samuel, who had replaced Burns, the outbreak of war ruined this effort.[36]

With the manifest failure of the town planning provisions of the 1909 Act to relieve the shortage of housing accommodation, the reformers of all parties were won over to the viewpoint of the Workmen's Council and accepted the necessity of large-scale municipal intervention to end the house famine. The lead in housing reform, however, was now taken by the Unionist Social Reform Council, a group of progressive Conservative MPs, including J. W. Hills, Leopold Amery, Steel-Maitland, F. E. Smith, Lord Henry Bentick and Waldorf Astor, some of whom, Hills and Amery included, had close links with Fabian circles. 'The younger school of Conservative thought', declared F. E. Smith, 'lays stress upon the undoubted fact that the party will never conquer a majority adequate to its purposes until it re-establishes itself in the confidence of the great industrial centres', illustrating that progressive Conservatism was a response to the earlier achievements of the Liberal governments of 1906–9.[37]

Apart from its forays into Poor Law and educational reform, the Unionist Council immersed itself increasingly in housing reform. Sir Arthur Griffith-Boscawen MP, an ex-chairman of the LCC housing committee, with the help of colleagues on the council and the advice of experts from nine major municipalities, drafted a Housing Bill on the model of the 1908 Housing of the Working Classes Ireland Act, which was introduced in 1912 and again in 1913 and 1914. Under the stimulus of cheap state loans and government grants provided by the Irish Act, 34,307 cottages were built up to 31 May 1911. The chief proposals of the Conservative bill were the establishment of a Housing Commission under the control of the Local Government Board, consisting of an urban and rural housing expert together with a medical officer of health, who would travel around the country, pointing out the necessity for slum clearance schemes and for the construction of more homes in rural areas; and the provision of an annual imperial grant of £500,000 to stimulate house building, accompanied by stringent powers to compel local authorities to carry out their responsibilities. To critics who suggested that a general rise in wages would be a better plan, Sir Ranulf Baker MP replied in 1913:

> [it] will take a long time to bring about. It is not going to be brought about at once by the proposal for a minimum wage or by Tariff Reform ... until economic

conditions obtain we shall not get a sufficient increase in wages to enable the working classes in rural districts to pay an economic rent.[38]

Despite the fact that the second reading of the bill in 1912 and 1913 was carried by large majorities, despite the fact that all the land and housing associations, organizations mostly aligned to the Liberal party, supported the measure, including the National Housing Council, the National Land and Home League and the Workmen's Council, Burns succeeded in blocking the bill in committee; but his victory was more than a personal triumph in parliamentary skirmishing and represented both the considered view of his Cabinet colleagues and divisions and discord rife among land reformers. 'I dislike the Bill', Burns confided in his diary for 1912, 'hate the Grant and abominate Commissioners for this purpose', which indicated a considerable hardening of his views under departmental pressures since 1906.

As I expected Tories and socialists united against us. We were nervous in argument, deficient in numbers, failed by our friends and the result was a rebuff ... Personally I have been anxious to resign and resume my place in the Labour movement.[39]

In the Commons, Burns – in a tone that was to grow shriller in later years – argued from his experience as chairman of the Labour party on the LCC:

we all of us took the line that charity rents through rates or taxes were nothing less than a bonus to employers in aid of low wages ... In these days ... economic fledglings from East End settlements think that the last word in housing reform is said when they delivered a speech, after they have motored though a London slum in a taxi-cab.[40]

The bill was blocked in committee partly by Liberal anti-social reformers, partly by extreme single taxers; yet on the second reading, progressive Liberal MPs such as Christopher Addison, Byles, Carr-Gomm and Ponsonby trekked into the division lobbies against the bill – a fact which underscores the deep divisions among housing and land reformers on the issue.

Henrietta Barnett recalled:

It was with great reluctance that my husband ... came to see that municipal housing was necessary ... Among his reasons for deprecating the covering of large areas with town houses by the Municipality was his fear of creating a privileged class whose vote would be influenced by private needs, and when massed in one district, be unduly influential. He foresaw the evils of huge blocks of buildings without freedom for development of individuality.[41]

George Cadbury to the last opposed the principle of a state subsidy, maintaining that the solution to the housing problem lay in the decentralization of industry, combined with the policy of the compulsory purchase of land at its rateable value. So too, Seebohm Rowntree, Lloyd George's mentor on housing problems, still condemned the grant of a government subsidy in 1914.[42] It has been argued by H. V. Emy, in an attempt to bolster his reputation as a percipient social reformer, that had not the 1914 war intervened, Lloyd George would have embarked on a massive national anti-slum campaign by means of a state housing programme. Close scrutiny of the Land Enquiry Committee's Report and Lloyd George's subsequent action reveals that he had not broken out of the rigid mould of an orthodox and old-fashioned land campaigner, who believed that far-reaching land reforms could abolish all the problems of housing. The urban section of the Land Report, when examining the problem of how to provide decent housing accommodation for those whose income was deficient, concluded that if the government had decided that agricultural employers should give their workers a wage adequate to pay an economic rent, there was no reason why similar legislation should not be applied to all urban workers; and that the arguments against a subsidy for rural housing applied with equal force to urban housing. Instead of the government stimulating local authorities by positive means such as subsidies, it was to withhold block grants from local authorities that neglected their housing and other duties. Shifting from their preliminary position of providing a housing subsidy from the proceeds of a tax on land values, the Land Enquiry Committee claimed:

> Whatever the advantages which are claimed for throwing upon Local Authorities the work of building houses for all their working population, it is not likely that such a course will be adopted in the life-time of the present generation ... On one point, certainly, all reformers will be agreed, viz, that if the adequate supply of houses is to be ensured the public authorities must provide them, should other agencies [meaning public utility companies] fail.[43]

Lloyd George's speech at Middlesbrough on 9 November 1913 outlining the government's policy for the town worker closely followed this line of thinking and was no doubt based on the recommendations of the Land Enquiry Committee, which was certainly in his hands by then. 'The housing problem is very largely a question of relieving the pressure on the centre of town. Congestion means overcrowding, overcrowding means excessive rents, and overcrowding and excessive rents mean between them slums', was how Lloyd George began his reflections on housing reform. He continued that '[i]t means cheap quick transit facilities', and ensuring that town councils should be able to buy land at market value in anticipation of future needs. 'And then we come to the poor residuum of the population who, if you gave them a new house, could not pay for it ... we propose to deal with that by extending our wages boards so far as to give the people who labour a fair day's wage for a fair day's work.' As he advised Asquith in November: 'The Trade Boards Act (1909) to be extended to other trades so as to reduce the number of those whose wages are insufficient for them to pay a commercial rent for decent houses.' For the chancellor 'was in favour of giving the working class a living wage. But he was against giving them charity rents.' In the next chapter we shall see that while trade boards raised existing wage levels, they did not necessarily provide a living wage that enabled tenants to afford market rents. Lloyd George also wanted '[m]easures to be taken to secure greater regularity of employment among those who are non-casual labourers, to enable them to pay a commercial rent. The opening up of the unused resources of the land would contribute to this result' – another example of misplaced optimism and not a coherent policy.[44] Again, Lloyd George deliberately obstructed the Conservative Housing Bill by refusing an Exchequer grant, indicating that he had scant regard for government housing subsidies. In fact, it is doubtful whether Lloyd George, like so many middle-class reformers, had a proper comprehension of the housing conditions and needs of the working class. As late as the end of April 1914, Riddell noted a conversation in his diary which does much to undermine the credibility of Lloyd George as an ardent housing reformer:

> Long talk regarding cottage accommodation, L.G. contending that one living-room is sufficient for all purposes. I said we should try to create a higher standard, and that people should not be required to live, cook, and do washing in one room. In twenty or ten years' time, I am confident that leading democratic statesmen will express very different opinions about housing. Millions of people are living under deplorable conditions.[45]

Within the National Housing Council, there was a growing body of opinion in favour of government aid to local authority house building schemes from 1912 onwards, but the fact that a coherent policy evolved so slowly is a clear indication that there was an inner conflict in the society. Alderman Thompson, its chairman, told a parliamentary select committee in 1906:

> I think if we are going to deal with the very poorest labourers living in the cheapest cottages, it cannot be done except by government subsidies such as those proposed in the Irish Labourers Bill ... If you have classes, as there are in our large centres, who are not economically self-supporting, there must be a subsidy for dealing with them.[46]

By securing the erection of 132 two-storey cottages in Richmond in 1903 under Part 3 of the 1890 Housing Act, Thompson was a pioneer of council house building. Although T. R. Marr had urged, in an important survey of Manchester's housing needs, as early as 1904 that as private enterprise could not supply the deficiency of house accommodation at rents within reach of the working class, town councils should provide this service, by acquiring fresh powers if necessary and by building model dwellings, he did not carry much weight as yet in the inner counsels of the National Council for another decade.[47]

Until the failure of the 1909 Housing Act became obvious, Thompson, Alderman Marr and Henry Aldridge, the secretary of the National Council, were not able to convince the chief policy makers in their organization to support an urban housing policy along the lines of the Griffith–Boscawen bill. For to the expected ideological opposition to municipal housing from laissez-faire apologists, expressed in a sophisticated form by the American Professor Dewsnap in *The Housing Problem in England* (1907), there was a strong resistance from the single taxers and certain distinguished land reformers and hostility and apathy from the Fabians, apart from Leo Chiozza Money MP, who advocated a massive scheme of slum clearance, instead of the timorous proposals so current among housing reformers. Moreover, Professor Dewsnap, while repeating the well-known arguments of those opponents of municipal projects who claimed that council housing would be an unfair wage subsidy in aid of employers and that council tenants would become a privileged and corrupt electoral influence, also stated that it was a weakness of supporters of council housing, to imagine that public services must necessarily be preferable to and cheaper than private service. Can the idea be seriously entertained that the municipality, as house-builder, house-owner, and landlord on such a scale, would be a success? Already, local authorities are overburdened with responsibilities, which are varied and so intricate that proper supervision is impossible, and far too large a dependence has to be placed on hired servants, the permanent staff, whose interests, under such lax conditions, have not always proved themselves to be identical with economy and efficiency.[48]

So too, before the war Seebohm Rowntree continued to rely on the Public Work Loan Commissioners for cheap loans to encourage house building, combined with a reliance on the extension of the minimum wage for workers for them to be able to afford the rent.[49] On the whole, it was a major weakness of the Fabian Society, guided by the Webbs, that it devoted so little attention to framing a viable urban housing policy, and the section in *The Case for a National Minimum* (1912) on housing requirements was a ludicrously inadequate statement, which showed the inability of well-meaning middle-class intellectuals to be moved by the desperate housing situation of sections of the working class.

> The housing of the casual labourer, the Sweated labourer, the semi-destitute and the vagrant, must after all remain an economic problem, not a housing problem. Municipal and philanthropic effort would be better expended in trying to reduce the numbers of this class, than in endeavouring to make possible a degraded condition of life which ought not to be allowed to continue.[50]

Even the parliamentary Labour party was divided as to the merits of a state housing subsidy, despite the consistent support of the Workmen's National Housing Council for the Boscawen bill.

In June 1912 when the Griffith–Boscawen bill came before Parliament, the National Housing Council issued a press statement to clarify its position on the question of a state housing subsidy, emphasizing:

> whilst we are on general principles opposed to the spending of either municipal or state money on the work of housing one part of the community at the expense of the rest, yet we are convinced that until the wages of the poorest are sufficient to enable them to pay reasonable rents for proper accommodation, the price of past neglect must be paid and houses – especially in rural districts – must be provided below cost. Until Parliament decides to take action to secure this end ... action which seems to be uneconomic must, as a temporary measure, be taken in order that much greater evils may be averted.[51]

In October 1913 the secretary of the National Council drafted a memorandum to assist the executive in formulating a fresh policy, concluding:

> It is useless to hope that private enterprise will meet the needs of the poorest. Builders have given up hope of doing this, as not likely to pay, and many of them welcome the proposal that local authorities should build to meet the housing needs of the poorest class of workers ... The exercise of compulsion by the Central

Authority in regard to local authorities will be rendered ten times more effective and valuable if the Central Authority can give financial aid in such cases.⁵²

At the same time, in October 1913, Aldridge, when discussing a Labour party proposal to give temporary Treasury grants for the building of rural cottages, remarked: 'In regard to the housing of the poorest in towns public opinion is by no means so far advanced.' Although Aldridge's memorandum was discussed several times, the executive, because of lack of unanimity on the vital question of a housing subsidy, could reach no more clear-cut decision than their previous policy of enquiring after the parliamentary prospects of the Boscawen bill and waiting for the publication of the Land Enquiry Report.⁵³

In February 1914 Herbert Samuel, a vigorous reforming minister who was close to the Webbs, was appointed president of the Local Government Board in order to carry out the government housing programme for the towns which had already been outlined by Lloyd George, but whose detailed provisions were only clarified when the urban volume of the Land Report was published in April 1914. Meanwhile, Runciman, the president of the Board of Agriculture, was obliged to introduce a measure for building cottages in rural districts in July 1914 by the introduction of the Conservative bill and Lloyd George's promises in his land campaign. Earlier Runciman set up an Advisory Committee on Rural Cottages which reported in April 1914 that it would be a great advantage if a sum of, say, £100,000 would be set aside in that year's Budget for building a few hundred cottages in order to gain experience in the best types of design and methods of building'; but a government member of the committee, Cecil Harmsworth MP, later explained why the proposal was unacceptable: 'I have myself toyed with the idea of State subsidised rents, but the more I contemplate it the more I am appalled by the possible economic results, and by its possible disastrous effects on the Exchequer of this country.' When Samuel took over from Burns at the Local Government Board, he clashed with Runciman by going over his head to Lloyd George and Asquith, and obtaining their consent to a national survey of both rural and urban housing to be undertaken by his own department. However, Runciman was not prepared to delay his bill while awaiting the findings of the survey of housing needs, and introduced a measure allowing the Admiralty to build 3,000 houses for its employees at Rosyth at a cost of £1 million and granting loans of £3 million at an as yet unspecified rate of interest to public utility societies and local authorities to build cottages with the proviso that if they failed to act, the Board of Agriculture would intervene. On 31 July 1914, the government decided to continue with their scheme for construction of homes for their employees at Rosyth, but postponed the other part of their bill for putting up cottages because the opposition wanted this to be debated at length.⁵⁴

Meanwhile, the urban housing programme of the land campaign made little public impact; and Samuel's restatement of government policy in a major address at Sheffield on 14 May 1914 was hardly inspiring, as there were few new proposals and the financial side of housing reform was scarcely touched upon. Seebohm Rowntree earlier complained to Hamilton, Lloyd George's private secretary, that 'the Campaign is being very seriously interfered with through our inability to make any statement with regard to the proposals of the Government in the matter of Urban Housing beyond the very general one that it is intended to make a survey'. Wallace Carter wrote confidentially:

> Urban housing and other purely Urban questions are continually being raised, and the fact that we have no authoritative answer is a very serious handicap to the whole campaign. In some districts they will not have other meetings or lectures until we know what the Government's Urban policy is. In London they have seriously discussed abandoning the whole campaign until we have more to tell them.[55]

Nevertheless, the *New Statesman*, the organ of the socialist followers of the Webbs, accepted the analysis of the Land Enquiry Report as regards housing, merely observing:

> We have no hesitation in saying that if the Government should attempt to deal with the question of urban housing without, at the same time, or indeed first, dealing with the question of urban wages and regularity of employment, it will be asking the House of Commons to waste its time.[56]

Almost alone among Liberal MPs, Chiozza Money declared: 'If we do not intend to tackle housing on a large scale, we simply mock the working classes by talking about the subject at all'; for he was fully aware that

> the lack of driving force behind politicians in this matter relegates housing bills to the position of minor matters. We may get excited about Home Rule, about Disestablishment, about the Franchise, about the House of Lords – even about Insurance – but we are quite incapable of getting excited about the question of making decent homes.[57]

The coming of the war on 4 August 1914 forced Samuel to accelerate his plans for implementing the proposals contained in the Land Enquiry Report, by hurriedly passing a Housing (No. 2) Act in August 1914 after conferences with the Conservative opposition, which empowered the Board of Agriculture in respect of rural districts and the Local Government Board in respect of urban areas to make arrangements with local authorities or authorized societies for the provision, maintenance, improvement and management of houses and gardens for the working class for the period of one year. The Treasury allotted £4 million to local authorities and non-profit-making housing organizations which they could borrow for capital expenditure on both urban and rural housing. For this purpose Runciman's plan for building rural cottages, which had been dropped from the previous housing bill, was incorporated into Samuel's measure. Neither government department was to authorize the building of houses, unless a public enquiry had revealed a shortage of accommodation. The aim of Samuel's bill was twofold: to provide housing for the working class and to mitigate the expected sharp rise in unemployment in the building trade. It was the government's considered opinion, Samuel reiterated, that

> in case there should be considerable distress through unemployment in this country that distress will very likely extend to the building trade, and that it would be absurd in such circumstances to spend great sums of public money in giving

relief to persons out of work instead of setting them to work at their own trade to make good the deficiency in housing accommodation, which has long been admitted on all sides to prevail both in town and country.[58]

By the time the First World War had broken out early in August 1914, the National Council was no closer to hammering out a viable policy on urban housing. To consider what changes should be introduced into the administration of housing policy during the war, a special committee of the National Council, including Horsfall, T. C. Marr, Seebohm Rowntree and Raymond Unwin, recommended that the government should stimulate the building of houses during the war by local authorities, as private capital would be restricted in wartime and there would consequently be much unemployment in the building industry, by allowing local authorities to build while borrowing at the same rates of interest as pre-war.

> We desire to add that, in the opinion of the majority of the members of our committee, it is most important that the Government should stimulate Local Authorities in undertaking Housing Schemes by making capital grants in aid of expenditure upon such schemes.[59]

When a deputation of the National Council met Herbert Samuel on 21 August 1914 to discuss the administration of the Act, under which the government would lend some £4 million to local authorities for approved building schemes at the rates at which they could themselves borrow, Marr and Wilkins raised the question of whether part of the loan of £4 million could be allocated for grants-in-aid. Samuel replied that

> [It] was not the intention of Government to use this £4,000,000 for the purpose of grants-in-aid. If they began to do this, every Local Authority borrowing money would expect to get a grant. Their great aim was to induce Local Authorities to undertake Housing Schemes.[60]

In the Commons, after persistent questioning from Chiozza Money, Samuel made it clear that Burns' opposition to the £1 million housing subsidy in the Conservative bill was the considered policy of the government, continuing:

> I think the further that we can keep away from the Irish example in this country the better, and we had better not set our foot on the slippery slope which leads from accepting the general principle that the able bodied labourer should be housed largely at the expense of the ratepayers and of the taxpayers.[61]

During the war so many workers from the building trade were absorbed in the army that the predictions of mass unemployment proved to be mistaken, so that the Treasury instructed local authorities to curtail their schemes, thereby rendering the Act a futile gesture.[62]

Already at the start of 1914 there was a clear recognition that the state had to act decisively to augment the existing stock of housing for the working class, though only the impact of the war quickened the resolve of the National Council to implement what was a national housing policy. Even in 1915 Rowntree had not advanced beyond his pre-war concept, declaring that a government committee should be appointed to consider the clearance of slum areas as a means of providing employment. In many towns this work is sorely needed, and the Government was just beginning to deal with it when war broke out ... And with energetic treatment, and the investment of a moderate amount of capital, every slum in England could be abolished within the next decade.[63]

In a memorandum on national housing policy in February 1916, Aldridge and Shawcross commented:

> The virtual stoppage of the building of new working class houses since the outbreak of the war has raised the question of housing accommodation in its acutest form, and the fact that this stoppage (so far as the building of houses by Local Authorities and Public Utility Societies is concerned) has been in some measure due to the refusal of the Government to lend money for this purpose, renders it imperative that we should consider the question ... on new lines.[64]

Further, the Rent and Mortgage Restriction Act of 1915, which froze rents, made the building of working-class houses an unattractive investment. Harold Shawcross steered the National Council in favour of a policy under which the government was to place capital of between £4 million and £20 million at the disposal of local authorities for housing on the same terms as the 1914 measure. However, when the National Council summoned a congress with 400 delegates from local authorities and trade unions in 1916 on Home Problems after the war, it was

> unanimous that the problem of housing the poor should, in the years following the war, be dealt with on stern and drastic lines. It was felt that the housing policies of the great political parties should be coalesced and merged in a joint policy of requiring employers to pay wages to ensure proper Housing Accommodation, and of aiding Local Authorities, by means of Grants, in the task of housing the poor in those cases in which meanwhile economic rents cannot be paid.[65]

What this survey seems to confirm is that with the slowdown in the construction of working-class housing in the years before the war and the standstill during the war, liberal housing policy on laissez-faire lines collapsed; and that the policy of government subsidies for council house building, which had been urged by trade unions, the Unionist Social Reform Council and certain radical housing reformers even before the onset of hostilities, triumphed.

15

# From Trade Boards to the Minimum Wage

## The Administration of the Trade Boards Act

Without the benevolent attention of the National Anti-Sweating League (NASL), even so modest a measure as the Trade Boards Act would have run aground over the difficulties of administration. The Act covered some 200,00 workers in four trades, whose wages were 'exceptionally low as compared with that in other employment', with power granted to the Board of Trade to extend the Act by provisional order to other such trades where low wage rates prevailed. The trades first included in the scheme were the male sector of the tailoring trade, paper box manufacture, some forms of chain making concentrated at Cradley Heath, and the lace industry of Nottingham. Each trade board consisted of an equal number of employers' and workers' representatives sitting together with a small number of independent members nominated by the Board of Trade, mostly university lecturers, lawyers and social workers. The NASL in cooperation with the trade unions, where they existed, held meetings and distributed leaflets to inform workers of their rights under the Act, helped to stage many of the meetings which elected representatives to serve on the boards in the interests of the workers, and aided the workers in the preparation and presentation of their case. Mary MacArthur was placed on the chain making and wholesale clothing boards; J. J. Mallon was put on the box making board. On the last board sixteen out of nineteen workers' representatives were inexperienced in negotiation, while the employers relied on eighteen heads of businesses and the legal adviser of the Box Makers Federation. The settlement as to minimum wage rates was arrived at after negotiations between the employers' and workers' representatives with the independent members only rarely taking the initiative in the fixing of scales.[1]

Almost the whole of the labour force engaged in the manufacture of chain was concentrated at Cradley Heath on the borders of South Staffordshire and East Worcestershire. Out of the 6,000 persons engaged in the trade, between 150 and 200 were small masters employing additional staff, another group numbering between 1,000 and 1,500 hammered out the chain at their own stalls, while of the 3,000 to 3,500 workers employed on the premises of the workshop owners, 2,000 were women; in contrast, all the factory employees were men. Other men toiling in their own sheds were, according to R. H. Tawney,

> at the mercy of an employer for his market, whether that employer is a factory occupier or middleman, and the apparent liberty of domestic employment has

hitherto been often little more than the liberty to work seventy or eighty hours a week for a subsistence wage.[2]

The owners of these small workshops, which were easy to set up, mushroomed in numbers, and when undertaking sub-contract work for large employers, they reacted to the excessive competition by 'beating down the worker's remuneration'.[3]

The chain-making industry was the first to establish minimum wage rates and under duress, the threat of mechanization, the workers' representatives accepted abysmally low rates of pay, thereby setting a poor precedent. Taking men's earnings first, Tawney computed from a sample of seventy-four outworkers and 148 journeymen that just over half the workers, some 50.4 per cent, earned between 20s. and 25s., 16.6 per cent earned less than 20s., 29.2 per cent earned between 25s. and 30s. and 3.6 per cent earned wages in excess of 30s., after the determination of minimum rates by the board. This meant that the majority of male workers were still earning less than a sum sufficient on Rowntree's subsistence scale of 25s. per week to keep a family consisting of a husband, wife and three children above the poverty line. As regards the weekly earnings of women, Tawney declared that after utilizing a sample of 588, he estimated that just over half the workers, some 53.8 per cent, earned between 5s. and 8s., 17 per cent earned less than 5s. and 29 per cent more than 8s., leading to his conclusion that 'the predominant earnings are, when measured by any reference to the idea of a "living wage", extraordinarily low'. When taking into account hours of labour and earnings, Tawney discovered that 17.5 per cent of the men were earning less than the minimum rate of 5d. per hour set by the board, 74.09 per cent of the women were earning less than $2^1/_2$d. per hour, the figures fixed as their minimum time rate, which was an alarmingly high proportion of them. This was even after strikes in 1910 and 1911 to force employers to implement the minimum rates.[4]

In the men's sector of the tailoring trade – the second such industry to be covered in an appraisal by Tawney – there were approximately 145,000 workers in Britain coming within the ambit of the trade board's operations. Between 75,000 and 80,000 were factory hands, principally concentrated in northern England, 50,000 were employed in 3,200 workshops, and there were an additional 15,000 to 22,000 female homeworkers. London was the chief centre of the workshop side of the trade. Once again, Tawney confirmed Beatrice Webb's conclusion that the Jewish section of the trade was not the source from which sweated production emanated, despite the sensational stories to the contrary. The cheapest section of the trade made garments for the black population of South Africa,

> largely in the East End, partly in Jewish workshops, where male labour is principally employed, and partly by non-Jewish sub-contractors working in a small way of business and employing almost exclusively female labour, sometimes in workshops, but principally in their own homes ... The male labour employed in Jewish shops, engaged in this class of work, is of almost incredible efficiency, and is able to earn reasonable wages at piece-prices which, when paid to a female homeworker, often provide the sensational instances of sweating with which the East London tailoring trade has been associated.[5]

The other branch of the tailoring trade which the Jews dominated was the better section of the wholesale bespoke trade, in which the retailer cut the customer's cloth but passed it on to a Jewish master tailor for fitting, machining and pressing by Jewish male assistants, helped by a few gentile women who did the finishing. If anything, the Jewish tailors with their careful subdivision of labour, as a result of the fixing of minimum rates by the board, ousted some of their competitors who paid the lowest rates. Thirdly, there was the juvenile trade, another cheap section of the trade, where the garments were produced in efficient factories or by homeworkers in East London or Colchester. Finally, there was the better class of ready-made tailoring for the home market and export, manufactured in London, Essex, and the districts around Abingdon and Bristol.[6]

Turning now to the question of whether there was an increase in the earnings of women workers, Tawney found that out of 177 indoor women workers, 113 (63.8 per cent) had experienced no change in earnings since the trade board's determination, while fifty-five (31 per cent) had gained an increase in their weekly earnings. 'It is evident from these figures', Tawney conceded, 'that the Tailoring Trade Board has not brought about any general increase in wages, such as the result of an advance secured by a Trade Union, or such as was effected by the Chain Trade Board', but this was to put an over-optimistic gloss on the figures for the chain-making trade. 'The workers affected are, roughly, the third of the trade which, prior to the issue of the Trade Board's determination, was the most poorly paid.' If the Board of Trade wage census in 1906 revealed that 58 per cent of all the women in the ready-made tailoring industry were earning less than 13s. $6^{1}/_{2}$d., it was estimated that the trade board, by fixing a minimum rate of this amount for women working a 50-hour week, increased the wages of 38 per cent of the female indoor workers. Although this weekly piece-rate for women was almost double the sum earned by half the women in the chain-making industry, the women workers in the tailoring trade in the north still regarded this minimum rate as far too low.

> The Trade Unions in Manchester and Leeds have ... established a standard rate for their members which is far above the minimum fixed by the Trade Board; the number of workers who protested that the Trade Board rate was a 'sweated wage', for which they would not dream of working except under compulsion, was considerable.[7]

As far as men's wages were concerned, some 24.4 per cent earned less than 25s. in 1906, the worst-paid areas being the eastern counties and Bristol, whereas after the trade board's determination at least a quarter of them obtained advances that brought almost all the male employees in the trade up to a 25s. wage level. More disturbing in illustrating the essential weakness of the boards in fostering the swift rise in the wages of the poorest section of the trade was the fact that less than half of a sample of 95 homeworkers in Colchester and only 45.6 per cent of a sample of 425 homeworkers in London could command minimum time rates, so that we would estimate that over the whole country 7,500 to 11,000 outworkers – invariably female – were receiving less than the minimum wage rates.[8] But an attempt by the employers in 1912–13 to have the flat rate of $3^{1}/_{4}$d. per hour overturned and fixed at a lower rate in Eastern

England because of alleged competitive disadvantages was overruled by the Tailoring Trade Board.[9]

As to the third trade covered by the Trade Boards Act, there were no exact figures as to the number of cardboard box makers in England and Wales, the total number lying somewhere between 4,068 and 10,660 for men and between 26,501 and 35,047 for women. Among them was a group of homeworkers some 2,000 strong, located in London and Birmingham, who were nearly all female, even if they enjoyed the assistance of their husbands from time to time. According to the Board of Trade returns, no fewer than 66.8 per cent of the female workers in the box-making industry earned less than a weekly wage of 13s.4d., a calculation based on a later trade board determination of 3d. per hour for women. As the trade board had stipulated that at least 855 of the workers in any factory should earn a minimum rate of 3d. per hour, 'it would appear that some 52 per cent of the workers must have experienced an increase of wages'. In certain towns, such as Nottingham and Leicester, the men gained marked advances in their wages through the trade board's determination of 6d. an hour, which, however, did not come into force until July 1913. Before the minimum rates were fixed, there were several instances of unskilled male workers in the Leicester area earning 15s. and the Board of Trade returns on earnings showed that 39.5 per cent of the unskilled male workers in the box-making industry earned 23s. or less. Of 300 homeworkers, an investigation summed up by Mildred Bulkley revealed that 126 (42 per cent) could not earn the minimum rate of 3d. per hour, while thirty-nine others (13 per cent) could only earn this amount on certain kinds of job. Related findings demonstrated that even when due allowance was made for the reduced earning capacity of the elderly and infirm, of 151 able-bodied women under forty-five years old, forty-three were earning less than 3d. per hour, while twenty-two others could only earn this amount on certain types of work – results which underscore our previous observation that the machinery established by trade boards was the least effective where it was the most urgently required.[10]

Briefly we must outline the impact which the coming of the trade boards had on the four industries concerned. The increase in wages was generally absorbed by the better organization of an industry, by an increase in prices and the reduction in the profits of the middlemen, and by an increased acceleration in the rate at which machinery was introduced. Although the latter feature was hardly significant as far as the installation of electric-wielding equipment for the manufacture of chain and machinery for the production of cardboard boxes was concerned, as existing trends were perpetuated; but in the tailoring trade the effect of trade board determination was to force the more backward firms to introduce power-driven machinery, while all sections of the trade purchased specialist equipment such as button-holing machines.[11] So too, apart from the box-making industry, where trade boards initially boosted union membership, but where 'generally speaking, attempts to organize the women workers and the more poorly paid sections of the male workers have not met with success', the setting up of trade boards stimulated trade union activity in the chain-making and even more markedly in the tailoring industry. The Jewish Tailors, Pressers and Machinists Trade Union witnessed an increase in its membership from 950 in 1910 to 4,465 in 1913; the membership of the National Federation of Women Workers rose from 8,000 in

1911 to 11,500 in 1913; and the membership of the Amalgamated Union of Clothiers' Operatives climbed in 1913 from 2,000 to 8,000. 'At the same time, the Unions have succeeded in several districts in securing advances which have raised the standard rates to be paid to their members considerably above the minimum fixed by the Trade Board', observed Tawney. So long as the lace industry in Nottingham was racked by a depression, the 10,000 female outworkers were too downtrodden to be organized effectively, so that little was achieved by the trade board before 1914, but even in the box-making and tailoring trades there was some evasion of the Act, particularly among employers of homeworkers, because there were only nine inspectors in 1914 to cover the whole country, with one more official who never left the central office.[12]

Central to any evaluation of the achievement of the trade boards is an assessment of their impact on wage movements. Before the amending act in 1918, trade boards were confined to localized sweated industries employing heavy pockets of female outworkers, such as the chain makers at Cradley Heath, the lace workers in Nottingham, the box makers in London and Birmingham, and the tailoring homeworkers concentrated strongly in London, whereas sweating prevailed also among factory hands and existed among a vast mass of unskilled male labourers with families to support, for whom the Act made little provision. Sometimes the male workers employed in these trades were marshalled in efficient trade unions, such as the men in the factories at Cradley Heath, the cutters and pressers in the tailoring factories of Manchester and Leeds, and the guillotine and shear cutters in the box-making factories, able to demand rates of pay well in excess of trade board determination because of the special skills of their members; or the trades scheduled under the Act were ones with only a small proportion of unskilled male factory hands, such as the box-making industry. Even so, the rates fixed for the overwhelming bulk of the male labour force in the chain-making and tailoring trades ranged from £1 to 25s. a week at the beginning of 1914, so that the trade board minimum rates dipped below Rowntree's calculation of a family income of 25s. a week required to keep a man with a wife and three children above the poverty line. For single women with trade board minimum rates ranging from 8s. to 13s. 6d., the struggle to maintain a standard of living above the Rowntree subsistence standard of 13s. a week was harder still.[13]

Yet we have seen that the most hard-pressed section of the women workers, the homeworkers, frequently found it difficult to earn these minimum rates. Against this rather harsh series of judgements of the effect of the trade boards on the movement of wages must be balanced the fact that the agitation at Cradley Heath had repercussions throughout the Midlands, 'where the hollow-ware makers, the clay-workers and certain sections of the metal trades have in the last year engaged in an agitation, with the result that the former have been brought within the scope of the Trade Boards Act, and the two latter have secured advances'. Further, if the shrinkage in the number of homeworkers was barely perceptible before 1914, the contraction in numbers occurred afterwards, the figures for West Ham starting at 1,600 in 1903, rising to 2,442 in 1913 and dwindling to 931 by 1923.[14]

What the trade boards set out to achieve was a series of gradualist wage adjustments in line with what each trade claimed it could bear – adjustments which were not linked to findings derived from scientific budget surveys. This was the position which

R. H. Tawney adopted after being appointed as director of the Ratan Tata Foundation, a unit of the London School of Economics, to study poverty in 1913, which enabled him to carry out detailed surveys of the impact of trade boards in the chain-making and tailoring industries. Tawney's research has been criticized as premature, because of the subsequent drastic change in conditions during the First World War and its aftermath; but this is not altogether a valid criticism, for how was he supposed to predict the timing, length and economic impact of the war? If his books and that of his colleague Mildred Bulkley are read carefully, they show that the achievements of the trade board legislation was limited, despite the positive spin presented by Tawney. Sheila Blackburn's overall conclusion is, however, convincing. While Tawney condemned the Webbs' national minimum wage for being too subsistence-based, he also dismissed a more generous minimum if it was considered to be above what the individual trade could bear. His opinions were so well received by contemporaries that they dominated propagandist literature for the subsequent decades, most notably that produced by the founders of the powerful anti-sweating group, the NASL, particularly J. J. Mallon. Tawney accepted that men and women should receive differentiated rates of pay for the same amount of work. Nor did he change his view in later life on the minimum wage; and despite being one of the foremost socialist thinkers in Britain, his position in this respect was somewhat rigid and 'conventional'.[15] Again, some of the civil servants within the Labour department of the Board of Trade shared similar backgrounds and assumptions to the propagandists of the trade board system, so that there was not always enough critical scrutiny on their part. Accordingly the trade board determinations were not a living wage in the sense of the later minimum wage legislation of New South Wales and the sixteen American states, a fact not fully grasped by Liberal politicians when they moved into the field of minimum wage reform before the 1914 war.[16]

## Towards the Minimum Wage

Swayed by the casual labour theory of unemployment which was much in vogue between 1907 and 1911, perhaps even hoping to cajole Mrs Webb's colleagues on the Poor Law Commission into lending their adhesion to her report by deliberately moderating their views, the Webbs in the Minority Report retreated from the radical posture on the connection between low earnings and poverty taken in the 1902 edition of *Industrial Democracy*. In the former, the Webbs claimed that

> The outcome of these investigations [the three special enquiries undertaken for the Poor Law Commission] is all the more impressive in that it was not what we anticipated. We do not exaggerate when we say that all these enquirers – numbering, with their assistants, more than a dozen, starting on different lines of investigation, and pursuing their researches independently all over the Kingdom – came, without concert, to the same conclusion, namely, that of all the causes or conditions predisposing to pauperism the most potent, the most certain and the most extensive in its operation was this method of

employment in odd jobs. Contrary to the expectations of some of our number and some of themselves, our investigators did not find that low wages could be described, generally speaking, as a cause of pauperism ... Thus the regularly employed railway porters, lowly paid as they are, contribute only infinitesimally to pauperism. Even the agricultural labourers in receipt, perhaps of the lowest money wages of any section of wage-earners, do not nowadays, so far as they belong to any section in regular employment, contribute largely to the pauperism of adult able-bodied life.[17]

Nonetheless, it is clear that the Webbs, through the hospitality they lavished on Rose Squire, Steel-Maitland, Cyril Jackson and the Revd Pringle, who were included among the six leading investigators for the series of special enquiries, had unwittingly focused the group's attention on hypotheses and areas of research to which the Webbs were themselves attracted. Rose Squire recalled:

I think Mrs Sidney Webb had, to some extent, stood sponsor for both my colleague and myself, and with her at the beginning, and from time to time during our inquiry, we specially discussed, not only our own particular subject, but the principles and problems of poor relief and its administration.[18]

Steel-Maitland and Rose Squire, who were specifically ordered to delve into the effects of insanitary conditions, long hours and low wages, concluded that '[t]hese are important causes of poverty and suffering, but do not actually create paupers to any marked extent', imperceptibly shifting the debate away from the recent sociological approach of defining the causes of poverty back to disputing the nature and extent of the different categories of pauper, an important concession to the upholders of the Poor Law Unions' point of view, in which they were followed by the Webbs.[19]

Against the general trend of their thesis concerning the link between casual labour and pauperism, Steel-Maitland and Rose Squire recorded several striking instances of the connection between low wages and pauperism. 'In our opinion', they admitted when reviewing the situation in Manchester, 'pauperism existing among foundry labourers and lesser paid workers in the engineering industry is not strikingly great, and in centres where casual labour predominates it would not arrest the attention. But it is considerable.' Even in Sheffield they conceded that '[p]aupers are nearly all ironworkers from among the labourers', whose earnings were meagre. 'Very few in proportion come from the other classes', although the general unhealthiness of the occupation plus low wages resulted in some pauperism among the cutlers.[20]

Within four years Beatrice Webb reversed back to her earlier position, by writing the preface for *The Case for the National Minimum*, in which the contributors pointed out:

Old Age Pensions, Labour Exchanges, State assistance for the Sick and the Unemployed, Housing schemes, School Feeding, and other forms of provision for special sections of the wage-earning class are desirable, even imperative, but the root factor in destitution is the factor of low wages, and until it is dealt with no substantial improvement in social conditions can be expected.[21]

So too, in the other industrial towns, as we tried to demonstrate in a previous chapter, where the incidence of casual labour was very low – although in our opinion slightly higher than the poverty surveys allowed – it was the poor earnings of the unskilled and semi-skilled workers, particularly the men, that engendered conditions of mass poverty. If London was an exceptional case, far more glutted with casual labour than distributive centres like Manchester and Liverpool, so numerous were the surveys conducted there by investigators that the finding that in London casual labour was rife was, because of unconscious bias, applied indiscriminately by these persons and their imitators to conditions in the rest of England and Wales. But even here we would add the qualification that in all probability the poverty prevalent in London, against the view of Booth and the Webbs, was due as much to low wages as to the incidence of casual labour, a point we have already examined. While East London was said to be dominated by a casual labour problem associated with the dock labourers, a later investigation appeared to indicate that the working population of South London was living in poverty and suffered principally from the blight of low wages. Research undertaken by the Fabian Women's Group from 1909–13 under the direction of Maud Pember Reeves in Lambeth indicated that

> The poorest people – the river-side casual, the workhouse in-and-out, the bar-room loafer, are anxiously ignored by ... respectable persons whose work is permanent ... and whose wages range from 18s. to 30s. a week. They generally are somebody's labourer, mate, or handyman. Painters' labourers, plumbers' labourers, builders' handymen, dustmen's mates, printers' labourers, potters' labourers, trouncers for Carmen, are common amongst them. Or they may be fish-fryers, tailors' pressers, feather-cleaners' assistants, railway-carriage washers, employees of dust contractors, Carmen for Borough Council contractors, or packers of various descriptions. They are respectable men in full work, at a more or less top wage, young, with families still increasing, and they will be lucky if they are never worse off than they are now. Their wives are quiet, decent, 'keep themselves-to-themselves' kind of women, and the children are the most punctual and regular scholars, the most clean-headed children of the poorer schools in Kennington and Lambeth.[22]

But many of these respectable London families, it was shown, despite the practice of thrift, were living on the brink of poverty.

Both Seebohm Rowntree's famous study of York (1899) and A. L. Bowley and A. R. Burnett-Hurst's *Livelihood and Poverty* (1915) were wide-ranging surveys into all the factors responsible for keeping families in a state of poverty, and conclusively proved contrary to the findings of the three special investigations for the Royal Commission on the Poor Laws that while casual labour only contributed towards poverty to a small degree, low wages were the major factor. Bowley was professor of statistics at the London School of Economics, but politically he was a sympathizer of the New Liberalism. The hiatus between the two studies was caused partly by the dominance of the casual labour theory of pauperism among social theorists in the years 1907–11, partly by the limited aims of the National Anti-Sweating League in its campaign for minimum wage regulation insofar as it did not sufficiently recognize the needs of the mass of unskilled male workers and concentrated its efforts on raising women's wages. A meeting of the Unionist Social Reform Council at Oxford in October 1911, including Lord Astor, Steel-Maitland and Leopold Amery, called to consider the onset of a wave of large-scale strikes, heard one paper which, at the same time as it blamed poverty for the unrest, stressed the sweated wages aspect of poverty, with the average male earning 24s. 6d. and the average woman factory hand taking home 11s. 6d. compared with the female outworker's wage of 7s. 6d. Taking 25s. per week to be the lowest possible wage to keep a family of five in a state of physical efficiency in London and 24s. or 23s. in provincial towns, according to the National Committee for the Prevention of Destitution, Bowley estimated in 1911 that of the eight million workers in regular occupations in the United Kingdom, some 2,560,000 (32 per cent) earned less than 25s. a week, which showed an alarmingly high percentage on the brink of poverty. Of these men, 320,000 earned under 15s. a week, 640,000 earned between 15s. and £1, and 1,600,000 earned between £1 and 25s. Yet evidence produced by the Board of Trade as a result of their exhaustive reports on the Earnings and Hours of Workers throughout industry indicated that even Bowley erred by overestimating the numbers of those earning 25s. and upwards a week, when, for example, 48.3 per cent of the adult men employed in the textile trades covering the cotton, woollen and worsted industries, and the jute and silk industries, earned under 25s. a week; and when the 230,423 adult males running the railway system (63 per cent of the total male staff) earned under 25s. a week.[23]

Turning to the industrial towns, Rowntree first demonstrated that in York, 2.83 per cent of the total population living in primary poverty did so on account of the irregular employment of the breadwinner, and that 51.96 per cent were in similar straits on account of the low wages of the head of the household – by far the greatest single cause of poverty. It should also be noted that Rowntree allowed a 'less generous' sum for food in his calculations than that stipulated in the dietary tables for workhouses prescribed by the Local Government Board. Bowley and Burnett-Hurst claimed that in Stanley, a mining village where special conditions prevailed, 9 per cent of the adult males earned less than 24s. a week, in Northampton 27 per cent, in Warrington 32 per cent and in Reading 50.5 per cent; and that according to their calculations 5.9 per cent of the families in Northampton, 10.9 per cent in Warrington and 15.1 per cent in Reading were living below the poverty line; that casual labour and unemployment did not rank as an important cause of poverty; that in all towns except Stanley low wages were the principal cause of poverty; and that the raising of the wages of the worst-paid section of the working class was the most pressing social task of the day.[24] At Middlesbrough Lady Florence Bell discovered in 1907 that out of 900 houses, 125 were 'absolutely poor', while 175 were 'so near the poverty line that they are constantly passing over it', or – put another way – that a third of the workers had to toil unremittingly for the basic essentials of life. Although she, like the other sociologists in the intermediate period, somewhat neglected the issue, Lady Bell cited figures to show that out of 1,197 adult ironworkers paid in a given week, ninety-six men – mainly labourers – received under 20s. and that 398 men received between 20s. and 30s., thereby lending support to the argument that low pay more than any other factor produced poverty. Adopting the Rowntree poverty standard, Arnold Freeman estimated that in Birmingham half the homes in the city were below or just above the poverty line in 1914, a grossly exaggerated figure.[25]

Driven on by the accumulated weight of evidence from their panel of investigators, the Liberal Land Enquiry volume on urban land, despite the fact that the subject of low wages was not strictly germane, buttressed the findings of the sociologists on the connection between low wages and poverty and, operating on a wider front, clearly demonstrated the nexus between low wages and slum dwellings. The Land Enquiry Committee concluded:

> While we cannot support our own view by statistics extending over a wide area, it is confirmed by enquiries made in London, Manchester, York, and other towns, and by the opinion expressed to us by social workers in different parts of the country. They agree that the majority of overcrowded and defective dwellings are probably occupied by families whose chief bread-winner is in regular employment at a wage which will not allow him to pay an economic rent for a sanitary dwelling.[26]

Again, they had earlier remarked that this point of view 'contradicts a theory still generally held, that insanitary and overcrowded dwellings are principally occupied by the socially diseased – such as the work-shy, the unemployable, the physically defective, families in misfortune from one cause or another, and criminals'.[27]

Having established a strong connection between low wages and poverty, we turn to two related problems, one being the fluctuating levels of women's employment in different parts of the country, the other being the degree to which the casual labour of male employees determined that their wives were driven into sweated labour occupations.

Apart from the London boroughs and parts of the Midlands, the highest levels of female employment were reached in the Lancashire cotton towns and in other towns where the textile industry was predominant. Next we come to a group of towns with a middle level in the proportion of women employed. These were industrial towns, often of ancient foundation and mainly concentrated in the southern half of the country, where women were employed on a large scale in the various branches of the food and clothing industries. Finally, we come to a group of towns with a small proportion of women employees, which were in the main towns in which there was a great concentration of heavy industry or its ancillary branches, including areas where there were mining communities. Examples of these towns were Sunderland where 23.14 per cent of the women worked, West Hartlepool where 21.23 per cent of the women were employed, and South Shields where only 19.36 per cent of the women had jobs. Thirdly, mining communities such as Stanley in Yorkshire and the Rhondda Valley in South Wales were capable of absorbing only the most limited number of women, a factor which made the coalfields front runners in pressing for a minimum wage for men. Fourthly, seaports and fishing communities were the last group of towns with low employment opportunities for women, such as Plymouth where 29.96 per cent of the women were employed, Southampton where 26.34 per cent of them were gainfully occupied, and Grimsby where 24.74 per cent were likewise engaged.[28] Accordingly, we may conclude, with Tawney, that as the level of employment of women fluctuated with the underlying industrial structure of the locality rather than strictly with the level of income of the male wage earners in the locality, any breakdown of the figures for earnings in a town to illustrate the reasons why its married women went back to work would not give us a complete picture of the financial circumstances of all its households.[29]

Having delineated the position as to the employment of women in the different types of community, we shall now investigate the relationship between casual labour and sweating, particularly the contention of W. H. Beveridge that

> casual employment is one of the most potent causes of sweating in the ordinary sense. When the head of the family cannot get enough work, his wife and children are driven to take what they can get at once. The tendency of low-grade women's industries – jam making, sack and tarpaulin work, matchbox making and the like – to get established in districts where casual labour for men is rife has often been noticed.[30]

Let us examine the problem in London. Although the results of two careful investigations in West Ham and in the London box-making trade seem to confirm the conclusion that where husbands were engaged in casual employments, their wives and children were forced to seek work in sweated occupations, there is a large mass of evidence which if it does not sharply contradict this hypothesis, clearly points to the fact that it requires serious modification, by reformulating it along lines suggested by Tawney. Homeworkers 'are predominantly the wives and daughters, usually the wives, of men whose employment is casual or whose wages are low, and who are described as "labourers" of one kind or another', he asserted.[31]

Beveridge seized on the study of West Ham to validate his theory: although in the summary of conclusions on which he rested his case, it was stated that 'there is a tendency for industries employing cheap women's and children's labour to arise in casual labour districts', in the main body of the text a rather different conclusion was reached:

> Undoubtedly in the great majority of cases the cause of taking in work is that the husband's work is casual, or ill-paid, or that he is in some trade, such as a carman's, where he is liable to work short time.[32]

Of 294 women giving the occupation of their husbands, 158 (53 per cent) declared that their spouses were employed in the building trade, as dock labourers or as general labourers, a generic term embracing a heterogeneous assortment of occupations. In another study of the box-making industry by Mildred Bulkley, it was demonstrated that out of a sample of 291 married homeworkers who were questioned, eighty-seven claimed to be dependent on their own exertions, 102 denied any dependence on their own work, while 102 said that they were partly dependent on their own labour; the vast bulk of the latter category, numbering some sixty persons, toiled at home because their husband's work was irregular, thirty-three of them because their husband's earnings were insufficient or they had too many children, and nine because their husbands were unemployed. In addition, Mildred Bulkley conceded that 'though a considerable proportion of the homeworkers state that they are not obliged to work, these households are as a rule comparatively poor' – a point that appears to confirm our hypothesis that the low earnings of the breadwinners attracted less attention than the more erratic and publicized misery of the casual labourer.[33]

Evidence patiently assembled by Clementina Black and her collaborators over several years allows us to go one step further, by suggesting that even in London, just as in the rest of the country, women were compelled to seek work, often of a sweated nature, because the wages of their husbands were inadequate. From their enquiry in 1908 into women's work in London in the tailoring, dressmaking and underclothing trades, Mrs Carl Meyer and Clementina Black, with additional information placed at their disposal by the Women's Industrial Council and the committee which supervised the West Ham Investigation, concluded after sifting through more than 1,000 cases that the largest group seen by them were 'formed by the wives of men who although in regular work do not receive a wage upon which it is possible to support a wife and children. To this group belong the larger number of married women visited in the course of this inquiry.' Further, they stated that the Women's Industrial Council was engaged in a thorough investigation of women's work, the preliminary findings of which seemed to indicate 'a marked preponderance of women whose reason for working is the inadequacy of the husband's wage for the support of his family'. In 1915 Clementina Black edited a volume entitled *Married Women's Work* summing up the results of an enquiry undertaken on behalf of the Women's Industrial Council and embodying both her general conclusions in light of the overall investigations and statistics relating to the employment of women which only make sense when discussed in connection with these conclusions. Out of a total of 616 women with jobs in London, it was found that 356 wives worked to supplement their husband's wage, 139 had to support themselves as they were widows, forty-three worked because their husbands were unemployed, thirty-six had to seek employment because their husbands were ill, while twenty-two worked as they were separated from their husbands or had been deserted.[34]

When the conclusions are carefully analysed and read in conjunction with the trend of thought revealed in her 1909 volume written with Mrs Carl Meyer, it is apparent that the emphasis of Clementina Black was on the low wages of the mass of unskilled labourers rather than on the insufficient family income brought about by casual employment and seasonal unemployment, nor did she see any reason to differentiate the position of London from the rest of the country in light of her findings. She reiterated:

> Now the present enquiry establishes beyond all question the fact that a considerable proportion – probably a very large proportion – of the working people of this country are receiving remuneration for their industry at rates that keep them and their families well below the standard of self support just set forth. Despite the current theory that wages of the men are reckoned not on an individual but on a family basis, thousands of men are paid at rates which (even if received – as is very seldom the case – regularly throughout the year), are in fact barely sufficient to support properly one adult and one child; while the wages of thousands of women (based theoretically on the needs of an individual) are wholly inadequate

to the proper support of one adult person. The earnings of man and wife together are, in thousands of households, inadequate, however industrious, however sober, however thrifty the pair, to the proper support of themselves and their children.[35]

Defining the wives in what she termed class B, she suggested in another passage that

> Such is the case with nearly all labourers' [income insufficient to support a family], whatever occupation subserved by their labour ... Altogether the army of underpaid men is a considerable one. Moreover, in many trades, employment is irregular; the money available for a man's housekeeping may drop from 20s. or 18s. to 10s. or even 8s., or may come altogether to an end, and that for a considerable number of weeks in every year.[36]

What else is interesting about the entire drift of these conclusions is that they neatly dovetail into the later Bowley findings about the causes of poverty in industrial towns.

There was mounting unrest among different sections of the working class in 1910, 1911 and 1912 in Britain, culminating in national strikes by seamen, dockers, railwaymen and miners. Utilizing data provided by A. L. Bowley, including indices for prices and wages, historians at first concluded that this revolt in the labour market was fuelled by a widespread perception of falling living standards; but when C. H. Feinstein reappraised this data, he concluded that real earnings rose until 1900 and that 'these gains were at least retained, if not marginally improved' until 1914. Hence it is more likely that labour militancy was stoked by the growth of the trade unions and the perception of different groups of workers that their incomes were falling, while other sections of the working class were enjoying a better standard of living.[37] Moreover, Roy Church, after examining Edwardian labour unrest concluded,

> There is little evidence of a major challenge to the *status quo*, except in respect of bargaining power – by the unions who challenged employers' associations, and by rank and file; those who envisaged as the outcome a transformation of society and the advancement of class, as distinct from industrial, trade union aims, were a small minority.[38]

The question of a minimum wage was not a leading item on the political agenda until the labour unrest in the years before the First World War. What pressure there was came from the ranks of the Labour party and the wider working-class movement. A small Labour pressure group had clamoured for a minimum wage of 30s., successfully passing a resolution at the 1906 TUC calling on the government to pay all workers directly employed by them a minimum wage of 30s. for a 48-hour week and recognized trade union rates for all trades employed on government work; and it was undoubtedly this group, the Labour Protection League, whose activities stimulated urgent pleas by the Labour party for a fixed minimum wage.[39] When the Labour party appointed a sub-committee to review future policy in 1912, it merely asked for an extension of the Trade Boards Act of 1909 to industries where wages were low. However, in 1911 and again in 1913 the Labour party sponsored resolutions, asking the Commons to affirm that the Trade Boards Act should be extended to provide for the establishment of a 30s. legal minimum wage for every adult worker in urban areas and that in rural areas there should be a minimum wage to secure an equivalent standard; further, it called on the government to adopt a legal minimum wage of 30s. in its own workshops. Between 1889 and 1894, 150 local authorities had adopted a fair wages resolution, leading to a situation in Edwardian times in which a number of London boroughs had fixed a 30s. minimum wage for unskilled workers, while in 1891 and 1893 the Commons had passed resolutions supporting the need for a minimum wage for state employees.[40]

Everything changed with the miners' strike in 1912, so Clifford Sharp alerted the Webbs, who had gone on an extended tour of Asia. The coal seams in South Wales were the most difficult to work and there had been disputes over wage rates in 1910–11 with limited violence in one area, when strike-breakers were utilized. The 1912 strike, which began on 1 March after members were balloted by the Miners' Federation, was national in scale and was over '"abnormal" places or other difficulties [which prevented pieceworkers] from earning wages at the ordinary tonnage or normal price list rates'. Until 1912,

> whenever the circumstances, such as bad roof, excessively hard or soft coal, shortage of tubs, or generally bad physical conditions in a working-place, occurred, the amount of allowance ... in addition to the agreed basis ... was arranged as a result of a very unsatisfactory system [of] 'haggling' between the management and the workmen in the particular working-place concerned. Complaints as to the amount of [the] allowance being altogether inadequate to compensate for the difficulties over which the workmen claimed to have no control were frequent.[41]

Following meetings between the colliery proprietors and the miners, the owners reiterated that only coal getters could receive a fair day's wage for a fair day's work, but not all underground pieceworkers could be given such a wage. This was rejected by the men, whose leaders insisted that no adult male working underground should receive less than 5s. per day, while boys' pay was to be no less than 2s. Asquith wrote to the Miners' Federation on 20 February 1912 that a prolonged stoppage in the coal industry was unacceptable to the government because of its repercussions on industry and consumers and summoned both parties to sessions with the Industrial Council in an attempt to resolve the differences between them. Further, he remarked that 'the principle of a minimum wage should become part and parcel of the organization and of the working of the coal mining industry of this country'.[42]

Asquith with the assistance of Lloyd George, Edward Grey and Buxton tried without success to negotiate a settlement between the parties. With the strike showing no indication of terminating, Asquith informed the parties on 15 April 1912 that the government was determined to introduce legislation

> (1) to make a reasonable minimum wage, adequately safeguarded, a statutory term of every contract of employment underground in coal mines, (2) to provide for the ascertainment of such wage locally, in each district, by a Board on which employers and men would be equally represented with a neutral Chairman.[43]

Four days later, Asquith introduced the Coal Mines (Minimum Wage) Bill in the Commons and it reached the statute book by 29 March 1912 with bi-partisan support, as Bonar Law, the leader of the opposition, was privately updated by Asquith on the state of the negotiations. The kernel of the bill was a Cabinet Paper drawn up by the chief inspector of mines and submitted by Reginald McKenna, the home secretary, which suggested extending the district boards extant in Durham and Northumberland, comprising six representatives of the colliery owners and six of the men plus an impartial chairman, to the rest of the country. In South Wales the coal getters hitherto besides the work of extracting coal had undertaken other tasks, such as taking the tubs into the face and setting the timber props, thus complicating the wages question. During Cabinet discussions of the proposed legislation, Lord Morley and Winston Churchill 'expressed doubts as to its expediency', but after further consideration the original proposals were modified. Hence 'the penal provision against employers paying less than the minimum, which was felt to be one-sided' was omitted, as it was indefensible 'in argument'.[44]

Another major point in contention was whether 5s. (for men) and 2s. (for boys) minimum wage rates should be incorporated in the schedule to the bill. Mrs Asquith wrote secretly to Robert Smillie, one of the most intransigent strike leaders, on 16 March, confiding in him that that she did not 'like to see … [her] husband suffer in his longing to be fair, just, and kind to both sides in this tragic quarrel' and pleading with him 'for an honourable settlement'. In her diary she confided: 'I don't mind prophesying that there will be terrible awakenings in a few years to the absolute necessity of giving a minimum or better said – *a living wage* to every worker in our islands.'[45] On Thursday 21 March, George Riddell, the newspaper proprietor, saw the prime minister.

> I told him plainly that the Bill would not go thro[ugh] unless 5s. & 2s. were included & showed him two of the amendments which I had prepared. He asked me to leave the paper with him & sd he would see what cd be done regarding the 5s. & 2s. He seemed worried and walked rapidly up & down the room. He was however gen[erally] genial & kind.[46]

The next day Riddell handed a letter to Lloyd George, proposing that the problem should be resolved by experts at the Board of Trade.

> L.G. showed it to Asquith & Sir Ed[ward] Grey but the former would not give way. He says that it is a question of principle. I cd understand the whole question of the minimum wage was a question of principle but I don't understand how the 5s. & 2s. can be so.[47]

Lunching with the chancellor, Rufus Isaacs, and Harold Spender on the Saturday, Lloyd George advised Riddell that

> he had strongly supported the inclusion of the 5s. & 2s. I sd they had missed a great opportunity, to which they admitted. L.G. looked worn out physically & mentally … Masterman told me that McKenna was opposed to the inclusion of the minimum 5s. & 2s. because he thought it wd lead to competition between Parliamentary candidates in mining districts at election times … During the past week … all sorts of influences had been brought to bear upon him [Asquith] & having gone $^7/_8$ths of the way he had stopped.[48]

Even as late as 18 March 1912 Lloyd George had stated that '[i]t is not Parliament's business to settle rates of wages'; only the miners' obduracy made him change his mind, but the majority of his Cabinet colleagues remained unconvinced. Despite the miners rejecting the settlement imposed by the new Coal Mines (Minimum Wage) Act after a vote, their leaders persuaded them to return to work early in April, as a two-thirds majority in favour of continuing the strike was not obtained on the ballot.[49]

Sydney Buxton, the president of the Board of Trade, appointed independent chairmen of the district boards which were set up under the Act, who by their tact and impartiality won the confidence of the employers and the miners. Everywhere there were significant wage rises in line with the underlying agreement. For instance, Judge J. K. Bradbury informed Buxton that in North Staffordshire,

> The Joint Board unanimously fixed the minimum wage for boys at a rate varying from 2s. a day at 14 to 4s. 6d a day at 21, and the minimum wage for the lowest paid classes of workmen has been fixed by myself, in default of agreement by the Board, at 5s. per day, except in the 5 collieries in the Cheadle District.[50]

During the summer of 1912 there was a transport strike involving the Port of London. Lloyd George and Haldane were 'inclined to favour' statutory powers 'either to make the rates of wages recognised in representative agreements compulsory in regard to all persons employed in the Port, or to give power to the Port Authority to fix a scale of wages from time to time'. Herbert Samuel was another minister who looked favourably on such initiatives. But Asquith and most of the Cabinet disagreed and 'subsequently [it] decided that there was no case for legislation'.[51] So too, when Asquith was asked by George Barnes, a Labour MP, in December 1912 whether he would facilitate the extension of the Trade Boards Act to all the sweated industries, he replied that 'the success of the experiment largely depends on any extension being of a gradual and cautious nature'.[52]

Clifford Sharp wrote to the Webbs in March 1912 about the new social and political climate prevailing in England, stating that during their long stay overseas 'the whole politico-economic situation' had changed. He told them of the strikes and their consequences. The 'upheaval must leave a permanent and a deep mark on our industrial and political history. The State within the state has suddenly come to its full power.' Further, '[w]ithin a week the Miners' Federation has converted Parliament and the nation to accept a legislative measure for which they would have had to fight 10 years if they had relied solely on political action through the Labour Party'. By September 1912, Sharp was advising them that '[i]t is in many respects, an awakened England which confronts us today. A new spirit and temper are being manifested by the industrial classes, and an entirely new group of questions has emerged' – above all, the minimum wage and adequate housing for the working class.[53]

## The Land Campaign

Despite his successes, Lloyd George's reputation remained on a roller-coaster. After he had steered the 1909 Budget and health insurance through Parliament, both very tricky pieces of legislation, his prestige suffered two blows. He had led a brilliant populist campaign in the country in favour of the Budget, winning the January 1910 election for the Liberals and thrashing the aristocratic–City alliance which had ruled the country for so long. Because national insurance required contributions from participants, it was thoroughly disliked by the electors. In December 1911 Lord Esher remarked:

> The Insurance Bill is very unpopular. Like the Education Act of 1870 it will drive its authors from office at the next General Election. I saw Lloyd George in the House of Lords this evening and he fully realises his position.[54]

The chancellor was very keen on a coalition with the Unionists in 1910 with the hidden intention of supplanting Asquith, though the negotiations foundered and came to nothing.[55] Meanwhile he had so alienated Sir Robert Chalmers, his resourceful civil servant at the Treasury, on both the Budget and health insurance that Chalmers had decided to take up the position of governor of Ceylon in September 1913. In conversation with Margot Asquith, Chalmers was scathing about Lloyd George's role in the Marconi affair, a scandal over the purchase of shares for which he had to apologize to the House of Commons:

> This is what I mind ... the truth [being dragged out of him] in driblets. Lloyd George is a treacherous man ... he thinks his brains make up for what you call trading ... not for me! But Mrs Asquith – people who think of themselves first are not really worth spending time on.[56]

Lloyd George thought he could redeem his position in the country by resurrecting the land campaign in a fresh and more incisive form and yet further undermine the power base of the aristocracy in the countryside. Just as he had appeared to be righting the situation for himself, Lloyd George's reputation plunged yet again by having to withdraw important sections of the 1914 Budget which had been ill prepared and too hurriedly introduced. On 9 May 1914 Margot Asquith noted: 'Lloyd George has distinctly slumped [in popularity] for what reason I don't quite know & his Budget hasn't caught on at all.'[57]

But Lloyd George was still determined to wrest the initiative from his Cabinet colleagues, particularly Haldane, who wanted to make education the big issue before the country, and shape the future course of Liberal social politics. A confidential memorandum which was submitted on 20 May 1912 to the Liberal leaders on 'Labour Unrest and Liberal Social Policy' by Seebohm Rowntree, J. A. Hobson, L. T. Hobhouse and Percy Alden urged:

> The time has come to have in view, as the distinctive objective of Liberal policy, the principle of a living wage for every worker, [for] the Railway workers, stimulated by the success of Coal Miners in securing a minimum wage, are certain to present in the very near future a demand for similar legislation.[58]

They suggested that in the transport and agricultural industries the provision of a minimum wage should be dealt with by special legislation, following the Coal Mines (Minimum Wage) Act, though in those industries,

> where the existing rates are in many cases decidedly lower, it might be well to consider whether they should be directed to have regard to the cost of maintaining an average family in physical efficiency, and in the case of any other workers where the wages are exceptionally low as compared with the wages of similar workers in other employments or with those of adult male workers in the same employment.[59]

Throughout 1912, Lloyd George, still steeped in the experience of the rural community in which he grew up, ridiculed the idea of a minimum wage for the town dweller, as opposed to his own scheme for a land campaign to regenerate national life. 'The Labour Party have never made any real progress. They have never made an appeal to the imagination. You can never run a great political campaign on wages ... It is too sordid', Lloyd George told Riddell on 2 July 1912. Around him, his advisers sedulously pressed for a minimum wage, particularly his political confidants Riddell and Charles Masterman, financial secretary to the Treasury from 1912–14, who was later joined by Seebohm Rowntree, whose influence was probably paramount on the urban section of the Land Enquiry Committee.[60] Nonetheless, Lloyd George overrode the advice of these urban experts because his knowledge of unfamiliar urban conditions lacked depth and his own analysis of the causes and extent of industrial poverty bore little resemblance to the findings of the sociologists. He advised the Commons on 8 May 1912:

> [Mr J. H. Thomas] says that there are 97,000 men in the railway world earning less than £1 per week ... unskilled labour, not merely on the railways but in the transport world generally, produces conditions of the same kind. Is he [another MP] quite sure that it is not very largely due to the fact that agricultural labourers, who constitute the reservoir from which railway labour, carters, dockers, and others are supplied, are very much underpaid in this country ... I am certain that it does have a very serious effect in depressing wages in the labour market in the industrial districts and towns of this country.[61]

As an analysis of the causes of industrial unrest, this statement smacks of enough truth to be superficially plausible, but its neglect of the situation in the towns meant it was misleading. However, by the summer of 1912 the chancellor was conceding that they might have compulsory arbitration by the state of wage disputes, though neither employers nor employed were as yet ready for this.[62]

In June 1912 Lloyd George informally opened his land campaign by inviting a group of radicals including Seebohm Rowntree, C. P. Scott, Charles Roden Buxton and Charles Masterman for breakfast, when it was decided to set up the Land Enquiry Committee with separate investigations into the rural and urban aspects of the problem.[63] Added impetus had been given to the movement for rural regeneration by the establishment of the Land and Home League – an amalgamation of the Cooperative Small Holdings Society, the Land Club Union and the Rural Development Society – in April 1911. It produced a new seven-point programme, whose principal objectives were the provision of small holdings, better housing in country districts, the encouragement of agricultural cooperation with the Agricultural Organization Society, and above all, the application of the Trade Boards Act to agricultural labourers, an idea zealously pursued by C. R. Buxton. Under the direction of St G. Heath as general secretary and H. L. Reiss as organizer, and aided by several paid assistants in the twelve districts into which the country was divided, the rural section of the Land Enquiry had made such swift progress that it had collected replies to its questionnaires by October 1912. At a meeting at Gaddesby Hall, Leicester, a secret memorandum was drafted between 27 and 30 September 1912, calling for a 'Minimum Wage. A living wage should be established by statute'; 'Housing Community should find houses eventually at economic rents – subsidy – out of National tax on Land values'; and 'Land Courts – to fix rents in view of the minimum wage – security of tenure for good husbandry', which was signed by Lloyd George and C. R. Buxton, among others.[64] To appease Haldane, whose education campaign had been sidelined, the chancellor later agreed to his proposal for an arbitration panel of Land Commissioners rather than land courts. Lloyd George, influenced by Rowntree, envisaged a national wages tribunal regulated by statute which would be able to 'award a wage which would secure the physical efficiency of the labourer and his family, and also enable him to pay a commercial rent for his cottage'. In contrast Walter Runciman at the Board of Agriculture held that a national minimum wage was impracticable.[65]

According to the 1901 census, there were more than 600,000 male farm labourers, servants and shepherds in England and Wales; of these 350,000 (60 per cent) were labourers who worked on the soil, while the remaining 250,000 looked after animals. Some 70 per cent of the agricultural workers in England and Wales were labourers with no direct interest in the land which they worked; only 30 per cent were farmers or smallholders. Here again Seebohm Rowntree's analysis of rural conditions was compelling. He estimated in 1913 that the average weekly wage of the ordinary male agricultural labourer in England, counting both payments in kind and cash, was 17s. 6d. per week, with cattlemen – whose work was slightly more skilled – earning 18s. 4d. He computed that if a family of five's total income was less than 20s. 6d. and their rent was 2s., they were not earning enough for the maintenance of physical efficiency and could be said to be living 'below the poverty line'. Of these male agricultural labourers above the age of twenty years, only 9.5 per cent drew an average wage of 20s. or more per week, leading to the conclusion that the overwhelming bulk of the rural population was racked by the curse of poverty.[66] Earlier surveys applying Rowntree's methodology to individual villages by P. H. Mann for Ridgmont in Bedfordshire in 1905 showed that out of a total population of 467 persons, 41.4 per cent of the population lived in poverty; secondly, in 1909 Maude F. Davies investigated Corsley in Wiltshire, finding that out of 220 households, 28.6 per cent of the families' standard of living fell below the poverty line. Thus Rowntree's later investigation conclusively proved that the dimensions of rural poverty were wider and more urgent than the two earlier pioneering surveys had assumed.[67] George Roberts, a Labour MP from a rural background, pointed out that he had relatives in Norfolk who were agricultural labourers earning 12s. and 13s. per week without any garden and also forbidden to keep a fowl or pig. Despite the fact that average earnings for these labourers in Norfolk were said to be 15s. 4d. on figures supplied by employers, he believed that in reality they were more in the region of 13s.[68]

Hence Lloyd George opened the land campaign in a speech at Bedford on 11 October 1913, which in Margot Asquith's opinion 'has worried every one a little & Mr Runciman [the minister involved] a good deal'.[69] He followed this up with a major address in Swindon on 22 October 1913, in which he announced that the government was establishing a Ministry of Lands and Forests to supersede the former department and that Land Commissioners would be entrusted with the valuation of land, the purchase of uncultivated land, and powers to afforest and reclaim such land. The government's intention was to build 120,000 cottages, by tapping into the money available in the Insurance Reserve Fund, and through the commissioners' regulation of wages fix a living wage to enable rural labourers to pay the rent. Excessive hours of labour would also be reduced. When there was a sale of land, the commissioners would have the power to order the vendor to grant compensation to the farmer for improvements. Walter Runciman, the minister of agriculture, was 'doubtful as to the [desirability of a] minimum wage' for agriculture. He was reluctant to concede that either the Trade Boards Act or the Coal Mines (Minimum) Wage Act was applicable to the case of agricultural labourers. Lloyd George, he informed Asquith, 'only wanted a living wage "because Rowntree has invented a protein standard"'.[70] Runciman feared that if such proposals were implemented in the countryside, landlords with a bigger wage bill to pay would reduce their labour force and that land would be converted into pasture. To conciliate Runciman, the chancellor permitted him to give priority to a bill to build 90,000 cottages in rural areas. Despite the Liberal administration's good intentions, the First World War delayed the government's legislative programme.[71] An attempt by the Labour party to introduce an Agricultural Labourers (Wages and Hours) Bill on 13 February 1914 did not proceed very far. Because of declining imports of food during the war, the Corn Production Act 1917 guaranteed the price of wheat and oats and imposed a minimum wage of 25s. for labourers – a reform enthusiastically endorsed by Lloyd George, who was now prime minister.[72]

So too, when Lloyd George came to present his urban proposals in a speech in Middlesbrough on 9 November 1913, despite the fact that he was fully briefed on what the urban land section of his investigating committee's report contained, he reversed their priorities by presenting the plight of the casual labourer as of wider dimensions than the distress of sweated workers – an endorsement of the somewhat jaded casual labour theory of pauperism:

> And then we come to that poor residuum of the population who, if you gave them a new house, could not pay for it, who working hard and incessantly cannot earn enough to pay for it – you would be amazed if you looked into it how many there are of them in our slums – we propose to deal with that by extending our wages boards so far as to give people who labour a fair day's work … Then there is the still larger problem of casual labour – the people who can only get a job for a day or two and then they cannot get anything.[73]

In sum, Lloyd George's message was circumscribed by a tendentious theory that the surplus labour generated by deteriorating conditions in the countryside caused it to flood into low-paid occupations in the towns, resulting in it ominously sinking into casual occupations and generating a rash of strikes; and that the shortest cut to abolishing poverty in towns was to regenerate rural life and create more employment opportunities to drain the surplus urban labour force. What this was to ignore was that the towns, by far the largest sector of the economy, generated their own conditions of distress which were responsible for producing casual labour, a minor sore, and poverty from low wages, a massive problem.

Nonetheless, the whole slant of Lloyd George's land campaign throughout the first half of 1914, even in urban areas, was on various aspects of the land problem; the specific reform issues were ill-defined, and in most of the boroughs the campaign aroused so little interest that the secretary of the Central Land and Housing Council wrote to Lloyd George on 28 May 1914: 'Speaking of the country as a whole I may say without any exception the Government's proposals are arousing unprecedented enthusiasm in the rural constituencies.' Apart from the north-east counties, Lancashire, East Anglia and the West Country, where the campaign was going 'fairly well', though not with the impact made in the countryside, 'the campaign in the boroughs has been disappointing'. He suggested that if the chancellor gave a clear public pledge that 'the principle of the Trade Boards Act will be extended to include all low-paid workers, it would place our urban campaign on an entirely different level'.[74] On 6 January 1914 Charles Trevelyan MP, an influential junior minister, reminded Lloyd George: 'Please don't forget that a large part of the best Liberals, especially where they are strongest, are remaining lukewarm about your Land Campaign till you are explicit about Land Values.' However, despite misgivings to the contrary, Lloyd George was never a single taxer and was contemptuous of the extremists on his side. Yet even so in June 1914 the government had still not reassured its supporters in the towns that a proportion of all municipal rates would be levied on land values, nor (as we have seen earlier) were its proposals on housing reform inspiring.[75] The secretary of the Home Counties Liberal Federation advised Lloyd George that '[s]o far, I should say, Greater London is quite unmoved. The Land Question has not touched it at all', while the secretary of the Yorkshire Federation declared that 'generally speaking town meetings have been small and dull, and little enthusiasm has been aroused'. 'But however satisfactory the progress of the agitation may be in the Rural Districts', Lloyd George told Runciman, 'it is quite clear that something more has to be done to educate the Urban population' – virtually an admission of failure. The concentration of the chancellor on rural issues even in towns blunted the Liberal propaganda drive.[76]

An added reason why the campaign did not gather momentum and sparkle was the dominance of the staple political issues in Parliament and the constituencies. The chief organizer of the Liberal campaign confided in Lloyd George: 'Public attention has been so occupied with Gun-running [in Ireland], Army revolts and Parliamentary manoeuvres that it had been difficult to arouse interest in Land and Housing.' On 29 April 1914, Edwin Montagu warned Lloyd George that he should take steps to make his Budget more popular, by dropping Herbert Samuel's elaborate rating bill, as the parliamentary timetable was congested with 'Home Rule, Welsh Disestablishment, Plural Voting, the Budget, the Revenue Bill and Education'.[77] Ernest Simon, a Manchester Fabian, was critical of C. P. Scott, the editor of the *Guardian*, for the same reasons, thinking it strange that he 'should feel more deeply about the wrongs of the captured Albanians or Armenians than of the starving slum dwellers of Manchester! And prefer Home Rule to a minimum wage.' All this meant that the politicians found it easy to shelve the new social questions year after year, protested the *New Statesman* in 1914:

> Then there are Poor Law Reform, the extension of Wages Boards, the drastic revision of Grants-in-Aid, and most important of all, perhaps, the general problem of Unemployment – all matters which have been waiting for years. The truth is, we fear, that with all our national awakening to the importance of the social, as distinguished from purely political questions, the politicians do not regard them as possessing any very great electioneering value, except in those instances in which they can be dealt with on large and spectacular lines.[78]

Seebohm Rowntree throughout the first half of 1914 pressed Lloyd George to spare him more time to confer on unsettled points of policy, including proposals on urban housing 'beyond the very general one that it is intended to make a survey' and some clearer definition of the 'Minimum Wage and some discussion as to the machinery to fix it'; and 'What is going to be done with regard to the fixing of a Minimum Wage in towns? This is most important.' But because traditional political issues continued to dominate the stage, it was not until the first days of June that the two men met to discuss a clarification of policy. Lloyd George informed Rowntree:

> It is almost impossible to find time up here for a prolonged discussion of the very important points that you put to me. Moreover, what between the Budget and the Irish question, there are too many distractions.'[79]

On 11 June 1914, Lloyd George and Edwin Montagu, the financial secretary to the Treasury, held talks on certain unresolved aspects of the land campaign before the chancellor sought the Asquiths' final endorsement of his programme. Montagu wrote to Lloyd George:

> It was, I think, agreed yesterday that the definition of a minimum wage in the country should be the definition in the Prime Minister's speech at the National Liberal Club; that a minimum wage in town should be secured by an early extension of the Trade Boards Act to embrace as far as possible all low-paid trades.[80]

He added that 'we also ought to decide whether Trade Boards or [Land] Commissioners shall fix the wages in the country districts' the appointment of a Cabinet Committee would resolve this. What Asquith outlined in his speech on 9 December 1913 was a definition of the minimum wage which would be payable in rural districts, which he took to mean 'a wage such as to ensure to the labourer of average industry and prudence reasonable conditions of living, among which I include the ability to pay commercial or economic rent for the house in which he lives'. If the farmer could show that an increase in the wages of his labourers would be an additional burden for him, he could apply to the commissioners for a reduction of the rent. Like Lloyd George, Asquith erroneously believed that the urban problem 'is in many ways less complex and demands shorter treatment than the rural one'.[81] One matter which Asquith clarified in this address was that business tenants with a twenty-one-year lease should have the right to apply for renewal on equitable terms, but improvements made at their own expense were not to be taken into account when fixing the new rent.[82]

Speaking in the Commons on 13 March 1913, Sydney Buxton, the progressive president of the Board of Trade, explained that the principle of a minimum wage had been

> conceded in regard to the less paid and the less organised sweated trades of the country. It has been conceded to a certain extent in regard to the coal-mining industry. But the principle of a minimum wage there applied was not necessarily a minimum living wage and there is a very considerable distinction. As regards the Trades Boards it has been a great success. As regards the question of mines, the minimum wage was still in its infancy, and it remains to be seen how far it is likely to be successful and so be extended to other industries ... Whether we adopt a flat rate or not – and it is quite obvious, if you have a minimum rate, it must be local and for trades and not general – I do not think myself, after carefully considering it, that it is for the House of Commons to fix such a rate.[83]

But in the same year Buxton was able to extend the trade boards to five new industries, embracing linen and cotton embroidery, holloware making, tin box making, sugar confectionery and food preserving, and shirt making. The familiar pattern was followed of introducing the boards mainly into trades with a high percentage of women workers.[84] So too, when replying to a deputation from the Miners' Federation in 1914, Asquith adamantly refused to extend the Coal Mines (Minimum Wage) Act to surface workers, adding that 'the principle of the Legal Minimum Wage was applicable only under comparatively rare and exceptional conditions'.[85]

Shortly afterwards, on 9 April 1913, Will Crooks, the Labour MP for Woolwich, moved a resolution in the Commons stating that

> the right of every family in the country to an income sufficient to enable it to maintain its members in decency and comfort should be recognised; that ... the Trade Boards Act should be so extended to provide for the establishment of a minimum wage of at least 30s. per week for every adult worker in urban areas and a minimum wage that will secure an approximately equal standard of life for every adult worker in rural areas; and that ... the Government should set an example by adopting the minimum of 30s. per week in its own workshops and insert it as a condition in all contracts.[86]

Percy Alden, a radical Liberal MP, moved an amendment welcoming 'the setting up of effective machinery whereby a Legal Minimum Wage might be secured to the worker in all those trades in which wages are below subsistence point'. Alden maintained that the only way to implement a minimum wage was 'by taking an individual trade and suiting yourself to the conditions and needs of that trade in each individual district and locality'. To introduce a 30s. minimum wage everywhere would only undermine the Trade Boards Act, as the schemes were based on inconsistent principles. In fact, 'there is nothing I want to see more than a minimum wage fixed in every trade where the workers have low pay'. He appealed to Labour members not to press ahead with their resolution, by omitting the 30s. minimum which makes it 'impossible for us [sympathisers on the Liberal benches], or for any Government, to apply it under the Trade Boards Act'. Despite pleas by Crooks, the debate was adjourned without a vote being taken.[87]

In March 1914 the Labour Party sponsored the Labour (Minimum Conditions) Bill which extended trade boards to every industry and also enabled them to deal with 'hours, meal-times, holidays, and juvenile labour as well as wages'. By stipulating that the normal minimum wage for adults was to be 25s., it attempted to gain maximum support from the Parliamentary Liberal party.[88]

All the talk of extending the field of operation of the trade boards meant very little without a re-evaluation of their functions, for the pre-1914 boards gave pay awards in line with what they assessed a trade could bear rather than with an ultimate aim of raising wage levels to a living wage. The trade boards possessed a number of flaws: 'The Boards so far have not yet as much courage as might have been hoped', proclaimed the National Committee for the Prevention of Destitution – and our own detailed examination of wage settlements made under their auspices substantiates this appraisal – 'and have been ready to listen to the pleas that large increases of wages would ruin the trades concerned'. Further:

> The application of the Act is too restricted. The Trade Board has power to extend it to other trades, but only to those in which wages are 'exceptionally low' compared to other trades; thus, many trades that ought to be brought in are excluded merely because others are in a worse plight.[89]

In addition, the boards did not have the power to deal with hours of work and other conditions of the wage contract. In 1914, J. A. Hobson argued that,

> apart from the great bulk of casual workers in all less skilled trades, there are a large strata of skilled and trained adult labour in the staple trades of the country which are not paid a full subsistence wage. Such are the large bodies of women employed in factories and workshops in the retail trade ... The same statement holds true of the wage of agricultural labour in most districts of the middle and southern counties of England.[90]

Even a progressive Liberal such as Seebohm Rowntree, who advocated a subsistence wage for all workers, demurred against excessive wage settlements:

> There is, therefore, a definite limit beyond which wages cannot be raised without throwing many workers out of employment. [Nonetheless] the limit is not so low as the average employer would often have us suppose. He does not allow for the economies in the cost of production which can, if necessary, be brought about in his own factory, nor for the increased efficiency on the part of better paid workers ... If in any industry it could be proved by the employers that the immediate raising of wages to an efficiency level would lead to widespread unemployment, it would be wise to make advances gradually, fixing however, a date, possibly two or even three years ahead, by which the efficiency maximum must be reached.[91]

Because of the clogging of the government's legislative programme by the Irish issue and the controversy over the 1914 Budget, there was no time to announce this clarification of urban policy in a major address by Asquith or Lloyd George before the onset of the war. Nor was it certain that either Asquith or the chancellor would have placed enough emphasis on the urban low wage problem in a future Liberal election campaign or that the land programme would be able to increase house production sufficiently for enough homes to be built and become available at an economic rent.

Increasingly towards the end of 1913 and into 1914 the Liberal administration, despite the land campaign, was growing increasingly unpopular and losing votes and seats to Labour among its working-class supporters. When Rufus Isaacs vacated his parliamentary seat in Reading to become Lord Chief Justice, the Liberal candidate G. P. Gooch, a radical and Fabian who campaigned on national health insurance and the extension of wages boards to rural areas, lost the by-election on 8 November 1913 to the Unionist candidate because many voters defected to the socialist candidate.[92] Similarly Masterman, on being promoted to the Cabinet, stood for Ipswich and was heavily defeated in May 1914. Masterman claimed that

> The result was chiefly due to the Insurance Act, which should have been voluntary and free to the poor. 'I am the victim', he concluded … M. said he had noted with surprise that all the poorest sections of the town were strongly opposed to him. The placards of his opponents were displayed in every window, and he [Masterman] was hissed and booed by women and children. His supporters were the mechanics, small shopkeepers, etc.[93]

Lloyd George's prestige had sunk to a low point: he had been humiliated by the Marconi scandal and the fiasco over his 1914 Budget, which had been assembled in a clumsy fashion.

The Webbs and the National Committee for the Prevention of Destitution pressed for the establishment of a minister of labour, who would set up trade boards in any industry in which 20 per cent of the workforce or employers desired him to do so. The minister would then decide whether there should be a single trade board or 'separate boards in separate districts'. Every part of the country would have a recognized minimum standard wage, based on the price of house room, food, clothing and other necessities and expressed in monetary terms, until such time as Parliament decided it needed to be raised.[94] This was a much more flexible scheme than the Labour party bills, and closer to the Liberal viewpoint, as embodied in a speech of J. M. Robertson, the parliamentary secretary to the Board of Trade.[95] Yet it was too extreme for the electorate to accept in 1914, and if there was to be a momentous shift in the distribution of the national income to the working class, it was found to be easier to achieve by implementing a wide range of social services, such as subsidies for council house building paid for out of the national Exchequer.

# Conclusion

Natty Rothschild, writing to his French cousins in January 1906 after the Liberal landslide in the general election and the emergence of a powerful group of Labour MPs, perceptively noted:

> Elections have gone one way [against the Unionists] although the number of Labour members in the new Parliament is small their influence will be great & they ask for a good many things, a large & comprehensive scheme of old age pensions, and a square meal once a day for every child in school, reversal of the Taff Vale decision ... so we shall have a lively time. Their best men say 'We are not Socialists or Anarchists who want to destroy wealth to be used for the benefit of all'.[1]

He also supposed 'next year we shall see some form of graduated income tax introduced, if only to satisfy the vanity of the radical Chancellor of the Exchequer for the time being'. Lord Rothschild was right in predicting that the influence of Labour MPs would lead to the advent of school meals subsidized by the local authority (1906) and non-contributory old age pensions (1908) and that Asquith as chancellor of the Exchequer would set in motion the reforms which would lead to the modernization of the tax system, thus paving the way for a form of graduated income tax and supertax to raise the funds needed for social reform. But this was not the whole story, and additional factors also came into play.

First there was the rise of the counter-elite recruited from the settlement movement, the proponents of the social gospel, women's organizations, the professional associations, the Webbs and the Fabian Society plus the London School of Economics, and the land associations – all these groups were responsible for the emergence of the New Liberalism and a new appetite for social reform among ministers and backbench MPs, while the same factors also influenced a new wave of young civil servants. Among these groups we would highlight the role of women in the reform of infant, child and juvenile welfare and the anti-sweating campaign, which was as invaluable as the support of Labour in implementing the government's new agenda. Secondly, the invention of applied sociology by such members of the business class as Charles Booth and Seebohm Rowntree, particularly the poverty survey, showed that the problems associated with destitution could be isolated and broken into component parts and solutions could then be found for each individual problem. In a looser sense Beatrice Webb, as a shrewd adviser of her father, a businessman with many financial interests, and as a protégé of Charles Booth, was also a member of this class.[2] An alliance of City and aristocratic interests had previously ruled Britain, espousing free trade, cheap food and low taxation and opposing big government. The top-ranking civil servants, mostly Oxbridge graduates with a classical education, had in the past had little understanding of the problems of poverty, thus happily serving this alliance, but some of these officials had undergone an uncomfortable encounter with the residents of the city slums while living in a university settlement and a few had their intellectual outlook changed by learning the methods of applied sociology and the new ideologies swirling around the universities. Idealist philosophy, which could lead either in the direction of collectivism or for intervention on an individual social casework basis, was a less important intellectual current than applied sociology and socialism in changing the outlook of later generations of university students. Thirdly, the new improved methods of communication, the telegraph and telephone, the railways and steamships meant that international congresses concerned with the various aspects of welfare met more frequently; and it was in these international gatherings that British reformers first became aware of the advances in social reform which had occurred overseas, especially in child welfare. Britain was in a fortunate geographical position, being close to the European continent and having good communications with the English-speaking world across the Atlantic and also excellent relations with its dominions in Australia and New Zealand, where many experiments had been carried out to stamp out sweating, to grant old age pensions and to introduce a graduated income tax. So too, much was borrowed from Germany, where officials were happy to discuss their thinking with Liberal reformers such as T. C. Horsfall on town planning and others on continuation education and ministers such as David Lloyd George with respect to social insurance.

What needs to be emphasized is the vital importance of two groups allied to the New Liberalism, and sometimes overlapping in its membership, in contributing to the government's social reform programme: the two wings of the Labour movement, comprising its working-class supporters and the Sociological Socialists on the one hand, and the women social reformers on the other. As mentioned in Chapter 2, I would place a much higher evaluation on the contribution of the Fabian Society and the Webbs to the reform achievements of the Liberal administrations than other historians might. At the same time, I would assess the political influence of the Edwardian women social reformers on at least an equal level to that of the suffragettes, and possibly on a significantly raised level. Beatrice Webb, who straddled both groups as a female reformer and Sociological Socialist, was one of the most influential women in twentieth-century British politics. Her sociological theorizing on sweating and the reconstruction of the public health system permanently changed the agenda of the Asquith administrations. As we indicated in the Introduction, the Liberal social reforms came in three waves: some barely noticed child welfare reforms in the period 1906 to the spring of 1908, when Campbell-Bannerman was serving as prime minister (Chapter 3); a spate of fundamental reforms when he was succeeded by Asquith from 1908 to 1911 (Chapters 4–12), each reform resting on a careful sociological analysis, without which any political action would have been stillborn; and a final attempt to rethink the agenda of the New Liberalism from 1911 until 1914 under the impact of rising labour discontent (Chapters 13–15), by slowly moving towards new goals in public health, housing, secondary education and the minimum wage.

Critical in the first phase of social reforms was a series of child welfare measures, particularly the medical inspection and treatment of schoolchildren and the provision of free school meals. Here we would regard the scouring of children from the city slums into the elementary schools in the 1880s and the following decade as crucial, rather than the national efficiency hypothesis which sees the reforms as flowing from the unfitness of the recruits to the armed services exposed by the Boer War. Nor did the impetus for such reforms come from a group of imperialist social reformers, but from the active campaigning of sections of the Labour movement and members of the NUT and the medical profession, particularly the Medical Officers of Health. Again, the child welfare reforms were across a very broad front, involving the introduction of special children's courts and probation officers, the Children's Act of 1908, and later the removal of state children from Poor Law barrack schools into scattered homes, the restrictions on the employment of children, and the opening of child labour bureaux to tackle the problem of blind-alley occupations. Moreover, the expansion of the child welfare services was influenced by the experiments taking place overseas. Much of this emulation of these more advanced foreign innovations was driven by a spirit of friendly cooperation, not a desire to triumph over competitors because of military or trade rivalry. If national efficiency was such an important factor driving the quest for reform, it is difficult to explain why the reforms for the medical inspection and treatment of schoolchildren and for free school dinners were so limited and tentative at first; and why Haldane, who was on the imperialist wing of the Liberal party, failed in 1914 to make educational reform the centrepiece of a future election programme. School medical inspection and dinners were demanded by pressure groups, but the Children's Act of 1908 was a government-sponsored bill and indicated a change of disposition among some ministers.

When Asquith became prime minister on 8 April 1908, he had already set in motion the machinery to secure two fundamental reforms: old age pensions, and the overhaul of the Inland Revenue to raise the taxes to pay for a non-contributory scheme costing £8 million; this inaugurated the second and more important phase of the Liberal social reform programme of 1908 to 1911. By staying at the head of the government and promoting Lloyd George to the office of chancellor of the Exchequer and Winston Churchill to become president of the Board of Trade, the balance of power within the Cabinet changed in a more radical direction, but Asquith also set the tone of the new administration by announcing that it would tackle the problems connected with infirmity and poverty. His calmness of manner and unemotional, rational form of discourse reassured the public, allowing for momentous changes to occur. Under the influence of the Webbs and Haldane, Asquith made the break-up of the Poor Law the supreme task of his new administration, so allowing for a fresh surge of creativity by Churchill and Lloyd George. Despite his junior Cabinet rank, Churchill became for a short while the senior ideologist of the new administration with his plea for unemployment and health insurance and minimum wage regulation. At the same time in 1908 there was a trade depression and an upsurge in unemployment, with a fresh outburst of activity by the grassroots Right to Work campaign of the Labour movement and a determined effort by Winston Churchill to alleviate the distress caused by unemployment, which resulted in the Labour Exchanges Act (1909) and unemployment insurance (1911). Following on from Charles Booth's demonstration of the necessity for old age pensions, the case for trade boards setting a minimum wage and for labour exchanges rested on the same solid sociological underpinning. Meanwhile in 1909 the Royal Commission on the Poor Law was reporting and the Minority Report of the Webbs was pushing the government in the direction of health reform. Lloyd George from his experience as chancellor became unhappy at the rising cost of providing an improved medical service and, perhaps having encountered a demand for a national insurance scheme while serving at the Board of Trade, ordered his officials to prepare such a scheme, in which employers, employees and the state would all share part of the cost. Because of the constitutional crisis with the House of Lords provoked by the radical Budget of 1909 and the premature death of William Blain, the civil servant in charge of the scheme, the reform was delayed until 1911. At the suggestion of William Harbutt Dawson, a civil servant at the Board of Trade, the health and unemployment insurance schemes were harnessed together and announced in the 1909 Budget as the Liberal answer to the reform of the Poor Law. Despite the intervention of Haldane, Asquith dropped Poor Law reform partly because the reform of the relationship between imperial and local taxation had not as yet been resolved and partly because the Webbs' Minority Report was dominated by their wrong-headed adoption of the casual labour theory of poverty, making it less radical than they believed. Because other government departments now took over many Poor Law functions, thus drastically shrinking these institutions in size, Poor Law reform also became less urgent.

After his initial stint as a reforming chancellor of the Exchequer, Asquith was content to leave new initiatives to his ministers, Lloyd George and Churchill, acting himself in the role of mediator and mentor. According to his wife Margot, writing in 1914: 'Henry knocks all the others into a cocked hat ... I feel proud of being near so great a man.'[3] Asquith encouraged Churchill to establish trade boards to regulate wages in low-paid industries (1909) and labour exchanges as an institutional base for unemployment insurance, and supported Lloyd George in his battles with the friendly societies and doctors when they threatened to disrupt the health insurance scheme.

Nevertheless, particularly in the years 1908–11, it was the positivist sociological analysis of the different aspects of poverty, rather than Idealist philosophy – however pervasive it was in the Edwardian era and the 1930s – that paved the way for far-reaching social reform. On pensions, on public health, on unemployment, on sweated industries, on the boy labour problem, on taxation, there would not have been sustained state action without scrupulous positivist sociological enquiry. José Harris admitted as much, by referring to 'the descriptive positivism often associated with the Webbs' and 'William Beveridge, who in social-scientific methodology was an out-and-out positivist', even if there were traces of an Idealist vision in some of their work. Harris conceded that

> Other political theories, such as new liberalism, ethical socialism, 'national efficiency' and the 'national minimum', contributed to this ... [legitimizing framework for modern social policy and the growth of the welfare state]; but they were often not so much rivals of idealist thought as offshoots or partners of it.[4]

Harris also conceded that idealist thought reached the peak of its influence in Britain in the burgeoning university social science departments after the First World War, when the era of social reform had gone by.[5] In these years 1908–11 positivist sociological investigation and the social forces propelling it resulted in a seismic shift in the role of the state as far as the welfare of its inhabitants was concerned.

In response to the industrial unrest and wave of strikes erupting in 1911, Lloyd George secured a minimum wage for the coal miners in 1912, though Asquith was unwilling to concede such a wage in all other industries, where large numbers of men were not receiving a living wage; and the period 1911–14 marked the third and final phase of the Liberal reform programme which was derailed by the First World War. Lloyd George learnt quickly on the job and expanded his initial health insurance scheme in new directions to provide dispensaries and sanatoria for persons suffering from tuberculosis and for the treatment of venereal disease and to provide increased medical services for infants and children. Here Lloyd George was ably assisted by his adviser on health issues, Dr Christopher Addison and doctors Newsholme and Newman. Returning to earlier concerns, Lloyd George with Asquith's consent opened the land campaign in 1913 to challenge the rule of the aristocracy and landed interest in the countryside and to argue the case for a minimum wage for rural labourers, as this would help the Liberal party to retain their thirty rural seats – and if the swing of 1.2 per cent persisted, might net them a gain of a further nine seats in a future election.[6] Slowly by the summer of 1914 Asquith and Lloyd George were persuaded of the necessity for paying workers in the towns a subsistence wage, but they both tended to regard the rural land problem as more important than urban poverty and to exaggerate the dimensions of the casual labour problem; and as yet they had failed to clarify how this new wage structure in the towns was to be instituted. In any case Lloyd George's adviser, Seebohm Rowntree was still opposed to subsidies for the building of houses by local authorities, which meant that little was done to alleviate the urban housing shortage and to provide homes for workers at a reasonable rent. Hence even if the minimum wage programme was implemented in stages over several years, wage earners would still not generate enough income to rent affordable housing. What could not be done in peacetime was quickly solved in war, when the acute labour shortage drove up wages and kept them at a higher level, so that A. L. Bowley, in his second 'Five Towns Survey' in 1923–4, found that primary poverty had halved to 6.5 per cent: 'Between 1906 and 1924 the average weekly earnings of adult male workers rose from 27s. ... to 57s. 6d. (a rise of 113 per cent), while the cost of living rose by only 88 per cent.' Put another way, after allowing for corrections to his data, Bowley stated that the reduction in family size combined with a rise in real earnings ensured that the 'incidence of primary poverty' was reduced to 'about one third of its pre-war level' by 1924.[7]

D. Vincent's conclusion as to the alleviation of poverty by the Liberal administrations of 1906–14 was too sweeping:

> Despite all the research, all the argument, all the planning and plotting by ministers and their civil servants, all the rhetoric which accompanied each Act on to the Statute Book, the incidence of poverty, and the basic features of the

strategies the poor adopted to cope with their problems, changed very little between the end of the Boer War and the outbreak of the Great War ... The neighbourhood remained for the poor as essential and as inadequate a means of support as it had done in the latter half of the nineteenth century. Pawnbroking reached its peak as the Edwardian period came to an end.[8]

By the early 1920s the pre-war rate of poverty running at around 10 per cent or less, following Ian Gazeley, had halved. Part of the drop in poverty levels was due to a significant wage rise during the war, but part was the cumulative effect of this social legislation and that which quickly followed in its aftermath, which together lifted a sizeable portion of the population out of poverty and laid the foundations of the Welfare State. There was a marked transfer of income to the poorest members of the community, so much so that the series of reforms in this period deserves the designation of the Welfare Revolution.

What were the continuities and what were the differences between what the Liberal administrations of 1906–14 accomplished and the record of the Attlee governments of 1945–51 in creating what became known as the Welfare State? Much of the reconstruction after the war sprang from plans initiated in the wartime coalition led by Winston Churchill, who had played a major role in bringing the previous Liberal social reforms to fruition; and many of the key personnel were the same, including Lord Beveridge, Lord Addison and Seebohm Rowntree. Whereas many of the Liberal reforms were experimental, small-scale initiatives, the Labour reforms after the Second World War were universal in approach and on a much larger scale. Nonetheless, the pre-1914 Liberal governments together with the radical thinkers in their ranks and the Sociological Socialists had demarcated all the areas of social deprivation that needed immediate attention, from social security to public health, unemployment, decasualization of dock labour, pensions, housing, continuation education and the minimum wage.

On the other hand, Robert Lowe asserted that 'there have always been "five core social services" central to the welfare state [first established by the Attlee governments]: social security, education, health, housing and the personal social services', to which we would add the minimum wage. The importance attached by Lowe to personal social services goes back to the debate within the 1909 Royal Commission on the Poor Law. Despite the wide areas of agreement between the two reports, most members of the commission, following Helen Bosanquet, favoured an overhaul of the existing system, by encouraging thrift and friendly societies and by relying on volunteers and the establishment of a Public Assistance Authority to deal with those seeking help. In contrast the Webbs sought more state intervention and the distribution of Poor Law functions to different public authorities; yet even here there was a wide degree of overlapping, with the majority favouring a system of labour exchanges and a government subsidy to trade unions to encourage the taking up of trade union schemes of insurance against unemployment; again both supported the detention of certain incorrigible social groups.[9] Between the two world wars there was a huge expansion of training facilities for social workers within university departments 'as a humane discipline' due to the influence of Idealist philosophy and casework courses became more professionalized, resulting in social workers being recruited by local authorities. Hence the viewpoint of Helen Bosanquet, an adherent of Idealist philosophy, was not discarded after 1945 either at the local level or by the state-sponsored National Assistance Authority, even if the Welfare State more closely resembled the model outlined by the Webbs.[10]

The early 1940s and the total engagement of the British population in the war effort and their shared experience led to sentiments demanding universal treatment for all, not the selective services which had been provided by the Liberal administrations of 1906–14. Evacuation and rationing during the Second World War, it was argued, produced a national consensus for thorough-going reform, though this view has been challenged by revisionist historians. The Beveridge Report on Social Insurance published in 1942 sold 635,000 copies; its impact was immense. Beveridge's plan was comprehensive and provided health, unemployment, industrial injury and funeral benefits and covered the entire population, unlike the previous Liberal experiment, which was partial in scope. The scheme itself rested on a prior set of assumptions: the establishment of full employment, a universal health service, and family allowances, all of which would involve a further series of reforms and more government social planning. In other words, by ensuring that the whole population would in cases of necessity be able to draw on subsistence benefits, Beveridge conferred a measure of protection on everyone and revived the Webbs' pre-1914 idea of a national minimum.[11] Like the National Insurance Act of 1911, Beveridge's plan also rested on the questionable assumption of the male breadwinner, who would be able to provide for a wife and child, and had a built-in bias, an anti-feminist slant.

Before the First World War, under the stimulus of A. L. Bowley's submission to the Poor Law Commission, Herbert Samuel as postmaster-general had tried to initiate building programmes when trade was slack to stimulate employment, though he had found the right timing difficult to achieve in practice. Lloyd George's attempt to boost employment through rural regeneration by means of the Development Commission and the Land Enquiry was an old-fashioned and somewhat outmoded approach. During the Second World War scarce manpower resources were carefully allocated, as under-utilized resources were exploited to increase war production and the lessons of Keynesian economics were absorbed by the coalition government. The old Labour slogan of the right to work was transmuted by Beveridge into the less emotive phrase of the government's obligation to maintain full employment for its citizens. In 1944 Lord Woolton, a former Fabian socialist but now the Conservative minister for reconstruction, issued a second White Paper in May called *Employment Policy* which accepted Keynes' economic theories and was called 'an updated version of the 1909 Minority Report' on the Poor Law, and put forward the remedy of public expenditure to counter cyclical trade depressions. In certain respects this was no more than a more sophisticated version of J. A. Hobson's attempt to stimulate demand by encouraging increased consumption, particularly among the working class. More important, Beveridge in his volume *Full Employment in a Free Society*, published later in the same year to much acclaim, declared that unemployment was due to weak demand, imperfect labour mobility and the poor organization of the labour market. He set out to keep unemployment below an 'irreducible' target of 3 per cent, by enabling a new Ministry of National Finance to increase expenditure when demand was low, by utilizing planning regulations and subsidies to direct industry near to concentrations of labour, and by ordering labour exchanges to encourage the mobility of young persons. The Labour government's economic policy, which was based on controls over the allocation of raw materials together with the nationalization of key industries and Keynesian methods of economic planning, was largely successful in eliminating unemployment.[12]

Another important area in which the wartime coalition government acted was education. R. A. Butler's Education Act of 1944 was based on a White Paper which he had introduced a year earlier and which had secured an inter-party consensus. Educational facilities were to be made available in primary and secondary schools and colleges of further education, all provided by local education authorities. The school leaving age was set at fifteen, while as soon as possible it was to be raised even further to sixteen. Free secondary education was to be provided for all in local authority schools. Liberal reformers had sought to extend secondary educational in a series of pre-war measures, culminating in H. A. L. Fisher's Education Act of 1918 which raised the school leaving age to fourteen and permitted local education authorities to provide day continuation schools until sixteen, but because of financial constraints the provision for compulsory continuation schools was abandoned.[13]

Clement Attlee won an overwhelming mandate at the 1945 election from the British electorate to implement reconstruction on the lines proposed by Beveridge and a series of White Papers issued by the wartime coalition government. But it was the coalition government that passed the Family Allowances Act in 1945 to alleviate poverty during the family life cycle, when there were children to feed and clothe – a problem first noted by Seebohm Rowntree almost fifty years earlier. In fact, Rowntree had introduced a voluntary scheme of family allowances in his own company in 1940 and in dialogue with Beveridge helped the latter to refine his ideas on social insurance. The first Labour measure to reach the statute book was the National Insurance (Industrial Injuries) Act of 1946, which was now made universal and the responsibility of the state, instead of being covered by private schemes and allowing contracting out, as was the case when Herbert Gladstone introduced his Workmen's Compensation Bill in 1906 extending previous legislation. What the TUC had been campaigning for since 1906, a compulsory state insurance scheme against industrial accidents was given concrete form. A month later on 1 August 1946, the National Insurance Act covering the whole population, as urged by Beveridge, became law. For a flat-rate contribution there were benefits 'safeguarding the insured' against 'disability, sickness, unemployment, old age and even death (in the form of widow's pensions)'. In contrast the social insurance legislation of Lloyd George and Churchill embraced only insured workers but not their wives and widows nor their orphaned children and in the case of unemployment insurance had only been extended to a few industries; industrial insurance for accidents had not become the concern of the state; access to doctors was limited to the insured but was not made available to their families. Again, the unemployed received insurance benefit for a limited period, after which they fell within the ambit of the Poor Law for relief; later they came under the Unemployed Assistance Board.[14]

Although there was a broad consensus for a scheme of health reform, there was no clear idea of its contours when Attlee handed the task over to Aneurin Bevan in 1945 as minister of health. Under the National Health Service Act 1948 he set out to promote the establishment of a comprehensive health service for the population of England and Wales to improve their physical and mental health and to provide services for the prevention, diagnosis and treatment of illness. To run the general practitioner, dental and ophthalmic services at the local level, executive councils were chosen to take over the functions of the insurance committees. But other services such as maternity and child care, home helps, health visiting and home nursing, vaccination and immunization and ambulances were put under the control of the local authority with much responsibility being entrusted to the MOHs. Local authority and voluntary hospitals were nationalized and placed under regional boards. Christopher Addison, now Labour leader in the Lords, assisted Bevan by helping him to overcome resistance to this move within the Cabinet. Once again Bevan, like Lloyd George in 1912, faced widespread and furious opposition from the doctors, which he overcame by splitting the profession and offering concessions to the consultants, by allowing them to continue private practice in NHS hospitals, and appeasing the general practitioners by dropping the demand for a state-salaried medical service and pouring in more resources. Hence Labour in power implemented the Webbs' plea for a public health service which was the 'natural continuation of a pre-existing trend'; it was chiefly paid for out of general taxation with a small contribution coming out of the state insurance fund.[15] Housing was another of Bevan's departmental responsibilities, but, like Addison after 1918, his rate of new construction was less than expected, leaving him with a somewhat blemished record.[16]

For all those who slipped through the state insurance scheme, the National Assistance Act of 1948 established Public Assistance Committees which provided supplementary allowances on a means tested basis. For the destitute and elderly local authorities were empowered under this Act to open reception centres and old age homes. The National Assistance Act proudly proclaimed that it was abolishing poverty and the Family Allowances Act of 1945 struck at one of the long-noticed causes of poverty, by making payments of 5s. a week to families with two or more children. Quite apart from this, the amount of benefit paid under the updated social insurance scheme was likewise not over-generous and placed the recipient near the margin of subsistence.[17] Trade boards were renamed as wages councils by a 1945 Act and extended to the retail trade with a high percentage of female employees, but once again there was no attempt to impose a 'clear minimum standard' as far as wage levels were concerned – a repetition of previous errors.[18] National Assistance when first implemented was regarded as a supplementary measure to the state social insurance scheme for those who fell through its safety net, but the numbers seeking its aid continued to expand, thus subverting 'the alleged universalism and insurance base of the post-war welfare state. Unsurprisingly, therefore, the stigma associated with poor relief has carried over into certain parts of the "welfare state".[19] While the Poor Law had long been abolished in name, many of the substandard facilities offered to the destitute and the elderly and the demeaning attitudes often shown towards them remain intact. At the same time, the growing number of elderly persons occupying beds for long-term stays in hospital because of the lack of suitable accommodation in residential institutions is undermining the viability of the National Health Service. Social insurance itself might yet have to be recast.

# Biographical Notes

**Percy Alden** (1865–1944) was a talented local boy encouraged by Jowett to study at Balliol College, Oxford. He was the first warden of the Mansfield House Settlement and became a Liberal MP from 1906 until 1918. He was a member of the Rainbow Circle which promoted collectivist causes and developed a particular interest in the unemployed, whom he believed should be assisted by the state.

**Herbert Henry Asquith** (1852–1928) was educated at Balliol College before becoming a barrister and Liberal politician. He held the offices of home secretary and chancellor of the Exchequer, assuming the position of prime minister on the illness of his predecessor in 1908, a post which he held until 1916. He presided over great reforming administrations before the First World War.

**Arthur James Balfour** (1848–1930) was prime minister from 1902 to 1905, and then served as opposition leader until he retired from this position in November 1911. Beatrice Webb was one of many women who fell under his spell and believed – mistakenly – that he would come out strongly for social reform.

**George Nicoll Barnes** (1859–1940) was general secretary of the engineering union and a Labour MP from 1906 until 1922. An influential figure in the trade union movement, he was active in the Right to Work organization and the campaign for old age pensions.

**Samuel Augustus Barnett** (1844–1913) and his wife **Henrietta Octavia Barnett** (1851–1926) were from its inception associated with Toynbee Hall, of which Canon Barnett was the warden 1884–1906. After breaking with the Charity Organisation, the Barnetts developed a philosophy of integrating all classes into a mixed community, where all would be encouraged to participate in high culture and orphan children could be fostered in individual homes, instead of being housed in barrack schools.

**William Henry Beveridge** (1879–1963) was educated at Balliol College, after which he became sub-warden of Toynbee Hall. An early social investigator and sociologist, he promoted the case for labour exchanges and unemployment insurance, after which he joined the Board of Trade. There he was appointed as director of Labour Exchanges, also helping to implement unemployment insurance. During the Second World War, he drew up the Beveridge Report, a master plan for social reconstruction at the war's end.

**William Blain** (1861–1908) was educated at Cambridge and became president of the Cambridge Union. Entering the civil service in 1884, he was transferred from the Post Office to the Treasury, where his remarkable abilities were quickly recognized and his advancement was rapid. In 1903 he became principal clerk of the Finance Division of the Treasury. Here he wrote an important memorandum on a supertax to pay for social reform for Asquith and was given the task of preparing social insurance legislation by Lloyd George. His premature death removed a great talent.

**Charles Booth** (1840–1914) was a shipowner and pioneer applied sociologist, who instituted a great enquiry into the *Life and Labour of the People of London* which he started publishing at his own expense in 1889 and which was completed in seventeen volumes. He devised the poverty line, which led to the mistaken belief that 30 per cent of the population of London was living below the poverty line, when it was a smaller but still significant percentage. One of his most outstanding protégés was Beatrice Webb, whom he hired as an investigator.

**Helen Bosanquet** (1860–1925) was married to **Bernard Bosanquet** (1848–1923) the Idealist philosopher and Charity Organisation enthusiast, sharing his views in both respects. Helen drafted the Majority Report of the Poor Law Commission and was intellectually formidable enough to stand up to Beatrice Webb. In her report, while accepting the necessity for some state-subsidized welfare schemes, she placed more emphasis on a one-to-one social casework approach for solving the problems of the poor.

**John Lyon Bowley** (1869–1957) studied at Cambridge and was a prized student of the economist Alfred Marshall. He was a part-time lecturer at the London School of Economics from 1895, becoming a full professor in 1915. His estimate of the size of the British national income convinced Liberal politicians that they could levy a graduated income tax. From 1910 he carried out social research on poverty, perfecting sampling techniques to quantify poverty levels in a number of towns. Despite his LSE affiliation, he was a lifelong Liberal.

**John Swanwick Bradbury** (1872–1950) was educated at Oxford and entered the Treasury in 1897, rising to become its joint permanent secretary 1913–19. From 1911–13 he was an insurance commissioner for England and served on the Joint Committee.

**William John Braithwaite** (1875–1938) was educated at Balliol College and was a member of Toynbee Hall. He was assistant secretary to the Board of Inland Revenue 1910–12, where he played a major role in devising the health provisions of the National Insurance Act 1911. He became secretary to the Joint Committee on National Health Insurance in 1912 before being sidetracked and shunted sideways to become a special commissioner of income tax.

**John Burns** (1858–1943) was a trade unionist who led the 1889 dock strike. From 1892 onwards he sat as an MP for Battersea but left Parliament in 1918. He was appointed by Campbell-Bannerman as president of the Local Government Board in 1906, staying there until 1914, when he was briefly moved to the Board of Trade, but resigned from the government in August 1914 because of his pacifist views. Vain and unwilling to listen to advice, he was an obstacle to the reform of the Poor Law while he held office.

**Sydney Charles Buxton** (1853–1934) was a radical politician and friend of Haldane, who sat as MP for Poplar 1905–14. He was in part responsible for the enactment of the unemployment insurance provisions of the National Insurance Act 1911, but was not a powerful voice in the Cabinet when its extension was discussed. In February 1914 he resigned his seat on being appointed as governor-general of South Africa.

**George Cadbury** (1839–1922) expanded the cocoa and chocolate factory founded by his father and built a model village in Bournville for his workers. Disgusted by the Boer War, he purchased the Liberal newspaper the *Daily News* and used it as a vehicle campaigning for social change. He generously donated to the organizations campaigning for old age pensions and legislation against sweating.

**Henry Campbell-Bannerman** (1836–1908), born in Glasgow, was Liberal prime minister from 1906 until the spring of 1908. He consolidated his position as Liberal leader by his opposition to the Boer War. A man of inherited great wealth and of great charm, he showed little enthusiasm for social reform, but supported traditional Liberal causes such as temperance and land reform.

**Robert Chalmers** (1858–1938) studied classics at Oxford and was a resident of Toynbee Hall. He joined the civil service, becoming chairman of the Board of Inland Revenue 1907–11 and permanent secretary to the Treasury 1911–13. He assisted Lloyd George on his great Budget and Braithwaite in drafting the health insurance scheme. Although sympathetic to social reform, he became tired of Lloyd George's wheeler-dealing.

**Austen Chamberlain** (1863–1937) was the son of Joseph Chamberlain and a prominent Conservative opposition figure under Arthur Balfour. He later served as foreign secretary 1922–9.

**Joseph Chamberlain** (1836–1914) was a businessman and mayor of Birmingham 1870–3, when he introduced many municipal reforms. He became the radical leader of the Liberals, but broke with Gladstone over home rule for Ireland in 1886. He formed the Liberal Unionist group of MPs and went into coalition with the Conservatives, but broke with Balfour over tariff reform. His name became associated with various schemes for old age pensions.

**Winston Spencer Churchill** (1874–1965), educated at Harrow and Sandhurst, emerged from the Second World War as Britain's greatest war leader. A Conservative MP, he crossed the floor of the House to become a great Liberal social reformer, but later returned to the Tory party. While serving under Asquith, he sponsored legislation on the minimum wage, labour exchanges and unemployment insurance. As leader of the coalition government in the 1940s, he agreed to the appointment of Beveridge, who produced a plan for post-war reconstruction.

**William Harbutt Dawson** (1860–1948) was author of *Social Insurance in Germany 1883–1911* and an expert on German social insurance legislation. As a civil servant, he drafted an early report in favour of a state and municipal subsidised scheme of unemployment insurance and he also had some input into the drafting of the health insurance legislation. During the 1930s, he still remained sympathetic to Nazi Germany, but he was unwelcoming to Jewish refugee members of his father-in-law's family. The latter, Emil Muensterberg, was a leading German social security expert.

**Sir Charles Wentworth Dilke** (1843–1911) was a leading radical, whose political career was damaged by a sexual scandal. He campaigned for many years for the Trade Boards Act of 1909 and strongly supported a graduated income tax and non-contributory old age pensions.

**Joseph Fels** (1854–1914) was an American millionaire socialist who manufactured the Fels-Naptha brand of soap. He purchased 1,300 acres of land at Hollesley Bay, Suffolk and another 600 acres in Maryland, Essex for unemployed labourers to be employed as agricultural workers. He was a single taxer and funded pressure groups campaigning for social change.

**Arthur Wilson Fox** (1861–1909) was educated at Cambridge and practised as a barrister for a short while before joining the labour department of the Board of Trade, where he rose to become comptroller-general. He settled labour disputes in the cotton, engineering and railway industries. He proposed a state-subsidised unemployment insurance scheme to the Poor Law Commission and participated in the framing of the legislation for labour exchanges. He died from the immense stress of work in his understaffed department.

**Alfred George Gardiner** (1872–1950) was appointed as editor of the Liberal *Daily News* and was a vigorous supporter of social reform, particularly the sweated labour campaign to protect women from exploitation.

**John Eldon Gorst** (1835–1916) was called to the Bar and was appointed by Disraeli as the central agent of the Conservative party, whose organization he modernized. He was a Tory democrat and formed the Fourth Party as a ginger group with Lord Randolph Churchill. Free of office from 1902, he campaigned on the health and nutrition of schoolchildren, writing a notable book on the subject. At the January 1910 election he stood for Parliament as a Liberal but was defeated.

**Richard Burdon Haldane** (1856–1928). Because he had doubts about his Christian faith, Haldane's parents decided not to send him to Balliol, as they believed that Idealist philosophy would further undermine his faith; instead he studied in Scotland and Germany. He was a friend of Asquith and a fellow lawyer. He was an outstanding secretary of state for war and later Lord Chancellor. A friend of the Webbs, he encouraged Asquith to replace the Poor Law and supported educational reform.

**Leonard Trelawny Hobhouse** (1864–1929) was educated at Oxford. He wrote a volume sympathetic towards the Labour movement in 1893 and a later work trying to redirect Idealist philosophy in more empirical directions. After doing a stint as a journalist at the *Manchester Guardian* from which he resigned in 1902, he turned to academic studies and was appointed as professor of sociology at the London School of Economics. He wrote a defence of Liberalism in 1911 and was a firm believer in minimum wage legislation and the rest of the government's social reform package.

**John Atkinson Hobson** (1858–1940), along with other new Liberal and socialist thinkers, was a member of the Rainbow Circle. He worked as a journalist for the *Manchester Guardian* and after a visit to South Africa gradually developed a grand theory of imperialism, which he believed was driven by under-consumption in the mother country. His theories of under-consumption anticipated Keynes and he developed a theory of economics in support of the heavier taxation of high-income earners.

**Cyril Jackson** (1863–1914) was educated at Oxford and was a resident of Toynbee Hall, where he stayed for ten years. As chief inspector of schools 1903–6, he was a firm adherent of the casual labour theory of unemployment and carried out an investigation for the Poor Law Commission.

**David Lloyd George** (1863–1945) – a Welsh Nonconformist, he irritated the Webbs, who did not appreciate his talents as an orator and political operator. He sat as an MP 1895–1945 and became a friend of Churchill. He was president of the Board of Trade 1906–8 and chancellor of the Exchequer 1908–15. He played a key role in promoting social insurance before moving on to the land campaign and the minimum wage. He served as prime minister of the coalition government 1916–22.

**Mary MacArthur** (1880–1921) was secretary of the Women's Trade Union League, a leading figure in the National Anti-Sweating League, and a powerful campaigner on health issues concerning women.

**Thomas James Macnamara** (1861–1931) was a school teacher and headmaster who joined the executive of the National Union of Teachers and became editor of their journal *The Schoolmaster*. On becoming an MP, he campaigned for the provision of school meals and medical inspection. Appointed as parliamentary secretary to the Local Government Board, he was moved in 1908 by Asquith to a similar position in the Admiralty. He stayed there for twelve years, where he was unable to utilize his enthusiasm for social reform.

**Margaret McMillan** (1860–1931) and her sister **Rachel McMillan** (1859–1917) were socialists, who were behind schemes to improve the health of the nation's children at the local level. Margaret instituted the medical inspection of schoolchildren in Bradford with Dr James Kerr, and later campaigned for medical inspection and school clinics across England. She opened the first school clinic at Bow in 1908, though a couple of years later it moved to larger premises in Deptford.

**James Joseph Mallon** (1874–1961) went to the Ancoats Settlement and became a member of the Independent Labour Party and the Fabian Society. He served on the executive of the Shop Assistants Union and championed the necessity for trade boards, becoming a member of thirteen different boards. From 1919–54 he served as Warden of Toynbee Hall.

**Charles Frederick Gurney Masterman** (1874–1927) was educated at Cambridge, where he became a fellow of Christ's College and contributed to a volume deploring empire. From Liberal journalism, he moved into politics and was returned for West Ham in 1906 and for Bethnal Green 1911–14. As under-secretary to John Burns, he assisted him in the passing of the Housing and Town Planning Act. He was promoted eventually, becoming chairman of the National Insurance Commission for England in 1912. He played an important role in shaping the administrative structure of the health provisions of the National Insurance Act.

**Leo Chiozza Money** (1870–1944) was a journalist on the *Daily News* and made a name for himself with the publication of *Riches and Poverty* (1905), which went through many editions. A Fabian, he argued in favour of redistributive taxation, particularly a graduated income tax which was to be used for social reforms. He became a Liberal MP in 1906, although his potential as a minister was ignored by Asquith, but not later by Lloyd George.

**Robert Laurie Morant** (1863–1920) was educated at Oxford and became tutor to the Crown Prince of Siam, where he established a modern system of education. From a post at Toynbee Hall, he moved to the Board of Education, where he became a ruthless operator and an important adviser of Balfour in the implementation of the 1902 Education Act. Under the Liberals he helped shape the legislation on school meals, medical inspection and school clinics. In 1912 he became chairman of the National Insurance Commission for England, where he stayed until 1919. He compelled Lloyd

George to recruit enough able administrators to run the new health insurance scheme and was author of the National Insurance Act of 1913, which corrected existing flaws.

**George Newman** (1870–1948) was chief medical officer to the Board of Education 1907–35, where he started the school meals programme and school clinics. He was a self-publicist who downplayed his colleague Newsholme's considerable achievements to become the chief medical officer at the new Ministry of Health.

**Arthur Newsholme** (1857–1943) was principal medical officer at the Local Government Board 1908–19, where he launched state-sponsored schemes for infant welfare and to curb tuberculosis and venereal disease.

**Benjamin Seebohm Rowntree** (1871–1954) became a director of Rowntree & Co. in 1897, when the family firm was converted into a company. His book *Poverty: A Study of Town Life* was published in 1901 and had a tremendous impact, as it confirmed Booth's earlier findings that urban destitution was widespread. Lloyd George appointed him to the Land Enquiry Committee and he became an important political adviser. His discovery of the family poverty cycle, when there were young children to maintain, led him many years later to institute a voluntary scheme of family allowances in the family company in 1940. His ideas influenced Beveridge when he compiled his Report.

**Michael Ernest Sadler** (1861–1943) was educated at Oxford, where he attended lectures by Toynbee and Ruskin. An ardent Christian and Liberal from his school days, he joined Acland's Inner Ring at Oxford. A brilliant scholar at university, he was soon an influential figure in the Board of Education but was ousted by the jealousy of Morant. Instead he helped shape educational policy from his university chair in a liberal direction with a plea for more continuation education.

**Herbert Louis Samuel** (1870–1963) was educated at Balliol College, Oxford. He had been struck by the poverty of the Jewish immigrant population in the East End and while an undergraduate, went into the surrounding countryside to unionize agricultural labourers. During the 1890s, he joined the Rainbow Circle with its collectivist ideas and became more radical, writing some Fabian pamphlets. As under-secretary in the Home Office, he pushed through the Children's Bill and was promoted to the Cabinet. He nationalized the telephone service, but his political career as a reformer was cut short by the war.

**Hubert Llewellyn Smith** (1864–1945) was educated at Oxford, where he participated in the Inner Ring, a group led by Arthur Acland, to discuss social and economic issues and with hosting workers from Bethnal Green. He was also influenced by John Ruskin's economic ideas on society and the visual arts. He participated in the activities of Toynbee Hall and in the Booth investigations into social deprivation in London. His work at the Board of Trade enhanced public recognition of unemployment as a structural problem of industry that required state intervention. However his construction of a viable scheme of unemployment insurance relied heavily on Beveridge and he insisted that the government legislation on sweating did not impose a statutory minimum wage.

**John Alfred Spender** (1862–1942) was educated at Balliol and a resident of Toynbee Hall, and trained as a journalist. He published a book setting out the case for non-contributory pensions which was liked by John Morley. From 1896–1921 he was the editor of the *Westminster Gazette*, a sober evening newspaper which defended the ministerial line, and he remained close to Asquith. His brother **Hugh Frederick Spender** (1864–1926), also a journalist, put across the views of Lloyd George.

**Richard Henry Tawney** (1880–1962) was educated at Balliol and a resident of Toynbee Hall, and taught economic history at classes run by the Worker's Educational Association. From these experiences, he developed an interest in the boy labour problem and put forward universal secondary education as a partial solution. He was appointed as director of the Ratan Tata Foundation attached to the LSE, where he wrote sociological studies supporting the case for the minimum wage.

**Margery Tennant** (1869–1946) became involved in the work of the Women's Trade Union League and was appointed as a factory inspector. She married **Harold John (Jack) Tennant** (1865–1935), a Liberal MP and later the brother-in-law of Asquith. She was on the executive of the National League for Physical Education and Improvement, while her husband, as an active backbench MP, tried to push forward legislation to protect children.

**Beatrice Webb** (1858–1943) and **Sidney Webb** (1859–1947) were joint authors of the Minority Report, which advocated the break-up of the Poor Law. Both shared the same philosophy of persuasion or permeation, of trying to influence the political elite through their writing on social problems and their conversation at the dinner table – a policy which was not wholly successful – and demanded a change of tactics after the First World War.

**John Howard Whitehouse** (1873–1955) was deeply influenced by the ideas of Ruskin and after a spell at Toynbee Hall, he was appointed as warden of the Ancoats Settlement in Manchester. Elected to Parliament as a Liberal in 1910, he became the parliamentary private secretary to Churchill and Lloyd George and specialized in the boy labour problem and education, becoming an important backbench MP and activist in children's pressure groups.

# Notes

## Introduction

1. G. R. Searle, *A New England. Peace and War 1886-1918* (Oxford, 2004), 358-61. Jose F. Harris and Cameron Hazlehurst, 'Campbell-Bannerman as Prime Minister', *History* 55 (1970): 360-83.
2. Derek Fraser, *The Evolution of the British Welfare State* (London, 1984), 37-55. Searle, *A New England*, 222-3, 227-8. M. A. Crowther, *The Workhouse System 1834-1929. The History of an English Social Institution* (London, 1981), 59, 65. Jose Harris, 'The Transition to High Politics in English Social Policy' in Michael Bentley and John Stevenson (eds), *High and Low Politics in Modern Britain. Ten Studies* (Oxford: Oxford University Press, 1983), 72.
3. Bentley B. Gilbert, *The Evolution of National Insurance. The Origins of the Welfare State* (London, 1966) and *British Social Policy 1914-1939* (London, 1970). John M. Eyler, *Sir Arthur Newsholme and British State Medicine, 1885-1935* (Cambridge, 1997). Simon Cordery, *British Friendly Societies, 1750-1914* (Basingstoke, 2003). David G. Green, *Working Class Patients and the Medical Establishment. Self-Help in Britain from the Mid-nineteenth Century to 1948* (Aldershot, 1985). Bernard Harris, *The Health of the Schoolchild* (Buckingham, 1995). Harry Hendrick, *Child Welfare in England 1872-1989* (London, 1994). E. P. Hennock, *British Social Reform and German Precedents: The Case of Social Insurance 1880-1914* (Oxford, 1987).
4. John Macnicol, *The Politics of Retirement in Britain* (Cambridge, 1998); Pat Thane, *Old Age in English History: Past Experiences, Present Issues* (Oxford, 2000).
5. Jose Harris, *Unemployment and Politics. A Study of English Social Policy 1886-1914* (Oxford, 1972) and *William Beveridge: A Biography* (Oxford, 1997). Thane, *Old Age in English History*. Kenneth D. Brown, *Labour and Unemployment, 1900-1914* (Newton Abbot, 1971).
6. A. L. Bowley and A. R. Burnett Hurst, *Livelihood and Poverty* (London, 1915). Ian Gazeley, *Poverty in Britain, 1900-1965* (Basingstoke, 2003). A. M. McBriar, *An Edwardian Mixed Doubles: The Bosanquets versus the Webbs. A Study in British Social Policy 1890-1929* (Oxford, 1987). Jane Lewis, *Women and Social Action in Victorian and Edwardian England* (Aldershot, 1991).
7. Martin Daunton, *Trusting Leviathan. The Politics of Taxation in Britain 1799-1914* (Cambridge, 2001) and Bruce K. Murray, *The Politics of the People's Budget, 1909/10: Lloyd George and Liberal Politics* (Oxford, 1980).
8. Anthony Wohl, *The Eternal Slum: Housing and Social Policy in Victorian London* (London, 1977). Kenneth D. Brown, *John Burns* (London, 1977). Anthony Sutcliffe, *Towards the Planned City: Germany, Britain, the United States and France 1780-1914* (Oxford, 1981).
9. H. V. Emy, *Liberals Radicals and Social Politics 1892-1914* (Cambridge, 1973). Ian Packer, *Lloyd George, Liberalism and the Land Issue and Party Politics in England 1906-14* (Woodbridge, 2001). Duncan Tanner, *Political Change and the Labour Party*

1900-1918 (Cambridge, 1990). Chris Wrigley, *David Lloyd George and the British Labour Movement* (Hassocks, 1976). Sheila Blackburn, *A Fair Day's Wage for a Fair Day's Work?* (Aldershot, 2007).

10   Bernard Harris, *The Origins of the British Welfare State. Society, State and Social Welfare in England and Wales, 1800-1945* (Basingstoke, 2004), 3-4, 154-5. Pat Thane, 'The Working Class and State "Welfare" in Britain, 1880-1914', JOURNAL NAME 27 (4) (1984): 877-900.

## Chapter 1: The Rise of the Counter-Elite

1   H. V. Emy, *Liberals Radicals and Social Politics 1892-1914* (Cambridge, 1973). G. R. Searle, 'The Edwardian Liberal Party and Business', *English Historical Review* (January 1983): esp. 32-4.
2   H. H. Gerth and C. Wright Mills, *From Max Weber: Essays in Sociology* (London, 1952).
3   David Cannadine, *The Decline and Fall of the British Aristocracy* (London, 1996), 25-7.
4   Sandra M. Den Otter, *British Idealism and Social Explanation. A Study in Late Victorian Thought* (Oxford, 1996), 48, 112, 166. Jose Harris, 'Political Thought and the Welfare State 1870-1940: An Intellectual Framework for British Social Policy', *Past and Present* 135 (May 1992): 116-41.
5   Otter, *British Idealism*, 1, 206. *Dictionary of National Biography*, entry on T. H. Green (Oxford, 2004), vol. 23, 535-40.
6   Michael Freeden, *The New Liberalism, An Ideology of Social Reform* (Oxford, 1986), 17-18.
7   Michael Freeden, *Ideologies and Political Theory: A Conceptual Approach* (Oxford, 1996), 200. Michael, *New Liberalism*, 256-7.
8   Freeden, *The New Liberalism*, 68-70. Freeden, *Ideologies and Politics*, 195-8. *Dictionary of National Biography* (Oxford, 2004) on L. T. Hobhouse, also his *Liberalism* (London, 1911), 157-63, 207-9, 248-50.
9   Freeden, *New Liberalism*, 19-20,70-1. *Dictionary of National Biography* entry on J. A. Hobson (Oxford, 2004), vol. 27, 424-9.
10   Victoria de Bunsen, *Charles Roden Buxton* (London, 1948), 52.
11   Emy, *Liberals Radicals and Social Politics 1892-1914*, 98-103
12   P. F. Clarke, *Lancashire and the New Liberalism* (Cambridge, 1971), 223. Burton J. Hendrick, *The Life and Letters of Walter H. Page* (New York, 1924), 145, 158.
13   Stephen E. Koss, *Sir John Brunner, 1842-1919: Radical Plutocrat* (Cambridge, 1970), 154.
14   E. P. Hennock, 'Poverty and Social Theory in England: The Experience of the Eighteen-eighties, *Social History* (January 1976), 73.
15   Ian Gazeley, *Poverty in Britain, 1900-1965* (Basingstoke, 2003), 26-7.
16   Canon Barnett Papers, Charles Booth to Canon Barnett, 22 October 1904.
17   J. A. Hobson, *Confessions of an Economic Heretic* (London, 1938), 30.
18   Harold Perkin, *The Rise of Professional Society. England. England Since 1880* (London, 2002), 32-5.
19   Ian Gazeley and Andrew Newell, 'Rowntree Revisited: Poverty in Britain, 1900', *Explorations in Economic History* 37 (2000): 174-88. Gazeley, *Poverty in Britain*, 31-2.

20  F. Musgrove, 'Middle-Class Education and Employment in the Nineteenth Century: A Rejoinder', *Economic History Review* (December 1961): 326.
21  R. H. Tawney, *Poverty as an Industrial Problem* (London, 1914).
22  Victor Branford, *Interpretations and Forecasts. A Study of Survivals and Tendencies in Contemporary Society* (London, 1914), 401–2.
23  Richard Titmuss, 'Health', in M. Ginsberg (ed.), *Law and Opinion in England in the 20th Century* (London, 1959), 313. Gordon Rose, *The Struggle for Penal Reform: The Howard League and its Predecessors* (London, 1961).
24  Emmeline W. Cohen, *The Growth of the British Civil Service 1780–1939* (London, 1941), 163–4. Moses Abramovitz and Vera F. Eliasberg, *The Growth of Public Employment in Great Britain* (New Jersey, 1957), 36, 38–9.
25  Élie Halévy, *The Rule of Democracy*, vol. 1 (London, 1952), 261–5; vol. 2, 445–8.
26  G. R. Searle, *A New England? Peace and War 1886–1918* (Oxford, 2004), 97. Perkin, *The Rise of Professional Society*, 117.

## Chapter 2: The Recruiting Grounds of the Counter-Elite

1  Canon Barnett Papers, Arnold Toynbee to Henrietta Barnett, 25 June 1879.
2  Henrietta Barnett, *Canon Barnett* (London, 1921), 3089. S. A. Barnett and H. Barnett, *Practicable Socialism* (London, 1915), 96–131. Seth Koven, *Slumming: Sexual and Social Politics in Victorian London* (New Jersey, 2004), 238.
3  Koven, *Slumming*, 4, 5, 244–5, 248.
4  Barnett and Barnett, *Practicable Socialism*, 105, 127; 1884 edn, 150.
5  Barnett, *Canon Barnett*, 307.
6  Barnett and Barnett, *Practicable Socialism*, 1894 edn, 99, 224.
7  S. A. Barnett, *Work and Worship* (London, 1914).
8  Barnett, *Work and Worship*, 100. Barnett, *Canon Barnett*, 285, 555, 543–71. Barnett and Barnett, *Practicable Socialism*, 1894 edn, 247–8. Earl Woolton, *Memoirs* (London, 1959), 24–5.
9  Barnett, *Canon Barnett*, 497–8. Barnett and Barnett, *Practicable Socialism*, 1894 edn; 1915 edn, 124–5.
10  E. J. Urwick, *Luxury and Waste of Life* (London, 1908).
11  Barnett, *Canon Barnett*, 500.
12  Cyril Jackson, *Report on Boy Labour* PP XLIV (1909). J. H. Whitehouse (ed.), *Problems of Boy Life* (London, 1912) and *A National System of Education* (London, 1913). O. Bolton King, *The Employment and Welfare of Juveniles* (London, 1925). Cyril Norwood and Arthur H. Hope, *The Higher Education of Boys in England* (Place, 1912).
13  Barnett, *Canon Barnett*, 500–6; Halévy, *The Rule of Democracy*, vol. 1, 86–90.
14  Micky Watkins, *Henrietta Barnett. Social Worker and Community Planner* (London, 2011), 52–3.
15  Barnett, *Canon Barnett*, 129–40, 702, 704–16. Henrietta Barnett, *Matters That Matter* (London, 1930), chapter on 'Housing'. M. Penelope Hall, *The Social Services of Modern England* (London, 1960), 330–5.
16  Prospectus for 'Universities' Settlement in East London' (1884). W. Reason (ed.), *University and Social Settlements* (London, 1898) essays of Percy Alden and Revd J. Scott Lidgett. Werner Picht, *Toynbee Hall and the English Settlement Movement* (London, 1914); and Barnett, *Canon Barnett*, 578.

17 Arthur Sherwell, 'Settlements and the Labour Movement', in Will Reason (ed.), *University and Social Settlements*. Barnett, *Canon Barnett*, 445-6. Cyril Jackson, 'Report on Boy Labour for *R.C. on the Poor Laws*' 1909. Arnold Freemen, *Boy Life and Labour* (London, 1914). M. D. Stocks, *Fifty Years in Every Street. The Story of the Manchester University Settlement* (London, 1945), 44-5. Cecile Matheson and George Shann, *Women's Work and Wages* (London, 1908). Edward G. Howarth and Mona Wilson, *West Ham. A Study of Industrial Problems* (London, 1907).

18 Picht, *Toynbee Hall*; Richenda Scott, *Elizabeth Cadbury 1858-1951* (London, 1955), 96-100.

19 W. A. Bailward, 'The Oxford House and the Organization of Charity', in John M. Knapp (ed.), *The Universities and Social Problems* (London, 1895). J. Scott Lidgett, *My Guided Life* (London, 1936), 129, 168-70.

20 John Gorst, 'Settlements in England and America', in John Knapp (ed.), *The Universities and the Social Problem*; and Picht, *Toynbee Hall*, 96. Barnett and Barnett, *Practicable Socialism*, 1915 edn, 144-5. Koven, *Slumming*, 286. Stocks, *The Story of the Manchester University Settlement*, 33. Woolton, *Memoirs*, 29.

21 E. J. Hobsbawm, *Labouring Men* (London, 1964), 251-2. A. M. McBriar, *Fabian Socialism and English Politics 1884-1918* (Cambridge, 1962), 29-118. Paul Thomson, *Socialists,Liberals, and Labour. The Struggle for London 1885-1914* (London, 1967), 96, 148, 208. Charles Albro Barker, *Henry George* (New York, 1955), 376, 471, 525-7, 595.

22 Margaret Cole, *Beatrice Webb* (London, 1945), 79,80, 124-5.

23 Emily Townshend (ed.), *Keeling Letters and Recollections* (London, 1918), 8-32. Oona Howard Ball, *Sidney Ball* (Oxford, 1923). McBriar, *Fabian Socialism*, 168-9. C. F. G. Masterman, *England After War* (London, 1922), 68.

24 Sidney Webb and Beatrice Webb, 'What is Socialism?', *New Statesman*, 26 April 1913.

25 LSE, Beveridge Papers, correspondence before First World War note of Beveridge.

26 R. H. Tawney, *Poverty as an Industrial Problem* (London, 1913).

27 Malcolm Warner, 'Sidney and Beatrice Webb', in Timothy Raison (ed.), *The Founding Fathers of Social Science* (London, 1969), 149. T. S. Simey, 'The Contribution of Beatrice and Sidney Webb to Sociology', *British Journal of Sociology* 12 (1961): 106-23.

28 Sidney Webb and Beatrice Webb, *The Case for the National Minimum* (London, 1913).

29 Jose Harris, 'The Webbs, the Charity Organization Society and the Ratan Tata Foundation', in Martin Bulmer et al. (eds), *The Goals of Social Policy* (London, 1989).

30 Francis Herbert Stead, *How Old Age Pensions Began to Be* (London, n.d.), 17-19, 45-6, 50, 54, 311-14. G. N. Barnes, *From Workshop to War Cabinet* (London, 1924), 68.

31 Harris, *The Origins of the British Welfare State*, 154. Henry Pelling, *Popular Politcs and Society in Victorian Britain* (London, 1979), 1-18. Pat Thane, 'The Working Class and State Welfare in Britain 1880-1914', *Historical Journal* 27 (4): 877-900. Elizabeth Roberts, 'The Recipients' View of Welfare', in Joanna Bornat et al., *Oral History, Health and Welfare 1890-1914* (London, 2000), 214 -15.

32 G. R. Searle, *A New England? Peace and War 1886-1918* (Oxford, 2004), 78. Stocks, *Fifty Years in Every Street,* 35. J. Ramsay MacDonald, *Margaret Ethel MacDonald* (London, 1929), 185-6. Ellen Ross, *Slum Travelers: Ladies and London Poverty (1860-1920)* (Berkeley, 2007), 8-9, 53-4.

33 William J. Braithwaite, *Lloyd George's Ambulance Wagon* (London, 1957), 234-5.

34  MacDonald, *Margaret Ethel MacDonald*, 23.
35  Anne Summers, *Female Lives, Moral States. Women, Religion and Public Life in Britain 1880-1930* (Newbury, 2000), 21-2.
36  Harry Hendrick, *Child Welfare in England 1872-1989* (London, 1994), 96. F. K. Prochaska, *Women and Philanthropy in 19th Century England* (Oxford, 1980), 224. Ross, *Slum Travelers*, 1-4.
37  Katharine Beauman, *Women and the Settlement Movement* (London, 1996), xx, xxi, 75, 224.
38  Picht, *Toynbee Hall*. Margaret A. Sewell and Eleanor G. Powell, 'Women's Settlements', in Will Reason (ed.), *University and Social Settlements* (London, 1898). Janet Penrose Trevelyan, *The Life of Mrs Humphrey Ward* (London, 1923), 123-42, 187-206; and *Evening Play Centres for Children* (London, 1920), 83-5. Violet R. Markham, *Return Passage* (London, 1953).
39  Rose E. Squire, *Thirty Years in the Public Service* (London, 1927), 17-18.
40  Roger Fulford, *Votes for Women* (London, 1957), 299.
41  Ross, *Slum Travelers*, 8-9. Squire, *Thirty Years*, 13, 35-9, 232-3. Violet Markham, *Return Passage* and Anne Freemantle, *This Little Band of Prophets* (New York, 1960), 29, 176.
42  *Women's Trade Union League* annual reports 1898-1910.
43  *Women's Industrial Council* leaflet and annual reports 1901-2 and 1910-11.
44  *Handbook and Report of the National Union of Women Workers of Great Britain* 1910-11 and 1911-12.
45  Richenda Scott, *Elizabeth Cadbury 1858-1951* (London, 1955) and Gervas Huxley, *Lady Denman 1854-1954* (London, 1961), 65-75.
46  Gertrude Tuckwell, *Constance Smith. A Short Memoir* (London, 1931). MacDonald, *Margaret Ethel MacDonald*, 139-42. Trevelyan, *Mrs Humphrey Ward*, 123-42, 187-206, 292-4; and *Evening Play Centres for Children*, 83-5.
47  Lambeth Palace, Randall Davidson Papers, Talbot Baines to Archbishop Davidson 24 October 1906. Peter D'A Jones, *The Christian Socialist Revival. Religion, Class and Social Conscience in Late-Victorian England 1877-1914* (Princeton, 1968), 60-3.
48  Jones, *The Christian Socialist Revival*, 99-163.
49  K. S. Inglis, *Churches and the Working Classes in Victorian England* (London, 1963), 278-86. Jones, *The Christian Socialist Revival*, 164-224. Maurice B. Reckitt, *Faith and Society* (London, 1932), 91.
50  Charles F. G. Masterman, *England After the War* (London, 1922), 202.
51  Revd Dr Fry, 'The Christian Social Union', *Economic Review* (October 1905).
52  Gertrude Tuckwell, *Constance Smith*. Bristol Right to Work Committee 1908 report. *Daily News*, 15 February 1909.
53  *Daily News*, 13 March 1905 and *Examiner*, 4 January 1906. *Free Church Year Book: Report of the Free Church Council* 1906. E. K. H. Jordan, *Free Church Unity* (London, 1956), 153-6.
54  Bentley B. Gilbert, *The Evolution of National Insurance in Great Britain. The Origins of the Welfare State* (London, 1906), 28-9. G. P. Gooch, *Under Six Reigns* (London, 1958), 68-9.
55  J. L. Paton, *John Brown Paton* (London, 1914). Earl Woolton, *Memoirs*, 59.
56  C. Silvester Horne, *Pulpit, Platform, And Parliament* (London, n.d.), 46, 48, 68-9, 72, 76, 81, 89-90, 93, 213.
57  Arthur Porritt, *John Henry Jowett* (London, 1924), 83-9.

58  Stead, *How Old Age Pensions Began to Be*, 17, 75, 79, 109, 146, 148, 183-4, 218, 220, 236. *Daily News*, 18 March 1907.
59  *National Housing Reform Council* report 1906-7. A. G. Gardiner, *The Life of George Cadbury* (London, n.d.), 177-8. Robert Forman Horton, *An Autobiography* (London, 1917), 81-3, and Revd R. J. Campbell, *Christianity and the Social Order* (London, 1907), x, xi.
60  *Land Tenure Reform Association* report 1871-2. J. Collings and J. L. Green, *Life of the Right Hon. Jesse Collings* (London, 1920). Eldwood P. Lawrence, *Henry George in the British Isles* (Michigan, 1957). *Land Values* March 1906, August 1907 and *Land and Liberty* June 1922.
61  Charles Albro Barker, *Henry George* (New York, 1955), 376, 471, 525-6, 595. *English Land Restoration League* reports 1891-1902. Robert Gathorne-Hardy, *Ottoline. The Early Memoirs of Lady Ottoline Morrell* (London, 1963), 134-5.
62  M. K. Ashby, *Joseph Ashby of Tysoe 1859-1919* (London, 1961), 157-64.
63  *Westminster Gazette*, 6 December 1913 and Gardiner, *George Cadbury*, 66.

# Chapter 3: Child Welfare

1  Bentley B. Gilbert, *The Evolution of National Insurance in Great Britain* (London, 1966), 72-3, 107, 124-6.
2  Gillian Sutherland, *Elementary Education in the Nineteenth Century* (London, 1971), 35, 39. Anon., *Can a Sufficient Midday Meal be Given to Poor School Children at a Cost for Material of Less than One Penny?* (London, 1883). M. E. Bulkley, *The Feeding of School Children* (London, 1914), 9-10.
3  Bulkley, *The Feeding of School Children*, 249-70.
4  Margaret McMillan, *Labour and Childhood* (London, 1907), 149-80.
5  *Third International Congress for the Welfare and Protection of Children*, 15-18 July 1902, 24.
6  Ethel Williams, *Report on the Condition of the Children who are in Receipt of the Various Forms of Poor Relief in England and Wales* PP, LII (1910). Tom Percival, *Poor Law Children* (London, 1911), 31-2,47.
7  I. Ellis, 'Diet, Cookery and Hygiene in Reformatory, Residential and Day Industrial Schools', in Charles E. Hecht (ed.), *Rearing an Imperial Race* (London, 1913).
8  Ibid .
9  *Report of the Departmental Committee on Reformatory and Industrial Schools* PP, XXXIX (1913), 24-5.
10  Jeanne L. Brand, *Doctors and the State. The British Medical Profession and Government Action in Public Health 1870-1912* (Baltimore, 1965), 134.
11  *Third International Congress for the Welfare and Protection of Children*, 15-18 July 1902.
12  Arthur Newsholme and Walter C. C. Pakes, *School Hygiene* (London, 1903), 174.
13  *Inter-Departmental Committee on the Employment of School Children PP*, XXV (1902), 8-9. *Third International Congress for the Welfare and Protection of Children*, 32.
14  Sidney Webb, *Twentieth Century Politics: A Policy of National Efficiency* (London, 1901). McBriar, *Fabian Socialism and English Politics*, 218.
15  Randolph Churchill, *Winston Churchill. Young Statesman 1901-1914 Vol. 2* (London, 1967), 31-2.

16  *Army and Navy Gazette* 1904-6, 30 July 1904 and 25 February 1905; and *The Broad Arrow. The Naval and Military Gazette* 1904-6 and 14 April 1906. *National Review*, August and November 1906.
17  Margaret McMillan, *The Life of Rachel McMillan* (London, 1927), 103-13.
18  Ibid.
19  Buckley, *Feeding of School Children*, 23. McBriar, *Fabian Socialism*, 217-18. *Select Committee on the Education (Provision of Meals) Bill* PP VIII (1906), *Evidence of Canon Moore Ede*, 190-1. G. P. Gooch, 'The Unemployed', *Contemporary Review* (January 1906).
20  Harry Hendrick, *Child Welfare in England 1872-1989* (London, 1994), 105.
21  Fenner Brockway, *Socialism Over Sixty Years. The Life of Jowett of Bradford* (London, 1946), 54-7. *Municipal Journal*, 15 April, 27 May, 26 August and 14 October 1904, and 5 May, 26 May and 9 June 1905. Gilbert, *Evolution of National Insurance*, 108-9.
22  John Stewart, 'Ramsay MacDonald, the Labour Party and Child Welfare, 1900-1914', *Twentieth Century British History* 4 (2) (1993): 105-25. *Daily News*, 21 January 1905 and *Schoolmaster*, 10 March 1906. Francis Countess of Warwick, *Life's Ebb and Flow* (London, 1929), 227-9 and *Afterthoughts* (London, 1931), 233.
23  *Hansard* (Commons), 27 March and 18 April 1905, cols 1231-74. *Daily News*, 28 March 1905.
24  *Daily News*, 16 March 1905. Sir John Gorst, *The Children of the Nation* (London, 1907), 86-8. Warwick, *Life's Ebb and Flow*, 228-30.
25  *Report of the Proceedings of the Conference Convened at the Guildhall on 22 and 23 May 1906 by the British Section of the International Congress for the Welfare and Protection of Children*. Papers by Eliott and Miss M. Frere on children's relief committees in elementary schools and the ensuing discussion.
26  Stewart, 'Labour Party and Child Welfare', 108, 119.
27  Gilbert, *The Evolution of National Insurance*, 109-11 and *Hansard* (Commons), 2 March 1906, cols 1436-9. *County Council Times*, April and November 1906. *Annual Reports of the SPCC* 1904-5 and 1905-6. *Poor Law Officers Journal*, 26 October and 14 December 1906.
28  *Select Committee on the Education (Provision of Meals) Bill* PP VIII (1906), iv-x, 41-51. Stewart, 'Labour Party and Child Welfare', 108-9.
29  *Poor Law Officers Journal*, 26 October and 24 December 1906.
30  *School Hygiene*, November 1916; and *Lancet*, 31 January, 14 February, 18 July 1903 and 14 January and 7 October 1905.
31  Lieut. Col. F. Maurice, *Sir Frederick Maurice. A Record of his Work and Opinions* (London, 1913), 5, 112-18.
32  Maurice, *Sir Frederick Maurice*, 118. *Interim report of the National League for Physical Education and Improvement* 1906.
33  National Archives, MH 139/1-6, George Newman Diary, 25 February 1908.
34  *Interim and Annual Reports of the National League for Physical Education and Improvement* 1906. National Archives, ED24/279 Deputation of the National League for Physical Education and Improvement, 27 February 1906. Violet Markham, *May Tennant* (London, 1949), 37.
35  *Daily News*, 17 July 2008. National Archives, ED24/279 Deputation of the B.M.A., 16 July 1906.
36  Gilbert, *The Evolution of National Insurance*, 117-18. J. David Hirst, 'The Growth of Treatment through the School Medical Service', *Medical History* 33 (1989): 318-42. N. D. Daglish, 'Robert Morant's Hidden Agenda? The Origins of the Medical

Treatment of Schoolchildren', *History of Education* 19 (1990): 139–48. Bernard Harris, *The Health of the Schoolchild* (Buckingham, 1995), 44–5.
37  *Annual Report of the League for Physical Education and Improvement* 1906 and *Daily News*, 17 July 1906. Mary Fels, *Joseph Fels* (London, 1920), 210–11. Margaret McMillan, *The Life of Rachel McMillan*, 114–16. Daglish, 'Robert Morant's Hidden Agenda', 146.
38  *Hansard* (Commons), 16 July 1906, cols 1390, 1392. Harris, *The Health of the Schoolchild*, 46.
39  Harris, *The Health of the Schoolchild*, 45.
40  *Hansard* (Lords), 21 November 1906, cols 745–7, 754–5.
41  Harris, *The Health of the Schoolchild*, 47.
42  G. R. Searle, *The Quest for National Efficiency. A Study in British Politics and British Political Thought 1899-1914* (Oxford, 1971), 236.
43  *Hansard* (Commons), 2 March 1906, cols 1420–3. Daglish, 'Robert Morant's Hidden Agenda', 147–8.

# Chapter 4: Old Age Pensions

1  Author, *Thrift and National Insurance as a Security against Pauperism with a Memoir of the late Revd. Canon Blackley and a Reprint of his Essays* (London, 1906), 1–43. Pat Thane, *Old Age in English History* (Oxford, 2000), 196–7.
2  J. A. Spender, *The State and Pensions in Old Age* (London, 1894), xvi, 145; and Thane, *Old Age*, 196–7.
3  *National Providence League for Promoting Insurance against Paperism*, annual report 1890–1 and circulars 15 December 1891 and 21 March 1893. *Thrift and National Insurance as a Security against Pauperism*, 1–43. Joseph Chamberlain, *A Political Memoir 1880-92* (London, 1953), 294–5.
4  Francis Herbert Stead, *How Old Age Pensions Began to Be* (London, n.d), 194.
5  Charles Booth, *Pauperism, a Picture, and the Endowment of Old Age, an Argument* (London, 1892), 45–50.
6  Charles Booth, *The Aged Poor in England and Wales* (London, 1894), 14–15. Charles Booth, *Old Age Pensions and the Aged Poor* (London, 1899), 15.
7  Booth, *The Aged Poor in England and Wales*, 331. Spender, *The State and Pensions in Old Age*, 37–43.
8  Thane, *Old Age in English History*, 194–5.
9  Booth, *Old Age Pensions and the Aged Poor*, 31.
10  Spender, *The State and Old Age Pensions*, 47–53, 154.
11  Thane, *Old Age in English History*, 199–200. Bentley. B. Gilbert, *The Evolution of National Insurance in Great Britain* (London, 1966), 266–99 and J. H. Treble, 'The Attitudes of Friendly Societies towards the Movement in Great Britain for State Pensions, 1878–1908', *International Review of Social History* 15 (2) (1970): 266–9.
12  Spender, *The State and Old Age Pensions*, 53–6, 59–60.
13  Thane, *Old Age in English History*, 199, 210.
14  Stead, *How Old Age Pensions Began to Be*, 26–7.
15  Stead, *How Old Age Pensions Began to Be*, 59–61. Thane, *Old Age in English History*, 205.
16  Stead, *How Old Age Pensions Began to Be*, 52, 81; and Thane, *Old Age in English History*, 209–12.

17  Spender, *The State and Old Age Pensions*, 48, Stead, *How Old Age Pensions Began to Be*, 124-5.
18  Treble, 'The Attitudes of Friendly Societies towards the Movement in Great Britain for State Pensions, 1878-1908', 280-5. Thane, *Old Age in English History*, 199-200.
19  *Daily News*, 17 June 1909. Frederick Rogers, *Labour, Life and Literature. Some Memories of Sixty Years* (1913, repr. Brighton 1973), 223-4. Stead, *How Old Age Pensions Began to Be*, 126-30.
20  Stead, *How Old Age Pensions Began to Be*, 107, 162-3, 183.
21  G. N. Barnes, *From Workshop to War Cabinet* (London, 1924), 68.
22  Stead, *How Old Age Pensions Began to Be*, 172-3. Treble, 'The Attitudes of Friendly Societies towards the Movement in Great Britain for State Pensions, 1878-1908', 293-4.
23  A. G. Gardiner, *Life of George Cadbury* (London, n.d.), 113. Rogers, 'Introduction', *Labour, Life and Literature*, xxviii.
24  Rogers, 'Introduction', *Labour, Life and Literature*, xxv, xxvii, 224. Stead, *How Old Age Pensions Began to Be*, 66, 70-4.
25  Stead, *How Old Age Pensions Began to Be*, 159, 175, 199-200. Thane, *Old Age in English History*, 216.
26  Rogers, *Labour, Life and Literature*, 243, 247-50. Stead, *How Old Age Pensions Began to Be*, 183-4. *Daily News*, 18 March 1907.
27  H.G. Hutchinson, *Life of Sir John Lubbock*, vol. 2 (London, 1914), 247-8.
28  BL, Balfour Papers Add MS 49736 Austen Chamberlain to Arthur Balfour, 24 October 1907, ff.29.
29  Austen Chamberlain, *Politics from the Inside* (London, 1936), 118.
30  *Daily News*, 16 February, 15 March and 5 April 1906. Stead, *How Old Age Pensions Began to Be*, 204-5, 207-9.
31  David Lloyd George, *War Memoirs*, vol. 2 (London, 1933), 409.
32  H. C. G. Matthew, *The Liberal Imperialists* (Oxford, 1973), 253.
33  Stead, *How Old Age Pensions Began to Be*, 212-14. *Daily News*, 14 June 1906.
34  Stead, *How Old Age Pensions Began to Be*, 219-22. *Daily News*, 21 November 1906.
35  Thane, *Old Age in English History*, 218.
36  Bodleian Libraries, Asquith Papers, *Memorandum on Old Age Pensions*, R. S. Meiklejohn and M. Sturges, 14 December 1906.
37  *Daily News*, 7 January and 30 January 1907. Stead, *How Old Age Pensions Began to Be*, 224, 233, 235-6.
38  Bodleian Libraries, Asquith Papers, box 75, fos. 126, 127. Francis Herbert Stead to Asquith, 14 December 1907.
39  Beatrice Webb, *Our Partnership*, Barbara Drake and Margaret Cole (eds) (London, 1948), 379. LSE Passfield Papers, General Correspondence Beatrice Webb to Reginald McKenna, 30 April 1907; and Reginald McKenna to Beatrice Webb, 2 May 1907 fos. 232-4, 238.
40  Webb, *Our Partnership*, 384.
41  Bodleian Libraries, Asquith Papers box 75, 'Suggestions on Old Age Pensions', memorandum by Sidney Webb 29 September 1907, and a further memorandum 'Some Arguments on Old Age Pensions', 12 December 1907; enclosure R. B. Haldane to Asquith, 17 December 1907, Asquith Papers box 75, fos. 137-58 and fos. 161-70.
42  Thane, *Old Age in English History*, 220.
43  Bodleian Libraries, Asquith Papers, Roderick Meiklejohn to Asquith, 27 November 1907. Pat Thane, *Old Age in English History*, 220-1.

44 Stephen Koss, *Asquith* (London, 1976), 88, 97, 104. S. D. Waley, *Edwin Montagu* (London, 1964), 26, 27.
45 *Daily News*, 8 May 1908.
46 *Daily News*, 27 May, 12 June, 19 June, 23 June, 24 June and 2 July 1908. Stead, *How Old Age Pensions Began to Be*, 263–5.
47 *Daily News*, 12 June and 16 June 1908. John Macnicol, *The Politics of Retirement in Britain* (Cambridge, 1998), 157–9.
48 Stead, *How Old Age Pensions Began to Be*, 255–6. Macnicol, *The Politics of Retirement in Britain*, 159–60.
49 *Daily News*, 29 July and 30 July 1908. Stead, *How Old Age Pensions Began to Be*, 285.
50 Macnicol, *The Politics of Retirement in Britain*, 162.
51 Thane, *Old Age in English History*, 227.
52 Hennock, *British Social Reform and German Precedents*, 146–7.

## Chapter 5: Sweating and the Minimum Wage

1 Beatrice Potter, 'Tailoring', in Charles Booth (ed.), *Labour and Life of the People*, vol. 1 *East London* (London, 1889), 209–40, esp. 228.
2 Beatrice Webb, 'How to Do Away with the Sweating System', in Sidney Webb and Beatrice Webb, *Problems of Modern Industry* (London, 1898), 139–55
3 Ibid.
4 Beatrice Webb, *My Apprenticeship*, vol.2 (Harmondsworth, 1938), 357–86, 372–6, 487–8. Webb, 'How to Do Away with the Sweating System', 142–5; and Mrs Carl Meyer and Clementina Black, *Makers of Our Clothes* (London, 1909), 158–65.
5 *Select Committee on Home Work* PP, viii (1908), Chiozza Money to Aves qq.3848–9.
6 *Select Committee on Home Work* (1908) evidence of E. G. Howarth, qq.358–550 and Clementina Black (1907) qq.2854–971. H. A. Mess, *Factory Legislation and Administration 1891–1924* (London, 1926), 160.
7 Meyer and Black, *Makers of our Clothes*, 150.
8 Clementina Black, *Sweated Industry and the Minimum Wage* (London, 1907), 100, 105–6.
9 Edward Cadbury and George Shann, *Sweating* (London, 1907), 100, 105–6. *Select Committee on Sweating* (1908) evidence of E. G. Howarth, qq.358–37 *Women's Trade Union League*, annual report 1905.
10 B. L. Hutchins, 'Proposed Regulations for German Home Industries', in Richard Mudie Smith (ed.), *Handbook of the Daily News Sweated Industries Exhibition* (London, 1906), 85–7. National Anti-Sweating League, *Report of the Conference on a Minimum Wage* (London, 1907), speech of Professor Stephen Bauer.
11 *Consumers League of New York*, annual reports 1897 and 1902.
12 Black, 'Suggested Remedies', in *Handbook of the Daily News Sweated Industries Exhibition*, 19–23. *Consumers League*, prospectus of inaugural meeting. Clementina Black, *Sweated Industry and the Minimum Wage*, 183–4. Peter D'A. Jones, *The Christian Socialist Revival 1877–1914* (London, 1968), 183–4.
13 Sir George Reid to Stella Mallon, 16 July 1961, letter in possession of author.
14 Cadbury and Shann, *Sweating*, 108–11 and National Anti-Sweating League, *Report of the Conference on a Minimum Wage,* speech of Dilke.
15 J. Ramsay MacDonald, *Margaret Ethel MacDonald* (London, 1929), 142–50. Select

*Committee on Home Work* PP VI (1907), evidence of Mary MacArthur, qq.2827–833. Mrs Ramsay MacDonald, 'A Bill for the Better Regulation of Home Industries', in Richard Mudie Smith (ed.), *Handbook of the Daily News Sweated Industries Exhibition*, 26–7.

16  S. and B. Webb, *Industrial Democracy* (London, 1902), xlii–l, 245–6, 814–15; and Black, *Sweated Industry and the Minimum Wage*, 231–9.
17  Ernest Aves, *Report on Wages Boards and Industrial Conciliation and Arbitration Acts of Australia and New Zealand* PP LXXI (1908). *Select Committee on Home Work* (1908), Chiozza Money to Aves, qq.3848–9. Phillip Snowden, *The Living Wage* (London, 1912), 104–11.
18  Aves, *Report on Wages Boards*, [page ref]; *Select Committee on Home Work* (1908), evidence of Dilke, qq.3920–6.
19  Webb and Webb, *Industrial Democracy*, xxxvi–xlii, 245–6. Black, *Sweated Industry and the Minimum Wage*, 246–57. *Select Committee on Home Work* (1908), Stuart Samuel to Aves. q.3817.
20  Ernest Aves, *Report on Wages Boards*, National Anti-Sweating League; *Report of the Conference on a Minimum Age*, speech of Revd John Hoatson. Dorothy Sells, *The British Trade Boards System* (London, 1923), 160–1, 259.
21  *Select Committee on Home Work* (1908), evidence of Dilke, qq.3926–7.
22  National Anti-Sweating League, *Report of the Conference on a Minimum Wage*, speech of Dilke.
23  Sheila Blackburn, *A Fair Day's Wage for a Fair Day's Work? Sweated Labour and the Origins of Minimum Wage Legislation in Britain* (Aldershot, 2007), 83.
24  Webb and Webb, *Industrial Democracy*, 749–66.
25  Cadbury and Shann, *Sweating*, 71–2.
26  Edward Cadbury, Cecile Matheson and George Shann, *Women's Work and Wages* (London, 1908), 39–40, 85, 149, 164, 283–4. Cadbury and Shann, *Sweating*, 80–2; *Select Committee on Home Work* (1908) evidence of George Shann, qq.551–693.
27  Webb and Webb, *Industrial Democracy*, xxxix.
28  Ibid., xli, xlii.
29  Reginald Bray, *The Town Child* (London, 1908), 89.
30  Webb and Webb, *Industrial Democracy*, li–liv.
31  Cadbury, Matheson and Shann, *Women's Work and Wages*, 300–2.
32  Ibid., 305.
33  National Anti-Sweating League, *Report of the Conference on a Minimum Wage*, speeches of J. A. Hobson and Clementina Black. *Select Committee on Home Work* (1908), evidence of Clementina Black, qq.2891–919.
34  National Anti-Sweating League, *Report of the Conference on a Minimum Wage*.
35  National Anti-Sweating League, *Report of the Conference on a Minimum Wage*, speeches of Mary MacArthur, Sidney Webb, Chiozza Money and J. A. Hobson. TUC Parliamentary Committee minutes, 18 March 1909.
36  *Select Committee on Home Work* (1907), evidence of Gertrude Tuckwell, qq.2333–34, 2396–2400; and evidence of Clementina Black, qq.2864–5. Cadbury, Matheson and Shann, *Women's, Work and Wages*, 252–3, 256–7.
37  Mary Hamilton, *Mary MacArthur: A Biographical Sketch* (London, 1925), 27–30, 56.
38  WTUL annual report 1901. *Select Committee on Home Work* (1908), evidence of Dilke. National Anti-Sweating League, *Report of the Conference on a Minimum Wage*, speech of Gertrude Tuckwell.
39  Mary Hamilton, *Mary MacArthur*, 65. Smith (ed.), 'Introduction', in *Handbook of the*

*Daily News Sweated Industries Exhibition*, 7-8, Tuckwell, 'Preface', [title], 10-17; and Smith, 'The German Home Workers Exhibition', 17-19. Women's Industrial Council, annual report 1905-6. A. G. Gardiner, *The Life of George Cadbury* (London, n.d.), 215-16.

40 *Report of the Conference on a Minimum Wage*, speech of Fenwick.
41 *Women's Industrial Council*, annual report 1905-6. WTUL annual reports 1907 and 1908. NASL annual report 1908. Blackburn, *A Fair Day's Wage*, 111. Stephen Koss, *Fleet Street Radical. A. G. Gardiner and the Daily News* (London, 1973), 77-8.
42 *The Memoirs of the Rt. Hon. The Earl of Woolton* (London, 1959), 10.
43 Margaret Stewart and Leslie Hunter, *The Needle is Threaded: The History of an Industry* (London, 1964), 135.
44 Ibid.
45 NASL annual reports 1907, 1912 and 1913. Lady Simon of Wythenshawe to the author 20 September 1965. Tuckwell, *Constance Smith. A Short Memoir*; C. R. Attlee, *As it Happened* (London, 1954), 27-8.
46 NASL, *Report of the Conference on a Minimum Wage*. Hamilton, *Mary MacArthur*, 67-9.
47 NASL annual report 1907. *Daily News*, 7 September 1906 and 7 September 1907. Black, *Sweated Industry and the Minimum Wage*, 258-9.
48 NASL annual reports 1907 and 1908. NASL, *Report of the Conference on a Minimum Wage*, speech of Barnes, 42-3. WTUL annual report 1910.
49 Sidney Webb and Beatrice Webb, *Industrial Democracy* (Place, 1902), xxxix-xlii. NASL annual reports 1908 and 1909. A. G. Gardiner, *Prophets, Priests and Kings* (London, 1917), 18. A. M. McBriar, *Fabian Socialism and English Politics 1884-1918* (Cambridge, 1962), 260.
50 NASL annual report 1907. Gervas Huxley, *Lady Denman 1884-1954* (London, 1961), 34-8. William Beveridge, *Power and Influence* (London, 1953), 50. C. V. Butler, *Social Conditions in Oxford* (London, 1912).
51 *Women's Industrial Council*, annual reports 1906-7, 1907-8 and 1908-9. *Handbook and Report of the National Union of Women Workers of Great Britain* (London, 1912), 69.
52 WTUL annual report 1905. NASL annual reports 1907 and 1908. *Daily News*, 29 January and 15 December 1908. Blackburn, *A Fair Day's Wage*, 104
53 NASL annual reports 1907, 1908 and 1909.
54 NASL annual report 1907.
55 NASL annual report 1908. William Beveridge, *Power and Influence* (London, 1953), 50. Koss, *A. G. Gardiner*, 78-9.
56 NASL annual reports 1907, 1908 and 1909.
57 Randolph S. Churchill, *Winston S. Churchill*, Companion vol. 4 (1907-11), 834-5. NASL annual reports 1907 and 1908.
58 Churchill, *Winston S. Churchill*, 864-5.
59 Ernest Aves, *Report on the Wages Boards and Industrial Conciliation and Arbitration Acts of Australia and New Zealand* PP LXXI (1908). *Select Committee on Home Work* (1908), iii-xviii.
60 NASL annual report 1908, *Select Committee on Home Work* (1908), iii-xiv. G. P. Gooch, *Under Six Reigns* (London, 1958), 147-8.
61 NASL annual reports 1907, 1908 and 1909. *Daily News*, 1 December 1908. *Manchester Guardian*, obituary of J. J. Mallon, 14 April 1961. Stewart and Hunter, *The Needle is Threaded*, 139-40.

62  Stewart and Hunter, *The Needle is Threaded*, 140-2.
63  *Nation*, 7 March 1908.
64  Lord Riddell, *More Pages from my Diary 1908-14*, 131.
65  Churchill, *Winston S. Churchill*, 860-1, 870. Blackburn, *A Fair Day's Wage*, 113.
66  NASL annual report 1909. *Daily News*, 25 March 1909. *Select Committee on Home Work* (1908), evidence of Dilke, qq.3926, 3929, 3931, 3936 and report, xvii.
67  NASL annual reports 1907 and 1909. *Select Committee on Home Work* (1908), evidence of Dilke, q.3936. WTUL annual report 1910.
68  National Archives, CAB 37/98/42 Memorandum of Churchill, 12 March 1909.
69  Sheila Blackburn, *A Fair Day's Wage*, 114, 127.
70  *Hansard* (Commons), col. 962, 24 May 1909; and col. 2479, 16 July 1909.
71  Gardiner, *Prophets, Priests and Kings*, 62.

# Chapter 6: The Webbs and the Minority Report on the Poor Law

1  Royden Harrison, 'Sidney and Beatrice Webb', in Carl Levy (ed.), *Socialism and the Intelligentsia* (London, 1987), 62-3.
2  *Municipal Journal*, 27 March and 8 May 1903.
3  Beatrice Webb, *Our Partnership*, Barbara Drake and Margaret I. Cole (eds) (London, 1948), 316-21.
4  *Poor Law Officers' Journal*, 12 January 1906.
5  Harris, *Unemployment and Politics*, 263.
6  Trevor Lumis, 'Charles Booth: Moralist or Social Scientist?' *Economic History Review* (February 1971): 100-5.
7  Harris, *Unemployment and Politics*, 349.
8  NA, CAB37/99/59 memorandum on the Poor Law Commission, June 1909.
9  Jane Lewis, *Women and Social Action in Victorian and Edwardian England* (Aldershot, 1991), 146-87.
10 *Majority Report*, 287.
11 Kathleen Woodroofe, 'The Royal Commission on the Poor Laws, 1905-9', *International Review of Social History* 22 (1977): 151.
12 Ibid., 151-3.
13 *Majority Report*, 221-2.
14 Woodroofe, 'Poor Law Commission', 158. Helen Bosanquet, *The Poor Law Report of 1909* (London, 1911), 242-8. Lewis, *Women and Social Action*, 180-1.
15 Harris, *Unemployment and Politics*, 254-5.
16 W. H. Beveridge, *Power and Influence* (London, 1953), 23-4, 61-4. W. H. Beveridge, *Unemployment: A Problem of Industry* (London, 1909), 160. Harris, *Unemployment and Politics*, 255-7. Charity Organisation Society, *Report of the Special Committee on Unskiled Labour* (London, 1908).
17 S. Webb and B. Webb, *Industrial Democracy* (London, 1902), xxxix-liv, 757-8.
18 Ibid.
19 Beveridge, *Unemployment*, 133-44, 205-6, 229.
20 Beveridge, *Power and Influence*, 27.
21 B. S. Rowntree, *Poverty: A Study of Town Life* (London, 1914), 154; and A. L. Bowley

and A. R. Burnett-Hurst, *Livelihood and Poverty* (London, 1915), 34–5, 41–2. N. B. Dearle, *Industrial Training* (London, 1914), 33–41.
22  Seebohm Rowntree, *The Way to Industrial Peace and the Problem of Unemployment* (London, 1914), 146.
23  Webb, *Our Partnership*, 341–2.
24  Webb and Webb, *Industrial Democracy*, liii.
25  Ibid., 772.
26  Woodroofe, 'Poor Law Commission of 1905–9', 163.
27  Webb, *Our Partnership*, 348–9. Interview with the late Dr McCleary.
28  Webb, *Our Partnership*, 351, 368, 370.
29  *Minority Report*, vol. 1, 228. LSE, Passfield Papers, Poor Law Collection, e.g. replies of the MOHs of the City of Westminster and Borough of Greenwich, both 6 September 1906.
30  John M. Eyler, *Sir Arthur Newsholme and State Medicine 1885–1935* (Cambridge, 1997), 209, 212, 219. Webb, *Our Partnership*, 292–3.
31  LSE, Passfield Papers, General Correspondence Beatrice Webb to Reginald McKenna, 30 April 1907, f.232.
32  LSE, Passfield Papers, General Correspondence Reginald McKenna to Beatrice Webb, 19 February 1908, ff.5, 6.
33  Webb, *Our Partnership*, 394, 402–3, 411.
34  LSE, Passfield Papers, General Correspondence R. B. Haldane to Beatrice Webb, 30 May 1907, f.44. Webb, *Our Partnership*, 418.
35  LSE, Passfield Papers, General Correspondence R. B. Haldane to Beatrice Webb, 30 May 1907, f.282. Bodleian Libraries, Asquith Papers, Old Age Pensions file, Cabinet Paper, 13 September 1907 by R. B. Haldane, 2–4.
36  Bodleian Libraries, Old Age Pensions file, R. B. Haldane to Asquith, 17 December 1907, enclosing a memorandum on old age pensions in Sidney Webb's hand plus a printed memorandum on the break-up of the Poor Law. *Daily News*, 19 June and 26 June 1908.
37  LSE, Passfield Papers, R. B. Haldane to Beatrice Webb, 16 August 1907, f.254.
38  Bodleian Libraries, Asquith Papers, General Correspondence, Churchill to Asquith, 26 December 1908.
39  Beatrice Webb, *Our Partnership*, 417.
40  Webb, *Our Partnership*, 399, 402. Bodleian Libraries, Asquith Papers, Old Age Pensions file, the Webbs printed memorandum on the break-up of the Poor Law, and General Correspondence, Beatrice Webb to Asquith, 2 March 1908, ff.1–4. LSE, Passfield Papers, J. Vaughan Nash to Beatrice Webb, 21 May 1908, f.30.
41  Webb, *Our Partnership*, 417.
42  *Daily News*, 1 May 1908.
43  *Daily News*, 13 June and 16 June 1908.
44  NA, CAB37/98/40 memorandum on the Poor Law Commission, 10 March 1909.
45  NA, CAB37/99/59 memorandum on the Poor Law Commission, June 1909.
46  Ibid.
47  Webb, *Our Partnership*, 418.

# Chapter 7: Asquith at the Exchequer

1. A. G. Gardiner, *Prophets, Priests and Kings* (London, 1917), 54–5, 58–60.
2. *Financial Reformer*, January–March 1906. Herbert Samuel, *Liberalism* (London, 1902), 189. Simon Maccoby, *English Radicalism 1886–1914* (London, 1953), 332–3.
3. *Daily News*, 26 January 1909. Herbert Samuel, *Liberalism*, 192. Richard Burdon Haldane, *An Autobiography* (London, 1929), 216. Peter Rowland, *The Last Liberal Governments: The Promised Land 1905–1910* (London, 1968), 342, 344.
4. *Colliery Guardian*, 24 January 1902, 27 January and 2 June 1905 and 26 February 1909.
5. *Colliery Guardian*, 5 January, 23 February and 4 May 1906.
6. *The Intermittent Message of the Free Tea League*, 24 March 1906. *Monthly Message of the Anti-Tea Duty League*, 31 January 1906.
7. *The Intermittent Message*, 24 March and 1 May 1906. *Monthly Message*, 9 April 1906.
8. *Confectionery*, 12 November 1901, 12 January and 13 March 1904, 12 January, 12 April and 12 September 1905 and 20 September 1906.
9. *Confectionery*, 12 January 1905, 12 March 1906 and 12 March 1907. Bodleian Libraries, Asquith Papers, Asquith to Edward VII, 1 May, ff.26 and 6 May, ff.27 1908. Austen Chamberlain, *Politics from Inside: An Epistolary Chronicle 1906–1914* (London, 1936), 153–4.
10. F. W. Kolthammer, *Some Notes on the Incidence of Taxation on the Working Class Family* (London, 1913).
11. Ibid.
12. Sir Charles Dilke, 'Finance in the new Parliament', *Financial Review of Reviews* (April 1906). Dilke draft report *Select Committee on Income Tax* 1906, xix. Simon Maccoby, *English Radicalism 1886–1914* (London, 1953), 59. Andrew Reid (ed.), *The New Party* (London, 1894).
13. Stead, *How Old Age Pensions Began to Be*, 214.
14. Erwin Esser Nemers, *Hobson and Underconsumption* (Amsterdam, 1956).
15. J. A. Hobson, *The Industrial System: An Inquiry into Earned and Unearned Income* (London, 1909), 218–41. *Daily News*, 10 November 1908.
16. McBriar, *Fabian Socialism and English Politics 1884–1918*, 23–4. John M. Robertson, *The Fallacy of Saving* (London, 1892).
17. Cambridge University Library, MS Add 9259.Chiozza Money, *Autobiography*, 388.
18. *Daily News*, 17 November 1906. BL, Dilke Papers Add MS 43919, Primrose to Dilke, 2 May 1906 and Dilke to Llewellyn Smith, 15 May 1906. *Select Committee on Income Tax* PP IX, 1906, 1–20, 78, 190–205.
19. BL, Dilke Papers Add MS 43919 McKenna to Dilke, 8 May and 9 September 1906. Lord Riddell, *More Pages from My Diary 1908–1914* (London, 1934), 174. *Daily News*, 30 November 1906.
20. L. G. Chiozza Money, *Riches and Poverty* (London, 1906), 8–52. *Select Committee on Income Tax*, 35.
21. *Select Committee on Income Tax*, xxii–xxviii. BL, Dilke Papers Add MS 43919 McKenna to Dilke, 29 October 1906. Cambridge University Library, Add MS 9259 Money Autobiography, 393–4. *Daily News*, 16 November 1906.
22. Chiozza Money, 'Mr Lloyd George's Opportunity and Responsibility', *Albany Review*, May 1908. Sir T. P. Whittaker, 'The New Income Tax Basis', *Financial Review of Reviews* (January 1907).

23 *Select Committee on Income Tax*, evidence of Snowden, 108–28, 237–9. J. Keir Hardie, 'A Labour Budget', *Financial Review of Reviews* (April 1906).
24 Sir T. P. Whittaker, 'The New Income-Tax Basis', *Financial Review of Reviews* (January 1907).
25 John Cooper, *The Unexpected Story of Nathaniel Rothschild* (London, 2015), 226–7.
26 BL, Dilke Papers Add MS 43919 Bernard Mallet to Dilke, 1 December 1906.
27 Treasury Papers, McKenna to Asquith, 17 December 1906 and Primrose to Asquith, 5 February 1907.
28 *Hansard*, cols 1203, 1206, 18 April 1907. Bruce K. Murray, *The People's Budget 1909/10: Lloyd George and Liberal Politics* (Oxford, 1980), 98–9. Martin Daunton, *Trusting Leviathan: The Politics of Taxation in Britain 1799–1914* (Cambridge, 2001), 361. *Daily News*, 19 April 1907.
29 *Hansard*, cols 474–5, 480, 7 May 1908.
30 Daunton, *Trusting Leviathan*, 333–4
31 Treasury Papers, Cabinet Paper signed by W.B[lain], 26 February 1907, 1.
32 Ibid., 2, 5.
33 *Daily News*, 8 May 1908. Austen Chamberlain, *Politics from Inside*, 109.
34 Bodleian Libaries, Asquith Papers General Correspondence 1908 memorandum of Haldane, 9 August 1908.
35 Richard Burdon Haldane, *An Autobiography* (London, 1929), 216.

# Chapter 8: The Great Budget of 1909

1 Kenneth O. Morgan, Lloyd George (London, 1974), 60.
2 Élie Halévy, *The Rule of Democracy 1905–14* (London, 1952), 14–15.
3 *Shipping World*, 4 December 1907. Board of Trade Papers, M12044, Havelock Wilson to Howell, 14 August 1903.
4 BOT Papers, M 15724, deputation of shipowners to Lloyd George, 3 August 1906. *Liverpool Journal of Commerce*, 24 February 1906 and 6 February, 9 February and 12 February 1907. *Shipping World*, 28 March 1907.
5 *Shipping World*, 21 March, 4 April and 30 May 1906. *Certain Questions Affecting the Mercantile Marine* PP LXII (1903). Report and Evidence of Havelock Wilson, 169, 172.
6 BOT Papers, M12366, deputation of seamen to Lloyd George, 28 May 1906. *Shipping World*, 30 May 1906.
7 BOT Papers, M15724, correspondence and deputation of Shipowners Parliamentary Committee to Lloyd George, 3 August [add year]; 24 August [add year] note of Howell.
8 BOT Papers, M14133, Cuthbert |Laws to Lloyd George, 4 July 1906, M14819, Mercantile Marine Service Association to Marine Dept. 13 July 1906, M105075 British Shipmasters and Officers Protection Association to Marine Dept 16 July 1906.
9 BOT Papers, M22003, Chamber of Shipping to Lloyd George, 26 October 1906, and M22603, Deputation of Chamber of Shipping to Lloyd George, 2 November 1906, 30–3, 41, 47.
10 BOT Papers, M22604, Conference between Lloyd George and Shipowners

deputation, 6 November 1906, 3, 4, 19, 33, 36–9 and 41; and M22603, Chamber of Shipping Deputation to Lloyd George on local marine boards, 5.
11  *Labour Leader*, 7 November 1908. *Certain Questions Affecting the Mercantile Marine* PP, lxii, 1903. Interview with Mr T. Roach, 25 September 1970. *Seaman*, November 1907. Fenner Brockway, *Jowett of Bradford* (London, 1946).
12  *Railway Companies Association*, minutes 17 December and 18 December 1907, 17 January and 11 February 1908.
13  *Mansion House Association*, annual report 1908.
14  J. A. Spender, *Journalism and Politics* (London, 1927), 157.
15  *Daily News*, 27 February and 5 March 1908. *Railway Companies Association*, 5 March, 8 April, 13 May and 3 December 1908. *Mansion House Association*, annual report 1908.
16  Lucy Masterman, *C. F. G. Masterman* (London, 1939), 226.
17  *Daily News*, 2 November 1906 and 20 March 1907; and *Alliance News*, 30 May 1907.
18  *Daily News*, 6 April, 16 April and 22 April 1907; and LSE Library, Cooperative Small Holdings Society, Minutes 19 December 1906 and 23 January 1907.
19  BL, Balfour Papers Add MS 49736 Austen Chamberlain to Balfour, 24 October 1907.
20  BL, Campbell-Bannerman Papers Add MS 41231 Whitely to Arthur Ponsonby, 20 December 1906, ff.220, 221. *Land Values*, October 1908. Francis Neilson, *The Churchill Legend* (Wisconsin, 1955), 107.
21  *Daily News*, 20 October, 27 October, 28 October and 25 November 1908. *Land Values*, November and December 1908. *The Times*, 11 February 1909.
22  *Land Values*, September 1908 and January 1909. *Daily News*, 10 November and 14 November 1908. J. C. Wedgwood, *Memoirs of a Fighting Life* (London, 1941), 78. Francis Neilson, *My Life in Two Worlds*, vol. 1 (Wisconsin, 1952), 247.
23  *Land Values*, February and March 1909.
24  *Daily News*, 26 January 1909. J. C. Wedgwood, *Memoirs of a Fighting Life*, 68. Bruce K. Murray, 'The Politics of the "People's Budget"', *Historical Journal* XVI2 (1973): 561.
25  Bodleian Libraries, Asquith Papers, Misc. Letters and Memoranda 1908–11, Cabinet Paper on the Taxation of Land Values, 23 January 1909, ff.115–20. *Land Values*, March 1909.
26  *Daily News*, 13 February 1907, 25 February, 2 May, 5 May and 11 November 1908.
27  John Cooper, *Nathaniel Rothschild*, 64–5, 232–9.
28  Bruce K. Murray, *The People's Budget 1909/10*, 101. Don M. Creiger, *Bounder from Wales. Lloyd George's Career before the First World War* (London, 1976).
29  Stephen Koss, *Asquith* (London, 1976), 113–14.
30  Ibid.
31  Margot Asquith, *The Autobiography of Margot Asquith*, vol. 2 (London, 1936), 88. Bodleian Libraries, Ms Eng.d 3206–7 Diary of Margot Asquith, 15 September 1909.
32  *D.N.B.* on Robert Chalmers and John Bradbury; and W. J. Braithwaite, *Lloyd George's Ambulance Wagon* (London, 1957), 68. Murray, *The People's Budget 1909/10*, 101.
33  Richard Lloyd George, *Lloyd George* (London, 1960), 110–13. Cameron Hazlehurst and Christine Woodland (eds), *A Liberal Chronicle: Journals and Papers of J. A. Pease* (Place, 1995), 102–4.
34  *Land Values*, June and August 1909. *Daily News*, 14 June 1909.
35  National Archives, CAB37/98/44 memorandum on the taxation of land values, 13 March 1909 of Lloyd George. Bernard Mallet, *British Budgets 1887–8 to 1912–13*,

306-7. Edgar Harper, 'Lloyd George's Land Taxes' reprinted from *Land & Liberty*. Murray, *The People's Budget 1909/10*, 134–5, 153–4.
36  Murray, *The People's Budget 1909/10*, 157–8.
37  *Daily News*, 14 December 1908.
38  Bodleian Libraries, Asquith Papers, Asquith to Edward VII, i, 5, 6 April 1909. Also Misc. Letters and Memoranda, memorandum of Sir George Murray, 25 March 1909. National Archives, CAB37/99/57 memorandum of Sir Robert Chalmers on Supertax, 27 March 1909, 2.
39  *Daily News*, 4 May and 14 September 1909.
40  Murray, *The People's Budget 1909/10*, 5, 137–8.
41  Joseph Rowntree and Arthur Sherwell, *The Taxation of the Liquor Trade* (London, 1909 abr. edn), 23–6,32–3, 49–50.
42  Rowntree and Sherwell, *The Taxation of the Liquor Trade*, 31–2, 37–8,64, 147.
43  Rowntree and Sherwell, *The Taxation of the Liquor Trade*, 95, 96, 138, 170. *Daily News*, 28 August 1909.
44  *Hansard*, 29 April 1909, cols 485–9.
45  *Hansard*, 29 April 1909, cols 489–94.
46  Ibid.
47  British Library, Balfour Papers Ms49860 office of the *Scotsman* to Balfour, 16 July 1909.
48  *Daily News*, 22 May, 24 May, 25 June and 24 July 1909.
49  *Daily News*, 27 July, 31 July and 2 August 1909.
50  *National Housing Reform Council*, minutes of the Land and Housing Joint Committee, 20 May 1909. *Daily News*, 26 May and 25 June 1909.
51  *Daily News*, 11 May, 16 June, 26 July, 31 July and 18 August 1909. *Land Values*, August 1909.
52  P. F. Clarke, *Lancashire and the New Liberalism* (Cambridge, 1971), 393–4, 398–400. Neal Blewett, *The Peers, the Parties and the People: The General Elections of 1910* (London, 1972), 398, 401–3, 405–6.
53  G. R. Searle, *A New England? Peace and War 1886–1918* (Oxford, 2004), 414–22. G. R. Searle, *The Quest for National Efficiency* (Oxford, 1971), 188–90.
54  Koss, *Asquith*, 125–6.
55  Michael Brock and Eleanor Brock (eds), *Margot Asquith's Great War Diary 1914–16* (Oxford, 2014), liv–lv.
56  Murray, *The People's Budget 1909/10*, 1. H. V. Emy, *Liberals, Radicals and Social Politics 1892–1914* (Cambridge, 1973), 224–6.
57  L. G. Chiozza Money, *The Future of Work* (London, 1914), 231, 240–1.
58  Ibid.

# Chapter 9: National Health Insurance

1  William J. Braithwaite, *Lloyd George's Ambulance Wagon* (London, 957), 71–2.
2  Braithwaite, *Lloyd George's Ambulance Wagon*, 68–9
3  *Daily News*, 2 May, 5 December and 6 December 1906. *Shipping World*, 11 April, 9 May, 23 May and 30 May 1906.
4  *TUC Parliamentary Committee Minutes*, 30 January, 20 February, 18 March, 15 April and 2 September 1908.

5   *Chamber of Commerce Journal* (April 1907). Virginia Berridge, 'Health and Medicine', in *The Cambridge Social History of Britain*, F. M. L. Thompson (ed.) (Cambridge, 1993), 218–19.
6   Interview with the late Dr George McCleary, 27 June 1961.
7   Edward Cadbury and George Shann, *Sweating* (London, 1907), 127.
8   *Chamber of Commerce Journal* (April/September/December 1907).
9   *Daily News*, 15 October 1909. G. F. McCleary, *National Health Insurance* (London, 1932), 79–80.
10  Alfred Cox, *Among the Doctors* (London, n.d.), 57, 60. McCleary, *National Health Insurance*, 80.
11  Gorst, *The Children of the Nation*, 142.
12  W. H. Beveridge, *Voluntary Action* (London, 1948), 29–34. Webb and Webb, *The Break-Up of the Poor Law*, vol. 1, 25–36.
13  Beveridge, *Voluntary Action*, 66–7.
14  *Daily News*, 23 October 1908. *Resolutions of the NCFS 1908*, 10.
15  *Resolutions of the NCFS 1909*, 11.
16  A. G. Gardiner, *Pillars of Society* (London, 1913), 290.
17  Chris Wrigley, *David Lloyd George and the British Labour Movement* (Hassocks, 1976), 61–2. Penelope Ismay, 'Between Providence and Risk: Odd Fellows, Benevolence and the Social Limits of Actuarial Science, 1820s–1880s', *Past and Present* (February 2015): 117–18.
18  Cadbury Research Library, Birmingham, William Harbutt Dawson Papers 2196 diary, 8 October and 27 December 1908.
19  *Resolutions of the NCFS 1909*, 12.
20  Ibid.
21  See also *Hansard*, 29 April 1909, cols 485–7.
22  *Daily News*, 31 May, 1 June, 2 June, 3 June and 17 June 1909.
23  Braithwaite, *Lloyd George's Ambulance Wagon*, 72–3.
24  NA, T170/76, Appendix to memorandum of George F. Hardy and Frank B. Wyatt, 21 March 1910, 50–5. Braithwaite, *Lloyd George's Ambulance Wagon*, 73–6
25  NA, T170/6, memorandum of Hardy and Wyatt, 27 August 1910, 1–3.
26  Braithwaite, *Lloyd George's Ambulance Wagon*, 79–80, 82–5.
27  Braithwaite, *Lloyd George's Ambulance Wagon*, 139, 149–51.
28  Braithwaite, *Lloyd George's Ambulance Wagon*, 243. A. S. Comyns Carr, W. H. Stuart Garnett and J. H. Taylor, *National Insurance* (London, 1912), 96–9.
29  *Hansard*, 4 May 1911, cols 621–3.
30  *Hansard*, 4 May 1911, col. 639.
31  Bentley B. Gilbert, *The Evolution of National Insurance in Great Britain. The Origins of the Welfare State* (London, 1966), 326–62, 368–9. Cordery, *British Friendly Societies*, 167.
32  Derek Fraser, *The Evolution of the British Welfare State* (London, 1984), 278–9.
33  Wrigley, *Lloyd George and Labour*, 39.
34  Cordery, *British Friendly Societies*, 168.
35  Harry Eckstein, *The English Health Service* (Cambridge, MA, 1959), 21.
36  Gilbert, *The Evolution of National Insurance in Great Britain*, 368–9. Frank Honigsbaum, 'Christopher Addison: A Realist in Pursuit of Dreams', in *Doctors, Politics and Society* (Amsterdam, 1993), 229–33.

37  Kenneth Morgan and Jane Morgan, *Portrait of a Progressive. The Political Career of Christopher, Viscount Addison* (Oxford, 1980), 14–15.
38  Gilbert, *National Insurance*, 325–6, 341–2, 378–83. National Archives, T170/6 Conference on the National Insurance Bill, 16 October 1911, 4–23, 45–7. Braithwaite, *Lloyd George's Ambulance Wagon*, 211–12.
39  E. W. Little, *History of the British Medical Association 1832–1932* (London, 1932), 79–88. Alfred Cox, *Among the Doctors* (London, n.d.), 72–8.
40  R. M. Titmuss, 'Health', in Morris Ginsberg (ed.), *Law and Opinion in the 20th Century* (London, 1959), 311.
41  McCleary, *National Health Insurance*, 81–2.
42  Gilbert, *National Insurance*, 401–16. Morgan and Morgan, *Christopher Addison*, 20.
43  David G. Green, *Working Class Patients and the Medical Establishment. Self-Help in Britain from the Mid-nineteenth Century to 1948* (Aldershot, 1985). Harris, *The Origins of the British Welfare State*, 4, 6.
44  William A. Brend, *Health and the State* (London, 1917), 223.
45  Braithwaite, *Lloyd George's Ambulance Wagon*, 134, 138, 142–3. Lucy Masterman, *C. F. G. Masterman. A Biography* (London, 1939), 217.

## Chapter 10: Unemployment Insurance

1  LSE, Executive committee of the Labour party, minutes (copy), 14 February 1906.
2  *Labour Leader*, 28 August, 4 September, 2 October, 9 October and 20 November 1908. *Daily News*, 14 March and 7 September 1908. Martin Petter, 'The Progressive Alliance', *History* 58 (February 1973).
3  Lucy Masterman, *C. F. G. Masterman* (London, 1939), 111–12; and Jose Harris, *Unemployment and Politics. A Study in English Social Politics 1886–1914* (Oxford, 1972), 275.
4  *Daily News*, 22 October 1908, and *Hansard* (Commons), 21 October 1908, cols 1160–72.
5  Christopher Hassall, *Edward Marsh* (London, 1959), 140. LSE, Passfield Papers, Sidney to Beatrice Webb, 21 February 1908, ff.159. Webb, *Our Partnership*; Barbara Drake and Margaret Cole (eds) (London, 1948), 404, 411.
6  E. P. Hennock, *British Social Reform and German Precedents. The Case of Social Insurance 1880–1914* (Oxford, 1987), 163.
7  Randolph S. Churchill, *Winston S. Churchill*, Companion vol. 4 (1907–11) (London, 1969), 754–6.
8  Ibid., 759.
9  Ibid., 761.
10  William Beveridge, *Power and Influence* (London, 1953), 68–9.
11  Winston Churchill to Beatrice Webb, 6 July 1908, ff.249, 250, Passfield Papers.
12  Beveridge, *Power and Influence*, 74. NA, LAB 8/821 Memorandum on Labour Exchanges by Beveridge and criticism of D. F. Schloss, 13 July 1907. CAB 37/97/17 Memorandum on Labour Exchanges and minutes, 27 January 1909.
13  Jose Harris, *William Beveridge* (Oxford, 1997), 170–5. TUC Parliamentary Committee: Minutes, 22 April, 7 July and 18 August 1909.
14  *Daily News*, 26 June 2008.
15  *The Times*, 17 August 1908.

16  Churchill, *Winston S. Churchill*, 860–1,
17  Ibid., 869–70.
18  TUC Parliamentary Committee: Minutes, 21 November 1906, and *Daily News*, 11 September 1908. Percy Alden, *The Unemployed. A National Question* (London, 1905), 65. David Schloss, *Insurance Against Unemployment* (London, 1909), 49–71. NA, LAB 8/821 Memorandum by D. F. Schloss, 13 July 1908. G. P. Gooch, 'The Unemployed', *Contemporary Review* (March 1906); and Masterman, *C. F. G. Masterman*, 226. Stephen Gwynn and Gertrude M. Tuckwell, *The Life of Rt. Hon. Sir Charles W. Dilke*, vol. 2 (London, 1917), 351–2.
19  NA, LAB 8/821 Memorandum on Labour Bureaux, 31 July 1908.
20  *RC on the Poor Laws* 1909, vol. xlix, 445–54.
21  Ibid.
22  Ibid.
23  Ibid.
24  H. N. Bunbury (ed.), *Lloyd George's Ambulance Wagon. Being the Memoirs of William J. Braithwaite 1911–12* (London, 1957), 139. Stefan Berger, 'William Harbutt Dawson, The Career and Politics of an Historian of Germany', *English Historical Review* 116 (2001): 78. Churchill, *Winston S. Churchill*, 860–1.
25  Cadbury Research Library, Birmingham, William Harbutt Dawson Papers, W. H. Dawson Diary, 1 October and 24 October 1908, WHD 2196.
26  Memorandum on assisted unemployment insurance in conjunction with labour exchanges by Dawson, 30 September 1908, WHD 2142.
27  Ibid.
28  Waley, *Edwin Montagu*, 26. Birmingham UL, W. H. Dawson Diary, 31 January and 8 October 1908, WHD 2196. George Riddell, *More Pages from My Diary 1908–14* (London, 1934), 3. Chris Wrigley, *David Lloyd George and the British Labour Movement* (Brighton, 1976), 29.
29  Birmingham UL, W. H. Dawson Diary, 27 December 1908, WHD 2196.
30  Birmingham UL, W. H. Dawson Diary, 19 November 1908, WHD 2196.
31  Harold Spender, 'Unemployment Insurance', *Contemporary Review* (January 1909).
32  Harris, *Unemployment and Politics*, 303.
33  NA, Memorandum on Unemployment Insurance: Labour Exchanges, 11 December 1908, CAB 27/96/159; and Memorandum on a Scheme for Unemployment Insurance, 19 April 1909, CAB 37/99/69. *Daily News*, 24 May 1909.
34  LSE, Beveridge Papers III, 37. Notes on Memorandum from Lewellyn Smith, 28 October 1908 by Beveridge. Beveridge, *Power and Influence*, 83, Harris, *William Beveridge*, 183 and Harris, *Unemployment and Politics*, 326, 328, 329, 331–2. Frank Tillyard and F. N. Ball, *Unemployment insurance in Great Britain 1911–48* (Leigh-on-Sea, 1949), 4.
35  NA, Memorandum on proposed extension of the National Insurance Act 1911 Part 2 by Sydney Buxton, November 1913, CAB 37/117/79. William Beveridge to Treasury, 30 December 1913 and G. S. Barnes to Treasury, 3 February 1914, T1/11659.
36  NA, T1/11659 Notes by C. F. G. Masterman, 10 February and 26 February 1914. Memorandum on Unemployment Insurance Extension Orders, 1 April 1914 by John Burns, March 1914 and note of Hamilton 11 March 1914 and further notes of Hamilton and Ross, 6 May 1914. Harris, *Unemployment and Politics*, 322–4.
37  H. A. Mess, *Casual Labour at the Docks* (London, 1916), 21–2.
38  Ibid., 88.
39  Ibid., 128.

40  Ibid., 132.
41  David F. Wilson, *Dockers: The Impact of Industrial Change* (London, 1972), 64.
42  Mess, *Casual Labour at the Docks*, 52, 137. R. Williams, *The First Year's Working of the Liverpool Docks Scheme* (London, 1914), 98, 103–4.
43  Gordon Phillips and Noel Whiteside, *Casual Labour: The Unemployment Question in the Port Transport Industry 1880–1970* (Oxford, 1985), 10.
44  Ibid.
45  David F. Wilson, *Dockers*, 62–3. Phillips and Whiteside, *Casual Labour*, 48–53.
46  Williams, *Liverpool Docks Scheme*, 5–15, 129–35. Phillips and Whiteside, *Casual Labour*, 90–2. Mess, *Casual Labour at the Docks*, 103–10.
47  Williams, *Liverpool Docks Scheme*, 84–6. Phillips and Whitehouse, *Casual Labour*, 92–5. Wilson, *Dockers*, 68–71.
48  Harris, *Unemployment and Politics*, 356. Phillips and Whiteside, *Casual Labour*, 88–9, 95–6.
49  NA, Memorandum on proposed extension of the National Insurance Act Part 2 by Sydney Buxton, November 1913, 4–7, and Treasury memorandum with comments, December 1913, CAB 37/117/79, T1/11659.
50  Phillips and Whiteside, *Casual Labour*, 103–6. Beveridge, *Power and Influence*, 79.
51  *RC on the Poor Laws*, Minority Report, 658–60. Webb, *Our Partnership*, 416–17. *Daily News*, 10 October 1908. Churchill, *Winston S. Churchill*, 862–4, 895–8. Harris, *Unemployment and Politics*, 344–5.
52  Churchill, *Winston S. Churchill*, 1037. *RC on the Poor Laws*, Minutes of Evidence, 1910, vol. XLVIII, 466–73.
53  *Hansard* (Commons), 29 April 1909, cols 488–9. Harris, *Unemployment and Politics*, 344–5, 357–9.
54  Memorandum on Labour Unrest and Liberal Social Policy signed by Seebohm Rowntree and others, c. 1913, C/21/1/17, Lloyd George Papers, HLRO.
55  *The Times*, 10 November 1913.
56  Frank Bealey and Henry Pelling, *Labour and Politics, 1900–1906* (London, 1958), 176. Herbert Samuel, *Liberalism* (London, 1902), 127–35, and John Hammond et al., *Towards a Social Policy* (London, 1905), 67–72.
57  LSE, Lansbury Papers Vol. 2, 1901–6, ff. 181–94, George Lansbury, 'Address on Unemployment to the Christian Union' May 1907.
58  *New Statesman*, 28 February 1914.
59  *New Statesman*, 4 April 1914
60  Churchill, *Winston S. Churchill*, 841.
61  *Daily News*, 6 August 1914. Edwin Montagu to Lloyd George, 2 October 1914, C/1/1/29, Lloyd George Papers. *Daily Chronicle*, 1 October 1914.
62  HLRO, Lloyd George Papers C/1/1/29, Edwin Montagu to Herbert Samuel, 1 October 1914. *Hansard* (Commons) 31 March 1914, col. 1153. *New Statesman*, 8 August and 22 August 1914.

# Chapter 11: Boy Labour and Continuation Education

1  Apprenticeship and Skilled Employment association reports for 1909 and 1913. Committee on Wage Earning Children, *A Record of Twenty-Five Years* (London,

1924). *Report of the Inter-Departmental Committee on the Employment of School Children* PP XXV, 1902, cols 3314–46, evidence of Nettie Adler.
2  Black, *Sweated Industry and the Minimum Wage*, 18, 104–31. Arnold Freeman, *Boy Life and Labour* (London, 1914), 86–8. *Royal Commission on the Poor Laws* PP XLIV, 1909, report by Cyril Jackson on Boy Labour, 10, 45, table 13. *Report of the Departmental Committee on the Employment of Children Act 1903*, xxviii, evidence of Constance Smith, cols 394–779.
3  Committee on Wage Earning Children, *A Record of Twenty-Five Years*. John Gorst, *The Children of the Nation* (London, 1907), 92–6. Frederic Keeling, *Child Labour in the United Kingdom* (London, 1914), xvi–xvii, xxv, xxvi.
4  Committee on Wage Earning Children, *A Record of Twenty-Five Years*.
5  *Report of the Inter-Departmental Committee on the Employment of School Children*, xxv, 1902.
6  Ibid.
7  Committee on Wage Earning Children 1903 report.
8  Committee on Wage Earning Children, *A Record of Twenty-Five Years* and their 1907–8 report.
9  J. G. Cloete, 'The Boy and his Work' in E. J. Urwick, *Studies of Boy Life in Our Cities* (London, 1904), 118–20.
10  Apprenticeship and Skilled Employment Association 1908 report. H. Winifred Jevons, 'Apprenticeship and Skilled Employment Committees' in M. Sadler (ed.), *Continuation Schools in England and Elsewhere* (London, 1908), 454–7.
11  Apprenticeship and Skilled Employment Association reports for 1907, 1908 and 1909. N. B. Dearle, *Industrial Training* (London, 1914), 458–63. Jevons, 'Apprenticeship Committees', 456–7.
12  Spencer J. Gibb, *The Irregular Employment of Boys* (London, 1903), 5.
13  Sidney Webb and Beatrice Webb, *Industrial Democracy* (London, 1913), 706, 768–71.
14  Gibb, *The Irregular Employment of Boys*, 5–12.
15  Spencer J. Gibb, *The Problem of Boy Work* (London, 1906), 94–6.
16  M. Ogilvie Gordon, 'Juvenile Employment Bureaux', *Contemporary Review* (June 1911).
17  Gibb, *Boy-Work, Exploitation or Training?* (London, 1919), 7–9.
18  LSE, Passfield Papers, Sidney to Beatrice Webb, 16 July 1907, f.139–40 and 3 November 1907 f.152.
19  *Report of the Committee on Compulsory Attendance or Otherwise at Continuation Schools*, xvii, 1909. Memorandum of R. H. Tawney on the Question of Compulsory Attendance at Continuation Schools 1907, 300–19.
20  F. J. Marquis, *Handbook of Employments in Liverpool* (Liverpool, 1916), xviii–xxii. Arnold Freeman, *Boy Life and Labour* (London, 1914), 201–2.
21  Florence Bell, *At the Works* (London, 1911), 198.
22  *Royal Commission on the Poor Laws* PP XLIX, 1910, memorandum by Henry Clay on Unemployment in Sheffield.
23  C. V. Butler, *Social Conditions in Oxford* (London, 1912), 38–61, 81, 93, 191, 206–12. *Royal Commission on the Poor Laws* PP XLIV, 1909, Report by Cyril Jackson on Boy Labour.
24  F. J. Marquis, *Handbook of Employments in Liverpool*, xxii.
25  *Royal Commission on the Poor Laws* PP XLIX, 1910. Memorandum of Reginald Bray and R. H. Tawney. N. B. Dearle, *Industrial Training* (London, 1914), 293. R. H. Best and C. K. Ogden, *The Problem of the Continuation School* (London, 1914), 42–4.

26 Frederic Keeling, *The Labour Exchange in Relation to Boy and Girl Labour* (London, 1910). Apprenticeship and Skilled Employment Association reports 1909–1912. Committee on Wage Earning Children 1909–10 report.
27 National Union of Women Workers 1910–11 report. M. Ogilvie Gordon, 'Juvenile Employment Bureaux', *Contemporary Review* (June 1911). Gibb, *Boy-Work, Exploitation or Training*, 11, 113. National Archives, HLG 29/103 draft of the Education (Choice of Employment) Bill 1910.
28 *School Child*, January 1912.
29 Dearle, *Industrial Training*, 466–8. *School Child*, September, October and December 1912.
30 *School Child*, April 1912, December 1912 and December 1913.
31 Gibb, *Boy-Work: Exploitation or Training?*, 65–6.
32 *School Child*, December 1911 and February 1912. Committee on Wage Earning Children 1911, 1912 and 1913 reports.
33 Apprenticeship and Skilled Employment Association 1912 report. *Departmental Committee on Van Boys*, xxxiii, 1913.
34 Samuel Smith, *My Life Work* (London, 1902), 245–7. Best and Ogden, *The Problem of the Continuation School*, 3.
35 Sadler, *Continuation Schools*, 524, 578, 657–77; and France, 576–642.
36 Sadler, *Continuation Schools*, 513–34, 569.
37 Sadler, *Continuation Schools*,513–34,535–47; and Best and Ogden, *The Problem of the Continuation School*, 9–24, 25, 30.
38 J. L. Paton, *John Brown Paton* (London, 1914). T. C. Horsfall (ed.), *Proceedings of the Conference on Education Under Healthy Conditions*, Manchester 14–17 April 1885. J. B. Paton, *Continuous Recreative Education in Evening Classes* (London, 1885). J. B. Paton, *Education for the Industrial Classes* (pamphlet), 1895.
39 National Association for the Promotion of Technical and Secondary Education final report 1907. Smith, *My Life Work*, 254.
40 E. J. Urwick (ed.), *Studies of Boy Life in Our Cities* (London, 1904), 285.
41 Frederic Keeling, *Child Labour in the United Kingdom* (London, 1914), xxviii.
42 *Chamber of Commerce Journal* (April 1907).
43 Royal Commission on the Poor Laws, xlix, 1910. Memorandum of Reginald Bray. Arnold Freeman, *Boy Life and Labour* (London, 1914), 3–5. Gibb, *Boy-Work, Exploitation or Training?*, 14–15.
44 Urwick (ed.), *Studies in Boy Life*, 285. Freeman, *Boy Life and Labour*, 1278. *Chamber of Commerce Journal* (April 1907).
45 Sadler, *Continuation Schools*, 183–4.
46 Ibid., 191–3, 294–7, 300–3, 307–8. The Consultative Committee on Attendance, Compulsory or Otherwise at Continuation Schools, xvii, 1909, vol. 1, 96–100. Richenda Scott, *Elizabeth Cadbury* (London, 1955), 110–11.
47 Apprenticeship and Skilled Employment Association 1909 report. *Daily News*, 10 October 1908 and 19 February 1909. Webb, *Our Partnership*, 404. Bodleian, Asquith Papers, General Correspondence Churchill to Asquith, 29 December 1908, ff. 252.
48 National Archives, ED31/183 Memorandum on the Education (School and Continuation Class Attendance) Bill, 28 March 1911.
49 NA, ED24/166 memorandum on compulsory attendance at continuation schools May 1911. Geoffrey Sherington, *English Education, Social Change, and War* (Manchester, 1981), 14. Committee on Wage Earning Children 1909–10 and 1911

reports. *School Child*, April 1912. Brian Simon, *Education and the Labour Movement 1870–1920* (London, 1965), 292.
50  *School Child*, April and May 1912.
51  NA, ED24/629 Memorandum of A. Abbot on compulsory day continuation schools, 17 January 1914.
52  National Archives, ED24/166 A. H. Gill to Jack Pease, 29 November 1911.
53  Sherington, *English Education*, 21–6. National Archives, ED24/628 L. A. Selby-Bigge to Jack Pease, 5 March 1913.
54  Sherington, *English Education*, 26–30, 34–6. National Archives, ED 24/129 Education Bill Cabinet Committee memorandum, 24 January 1913.
55  Addison, *Politics from Within*, vol. 1, 61.
56  *Hansard*, 22 July 1913, cols 1907–15.
57  Sherington, *English Education*, 30–1.
58  *Hansard*, 20 February 1914, cols 1296–7. Committee for Wage Earning Children 1914 report.
59  National Archives, ED 24/628 Haldane to Selby-Bigge, 20 April 1914.
60  National Archives, ED 24/628 Haldane to Selby-Bigge, 21 April 1914.
61  Sherington, *English Education*, 37.
62  *Hansard*, 28 July 1914, col. 1256.
63  Ausubel, *In Hard Times*, 202
64  Ibid.
65  National Archives, ED24/628 Selby-Bigge to Jack Pease, 24 February 1913.

# Chapter 12: A Partially Reformed Poor Law

1  Jose Harris, 'The Webbs, the Charity Organisation Society and the Ratan Tata Foundation: Social Policy from the Perspective of 1912' in Martin Bulmer, Jane Lewis and David Piachaud (eds), *The Goals of Social Policy* (London, 1989), 27–63.
2  A. M. McBriar, *An Edwardian Mixed Doubles: The Bosanquets versus the Webbs: A Study in British Social Policy 1890–1929* (Oxford, 1987), 308.
3  Ibid.
4  Beatrice Webb, *Our Partnership* (London, 1948), 430.
5  McBriar, *An Edwardian Mixed Doubles*, 319–21, 326–7, 329–30.
6  *Hansard*, 8 April 1910, col. 838.
7  *Hansard*, 8 April 1910, cols 839–40.
8  Webb, *Our Partnership*, 462.
9  *Hansard*, 3 May 1911, col. 431
10  *Hansard*, 18 December 1912, col. 1501.
11  McBriar, *An Edwardian Mixed Doubles*, 330. Harris, *Unemployment and Politics*, 267–72.
12  *Hansard*, 8 April 1910, col. 841.
13  Kenneth D. Brown, *John Burns* (London,1977), 162, 166,166
14  Harris, 'The Webb, COS and the Ratan Tata Foundation', 38–9.
15  McBriar, *An Edwardian Mixed Doubles*, 334, 339, 354–5, 365–7.
16  Micky Watkins, *Henrietta Barnett. Social Worker and Community Planner* (London, 2011), 191.
17  *State Childrens Aid Association*, annual reports for 1897 and 1898.

18 Henrietta Barnett, *Canon Barnett* (London, 1921), 688.
19 *State Children's Association*, reports for 1900, 1901–3 and 1910–12.
20 *National League for Physical Education and Improvement*, report for 1908. *State Children's Association*, reports for 1898, 1904–6 and 1910–12.
21 John Gorst, *The Children of the Nation* (London, 1907), 247. *State Children's Association*, reports for 1898, 1901–3, 1905–6, 1907–9 and 1910–12.
22 Gorst, *The Children of the Nation*, 238–40. *State Children's Association*, reports for 1901–3 and 1910–12.
23 Webb and Webb, *The Break-Up of the Poor Law* vol. 1, 148–67. Gorst, *The Children of the Nation*, 279.
24 *The Times*, 29 May 1962.

## Chapter 13: First Steps Towards a Health Service

1 Comyns Carr, Stuart Garnett and Taylor, *National Insurance*, v, vi.
2 Harris, *The Health of the Schoolchild*, 53–7.
3 PP XLIX 1910, evidence of Newman, 25 February 1908.
4 PP XXIII 1910, Newman annual report for 1908.
5 Harris, *The Health of the Schoolchild*, 63.
6 J. B. Hobman (ed.), *David Eder: Memoirs of a Modern Pioneer* (London, 1945), 74.
7 Ibid., 75.
8 *School Hygiene*, May and August 1910, March, May and October 1911; *The Child*, May 1911.
9 Countess of Warwick, *Life's Ebb and Flow*, 264.
10 Margaret McMillan, *The Child and the State* (London, 1911), 32. *School Hygiene*, February 1910 and February, March, May and October 1911. *The Child*, May 1911. Women's Labour League, *The Needs of Little Children* (London, 1912).
11 *School Hygiene*, February 1911.
12 Bernard Harris, *The Health of the Schoolchild*, 66. National Archives, ED31/167 correspondence.
13 *School Hygiene*, March 1911.
14 National Archives, MH139/2 Newman diary, 3 August 1911.
15 National Archives, MH139/2 Newman diary, 5 November 1911.
16 *Hansard* 31 October 1911, cols 787–8, 799–800, 816–17; 6 December 1911, col. 1460.
17 National Archives, MH139/2 Newman diary 1 February 1912.
18 Harris, *The Health of the Schoolchild*, 67–8, 71.
19 Lewis D. Cruickshank, *School Clinics at Home and Abroad* (London, 1913). National League for Physical Education and Improvement annual reports for 1913 and 1914.
20 Earl Woolton, *Memoirs* (London, 1959), 32–4.
21 Dr L. Haden Guest (ed.), *The Next Steps in Educational Progress* (London, 1915). J. H. Whitehouse, *A National System of Education* (London, 1913).
22 Richenda Scott, *Elizabeth Cadbury 1858–1951* (London, 1955), 105–10.
23 PP XVIII 1914–16 Newman annual report for 1914.
24 Honigsbaum, 'Christopher Addison', 231. Morgan and Morgan, *Christopher, Viscount Addison*, 24.
25 National Archives, MH139/2 Newman diary, 12 February and 13 February 1914.

26 *The Times*, 7 February 1914.
27 Christopher Addison, *Politics from Within 1911-1918*, vol. 1 (London, 1924), 28.
28 National Archives, MH139/2 Newman diary, 12 February and 16 February 1914.
29 Addison, *Politics from Within*, 29. *Hansard*, 4 May 1914, cols 75-82. National Archives, MH139/2 Newman diary 4 May 1914.
30 Phyllis Winder, *The Public Feeding of Elementary School Children* (London, 1913), 44-62. And Bulkley, *The Feeding of School Children*, 210-11.
31 Derek J. Oddy, 'Working-Class Diets in late Nineteenth- Century Britain', *Economic History Review* 23 (2) (August 1970): 314-22.
32 G. C. M. M'Gonigle and J. Kirby, *Poverty and Public Health* (London, 1936), 142-3, 190-1.
33 Arthur Greenwood, *The Health and Physique of School Children* (London, 1913), 48-50. The late Dr Letitia Fairfield to the author. Bulkley, *The Feeding of School Children*, 50-130.
34 K. Laybourn, 'The Issue of School Feeding in Bradford', *Journal of Educational Administration History* XIV (2) (July 1982): 36.
35 National Archives, HLG29/113 memorandum on Jowett's Bill, 13 February 1913; and L. A. Selby-Bigge to Horace Monro, 23 July 1913. *Hansard*, 28 March 1912 col. 598; and 27 March 1914 cols 716-67.
36 John Hurt, 'Feeding the Hungry Schoolchild in the First Half of the Twentieth Century', in Derek J. Oddy and Derek S. Miller (eds), *Diet and Health in Modern Britain* (London, 1985), 182-3. National Archives, ED24/1371 Newman to A. J. Pease 4 August 1914.
37 John Welshman, 'School Meals and Milk in England and Wales, 1906-45', *Medical History* 41 (1997): 11.
38 Jane Lewis, 'The Working-Class Wife and Mother and State Intervention, 1870-1918', in Jane Lewis (ed.), *Labour and Love. Women's Experience of Home and Family, 1850-1940* (Oxford, 1986), 99-120. Elizabeth Roberts, 'The Recipients' View of Welfare', in Joanna Bornat et al. (eds), *Oral History, Health and Welfare 1890-1914*, 214.
39 PP XLII 1909, *R. C. on Poor Laws*, evidence of Dr McVail.
40 Ibid.
41 William Harbutt, *Dawson, Social Insurance in Germany 1883-1911* (London, 1911).
42 Comyns Carr, *National Insurance*, 90-1.
43 *Hansard*, 7 July 1911, cols 1534-5.
44 Braithwaite, *Memoirs*, 71.
45 *Hansard*, 24 May 1911, cols 322-7 and 7 July 1911, cols 1520-3.
46 Arthur Newsholme, *The Last 30 Years in Public Health* (London, 1936), 72.
47 John M. Eyler, *Sir Arthur Newsholme and State Medicine 1885-1935* (Cambridge, 1997), 239-40.
48 Newsholme, *The Last 30 Years*, 138-48. Eyler, *Sir Arthur Newsholme and State Medicine 1885-1935*, 240
49 Eyler, *Sir Arthur Newsholme and State Medicine 1885-1935*, 241.
50 National Archives, MH55/522 memorandum, 6 February 1913. Newsholme, *30 Years*, 259.
51 National Archives, MH 48/32 Newsholme memorandum on Administrative Measures against Tuberculosis, February 1912.
52 Ibid.
53 PP XLVIII, *Departmental Committee on Tuberculosis*, 1912-13.

54 National Archives, MH 55/522 memorandum on Assistance from the Exchequer towards the cost of Sanatorium Treatment, 31 July 1912.
55 National Archives, MH55/522 John Burns to Lloyd George, 19 June 1912.
56 National Archives, MH 55/522 L.G.B memorandum, February 1913.
57 National Archives, MH 55/522 John Burns to Lloyd George, 24 January 1913.
58 National Archives, MH 55/522 deputation of the County Councils Association and others to Lloyd George, 6 February 1913.
59 Ibid.
60 Parliamentary Archives, Lloyd George Papers, C/6/2/2 memorandum of Robert Morant for Lloyd George, 22 May 1913.
61 Ibid.
62 Parliamentary Archives, Lloyd George Papers, C/5/15/2 S. P. Vivian to Hamilton, 27 April 1911.
63 Eyler, *Newsholme*, 261.
64 Parliamentary Archives, Lloyd George Papers, memorandum of the L.G.B on institutional treatment of tuberculosis, 22 May 1913. Eyler, *Newsholme*, 260–1.
65 PP XXXIX 1914 Report of the Medical Officer of the L.G.B. 1914, lxvii.
66 Newsholme, *30 Years*, 143–5.
67 NAPC annual reports 1913 and 1914.
68 NAPC annual reports 1913 and 1915.
69 NAPC annual report 1915.
70 NAPC annual report 1916.
71 PP XI 1918 Report of medical officer of L.G.B., 1917–18, lx.
72 Ibid.
73 PP XI 1918 Report of medical officer of L.G.B., 1917–18, lx, lxi.
74 NAPC annual report 1922.
75 *Royal Commission on Venereal Diseases*, PP XVI, 1916, 44–5.
76 Author, *R. C. on Venereal Diseases*, 43–4.
77 Eyler, *Newsholme*, 285.
78 Eyler, *Newsholme*, 288–9. Newsholme, *The Last 30 Years*, 156–7.
79 Newsholme, *The Last 30 Years*, 155–6, 161–2. *National Council for Combating Venereal Diseases* 1917 report.
80 Newsholme, *The Last 30 Years*, 163–4 reports. *National Council for Combating Venereal Diseases* 1918, 1919 and 1920.
81 Eyler, *Newsholme*, 293.
82 Eyler, *Newsholme*, 293–316.
83 G. F. McCleary, *The Early History of the Infant Welfare Movement* (London, 1933), 37–52.
84 McCleary, *The Early History of the Infant Welfare Movement*, 69–83, 93, 135. Harry Hendrick, *Child Welfare in England 1872–1989* (London, 1994), 96–100. Deborah Dwork, *War is Good for Babies and Other Young Children. A History of the Infant and Child Welfare Movement in England 1898–1918* (London, 1987), 104–23. Frank Honigsbaum, *The Struggle for the Ministry of Health 1914–19* (London, 1970), 21.
85 Eyler, *Newsholme*, 322–5.
86 *Second Report on Infant and Child Mortality 1912–13*, PP XXXII, 1913. Eyler, *Newsholme*, 322. Honigsbaum, *The Struggle for the Ministry*, 21.
87 Norman MacKenzie and Jeanne MacKenzie (eds), *The Dairy of Beatrice Webb 1905–24*, vol. 3 (London, 1984), 199–200. Christopher Addison, *Four and a Half*

*Years*, vol. 1 (London, 1934), 44, 74. Honigsbaum, *The Struggle for the Ministry*, 20–3.
88  *Women's Labour League* Central London branch. Conference on Babies and Young Children 1912.
89  Addison, *Four and a Half Years*, 16–18.
90  Harry Hendrick, *Child Welfare*, 101. Newsholme, *The Last 30 Years*, 196, 202.
91  Hendrick, *Child Welfare*, 102. Dwork, *War is Good for Babies*, 211.
92  Dwork, *War is Good for Babies*, 166. Jane Lewis, *The Politics of Motherhood. Child and Maternal Welfare in England, 1900–1939* (London, 1980), 13–14, 219–20.
93  *Departmental Committee on Sickness Benefit Claims* memorandum of Mary MacArthur, 78. PP XXX, 1914–16.
94  Honigsbaum, *The Struggle for the Ministry*, 30–2 *New Statesman*, 21 March 1914. National Union of Women Workers 1915–16 and 1916–17 report, 151. Women's Trade Union League 1914 report.
95  National Archives, MH139/2 Newman diary, 18 December 1913; and Eyler, *Newsholme*, 335.
96  Hendrick, *Child Welfare*, 102. Honigsbaum, *The Struggle for the Ministry*, 12, 31. *The Times*, 27 June 1914.
97  National Archives, MH139/2 Newman diary, 8 July and 27 July 1914.
98  National Archives, MH 139/2 Newman diary, 6 July and 8 July 1914.
99  *New Statesman*, 24 January 1914.

# Chapter 14: Municipal Housing and Town Planning

1  *Report of the Land Enquiry Committee*, vol. 2 (London, 1914), 108–25. P. Alden and E. E. Hayward, *Housing* (London, 1907), 76. *Conference of Delegates on Questions Concerning the Housing of the People*, report of the Financial and Compensation Committee (London, 1890).
2  E. D. Simon, *A City Council from Within* (London, 1926).
3  Workmen's National Housing Council annual reports, 1899–1900, 1904–5, 1908 and 1909. Anthony S. Wohl, *The Eternal Slum. Housing and Social Policy in Victorian Britain* (London, 1977), 325–30.
4  Workmen's National Housing Council annual reports 1899–1900 and 1904–5.
5  Workmen's National Housing Council annual reports 1908 and 1909. Wohl, *The Eternal Slum*, 329.
6  *Report of the Land Enquiry Committee*, vol. 2, 116–17. Alden and Hayward, *Housing*, 90. J. S. Nettlefold, *Practical Town Planning* (London, 1914), 14.
7  Meyer and Black, *Makers of Our Clothes*, 158–65.
8  *Report of the Land Enquiry Committee*, vol. 2, 120–30. Alden and Hayward, *Housing*, 41. *Municipal Journal*, 30 December 1904.
9  *Conference of Delegates Concerning the Housing of the People*, report of the Financial and Compensation Committee.
10  D. Macfayden, *Sir E. Howard and the Town Planning Movement* (London, 1933), 37. National Housing Reform Council, minutes 19 December 1907. *Municipal Journal*, 21 September 1900 and 30 December 1904.
11  Land Law Reform Association, *National Conference on Housing*, 3 December 1901,

1902. Herbert Samuel, *Liberalism* (London, 1902), 52–7. *Municipal Journal*, 30 December 1904. Workmen's National Housing Council annual report 1899–1900.
12 *Municipal Journal*, 27 November 1903 and 29 April and 15 July 1904. T. C. Horsfall, *The Improvement of the Dwellings and Surroundings of the People: The Example of Germany* (Manchester, 1904).
13 *Report of the Inter-Departmental Commission on Physical Deterioration* PP XXXII, 1904, 19, 220–30. *Municipal Journal*, 15 July and 26 August 1904.
14 *Municipal Journal*, 28 July 1905.
15 Henry R. Aldridge, *The Case for Town Planning* (London, 1917), 76–113.
16 John R. Kellett, *The Impact of Railways on Victorian Cities* (London, 2005).
17 Aldridge, *The Case for Town Planning* [PAGE?].
18 Horsfall, *The Example of Germany*, 36–46.
19 Horsfall, *The Example of Germany*, 2–3, 24–9, 36–46.
20 National Housing Reform Council, minutes 6 January 1910. Henry Aldridge to George Cadbury, 20 December 1909.
21 National Housing Reform Council, minutes 6 January 1910. T. C. Horsfall to George Cadbury, 26 December 1909.
22 National Housing Reform Council, annual reports 1906–7 and 1907–8; and minutes 26 July 1911 and 6 November 1912.
23 National Housing Reform Council, annual report 1906–7 and minutes 23 October 1908. *Daily News*, 26 October 1909.
24 National Housing Reform Council, annual report 1907–8 and minutes 21 September and 29 November 1906 and 23 November 1908. *Daily News*, 29 October 1906 and 8 August 1907. *Municipal Journal*, 27 November 1903 and 30 December 1904. Anthony Sutcliffe, *Towards the Planned City: Germany, Britain, the United States and France 1780–1914* (Oxford, 1981), 61, 72–82.
25 National Housing Reform Council, minutes 6 July 1910. Henry Aldridge to George Cadbury, 20 December 1909.
26 *Daily News*, 26 October 1907. *Municipal Journal*, 13 October 1905.
27 *Daily News*, 7 November 1906. National Housing Reform Council, minutes 6 January 1910. T. C. Horsfall to George Cadbury, 26 December 1909. Alden and Hayward, *Housing*, Appendix 1.
28 *Daily News*, 5 May 1908.
29 BL, John Burns Diary Ms 46330 22 October and 29 October 1908.
30 National Housing Reform Council, minutes 2 April 1908. *Daily News*, 31 August, 1 September and 3 September 1909.
31 Workmen's National Housing Council, 1910, 1911 and 1913 reports. *Report of the Land Enquiry Committee*, vol. 2, 179–80.
32 Workmen's National Housing Council 1909 report. *Daily News*, 7 November 1906, and 26 October, 4 November and 20 November 1909. Bodleian, Asquith Papers, misc. letters and memoranda 1908–11, memorandum of John Burns on the arrangements with the Lords re. Housing and Town Planning Bill.
33 National Housing Reform Council, minutes 6 July 1910 secretary of the Garden Cities Association to the Council, 16 December 1909; also, minutes 24 July and 4 November 1909, and 23 February and 14 April 1910. Workmen's National Housing Council 1911 report.
34 Nettlefold, *Practical Town Planning*, 155.
35 *Report of the Land Enquiry Committee*, vol. 2, 149.
36 Nettlefold, *Practical Town Planning*, 152, 156–8, 189–90. George Cadbury, *Town*

*Planning* (London, 1915), 58-9. Kenneth D. Brown, *John Burns* (London, 1977), 171-2.
37 Jane Ridley, 'The Unionist Social Reform Committee, 1911-14: West before the Storm', *Historical Journal* (1987): 391-413.
38 *Hansard*, 15 March 1912, cols 1414-27, 18 April 1913, col. 2239, and 24 July 1914, col. 807. Arthur Griffith-Boscawen, *Memories* (London, 1925), 154-5. Anthony S. Wohl, *The Eternal Slum. Housing and Social Policy in Victorian Britain* (London, 1977), 336-8.
39 BL, Burns Diary, 14 and 15 March 1914 Ms 46334.
40 Brown, *John Burns*, 169-70. *Hansard*, date 1912, cols 1485-2.
41 Barnett, *Canon Barnett*, 702-3.
42 Seebohm Rowntree and A. C. Pigou, *Lectures on Housing* (Manchester, 1914), 28-31.
43 H. V. Emy, *Liberals Radicals and Social Politics 1892-1914* (Cambridge, 1973), 297-8. *Report of the Land Enquiry Committee*, vol. 2, 108, 114-15.
44 Parliamentary Archives, Lloyd George Papers, Lloyd George to Asquith November 1913. Wrigley, *Lloyd George and British Labour*, 41.
45 George Riddell, *More Pages from My Diary 1908-14* (London, 1934), 210.
46 T. R. Marr, *Housing Conditions in Manchester and Salford* (Manchester, 1904), 81
47 Ibid., 81-5.
48 Ernest Ritson Dewsnap, *The Housing Problem in England* (London, 1907), 239-42. Mauritz Kaufman, *The Housing of the Working Classes and of the Poor* (London, 1907), 109. L. G. Chiozza Money, *The Future of Work* (London, 1914), 17-18, 118-19.
49 Rowntree and Pigou, *Lectures on Housing*, 28-31.
50 Webb and Webb, *The Case for a National Minimum* (London, 1913), 50.
51 National Housing Reform Council, minutes 14 June 1912.
52 National Housing Reform Council, minutes 4 October 1913.
53 National Housing Reform Council, minutes 30 April 1914.
54 *Hansard*, 31 July 1914, cols 1784-6.
55 Parliamentary Archives, Lloyd George Papers, Seebohm Rowntree to Hamilton and Wallace Carter to Rowntree, 4 February 1914 C/2/4/6.
56 *New Statesman*, 4 April 1914.
57 Chiozza Money, *The Future of Work*, 116.
58 *Hansard*, 8 August 1914, cols 2208-9.
59 National Housing Reform Council, minutes 20 August 1914.
60 National Housing Reform Council, deputation to Samuel 21 August 1914.
61 *Hansard*, 8 August 1914, cols 2208-9,
62 *Hansard* 20 March 1914, cols 2459-62.
63 National Housing Reform Council, minutes 14 October 1915.
64 National Housing Reform Council, minutes 19 February and 20 February 1916
65 National Housing Reform Council, minutes 15 May 1916.

# Chapter 15: From Trade Boards to the Minimum Wage

1 NASL annual reports 1910, 1911 and 1913. L. G. Chiozza Money, *The Future of Work* (London, 1914), 179-87. Dorothy Sells, *The British Trade Boards System* (London, 1923).

2   R. H. Tawney, *The Establishment of Minimum Rates in the Chain-Making Industry under the Trade Boards Act of 1909* (London, 1914), 1.
3   Ibid., 1–9.
4   Tawney, *The Establishment of Minimum Rates in the Chain-Making Industry*, 75–99 and Blackburn, *A Fair Day's Wage*, 147.
5   R. H. Tawney, *The Establishment of the Minimum Rates in the Tailoring Industry under the Trade Boards Act of 1909* (London, 1915), 6–7.
6   Ibid., 11–13, 19–21.
7   Ibid., [PAGE?]
8   Ibid., 67–86, 201–10.
9   National Archives, LAB11/153 George Reid to the Board of Trade, 17 February 1913.
10  Mildred E. Bulkley, *The Establishment of Legal Minimum Rates in the Boxmaking Industry under the Trade Boards Act of 1909* (London, 1915), 1–3, 27–39, 68–74.
11  Tawney, *The Establishment of Minimum Rates in the Chain-Making Industry*, 113–17, Bulkley, *The Establishment of Legal Minimum Rates in the Boxmaking Industry*, 52–3, and Tawney, *The Establishment of the Minimum Rates in the Tailoring Industry*, 148–55.
12  Bulkley, *The Establishment of Legal Minimum Rates in the Boxmaking Industry*, 41, 83–7, Tawney, *The Establishment of Minimum Rates in the Chain-Making Industry*, 101–2, Tawney, *The Establishment of the Minimum Rates in the Tailoring Industry*, 90–6, 221–51; and Constance Smith, 'The Working of the Trade Board Act', *Report of the 7th General Meeting of the International Association for Labour Legislation* (1912).
13  Sells, *British Trade Boards*, 77–120.
14  Tawney, *The Establishment of Minimum Rates in the Chain-Making Industry*, 103. Mess, *Factory Legislation and Administration 1891–1914*, 98. Sells, *British Trade Boards*, 149–53, 160–1.
15  Blackburn, *A Fair Day's Wage*, 147, 162, 165, 170, 172.
16  Sells, *British Trade Boards*, 160–1.
17  *RC on the Poor Laws, Minority Report* Part 2, 597–8.
18  *Report by A. D. Steel-Maitland and Rose Squire on the Relation of Industrial and Sanitary Conditions to Pauperism* PP XL111, 1909, 58.
19  Constance Williams and Thomas Jones, *Interim Reports of an Inquiry into the Effects of Outdoor Relief on Wages and the Conditions of Employment in certain Unions in England* PP XLIII 1909 and *Report by Cyril Jackson and Revd J. C. Pringle on the Effects of Unemployment or Assistance given to the 'Unemployed' since 1886 as a Means of Relieving Distress Outside the Poor Law* PP XLIV, 1909. Squire, *Thirty Years in the Public Service*, 116. Webb, *Our Partnership*, 342, 388.
20  Steel-Maitland and Squire, *Report on Pauperism*.
21  Webb and Webb, 'Preface', in *The Case for the National Minimum* (London, 1913).
22  Maud Pember Reeves, *Round About a Pound a Week* (Place, 1999), 2–3, 211–14.
23  Unionist Social Reform Council, 'The Wages Aspect of Poverty', in *Papers on Unrest Among the Working Classes* (London, 1911). Philip Snowden, *The Living Wage* (Place, 1912), 28–34. Webb and Webb, *The Case for a National Minimum*, 2–3.
24  B. S. Rowntree, *Poverty. A Study of Town Life* (Place, 1914), 97–9, 154; and A. L. Bowley and A. R. Burnett-Hurst, *Livelihood and Poverty* (Place, 1915), 34–5, 38, 41–2.
25  Florence Bell, *At the Works* (London, 1911), 81–6 and Freeman, *Boy Labour*, 86.
26  Author, *The Land*, vol. 2 Urban (London, 1914), 16,

27  Ibid., 160.
28  *1911 Census. General Report*, 158-9.
29  R. H. Tawney, *The Establishment of the Minimum Rates in the Tailoring Industry*, 110-11.
30  W. H. Beveridge, *Unemployment, a Problem of Industry* (Place, 1909), 108-9.
31  Tawney, *The Establishment of the Minimum Rates in the Tailoring Industry*, 194-5.
32  Mona Wilson and Edward G. Howarth, *West Ham* (London, 1907), 269, 400.
33  Bulkley, *The Establishment of Legal Minimum Rates in the Boxmaking Industry*, 67.
34  Meyer and Black, *Makers of Our Clothes*, 148; Clementina Black, 'Introduction', in C. Black (ed.), *Married Women's Work* (London, 1915), 3-4 and Clementina Black, 'London', in C. Black (ed.), *Married Women's Work* (London, 1915), 12.
35  Black, 'Introduction', *Married Women's Work*.
36  Ibid.
37  Peter Wardley, 'Edwardian Britain: Empire, Income and Political Discontent' in Paul Johnson (ed.), *Edwardian Britain: Empire, Income and Political Discontent* (London, 1994), 64-6.
38  Roy Church, 'Edwardian Labour Unrest and Coalfield Militancy, 1890-1914', *Historical Journal* 30 (4) (1987): 841-57.
39  *Daily News*, 7 September 1906.
40  LSE, Labour Party executive, memorandum on future policy c. 1912, 1. TUC Parliamentary Committee minutes 18 March 1909. Snowden, *The Living Wage*, 18-19.
41  Chris Wrigley, *David Lloyd George and the British Labour Movement* (Hassocks, 1976), 67-8
42  National Archives, POWE 20/17 Historical Statement on Coal Mines Act 1912 W.L.C. August 1923.
43  Wrigley, *Lloyd George and British Labour*, 69.
44  National Archives, CAB37/109/37 Methods of settling wage questions in coal-mining industry. Comparisons between the North of England and South Wales, 4 March 1912; and CAB41/33/41 Asquith's Cabinet reports to the King, 16 March and 20 March 1912.
45  Robert Smillie, *My Life for Labour* (London, 1924), 218-20, 222. Bodleian Libraries, Ms 3210-11 Eng. Margot Asquith diary, 22 February 1912.
46  BL, Add. Ms 62955 diary of George Riddell, 24 March 1912, f.35.
47  BL, Add. Ms 62955 diary of George Riddell, 24 March 1912, f.36
48  BL, Add. Ms 62955 diary of George Riddell, 24 March 1912, f.37.
49  George Riddell, *More Pages from My Diary 1908-1914* (London, 1934), 45-6. Wrigley, *Lloyd George and British Labour*, 72.
50  National Archives, LAB2/76 J. K. Bradbury to Sydney Buxton with copy of the award, 11 May 1912; and POW20/9 George Askwith memorandum on South Wales award, 5 July 1912.
51  H. V. Emy, *Liberals, Radicals and Social Politics 1892-1914* (Cambridge, 1973), 270.
52  *Hansard*, 18 December 1912, cols 1499-50.
53  J. M. Winter, *Socialism and the Challenge of War: Ideas and Politics in Britain 1912-18* (London, 1974), 2931.
54  Ian Packer, *Lloyd George, Liberalism and the Land: The Land Issue and Party Politics in England 1906-14* (Woodbridge, 2001), 80.
55  Stephen Koss, *Asquith* (London, 1976), 123.
56  Bodleian, Ms Eng. 3210-11 Margot Asquith diary, 3 June and September 1913.

57 Bodleian, Ms Eng. 3210-11 Margot Asquith diary, 9 May 1914.
58 Parliamentary Archives, Lloyd George Papers, C/21/1/17 'Labour Unrest and Liberal Social Policy', 20 May 1912.
59 Ibid.
60 Riddell, *My Diary*, 75-6, 213.
61 *Hansard*, 8 May 1912, col. 524.
62 Riddell, *My Diary*, 76.
63 H. V. Emy, 'The Land Campaign: Lloyd George as a Social Reformer, 1909-14', in A. J. P. Taylor (ed.), *Lloyd George. Twelve Essays* (London, 1971), 49.
64 Richard Winfrey, *Great Men and Others I Have Met* (Kettering, 1943), 25-6.
65 Emy, 'The Land Campaign', 52. Ian Packer, *Lloyd George, Liberalism and Land*, 118-19.
66 B. Seebohm Rowntree and May Kendall, *How the Labourer Lives. A Study of the Rural Labour Problem* (London, 1913), 16-18, 21-3, 27-35.
67 Maude E. Davies, *Life in an English Village* (London, 1909); and H. H. Mann, 'Life in an Agricultural Village in England', in *Sociological Papers* (London, 1904).
68 *Hansard*, 13 March 1913, col. 476.
69 Bodleian, Ms Eng. 3210-11, Margot Asquith diary, 27 September 1913.
70 Duncan Tanner, *Political Change and the Labour Party 1900-1918* (Cambridge, 1990), 61.Emy, 'The Land Campaign', 52.
71 Emy, 'The Land Campaign', 58. *The Times*, 23 October 1913. Packer, *Lloyd George, Liberalism and the Land*, 120-1.
72 *Hansard*, 13 February 1914, col.472. Robin Gowers and Timothy J. Hatton, 'The Origins and Early Impact of the Minimum Wage in Agriculture', *Economic History Review* (1997): 83.
73 *Daily News*, 3 November and 10 November 1913. *The Land. The Report of the Land Enquiry Committee. Urban*, vol. 2 (London, 1914), 160-1.
74 Parliamentary Archives, LG Papers C/2/4/22 G. Wallace Carter to Lloyd George, 28 May 1914.
75 Parliamentary Archives, LG Papers C/4/ 12/4Charles Trevelyan to Lloyd George, 6 January 1914. Wrigley, *Lloyd George and British Labour*, 40.
76 Parliamentary Archives, LG Papers C/2/4/28 W.M. Crook to Lloyd George, 31 May 1914; C/2/4/27 Harold Storey to Lloyd George, 29 May 1914 and C/7/5/8 Lloyd George to Walter Runciman, 12 June 1914.
77 Parliamentary Archives, LG Papers C/2/4/22 G. Wallace Carter to Lloyd George, 28 May 1914, and C/1/1/16 Edwin Montagu to Lloyd George, 29 April 1914.
78 P. F. Clarke, *Lancashire and the New Liberalism* (Cambridge, 1971), 196. *New Statesman*, 7 February 1914.
79 Parliamentary Archives, LG Papers Seebohm Rowntree to C/2/4/6 Hamilton, 4 February 1914; C/2/4/16 Seebohm Rowntree to Lloyd George, 12 May 1914; C/2/4/17 Lloyd George to Rowntree, 14 May 1914; and C/2/4/19 Rowntree to Lloyd George, 18 May 1914.
80 Parliamentary Archives, LG Papers, C/1/1/18 Edwin Montagu to Lloyd George, 12 June 1914.
81 *Daily News*, 10 December 1913.
82 *The Times*, 10 December 1913.
83 *Hansard*, 13 March 1913, col. 520.
84 Ibid., col. 521.
85 *New Statesman*, 4 April 1914.

86  *Hansard*, 9 April 1913, col. 1280.
87  *Hansard*, 9 April 1913, cols 1304–9, 1324.
88  *New Statesman*, 4 April 1914.
89  S. Webb and B. Webb, *The Case for a National Minimum* (London, 1913), 11.
90  Blackburn, *A Fair Day's Wage*, 176.
91  Seebohm Rowntree, 'The Effect of Minimum Wage Legislation upon British Industry', *Financial Review of Reviews* (July 1914): 774–85. H. V. Emy, *Liberals, Radicals and Social Politics 1892-1914* (Cambridge, 1973), 238. Bentley B. Gilbert, *Lloyd George. A Political Life.The Organizer of Victory 1912-16* (London, 1992), 64.
92  *The Times*, 22 October 1913.
93  Riddell, *My Diary*, 213.
94  Webb and Webb, *The Case for the National Minimum*, 12–14.
95  *Hansard*, 9 April 1913, cols 1316–28.

# Conclusion

1   Cooper, *The Unexpected Story of Nathaniel Rothschild*, 224–5.
2   Beatrice Webb, *My Apprenticeship*, vol.1 (Harmondsworth, 1938), 61–3,135–6.
3   Michael Brock and Eleanor Brock (eds), *Margot Asquith's Great War Diary 1914-16* (London, 2015), lxxxiii.
4   Harris, 'Political Thought and the Welfare State 1870–1914', [PAGE?]
5   Ibid., 123, 125, 133, 137, 139.
6   Packer, *Lloyd George, Liberalism and the Land*, 136.
7   Mark Abrams, *Social Surveys and Social Action* (London, 1951), 44–5. Gazeley, *Poverty in Britain. 1900-1965*, 65.
8   Vyvyen Brendon, *The Edwardian Age* (London, 1996), 46–7.
9   John Stewart, 'The Twentieth Century an Overview', in Robert M. Page and Richard Siburn (eds), *British Social Welfare in the Twentieth Century* (Basingstoke, 1999), 27.Crowther, *The Workhouse System 1834–1929*, 55–6.
10  Harris, 'Political Thought and the Welfare State 1870–1940', 124–5, 138.
11  Fraser, *The Evolution of the British Welfare State*, 215–16. Page and Silburn (eds), *British Social Welfare in the Twentieth Century*, 7, 25–7.
12  Fraser, *The Evolution of the British Welfare State*, 220. Harris, *William Beveridge*, 438–9.
13  Fraser, *The Evolution of the British Welfare State*, 221–2. Page and Silburn (eds), *British Social Welfare in the Twentieth Century*, 135–6.
14  Fraser, *The Evolution of the British Welfare State*, 227–9. Peter Clarke, *Hope and Glory. Britain 1900-1990* (London, 1996), 221.
15  Fraser, *The Evolution of the British Welfare State*, 232–8. Kenneth O. Morgan, *The People's Peace: British History 1945-89* (Oxford, 1990), 37–9. Clarke, *Hope and Glory. Britain 1900-1990*, 222–4.
16  Kenneth O. Morgan, *Labour in Power 1945-1951* (Oxford, 1984), 163–70. Page and Silburn (eds), *British Social Welfare in the Twentieth Century*, 29.
17  Fraser, *The Evolution of the British Welfare State*, 226–7, 229–30.
18  Blackburn, *A Fair Day's Wage for a Fair Day's Work*, 184–5.
19  Stewart, 'The Twentieth Century: An Overview', 29–30.

# Bibliography

## Principal Archives, Libraries and Manuscript Collections

H. H. Asquith Papers, Weston Library, Bodleian Libraries
Margot Asquith diary, Weston Library, Bodleian Libraries
Balfour Papers, British Library
Beveridge Papers, London School of Economics
John Burns Papers, British Library
Campbell-Bannerman Papers, British Library
Canon Barnett Papers, Hampstead Garden Suburb Institute
Leo G. Chiozza Money, Autobiography, Cambridge University Library
Randall Davidson Papers, Lambeth Palace
Dilke Papers, British Library
Lloyd George Papers, Parliamentary Archives
William Harbutt Dawson Papers, Cadbury Research Library, Birmingham University
Labour Party Executive Committee, minutes
George Lansbury Papers, London School of Economics
*National Housing Reform Council*, minutes
George Newman Diary, National Archives
Passfield Papers, London School of Economics.
*Railway Companies Association*, minutes, National Archives.
*TUC Parliamentary Committee*, minutes.

## UK Parliamentary Papers

*Inter-Departmental Committee on the Employment of School Children* PP XXV (1902)
*Certain Questions Affecting the Mercantile Marine* PP LXII (1903)
*Select Committee on the Education (Provision of Meals) Bill* PP VIII (1906)
*Select Committee on Income Tax* PP IX (1906).
*Select Committee on Home Work* PP VI (1907).
*Select Committee on Home Work* PP VII (1908).
Ernest Aves, *Report on Wages Boards and Industrial Conciliation and Arbitration Acts of Australia and New Zealand* PP LXXI (1908).
*Report of the Committee on Compulsory Attendance or Otherwise at Continuation Schools* PP XVII (1909)
*Report of the Royal Commission on the Poor Laws and Relief of Distress* PP XXXVII (1909)
*Royal Commission on the Poor Laws evidence* PP XLII (1909)
*Report by A. D. Steet-Maitland and Rose Squire on the Relation of Industrial and Sanitary Conditions to Pauperism* PP XLIII (1909)

Constance Williams and Thomas Jones, *Interim Reports of an Inquiry into the Effects of Outdoor*
*Relief on Wages and the Conditions of Employment in certain Unions in England* PP XLIII (1909)
*Report by Cyril Jackson and Revd J. C. Pringle on the Effects of Unemployment or Assistance given to*
*the 'Unemployed' since 1886 as a Means of Relieving Distress Outside the Poor Law* PP XLIV (YEAR)
Cyril Jackson, *Report on Boy Labour* PP XLIV (1909)
*Report of the Chief Medical Officer of the Board of Education 1908* PP XXIII (1910)
*Report of the Departmental Committee on the Employment of Children Act 1903* PP XXVIII (1910)
Ethel Williams, *Report on the Condition of the Children who are in Receipt of the Various Forms*
*of Poor Relief in England and Wales* PP LII (1910)
*Royal Commission on the Poor Laws Evidence* PP XLIX (1910)
*Departmental Committee on Tuberculosis* PP XLVIII (1912–13)
*Second Report on Infant and Child Mortality 1912–13* PP XXXII (1913)
*Departmental Committee on Van Boys* PP XXXIII (1913)
*Report of the Departmental Committee on Reformatory and Industrial Schools* PP XXXIX (1913)
*Report of the Chief Medical Officer of the Board of Education 1914* PP XVIII
*Departmental Committee on Sickness Benefit Claims* PP XXX (1914–16)
*Royal Commission on Venereal Diseases* PP XVI (1916)

## Newspapers and Periodicals

*Albany Review*
*Army and Navy Gazette*
*Chamber of Commerce Journal*
*Colliery Guardian*
*Confectionery*
*Contemporary Review*
*County Council Times*
*Daily News*
*Economic Review*
*Examiner*
*Financial Reformer*
*Financial Review of Reviews*
*Labour Leader*
*Lancet*
*Land and Liberty*
*Land Values*
*Liverpool Journal of Commerce*
*Monthly Message of the Anti-Tea Duty League*
*Municipal Journal*
*New Statesman*

*Poor Law Officers Journal*
*School Child*
*School Hygiene*
*Schoolmaster*
*Shipping World*
*The Broad Arrow. The Naval and Military Gazette*
*The Intermittent Message of the Free Tea League*
*The Times*

## Annual Reports

*Bristol Right to Work Council*
*Committee on Wage Earning Children*
*English Land Restoration League*
*Free Church Year Book*
*Land Tenure Reform Association*
*Mansion House Association*
*National Association for the Prevention of Consumption*
*National Association for the Promotion of Technical and Secondary Education*
*National Council for Combating Venereal Diseases*
*National Housing Reform Council*
*National League for Physical Education and Improvement*
*National Providence League against Pauperism*
*National Union of Women Workers of Great Britain*
*Resolutions of the National Conference of Friendly Societies*
*Society for the Prevention of Cruelty to Children*
*State Children's Association*
*Workmen's National Housing Council*
*Women's Industrial Council*
*Women's Trade Union League*

## Works Cited

Abramovitz, Moses and Vera F. Eliasberg. *The Growth of Public Employment in Great Britain* (New Jersey, 1957).
Abrams, Mark. *Social Surveys and Social Action* (London, 1951).
Addison, Christopher. *Politics from Within 1911-1918*, vol. 1 (London, 1924).
Addison, Christopher. *Four and a Half Years*, vol. 1 (London, 1934).
Alden, Margaret. *Child Life and Labour* (London, 1909).
Alden, Percy. *The Unemployed. A National Question* (London, 1905).
Alden, Percy and E. E. Hayward. *Housing* (London, 1907).
Anon. *Can a Sufficient Midday Meal be Given to Poor Children at a Cost for Material of Less than One Penny?* (London, 1883).
Ashby, M. K. *Joseph Ashby of Tysoe 1859-1919* (London, 1961).
Asquith, Margot. *Autobiography*, vols 1 and 2 (London, 1936).

Attlee, C. R. *As It Happened* (London, 1954).
Ball, Oona Howard *Sidney Ball* (Oxford, 1923).
Barker, Charles Albro. *Henry George* (New York, 1955).
Barnes, G. N. *From Workshop to War Cabinet* (London, 1924).
Barnett, Henrietta. *Canon Barnett* (London, 1921).
Barnett, Henrietta. *Matters That Matter* (London, 1932).
Barnett, A. A. and Henrietta Barnett. *Practicable Socialism* (London, 1894 [1915 edn]).
Bealey, Frank and Henry Pelling. *Labour and Politics, 1900–1906* (London, 1958).
Berger, Stefan. 'William Harbutt Dawson: The Career and Politics of an Historian of Germany', *English Historical Review* 116 (2001): 78–113.
Berridge, Virgina. 'Health and Medicine', in F. M. L. Thompson (ed.), *The Cambridge Social History of Britain 1750–1950*, vol. 3 (Cambridge, 1993).
Berridge, Virgina, Martin Gorsky and Alex Mold (eds). *Public Health in History* (London, 2011).
Best, R. H. and C. K. Ogden. *The Problem of the Continuation School* (London, 1914).
Beveridge, W. H. *Unemployment. A Problem of Industry* (London, 1909).
Beveridge, W. H. *Voluntary Action* (London, 1948).
Beveridge, W. H. *Power and Influence* (London, 1953).
Black, Clementina. *Sweated Industry and the Minimum Wage* (London, 1907).
Black, Clementina (ed.). *Married Women's Work* (London, 1915).
Blackburn, Sheila. *A Fair Day's Wage for a Fair Day's Work?* (Aldershot, 2007).
Blewett, Neal. *The Peers, the Parties and the People. The General Elections of 1910* (London, 1972).
Booth, Charles (ed.). *Labour and Life of the People. East London*, vol. 1 (London, 1889).
Booth, Charles. *Pauperism, a Picture, and the Endowment of Old Age, an Argument* (London, 1892).
Booth, Charles. *Old Age Pensions and the Aged Poor* (London, 1899).
Bosanquet, Helen. *The Poor Law Report of 1909* (London, 1911).
Bowley, A. L. and A. R. Burnett Hurst. *Livelihood and Poverty* (London, 1915).
Braithwaite, William J. *Lloyd George's Ambulance Wagon* (London, 1957).
Brand, Jeanne L. *Doctors and the State. The British Medical Profession and Government Action in Public Health 1870–1912* (Baltimore, 1965).
Branford, Victor. *Interpretations and Forecasts. A Study of Survivals and Tendencies in Contemporary Society* (London, 1914).
Bray, Reginald. *The Town Child* (London, 1908).
Brend, William A. *Health and the State* (London, 1917).
Brock, Michael and Eleanor Brock (eds). *Margot Asquith's Great War Diary 1914–16* (Oxford, 2014).
Brockway, Fenner. *Socialism Over Sixty Years. The Life of Jowett of Bradford* (London, 1946).
Brown, Kenneth D. *John Burns* (London, 1977).
Bulkley, M. E. *The Feeding of School Children* (London, 1914).
Bulkley, M. E. *The Establishment of Legal Minimum Rates in the Boxmaking Industry under the Trade Boards Act of 1909* (London, 1915).
Bulmer, Martin (ed.). *The Goals of Social Policy* (London, 1989).
Bunsen, Victoria de. *Charles Roden Buxton* (London, 1948).
Butler, C. V. *Social Conditions in Oxford* (London, 1912).
Cadbury, Edward and George Shann. *Sweating* (London, 1907).

Cadbury, Edward, Cecile Matheson and George Shann. *Women's Work and Wages* (London, 1908).
Cadbury, George. *Town Planning* (London, 1915).
Campbell, R. J. *Christianity and the Social Order* (London, 1907).
Cannadine, David. *The Decline and Fall of the British Aristocracy* (London, 1996).
Chamberlain, Austen. *Politics from Inside: An Epistolary Chronicle 1906-1914* (London, 1936).
Chamberlain, Joseph. *A Political Memoir 1880-92* (London, 1953).
Charity Organization Society. *Report of the Special Committee on Unskilled Labour* (London, 1908).
Chiozza Money, L. G. Riches and Poverty (London, 1906).
Chiozza Money, L. G. *The Future of Work* (London, 1914).
Church, Roy 'Edwardian Labour Unrest and Coalfield militancy, 1890-1914', *Historical Journal* 30 (4) (1987): 841-57.
Churchill, Randolp. *Winston S. Churchill. Young Statesman 1901-1914*, vol. 2 (London, 1967).
Churchill, Randolph. *Winston S. Churchill*, Companion vol. 4 (1907-11).
Clarke, P. F. *Lancashire and the New Liberalism* (Cambridge, 1971).
Cohen, Emmeline W. *The Growth of the British Civil Service 1780-1939* (London, 1941).
Cole, Margaret. *Beatrice Webb* (London, 1945).
Collings, J. and J. L. Green. *Life of the Right Hon. Jesse Collings* (London, 1920).
Comyns Carr, A. S., W. H. Stuart Garnett and J. H. Taylor. *National Insurance* (London, 1912).
*Conference of delegates on questions concerning the Housing of the people* (London, 1890).
Cooper, John. *The Unexpected Story of Nathaniel Rothschild* (London, 2015).
Cordery, Simon. *British Friendly Societies, 1750-1914* (Basingstoke, 2003).
Cox, Alfred. *Among the Doctors* (London, n.d.).
Creiger, Don M. *Bounder from Wales. Lloyd George's Career before the First World War* (London, 1976).
Crowther, M. A. *The Workhouse System 1834-1929* (London, 1981).
Cruickshank, Lewis D. *School Clinics at Home and Abroad* (London, 1913).
Daglish, N. D. 'Robert Morant's Hidden Agenda? The Origins of the Medical Treatment of Schoolchildren', *History of Education* 19 (1990): 139-48.
Daunton, Martin. *Trusting Leviathan. The Politics of Taxation in Britain 1799-1914* (Cambridge, 2001).
Davies, Maude E. *Life in an English Village* (London, 1909).
Dearle, N. B. *Industrial Training* (London, 1914).
Mause, Lloyd de (ed.), *The History of Childhood* (London, 1971).
Dewsnap, Ernest Ritson. *The Housing Problem in England* (London, 1907).
Dwork, Deborah. *War is Good for Babies and Other Young Children: A History of the Infant and Child Welfare Movement in England 1898-1918* (London, 1987).
Eckstein, Harry. *The English Health Service* (Cambridge, MA, 1959).
Emy, H. V. 'The Land Campaign: Lloyd George as a Social Reformer, 1909-14', in A. J. P. Taylor (ed.), *Lloyd George. Twelve Essays* (London, 1971).
Emy, H. V. *Liberals, Radicals and Social Politics 1892-1914* (Cambridge, 1973).
Eyler, John M. *Sir Arthur Newsholme and State Medicine 1885-1935* (Cambridge, 1997).
Fels, Mary. *Joseph Fels* (London, 1920).
Fraser, Derek. *The Evolution of the British Welfare State* (London, 1984).
Freeden, Michael. *The New Liberalism. AnIdeology of Social Reform* (Oxford, 1986).

Freeden, Michael. *Ideologies and Political Theory: A Conceptual Approach* (Oxford, 1996).
Freeman, Arnold. *Boy Life and Labour* (London, 1914).
Freemantle, Anne. *Little Band of Prophets* (New York, 1960).
Fulford, Roger. *Votes for Women* (London, 1957).
Gardiner, A. G. *Prophets, Priests and Kings* (London, 1917).
Gardiner, A. G. *George Cadbury* (London, n.d.).
Gathorne-Hardy, Robert. *Ottoline. The Early Memoirs of Lady Ottoline Morrell* (London, 1963).
Gazeley, Ian and Andrew Newell. 'Rowntree Revisited: Poverty in Britain, 1900', *Explorations in Economic History* 37 (2000): 174–88.
Gazeley, Ian. *Poverty in Britain, 1900–1965* (Basingstoke, 2003).
Gerth. H. H. and C. Wright Mills (eds). *From Max Weber: Essays in Sociology* (London, 1952).
Gibb, Spencer J. *The Irregular Employment of Boys* (London, 1903).
Gibb, Spencer J. *The Problem of Boy Work* (London, 1906).
Gilbert, Bentley B. *The Evolution of National Insurance. The Origins of the Welfare State* (London, 1966).
Gilbert, Bentley B. *British Social Policy 1914–1939* (London, 1970).
Gilbert, Bentley B. *Lloyd George. A Political Life. The Organizer of Victory 1912–16* (London, 1992).
Ginsberg, Morris (ed.). *Law and Opinion in England in the 20th Century* (London, 1959).
Gooch, G. P. *Under Six Reigns* (London, 1958).
John Gorst, John *Children of the Nation* (London, 1907).
Robin Gowers. Robin and Timothy J. Hatton. 'The Origins and Early Impact of the Minimum Wage in Agriculture', *Economic History Review* (1997).
Green, David. G. *Working Class Patients and the Medical Establishment. Self-Help in Britain from the Mid-nineteenth Century to 1948* (Aldershot, 1985).
Greenwood, Arthur *The Health and Physique of School Children* (London, 1913).
Griffith-Boscawen, Arthur *Memories* (London, 1925).
Guest L. Haden (ed.), *The Next Steps in Educational Progress* (London, 1915).
Gwynn, Stephen and Gertrude M. Tuckwell. *The Life of the Rt. Hon. Sir Charles W. Dilke*, vol. 2 (London, 1917).
Haldane, Richard Burdon. *An Autobiography* (London, 1929).
Halévy, Éli. *The Rule of Democracy*, vol. 1 (London, 1952).
Hall, M. Penelope. *The Social Services of Modern England* (London, 1960).
Hamilton, Mary. *Mary MacArthur: A Biographical Sketch* (London, 1925).
Hammond, John et al., *Towards a Social Policy* (London, 1905).
Harris, Bernard. *The Health of the Schoolchild* (Buckingham, 1995).
Harris, Bernard. *The Origins of the British Welfare State. Society, State and Social Welfare in England and Wales, 1800–1945* (Houndmills, Hants, 2004).
Harris, José. *Unemployment and Politics. A Study of English Social Policy 1886–1914* (Oxford, 1972).
Harris, José. 'The Transition to High Politics in English Social Policy', in Michael Bentley and John Stevenson, *High and Low Politics in Modern Britain. Ten Studies* (Oxford, 1983).
Harris, José. 'The Webbs, the Charity Organization Society and the Ratan Tata Foundation. Social Policy from the Perspective of 1912', in Martin Bulmer, Jane Lewis and David Piachaud (eds), *The Goals of Social Policy* (London, 1989).
Harris, José. 'Political Thought and the Welfare State 1870–1940: An Intellectual Framework for British Social Policy', *Past and Present* 135 (May 1992): 116–41.

Harris, José. *Private Lives, Public Spirit: Britain 1870-1914* (London, 1994).
Harris, José. *William Beveridge* (Oxford, 1997).
Hazlehurst, Cameron and Christine Woodland (eds). *A Liberal Chronicle. Journals and Papers of J. A. Pease* (London, 1995).
Hecht, Charles E. (ed.). *Rearing an Imperial Race* (London, 1913).
J. Hendrick, Burton J. *The Life and Letters of Walter H. Page* (New York, 1923).
Hendrick, Harry. *Child Welfare in England 1872-1989* (London, 1994).
Hennock, E. P. 'Poverty and Social Theory in England: The Experience of the Eighteen-eighties', *Social History* (January 1976).
Hennock, E. P. *British Social Reform and German Precedents: The Case of Social Insurance 1880-1914* (Oxford, 1987).
Hirst, J. David. 'The Growth of Treatment through the School Medical Service', *Medical History* 33 (1989): 318-42.
Hobman, J. B. (ed.). *David Eder. Memoirs of a Modern Pioneer* (London, 1945).
Hobsbawm, E. J. *Labouring Men* (London, 1964).
Hobson, J. A. *The Industrial System. An Inquiry into Earned and Unearned Income* (London, 1909).
Hobson, J. A. *Confessions of an Economic Heretic* (London, 1938).
Honigsbaum, Frank. *The Struggle for the Ministry of Health 1914-19* (London, 1970).
Honigsbaum, Frank. *Doctors, Politics and Society* (Amsterdam, 1993).
Horne, C. Silvester. *Pulpit, Platform and Parliament* (London, n.d.).
Horsfall, T. C. *The Improvement of the Dwellings and Surroundings of the People. The Example of Germany* (Manchester, 1904).
Horton, Robert Forman. *An Autobiography* (London, 1917).
Howarth, Edward G. and Mona Wilson. *West Ham. A Study of Industrial Problems* (London, 1907).
Hurst, John. 'Feeding the Hungry Schoolchild in the First Half of the Twentieth Century', in Derek J. Oddy and Derek S. Miller (eds), *Diet and Health in Modern Britain* (London, 1985).
Hutchinson, H. G. *Life of Sir John Lubbock*, vol. 2 (London, 1914).
Huxley, Gervas. *Lady Denman 1884-1954* (London, 1961).
Inglis, K. S. *The Churches and the Working Classes in Victorian England* (London, 1963).
Ismay, Penelope. 'Between Providence and Risk: Odd fellows, Benevolence and the Social Limits of Actuarial Science, 1820s-1880s', *Past and Present* (February 2015).
Jones, Peter D'A. *The Christian Socialist Revival. Religion, Class and Conscience in Late-Victorian England 1877-1914* (Princeton, NJ, 1968).
Jordan, E. K. H. *Free Church Unity* (London, 1956).
Kaufman, Mauritz. *The Housing of the Working Classes and of the Poor* (London, 1907).
Keeling, Frederic. *The Labour Exchange in Relation to Boy and Girl Labour* (London, 1910).
Keeling, Frederic. *Child Labour in the United Kingdom* (London, 1914).
Kellett, John R. *The Impact of the Railways on Victorian Cities* (London, 2005).
King, O. Bolton. *The Employment and Welfare of Juveniles* (London, 1925).
Knapp, John M. (ed.). *The Universities and Social Problems* (London, 1895).
Kolthammer, F. W. *Some Notes on the Incidence of Taxation on the Working Class Family* (London, 1913).
Koss, Stephen E. *Sir John Brunner, 1842-1919: Radical Plutocrat* (Cambridge, 1970).
Koss, Stephen E. *Fleet Street Radical. A. G. Gardiner and the Daily News* (London, 1973).
Koss, Stephen E. *Asquith* (London, 1976).

Koven, Seth. *Slumming. Sexual and Social Politics in Victorian London* (New Jersey, 2004).
Laybourn, K. 'The Issue of School Feeding in Bradford', *Journal of Educational Administration History* XIV (2) (July 1982).
Lawrence, Eldwood P. *Henry George in the British Isles* (Michigan, 1957).
Levy, Carl (ed.), *Socialism and the Intelligentsia* (London, 1987).
Lewis, Jane. *The Politics of Motherhood. Child and Maternal Welfare in England 1900-1939* (London, 1980).
Lewis, Jane. (ed.), 'The Working-Class Wife and Mother and State Intervention, 1870-1918', in *Labour and Love. Women's Experience of Home and Family, 1850-1940* (Oxford, 1986).
Lewis, Jane. *Women and Social Action in Victorian and Edwardian England* (Aldershot, 1991).
Lidgett, J. Scott. *My Guided Life* (London, 1936).
Little, E. W. *History of the British Medical Association 1832-1932* (London, 1932).
Lloyd George, David. *War Memoirs*, vol. 2 (London, 1933).
Lloyd George, Richard. *Lloyd George* (London, 1960).
Lumis, Trevor. 'Charles Booth: Moralist or Social Scientist?', *Economic History Review* (1971): 100-5.
MacDonald, J. Ramsay. *Margaret Ethel MacDonald* (London, 1923).
Macfayden, D. *Sir E. Howard and the Town Planning Movement* (London, 1933).
Macnicol, John. *The Politics of Retirement in Britain* (Cambridge, 1998).
Maccoby, Simon. *English Radicalism 1886-1914* (London, 1953).
MacKenzie, Norman and Jeanne MacKenzie (eds). *The Diary of Beatrice Webb 1905-24* (London, 1984).
Mallet, George Bernard. *British Budgets 1887-8 to 1912-13* (London, 1914).
Mann, H. H. 'Life in an Agricultural Village in England', *Sociological Papers* (London, 1904).
Margaret McMillan, Margaret. *Labour and Childhood* (London, 1907).
Markham, Violet R. *May Tennant* (London, 1949).
Markham, Violet R. *Return Passage* (London, 1953).
Marquis, F. J. *Handbooks of Employments in Liverpool* (Liverpool, 1916).
Marr, T. R. *Housing Conditions in Manchester and Salford* (Manchester, 1904).
Masterman, C. F. G. *England After the War* (London, 1922).
Masterman, Lucy. *C.F.G. Masterman* (London, 1939).
Matheson, Cecile and George Shann. *Women's Work and Wages* (London, 1908).
Maurice, F. *Sir Frederick Maurice. A Record of his Work and Opinions* (London, 1913).
Mause, Lloyd de (ed.), *The History of Childhood* (London, 1971).
McBriar, A. M. *Fabian Socialism and English Politics 1884-1918* (Cambridge, 1962).
McBriar, A. M. *An Edwardian Mixed Doubles. The Bosanquets versus the Webbs. A Study in British Social Policy 1890-1929* (Oxford, 1987).
McCleary, G. F. *National Health Insurance* (London, 1932).
McCleary, G. F. *The Early History of the Infant Welfare Movement* (London, 1933).
McMillan, Margaret. *Rachel McMillan* (London, 1927).
Mess, H. A. *Casual Labour at the Docks* (London, 1916).
Mess, H. A. *Factory Legislation and Administration 1891-1924* (London, 1926).
Meyer Carl (Mrs) and Clementina Black. *Makers of Our Clothes* (London, 1909).
M'Gonigle, G. C. M. and J. Kirby. *Poverty and Public Health* (London, 1936).
Morgan, Kenneth. *Labour in Power 1945-1951* (Oxford, 1984).

Morgan, Kenneth. O. *Lloyd George* (London, 1974).
Morgan, Kenneth and Jane Morgan. *Portrait of a Progressive. The Political Career of Christopher Viscount, Addison* (Oxford, 1980).
Murray, Bruce K. 'The Politics of the "People's Budget"', *Historical Journal* (1973).
Murray, Bruce K. *The People's Budget 1909/10. Lloyd George and Liberal Politics* (Oxford, 1980).
Musgrove, F. 'Middle Class Education and Employment in the Nineteenth Century: A Rejoinder', *Economic History Review* (December 1961).
National Anti-Sweating League, *Report of the Conference on a Minimum Wage* (London, 1907).
Neilson, Francis. *My Life in Two Worlds*, vol. 1 (Wisconsin, 1952).
Neilson, Francis. *The Churchill Legend* (Wisconsin, 1955).
Nemers, Erwin Esser. *Hobson and Underconsumption* (Amsterdam, 1956).
Nettlefold, J. S. Practical Town Planning (London, 1914).
Newsholme, Arthur. *The Last 30 Years in Public Health* (London, 1936).
Newsholme, Arthur and Walter C. C. Pakes. *School Hygiene* (London, 1903).
Norwood, Cyril and Arthur H. Hope. *The Higher Education of Boys in England* (1912).
Oddy, Derek J. 'Working Class Diets in Late Nineteenth-century Britain', *Economic History Review* 23 (2) (August 1970): 314–22.
Otter, Sandra M. Den. *British Idealism and Social Explanation. A Study in Late Victorian Thought* (Oxford, 1996).
Packer, Ian *Lloyd George, Liberalism and the Land Issue and Party Politics in England 1906–14* (Woodbridge, 2001).
Paton, J. B. *Continuous Recreative Education in Evening Classes* (London, 1885).
Paton, J. L. *Education for the Industrial Classes* (London, 1895).
Paton, J. L. *John Brown Paton* (London, 1914).
Pelling, Henry. *Popular Politics and Society in Victorian Britain* (London, 1979).
Percival, Tom. *Poor Law Children* (London, 1911).
Perkin, Harold. *The Rise of Professional Society: England Since 1880* (London, 2002).
Petter, Martin. 'The Progressive Alliance', *History* 58 (February 1973).
Phillips, Gordon and Noel Whiteside. *Casual Labour. The Unemployment Question in the Port Transport Industry 1870–1970* (Oxford, 1985).
Picht, Werner. *Toynbee hall and the English Settlement Movement* (London, 1914).
Porritt, Arthur. *John Henry Jowett* (London, 1924).
Raison, Timothy (ed.). The Founding Fathers of Social Science (London, 1969).
Reason, W. (ed.). *University and Social Settlements* (London, 1898).
Reeves, Maud Pember. *Round About a Pound a Week* (London, 1999).
*Report of the Land Enquiry Committee* vol. 2 (London, 1914).
Ridley, Jane. 'The Unionist Social Reform Committee, 1911–14: West before the Storm', *Historical Journal* (1987): 391–413.
Riddell, Lord. *More Pages from My Diary 1908–1914* (London, 1934).
Roberts, Elizabeth. 'The Recipients' View of Welfare', in Joanna Bornat, Robert Perks, Paul Thompson and Jan Walmsley (eds), *Oral History, Health and Welfare 1890–1914* (London, 2000).
Rogers, Frederick. *Labour, Life and Literature. Some Memories of Sixty Years* (Brighton, 1973).
Rose, Gordon. *The Struggle for Penal Reform. The Howard League and its Predecessors* (London, 1961).
Ross, Ellen. *Slum Travelers. Ladies and London Poverty (1860–1920)* (Berkeley, 2007).

Robertson, John M. *The Fallacy of Saving* (London, 1892).
Rowland, Peter. *The Last Liberal Governments. The Promised Land 1905–1910* (London, 1953).
Rowntree, B. S. *Poverty. A Study of Town Life* (London, 1901).
Rowntree, B. S. *The Way to Industrial Peace and the Problem of Unemployment* (London, 1914).
Rowntree, B. S. and May Kendall. *How the Labourer Lives. A Study of the Rural Problem* (London, 1913).
Rowntree, B. S. and A. C. Pigou. *Lectures on Housing* (Manchester, 1914).
Rowntree, Joseph and Arthur Sherwell. *The Taxation of the Liquor Trade* (London, 1909).
Sadler, Michael (ed.). *Continuation Schools in England and Elsewhere* (London, 1908).
Samuel, Herbert. *Liberalism* (London, 1902).
Schloss, David. *Insurance Against Unemployment* (London, 1909).
Scott, Richenda. Elizabeth Cadbury 1858–1951 (London, 1955).
Searle, G. R. *The Quest for National Efficiency. A Study in British Politics and British Political Thought 1899–1914* (Oxford, 1971).
Searle, G. R. 'The Edwardian Liberal Party and Business', *English Historical Review* (January 1983).
Searle, G. R. *A New England? Peace and War 1886–1918* (Oxford, 2004).
Sells, Dorothy. *The British Trade Board System* (London, 1923).
Sherington, Geoffrey. *English Education, Social Change, and War* (Manchester, 1981).
Simey, T. S. 'The Contribution of Beatrice and Sidney Webb to Sociology', *British Journal of Sociology* 12 (1961): 106–23.
Simon, Brian. *Education and the Labour Movement 1870–1920* (London, 1965).
Simon, E. D. *A City Council from Within* (London, 1926).
Smillie, Robert. *My Life for Labour* (London, 1924).
Smith, Richard Mudie (ed.). *Handbook of the Daily News Sweated Industries Exhibition* (London, 1906).
Samuel Smith, Samuel. *My Life Work* (London, 1902).
Philip Snowden Philip., *The Living Wage* (London, 1912).
Spender, J. A. *The State and Pensions in Old Age* (London, 1894).
Spender, J. A. *Life, Journalism and Politics* (London, 1927).
Squire, Rose E. *Thirty Years in Public Service* (London, 1927).
Stead, Francis Herbert. *How Old Age Pensions Began to Be* (London, n.d.).
John Stewart, John. 'Ramsay MacDonald, the Labour Party and Child Welfare, 1900–1914', *Twentieth Century British History* 4 (2) (1993): 105–25.
Stewart, Margaret and Leslie Hunter, *The Needle is Threaded. The History of an Industry* (London, 1964).
Stocks, M. D. *Fifty Years in Every Street. The Story of the Manchester University Settlement* (London, 1945).
Summers, Anne. *Female Lives, Moral States. Women, Religion and Public Life in Britain 1880–1930* (Newbury, 2000).
Sutcliffe, Anthony. *Towards the Planned City: Germany, Britain, the United States and France 1780–1914* (Oxford, 1981).
Sutherland, Gillian. *Elementary Education in the Nineteenth Century* (London, 1971).
Tanner, Duncan. *Political Change and the Labour party 1900–1918* (Cambridge, 1990).
Tawney, R. H. *Poverty as an Industrial Problem* (London, 1914).
Tawney, R. H. *The Establishment of Minimum Rates in the Chain-Making Industry under the Trade Boards Act of 1909* (London, 1914).

Tawney, R. H. *The Establishment of Minimum Rates in the Tailoring Industry under the Trade Boards Act of 1909* (London, 1915).
Thane, Pat. 'The Working Class and State Welfare in Britain 1880–1914', *Historical Journal* 27 (4) (1984): 877–900.
Thane, Pat. *Old Age in English History: Past Experiences, Present Issues* (Oxford, 2000).
*Third International Congress for the Welfare and Protection of Children* (London, 1902) and *Report of British Section* (1906).
Thompson, Paul. *Socialists, Liberals and Labour. The Struggle for London 1885–1914* (London, 1967).
*Thrift and National Insurance as a Security against Pauperism with a Memoir of the Late Revd Canon Blackley and a Reprint of his Essays* (London, 1906).
Tillyard, Frank and F. N. Ball. *Unemployment Insurance in Great Britain 1911–48* (Leigh-on-Sea, 1949).
Titmuss, R. M. 'Health', in Morris Ginsberg (ed.), *Law and Opinion in the 20th Century* (London, 1959).
Treble, J. H. 'The Attitudes of Friendly Societies towards the Movement in Great Britain for State Pensions, 1878–1908', *International Review of Social History* 15 (2) (1970): 266–99.
Trevelyan, Janet Penrose. *Evening Play Centres for Children* (London, 1920).
Trevelyan, Janet, Penrose. *The Life of Mrs Humphrey Ward* (London, 1923).
Tuckwell, Gertrude. *Constance Smith. A Short Memoir* (London, 1931).
Unionist Social Reform Council. *Papers on Unrest Among the Working Classes* (London, 1911).
Urwick, E. J. ed., *Studies of Boy Life in Our Cities* (London, 1904).
Urwick, E. J. *Luxury and Waste* (London, 1908).
Waley, S. D. *Edwin Montagu* (London, 1964).
Wardley, Peter. 'Edwardian Britain: Empire, Income and Political Discontent', in Paul Johnson (ed.), *Edwardian Britain: Empire, Income and Political Discontent* (London, 1994).
Warwick, Countess of *Life's Ebb and Flow* (London, 1929).
Warwick, Countess of. *Afterthoughts* (London, 1931).
Watkins, Micky. *Henrietta Barnett. Social Worker and Community Planner* (London, 2011).
Webb, Beatrice. *My Apprenticeship*, vols 1 and 2 (Harmondsworth, 1938).
Webb, Beatrice. *Our Partnership*, Barbara Drake and Margaret Cole (eds) (London, 1948).
Webb, Sidney. *Twentieth Century Politics. A Policy of National Efficiency* (London, 1901).
Webb, Sidney and Beatrice Webb, *Problems of Modern Industry* (London, 1898).
Webb, Sidney and Beatrice Webb, *Industrial Democracy* (London, 1902).
Webb, Sidney and Beatrice Webb, *The Break-Up of the Poor Law* (London, 1909).
Webb, Sidney and Beatrice Webb, *The Case for the National Minimum* (London, 1913).
Whitehouse, J. H. (ed.). *Problems of Boy Life* (London, 1912).
Wedgwood, J. C. *Memoirs of a Fighting Life* (London, 1941).
John Welshman, John. 'School Meals and Milk in England and Wales, 1906–45', *Medical History* 41 (1997).
Whitehouse, J. H. *A National System of Education* (London, 1913).
Williams, R. *The First Year's Working of the Liverpool Docks Scheme* (London, 1914).
Wilson, David F. *Dockers. The Impact of Industrial Change* (London, 1972).
Winder, Phyllis. *The Public Feeding of Elementary School Children* (London, 1913).
Winfrey, Richard. *Great Men and Others I Have Met* (Kettering, 1943).

Winter, J. M. *Socialism and the Challenge of War. Ideas and Politics in Britain 1912–18* (London, 1974).
Wohl, Anthony S. *The Eternal Slum. Housing and Social Policy in Victorian Britain* (London, 1977).
Woodroofe, Kathleen 'The Royal Commission on the Poor Laws, 1905–9', *International Review of Social History* 22 (1977).
Woolton, Earl. *Memoirs* (London, 1959).
Wrigley, Chris. *David Lloyd George and the British Labour Movement* (Hassocks, 1976).

# Index

able-bodied unemployed 1–2
Abramovitz, Moses, and Eliasberg, Vera 14
accommodation, on merchant vessels 137–8
*Active Innovator* 85, 191
actuaries 157
Addison, Christopher 116, 160–1, 219, 220, 240, 291, 292, 295
Adler, Nettie 185–6
adult Sunday Schools 36
afforestation 147, 180, 280
after-care, for apprentices
aged 1, 2
agricultural labourers 279–80, 283
alcohol, ban on sale to children 60
Alden, Percy 20, 23, 27, 170, 219, 277–8, 283, 297
Aldridge, Henry 246, 247, 255, 256–7, 260
aliens, pensions ban 74, 76
American, licensing system for workshops 83–4, 93–4, 96
Ancoats, Settlement 17
Anson, Sir William 46, 48
ante-natal clinics 239
Anti-Tea Duty League 122–3
apprenticeship 189–90, 192, 193–4, 202
Apprenticeship and Skilled Employment Association 31–2, 55, 185, 189, 194, 198
Aristocratic-City elite 7, 142, 147–8, 287
Aristocratic-Civil Service alliance 7–8, 288
Army and Naval Journals 44
Askwith, George 98, 99
Asquith, Herbert, Henry 5, 8, 26, 27, 30, 43
  as Chancellor of the Exchequer 122–4, 126, 130–2
  and old age pensions 63, 70–2, 73–4, 76
  and Poor Law reform 115–17, 167, 173, 210–11
  as Prime Minister 103, 142–3, 148, 149, 197, 203, 205, 207, 274–5, 276, 280, 282–3, 287, 288, 289, 290, 297
  and trade boards 100, 101
Asquith, Margot 143, 149, 275, 277, 280, 290
Associated Chambers of Commerce 152, 153, 201
Association of Municipal Corporations 228, 248, 249
Astor, Waldorf 220, 225, 226, 227
Australia, anti-sweating legislation 79, 84–5, 94, 101
Australia and New Zealand 288
Atlantic 288
Attlee, Clement 15, 22, 24, 26, 292, 294
Aves, Ernest 11, 85, 96, 98, 99

Baker, Harold 117
Balfour, Arthur James 55, 66–7, 70, 75, 105, 140, 297
Balfour, Gerald 105, 246
Balliol College, Oxford 8, 16
Barnes, George Nicoll 65, 68, 74, 75, 94, 141, 165, 276
Barnett, Canon Samuel Augustus 11, 16–20, 22, 38, 109, 200, 253, 297
Barnett, Henrietta 16–17, 19–20, 22, 28, 31, 212–14, 253
Barrack schools 212, 214
Bedford, Duke of 230
Belgium 181
Bell, Lady 11, 193, 269
Bermondsey Settlement 20, 22
Best, Robert 198
Bevan, Aneurin 294–5
Beveridge, William Henry 11, 24, 25, 107, 109–11, 112, 167–8, 174, 175, 179, 194, 274, 290, 292, 293, 297
Birmingham 21, 269–70
Birrell, Augustine 50–1, 52

birth and pregnancy, state schemes 238–9
Black, Clementina 31, 81, 82, 92, 96, 97, 99, 100, 272–3
Blackburn, Sheila 3, 266
Blackley, Canon 62, 63, 70
Blain, William 115, 131, 155, 173, 298
Blewett, Neal 149
Blind-Alley Occupations 6, 185, 191, 192, 196, 198
Board of Education 195
Board of Trade 195
boarding out of children
Boards of Guardians 47, 48–9, 105
Boer War 39
Booth, Charles 10–11, 21, 25, 35, 36, 63–4, 66, 72, 75, 79, 106, 109–11, 177, 190, 210, 222, 268, 287, 290, 298
Bosanquet, Helen 107–8
Bow School Clinic 217
Bowerman, C. W. 242
Bowley, Arthur Lyon 11, 25, 27, 111, 121, 125, 126, 127, 147, 268–9, 273, 291, 293, 298
boy labour problem 6, 110, 189–98
Bradbury, John Swanwick 143, 298
Bradford 44–6, 217
Braithwaite, William 151, 157–8, 159, 162–3, 225, 298
Brand Jeanne L. 42
Branford, Victor 13, 15
Bray, Reginald 88, 185
brewers 142
Britain, decline of 207
British Medical Association 51, 55, 161, 233, 234
Broadbent, Benjamin 236
Brown, Kenneth 211–12
Browning Settlement 35, 65, 76
Brunner, Mond & Co. 202
Brunner, Sir John 7, 10
Brunton, Sir Lauder 49, 50
Bryce, James
Budget
    1907 130
    1908 130–2
    1909 6, 118, 139–50, 290
    1914 150, 277
Budget Protest League 147

Bulkley, Mildred 24, 26, 222, 271
Bunsen, Victoria de 9–10
Burnett-Hurst, A. R. 11, 268–9
Burns, John 68, 73, 76–7, 153, 155, 165–6, 179, 213, 226, 227, 236, 249, 253, 299
Burt, Sir Cyril 18
business, MPs in 7, 10
businessmen, attitude to health insurance 152–3
Butler, R. A. 294
Buxton, Charles Roden 139, 244, 279
Buxton, Sydney 31, 166, 175, 179, 274, 276, 283

Cabinet Committee 73, 114, 165–6
Cadbury, Edward 21, 68, 80, 87–8, 152–3, 170
Cadbury, Elizabeth 28, 31, 220
Cadbury, George 38, 79, 91, 92, 96, 98, 102, 247, 248, 299
Cadbury and Rowntree families 23, 38
Campbell-Bannerman, Sir Henry 1, 2, 4, 5, 39, 70, 97, 103, 153, 248, 288, 299
Canterbury, Archbishop of 248
cardboard box makers 264
care committees 195–6
Carpenter, Edward 30
casual labour, theory of pauperism and under-employment 5, 107, 108, 109–12, 222, 266–7, 268–9, 271–3, 280–1
chainmaking 101, 261–2, 263, 265
Chalmers, Robert 131, 143, 145, 157, 172, 219, 277, 299
Chamber of Shipping 136
Chamberlain, Austen 70, 123, 124, 131, 140, 299
Chamberlain, Joseph 63, 66–7, 152, 299
character test 72–3, 75, 175
Charity Organization Society 8, 22, 48, 75, 106, 107, 109, 111, 112
Cheap Trains Act (1883) 243
child labour, limitation of 54, 186–8, 196–8
children
    from the slums 40
    medical inspection of 42–4, 49–53
    medical treatment of 44–5, 52–4, 215–21

new attitudes towards 54
    in Poor Law institutions 6, 20, 212–14, 289
Children's Act (1908) 59–60
children's courts 55–9
Choice of Employment Act (1910) 195
Christian Social Union 33–4, 80, 82, 96
Christian Socialism and the Social Gospel 32–6
Church, Roy 273
Church Socialist League 34
Churchill, Winston Spencer 5, 25, 44, 74, 79, 100–1, 102–3, 106, 114, 115, 118, 147–8, 166, 167–70, 172–5, 179–80, 194, 197, 203, 204, 275, 289, 290, 300
Civil Service 8, 13–14, 30
Clarke, P. F. 148
class 38
Clifford, Dr 35, 52, 205
clinics and laboratories
Clynes, J. R. 46, 94, 165
Coal Mines (Minimum Wage) Act (1912) 274–6
coalowners and shipowners 122
Co-efficients 105
Coghlan, T. A. 127, 128
Cohen, Emmiline W. 14
collective bargaining, impediments to 88
Committee on Wage Earning Children 32, 55, 56–9, 185–6, 187–8, 194, 196–8
communications, better 55, 288
Comte, Auguste 13
confectionery trade 123–4
Conservative party 46, 66, 74, 105, 218
Conservative philanthropic opinion 47, 48
consultants 221, 295
Consumer Leagues 82–3
construction and sawmilling 176, 182
continuation education 6, 18, 32, 198–208
contract practice 161–2
Cooperative Small Holdings Society 37–8, 278–9
cotton and woollen industries 203–5
Counter-Elite, recruiting grounds of 4–5, 15–38
County Councils Association 48, 227, 228
Crewe, Lord 57, 176, 220

Crooks, Will 283
Cruickshank, Dr Lewis 220
crusade 26, 210, 212
culture, popular and high 16–18
cyclical trade depression 45, 79, 98–9, 100–3, 106, 118, 138, 139, 147–8, 165, 166–70, 172, 173–5

Daglish, N. D. 52
*Daily News* 91, 96, 139, 141
Davies, Margaret Llewellyn 95
Davies, Maude F. 279
Dawson, William Harbutt 118, 146, 158, 168, 170, 171–4, 300
Deakin, Alfred 85, 86, 91
Dearle, N. B. 21, 6
death duties 130, 145
Denman, Lady 32
dental treatment 41, 42, 218
Departmental Committee on Tuberculosis 226–7
Deptford school clinic 217
Development Commission 147, 179–83
Dewsnap, E. R. 255
Dickson-Poynder, Sir John 249
dietary scale on merchant ships 134–5, 137
diets 222
differentiation of income 128–30
Dilke, Lady 30, 90, 95
Dilke, Sir Charles 85, 86, 99, 124, 126, 127–30, 300
direct taxation 124–32
distress committees 166
Dock Labourers Union 178
dockers, decasualization 176–9
doctors 161–2, 294–5
dreadnoughts 122

*Economic Journal* 31
*Economic Review* 34
Eder, Dr David 26, 218
Education Act (1902) 105
Education (Administrative Provisions) Act (1907) 53
Education (Provision of Meals) Act (1906) 49
Education (Scotland) Act (1908) 191
Ehrlich, Paul 232

Eichholz, Dr Alfred 43
Eight Hours League 27
elections
    December 1910 149
    January 1910 149
elementary schools 40
Ellis, Havelock 30
Employment of Children Act (1903) 188
Emy, H. V. 3, 7, 253–4
English Land Restoration League 37
English Land Values League 140
European anti-sweating movement 82
Evans, Samuel 129, 144–5
Eyler, John 2, 234

Fabian Society 23–7, 30, 38, 43, 45, 95, 218, 220, 243, 256, 287, 288
Factory and Workshop Acts 81–2
Family Allowances 294
family casework approach 108, 117, 288, 292–3
Fawcett, Millicent 28, 31
Feinstein, C. H. 273
Fels, Joseph 141, 217, 300
females, number not in employment in Britain 29
Financial Reform Association 121
Fisher Education Act (1918) 207–8, 294
Foster, Sir Walter 139
Fox, Arthur Wilson 170–1, 172, 173, 174, 300
France, infant welfare reform 235
free breakfast table 122
Free Church Council 248
Freeman, Arnold 138, 192–3, 269–70
Friendly Societies 153–6, 159, 160–1
Fulford, Roger 30

Garden City Association 244, 248–9, 251
Gardiner, A. G. 91, 102, 103, 152, 155, 300
George, Henry 23, 37, 142, 144
German continuation education 199–200
German invalidity insurance 151, 158–9
German town planning 244–7
Gibb Revd Spencer J. 34, 191
Gilbert, Bentley 2, 39–40, 51–2
Gladstone, Herbert 39, 57–8, 97, 98–9, 100, 169

Gooch, George Peabody 35, 45, 99, 170, 285
Gordon, Mrs Ogilvie 191
Gore, Bishop Charles 33, 96
Gorst, Sir John 17, 19, 22, 39, 154, 167, 300–1
graduated income tax 124–5, 126–30, 145
*Great Disseminator* 34, 36, 50, 75, 79, 86, 191, 244
Green, T. H. 8–9
Greenwood, Arthur 24, 26
Grey, Sir Edward 8, 43, 46, 47, 53, 105, 169, 275
Griffith-Boscawen, Sir Arthur 255, 256–7
Guild of St. Matthew 12, 33

Hadleigh farm colony 109
Haldane, Richard Burdon 105, 115, 116, 118, 132, 166, 169, 205, 207, 209, 237, 289, 301
Halévy, Élie 14
half-time 187, 188, 201, 203–5
Hamilton, Lord George 50, 106, 210
Hamilton, Sir Edward 66, 130, 131
Harcourt, Louis 145
Harcourt, Robert 211
Harcourt, William Vernon 124, 145
Hardie, James Keir 94, 128, 129
Hardy, George 157
Harris, José 3, 54, 106, 174, 290
Harvey, T. Edmund 182, 185, 216, 219
Hay, Claude 46
Headlam, Stuart 33, 34
health insurance 152–63
health committees 160–1
Heath, St G. 279
Henderson, Arthur 46, 48, 94, 101, 166
Hennock, E. P. 2, 77, 167
Herbert, Jesse 10
Higgling of the market 87
Hill, Octavia 19
Hoatson, Revd John 85, 86
Hobhouse, Henry 227, 301
Hobhouse, L. T. 9, 277, 301
Hobsbawm, Eric 23
Hobson, J. A. 9, 90, 125, 277, 293, 301
Holland, Canon Scott 33, 34
Home Industries Bill 83
home workers 81–2, 265

Horne, Revd C. Silvester 35, 36
Horsfall, T. C. 17, 51, 247, 249, 288
Horsley, Sir Victor 51, 161
Horton, Dr 36, 69, 96
housing, movement for municipal intervention 241, 252–60
Housing and Town Planning reform 241–52
Housing of the Working Classes Ireland Act (1908) 252
Howard League 56, 59
Howell, Walter J. 133, 137
Hyndman, Henry Myers 23

Income Tax 6, 124–32, 145
Independent Labour party (ILP) 44, 45, 107
indirect taxation 121–4
*Industrial Democracy* 87, 88
industrial assurance companies 159, 160
industrial schools 41–2, 60
infant and child protection 59–60
infant, deaths, causes of 235
infant welfare 32, 235–8
Inglis, M. R. 59
institutional churches 35–6
insurance committees 160
Inter-Departmental Committee on Physical Deterioration 43, 46
Inter-Departmental Committee on the Employment of School Children 43
International Association for Labour Legislation 82
International Congress for School Hygiene 55
International Congress for the Welfare and Protection of Children 55
International Congress on Infant Welfare 55
Irish party 69, 149
Irwin, Margaret 101
Isaacs, Rufus 275, 285

Jackson, Sir Cyril 18, 21, 185, 192, 267, 301
Jewish Board of Guardians 189
Jews 79–80, 235, 262–3
Joint Committee for the Abolition of Half-Time 203–4

Jowett, F. W. 45, 223
juvenile
  employment 189–98
  employment bureaux 191, 194, 195
  offender 55–9

Keeling, Frederic
Kellett, John R. 246
Kerr, Dr James 44
Kerschensteiner, Dr 199
Knee, Fred 241
Kolthammer, F. W. 124
Koss, Stephen 142

laboratories, for diagnosis 221
Labour Exchanges 167–70
Labour party 10, 48, 69, 71, 72, 74, 76, 94–5, 141, 148, 149, 152, 160, 166, 181, 241, 256, 257, 273–4, 283, 284, 287
Labour Protection League 273
Lancashire cotton towns 203, 204
Lancashire and London constituencies 148
land associations 36–8, 278
land campaign 277–85
land, cheap, 243
Land and Home League 37–8, 278–9
Land and Housing Joint Committee 148
Land Law Reform Association 139, 140, 243–4
Land Nationalization Society 27, 244
land taxes 139–44
Land Tenure Bill 140
Land Tenure Reform Association 36
Lansbury, George 22, 106, 165, 181, 241–2
Lansdowne, Lord 70, 75
Lascars (Indian seamen) 135
legal aid 23
*Lesser Disseminators* 86, 88, 245, 248
Lever Brothers 202
Lewis, Herbert 116
Liberal England, death of 143
Liberal imperialists 40, 43, 44, 105
Liberal party 7, 10, 37, 38, 46, 48, 68, 74, 141–2, 148–9, 291
Liberal Unionist party 11, 147, 149
liberal women 30–1, 185–6
licence duties 130, 142, 144, 145–6

Licensing Bill (1908) 142
Lidgett, Dr Scott 20, 22, 35
Lipset, Seymour 13
Liverpool docks scheme 178
Liverpool, employment situation 192
Liverpool University Settlement 22–3
living wage 275, 277, 283–5
Lloyd George, David 5, 6, 25, 27, 61, 70–1, 74–5, 77, 100, 114, 115, 116, 289, 290, 291, 293, 301
　at the Board of Trade, shipping reform and railways 133–9
　and Coal Mines (Minimum Wage) Bill 274–5
　at the Exchequer, land taxation 141–2
　the Great Budget 142–50
　and health insurance 154–63
　and health service 218–21, 223, 224–9, 233, 236, 237–8, 239–40
　and housing 254–5, 257–8
　unemployment insurance 166, 169, 172, 173, 175–6
load-line, modification of 133–4
local authorities, inactive in housing 250
Local Government Board 210, 226, 228, 229, 233, 236, 246, 251
local marine boards 136–7
local opinion leaders 36, 97, 245
Loch, C. S. 108, 112
London and India Docks Company 177–8
London, industries in 110
London, poverty in 268, 271–3
London School of Economics 26–7
Long, Walter 105, 233, 246
Lords, House of 75, 140, 142
low wages 88–9, 222, 266–70, 272–3, 280–1
Lowe, Robert 292
luxury, nationalization of 18

Majority Poor Law Report 107, 108, 109, 112, 117, 118, 209, 210
Mallon, James Joseph 22, 92, 92–3, 94, 97, 100–1, 261, 266
MacArthur, Mary 28, 31, 84, 89, 91–2, 94, 97, 99, 100, 102, 238, 301
MacDonald, Margaret 28, 29, 84, 92, 93, 94, 96
MacDonald, Ramsey 48, 84, 93, 94, 99, 141, 160, 165, 175
machinery, delay in introduction 87–8
Macnamara, Thomas 24, 46, 47, 52, 53, 302
Malborough, Duchess of 93
Mallet, Bernard 129–30, 131
*Manchester Guardian* 9, 141, 205, 281
Manchester Health Society 29
Manchester University Settlement 17, 22
Mansbridge, Albert 19
Mansfield House Settlement 20, 23
Marconi scandal 277
Marquis, Frederick (Lord Woolton) 17, 22, 24, 193
Marr, T. R. 21, 255, 259
married women 29, 157, 158
Marshall, Alfred 87, 117
Marx, Karl 7, 87
Masterman, Charles 20, 33, 52, 139, 162–3, 175, 219, 238, 285
Maurice, Frederick Dennison 49
Maurice, Sir Frederick 49–50
Maxse, Leopold 44
McBriar, A. M. 3, 23
McClearly, Dr George 25, 113, 152, 235
McKenna, Reginald 25, 54, 72–3, 126–9, 141, 197, 275
McMillan, Margaret 28, 34, 44–5, 49, 53, 217–18
McMillan, Rachel 44–5, 49, 53
McVail, Dr J. C. 224
Mearns, Revd Andrew 35
medical
　inspection of schoolchildren 39–45, 49–54
　institutes 161
　officers of health 42, 50, 113, 216, 220 225, 230, 235, 236
Medical Officers of Schools Association 51
Medical Practitioners Union 152
Medical Treatment Act (1909) 218–21
medical treatment of schoolchildren 52–3, 215–21
Meiklejohn, Roderick 72, 73
Merchant Shipping Act (1906) 133–8
Mess, Henry 176
Meyer, Adele 31, 82, 272

M'Gonigle and Kirby Drs 222
middleman, as sweater 80, 84
Middlesbrough 269, 280
midwives 158
Mill, John Stuart 144
Milner, Lord Alfred 97
miners, strike of 274, 275–6
minimum wage for agricultural labourers 279–80
Ministry of Health 239–40
Ministry of Labour 209
Ministry of Lands, 180, 280
Minority Poor Law Report 22, 23, 26, 107, 108, 112, 117, 209–10, 212
Money, Sir Lee George Chiozza 27, 71, 81, 89–90, 99, 102, 121, 126, 127, 128, 131, 144, 149–50, 255, 258, 259
Montagu, Edwin 74, 173, 182, 282
Montagu, Lily 29, 31
Morant, Robert 18, 45, 51–2, 162, 216, 220, 221, 228–9, 238, 302–3
Morgan, Kenneth 142–3
Morley, Lord 275
municipal housing 242, 254–60
*Municipal Journal* 248
Mundella, A. J. 40
Munich, continuation education 199–200
Murray, Alec 140
Murray, Bruce 145
Murray, Sir George 131, 143, 157

Nash, J. Vaughan 116
*Nation* 203, 207
National Anti-Sweating League 92–103
National Association for the Prevention of Consumption 230–1
National Association for the Prevention of Infant Mortality 236
National Association for the Promotion of Technical and Secondary Education 200
National Committee for the Break-Up of the Poor Law 209
National Committee for the Prevention of Destitution 105, 212, 285
National Committee of Organized Labour on Old Age Pensions 65–77
National Conference of Friendly Societies 153–6, 158–9, 160–1

National Conference on Infant Mortality 235
National Council for Combating Venereal Disease 233, 234
national efficiency movement 39–40, 206, 289, 290
National Health Service 112, 294–5
National Insurance Act (1911)
  health provisions 157–63
  unemployment provisions 170–6
National Land and Housing Demonstration (1907) 139
National League for Physical Education and Improvement 50–3
national minimum 89, 101, 112
National Old Age Pensions League 69
National Order of Oddfellows 67
National Poor Law Reform Association 210
National Providence League 63
National Union of Teachers (NUT) 46, 289
National Union of Women Workers 31–2, 195, 220
National Workmen's Housing Council 241–2, 251
Newcastle, Duke of 230
New Liberalism 5, 6, 23, 48, 53, 61, 75, 105, 125, 220, 287, 288
*New Statesman* 182, 212, 238, 258
New Zealand, anti-sweating legislation 80, 84, 86, 93
New Zealand, pensions scheme 62, 73
Newman, Dr George 50, 54, 215, 216, 218–21, 223–4, 235–7, 239–40, 303
Newsholme, Dr Arthur 42, 50, 215, 226–7, 229–32, 233–4, 235–7, 239–40, 303
Nonconformists 34–6, 69, 200, 205
Northampton 269
Norwood, Sir Cyril 18
Notification of Births Act (1907 and 1915)
Nottingham 264, 265

Oddy, Derek 222
Ogden, C. K. 198
old age pensions 61–77
Old Age State Pensions League 67
Orr, Sir John Boyd 222

Outdoor Relief (Friendly Societies) Act (1904) 67
outworkers 81
Oxford and Cambridge Universities 8, 10, 19
Oxford House 22

parasitic trades 79, 87, 88–9
'particulars clause' 82
panel system of doctors 161, 162
Paton, Revd Dr John Brown 35, 200
pauperism 1–2, 26, 117, 268
Pearson, Karl 26
Pease, Jack 7, 165, 204–7, 220, 223, 236
*People* 143
Perkin, Harold 11, 14
Phillips, Gordon and Whiteside, Noel
Picht, Werner 21
Pleasant Sunday Afternoon Associations 36
Poor Law, break-up 109, 114–15, 116, 118
Poor Law Commission 105–6
Poor Law institutions 1–2, 4, 41, 209–14
Poor Law medical service 216
Poor Law Unions Association 48, 49, 115
poor relief and pensions 72, 73, 75, 76
Port of London Authority 177–8
Port of London strike 276
poverty, line, and poverty surveys 10–12, 111–12, 268–73, 279–80
practicable socialism 22, 38
Price, Sir Robert 210
Primrose, Sir Henry 126, 130, 131
Probation of Offenders Act 57–9
Probation Service for juveniles 57–9
professions 9, 14
public health authority 113–15
public works 179–83

railway
  companies 138, 160
  nationalization 138
  workers 175, 273
Ratan Tata Foundation 26
Rea, Walter Russell 53
Reading 12, 269
reclassification of the poor 117
Recreative Evening Schools Association 200

Reeves Maud 86, 92, 268
Reeves, William Pember 65, 84, 86
Reiss, H. L. 279
religious settlements 21–2
reserve army of labour 87
Riddell, George 101, 275, 278
Right to Work National Council 27, 34, 165, 289
Ripon, Bishop of 53
roads 147, 180
Roberts, George 279–80
Robertson, John M. 125, 285
Rockcliff, Percy 160
Rogers, Frederick 67–9, 76
Romilly Society 59, 185
Roscoe, Sir Henry 207
Rothschild, Lord Nathaniel 63, 144, 287
Rowland, Peter 122
Rowntree, Arnold 216, 219
Rowntree family 123, 202
Rowntree, Joseph 145–6
Rowntree, Seebohm 3, 11, 12, 25, 37, 44, 180–1, 256, 257–8, 259–60, 269, 277–8, 279, 282, 284, 291, 292, 294, 303
Royal Commission on Venereal Diseases 232–3
Runciman, Walter 203, 204, 257, 258, 279, 280
rural housing 257, 258, 280
Ruskin, John 18

Salvarsan 232
Samuel, Herbert 57, 59, 121, 139, 182–3, 252, 257, 258–9, 276, 303
Say's Law 125
scattered homes 213, 214
school
  clinics 216–21
  dinners 39–42, 45–9, 53–4, 222–4
  medical inspection 39–40, 42–5, 49–53, 216
School Boards 105
Scott, A. H. 249
Scott, C. P. 205, 281–2
Scottish Land Values Bill 140
seamen, wages of 137–8
Searle, G. R. 7, 53
secondary education 19, 198–208

Select Committee on the Education (Provision of Meals) Bill 48
Select Committee on Home Work 99
Select Committee on Income Tax 124, 126–30
Shaw, Bernard 43–4, 95
Sherwell, Arthur 21, 145–6, 219
sexual sphere, 30
Simey, T. S. 25
Smith, Constance 28, 31, 34, 93, 96, 196
Smith, Samuel MP 40, 198, 201
Smith, Sir Hubert Llewellyn 7, 11, 167, 170, 174, 176, 185, 200, 303–4
smoking, ban on children 60
Social Democratic Federation 23, 45, 46
Social Gospel 4, 33, 34–6
Social Services 13, 26, 108, 150
social work 107–8, 117–18, 292–3
Socialists 9, 38, 105, 212
Society for the Prevention of Cruelty to Children 48
sociological analysis 4, 6, 10–12, 287
Sociological Socialism 23–27
South Place Ethical Society 125
Spender, Harold 173–4, 304
Spender, J. A. 38, 63, 65, 138, 167, 304
Squire, Rose 28, 30, 81, 102, 267
State Children's Association 20, 56, 57, 212–14
Stead, Revd Francis Herbert 36, 65–6, 68, 76
Suffragette movement 28
sugar duty 123–4
Summary Jurisdiction Children's Bill 57
Supertax 129, 130, 131, 132, 145
Sutherland, Gillian 40
sweating 79–103, 210, 272–3
Sydenham, Lord 232–4

tailoring trade 79–80, 262–3
Tariff Reform Women's Liberal Federation 95
Tawney, R. H. 13, 18, 19, 22, 24–5, 26, 109, 192, 262–3, 265, 266, 304
Taylor, A. J. P. 155
Taylor, Austin 134, 135–6
tea duty 122–3
Tennant, Jack 51, 52, 57, 92

Tennant, May 28, 50, 51, 57, 86, 92, 96, 304
Thane, Pat 3, 28, 64, 67
theatres, safeguards for children 59
Thompson, Paul 23
Thompson, William 248, 250, 255
Thorne, Will 46
Titmuss, Richard 13
Town Planning 243, 244–9, 250, 251–2
Toynbee, Arnold 15
Toynbee Hall 15–20, 22
Trade Boards 14, 32, 79, 84–8, 90–103, 261–6, 282, 283–4
Trade schools, German 199–200
Trade Unions 27, 65, 94, 165, 171
Trades Union Congress 65, 94, 168, 171
Treasury 126, 127, 131, 143
Trevelyan, Sir Charles 129, 139, 281
tuberculosis, treatment of 224–32
Tuckwell, Gertrude 28, 30, 80, 90, 92, 99

unearned income 145
unemployment
    insurance 167–76
    reform 165–6, 179–83
*Unemployment: A Problem of Industry* 109–11
Unionist Social Reform Council 252–3, 255, 256, 269
United Committee for the Taxation of Land Values 37, 140, 141
United States, secondary education 199
university graduates 12–13
University Settlements 15–23
urban land reform 241–60, 280–3
Urwick, E. J. 18, 201

van boys 198
venereal diseases, treatment of 232–4
Victoria, Australian state and wages boards 84–5, 86, 91
Vincent, D. 291–2

York 11, 111, 268, 269
youth employment exchanges 32, 34, 191

Wages Board Bill of Dilke 86, 91
Wallas, Graham 43, 243
Warner, Lloyd 9

Warner, Malcolm 25
Warwick, Lady 24, 28, 39, 46, 53, 218
Webb, Beatrice 24, 25, 26, 79–80, 86, 87, 88–9, 95, 105–6, 107, 108, 109, 110, 112–16, 118, 166, 167, 168, 181–2, 209–12, 214, 238, 239, 287, 288, 290, 293, 295, 304
Webb, Sidney 23, 24, 25, 26, 79, 86, 87, 88–9, 95, 100, 106, 107, 108, 110, 112, 114–16, 166, 167, 181–2, 209–12, 214, 238, 239, 290, 293, 295, 304
Weber, Max 7–8
Wedgewood, Josiah 141, 142
Welfare Revolution 1, 13, 166, 293
Welfare State 292, 293
Wells, H. G. 95
*Westminster Gazette* 167
Whitehouse, J. H. 18–19, 220, 304
Whittaker, Thomas 128
widows 157
Williams, Richard 178
Willis, F. J. 226, 233
Wilson, David 178
Wilson, J. Havelock 135
Winder, Phyllis 222

women
    employment of 270–1
    in local government 30
    as social reformers 28–32
Women's Cooperative Guild 29, 95
Women's Industrial Council 31, 32, 95–6, 185, 186
Women's Institutes 32
Women's Labour League 237
Women's Liberal Federation 95
Women's Trade Union League 30–1, 32, 79, 86, 90–4, 96
women workers, slow recruitment into unions 90–1
Wood, Kingsley 160
Woodbrooke Settlement 21
Workers Educational Association 19
workhouses 1–2, 107, 211, 295
working class, diet 222
Workmen's Compensation Acts 151–2, 294
Workmen's National Housing Council 241–2, 244, 250, 252, 253
workshops, improvements in sanitary conditions 81–2
Wyatt, Frank 157